Religion in America

ADVISORY EDITOR

Edwin S. Gaustad

Boehm, John Philip, 1683-1749.

LIFE AND LETTERS

OF THE

REV. JOHN PHILIP BOEHM

FOUNDER OF THE REFORMED CHURCH
IN PENNSYLVANIA

1683-1749

EDITED BY THE

REV. WILLIAM J. HINKE, PH. D., D. D.

ARNO PRESS
A NEW YORK TIMES COMPANY
New York • 1972

BX
9593
B6A3
1972

Reprint Edition 1972 by Arno Press Inc.

Reprinted from a copy in
The Pennsylvania State Library

RELIGION IN AMERICA - Series II
ISBN for complete set: 0-405-04050-4
See last pages of this volume for titles.

Manufactured in the United States of America

———◆◆◆———

Library of Congress Cataloging in Publication Data

Boehm, John Philip, 1683-1749.
  Life and letters of the Rev. John Philip Boehm.

  (Religion in America, series II)
  1. Reformed Church in the United States--Pennsylvania. I. Hinke, William John, 1871-1947, ed.
BX9593.B6A3 1972   285'.7'0924 [B]   71-38784
ISBN 0-405-04069-5

REV JOHN PHILIP BOEHM

351787

BOEHM'S CHURCH, FIRST STONE STRUCTURE, ERECTED 1747.
Drawing made by J. Irwin Yost, of Centre Square, Pa., according to directions given by Jonas Detweiler, who had seen the original building.

BOEHM'S CHURCH, PRESENT BUILDING, REMODELED 1890.

LIFE AND LETTERS

OF THE

REV. JOHN PHILIP BOEHM

FOUNDER OF THE REFORMED CHURCH IN PENNSYLVANIA

1683-1749

EDITED BY THE

REV. WILLIAM J. HINKE, PH. D., D. D.

PROFESSOR OF SEMITIC LANGUAGES AND RELIGIONS IN AUBURN
THEOLOGICAL SEMINARY

Philadelphia
PUBLICATION AND SUNDAY SCHOOL BOARD OF THE
REFORMED CHURCH IN THE UNITED STATES
1916

Copyright, 1916
BY
Rev. William J. Hinke, Ph. D., D. D.

PRESS OF BERGER BROTHERS
PHILADELPHIA

To
THE REV. PROF. JAMES I. GOOD, D.D., LL.D.,
My Esteemed Teacher, Colleague and Friend,
Who first kindled in me the love for church history, and through whose liberality the historical records of the Reformed Church of this country, preserved in Holland, were made accessible, this volume is gratefully dedicated.

PREFACE

Most of the letters and reports, contained in this volume, were sent by the Rev. John Philip Boehm, the founder of the Reformed Church in Pennsylvania, to the Classis of Amsterdam and the Synods of North and South Holland. It was the earliest of these letters that first attracted the attention of the Reformed Church of Holland to the German Reformed settlers in the Colony of Pennsylvania. The letters cover a period of twenty years. The first of them was written in 1728, the last in 1748. They are twenty-five in number, many of which are lengthy and elaborate. They throw a flood of light upon the founding of the earliest Reformed congregations. Of the more than sixty Reformed congregations in the colony in 1750, reference is made by Boehm to twenty-four, thirteen of which he served for longer or shorter periods, and of twelve of which he may be regarded as the founder. They also contain references to many of the itinerant preachers and school teachers of that early period, besides, the names of a large number of elders, deacons and influential laymen. In addition, the collection, published in this volume, contains also the letters sent to Boehm from Holland, by the Classis as well as the Synods.

It was mainly upon the urgent appeals of these letters from Boehm that the Reformed Church of Holland in 1746 commissioned the Rev. Michael Schlatter, to go to Pennsylvania to organize the scattered congregations and ministers into a Coetus or Convention. This was accomplished with the aid of Boehm; and, on September 29, 1747, four ministers and twenty-eight elders, the latter representing twenty congregations, met in Philadelphia and organized the Coetus of the Reformed Congregations of Pennsylvania. For forty-five years (1747-1792) the Coetus of Pennsylvania stood in filial relation to the Church of Holland, being one of the many mission fields of that great missionary church. It transmitted to the parent body copies of its minutes, letters and reports, setting forth the condition and needs of the congregations in the province.

The correspondence from the Churches in Pennsylvania has been carefully preserved in the archives of the Reformed Church of Holland, in the Classical archives at Amsterdam and in the Synodical archives at The Hague. There it was carefully treasured, unknown however to the American churches, till in July, 1895, the Rev. Dr. James I. Good visited Amsterdam, where he found and had copies made of a portfolio of Pennsylvania letters, in the archives of the Classis. In January, 1896, the late Henry S. Dotterer, having gone abroad in search for data for the "Perkiomen Region", a magazine devoted to the history of the Perkiomen valley, of which publication he was the editor, discovered the second great depository of Pennsylvania documents, the archives of the General Synod of the Reformed Church of Holland, at The Hague. Mr. Dotterer spent nearly two months at The Hague, making extracts which he published in his magazine, and later in that delightful, but now very rare publication, "Historical Notes Relating to the Pennsylvania Reformed Church." Mr. Dotterer called the attention of Dr. Good, who had spent a number of summers in Europe in search of materials for the history of the Reformed Church in the United States, to this collection of Pennsylvania manuscripts. Dr. Good visited The Hague in the summer of 1896, and to his great joy discovered that there, in the archives of the General Synod, had been preserved many of the minutes of the Coetus, together with a large number of the letters and reports from the Churches in Pennsylvania. The next summer he sent Prof. W. J. Hinke, Ph.D., D.D., to The Hague to copy them. The task was not an easy one, nor was one summer sufficient time for the work. Not only did Doctors Good and Hinke copy and photograph all that was available at The Hague and at Amsterdam, but Dr. Hinke also visited the Reformed centers in Germany and Switzerland, in search for data relating to the churches in Pennsylvania and the ministers, who left the fatherland to serve them. This prodigious, self-imposed, task was completed in 1898; and its fruits are contained in upwards of four thousand pages of manuscript and one thousand photographs, which were brought to this country, and by which the history of our church has been remarkably enriched. The expenditure involved, in copying and translating these documents, which was upwards of four thousand dollars, was most generously borne by Dr. Good. To him the church owes a lasting debt of gratitude, and Dr. Hinke, the editor of this work, has fittingly dedicated it to him.

In 1903, the Eastern Synod published the Coetal Minutes, prefaced by three of the letters of Rev. Mr. Boehm. They immediately attracted widespread attention and stimulated historical efforts within the church, by furnishing the documents necessary for the study of the Coetal period. But the pre-coetal period (1725-1747), the period of the founding of the congregations, remained practically untouched.

The happy custom of many of the early congregations of celebrating anniversaries, of erecting markers and placing tablets upon the walls of churches, together with the approaching bi-centenary of the founding of the church in Pennsylvania, began to call more strongly than ever before for definite data and reliable information, relative to the origin of the congregations and the labors of the early pastors. In answer to this increasing call for more definite and accurate information concerning the earlier period in the history of our church, Dr. Hinke began to translate and to edit the letters and reports of Rev. Mr. Boehm and to publish them in "The Journal of the Presbyterian Historical Society." The first installment appeared in the December number of 1902 of that journal. The timeliness and importance of this work of Dr. Hinke was immediately recognized both within and without the church. Hence, the Classis of East Pennsylvania, at its annual session at Easton, May 25-28, 1914, overtured the Eastern Synod to publish these letters and reports in a memorial volume. The Synod, at its meeting in Allentown, October, 1914, approved the overture and appointed Rev. John B. Stoudt, Rev. James I. Good, D.D., Rev. James A. Boehm, B. F. Fackenthal, Jr., Sc.D., and S. P. Heilman, M.D., a committee to co-operate with the Publication and Sunday School Board in this work, and to solicit advance subscriptions. At the subsequent meeting of the Synod in Philadelphia, the committee reported; that it had obtained the consent of Dr. Hinke to edit the letters and reports of Mr. Boehm and to add an account of his life and services in the church; and that they had succeeded in procuring a number of advance subscriptions and several gifts towards the work. The Synod accordingly endorsed the publication of the work and continued the committee.

This volume is made uniform with "The Minutes of the Coetus", its companion. The two together contain the documents necessary for the study of the history of the Reformed Church in Pennsylvania during the colonial period. Not of least importance are the many interesting and valuable annotations by the editor, which illuminate not only many of the otherwise obscure statements or references, but contain also much additional information relative to the early congregations, ministers, school teachers, elders, deacons, and the other denominations and sects, some of which are now extinct, but flourished during the period of Mr. Boehm's ministry. Thus, in addition to setting forth the life and labors of the founder of the Reformed Church in Pennsylvania, this work becomes a general contribution to the colonial history of the great Keystone State. Another valuable feature of the work is the map, which shows the location of all the Reformed congregations in Pennsylvania, founded before the year 1750, and the list of congregations accompanying it, which gives, as far as possible, documentary evidence for the dates of the founding of the congregations and of the building of the first churches. From this list it appears that a much larger number of Reformed churches was in existence in 1750, than was formerly realized.

The committee on behalf of the Synod acknowledges its obligations to the advance subscribers and the special donors, whose subscriptions and gifts made the publication of this volume possible; also to Dr. Hinke for his unselfish service in translating and editing these letters and reports and in prefacing them with a biography of Mr. Boehm, setting forth his labors in a manner in keeping with the important services which he rendered to the Church and the Colony.

That this story of faithfulness and devotion in the labor of planting the vineyard of the Master in this country, may inspire others to equal and perhaps still greater faithfulness and devotion in the labor of watering, is the hope and prayer of the Committee.

JOHN BAER STOUDT,
Chairman of the Committee of Synod.

INTRODUCTION

The publication of this volume is not the first evidence which the old Mother Synod of the Reformed Church in the United States has given of her interest in the preservation of her history. As early as 1817, the president of Synod, Rev. Wm. Hendel, Sr., proposed that an investigation be made into the origin and growth of Synod, and that a historical statement regarding it be printed. As a result, Synod appointed the president, the clerk, John Henry Hoffmeier and Caspar Wack, Sr., a committee to prepare such a sketch, print it and sell 5000 copies of it (Minutes, 1817, p. 12). A member of the committee (no doubt the chairman, Mr. Hendel, Sr.), then remembered that he had in his possession a copy of Michael Schlatter's Diary in Dutch, which had been published by the Classis of Amsterdam in 1751. Of this document the committee gave a short summary, covering six and a half pages, which was printed as an appendix to the minutes of 1817 (pp. 14-20) and 3000 separate copies were issued, because, as the committee reported in the following year, "there was no evidence of a desire for a larger number". (Minutes, 1818, p. 7.)

At the same meeting of Synod at York, in September, 1817, it was resolved to deposit the letters and other documents of Synod in the archives of the Reformed congregation at Lancaster, "where several are already kept", and to ask the pastor, Mr. Hoffmeier, then clerk of Synod, to entrust them to his consistory, with instructions not to hand over any of them, without the express order of the Synod (Minutes, 1817, p. 10f).

The archives of Synod remained in Lancaster till 1833, when Synod resolved to remove them to York and to deposit all the Synodical papers there (Minutes, 1833, p. 12). In the following year, the parsonage of the Reformed congregation at York was designated as the depository of the archives and the pastor of that church as its custodian (Minutes, 1834, p. 13). In 1836, the committee entrusted with the removal of the archives, reported that they had carried out in part their instructions and had deposited at York all the documents of Synod, extending back as far as the year 1821, but that there were other documents at Lancaster, in "Low Dutch", which they were unable to read and of which they did not know whether they belonged to Synod or to the congregation (Minutes, 1836, p. 8f). In 1838, when Synod met at Lancaster, a committee, consisting of Dr. Willers, M. Bruner and H. Dorwert, were appointed to examine the papers in the "Low Dutch language", still remaining in the archives of the congregation at Lancaster. Later in the sessions, the committee asked for more time to examine these documents (Minutes, 1838, pp. 12, 54). In the following year, Dr. Willers reported at length about nine of these Dutch letters, which had been written from Holland to the Coetus of Pennsylvania between the years 1775-1786. His recommendation to print seven of them as a part of the Synodical minutes was adopted (Minutes 1839, pp. 77-80). But, when in the following year objection was made by Zion's Classis to this plan, they were ordered to be printed in pamphlet form and the expense of the publication to be covered by the proceeds of the sale of the work (Minutes, 1840, pp. 20, 65-66). They appeared in 1841, printed by the Publication Office of the Reformed Church at Chambersburg, under the title: "Letters from Holland connected with the first Organization of the German Reformed Church in the United States". This, now exceedingly rare, little pamphlet constitutes the first effort of Synod to make its historical documents accessible to its members. It contained seven letters, written in answer to the Coetus Minutes. The originals are at present preserved in the Harbaugh Collection of Mss.

On September 29, 1839, while Synod was in session in the Reformed Church at Philadelphia, that congregation celebrated the centennial anniversary of its organization. Its pastor, the Rev. Joseph F. Berg, preached a "centenary sermon" from Proverbs 22:28, on the subject "The Ancient Landmark". In this sermon he informed his hearers that "the first building, in which our forefathers worshipped in this city, was completed A. D. 1739". He also regarded it as peculiarly appropriate that this centennial anniversary of the church should be commemorated whilst Synod was meeting with them, because it might in some measure be regarded "as the centenary anniversary of our existence as a denomination in this country". We now know that Dr. Berg was entirely mistaken in his interpretation of the congregational records, for no church had been begun in 1739, and hence no church could have been completed in that year. Of this, however, he and his contemporaries were in blissful ignorance. But his celebration in 1839, and the booklet he published in 1840 regarding it, induced Maryland Classis in 1840 to overture Synod, "whereas it is about one hundred years since our Church commenced its existence in this country, and whereas, it must be regarded both as proper and important that a centenary celebration should be observed throughout the churches", that Synod be requested to resolve upon the observance of such a centenary celebration (Minutes, 1840, p. 20). In answer to this request, Synod appointed the year 1841 to be observed by a centenary celebration and ordered that the celebration close on the 25th of December of that year with a solemn festival of thanks, and further that united efforts be put forth to raise at least $100,000 for the Institutions of the Church (Minutes, 1840, p. 72). At the same time a "Circular to the Ministers, Consistories and Members of the German Reformed Church", was prepared, printed in the minutes (pp. 75-82), also in the church papers and as separate pamphlets, which were ordered to be read from all the pulpits. As a result, numerous congregations observed the "Centenary Anniversary", but the hopes of gathering a large centenary fund for the institutions of the church were not realized (Minutes, 1842, p. 70ff).

At the meeting of Synod in 1841, Susquehanna Classis requested Synod to publish a short history of the German Reformed Church (German Minutes, 1841, p. 17). But, in the following year the request of East Pennsylvania Classis was granted to postpone the publication of this history, "until more satisfactory facts have been procured" (Minutes, 1842, p. 11).

At the Synod of 1842, the delegates to the Synod of the Dutch Reformed Church were instructed, "respectfully to ask that body, the use of the documents recently received by them from Holland, so far as they may be calculated to throw light upon the early history of the German Reformed Church in this country" (Minutes, 1842, p. 19). These were the documents from the Classis of Amsterdam, brought to America by the Hon. J. R. Brodhead (See Coetus Minutes, p. XIV). As the delegates failed to attend to this duty, a special committee was appointed in 1843, to secure the use of these documents (Minutes, 1843, p. 27). This committee reported in 1844 that they were informed that "these documents had been in possession of the Rev. Lewis Mayer, D.D., of York, Pa., who is engaged in preparing a history of the German Reformed Church, and they consequently felt that further action on their part in relation to these documents was precluded" (Minutes, 1844, p. 13). The committee was, however, continued to carry out its original instructions. In 1845, it reported that the original documents had been returned by Dr. Mayer to their owners, but that copies were in his possession, "which throw much light on the early history of the German Reformed Church in this country" (Minutes, 1845, p. 135).

In 1846, the first printed history of the German Reformed Church in the United States appeared, not however, in America, but in Germany. The Rev. Dr. J. G. Buettner, who in 1838 and 1839 had been professor in the Theological Seminary of the Synod of Ohio, at Canton, Ohio, and who had returned to Germany in 1840, published in 1846, at Schleiz, Germany, a small book of 154 pages, entitled: "Die Hochdeutsche Reformirte Kirche in den Vereinigten Staaten von Nord Amerika, von ihrer Gründung bis auf die neueste Zeit". It is a mere sketch, the early history of the Coetus being covered on nine pages. The later history, however, from 1826-1841, is fairly complete.

In the same year, 1846, Synod appointed a new committee, in answer to an overture of Maryland Classis, "to make arrangements to secure certain documents from Holland, in the hands of the Rev. Dr. Mayer" (Minutes, 1846, p. 70). They reported, in the following year, that Dr. Mayer was using these documents for a history of the German Reformed Church in America, upon which he was engaged and that he was, for that reason, not prepared to make a transfer of them to other hands. He had, however, expressed the expectation, that they would eventually become the property of Synod (Minutes, 1847, p. 89).

At the meeting of Synod in October, 1849, at Norristown, Rev. Elias Heiner called the attention of Synod to the fact that Dr. Mayer had died at York August 25, 1849. Whereupon a committee was appointed, with Dr. Heiner as chairman, to express the feelings of Synod with regard to his decease In the minute, prepared by the committee, the suggestion was made, "to confer with the family of the deceased on the subject of the Dr.'s papers generally, but especially on the subject of his History of the Reformed Church" (Minutes, 1849, p. 88). A new committee was entrusted with this task. It reported in the following year, that they had examined the Rev. Dr. Mayer's Manuscript History of the German Reformed Church and they found that "the first volume, embracing the history of the Reformed Church in Switzerland and Germany, and which will probably make, if published some five or six hundred octavo pages, is ready for the press. The second volume, designed to embrace the history of the Reformed Church in this country, is incomplete. Most of the necessary materials are collected and its history down to the year 1756, is partly written out. Great labor and much time have been expended on this important work, and it is deeply to be regretted that Dr. Mayer was not spared to complete it with his own hand. As it is, your committee recommend the publication of the first volume, and suggest the expediency of having the second volume completed by another hand" (Minutes, 1850, p. 78). At the Synod of 1851, four copies of Dr. Mayer's History of the German Reformed Church were presented by Dr. Elias Heiner (Minutes, 1852, p. 99). The book had been published by Lippincott, Grambo and Co., as a stately octavo volume of 461 pages, under the title: "The History of the German Reformed Church by Rev. Lewis Mayer, D.D., Volume I". A life of Dr. Mayer, written by Dr. Elias Heiner, formed the introduction to it. In the preface (p. XV) it is stated that of the second volume "perhaps three hundred pages" had been written out, bringing the history down to the year 1770.

In 1854, Synod appointed a committee of five members to

endeavor to secure from the heirs of the late Rev. Dr. Mayer "the important papers relating to the history of the German Reformed Church in this country" (Minutes, 1854, p. 71). After several years of negotiations, the committee reported in 1856, that they had "secured the said documents consisting of the manuscript volumes, transcribed with great labor and care, from original sources, by Dr. Mayer, together with original letters, copies of minutes of Coetus, etc. On condition that the remaining copies of Volume I, of Mayer's History be sold, and the volume of manuscript history, be published in a given time the heirs of Dr. Mayer donated these manuscript volumes, papers, letters, etc., to Synod, through its committee for its archives as the last legacy of their beloved father" (Minutes, 1856, p. 90). The Mayer Mss. are preserved in the library of the Theological Seminary of the Reformed Church at Lancaster, but the second volume of Dr. Mayer's History was never published. Even the Ms. itself seems to have been lost or mislaid.

On the basis of the Coetus Minutes and other original documents which had thus passed into the possession of Synod, Dr. Harbaugh published in 1857 his excellent "Life of Rev. Michael Schlatter" and two volumes of "The Fathers of the German Reformed Church in Europe and America."

No general and connected history of the Reformed Church was, however attempted till 1885. The story of its composition carries us back till 1875, when Eastern Synod overtured the General Synod to observe "the approaching National Centennial Celebration, in A. D. 1876". In response to this overture a special committee was appointed which recommended that "a record of the historical origin of the Reformed Church be prepared, together with a statement of her doctrine and government" (General Synod Minutes, 1875, pp. 68-70). After a delay of several years and repeated requests from Classes that this recommendation be carried out, the General Synod of 1881 appointed the Rev. Joseph H. Dubbs, D.D., to prepare a "Manual of the origin, history, doctrines, government and customs of the Reformed Church in the United States" (General Synod Minutes, 1881, p. 161). In obedience to this request, Dr. Dubbs published in 1885 at Lancaster the "Historic Manual of the Reformed Church in the United States", in which he gave for the first time a readable and interesting account of the history of the church, having made good use of the original documents at his disposal. Later researches enabled Dr. Dubbs to correct, enlarge and complete this record in the "History of the Reformed Church, German", which he contributed in 1895 to the "American Church History Series", edited by Dr. Philip Schaff, Vol. VIII, pp. 213-423. He prefaced this contribution by the first useful, though brief, bibliography of German Reformed publications in this country.

At its meeting in October, 1895, at Shamokin, Eastern Synod resolved on final adjournment, "to meet in 150th sessions on Wednesday, October 7, 1896, and to devote a portion of its time to the Sesqui-Centennial Celebration of said event, that also in connection therewith the 50th Anniversary of the adoption of the Constitution be observed at the services appointed by the committee" (Minutes, 1895, p. 84). In compliance with this resolution the committee appointed for this purpose prepared a Sesqui-Centennial program, which was carried out during the sessions of Synod at Bethlehem, October 7-11, 1896. The historical addresses and sermons, delivered on this occasion, were published in a small pamphlet, under the title: "Addresses delivered on the Occasion of the One Hundred and Fiftieth Anniversary of the Founding of the Eastern Synod of the Reformed Church in the United States", pp. 131.

Similar Sesqui-Centennial services were held by Potomac Synod. The memorial addresses then delivered, were published by Daniel Miller, at Reading, in 1900, entitled: "Michael Schlatter Memorial Addresses at the Sesqui-Centennial Services, held in Hagerstown, Md., by the Synod of the Potomac, October 20, A. D. 1897, in honor of the Pioneer Organizer of the Reformed Churches in America", pp. 61. The example thus set by the Synods was followed by many Classes and individual congregations. Some of these Sesqui-Centennial Addresses were published, as *e. g.*, the "Sesqui-Centennial Services of the Evangelical Reformed Church, Frederick, Maryland, May 9, 14, and 16, 1897, Rev. E. R. Eschbach, D.D., Pastor", Frederick, 1897, pp. 91. Among other books and pamphlets, called forth by the Sesqui-Centennial Celebration, may be mentioned: "The Early Fathers of the Reformed Church in the United States", by Rev. James I. Good, D.D., Reading, Daniel Miller, Publisher (1897), pp. 75, and "The Historical Hand

Book of the Reformed Church in the United States", by Rev. James I. Good, D.D., Philadelphia, Reformed Church Publication Board, 1897, pp. 95, the latter being a brief sketch for the use of young people's societies.

In all these publications use had been made almost exclusively of the well-known documents and sources, gathered with much labor and zeal by Drs. Mayer and Harbaugh. No further progress was possible unless new manuscript material be made accessible. This was accomplished by the Rev. Dr. James I. Good, who, in July, 1895, had a portfolio of Pennsylvania papers, preserved in the Classical archives at Amsterdam, copied. Still more documents were found by the late Mr. Dotterer at The Hague, in January 1896, which were copied and photographed in full during the next three summers by Dr. Good and the writer. The results of these new finds were presented by Dr. Good in his "History of the Reformed Church in the United States, 1725-1792", Reading, Daniel Miller, Publisher, 1899, pp. 701. Other writers also made use of this new material. Dr. Dubbs embodied the new finds in his interesting and beautifully illustrated book (published by the Pennsylvania-German Society), "The Reformed Church in Pennsylvania", Lancaster, 1902, to which the writer contributed an extensive bibliography (pp. 341-380). Many local histories, monographs and sketches, which have appeared since 1900, have profited by the new documents, as *e. g.*, the "Early History of the Reformed Church in Pennsylvania", by Daniel Miller, Reading, 1906, pp. 280.

The publication of the new manuscripts thus brought to light was undertaken by Eastern Synod in 1901, when a committee was appointed to superintend the publication of the most important of these documents, the Coetus Minutes. This volume was brought out in 1903, under the title: "Minutes and Letters of the Coetus of the German Reformed Congregations in Pennsylvania, 1747-1792, together with three preliminary reports of Rev. John Philip Boehm, 1734-1744", Reformed Church Publication Board, Philadelphia, 1903, pp. 463. To this book the present volume forms a fitting sequel and complement, because it covers fully the earliest period before the organization of the Coetus of Pennsylvania in 1747.

The manuscript material, which has been made use of in

INTRODUCTION xix

the Life of Boehm, has been gathered from many different sources.

Regarding the career of Boehm's father, Rev. Philip Lewis Boehm, numerous documents were secured from the Royal State Archives at Marburg. They are chiefly extracts from the protocols of the Reformed Consistory of Hanau. In addition, the records of the Latin school at Hanau were consulted.

Regarding Boehm's life in Europe, the city archives of Worms furnished most of the material. Copies of no less than thirty-two separate documents were secured from Worms and three documents from the town archives of Lambsheim. Besides, the church records of Reformed congregations at Worms, Hanau, Wachenbuchen and Hochstadt were examined and extracts, touching the family of Boehm, were made.

Similar investigations were made by the writer into the antecedents of the other early Reformed ministers, who were contemporaries of Boehm. The matriculation books of the following universities were consulted: those of Leyden and Utrecht in Holland, of Duisburg, Marburg, Herborn and Heidelberg in Germany and of Basel in Switzerland. Moreover, Reformed church records were explored, those at Heidelberg and Weinheim for Tempelman and Bartholomaeus, at Eppingen fo' Weiss, at Oberingelheim for Rieger, at Zurich for Goetschy and Wirtz, at St. Gall for Schlatter and Hochreutner, at Berne for Guldin and at Muelhausen for Lischy. Through correspondence, additional information was secured at Moers regarding the family of Dorsius, at Alsenborn, regarding the family of Peter Miller and at Zurich regarding John Henry Goetschy.

Boehm's life and activity in Pennsylvania is based almost entirely upon his own letters and pamphlets, as published in this volume, and upon the church records of the congregations which he founded. Finally, the county records at Philadelphia, in the recorder of deeds and the register of wills offices, furnished information regarding the extent and disposition of his property.

The correspondence of Mr. Boehm has been derived from five different sources. The earliest letters, of the years 1728-1730, referring to the ordination of Boehm, were taken from a record book of the Collegiate Reformed Church at New York. Most of the later letters and reports (14 in all, namely, Nos.

10, 11, 12, 13, 23, 25, 26, 28, 29, 30, 32, 40, 44, 45) were copied from the Pennsylvania Portfolio, in the archives of the Classis of Amsterdam, fourteen letters addressed to Boehm or to his congregations by the Classis (namely, Nos. 3, 4, 5, 6, 7, 14, 15, 16, 17, 18, 24, 27, 33, 47) were taken from the Classical Letter Books, Vols. XXIX and XXX. The Synodical archives furnished also fourteen documents, among which are eight letters and reports written by Boehm (namely, Nos. 21, 22, 36, 37, 38, 39, 42, 43), two pamphlets (Nos. 34, 46) and four letters addressed to Boehm (Nos. 19, 20, 35, 41). One document (No. 44) was taken from the Mayer Ms., the original, at one time in the archives at New Brunswick, seems to have been lost. Finally of No. 31, Boehm's book against the Moravians, the only surviving copy, in possession of Dr. Good, was used.

This brief account of the manuscript sources, used in this volume, emphasizes once more the indebtedness of the Reformed Church in the United States to the Church of Holland. But for her care in preserving these records, it would have been impossible to reconstruct Boehm's life and labors so fully after a lapse of more than a century and a half. How much more could have been presented, if all the congregations, founded and served by Boehm had shown an equal care in preserving their church records. Some of them, like Boehm's own private records, are irrecoverably lost, one or two of them being lost within the last twenty years. If we wish to honor the memory of our fathers, we must preserve the records which they kept with conscientious care and handed down to us as a precious heritage.

WILLIAM J. HINKE.

Auburn, August 1, 1916.

CONTENTS

PART I

LIFE OF THE REV. JOHN PHILIP BOEHM

	PAGE
CHAPTER I. BOEHM'S PARENTAGE AND BIRTH	1
CHAPTER II. BOEHM AS SCHOOLMASTER AT WORMS AND LAMBSHEIM	6
CHAPTER III. THE ORDINATION OF BOEHM	20
Earliest Reformed Settlers in Pennsylvania	20
Beginning of Boehm's Ministry	28
Arrival of Rev. George Michael Weiss	29
Ordination of Boehm	35
CHAPTER IV. BOEHM'S EARLY OPPONENTS	38
The Reiff Collecting Tour	39
John Peter Miller	44
John Bartholomew Rieger	49
John Henry Goetschy	51
Peter Henry Dorsius	54
CHAPTER V. BOEHM AS THE ORGANIZER OF CHURCHES	58
Whitemarsh Reformed Church	58
Skippack Reformed Church	59
Falkner Swamp Reformed Church	61
Conestoga Reformed Churches	62
Tulpehocken Reformed Churches	66
Philadelphia Reformed Church	70
Oley Reformed Church	73
Providence Reformed Church	74
Boehm's Reformed Church	75
Egypt Reformed Church	77
Coventry Reformed Church	79
CHAPTER VI. BOEHM'S OPPOSITION TO THE UNION MOVEMENT	82
German Sects in Pennsylvania	84
Visit of Zinzendorf to Pennsylvania	89
Pennsylvania Synods	92
Opposition to the Union Movement	101

CONTENTS

	PAGE
CHAPTER VII. BOEHM'S OPPONENTS IN THE UNION MOVEMENT	109
Henry Antes	109
John Bechtel	115
Jacob Lischy	119
Christian Henry Rauch	125
John Brandmiller	127
David Bruce	129
CHAPTER VIII. BOEHM'S LAST LABORS	132
Arrival of Michael Schlatter	132
The First Coetus	134
The Second Coetus	135
Boehm Surrenders His Churches	137
Summary of Boehm's Work	140
CHAPTER IX. BOEHM'S FAMILY AND DESCENDANTS	145

PART II

CORRESPONDENCE OF REV. JOHN PHILIP BOEHM

1. 1728, July, The Consistories of Mr. Boehm to Classis........ 155
2. 1728, Aug. 15, New York Ministers to Classis................ 170
3. 1728, Nov. 28, The Classis to the Churches in Pennsylvania.. 170
4. 1728, Dec. 1, Classis to the New York Ministers............. 172
5. 1729, June 20, Classis to the Brethren in Pennsylvania....... 172
6. 1729, June 20, Classis to Mr. Boehm 174
7. 1729, June 20, Classis to the New York Ministers........... 176
8. 1729, Nov. 23, Ordination of John Philip Boehm............ 177
9. 1729, Nov. 24, Reconciliation between Boehm and Weiss..... 180
10. 1730, Jan. 29, Mr. Boehm to the Classis.................... 183
11. 1730, Jan. 29, Mr. Boehm and His Consistories to the Classis. 186
12. 1730, Apr. 21, New York Ministers to the Classis........... 192
13. 1730, Nov. 12, Mr. Boehm to the Classis, with Enclosures.... 198
    - a. 1730, May 17, Mr. Boehm to the Ministers of New York.. 207
    - b. 1730, July 17, New York Ministers to Mr. Boehm........ 210
    - c. 1727, Nov. 28, Mr. Weiss to Mr. Boehm................. 211
    - d. 1727, Oct. 2, Mr. Weiss to Mr. Schwab, of Canastocka... 212
    - e. 1730, Nov., Complaints of Mr. Boehm against Mr. Weiss.. 214
    - f. 1730, Nov. 5, Mr. Boehm and Skippack Elders to New York Ministers 219
14. 1730, Dec. 5, Classis to Mr. Boehm 220
15. 1730, Dec. 5, Classis to Churches of Mr. Boehm............. 222
16. 1730, Dec. 5, Classis to Church of Skippack................. 223
17. 1730, Dec. 5, Classis to New York Ministers................. 226
18. 1731, Oct. 19, Classis to Mr. Boehm 228

CONTENTS   xxiii

		PAGE
19.	1731, Dec. 1, Synodical Deputies to Mr. Boehm	230
20.	1734, Apr. 20, Reformed Church of Philadelphia to Mr. Boehm	231
21.	1734, Oct. 28, Mr. Boehm and Phila. Consistory to Synods	234
22.	1734, Oct. 28, First Report of Mr. Boehm to Synods	250
23.	1738, Mar. 10, Mr. Boehm and his Consistories to Classis	258
24.	1739, Jan., Classis to Mr. Boehm	261
25.	1739, Mar. 16, Mr. Boehm to Classis	262
	Mar. 18, Postscript	267
26.	1740, Mar. 26, Mr. Boehm to Classis, with enclosures	269
	a. 1738, Nov. 28, Mr. Dorsius to Mr. Boehm	271
	b. 1739, Jan. 14, Report of Mr. Boehm to Classis	272
	c. 1739, Dec. 6, Mr. Dorsius to Mr. Boehm	284
	d. 1740, Mar. Certified Pledges of Reformed Churches	285
	including (a) A Summary	294
	(b) An Additional Report	295
	e. 1740, Mar. Repartition of Reformed Churches	297
27.	1740, Apr. 1, Classis to Mr. Boehm	298
28.	1740, Apr. 4, Mr. Boehm to the Classis	300
	including: Letter of Wilhelmius to Pa. Churches	303
29.	1741, May 3, Defense of Mr. Boehm by his Consistories	311
30.	1741, July 25, Mr. Boehm to the Classis, with enclosures	318
	a. 1740, Oct. 20, Visit of Dorsius to Goshenhoppen	338
	b. 1740, Nov. 30, Defense of Mr. Boehm by his Elders	339
	c. 1740, Apr. 20, Tulpehocken Consistory to Mr. Boehm	342
	d. 1735, Feb. 27, Statement of Rev. John B. Rieger	343
	e. 1741, June 20, Mr. Weiss to C. Ulrich of Philadelphia	344
	f. 1738, May 8, Account of Collection Money, by Weiss	345
	g. 1741, Declaration of Allegiance to King	346
31.	1742, Aug. 23, Boehm's Faithful Letter of Warning	348
	1742, July 18, Commotion in Philadelphia Meeting House	366
32.	1742, Nov. 17, Mr. Boehm to the Classis	370
33.	1743, May 9, Classis to Mr. Boehm	372
34.	1743, May 19, Boehm's Second Faithful Warning	373
35.	1744, Mar. 27, Tulpehocken Congregation to Mr. Boehm	385
36.	1744, Mar. 18, Mr. Boehm and his Consistories to the Synods. with enclosures:	386
	a. 1743, Sept. 20, Synodical Deputy to Reformed Churches	396
	b. 1739, Jan. Report of Mr. Boehm to the Synods	397
	c. 1740, Mar. 26, Mr. Boehm to Synods	397
	d. 1743-1744, Statistics of Mr. Boehm	397
	e. 1744, Mar. 18, Church Order of Mr. Boehm	400
37.	1744, July 8, Mr. Boehm and Phila. Consistory to Synods	405
38.	1744, July 8, Report of Mr. Boehm to the Synods	408
39.	1744, July 9, Mr. Boehm to Deputies of Synods	426
40.	1746, Nov. 23, Mr. Boehm to the Classis	428

CONTENTS

		Page
	Nov. 25, Postscript	433
41.	1746, Nov. 29, Mr. Schlatter to Mr. Boehm	435
42.	1746, Dec. 12, Mr. Boehm to Deputies of Synods	436
43.	1748, Nov. 21, Mr. Boehm sending Minutes of Coetus	438
44.	1748, Nov. 22, Mr. Boehm to Classical Deputy	441
45.	1748, Dec. Mr. Boehm to Classical Deputy	442
46.	1748, Preface to Church Order	463
47.	1749, June 2, Classical Deputies to Mr. Boehm	468

APPENDIX I

Documents Relating to Boehm's Death and Property

48.	1749, Mar.-May, Notices of Mr. Boehm's Last Labors	469
49.	1749, May 16, Obituary Notice of Mr. Boehm	469
50.	1749, May 6, Widow renouncing right of administration	470
51.	1749, May 6, Letters of administration granted to Son	470
52.	1749, May 6, Bond of Administrator	471
53.	1749, July 13, Inventory of Estate	472
54.	1749, July 13, Account of Administrator of Estate	475
55.	1749, July 1, Deed given by Daughters to youngest Son	476

APPENDIX II

List of Reformed Congregations founded before 1750 481
Index 491

ILLUSTRATIONS ON PLATES

1. Boehm's Church, First Structure................*Frontispiece*
2. Boehm's Church, Present Building................*Frontispiece*

Facing Page

3. Hochstadt, the Birthplace of Boehm....................... 6
4. Lambsheim, where Boehm taught School.................... 6
5. First Page of Neshaminy Record.......................... 24
6. The Dutch Reformed Ministers at New York, who ordained Boehm 36
7. First Printed Report about the Reformed Church of Penna... 40
8. House of Wm. De Wees, in which the Whitemarsh Congregation met 58
9. Cornerstone of Old Goshenhoppen Church 58
10. Title Page of the Book of Weiss against the Newborn...... 72
11. Portrait of Count von Zinzendorf........................ 82
12. Market Place at Germantown, showing the Reformed Church. 100
13. The Tomb of Henry Antes 114
14. Historic Houses in Germantown, showing John Bechtel's House 118
15. Monument of Buettner and Rauch, at Shekomeko, N. Y....... 126
16. Portrait of Rev. Michael Schlatter 132
17. Minutes of First Coetus, September 29, 1747................ 134
18. House of Peter Troxell, at Egypt, in which Boehm held his last Communion 140
19. The old "Boehm Homestead," in Hellertown, in which Boehm died 140
20. Letter of Boehm, showing his Penmanship 142
21. Boehm's Second Letter of Warning against Moravians........ 374
22. Title Page of Boehm's Church Order of 1748............... 464
23. Map of Pennsylvania, showing location of Reformed Churches founded before 1750 489

ILLUSTRATIONS IN THE TEXT

		PAGE
1.	Signature of Boehm, as Schoolmaster at Lambsheim	16
2.	Signature of Rev. George M. Weiss	30
3.	Signatures of Boehm's Elders in 1730	36
4.	Signature of Peter Miller	46
5.	Signature of Rev. John B. Rieger	49
6.	Signature of John Henry Goetschy, from Egypt Record	52
7.	Signature of Conrad Tempelmann	62
8.	Title Page of Boehm's Letter of Warning against the Moravians	103
9.	Signature of Jacob Lischy	120
10.	Signature of Rev. John P. Leydich	139
11.	Signature of Rev. John Philip Boehm	143
12.	Signature of John Conrad Wurtz, from Egypt Record	447

ILLUSTRATIONS ON PLATES

1. Boehm's Church, First Structure....................*Frontispiece*
2. Boehm's Church, Present Building..................*Frontispiece*

Facing Page

3. Hochstadt, the Birthplace of Boehm........................ 6
4. Lambsheim, where Boehm taught School..................... 6
5. First Page of Neshaminy Record........................... 24
6. The Dutch Reformed Ministers at New York, who ordained Boehm 36
7. First Printed Report about the Reformed Church of Penna... 40
8. House of Wm. De Wees, in which the Whitemarsh Congregation met 58
9. Cornerstone of Old Goshenhoppen Church 58
10. Title Page of the Book of Weiss against the Newborn...... 72
11. Portrait of Count von Zinzendorf.......................... 82
12. Market Place at Germantown, showing the Reformed Church. 100
13. The Tomb of Henry Antes 114
14. Historic Houses in Germantown, showing John Bechtel's House 118
15. Monument of Buettner and Rauch, at Shekomeko, N. Y....... 126
16. Portrait of Rev. Michael Schlatter 132
17. Minutes of First Coetus, September 29, 1747.................. 134
18. House of Peter Troxell, at Egypt, in which Boehm held his last Communion 140
19. The old "Boehm Homestead," in Hellertown, in which Boehm died 140
20. Letter of Boehm, showing his Penmanship 142
21. Boehm's Second Letter of Warning against Moravians........ 374
22. Title Page of Boehm's Church Order of 1748................ 464
23. Map of Pennsylvania, showing location of Reformed Churches founded before 1750 489

ILLUSTRATIONS IN THE TEXT

		PAGE
1.	Signature of Boehm, as Schoolmaster at Lambsheim..........	16
2.	Signature of Rev. George M. Weiss........................	30
3.	Signatures of Boehm's Elders in 1730	36
4.	Signature of Peter Miller	46
5.	Signature of Rev. John B. Rieger	49
6.	Signature of John Henry Goetschy, from Egypt Record......	52
7.	Signature of Conrad Tempelmann	62
8.	Title Page of Boehm's Letter of Warning against the Moravians	103
9.	Signature of Jacob Lischy	120
10.	Signature of Rev. John P. Leydich.........................	139
11.	Signature of Rev. John Philip Boehm	143
12.	Signature of John Conrad Wurtz, from Egypt Record........	447

LIFE OF THE REV. JOHN PHILIP BOEHM

CHAPTER I.

BOEHM'S PARENTAGE AND BIRTH.

The name Boehm indicates that the family originated in Bohemia, for it means "the Bohemian." At present we are unable to trace the family farther back than the father of John Philip Boehm. His name was Philip Lewis [Ludwig] Boehm. The older Boehm was born in the year 1646 at Dorheim, a village in the Wetterau, a district which is now a part of the Grand-duchy of Hesse, between Frankfort-on-the-Main and Giessen. When the Latin school at Hanau-on-the-Main was opened in March, 1665, "Philippus Ludovicus Bohemus, Dorheimensis," matriculated as the thirty-fourth student of the first class.[1] A year and a half later, on August 27, 1666, he matriculated with the same signature in the university of Marburg. Sometime afterwards he became the Dutch schoolmaster of the Walloon congregation in the new-town of Hanau. On October 22, 1679, the protocol of the Reformed Consistory of Hanau states: "Inasmuch as the present Dutch schoolmaster in the new-town [Hanau] has been accepted as pastor of the vacant congregation at Hochstadt, it has been deemed proper to address, according to usual custom, a letter of recommendation to Messrs. Von Carben,

---

[1] The matriculation book of the Latin school at Hanau has been printed: *Illustris Scholae Hanoviensis Leges et Album Civium Academicorum inde ab anno 1665 usque ad annum 1812*. Particula I, 1665-1724, Hanau 1895, Programm No. 397; Particula II, 1724-1812, Hanau 1896, Programm No. 399. Published by the Director, Dr. Ph. Braun. The entry of Philip Ludwig Boehm occurs in the first of these publications, p. 6.

patrons of this parish."[2] Shortly afterwards Boehm was ordained and entered upon his pastoral activity. He officiated at the first wedding at Hochstadt on February 19, 1680.

His pastorate at Hochstadt was quite stormy. The records of the Consistory of Hanau[3] refer repeatedly to quarrels and troubles in which he was involved. In August, 1682, John Hoerst, one of the members of the village board, complained that his pastor, Mr. Boehm, had scolded him publicly from the pulpit for allowing his son to haul earth during the prayer meeting, which, Mr. Hoerst explained, his son had done contrary to his orders and unknown to him. The Consistory gave Boehm a reprimand and made him promise to attend to the duties of his office more peaceably. In August, 1684, the Consistory heard that the pastor of Hochstadt was daily running with his gun through the vineyards, after game, a misdemeanor, which was strictly forbidden. A written reprimand was sent to him. In September, 1684, the burgess of the village complained to the Consistory about the language Boehm had used when speaking of him and the village officials. When e.g., in the course of a conversation Boehm had been asked why ministers nowadays were riding beautiful horses, he had answered sarcastically that the great Lords had made all the asses their servants, hence ministers were compelled to take horses. Boehm was put through a rigorous examination by the Consistory, in which he was compelled to confess that he had a slippery tongue and had spoken in anger. He had to beg the burgess' pardon and had to promise to live in peace with his parishioners. The case was reported to the noblemen, who were the patrons of the parish. They decreed that Boehm should be suspended from office for four weeks.

[2] The extracts from the minutes of the Consistory of Hanau, quoted in this chapter, are taken from the original minute books, preserved in the Royal State Archives at Marburg. They were made for the writer with the kind permission of the present director of these archives.
[3] It may be well to add that the term "Consistory" is not used in Germany in the same sense as in this country. It does not refer to a congregational consistory. It is the supreme ecclesiastical judicatory of a province. At present a provincial consistory consists of six pastors and six theological professors of the university of the province, appointed by the government.

In spite of this severe sentence, Boehm was unable to control his tongue. On two later occasions suspensions from office were imposed upon him. In July, 1686, he preached a sermon against heretics and heretical books, in which he insinuated that the Consistory was not doing its duty with regard to them. On another occasion he again attacked the village officials, calling one of them a spider, sucking poison out of his sermons. After his third suspension the Consistory considered it better for him to take another charge. He was, therefore, transferred to Kesselstadt, near Hanau, in 1688.

During his pastorate at Hochstadt several children were born to him. A daughter, Margaretha, born October 4, 1681, was baptized at Hanau October 9, 1681. His wife's Christian name is given as Maria. Two years later, in November, 1683, his son, John Philip, was born at Hochstadt and baptized there on November 25, 1683.[4] In the following year, on June 6, 1684, two older sons, John Daniel Boehm and Clement Lewis (Ludwig) Boehm, entered the Latin school at Hanau. They are called in the matriculation book: "fratres et filii Philippi Ludov. Boehm, p.t. pastor Hochstadiensis," *i.e.*, "brothers, sons of Philip Lewis Boehm, p.t. pastor at Hochstadt."

After a brief pastorate at Kesselstadt, about which nothing is known at present, Mr. Boehm, Sr., returned again to his former congregation at Hochstadt. The records of the Consistory of Hanau state, under date January 14, 1691: "Inasmuch as the congregation at Hochstadt has again asked for its former pastor, Rev. Philip Lewis Boehm, hitherto pastor

[4] The writer himself examined the church records of the Reformed churches at Hanau and Hochstadt in August, 1898. Boehm was *not* born on November 25, 1683, but that day was the date of his baptism. The date of his birth is not given. It was most likely from three to five days earlier, according to the usual custom prevailing at that time. Note the dates in the case of Boehm's own children, in the next chapter, p. 8. The entry relating to John Philip Boehm's baptism reads, literally translated, as follows:

"In the village of Hochstadt, township of Hanau, Philippus Ludovicus Boehm, pro tempore pastor of this place, and Maria, his wife, brought a son to baptism on November 25, 1683. His name is 'Johannes Philipp.' Sponsors were: Mr. Johannes Hassenpflug, pro tempore praeceptor in the third Class [of the Latin school] at Hanau-on-the-Main, a brother-in-law."

of Kesselstadt, and his Reverence is also willing and has entered into an agreement with the congregation accordingly, he shall be transferred to that place, upon the ratification of the noble Lords."

During his second pastorate at Hochstadt, Boehm married a second time, on January 11, 1694, a widow, daughter of Jacob Bernes, then in Brazil. This union seems to have been very unhappy. There were frequent quarrels. Twice Boehm was cited before the Consistory because of his domestic troubles. At the second citation, in November, 1700, a reconciliation between him and his wife was effected before the Consistory, but in view of what had occurred it was considered more expedient to transfer Boehm to Rumpenheim on the Main, near Frankfort. This change was made in January, 1701.

Of his older sons the following facts are on record during this period. His son, John Daniel, matriculated at the university of Marburg on June 17, 1691. In May, 1694, Mr. Boehm requested assistance of the Consistory for his son, John Daniel, to prosecute his studies at Bremen. Six rixdollars were granted to him on May 23, 1694. On February 26, 1696, the father asked the Consistory to intercede, on behalf of his son, with the Consistory of Budingen, to give his son a pastorate. The request was granted. On June 12, 1705, John Daniel Boehm reported to the Hanau Consistory that he had accepted the position of Court preacher to the Count von Donau at Guntersblum, but he asked that if a vacancy should occur in his native land he be remembered.

In October, 1708, complaints were preferred against Mr. Boehm, Sr., to the Consistory of Hanau, by the officers of his congregation. As a result he was transferred from Rumpenheim to Wachenbuchen, a village but a few miles north of his former parish at Hochstadt. The transfer took place in February, 1709, but his ministry there was not of long duration. In 1712, he was stricken with the grey cataract on both eyes. As a result his congregation asked the Consistory, in April, 1713, for an assistant to their pastor. In answer to their request Candidate Roediger was sent to them. On June 18, 1713, a famous eye specialist, Dr. Hieronymus Siegfried of Langenselbolt, operated on his right eye. Five days later a severe sickness came upon him, as a result of which he was incapacitated for further work. He was, therefore, retired from the ministry, at his own request, towards the end of the year 1713, with the understanding that his successor pay him annually 15 fl. in money and five-eighths of a hundred weight of grain. To this, at Boehm's urgent request, ten florins were added from the funds of the Consistory. This arrangement continued till 1718, when Boehm petitioned the Consistory for an increase of his pension. His connection with Wachenbuchen was then severed and fifty florins annually were voted to him by the Consistory. In this petition, submitted by Boehm on July 20, he related at length his unfortunate experiences, dating from the year 1712. He also stated that at that time, July, 1718, he was 72 years of age.

His name occurs for the last time in the records of the Hanau Consistory on May 15, 1726, when he is mentioned as "the lately deceased pastor."

The older Boehm during his somewhat checkered career had evidently belonged to the church militant, and his son, John Philip, was destined to follow his footsteps.

CHAPTER II.

BOEHM AS SCHOOLMASTER AT WORMS AND LAMBSHEIM.

John Philip Boehm was born at Hochstadt, near Frankfort-on-the-Main, in the year 1683. On November 25, 1683, "Philippus Ludovicus Boehm, p.t., pastor of this place, and Maria his wife, brought a son to baptism, John Philip. Sponsors were Mr. John Hassenpflug, p.t., teacher of the third Class at Hanau-on-the-Main, a brother-in-law."

Nothing is known at present about the youth of John Philip Boehm, nor of the place where he received his education. It was not in the Latin school at Hanau, in which his brothers studied, nor at Bremen. The matriculation books at these places have been examined, but his name is not found in them.

The first trace of John Philip Boehm has come to light in the city of Worms.[5] In February, 1708, he was engaged as schoolmaster of the Reformed congregation there. When Boehm came to Worms the Reformed congregation in that city was of recent origin.

In the year 1689 Worms, together with many other cities along the Rhine, had been totally destroyed by the troops of King Louis XIV of France.[6] Till 1697, when the peace of Ryswick closed the war with France, Worms lay in ruins. Immediately afterwards energetic measures were taken for the rebuilding of the city. In order to encourage outsiders to help in restoring the city, certain privileges were granted to them. Thus the Reformed, who had worshipped at Neuhausen, a neighboring village, were invited to settle in Worms. On June 13, 1699, a formal agreement was drawn up between

---

[5] The documents relating to Boehm were found by the writer in the city archives of Worms, in the summer of 1897. All together, copies of thirty-two documents relating to Boehm were secured.

[6] A monograph on the destruction of Worms in 1689 appeared at Worms in 1889, entitled: *Die Zerstoerung der Stadt Worms im Jahre 1689*, von F. Soldan, 4 to, pp. 68, with twelve plates of pictures. From this book some of the facts noted in this paragraph are taken.

HOCHSTADT, THE BIRTHPLACE OF BOEHM

LAMBSHEIM, WHERE BOEHM WAS SCHOOLMASTER

the City Council and the Reformed congregation, by which Reformed services were permitted in Worms. By it the Reformed people were also allowed to build a church and a schoolhouse within the city, but not on the main street nor adjoining the market place, and in the suburbs a site for a cemetery was granted to them. The Reformed on their part had to promise that they would never seek public offices, but give their support to Lutheran candidates, nor demand more liberties than had already been granted to them. They were allowed to call their own ministers and schoolmasters, but these were to render an oath of allegiance to the magistrates and be subject to their jurisdiction. The Reformed agreed also to appeal to their co-religionists in other parts of the empire for funds to rebuild the city.

The first Reformed service in Worms was held June 25, 1699.[7] It was an open air service, conducted by the Rev. Prof. Gottfried Juengst, pastor and church councillor at Hanau. On January 1, 1700, the newly built Reformed church in Worms was dedicated by the first pastor of the congregation, the Rev. Henry Schmedes, Doctor of Theology, and formerly pastor of the Holy Ghost church in Heidelberg. When Boehm came to Worms in 1708, the Reformed pastor was the Rev. John Caspar Cruciger, who later on, as Electoral Councillor at Heidelberg, was instrumental in sending Schlatter to Pennsylvania.

During the first years of its existence, the Reformed congregation in Worms was small in number. According to a list, drawn up in 1714, it numbered at that time eighty-three members. The seal of the congregation fittingly represented its condition. It was a candle standing on a table, being lighted by a torch.

Boehm was not the first parochial teacher of the congregation. He was preceded in Worms by Jacob de Malade, a Huguenot, who resigned, as the pastor informs us in a long report, because he had become an adherent of pietism.

Before Boehm came to Worms he had been married to

---

[7] The statements regarding the Reformed church at Worms are based on the old church record of the congregation, preserved in Ms. in the city archives of Worms.

Anna Maria Stehler. Four children were born to them during their stay in Worms, as follows:

(1) Johanna Sabina, born May 2, baptized May 4, 1709. Sponsor: Sabina Cruciger (née Zwengelin) wife of the Rev. John Caspar Cruciger.

(2) Franciscus Ludovicus, born July 24, baptized July 26, 1711. Sponsors: Philip Lewis Boehm, pastor at Wachenbuchen near Hanau, the grandfather of the child and Franz Cæsar, citizen and merchant here.

(3) John Christopher, born May 4, 1713. Sponsor: John Christopher Erb, baker here.

John Christopher, son of John Philip Boehm, schoolmaster of the Reformed congregation here, died August 2, and was buried August 4, 1713.

(4) Anthony William, born April 27, baptized April 29, 1714. Sponsors: Anthony Wilkhaus, citizen and merchant, and his son William Wilkhaus.

Not only the third but also the second child must have died in infancy, because their names do not appear in later documents.

After Boehm had served six weeks on trial, he was formally elected as schoolmaster March 11, 1708. His salary was 100 gulden for the first year, and, if satisfactory, 100 rix-dollars[8] later on. The baptismal fees were to be his perquisites. His election took place not without considerable opposition, led by Christopher Schmidt, president of the consistory and the most influential member of the congregation. He had urged the election of another candidate, Matthias Dirl[9] of Kesselstadt. Failing in securing his election, he turned his displeasure against Boehm. As a result the life of Boehm in Worms was made unpleasant by several quarrels, in which he was involved by his enemy. We are perhaps not justified in calling Boehm quarrelsome, like his father, for he was apparently the innocent party in these quarrels, but he always fought with

[8] A German gulden was approximately 48 cents in American money. A rix-dollar varied in value in the different states, but it approximated one American dollar.

[9] The name is Dirl, not Diel, as formerly given, in articles of the writer on "John Philip Boehm," in the *Reformed Church Messenger* of May 19, 1898.

determination and ability for what he considered his rights. He was not a man to suffer injustice in silence. Hence we find numerous documents in the city archives at Worms, which show that Boehm was able to make a spirited defense when he was attacked.

The first quarrel arose about the perquisites of the schoolmaster. In March, 1710, Schmidt urged the election of a new sexton and proposed that the baptismal fees be given to him as a part of his salary. Failing in this, he urged that the baptismal fees be laid no more on the table in the church, but be carried into the house of the schoolmaster. When this suggestion also failed to meet with approval, he demanded that the fees be put into the alms fund. Although this demand was never made legal by a formal resolution of the consistory, Schmidt and his friends proceeded to enforce this regulation, which was naturally regarded by Boehm as a breach of the contract made with him.

When on May 17, 1711, a child of the pastor, Rev. Mr. Cruciger, was baptized in the church, and Mr. Fuchs, the sponsor of the child, laid half a gulden on the table for the schoolmaster, Bassermann, a deacon and friend of Schmidt, took the money and put it into the alms box. This action was repeated by Bassermann at a later occasion. Hence on Monday after Pentecost, 1711, Mr. Fuchs and fifteen other members of the congregation appeared before the consistory to complain and protest against such actions. One of the elders insisted that a resolution to that effect had been passed by the consistory, but others declared that this was not the case, there being no record of it in the minutes. Boehm was also present and demanded to know of Bassermann why he had kept back his salary for eleven weeks and finally had deducted a certain amount from it. Bassermann became very angry and abusive and would have struck Boehm in front of the church, if others had not interfered. On July 5, 1711, Basserman took again a baptismal fee and put it into the alms box, in spite of the protests of the pastor and the giver.

Unable to secure redress from the consistory, Boehm appealed to the City Council on July 6th, accompanying his complaint with the testimony of 48 members of the congregation, who declared that they were satisfied with Boehm and wished to leave the custom of the baptismal fees unchanged. On July 17th, the Council voted that matters be left in statu quo, until a final decision could be reached.

Schmidt was determined to disregard the action of the Council, or at least to interpret it in a way that suited his fancy. On August 2, he himself took the money that had been given at a baptism, although it was wrapped in paper with Boehm's name on it. The pastor protested and Boehm called his attention to the decision of the Council. Schmidt answered cooly that he understood the decision of Council to mean that everything should remain as he (Schmidt) had decided it. When Boehm declared that such was not the decision of the Council, Schmidt became so angry that he ran towards him, held his fist before Boehm's face, and called him a pedant and other worse names. Shortly afterwards Boehm appealed to the City Council, because his salary was again kept back by Bassermann. The Council ordered Bassermann to pay the salary, but he made all kinds of excuses and delayed payment. Another appeal of Boehm brought matters to a climax. The Council now insisted that the various parties come together and settle their differences. Finally, on November 2, 1711, a compromise was arranged in the presence of the Council. On the question of the fees the votes were equally divided. At the suggestion of one of the city magistrates, it was then decided to make the giving of baptismal fees optional, with which both parties were satisfied. The compromise contained a clause that Schmidt should deliver to the Consistory all church records, cash books, etc. This led to a new controversy between him and the majority of the Consistory, headed by the pastor, which was not concluded till April, 1714, when an agreement was signed. Thus the first controversy came to an end.

The second quarrel in which Boehm was involved had a cause even more trifling than the first. But, in spite of the insignificance of the issue, the congregation was deeply stirred over it.

Article fourteen of the constitution of the congregation prescribed: "Whereas the office of deacons includes the duty to provide for the Holy Supper, they shall from their own means procure the bread, and, baked in good time, hand it to the schoolmaster that he may cut it; and moreover, they shall see to it that the table be ready and, whenever the tankard becomes empty, they shall fill it".

On Sunday, August 5, 1714, the communion was to be celebrated. For that occasion Mr. Christopher Erb, a baker, had to provide the bread. On Saturday preceding he sent the bread, through a maid servant, to Boehm's house. His wife received it and put it into the cellar. When Boehm rose up early the next morning to cut this bread, he found it too brittle to be cut into little squares. As he did not know what to do, he opened the window, called the minister, who lived next door, and asked him what to do under the circumstances. The minister advised him to notify the deacons and secure if possible other bread.

Boehm then sent a notice to Erb, through his maid servant, telling him of the condition of the bread and asking him for another loaf of bread. When the servant returned, she brought a loaf, half as large as the first and just as brittle. In this extremity Boehm did not know what else to do but to cut up a loaf of rye bread which he had in his house. Meanwhile the time for the church services was approaching and Boehm proceeded, therefore, to make all other necessary preparations. Erb did not come to church till the bells were ringing and then it was too late to secure other bread. The rye bread was, therefore, actually used in the communion service, without offense to anybody, as Boehm claims. This harmless act of Boehm, made necessary by the carelessness of others, was the opportunity for which his enemies had waited to attack him.

On Wednesday, August 29th, 1714, after the midweek services, the deacons came to the minister and informed him that there would be a meeting of the Consistory, but they had the impudence to add, that his presence would not be required. Nor did they invite the elders, who were friendly to Boehm, to be present. The rest, four in number, Schmidt, Clementz, Schaum and Schertz, constituted themselves into a committee of investigation. Paper and ink were ordered to be brought over from the house of the schoolmaster, and then the investigation began. Erb was the first witness called. He was asked about the bread used at the last communion service.

Then the schoolmaster was called in to give testimony, of which also a record was made in a book. This was signed by the members of the consistory present. The peculiar thing about this investigation was, as Boehm remarks in a later appeal to the City Council, that it was begun by a man, who had not been inside of the church for nineteen months and had not taken part in a communion service for four years.

The report thus drawn up was circulated through the congregation, and when the members were sufficiently stirred up, the deacons asked the minister on Sunday, September 9th, to announce a congregational meeting after the services. In spite of all protests they insisted upon it, declaring that the members of the congregation demanded it. After the service the minister was asked to retire, which he did. Schmidt then read the report of the investigating committee. Schmidt had been careful to gather all his followers and they had been instructed what to do. A number of speeches were made after the reading of the report, in which the speakers demanded the dismissal of Boehm as schoolmaster. One of them went even so far as to declare that whoever would not vote for the dismissal could not be saved. But the supporters of Boehm did not remain silent under these accusations. They answered the harangues of his enemies. As a result a regular tumult arose, which caused many of the good members to leave the church. The rest brought the question to a vote, and, according to the statement of Boehm, counted even the votes of absent members, which they claimed had been sent in. Schmidt announced as the result of the vote, that the majority were in favor of the dismissal of the schoolmaster. This was denied by Boehm afterwards, on the ground that no definite number of votes had been announced and that after the meeting some of the elders went around in the congregation soliciting votes. But Schmidt claimed the victory and was determined to make the most of it.

On Tuesday, September 11, 1714, the consistory, or rather the faction of it hostile to Boehm, sent a delegation of four to Boehm's house, of whom deacon Schertz was the speaker. He announced to Boehm, in the name of the congregation, that he had been dismissed, and demanded that he vacate the schoolhouse within six weeks.

Boehm astonished them, however, by his cool answer. He replied: "In the first place I do not accept my dismissal from you. I demand that it be given to me in writing with the reason for such action stated in full. Moreover, I shall appeal to the City Council and lay the whole matter before them. You claim that you act in the name of the congregation. That I want to find out".

Mr. Clementz, one of the delegates, remarked: "God forbid, that we should tell you a lie". Boehm answered: "I do not say that, but I want to know whether this case has been properly laid before the congregation. In a word, I do not accept my dismissal in this way. I demand it in writing with the reasons attached to it". Clementz remonstrated that there was no occasion for that, the use of rye bread in the last communion was the main reason. "Very well", said Boehm, "let me have that black on white, that I can lay it before the Council". "Never mind", interrupted another, "we are on the way to the mayor to notify him of our decision". "Oh", said Boehm, "so you have dismissed me without the knowledge and consent of the Council". "What does that matter"? asked another delegate. "We shall see", replied Boehm. "Meanwhile I assure you, I shall not concern myself about this action during the next six weeks, but I shall continue my work, perhaps for more weeks than some of you like. Good bye".

The climax of the affair was reached on Wednesday, September 12th. In the morning of that day, Boehm went to the pastor to get the hymns for the evening service. The pastor informed him, that the deacons had waited on him and, in the name of the congregation, had asked him not to give the hymns to the schoolmaster. Boehm asked whether he (the pastor) would forbid him to lead the singing. He answered, no. Boehm then went into the church. When, after the ringing of the bells, he arose to read the Scriptures, as was customary, and had read only a few words, one of the members, Mr. Emrich, came up and told him, in the name of the congregation, to stop, as he was no longer their teacher. Boehm answered: "I am here at my place, which God and the church have entrusted to me, and I ask you to be quiet, so that I can fulfil my duty. I have not yet received my dismissal, nor do I accept it now". But the man shouted: "You are dismissed". Meanwhile another member, Mr. Sauerwein, had come up, closed the Bible and tried to take it away from him. But Boehm took the Bible with both of his hands and held it up. The excitement became now general, ending in great confusion. During the tumult an old woman fainted and had to be carried out of the church. She was taken to the parsonage, where she died during the night.

Two days afterwards, September 14th, Boehm laid the whole case before the City Council. He received a favorable decision, that he should be retained in his office. As the consistory took no notice of this decision, Boehm wrote a lengthy report, entitled "Species Facti", which he submitted to the Council on the 12th of October, demanding at the same time that his opponents be compelled to state their reasons for his dismissal in full, so that he might answer them. After repeated requests of Boehm and repeated decrees of the Council, the charges were finally produced, laid before the Council and sent to Boehm for answer.

On November 14, 1714, Boehm answered the charges in full. His opponents had tried first to prove that as a consistory they had a right to dismiss their preacher and schoolmaster, if their life and conduct prove offensive. Boehm answered their claim with the statement that, if the Council had the privilege of confirming the election of pastor and schoolmaster, they could not be dismissed without its approval. He then took up the charges preferred against him and answered them seriatim:

1. They charged Boehm that three years before he had forcibly entered the church and taken money out of the alms box. Boehm answered, that not he but his friends had opened the alms box to take the money that had been given to him. It had, however, been restored afterwards.

2. The fact that he substituted rye bread at the communion service, was not due to his fault, but to the neglect of Mr. Erb.

3. They claimed that he was a poor teacher and that his school was becoming smaller every day. To this Boehm answered that this was not his fault, but was rather due to his enemies, who had taken their children out of his school and had influenced others to do the same. Yet he claimed that

his school was stronger than at the time of his predecessor, for he had forty children of good citizens in it.

4. They charged him with discontinuing his private instruction. Boehm replied that this was his private affair, in which he could do as he pleased. He had not been required by his call to hold these private instructions, and now they could not compel him to continue them.

5. They objected to the fact that he had admitted Jewish children into his school. Boehm answered that his enemies ought to be ashamed to make such a complaint. They ought rather be glad that they were coming, which they would certainly be, if they were not actuated by jealousy, being afraid that he might earn some extra money.

6. They charged that Boehm had gotten into a lawsuit. He answered that he was sorry for that. However, it was not his doing, but had been caused by some who had slandered him. Besides, the case had been settled.

7. They complained about his indistinct reading and speaking. Boehm answered that this was a peculiar charge to make now after six years, when in the beginning of his service they had given him a trial of six weeks, without finding any fault with him then.

8. Lastly they charged that the favorable decision of the Council had been secured by "sneaky" conduct. Boehm replied curtly that that charge was too mean to answer.

The case was hanging fire before the Council for more than a year. Boehm appealed to them time and again for a speedy termination, without result. Schmidt had evidently his friends in the Council, through whom favorable action was prevented. Finally Boehm became tired of waiting and fighting for his rights. Accordingly he handed in his resignation to take effect on November 22, 1715. After leaving Worms he went to Lambsheim, a neighboring town, whence he continued to implore the Council of Worms for a favorable decision. But, as far as the records go, it was never given.[10]

Lambsheim is a little town, south-west of Worms, near

[10] The story of Boehm's life in Worms was first given by the writer in a series of three articles on "John Philip Boehm," which appeared in the *Reformed Church Messenger,* May 12, 19, 26, 1898.

Frankenthal. There Boehm served also in the capacity of Reformed schoolmaster. One of his fellow-citizens there was Matthias Baumann, who came to Pennsylvania about 1718 and started in Oley, Pennsylvania, the sect of the New Born. Boehm, who probably knew him in Lambsheim, came in contact with him at Oley.

In the town records of Lambsheim[11] Boehm's name appears repeatedly. The tax records show that his salary as schoolmaster for the year 1717 was 145 fl., on which he paid 46 Kreutzer and four Heller[11a] as tax. In 1718, the salary is given as 150 fl., on which he paid a tax of 42 Kreutzer. The position which Boehm held in the community is seen by the fact that in 1718 fifty citizens were assessed on a larger sum

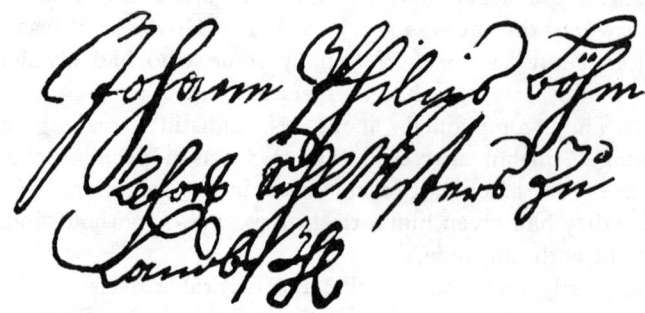

SIGNATURE OF BOEHM AS SCHOOLMASTER AT LAMBSHEIM.

than Boehm, while 116 citizens were assessed on a smaller income than he.

In 1718, some trouble arose over the distribution of the community lands belonging to the town. On May 12, 1718, Boehm addressed a complaint to the Electoral "Ober-Amt" at Neustadt, claiming that the heathlands which were his share had been taken away from him and given to others who were not even citizens. Having married a daughter of a citizen and being a citizen himself, who paid his taxes regularly, he petitioned that he be treated like other citizens.

[11] These records were examined by the writer in August, 1898.
[11a] A Kreutzer is one-fifth, a Heller one-eighth of a cent; a German florin (fl.) about 48 cents.

The petition of Boehm, which the town council of Lambsheim turned over to the writer at the time of his visit there in 1898,[12] is interesting enough to be inserted in full:

LETTER OF JOHN PHILIP BOEHM.

To the Esteemed Upper Department [*at Neustadt*]:

I cannot forbear addressing to your Most Noble and Gracious Lordships the following complaint, namely, that two years ago the so-called heath-rights were renewed, which, according to ancient custom, had been distributed in such a way that a citizen with a family received three, but one without a family two lots because of his citizenship. Now for many years ministers as well as schoolmasters had received equal shares with the other citizens, which appears from the indisputable fact that the Rev. Moock, who has been pastor here thirty or more years ago, had cleared vineyards out of these heath-lots. Nevertheless, in the renewal of these lots two years ago, ministers and schoolmasters were deprived of their lots and they were given to others, even to those who were mere residents. But inasmuch as I have settled here with my family and have married a daughter of a citizen here, and was at once held to a strict payment of my taxes as a citizen, which, according to the records, were paid at once by me, I have repeatedly complained about this, inquiring why that which was given to others was not accorded to me. I stated, moreover, that as a citizen I had the same rights as others, because I had paid assessments on 150 fl. and had not been passed over with any taxes. But I was always answered by the Assistant Mayor, that the town did not owe this to the clericals. It was under no compulsory service [to the clericals], and I was only a schoolmaster. This state of affairs has continued until now, when on the 6th of this month the heath-rights were again allotted and were granted even to those who had not paid their citizens' tax.

I again appealed to the town council, which also promised to assist me. But, owing to the Assistant Mayor, they were

[12] It is now, together with the second petition of May 28, 1718, and the joint petition of May 29th, in possession of the Rev. Prof. J. I. Good, D.D.

unable to help me in my just request. He, according to report, answered that I was a mere schoolmaster and that, if they would accede to the demands of every minister and schoolmaster, they would have to give them half of the heath. In view of this I may justly complain to the highly esteemed Upper Department.

My most submissive request to your noble and gracious Lordships is, therefore, to the effect, that you will urgently command the burgomasters, without regard to the Assistant Mayor, because of the reasons given above, that they will in future regard me in all things as equal to the other citizens, and with respect to my office as schoolmaster will treat me like the Catholic schoolmaster, inasmuch as I have always been willing to pay my dues to the manor, as all know who enter the mayor's office, and I am not found on any lists of arrears. I, therefore, live in expectation of your very gracious and favorable answer.

Highly Esteemed and Gracious Lordships of the Upper Department,

Your most submissive Servant,
JOHANN PHILIPS BOEHM,
Reformed Schoolmaster.

One statement of this petition deserves special notice. It is the reference to the fact that Boehm had married the daughter of a citizen of Lambsheim. In view of the fact that in Pennsylvania the name of his father-in-law appears as Philip Scherer, while his wife's name in Worms was Anna Maria Stehler, we are forced to the conclusion, that his first wife had died and that he had married a second wife, whose name was Anna Maria Scherer. In corroboration of this it may be mentioned that the name Philip Scherer appears among the citizens of Lambsheim at that time. Unfortunately the church records of Lambsheim covering that period are lost.

On May 14, 1718, the Electoral government ordered that ministers and schoolmasters in matters of public lands be treated like other citizens. When the town authorities did not comply with this decision at once, Boehm addressed a second petition to the government on May 28, 1718, in which he repeated the statement that for two years the assistant mayor had withheld the heath lands from the ministers as well as the schoolmasters. On the following day the Catholic and Reformed pastors as well as the Catholic schoolmaster joined Boehm in a common petition, in which they notified the government that its decision of May 14th had been ignored by the Council. In reply the government decreed that, unless the Council complied with the decree within eight days its members would be fined ten rix-dollars. Then the Council yielded and accorded to ministers and schoolmasters their rights as citizens.

The last reference to Boehm in Lambsheim occurs on April 6, 1720. Shortly afterwards he must have left Lambsheim and his native land, for in that very year 1720 he made his appearance in Pennsylvania.

CHAPTER III.

THE ORDINATION OF BOEHM.

There can be no doubt that Boehm arrived in Pennsylvania in the year 1720. The appeal to the Classis of Amsterdam, made by the Pennsylvania churches in July 1728, states definitely: "Indeed, as early as the year 1720, there came over to us John Philips Boehm". This is supported by other statements. When the appeal was made in 1728, Boehm, we are told, had served as Reader for five years and as Pastor for three years, which carries us back to the year 1720. Moreover, in January 1739, Boehm stated that he had been in this country for eighteen years. This too points back to the year 1720. The question arises whether the date can be determined still more exactly. This seems indeed to be the case. An examination of the "American Weekly Mercury" for the year 1720 shows that it announces for that year the arrival of but one ship with Palatines in the harbor of Philadelphia. On September 1, 1720, the "Mercury" states: "On the 30 [arrived] the ship Laurel, John Coppel [captain], from Liverpoole and Cork with 240 odd Palatine Passengers come here to settle".[13] This is the first ship carrying Palatines noticed in the "Mercury". It is therefore probable that John Philip Boehm arrived at Philadelphia on August 30, 1720, with the ship "Laurel", from Liverpool.

EARLIEST REFORMED SETTLERS.

When Boehm arrived in Pennsylvania in 1720, there must have been a considerable number of German Reformed people in the province. It will be of interest to gather together the scattered references to these earliest Reformed settlers.

Among the earliest of these settlers was perhaps Henry

---

[13] See Diffenderffer, *German Immigration into Pennsylvania*, Lancaster, 1900, p. 202.

Frey, who settled in Germantown about 1680.[14] Rev. H. M. Muhlenberg refers to him in 1754. He writes: "In the first period [of immigration] from 1680 to 1708, a few arrived by chance, among whom was one, named Henrich Frey, whose wife is said to be still living. He arrived about the year 1680".[15] In 1689, Henry Frey occupied lot No. 18 in Germantown, on the west side of Main street.[16] In 1713, Henry Frey took up 200 acres of land at Skippack, on which he paid quitrent for twelve years on January 14, 1725.[17] Conrad Frey, perhaps a son, was a member of the Goshenhoppen Reformed Church in 1740.[18]

There is said to be a tradition in the Reiff family that their ancestor, Hans Georg Reiff, arrived in Pennsylvania "before Penn set up his government".[19] In 1730, Hans Georg Reiff was a member of the Reformed Church at Skippack.[20]

In 1683, Isaac Dilbeck, later one of the leading members of the Reformed Church at Whitemarsh, came with Francis Daniel Pastorius, the founder of Germantown. In an interesting letter of Pastorius, which the writer had the good fortune to find in the city library of Zurich, Switzerland, Pastorius writes: "Among my servants I have such as hold to the Roman, to the Lutheran, to the Calvinistic, to the Anabaptist and to the Anglican Church, but only one Quaker".[21] The names of these servants are given by Pastorius in his *Beehive,* in which he writes: "I, with Jacob Shoemaker (who came with me from Mentz), George Wertmüller, Isaac Dilbeck, his wife Marieke and his two boys Abraham and Jacob, Thomas Gasper, Conrad Backer (alias Rutter) and an English maid, called Frances Simson, went on board of a ship, which had the name America (the captain whereof was Joseph Wasey) and being

---

[14] According to Mr. Dotterer, Henry Frey came to Pennsylvania in 1675. On what authority this date rests is not stated. See *Perkiomen Region,* II, 122. The claim that Frey was Reformed is made with much reservation. It is not at all certain.

[15] See *Hallesche Nachrichten,* new ed., Vol. II, p. 194.

[16] See Keyser, *History of Old Germantown,* Vol. I, p. 40.

[17] See *Perkiomen Region,* Vol. I, p. 53.

[18] See *Perkiomen Region,* Vol. III, p. 112.

[19] Cited by Mr. Dotterer in *Historical Notes,* Vol. I, p. 14.

[20] See *Historical Notes* of Dotterer, Vol. I, p. 103.

[21] See Pennypacker's *Settlement of Germantown,* p. 136.

gone the 6th of June [1683] from Gravesand, we arrived the 7th ditto at Deal and left England the 10th of the said month of June".[22] They reached Philadelphia August 20, 1683. On May 27, 1686, Pastorius conveyed to Dilbeck a lot of twenty five acres in Germantown. Dilbeck was naturalized May 7, 1691. In 1696, he sold his lot in Germantown, buying in 1700 a large farm of 500 acres in Whitemarsh township.[23] In 1710, he was a member and deacon of the Dutch Reformed congregation of Dominie Paulus Van Vlecq at Whitemarsh.

Regarding the year 1684 we have an interesting statement in a letter, written from Germantown on February 12, 1684: It reads: "There are in Pennsylvania (besides ourselves) Lutherans and Reformed. The former have two preachers, but their fruits bear testimony that they are teachers without spirit. In New Castle most of the inhabitants are Hollanders. The Reformed have at present no preacher there. The Papists at that place have no congregation".[24]

This statement that, besides the sect people, there were Lutherans and Reformed in the province in 1684, is the first direct evidence which we have that the Reformed were numerous enough to call for a definite reference to them. As to the Reformed in New Castle we know that this refers to the Dutch Reformed congregation there, which was organized in 1654 by Rev. John Theodore Polhemus.[25]

Another early settler of Germantown was William De Wees, who came to America about 1689. On May 29, 1689, Wilhelmina Dewees, his sister, was married in the Dutch Reformed church of New York to Nicholas Rittenhouse. On March 1, 1700, Gerrit Hendricks De Wees (possibly his father) bought a lot of land on Main street, in Germantown, which on February 10, 1703, passed into the possession of William De Wees. In 1704, De Wees was chosen sheriff and in 1706 member of the Council of Germantown. In 1710, he erected the second paper mill in Pennsylvania, on the west side of the

---

[22] See Prof. Learned's *Pastorius*, p. 111.
[23] See Dotterer in *Historical Notes*, p. 15f.
[24] Letter quoted by Dr. Dubbs, in *Reformed Church in Pennsylvania*, p. 63.
[25] See Corwin, *Manual of the Reformed Church in America*, fourth ed., pp. 663, 991.

Wissahickon, in that part of Germantown, called Crefeld. In the same year 1710, he was made deacon of the Dutch Reformed congregation of Whitemarsh. When Boehm organized his congregation at Whitemarsh, William De Wees became one of the elders, in whose house Boehm held his services at Whitemarsh.[26]

Cornelius De Wees and Garret De Wees, relatives (possibly brothers) of William De Wees, also located at or near Germantown. On May 29, 1710, Cornelius De Wees and his wife Margaret Koster brought their son John to Dominie Paulus Van Vlecq for baptism at Skippack.

In 1698, Evert ten Heuven (In De Haven) came from Mühlheim on the Ruhr. On June 4, 1710, he was installed Junior elder of the Dutch Reformed congregation at Whitemarsh. His wife, Elizabeth Schipbouwer, was also a member of that congregation. Gerhart In de Haven doubtless a son, was in 1730 elder of the German Reformed congregation at Skippack. Herman ten Heuven (a brother of the last) and Annecken Op den Graf were married on February 12, 1711, by Dominie Van Vlecq at Whitemarsh.[27]

As early as 1699, Hendrick Pannebecker lived in Germantown, for he was married there in that year to Eva, the daughter of Hans Peter Umstatt. In 1702, he settled at Skippack. On May 29, 1710, they brought to Dominie Van Vlecq at Skippack three children for baptism, Adolf, Martha and Peter. A relative, Frederick Pannebecker, was in 1736 member of the New Goshenhoppen Reformed Church.[28]

On December 23, 1701, Hans Hendrick Meels bought half a lot of land, on Main street in Germantown. In the same year he was chosen Recorder of Germantown. On June 4, 1710, he was installed Senior elder of the Reformed congregation of Whitemarsh.[29]

Of the year 1701 we have Lutheran testimony regarding the Reformed people in the province. On August 1, 1701, Rev.

---

[26] For a sketch of William Dewees see Dotterer's *History of the Church at Market Square, Germantown*, in *Historical Notes*, pp. 23-25.

[27] See Dotterer, *Historical Notes*, p. 25.

[28] See the *Life of Hendrick Pannebecker, 1674-1754*, by Hon. Samuel W. Pennypacker, Philadelphia, 1894.

[29] See Dotterer, *Historical Notes*, p. 26.

Justus Falckner wrote to Rev. Henry Muhlen in Holstein, Germany:

"According to their confession the local Protestants, as they are comprehended under that name in the European Roman Empire, are either Evangelical Lutherans or of the Presbyterian and Calvinistic Church. And as the Protestant church is here also divided into three nations, so there are here an English Protestant church and a Swedish Protestant Lutheran church, and also persons of the German nation of the Evangelical Lutheran and Reformed churches. About these more at another time".[30]

In 1702, John Rebenstock came to Germantown. He owned lot No. 2, containing two hundred acres, in the section of Germantown called Sommerhausen. In 1711, he was a member of Dominie Van Vlecq's Whitemarsh congregation. In 1728, he was an officer of Boehm's Whitemarsh church.[31]

In the same year 1702 arrived Michael Renberg, with his sons Dirck and Wilhelm, from Mühlheim on the Ruhr. On November 3, 1711, William Renberg and Jannetye Van Sandt were married by Dominie Van Vlecq. Dirck Renberg and his wife Stijntje (Christina) Hendricks had their son Jan baptized by pastor Van Vlecq on May 29, 1710. Another child of theirs, Gertruy, was baptized by Van Vlecq on May 25, 1712.[32]

Another person who arrived in Germantown in 1702 was Peter Bon. On May 29, 1710, Pieter Bon and Elizabeth Op de Graf, brought a daughter to Dominie Van Vlecq for baptism at Skippack. On April 1, 1711, Pieter Bon, widower of Elizabeth Op de Graf, and Gerretye Jansen were married by the Dutch Dominie.[33]

On June 4, 1710, Dominie Paulus Van Vlecq organized a Reformed Church at Whitemarsh, installing on that day the

---

[30] Quoted in part by Dr. Schmauk in his *History of the Lutheran Church in Pennsylvania*, p. 128.

[31] See Dotterer, *Historical Notes*, p. 26.

[32] Pennypacker, *Settlement of Germantown*, p. 191; and *Journal of Presbyterian Historical Society*, Vol. I, pp. 122, 128.

[33] Pennypacker, *Germantown*, p. 191; *Journal of Presbyterian Hist. Society*, Vol. I, pp. 122, 124.

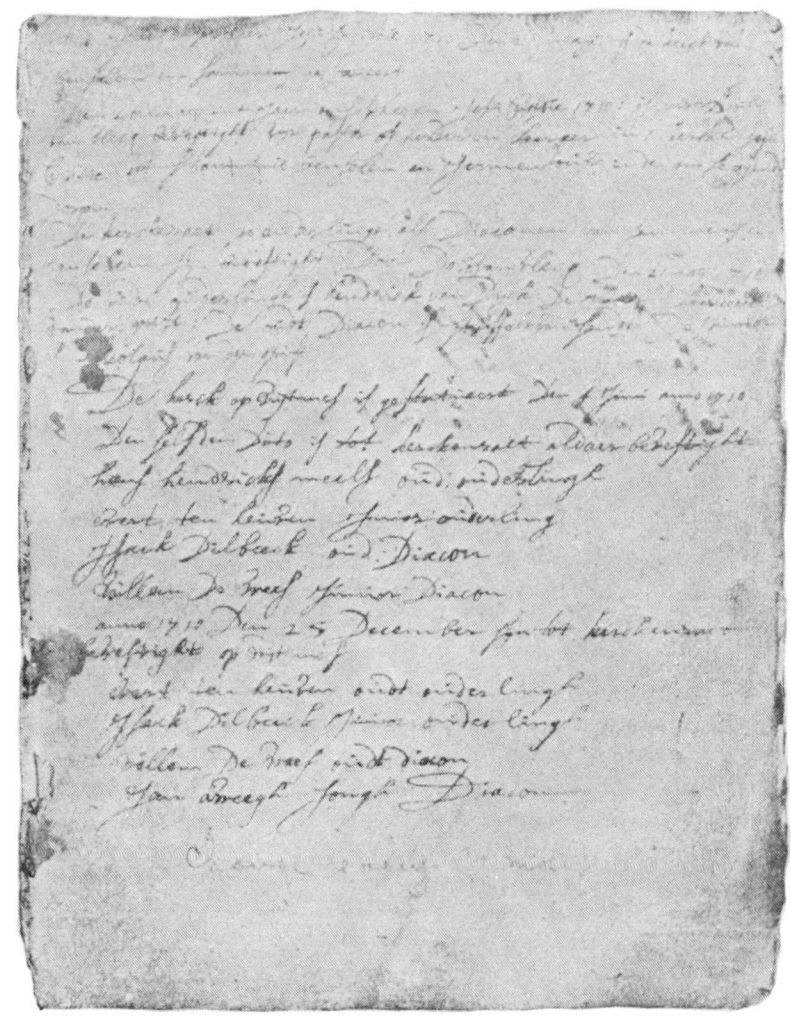

FIRST PAGE OF NESHAMINY AND BENSALEM RECORD, THE OLDEST (DUTCH) REFORMED RECORD IN PENNSYLVANIA, RECORDING ORGANIZATION OF WHITEMARSH CHURCH, JUNE 4, 1710
(*By Courtesy of Presbyterian Historical Society*)

following elders and deacons: Hans Hendrick Meels and Evert ten Heuven as elders, Isaac Dilbeck and William De Wees as deacons. The congregation at Whitemarsh consisted in 1710 of the following members:[34]

Hans Hendrick Meels, Evert ten Heuven, Isaac Dilbeck, William De Wees, Jan Aweeg, Johannes Yodder, Antonie Gerckes, Johannes Revenstock, Gertruy Rembergh, Elisabet Schipbouwer, wife of E. ten Heuven, Marritye Bloemers, wife of I. Dilbeck, Catrina Meels, wife of W. De Wees, Gertruy Aweeg, Anneken Barents, wife of J. Pieterse, Maria Selle, wife of G. ten Heuven. On December 25, 1710, were received by profession: Sebastian Bartels and his wife Marytye Hendricks, and Kaspar Staels. On March 31, 1711, were received: Elsye Schol, Sibilla Revenstock, wife of Hendrick Tibben and Margriet Bon, wife of Kasper Staels.

These twenty-one Reformed church members at Whitemarsh were among the earliest Reformed settlers in the province.

To these members should be added Gabriel Schuler. In September, 1711, Gabriel Schuler and Margriet Aweegh were married by Dominie Van Vlecq. On September 28, 1734, he paid quitrent on one hundred acres of land in Skippack, for sixteen years in full. Hence he must have settled there as early as 1718. In 1728, Gabriel Schuler was one of the officers of Boehm's congregation at Skippack.

A fact worthy of special note and emphasis is that among these people who belonged to Van Vlecq's Whitemarsh congregation in 1710, John Philip Boehm found the nucleus for his congregations in 1725. Isaac Dilbeck, William De Wees and John Rebenstock were the three most prominent members of Boehm's Whitemarsh congregation, while Gerhart ten Heuven and Gabriel Schuler became the two leading members in the Skippack congregation.

Two other early Reformed settlers deserve to be mentioned:

---

[34] The church record of Van Vlecq was published by the writer in the *Journal of the Presbyterian Historical Society*, Vol. I, pp. 118-134.

On January 15, 1718, Peter Wents (Wentz)[35] paid quitrent on one hundred acres for ten years and on fifty acres for fourteen years, located near Skippack. Hence he must have settled there as early as 1704. In 1730, Peter Wentz was a member of the Skippack Reformed church, an adherent of Rev. George Michael Weiss. Members of the Wentz family were among the founders of Wentz's church in Worcester township, the successor of the old Skippack church.

In 1719, John Lefeber took up 500 acres of land in Worcester township, for which he paid quitrent on February 6, 1734, for fifteen years.[36] John Lefeber was one of the officers of Boehm's congregation at Skippack in 1728. In 1730, he sided with Rev. G. M. Weiss.

Toward the close of the second decade of the eighteenth century immigrants from Germany had become so numerous that they attracted the attention of the government. On September 7, 1717, Governor William Keith reported to the Provincial Council, "that great numbers of foreigners from Germany, strangers to our Languages and Constitutions, having lately been imported into this Province daily dispersed themselves immediately after Landing, without producing any Certificates from whence they came and what they were". The

---

[35] Peter Wentz was an extensive landowner. April 11, 1711, Thomas Fairman, of Shackamaxon, sold 100 acres in Bristol, Phila. Co., to Peter Wentz, of Chestnut Hill, Germantown. In 1713 he signed petition for Skippack road. August 11, 1715, William Willis sold to Peter Wentz 250 acres in Bristol township for £85. His will is dated June 7, 1745. It was probated December 5, 1749. His wife's name was Elizabeth. Their children were: (1) Jacob, married, Elizabeth; (2) Peter, born November 19, 1719; died Sept. 13, 1793; married Rosanna; (3) Philip, born Oct. 1, 1722; died Dec. 30, 1803; married Appolonia Hartman; (4) Abraham, died about 1781; married Mary Wentz; (5) Catharine, died 1745; married (a) Henry Snyder, (b) Simon Hurdy Haker. Peter Wentz, Sr., his wife, his children and grandchildren to the number of 36, are buried in the cemetery near Skippackville. Peter Wentz, Jr., and Philip Wentz were among the trustees of the Wentz Reformed Church property in Worcester township, when that was acquired in January, 1762. See "Early History of Wentz's Reformed Church," in *Journal of Presb. Hist. Soc.*, Vol. III, pp. 332-346.

[36] See "Payments for Land in Perkiomen County" in Dotterer's *Perkiomen Region*, Vol. I, p. 104.

Council ordered that no vessel be admitted to entry, "until the master shall first give an exact List of all their passengers imported by them".[37] Never had a government scare more beneficial results, for to it we owe the preservation of more than thirty thousand names of immigrants, who entered the harbor of Philadelphia from 1727-1775.

The year 1710 is named as the beginning of a larger influx of Reformed settlers, in the appeal of Boehm's congregations, sent to Holland in 1728. They write:

"In this widely extended region, Pennsylvania, where the first settlers bearing the name of Christians were Quakers, and whither men of all sorts of sentiments have come, about eighteen years ago [1710] there came from time to time here and there, widely separated from one another, some of the Reformed faith, from different parts of Germany and other places, and also some few from the neighboring Provinces of New York and New Jersey".

Regarding the religious condition of these earliest arrivals the same writers continue:

"These, having in time grown to a number, in order not to fall into the errors of those among whom they dwelt, stirred up and encouraged each other to hold religious meetings on the Lord's day, etc., according to the doctrine and order of the Reformed Church, so far as it was known to them".

A report regarding the Reformed Church of Pennsylvania, printed in Holland in 1731, refers to this earliest period as follows:

"The German Palatines migrating from their own country to Pennsylvania were unable to provide themselves with ministers. Finding no religious worship many, attracted by the good morals and blameless conduct of the Quakers, joined themselves to them, preferring their worship to none".

Rev. Jedidiah Andrews, pastor of the old Buttonwood Presbyterian Church in Philadelphia, writes to a friend in Boston, under date October 14, 1730. He also throws light on the religious condition of the earliest Reformed settlers. He writes:

"There is besides, in this Province, a vast number of Pala-

---

[37] See *Colonial Records,* First Series, Vol. III, p. 29.

tines, and they come in still, every year. Those who have come of late years, are, mostly Presbyt'n, or as they call themselves, Reformed . . . they did use to come to me for baptism for their children, and many have joined with us in the other sacram't".[38]

This statement of Rev. Mr. Andrews is corroborated by Boehm's report of 1744, in which he writes: "Formerly, when there were no Reformed services in this country, the Reformed people at Falckner Schwam, Schipbach and Witmarsh came together and when they took communion it was with the Presbyterians in Philadelphia, up to the year 1725".

When John Philip Boehm arrived in Pennsylvania in 1720, and settled in the Perkiomen valley, his Reformed neighbors persuaded him, "shortly after his arrival", to hold religious services for them, in which he acted as their reader. Thus he "maintained the ministry of the Word, to the best of his ability, and to the great satisfaction of the people, for five years, without any compensation".

When in 1725 the number of Reformed settlers in the Perkiomen valley had grown to fifty men, they urged upon Boehm the necessity of assuming the office of minister among them, as there was apparently no prospect of securing the services of a regularly ordained pastor. Boehm objected at first strenuously, interposing to their arguments the plea that his family needed his services. But, as his friends continued to urge him, offering to support him with voluntary contributions to the best of their ability, and pleading with tears in their eyes, that he could not justify his refusal before God, he felt constrained to yield to their entreaties. The urgent need as represented by the delegates and their own earnest plea are recorded vividly in Boehm's report of 1744. He then wrote: "Accordingly they resolved once more urgently to request me, although for full five years I had declined to do so that I would become their pastor. This was so touchingly represented to

---

[38] The letter of Rev. Mr. Andrews was first printed in *Hazard's Register*, Vol. XV, p. 200f. Rev. Jedidiah Andrews was pastor of the Old Buttonwood Presbyterian Church (built 1704, enlarged 1729) from his arrival in Philadelphia in the fall of 1698 to his death in 1747.

me by two of their number thereunto commissioned,[38a] that our hearts melted together in tears, and in the name of all the people it was pressed upon my conscience whether I had the courage to answer for it at the last judgment, if I should leave them thus without help and allow so many souls to remain scattered among all kinds of sects, of which this country is filled. I thought indeed that it would be better for me if I could escape this yoke and support my family with my work and agriculture, but I was convinced by my conscience that I could not do otherwise. I allowed myself therefore to be persuaded to this work".

The first act of the new pastor was to draw up a constitution, which he read before his people and caused them to subscribe individually. The charge was then (in 1725) divided into three congregations, one at Falkner Swamp, the second at Skippack and the third at Whitemarsh. As soon as the congregations were constituted, Boehm was elected as pastor by each one of them. A regular call was issued to him, which he accepted. Thus he "began the ministry of the Lord in His name". After preaching a few times to his congregations, the Lord's Supper was celebrated. At Falkner Swamp forty members communed on October 15, 1725, at Skippack thirty-seven members in November, 1725, and at Whitemarsh twenty-four members on December 23, 1725. These services were the beginning of regular Reformed worship in Pennsylvania.

But hardly had this auspicious beginning been made, when all future progress was blocked, at least temporarily, by an important event. It was the arrival of the first ordained Reformed minister in Pennsylvania.

REV. GEORGE MICHAEL WEISS.

On September 21, 1727, there appeared in the Court House at Philadelphia the Rev. George Michael Weiss at the head of a colony of one hundred and nine Palatines, who together with their families numbering about four hundred persons, had come with the ship "William and Sarah", Captain William Hill, from Rotterdam. They were the first immi-

---

[38a] One of the men was certainly Henry Antes, as we know from Boehm's book of 1742. The other was most likely William DeWees.

grants to sign the oath of allegiance to the English king, George II.[39]

Mr. Weiss had in his possession a Latin certificate from the Upper Consistory of Heidelberg, dated Heidelberg, May 1, 1727, which showed that planning "with some of his fellow-citizens and other friends well known to him, to undertake a journey to the parts of the world across the sea", he had petitioned the Consistory for ordination and had secured the same, so that he might be fully qualified to minister to the spiritual needs of his countrymen in Pennsylvania.[40]

Judging from Boehm's report of 1744, the real leader of the colony was Frederick Hillegas, who with his two brothers had been a resident of Pennsylvania and who had evidently gone back to Germany to organize this colony. This inter-

SIGNATURE OF REV. G. M. WEISS.

pretation gives full significance to the words of Boehm: "After that time Frederick Hillegas arrived in this country with a companion. He had also two brothers, called Peter and Michael, residing at Philadelphia, but he himself resided at New Goshenhoppen. He brought with him the well known Mr. George Michael Weiss, a youthful preacher . . ., whom he sought to force in a violent manner and in a shameful way into all my congregations here".

Weiss at once proceeded to establish himself as the chief Reformed minister of the province. He visited the various

[39] Rupp's, *Thirty Thousand Names of Immigrants*, Philadelphia, 1880, p. 49; *Pennsylvania Archives*, Second Series, Vol. XVII, p. 7.

[40] Weiss placed a transcript of this certificate into the old church record of the Catskill Reformed Church, N. Y., from which the writer copied it recently.

Reformed settlements and organized the Reformed people there into regular congregations. Thus he visited Goshenhoppen and administered the Lord's Supper there on October 12, 1727. This is the first date in the history of that congregation. A week later, on October 19th, he preached at Skippack, and on the next Sunday, October 26th, at Philadelphia. In Philadelphia a regular organization was effected before the close of the year 1727. "In the year of our Lord one thousand seven hundred and twenty-seven, they formed themselves into a religious society, as near as they could upon the model of the German Reformed Church, and they unanimously chose to themselves George Michael Weitzius (alias Weiss) in the bill named for their pastor . . . Peter Lecolie, Johan Wilhelm Röhrig, Hendrick Weller, and Geo. Peter Hillegas were then elected church wardens or elders for the German Reformed Church of Philadelphia".[41] In the same year 1727 the congregation of Germantown was organized by Weiss. Shortly afterwards Weiss visited Oley, where he preached and baptized children, among them even some Indian children. This is undoubtedly one of the earliest Indian baptisms in Pennsylvania on record.

But Weiss was not satisfied with simply occupying new fields. When he heard that Boehm, a farmer and layman, was preaching to various Reformed congregations, he at once declared his work illegal. Wherever he preached he notified the people that Boehm was "an incompetent preacher whom he did not regard fit to administer the sacraments". He also invaded the congregations of Boehm, in order to convince his people that he had no right to persist in his unlawful ministry. On October 2, 1727, he wrote a letter to Hans George Schwab, one of his traveling companions on his journey across the ocean. He, with some of his friends, had settled in the Conestoga valley. Weiss informed him that he was ready to hold a communion service in the Conestoga region and he asked that he be notified as to the time when and the place where such service could be held. In the same letter he also warned the people of Conestoga against Boehm, telling them

---

[41] See "Papers in the Reiff Case, 1730-1749," printed by Prof. Jos. H. Dubbs, in the *Reformed Quarterly Review*, Vol. XV, (1893), p. 60.

that he could not recognize him as a Reformed teacher and preacher, until he had submitted to an examination and had been regularly ordained, which, however, he declared, "he will never be able to do".

Not satisfied with this, Weiss went even a step farther. In order to compel Boehm to desist from his ministry, he summoned him, on November 28, 1727, to appear in the manse of the Presbyterian minister of Philadelphia, the Rev. Jedidiah Andrews, that he might be examined as to his qualifications. As Weiss had no legal power to issue such a summons, Boehm paid no attention to it.

The most serious clash between the two men occurred at Skippack. With the aid of his friends Weiss organized a separate congregation there. When he preached there February 11, 1728, he brought with him some of his adherents from Philadelphia, Peter and Michael Hillegas and Michael Schmidt, "who persuaded the people to the utmost of their power to give me up, and subscribe an annual salary for Mr. Weiss. This was done by many whose names are also found on my voluntary subscription list". The result was that Boehm was compelled to serve those who were faithful to him at Skippack without any salary.

An open break occurred on March 10, 1728, when Weiss with his Philadelphia adherents came to Skippack on a Sunday when Boehm was to preach there. The Philadelphians then expelled Boehm from his usual meeting place, the private house of Jacob Reiff. By this act Boehm was compelled to meet with his faithful friends in other houses here and there. Reiff was also persuaded by the opponents of Boehm to secure in his name a deed to the land, on which Boehm and his elders had begun to build a little log church. This church, the first Reformed church in Pennsylvania, was dedicated on June 22, 1729, by Weiss and his followers. The separate organization of Weiss's friends at Skippack was completed by the election of a consistory. The new elders were: Wendel Keiber, Gerhart In de Haven, Christopher Schmidt and Hans George Reiff.[42]

---

[42] See letter of the followers of Weiss at Skippack, dated May 10, 1730. Signatures printed in Dotterer, *Historical Notes*, p. 103.

When the adherents of Weiss attacked the validity of Boehm's ministry, the friends of Boehm retaliated by questioning Weiss' ordination. This compelled Weiss to produce his certificate of ordination, issued by the Palatinate Consistory, on May 1, 1727. But it was in Latin which none was able to read. It was therefore rejected as unsatisfactory. Hence Weiss was compelled to write to Heidelberg, on December 2, 1727, for a German certificate, which was sent to him on April 26, 1728. In his letter to Heidelberg Weiss "gave information to the Ecclesiastical Council of the Palatinate concerning the present condition of religious and ecclesiastical affairs there."[43] The effect of this letter was that the Upper Consistory of the Palatinate wrote to the Synod of South Holland, requesting aid for the poor German fellow believers in Pennsylvania. This was the first time that the condition of the German Reformed people of Pennsylvania was brought to the attention of the Reformed Church of Holland.

When the Synod of South Holland met at Woerden, from July 6-16, 1728, "a letter was read by the president, written by the Great Consistory of Heidelberg, in which a request was made for a charitable contribution towards the building of a church in Pennsylvania for our fellow-believers, who have removed thither, inasmuch as they are compelled to hold their divine services under the blue sky." This appeal of the Heidelberg Consistory was the first link in the chain, which was to bind together the Reformed churches of Pennsylvania and the Church of Holland for more than sixty years.

But even before the German certificate of Weiss could reach Pennsylvania, the friends of Boehm, instead of forsaking their leader, determined to remove, if possible, the objection to his ministry as that of an unauthorized layman. To that end Boehm and his most prominent elder, William De Wees, were sent to New York to confer with the Dutch Reformed ministers of New York and Long Island, Revs. Gualtherus Du Bois, Henricus Boel and Vincentius Antonides. They met them in New York on May 16, 1728, and laid before

[43] See the text and translation of the German certificate, printed in C. Z. Weiser, *Monograph of the New Goshenhoppen and Great Swamp Reformed Charge,* Reading, 1882, pp. 28-31.

them their whole situation. The New York ministers informed them that, upon their own authority, they were unable to help them, but they advised them to report their case at length to the Classis of Amsterdam and to petition the Classis to legitimize the ministry of Boehm by ordination. In compliance with this advice the consistories of Boehm's congregations drew up an elaborate petition to the Classis, in which they reviewed their religious life in Pennsylvania, explained why Boehm had been forced by circumstances to assume the duties of the ministry, spread before them the constitution which they had adopted for the government of their churches, and requested the Classis to assist them in making the ministry of Mr. Boehm legitimate by conferring ordination upon him. They describe Boehm as "a man of more than common knowledge in the sound doctrine of truth, of praiseworthy life and of exemplary zeal in resisting error and guarding the ignorant against it."

This petition to the Classis, accompanied by a separate letter of Boehm as well as by his written confession of faith,[44] was sent to Holland by the ministers of New York on August 15, 1728. These documents reached Holland in November, 1728. On November 14, 1728, the Classical minutes state: "It was reported by Rev. Houthof that the Deputati ad res exteras had received a communication from New York in regard to the German churches in Pennsylvania. The Deputati were thereupon requested to write comfortingly to those congregations, and to assure them of the future consideration of this case, and an answer thereto and to furnish this Classis with a report thereon".[45]

In accordance with this resolution the Deputies wrote on November 28, 1728, to the churches of Boehm, expressing sympathy with them in their distressed condition and assuring them that their petition would receive the careful consideration and mature judgment of the Classis at its next meeting. On December 1, 1728, a similar letter was sent to the ministers at New York. The Deputies of the Classis reported their

[44] This important document is no longer in existence.

[45] See *Ecclesiastical Records of State of New York*, Vol. IV, p. 2440.

opinion on January 11, 1729, which was adopted by Classis. But, as there was no opportunity to send a letter during the winter, the answer of Classis to the Pennsylvania churches was delayed till June, 1729.

Finally on June 20, 1729, the Classis through its deputy, J. Bakker, sent off three letters, one to the brethren in Pennsylvania, one to Mr. Boehm and one to the ministers of New York. The answer of Classis was to the effect that the call extended to Boehm had all the inherent elements of a legal call, that therefore his ministerial acts should be recognized as legal, that his ordination should be consummated by one of the ministers of New York, either in Pennsylvania or in New York or at a place agreed upon by both parties, that Boehm before his ordination should accept the Heidelberg Catechism and the Formulas of Unity of the Synod of Dort, and that the constitution adopted by the Pennsylvania churches was regarded useful and effective for their government and hence its use was permitted by Classis. When this answer reached Pennsylvania, on November 4, 1729, (having been sent from New York to Philadelphia by special messenger), it created the greatest joy in the congregations of Boehm, as can be seen from Boehm's letter to the Classis, dated January 29, 1730: "We could not receive this letter without tears, because of our surprize and heart-thrilling joy, considering that the Reverend Classis had so graciously listened to the prayers of us poor people".

Steps were at once taken to secure the ordination of Boehm as speedily as possible. Three commissioners were appointed on November 4, one from each congregation, to accompany Boehm to New York, Frederick Antes of Falkner Swamp, Gabriel Schuler of Skippack and William De Wees of Whitemarsh. The delegates appeared with Boehm before the Dutch ministers in New York, November 18, 1729. The letter of the Classis was duly considered. Boehm and his delegates declared their adherence to the Heidelberg Catechism and the Formulas of Unity. They promised to maintain correspondence with the Classis and to exert themselves to secure the regular payment of Boehm's salary.

On November 20, 1729, the consistory of the Dutch Reformed Church of New York met and resolved that its ministers should proceed to carry out the commission of Classis, with the stipulation that "nothing of the kind should ever be undertaken or performed hereafter, without an express order from the Classis". In compliance with this resolution the ordination

SIGNATURES OF BOEHM'S ELDERS IN 1730.

of Mr. Boehm "was performed by Domine Henricus Boel, and the consecration by the laying on of hands by Domine Gualtherus Du Bois, in the presence of said consistory, publicly,

REV. GUALTHERUS DU BOIS

REV. HENRICUS BOEL

THE DUTCH REFORMED MINISTERS AT NEW YORK WHO ORDAINED BOEHM

in the Dutch Reformed Church in New York, on Sunday afternoon, November 23, 1729".

On the following day a reconciliation took place between Boehm and Weiss, who had come over to New York to be present at the ordination. They agreed to forgive each other for what had taken place in the past, and promised to live henceforth together in brotherly love and friendship. Weiss, on his part, promised to recognize Mr. Boehm as a lawfully ordained minister, to give up Skippack altogether and to leave to Boehm also Falkner Swamp and Whitemarsh as his congregations. Boehm, on the other hand, promised to recognize the ministry of Weiss and to leave to him Philadelphia and Germantown as his field. This action was ratified by Boehm's elders, but the adherents of Weiss refused to live up to it. Indeed through them it was largely nullified. Especially the people of Skippack were so set against Boehm that they not only refused to accept Boehm as their minister, but they also insisted that Weiss should not read in their church the act of reconciliation made between him and Boehm. Weiss yielded weakly to their demands and through his weakness encouraged his followers to continue in their opposition to Boehm.

In May, 1730, Weiss determined to go to Holland, to take charge of the moneys collected there in behalf of the Pennsylvania churches, in answer to an appeal sent by him to Holland in 1727. His congregations associated with him Jacob Reiff, one of his members at Skippack, an experienced business man, who had been in Holland in 1727. When Weiss left Philadelphia, two protests against Boehm's ordination were given to him by the seceders at Skippack, dated May 10, 1730. One was handed to Do. Wilhelmius, who laid it before the Classis of Rotterdam and the Deputies of the South Holland Synod. The other protest was laid before the Classis of Amsterdam.[46] But, instead of nullifying Boehm's ordination, as the petitioners requested, the Classis confirmed his ordination on December 5, 1730.

---

[46] The protest submitted to the Synod of South Holland is now, in a Dutch translation, in the archives at The Hague, 74, II, 1. The protest to the Classis is in the "Pennsylvania Portfolio" at Amsterdam.

CHAPTER IV.

BOEHM'S EARLY OPPONENTS.

The ordination of Boehm in New York and his reconciliation with Weiss seemed at first sight to be the end of all his troubles, but in reality they were the beginning of a ministry filled with difficulties and obstacles, largely created by persons who opposed his work.

Even Weiss, who had been reconciled to him at New York, was not faithful to the promises he then made. The most that can be said in extenuation of his later course of action is that it was dictated by his parishioners. Nevertheless, it called forth the indignant resentment of Boehm, to which he gives utterance in his letter to the New York ministers, dated May 17, 1730. He writes: "To sign such a covenant with his own hand, before such reverend men, who for the glory of Jesus labored so zealously to restore everything to good order, and then to break the same in such a disgraceful manner,—such conduct is not only devoid of honor, but far removed from godliness, nor is it worthy of a minister to set such an example." Nor was the attitude of Weiss to Boehm in Holland more friendly. The Acts of the Deputies bear evidence of the fact that he spoke slightingly of Boehm before the deputies.[47]

But of far greater importance for the whole ministry of Boehm was the ill-fated collecting tour of Weiss to Holland. For sixteen years it prevented any material help reaching Pennsylvania from Holland. Therefore, although Boehm was not directly involved in this tour, a brief account of it is necessary

[47] When Weiss appeared before the Deputies of the Synods at Rotterdam, on August 16, 1730, he gave them "an account of the large number of Reformed people in Pennsylvania, who hitherto have been served by him alone and by a certain Philip Boehm, who has set himself up as a teacher, although being without education and having no proper call, but who through wrong information was examined, it seems, and admitted to the ministry by one of the ministers of New Netherland, upon the order of the Reverend Classis of Amsterdam."

to understand much of the later correspondence of Boehm, which reverted continually to this all-absorbing topic.

THE REIFF COLLECTING TOUR.

In 1727, Jacob Reiff, then a resident of Skippack,[48] went to Germany "to fetch his relations", and at the same time, he tells us, he took with him a petition, which "the said congregation of Philadelphia and Skippack in conjunction with their minister, George Michael Weitzius (alias Weiss), did prefer to the excellent Classis of Divinity in the United Provinces, which petition . . . was signed and subscribed by the church wardens and elders of both the said congregations of Philadelphia and Skippack, and it set forth the unhappy and necessitous condition of the said congregations and prayed the charitable donations of the said Classis, and this defendant delivered the said petition to Dr. Wilhelmus". The reason why the petition was handed to the Rev. John Wilhelmius, then pastor at Rotterdam,[49] was most likely because Weiss had come in contact with him when he passed through Rotterdam on his way to Pennsylvania. In corroboration of this conclusion it may be pointed out that in a later report Wilhelmius stated that "the ministry of these churches [in Pennsylvania] has been in charge of the Rev. Mr. Weiss, who went over *with a colony of these Palatines"*. Wilhelmius was apparently the only minister in Holland acquainted with this fact. This too points to a personal contact between him and Weiss.

In answer to this petition of Weiss "a collection was made in favor of said congregations of the German Reformed Church of Philadelphia and Skippack to the amount of about

[49] John Wilhelmius, the son of William Wilhelmius, was born December 4, 1671, at Hardwyk. He studied at Leyden, where he also took the degree of doctor of philosophy. He became minister at Twisk, then professor of theology in the Reformed university at Lingen and finally pastor at Rotterdam, 1713-1748. He was a faithful friend, of the Palatines and especially of the Reformed people of Pennsylvania. See *Biographisch Wordenboek der Nederlanden*, 20ste Deel, Haarlem 1877.

[48] Jacob Reiff was the youngest son of John George Reiff and his wife, Anna Maria. He was born November 15, 1698, and died February 16, 1782. He is buried with his wife in the Mennonite burial ground at Skippack. The first reference to him in Pennsylvania is

200 guilders".[48a] When Reiff returned to Pennsylvania in 1729, he was requested to take charge of the money thus collected. But, as he had heard that his honesty had been questioned, he refused to have anything to do with it. The congregations of Weiss, therefore, determined to send their pastor to Holland to receive this money. And, as they were afraid that Weiss might be persuaded to stay in Germany, they associated with him Jacob Reiff. Another event prepared the way for the visit of Weiss to Holland. At the meeting of the South Holland Synod, held at Breda, July 4-14, 1730, its president, Rev. John Wilhelmius, read a lengthy report on the condition of the Reformed people in Pennsylvania. As a result Synod resolved to call upon its churches for a contribution to the Reformed people in Pennsylvania.

When Weiss, therefore, with his companion appeared in Holland, they were received with open arms. We find them first, on August 10, 1730, at Haarlem, where they received of Rev. Jacob Geelkerke fl. 390, from the Synod of North Holland. A few days later, on August 15th and 16th, they were at Rotterdam, where Rev. Alardus Tiele gave them the contributions of the Synod of South Holland, held at Kuylenberg in 1729, in all fl. 696.12, and the Rev. Barth. Van Velse gave the contributions of the Synod just held at Breda, namely fl. 79.

At the same time they appeared before the Synodical Deputies, at the house of Rev. J. Wilhelmius in Rotterdam. Here Weiss presented his credentials, gave the deputies an account of the Reformed people in Pennsylvania, handed over to them the protest of the seceders at Skippack against Boehm and accepted the request of the deputies to prepare a chart, showing the different settlements and a report "of the whole condition of

---

made on July 2, 1723, when he is mentioned in the diary of Gerhart Clemens. See Heckler, *History of Lower Salford Township*, p. 98. On December 1, 1727, Jacob Reiff, of Skippack, yeoman, bought three tracts of land containing five hundred and forty-six acres. The plantation on which he himself lived was located near the southeastern corner of the present township of Lower Salford, near the Skippack Creek. This was the property on which the Reformed Church was erected. See Heckler, l. c., p. 99; also p. 111.

[48a] A Dutch guilder, also called florin (fl.), is worth about 40 cents. Twenty stuivers (st.) make a guilder.

BERIGT,
EN
ONDERRIGTINGE,
NOPENS EN AAN DE COLONIE EN KERKE
VAN
PENSYLVANIEN.

Opgestelt en Uytgegeven door de Gedeputeerden van de E. Christelyke Synodus van Zuyd-Holland, benevens de Gecommitteerden van de E. Classis van Delft en Delfsland, en Schieland.

THE FIRST PRINTED REPORT ABOUT THE REFORMED CHURCH
OF PENNSYLVANIA, 1731

the land and the Palatines living there".[50] Upon this report of Weiss, which was submitted in September, 1730, was based the first printed report regarding the Reformed Church of Pennsylvania, laid before the South Holland Synod at Dort in July, 1731.

On September 4, 1730, Weiss and Reiff were at Amsterdam, where they appeared before the Classis. They "made known that the congregation at Schibach, from which also a lettter has been received, is very much disturbed and in great confusion, because the congregation refuses to recognize Do. Boehm as a properly ordained minister". The deputies were asked to investigate the matter carefully and report to the Classis. Weiss also asked for a contribution to build a church in Philadelphia. In answer to this request "the congregation was recommended to the charity of all congregations under the jurisdiction of this Classis".

The two travelers remained in Amsterdam several months. On October 18, 1730, the burgomasters permitted them[51] to collect fl. 600 in the city, while on the next day the Amsterdam diaconate voted them fl. 150, and on October 20th, the diaconate gave fl. 600. These gifts, together with contributions from private parties, amounted in all to fl. 2132.12.

The last reference to the presence of Weiss in Holland is found in the minutes of the Classis of the Hague, which refer, under date November 6, 1730, to a Latin letter of Weiss to the Classis, asking for its help. According to a statement made by Weis in 1738, he stayed in Holland six months. Hence his stay lasted from August, 1730, to February, 1731. Before he left, he received from Reiff, who had taken charge of the money, fl. 250, for his return journey. Weiss returned by way of London to Baltimore, in the summer of 1731, but shortly after his arrival in Philadelphia, he accepted a call to Huntersfield, Schoharie County, N. Y. On September 22, 1731, his elders in Philadelphia gave him a letter of recom-

[50] These valuable documents do not seem to be preserved. At least they are not in the archives at the Hague.

[51] The permit of the burgomaster is printed in Dr. Good's *History of the Reformed Church in the U. S.*, 1725-1792, p. 142.

mendation to his new field of labor.[52]

Meanwhile affairs had taken a remarkable turn in Holland. The evidence is somewhat contradictory, coming to us from Weiss, Reiff and Boehm.[53] Selecting the statements of Boehm as giving us most likely the true version of what happened, we learn from him, that, before Weiss left Holland, Reiff received a lettter from seven prominent members of the Philadelphia congregation, which took away the power of attorney, given to Weiss by the whole congregation, and transferred it to Reiff. This accounts for the fact that instead of taking the money with him when he left, Weiss turned it all over to Reiff, receiving from him only fl. 250 for the return journey. In the same letter Reiff was advised to invest the money received in merchandise. This was a fatal move, as future events plainly showed.

In accordance with the instructions received, Reiff bought merchandise, which he put on board of the ship Britannia, bound from Rotterdam for Philadelphia. About that time, from July 3-13, 1731, the Synod of South Holland met at Dort. Rev. J. Wilhelmius persuaded Reiff (so the latter claims) to attend its sessions, but when he returned to Rotterdam he found the ship with his goods had left. It was the same ship which brought Rev. J. B. Rieger to America. When the ship arrived in England, the goods were detained "by the collector of His Majesty's customs at Cowes, in the Isle of Wight, where the ship went to clear". Reiff, however, instead of following with the next ship, delayed his departure till the next spring. During this interval he probably went to the Palatinate.[54] In June, 1732, we find that Reiff had boarded another ship and was at Cowes, trying to free his goods from the custom house. But, before he could make a settlement

[52] A copy of the letter was spread by Weiss upon the church record of the old Catskill Reformed Church.

[53] The evidence of Reiff is given in paper which he presented to the Court of Chancery, in answer to a bill of complaint made against him. It was printed by Dr. Dubbs in the *Reformed Quarterly Review*, Vol. XV (1893), pp. 60-66.

[54] So Reiff claimed before Schlatter, when he made his settlement with him. See "Diary of Schlatter," printed in *Journal of the Presbyterian Historical Society,* Vol. III, p. 112.

with the collector, the ship was ready to sail and he was forced to leave the goods in England.

When Reiff returned to Pennsylvania, in the fall of 1732, he threw the members of the congregations at Philadelphia and Skippack into great consternation by denying that he had ever received more than fl. 750 in Holland, although letters of Weiss, received by them, showed that more than fl. 2100 had been given in Holland. Moreover, a rumor was circulated that Reiff intended to leave the province. To prevent him doing this and to compel him to render an account, several of the Philadelphia members cited him before the Court of Chancery.[55] On November 23, 1732, Jacob Diemer, Michael Hillegass, Peter Hillegass, Jost Schmidt, Hendrick Weller, Jacob Sigel and Wilhelm Rohrich appeared before Governor Keith in the Court of Chancery at Philadelphia and laid before him a complaint and petition, in which they stated their whole case, the story of the collection, the moneys received by Reiff, his unwillingness to render an account and his apparent intention to leave the province, and hence they prayed the Court "to restrain the said Jacob Reiff from departing this province, until he has answered the bill of complaints of these deponents who prosecute in behalf of the said Reformed German Church of Philadelphia". Their petition was granted and Reiff was compelled to give bail. On June 20, 1733, the attorney of Reiff asked the Court to discharge Reiff and his securities from bond. When the case was called up it was found that the petitioners had failed to lodge a formal bill of complaint against Reiff, having thought perhaps that their petition and affidavit were sufficient. They were given time to file their bill of complaint till July 3rd, and when they were not ready at that time, till July 12th, when the bill of complaint was presented. Two days later Reiff filed his answer. On February 20, 1734, the bond of Reiff was reduced from £1000 to £500. This ended the case before the court. Nothing else at least is found in the record which closes in 1735. The complainants failed to prosecute, perhaps because they were unable to prove their contentions.

[55] The Registrar's Book of Governor Keith's Court of Chancery, 1720-1735, has been printed by Wm. H. Rawle in his *Equity in Pennsylvania*, Philadelphia, 1868, Appendix p. 33f.

In April, 1734, however, an important event occurred, which revealed the hidden cause of the whole unfortunate affair. A congregational meeting was held by the Philadelphia congregation. There, in the presence of thirty members, Reiff openly charged the prosecuting members with being the cause of the whole trouble, in that they had advised investing the money in merchandise. He produced the letter which they had written to him while he was in Holland, ordering him to invest the money in that way. He also claimed to have sent them the goods, but they flatly denied having seen anything of them.

The result of this "discovery" (as Boehm calls it) was that these men were deposed by the congregation as members of the consistory. A new consistory was at once chosen, which appealed to Boehm to help them. Boehm consented and became the pastor of the Philadelphia congregation in August, 1734. But the Reiff affair was no nearer a solution than it was before. The secret of the whole trouble was that when the investment of the money in merchandise proved a total failure, none of the participants was willing to shoulder the loss, hence Reiff was unwilling to make a settlement. The case remained unsettled till the arrival of Schlatter in 1746.

For Boehm the consequences of the "Reiff Case" were threefold: In the first place, it deprived him for years of the much-needed help from Holland; in the second place, it made him pastor of the Philadelphia congregation, and in the third place, it alienated the seceders at Skippack from him for ever, since they continued to be under the influence of Jacob Reiff, until the congregation ceased to exist in 1746. Weiss and Reiff, however, were not the only opponents of Boehm in his pastoral activity. The disturbance and division, caused by Weiss at Skippack and other places, were continued by others. The first of these successors of Weiss, opposing Boehm's work, was John Peter Miller.

JOHN PETER MILLER, 1730-1734.

John Peter Miller (Mueller) was born December 25, 1709, probably at Zweikirchen, near Zweibruecken, Germany. His father was the Rev. John Mueller, who from 1707-1714 was pastor at Zweikirchen and Wolfstein near Kaiserslautern, from 1714-1726, pastor at Alsenborn and from 1730-1741, pastor at

Altenkirchen, near Homburg in the Palatinate. He died at Altenkirchen May 11, 1741.[56]

His son, John Peter Mueller, entered the university of Heidelberg, where he registered December 29, 1725, as "Johannes Petrus Mullerus, Altzbornensis". This does not mean that he was born at Alsenborn, as was thought hitherto, but Alsenborn was his temporary home, where his father was pastor when he entered the university. According to a statement in the *Berliner Monatsschrift* of 1784:[57]

"Peter Miller the only educated man (in the society at Ephrata) studied in Heidelberg and was authorized to preach, but not to baptize. With thirty guldens in his pocket he left his father".

On August 29, 1730, Miller arrived in Philadelphia on "the ship Thistle, of Glasgow, Colin Dunlap, master, from Rotterdam, last from Cowes" with 260 Palatines.

Soon after his arrival he was engaged by the Reformed people of Philadelphia and Germantown, and also by the seceders at Skippack, to preach for them. In order to qualify himself for this work, he applied to the Presbyterian Synod of Philadelphia for ordination. On September 19, 1730, the Synod voted that he "be left to the care of the Presbytery of Philadelphia, to settle him in the work of the ministry".[58]

The minutes of the Presbytery of Philadelphia covering this period are unfortunately lost, but a letter of Rev. Jedidiah Andrews, pastor of the old Buttonwood Presbyterian Church, supplies the deficiency, at least in part. On October 14, 1730, Mr. Andrews wrote to the Rev. Thomas Prince, pastor of the Old South Church of Boston:[59]

"There is lately come over a Palatine candidate of the ministry, who having applied to us at the Synod, for Ordin'n,

[56] This information about Peter Miller's father was kindly communicated to the writer by the present pastor of the Reformed Church at Alsenborn, in a recent letter, dated June 5, 1914. The church records of Wolfstein are unfortunately no longer in existence. The Reformed church at Zweikirchen is no longer in existence.

[57] Quoted by Dr. Dubbs in his *Reformed Church in Pennsylvania*, p. 98, note 99.

[58] See *Records of Presbyterian Church in U. S. A.*, Vol. I, p. 99.

[59] First printed in Hazard's *Register*, Vol. XV, p. 200f.

t'is left to 3 ministers to do it. He is an extraordinary person for sense and learning. We gave him a question to discuss about Justification, and he has answered it, in a whole sheet of paper, in a very notable manner. His name is John Peter Miller, and speaks Latin as readily as we do our vernacular tongue, and so does the other, Mr. Weis".

Shortly afterwards, on October 19, 1730, Miller visited Boehm in his home at Whitpain. When Miller told him that he had applied to the Presbyterians for ordination, Boehm advised him to go rather to the Dutch Reformed ministers of New York, that his ordination might take place in accordance with Reformed custom. But Miller refused, saying that this was too round about a way for him. He preferred to take the easier way. He questioned the authority of the Church of Holland to control church affairs in America. Boehm retorted sharply that, if the Classis did not have this right she would not have assumed it. Miller also deprecated the attempt to

Peter Miller

SIGNATURE OF JOHN PETER MILLER.

deprive the Pennsylvania churches of their liberty by subjecting them to the Classis of Amsterdam, to which remark Boehm made a spirited reply. Towards the end of the year 1730, Miller was ordained in the Presbyterian Church by three Presbyterian ministers, Andrews, Tennent and Boyd.[60] Boehm complained repeatedly in his letter about the harmful activity of Miller, which, from his point of view, produced only division and the spirit of independence in the Reformed congregations.

Miller preached at Philadelphia, Germantown and Skippack till the fall of 1731. He then withdrew to the interior

[60] Miller himself preserved this fact in a letter which he wrote to a friend late in life, dated December 5, 1790. In it he writes: "In August, 1730, I arrived in Philadelphia, and was there at the end of the said year, upon the order of the Scotch Synod, ordained in the old Presbyterian Meeting House, by three eminent ministers, Tennent, Andrews and Boyd." See Hazards *Register*, Vol. XVI, p. 254.

settlements. He became Weiss' successor at Goshenhoppen. The first sixty-nine baptisms in the New Goshenhoppen record, from June, 1731, till July, 1734, were performed by Peter Miller.[61] At one of these baptisms, on April 16, 1732, "Johann Peter Mueller", acted as sponsor. Boehm refers to Miller's activity in his report of 1739. In a paragraph treating of Goshenhoppen he writes: "When Weiss traveled to Holland in order to obtain the well known moneys collected there, they immediately clung to Miller, who, assisted by another person, continued to serve Goshenhoppen". Beside Goshenhoppen Miller was also serving Conestoga and Tulpehocken, which he took away from Boehm. On March 4, 1733, Rev. John B. Rieger wrote to the Synods:

"The church at Conestoga and vicinity has a preacher by the name of Johann Petrus Mueller, who was ordained in the Presbyterian church here. He holds divine services there [at Conestoga]".

Boehm himself also refers to Miller's activity at Conestoga and Tulpehocken. In his report of 1739 he states: "But soon afterwards Weiss left them again, whereupon Miller went there to carry on the work of Weiss. At that time Miller drew also Tulpehocken to himself". According to a letter of Conrad Tempelman, dated February 13, 1733, Miller had three preaching places in the Conestoga valley.

As early as 1732, Miller showed inclinations towards the Seventh Day Dunkers. Boehm reports that at that time he went into the house of a Seventh Day Dunker, with one of his elders from Goshenhoppen, and had his feet washed by him. It is therefore not surprising that when Conrad Beissel, their leader, set out to win one of the Reformed preachers for his work, "aware of his own inability in view of the important work before him", he succeeded with Peter Miller. On the occasion of a visit to Tulpehocken with several of his disciples, Beissel "was received by the teacher [Miller] and elders with the consideration due to him as an ambassador of God".[62] The result of this visit of Beissel was that Miller, the school-

---

[61] Published by the writer in Mr. Dotterer's *Perkiomen Region*, Vol. III, pp. 94-95.

[62] See *Ephrata Chronicle*, Engl. Ed., p. 71.

master, three elders and various other households determined to go over to the new faith. But his efforts to win the whole congregation proved unsuccessful, for Boehm reports: "When he could not persuade the people to follow his example, he gave up the ministry and became an oil-miller". Miller himself writes in a later letter about this event: "Having officiated among the Germans several years, I quitted the ministry and returned to private life". The separation of Miller from the Reformed Church was made as dramatic as possible. Boehm has recorded the strange scene for us. The four leaders in the movement, Peter Miller, Michael Miller, Conrad Weiser and Gottfried Fidler, gathered, no doubt with their sympathizers, in the house of Gottfried Fidler, and there they burnt the Heidelberg Catechism, the Lutheran Catechism, the Psalms of David, and several books of devotion, in all 36 volumes, "in derision and disparagement." Shortly afterwards, Miller and his followers completed their renunciation of the Reformed Church by being baptized in Dunker fashion, through trine immersion in a river. This took place on a Sabbath in May, 1735. According to Boehm "he took with him about ten families, Lutheran and Reformed, from the congregation of Tulpehocken who followed his example". As the Seventh Day Dunkers lived at that time dispersed through the Conestoga valley as hermits, Miller, so he tells us, followed their example and set up his "hermitage in Dulpehackin, at the foot of a mountain, on a limped spring, the house is still [in 1790] extant there with an old orchard". There Miller lived till November, 1735, when the cloister at Ephrata was begun and all the "solitary brethren" were called in. He then removed to Ephrata, where he spent the rest of his life behind cloister walls.

This conversion of Miller and his friends caused such an alarm among the Reformed congregations, that they appealed again to Mr. Boehm to save them. Accordingly he went to Conestoga, on May 11, 1735, and administered there the Lord's Supper to two congregations. Tulpehocken also engaged him again to hold communion services for them twice a year.

When Miller withdrew from Philadelphia and Skippack, his place was taken by Rev. John Bartholomew Rieger.

JOHN BARTHOLOMEW RIEGER, 1731-1734.

John Bartholomew Rieger, the son of John Adam Rieger, a tax-collector, and of his wife Anna Magdalena, was born at Oberingelheim in the Palatinate, January 23, 1707.[63] He took his Christian name from his sponsor, John Bartholomew Eberth. Young Rieger matriculated in the university of Heidelberg, as student of philosophy, on February 14, 1724. For some unknown reason he left Heidelberg after a stay of a few months and, on April 20, 1724, matriculated in the university of Basel. After that date we lose sight of him till September 21, 1731, when he appears at the Court House in Philadelphia, at the head of a colony of 104 Palatines, to sign the oath of allegiance to the English king. They, together with their fami-

SIGNATURE OF REV. JOHN B. RIEGER.

lies, in all 269 persons, had been imported in the ship Britannia, of London, Michael Franklyn, captain, from Rotterdam. Like Weiss, Rieger came as the leader of this colony. This is distinctly asserted by Rev. John Wilhelmius, the friend of the Palatines in Rotterdam. In a report, submitted to the deputies on October 31, 1735, he states that the third minister serving the Reformed people in Pennsylvania is "Candidate Rieger, who went over with another colony and became minister there." This statement is supported by the fact that the original list of immigrants, who signed the declaration of allegiance on September 21, 1731, is headed by "Johannes Bartholomay Rieger, Hochteutscher Prediger".[64]

[63] The data regarding Mr. Rieger's life in Germany were collected by the writer at Heidelberg and Oberingelheim in August, 1898.

[64] This is not the case in the printed list, Rupp's *Thirty Thousand Names*, p. 68; *Pennsylvania Archives*, Second Series, Vol. XVII, p. 29; but in the original document his name stands first.

Shortly after his arrival Rieger was elected pastor of the Reformed congregations in Philadelphia and Germantown. On November 22, 1731, the members at Philadelphia wrote to the Synods: "As Mr. Weiss has left us, in order not to allow our pulpit to remain vacant, we have chosen the newly arrived candidate Rieger as our minister, to whose planting and sprinkling among us the Lord may graciously grant His blessing from above".[65]

Rieger, like his predecessors, opposed the ministry of Boehm at Skippack. In his report of 1744, Boehm writes to the Synods: "When Weiss went to Holland, Peter Miller preached there [at Skippack], who now for a long time has been a Seventh Day Dunker. After him came Bartholomew Rieger, whom I never considered, on account of certain evidence, to be different from, or more sound in the Reformed doctrine, than Miller. He preached there for some time". A few details about the ministry of Rieger at Philadelphia and neighboring places can be learnt from a letter of Rieger and Dr. John Diemer of Philadelphia, dated March 4, 1733.[66] They write: "The congregations of Schippach, Germantown and Philadelphia have as their minister Bartholomew Rieger, who arrived a year and a half ago. He preaches one Sunday at Schippach, the second at Germantown and the third at Philadelphia." As to the condition of the Reformed people at that time they write: "At Philadelphia, which is the capital and from which most of the grain is shipped to other countries, are only ten [Reformed] families that are settled, all the others are in service. Among the townships Schippach is the most densely populated. There they count about forty families, but they are mostly poor and about thirty miles from the city. The other places are still farther away".

It was during the ministry of Rieger that the Reiff case was taken into court. When the men implicated in this affair were forced out of the consistory, Rieger also resigned, probably because he sympathized with them. His withdrawal led to the election of Boehm at Philadelphia. The elders of Boehm describe these events as follows:

[65] Original letter in archives at The Hague, 74, I, 10.
[66] Letter at The Hague, 74, I, 15.

"When Mr. Rieger had left the congregation, thinking perhaps that because of his absence we would not know what to do, and we would have to unite again with the deposed persons, with whom he was in harmony, which the congregation, however, regarded as extremely harmful, because of the evident deception which they had practised,—then another plan was thought of, and they resolved unanimously (in order to prevent the entire ruin of the congregation) humbly to ask aid and assistance of Mr. John Philip Boehm. . . . This was done immediately by means of a letter, dated April 20, 1734, signed by forty-two persons and conveyed to him by two of our members".

From Philadelphia Rieger went to Amwell, N. J. But, before that congregation was willing to accept him, he had to confess that he had done wrong in breaking into Boehm's congregations, ask Boehm's forgiveness and promise that it should not happen again. Nevertheless, Boehm complained, "he has not been ashamed to act against his pledge and promise in the congregation at Tulpehocken, without speaking to me about it". When Rieger had withdrawn, another young minister appeared to continue the opposition to Boehm. It was John Henry Goetschy.

JOHN HENRY GOETSCHY, 1735-1740.

On May 29, 1735, the ship Mercury, William Wilson, master, arrived in Philadelphia, from Rotterdam, with 186 passengers. Among them was the Goetschy family, consisting of ten members. The head of the family, who was also the leader of the colony, was the Rev. Maurice Goetschy, who had been pastor at Saletz, Switzerland. His son, John Henry, had been born March 8, 1718. He matriculated in the Latin school at Zurich March 23, 1734. But, before he had spent half a year at school, his father with his whole family left for Pennsylvania.[67]

When the ship Mercury reached Philadelphia with the immigrants, Rev. Maurice Goetschy was so sick that he had to be carried ashore. He died on the following day and his

---

[67] Documents relating to the Colony of Goetschy are in the city library at Zurich.

funeral took place on the third day following in the "principal English Presbyterian Church in Philadelphia".

On July 21, 1735, young Goetschy, then a boy of seventeen years, wrote to one of his relatives at Zurich: "When the people saw that I had been engaged in study, they almost compelled me to preside over the congregations to the best of my ability. Hence, through the goodness of God, I preach twice every Sunday and teach two catechetical lessons. For this I make use of the books which I have brought with me and through diligence I am enabled, thank God, to perform this work in such a way, that each and every person is well satisfied with me. Now the first Sunday I preach in Philadelphia, both in the forenoon and afternoon and I give always along with it catechetical instruction. On the second Sunday

22. Märtii 1739.
J. Henricus Goetschius. A
Helvetico - Tigurinus.

SIGNATURE OF JOHN H. GOETSCHY FROM EGYPT RECORD.

in Schippach, which is a very large congregation, I have a sermon and catechetical instruction in the forenoon. In the afternoon at Old Goshenhoppen, two hours [six miles] from Schippach, I have a sermon and catechetical instruction. It is also a pretty large congregation, as large as any in the canton of Zurich. On the third Sunday I preach in New Goshenhoppen and hold catechetical instruction there in the forenoon. In the afternoon I am at Great Swamp, which is also one of the large congregations".

On May 27, 1737, Goetschy applied to the Presbyterian Synod of Philadelphia for ordination.[68] He was referred to the Presbytery of Philadelphia for examination. The Presbytery met on the following day, but the examiners came unani-

---

[68] See *Records of the Presbyterian Church*, Vol. I. p. 133.

mously to the conclusion "that tho' he appeared well skilled in the learned languages, yet inasmuch as they found him altogether ignorant in college learning and but poorly read in Divinity, his ordination to the ministry must at present be deferred". He was, therefore, advised to put himself under the care and instruction of some minister. Meanwhile he was given a license to preach.

From Goshenhoppen as a center, young Goetschy soon developed an extensive missionary activity. On the title page of the New Goshenhoppen record he mentions eleven congregations as included in his charge, although in some of them he probably preached only occasionally. These were: Skippack, Old Goshenhoppen, New Goshenhoppen, Great Swamp, Saucon, Egypt, Maxatawny, Moselem, Oley, Berne and Tulpehocken. At Skippack, Oley and Tulpehocken, Goetschy came in conflict with Boehm, because they were Boehm's congregations, and he attempted to enter them without consulting him. He further caused Boehm much annoyance by circulating a letter of Rev. John Wilhelmius, forged in part by Reiff or his adherents. But on February 21, 1740, a reconciliation was effected between Boehm and Goetschy at the home of Rev. P. H. Dorsius at Neshaminy, Bucks County. The words of Boehm describing this reconciliation are worth quoting. They show that there was nothing mean in his character, but that he was ready to extend the hand of brotherly fellowship to any one who was anxious to live and labor peacefully with him. He writes: "Henry Goetschy has shown this letter [of Wilhelmius] everywhere and thereby caused me much persecution, until he learned differently from his Reverence, Inspector Dorsius. Then he heartily repented and asked my forgiveness in the presence of his Reverence, which I granted him with all my heart. I also wish him success and intercede for him with God and our Reverend Church Fathers. He obediently submitted to the decision of the Reverend Christian Synods and desisted immediately. May God give him blessing and grace that he may become an efficient instrument to edify others".

Goetschy had stopped preaching because the Synods had notified the Reformed churches of Pennsylvania that they could expect no help from them, "unless they refused to hear the unordained ministers and hirelings and refused to accept them for the administration of the sacraments, etc., among whom are included the young Goetschy and Van Basten, who while students presume to do everything that belongs to a regular minister".

As a result of this notice, Goetschy gave up his preaching, went to Neshaminy and put himself there for a year under the instruction of the Rev. P. H. Dorsius. On April 7, 1741, he was ordained as minister of Jamaica and Long Island, by Dorsius with the assistance of the Dutch Reformed minister, Theodore Jacob Frelinghuysen and the Presbyterian minister of New Brunswick, N. J., Gilbert Tennent. Thus his activity in Pennsylvania came to an end.

Even before Goetschy left Pennsylvania, the congregation at Skippack was still further divided by another adventurer, John William Straub. He had been schoolmaster at Gronau in the Palatinate (now in the Grandduchy of Hesse, south of Darmstadt), where he had been dismissed because of immorality. He arrived at Philadelphia September 21, 1732. His age at that time is given as 44 years. Hence he was born in 1688. We first meet him at Skippack in 1739. He seems to have stayed there till 1741. In 1742 we find him at Western Salisbury, Lehigh County, where he preached apparently till 1744.[69] In 1746 Schlatter reports him as preaching at Indian Creek.[70] After that he disappeared.

PETER HENRY DORSIUS, 1737-1743.

More important for Boehm was his contact with Rev. Peter Henry Dorsius, pastor of the Dutch Reformed congregation at Neshaminy, Bucks County.

As early as May 3, 1730, the Dutch Reformed people of Bucks County wrote to Messrs. David Knibbe and John Wilhelmius, Reformed pastors in Rotterdam, requesting them to assist them in securing a minister. On May 29, 1734, Rev. John Wilhelmius wrote them that he had found "a certain young man, suitable and pious, 24 years of age, who still needs

---

[69] See *History of Western Salisbury Church*, 1911, p. 9.
[70] According to private "Diary of Schlatter," printed in *Journal of Presbyterian Historical Society*, Vol. III, p. 161.

one year to complete his studies". His name was Peter Henry Dorsius. He had been born at Moers near the Lower Rhine, and was baptized there January 2, 1711.[71] On April 5, 1734, he matriculated in the university of Groningen and on September 17, 1736, in the university of Leyden. He was examined by the Classis of Schieland April 30, 1737, and ordained by the theological faculty at Groningen July 11, 1737. Shortly afterwards he embarked for America. He landed at Philadelphia September 26 (or October 5, new style), 1737.

A year after his arrival Dorsius asked Boehm to visit him, which Boehm did on November 28, 1738. Dorsius then showed him letters from the two Synods of North and South Holland, in which he was asked to secure information about the Reformed churches in Pennsylvania. Dorsius asked Boehm to cooperate, which he promised on receipt of a written request. There was the best of feeling between the two men, as is evident from the words of Boehm, written to the Classis on November 16, 1739:

"His Reverence, Mr. Dorsius, whom the Christian Synods have now been pleased to appoint superintendent of our true Church in Pennsylvania, shows indeed a real zeal faithfully to do all he can for the Church of Jesus in this country. To this end God has blessed him with much wisdom". In a similar strain Boehm wrote to the Classis regarding Dorsius on March 26, 1740. But the good feeling did not last very long. When Boehm had gathered his information with great difficulty in the depth of the winter, had prepared his report and had handed it to Dorsius, in March, 1740, to send it to the Synods, he heard shortly afterwards, that, instead of sending the report, Dorsius had himself prepared a report on its basis and had sent it to Holland, keeping meanwhile Boehm's origi-

[71] A series of extracts from the church records of the Reformed Church at Moers were secured by the writer with the kind assistance of the present pastor of that church, the Rev. W. Rotscheid. September 15, 1708, John Henry Dorschius, widower, of Meurs and Petronella Gravers, of Altkirch, were married. Their children were: (1) Alethea bapt. November 15, 1709; (2) Peter Henry, bapt. January 2, 1711; (3) Abraham, bapt. August 5, 1712; (4) Isaac, bapt. Dec. 22, 1713, died in infancy; (5) Isaac, bapt. March 8, 1715. The old spelling of the city was Meurs, but the present spelling is Moers.

nal report in his home. This displeased Boehm very much and led to an argument between them, in which Dorsius maintained that he was the only medium of communication between the Synods and the Pennsylvania churches. The tension was aggravated when Boehm mentioned the fact of Dorsius having retained the original report at home to some elders from Goshenhoppen. When Dorsius visited Goshenhoppen, September 24, 1740, he was asked whether he had sent the report of Boehm to Holland. Replying in the affirmative, he was confronted with the statement of Boehm that it had not been sent. This angered Dorsius exceedingly and he poured out his anger in unrestrained language. When this incident was reported to Boehm, he felt much aggrieved. He reported it to the Classis July 25, 1741, accompanying his statement with an affidavit of some of the elders, who had been present at Goshenhoppen at the time of Dorsius' visit and had heard his outburst against Boehm.

Another cause of friction was the fact that Dorsius, together with Dr. Diemer, one of Boehm's arch-enemies, had been appointed by the Synods to settle the Reiff case. This was regarded by Boehm as a slight to himself, as Dorsius knew practically nothing about the case, while Diemer had been one of the conspirators, who, through his scheme of investing the funds in merchandise, had caused the whole trouble. The result of their united efforts was of course absolute failure, as Boehm had predicted. The indifference of the two prosecuting agents of the Synods is fully set forth by Boehm's elders, in March, 1741.

In 1743, when his salary had been reduced from 69 to 40 pounds, Dorsius felt that he had to do something. As a result he determined to visit Holland. He left Pennsylvania in May, 1743. On September 17-19, 1743, he appeared before the deputies of the Synods at The Hague. When they asked him what had brought him to Holland, he answered that he wished to consult the deputies about his work and find out whether he might be permitted to leave his congregation and accept another, or whether he could organize a congregation in Philadelphia, in order to increase thereby his salary. He also made a long report about the condition of the Pennsylvania churches, "from which it appeared clearly that the same was getting worse all the time, the number of the Reformed people were growing less constantly, through the great increase of the Moravians and the powerful agitation of Romish missionaries". This unfortunate and very misleading report of Dorsius was probably inspired through the ill-feeling that existed between him and Boehm. After Dorsius had returned to Pennsylvania in January, 1744, he wrote a letter to the deputies, dated February 16, 1744, enclosing a report by him, entitled "Some Means which Do. Dorsius considers as useful for the establishment and preservation of our Reformed Church in the Government of Pennsylvania."[72] In it he grouped the Reformed churches into six charges, and stated in connection with each how much it was willing to pay toward a minister's salary. But he failed to hint even with a single word that the whole plan was but a reproduction of Boehm's report of 1739, together with the congregational pledges of 1740, which he had failed to send to Holland in 1740, and which now in 1744 he palmed off as his own work. This was but the beginning of his complete moral collapse a few years later.

The decade from 1730-1740 had been to Boehm a period of great stress and strain, but with the perseverance peculiar to him, he emerged from it victorious, being the only Reformed minister who during the whole time had maintained his position.

There is one interesting event in the life of Boehm during this decade which had nothing of a controversial character. On April 27, 1738, Mr. Boehm and his elder, Sebastian Reiffschneider, attended a meeting of the Dutch Reformed ministers of New York, which had been called to deliberate about the advisability of organizing a Coetus (Convention) of the Reformed Churches in the colonies. The draft of a constitution was drawn up and signed by those present,[73] but the organization itself did not materialize.

[72] Preserved at The Hague, 74, I, 21.
[73] Published by Dr. E. T. Corwin in *Ecclesiastical Records of the State of New York*, Vol. IV, pp. 2706-2708.

CHAPTER V.

BOEHM AS THE FOUNDER OF CHURCHES.

It would be altogether unfair to Boehm to think or write of his work as entirely or even mainly polemical. The most outstanding and enduring feature of his life-work is the part he took in the founding of Reformed churches in Pennsylvania. There are at least eleven, perhaps twelve, congregations, in whose organization he was directly interested and which he served from time to time.

Reference has already been made to Boehm's three original congregations, which he organized in the year 1725, Falkner Swamp, Skippack and Whitemarsh. The number of men in these three congregations was about fifty in 1725, the number of communicant members about one hundred, in 1728 the number of men had increased to fifty-eight, namely twenty-four at Falkner Swamp, about twenty at Skippack and fourteen at Whitemarsh.

WHITEMARSH REFORMED CHURCH.

The congregation at Whitemarsh met at all times in the house of William De Wees. The house was still standing recently opposite St. Joseph's Convent, on the west side of the Germantown and Perkiomen turnpike, after it has passed the bridge across the Wissahickon.[74] The number of communicants at Whitemarsh was twenty-four in 1734, fifteen in 1730, fifty-nine in 1740, fifty-one in 1743. In 1744, Boehm reported of elder William De Wees: "That honest man cherishes a steadfast and pious hope that God will yet furnish means (to build a church)". But his hope was not realized. He died March 3, 1745. In November, 1746, Boehm reported to the

---

[74] See Keyser, *Old Historic Germantown* (Proceedings of Pa. German Society, Vol. XV), p. 34; for a picture of the house see Keyser, l. c., pl. facing p. 72. The house was only a few hundred feet to the west of the Dewees paper mill. See Keyser, l. c., p. 38.

HOUSE OF WILLIAM DE WEES, IN WHICH THE WHITEMARSH CONGREGATION MET

CORNERSTONE OF THE OLD GOSHENHOPPEN CHURCH, 1744

Synods, "the congregation at Whitemarsh, which at all times consisted of but few members, through the death of the aged, faithful elder William De Wees, has come to a standstill [has been discontinued], because his house was at all times our church, but since his death it can be so no longer, nor is there any opportunity to worship elsewhere, much less are there the means to build a church". The lower part of the congregation was then joined to Germantown, the upper part to Old Goshenhoppen.

SKIPPACK REFORMED CHURCH.

Sixteen miles from Whitemarsh in a northwesterly direction, in what is now Lower Salford township, was founded the Skippack congregation in the year 1725. The congregation met at first in the house of Jacob Reiff, from which Boehm and his adherents were expelled on Sunday, March 10, 1728. Even before that time Boehm and his elders had started to build a church. But Jacob Reiff and his brothers succeeded in securing a title to the land in their own name[75] and hence, when the church was dedicated on June 22, 1729, as the first German Reformed church in the province, it was held by Reiff and his followers. Rev. George Michael Weiss was the first pastor, who preached in this church till his departure for Holland in May 1730. On May 1, 1730, Weiss held his last communion at Skippack, while on May 7th and May 17th two farewell services were held there by him. Mr. Dotterer describes the location of the Skippack Reformed church as follows:

"The plantation which Jacob Reiff retained for his home was located near the south east border of the present township of Lower Salford, on both sides of the Little Branch creek, near the Skippack. This property became famous as the place upon which the Skippack Reformed Church was erected. . . . About two hundred yards east of the graveyard is the spot on which stood the log church. The site of the old church is at the edge of the woods, where is still to be seen something of a glebe, such as betrays a venerable place. The logs of the church were used in the erection of what is

---

[75] The land was secured by Jacob Reiff, December 1, **1727, see** Heckler, *History of Lower Salford Township,* p. 99.

now Allebach's mill, on the Schippach, where they still form the walls of that old building".[76]

During Boehm's lifetime there were two Reformed congregations at Skippack. The Reiff faction which worshipped in the church on the Reiff property and the adherents of Boehm. The party of Reiff had the following pastors: George Michael Weiss, 1727-1730; John Peter Miller, 1730-1731; John Bartholomew Rieger, 1731-1734; John Henry Goetschy, 1735-1739; and John William Straub, 1739-1741. After that they were apparently without a regular pastor.

Boehm and his followers worshipped at first in private houses. But on March 20, 1735, Boehm and two of his elders, Gabriel Schuler, of Salford, and Ulrich Stephen of Skippack, bought a tract of 150 acres and 154 perches from Christian Allebach and Christian Myers, Jr., executors of the last will of Christian Stauffer.[77] This land is now a part of the village of Harleysville. On it was a well-built house, in which the congregation worshipped till December, 1745, when Boehm was compelled to sell the land again, as no help came to him from Holland. Under date October 20, 1746, Schlatter reports in his private diary: "If the scattered Skippack congregation, which I have not yet visited, could again be brought together, it could be most advantageously united with it [Indian Creek], for they are only six miles apart and no river is between them. Hitherto a linen weaver, named Straub, has preached every three weeks in this congregation [Indian Creek], and has performed ministerial acts, but he has now promised me to administer the sacraments no more".[78] A report of Boehm, made in November, 1746, is similar: "The congregation has been scattered by past divisions, so that, according to all appearance, there is no more hope of maintaining a congregation there. The few members of the upper part can conveniently go to Old Goshenhoppen". In 1747, there were 18 men at Skippack, who promised eight pounds and eight shillings for a pastor, who would minister to them.[79] In November, 1748, Boehm

---

[76] See Heckler, *History of Lower Salford*, pp. 99, 109.
[77] See Heckler, l. c., pp. 4-6.
[78] See "Diary of Schlatter," printed in *Journal of Presbyterian Historical Society*, Vol. III, p. 161.
[79] See *Coetus Minutes*, p. 38.

informed Schlatter that "Skippack had scattered of itself and was no more". Nevertheless, the congregation continued its shadowy existence in some form, for in 1755 Schlatter gave 100 fl. of the Reiff money to the congregation at Skippack.[80] This is the last reference to it. In 1762, Wentz's Reformed Church in Worcester township was organized as the successor of the Skippack Church.

FALKNER SWAMP REFORMED CHURCH.

The Falkner Swamp congregation is the only one of the three original congregations of Boehm, which has survived to the present day. It is located in what is now New Hanover township, Montgomery County, about twelve miles north-west from the former Skippack church. This congregation also, like that of Whitemarsh, met at first in private houses. Its first officers in 1728 were: Frederick Antes, George Philip Dotterer, Jacob Meyer, John Berkenbeil, Sebastian Reifsnyder and George Klauer. The congregation grew rapidly. In 1738, the number of communicants was 89, in 1740 it had increased to 152, and in 1743 to 236. In 1741, the elders of the congregation bought three quarters of an acre for church and cemetery, on which they erected a church. On June 21, 1741, the first services were held in this church. In 1744, Boehm speaks of it as a "well built frame church", on which the congregation owed nearly sixty pounds. In 1746, Boehm reported that Falkner Swamp, being twenty miles from his home in Whitpain, was very difficult for him to supply, as he was geting feeble, but in the fall of 1748, he had the joy of installing his successor, the Rev. John Philip Leydich, who had arrived in Philadelphia September 15, 1748. The installation of Leydich took place on October 16, 1748.[81]

---

[80] See *Coetus Minutes*, p. 128. A detailed history of the "Skippack Reformed Church," was published by Mr. Dotterer in the *Lansdale Reporter*, beginning February 25, 1886. See Dotterer, Historical Notes of Montgomery County, pp. 117-125. (A book of clippings in the library of the Pa. Hist. Society, at Philadelphia.)

[81] For the history of the Falkner Swamp Reformed Church, see the address of Mr. Dotterer, printed in his *Historical Notes*, pp. 86-89, 106-109; also G. W. Roth, *History of the Falkner Swamp Reformed Church*, New Hanover, 1904, pp. 71.

CONESTOGA REFORMED CHURCHES.

While Boehm was organizing the Reformed people in the Perkiomen valley into three congregations in 1725, another Reformed leader was doing the same thing in the Conestoga valley, in Lancaster County. It was John Conrad Tempelman, a pious tailor from Heidelberg, Germany. He was born at Weinheim in the Palatinate and was baptized there March 22, 1692. In 1717, we find him at Heidelberg, where he lived at the foot of the castle hill. He was married September 22, 1717, to Anna Maria Barth. They had two children, Anna Margaret, baptized September 11, 1718, and Anna Maria, baptized March 16, 1721. Shortly afterwards and before 1725, Tempelman with his family reached Pennsylvania and settled in the Conestoga valley. In a most important letter, which he wrote to the Synods of North and South Holland on February

SIGNATURE OF CONRAD TEMPELMAN.

13, 1733, he relates the origin of the Reformed Church in the Conestoga valley:[82]

"The church at Chanastocka had its origin in the year 1725, with a small gathering in houses here and there, with the reading of a sermon and with song and prayer, according to their High German Church Order upon all Sundays and holidays, but, on account of the lack of a minister, without the administration of baptism and the Lord's Supper.

"Thereafter Dom. Boehm served them, at first [1727] voluntarily at the request of the people, later, after being fully ordained, he administered baptism and communion to them for the space of two years [1730-1731], upon a yearly call, although he lived a distance of twenty-one hours [about 63 miles] away from them, being satisfied with their small voluntary gifts. Subsequently he also established a church order

---

[82] The original letter of Tempelman is lost, but an abstract in Dutch is preserved in the archives at The Hague, 74, I, 14.

[constitution] among them and the congregation chose elders, and he himself [Tempelman] exercised a strict and careful supervision, so that all things went on in a good order in this congregation.

"Further, the writer reports that the congregation, on account of enlargement and great distance between the members, has divided itself into six meeting places in Chanastocka, three of which places are served by a Reformed minister, Johann Peter Muller by name, by whom also another strong congregation is served about seven hours [21 miles] distant, called Dalbenhacken [Tulpehocken].

"But that they now, by reason of the division of the congregation, can no longer be served by Do. Boehm, nor by the aforesaid Muller, both by reason of the great extent of the localities and because of the manifold occupations and heavy labor wherewith he is overburdened. . . .

"The entire north side, twenty-four hours [sixty miles] distant from Philadelphia, named Chanastocka (which is not a town but a tract of land so named after a certain creek) is settled by Germans and English. Three of the meeting places of the Reformed people cover an area, seven hours [21 miles] long and seven hours wide. But they say that they can give no report to the Christian Synods regarding the three places ministered unto by Do. Muller. Nevertheless, they hope that the said preacher will make known his own needs (inasmuch as he cannot well subsist by the free will gifts of the people) as well as the condition of his congregation and his elders. . . .

"Regarding the three first-named meeting places they give further report to the Reverend Christian Synods [Classes] of Amsterdam and Rotterdam, concerning the members and elders belonging to them, with the autograph signatures of the latter.

"It is signed Conrad Tempelman,
"Reader of the Congregation."

(N. B. He seems to be the writer of the letter).
Members 55, Elders:
    Rudolf Heller (l. s.)
    Michael Albert (l. s.)
    Andries M —— (l. s.)

"At the second meeting place are the following number of members and elders:

Members 51, Elders:
> Hans Georg Swab (L. S.)
> Johannes Göhr (L. S.)
> Conrad Werns (L. S.)

"At the third meeting place are the following members and elders:

Members 30, Elders:
> Johann Jacob Hook (L. S.)
> Andries Halsbrun (L. S.)
> Nicolaus —— (L. S.)".

The fact that Tempelman has given us the names of the elders of these congregations enables us to identify them. The first of these preaching places is identical with what Boehm calls the Hill Church in Conestoga. Michael Albert is given by him as one of the elders in 1740. The modern name is Heller's Reformed Church in Upper Leacock township, Lancaster County.[83] The second preaching place is identical with Cocalico. The names of Conrad Werns and Johannes Gehr are found in the old Cocalico record. Moreover, we know from the printed defense of Jacob Lischy that Conrad Werns lived near Ephrata in 1743. The third preaching place is Lancaster, whose elder, John Jacob Hock, was elected in 1736 as the first regular pastor of the Lancaster congregation.

About these congregations we learn many interesting details from the reports of Boehm. According to his report of

---

[83] At the Coetus of 1748, the first Conestoga church was represented by John "Lein." In 1746 John "Leyn" and Michael Weidler signed the pledge of the Conestoga church for eight pounds and twenty-five bushels of oats, towards a minister's salary. Both of these men are found on the deed of the Heller church property. On February 11, 1743, Philip Scot, of Leacock township, Lancaster County, sold to John Line, Jr., and Michael Widler two acres of land for the sum of eight shillings. This land, "whereon the meeting house now stands," was deeded "for the use of the Presbiteirian Congregation of the said Church in Leacock aforesaid." In the cemetery, adjoining Heller's Church, Michael Weidler was buried, having died July 23, 1770. His tombstone is still preserved. See D. W. Gerhard, *History of the New Holland Charge,* New Holland, 1877, p. 119.

1744, he celebrated his first communion at Conestoga on October 14, 1727, when 59 members communed. Having visited the congregation a few times, Weiss took it away from him, but he soon left it again. After his ordination the congregation in Conestoga invited Boehm again to visit them. This he did on May 30, 1730, when he told them about his ordination in New York and about the constitution his churches had agreed to accept. They then expressed their readiness to be taken under the care of the Amsterdam Classis. To that end they drew up a petition, which Boehm agreed to send to Holland. From 1731-1732 John Peter Miller ministered to the congregation. Then the division into six preaching places was effected, of which Tempelman speaks in his letter. Three of these were served by Miller and three by Tempelman. The former included perhaps Muddy Creek, White Oaks and Seltenreich.

When Miller had gone over to the Seventh Day Dunkers, Boehm was again invited by the Conestoga congregations. He went there again, and on May 11, 1735, ninety-two members communed at the Hill Church in Upper Leacock township, and sixty members at Cocalico, "which had been gathered previously". The Cocalico congregation, near Ephrata, originated most likely during the ministry of Boehm from 1730-1731.[84]

After the year 1735, the congregations in the Conestoga valley made Conrad Tempelman their pastor. Boehm says of him in 1744: "Of the same I noticed at that time nothing wrong in his life and conduct, and since have heard of him nothing but what was praiseworthy, especially that he is very watchful against the sects and that his congregations are very much united". When Schlatter visited Lancaster County in June, 1747, Muddy Creek, Cocalico and White Oaks were still served by Tempelman.

[84] For a detailed account of the early history of the Conestoga and Cocalico Churches, see the writer's articles in the *Reformed Church Messenger*, entitled "Early History of the Reformed Church in the Conestoga Valley," *Messenger* of January 4, 11, 18, 1900; also the "History of the Cocalico Charge," from 1750-1800, in the *Reformed Church Record*, of February 15, 22, and March 1, 1900.

TULPEHOCKEN REFORMED CHURCHES.

Another congregation, which Boehm organized in 1727, was Tulpehocken. It had been settled by Palatines coming from the State of New York in 1723. Conrad Weiser describes its origin as follows:

"The people got news of the land on the Swatara and Tulpehocken in Pennsylvania. Many of them united and cut a road from Schoharie [N. Y.] to the Susquehanna River, carried their goods there, made canoes and floated them down the river to the mouth of the Swatara creek [where Middletown is situated at present], and drove their cattle over land. This happened in the spring of the year 1723. From there they came to Tulpehocken, and this was the beginning of the Tulpehocken settlement". The original colony consisted of thirty-three families, which were soon followed by others. How many of them were Reformed cannot be determined at present. The Lutheran settlers induced their former minister at Schoharie, Bernhard von Thieren, to visit them occasionally. They were also visited by Rev. Anthony Jacob Henckel of Falkner Swamp. At the suggestion of the latter a church was built in 1727. This church was at first a union church. This is distinctly asserted by a number of contemporaneous documents. In 1747, Conrad Weiser wrote to Rev. Peter Brunholtz, a Lutheran minister:

"In 1729, I began to live at this place. A few years previously the Lutherans had built a little church or meeting house, in which Lutherans *as well as so-called Reformed people came together,* and were led by a reader in their divine services".[85]

A similar statement is found in Saur's Paper, under date October 16, 1747: "About twenty years ago the Lutherans at Dolpehocken built a little church and laid out a cemetery, where Lutherans, as well as Reformed, buried their dead".

Finally a document presented to the court of Berks county

---

[85] See *Heinrich Melchior Muehlenberg, Selbstbiographie*, 1711-1743, Allentown, 1881, p. 232; also Fresenius, *Bewaehrte Nachrichten*, Vol. III, p. 848.

in 1755, is still clearer in its statements:[86] "In the year 1725, Tulpehocken was first settled by about fifty families, who came from the County of Albany, in the Province of New York, chiefly Lutherans and (so called) Reformed or Calvinists. A few years after the Lutherans built a church (the Reformed assisting them) in the heart of Tulpenhocken".

Boehm visited Tulpehocken for the first time October 18, 1727, when thirty-two members communed. But on June 28, 1728, only twenty-seven communicants were present. That may have been due to the interference of Weiss, who entered all of Boehm's congregations to protest against his ministry. A year after his ordination Boehm went again to Tulpehocken, on November 23, 1730. A year later, John Peter Miller was called by the Reformed people of Tulpehocken "to be their teacher, which office he served among them and in other places during four years". During Miller's ministry the services were still held, part of the time, in the Lutheran church, for the Lutheran Tulpehocken record, now in the archives at Bethlehem, states: "Peter Mueller, a Reformed minister, came also to us and preached almost two years". But a church was built for the Reformed people during the latter part of Miller's ministry. This is implied in the Ephrata Chronicle[87] which refers to a conversation between Conrad Weiser and Conrad Beissel, in which the latter asked his visitor: "What is the other [Miller] doing? He was told that he was engaged in building. Ay, Ay, he replied, let him build on; he has but little more time left".

As soon as Miller withdrew, Boehm was again called by the congregation to visit them twice a year, in order to hold communion services for them. In 1737, the number of communicants was one hundred and three, in 1740, they numbered one hundred and nineteen. In 1736, Goetschy tried to break into the congregation by "three uncalled-for visits". Similar visits were made by him in 1740, but he did not succeed in taking the congregation away from Boehm. In 1738, there

---

[86] Printed in full in Dr. Schmauk's *History of the Lutheran Church in Pennsylvania*, p. 570f. Compare also the statement in the "Tulpehocken Confusion," in which reference is made to "the Reformed at that time [1733] dwelling with us," see Schmauk, l. c., p. 476.

[87] See *Ephrata Chronicle*, Engl. Ed., p. 71f.

was a division, on account of the wide extent of territory covered by the congregation. On October 19th and 22, 1738, communion services were held for the first time at two places in Tulpehocken. In January, 1739, Boehm reported that at Tulpehocken there was a log church, not serviceable for public worship nor centrally located.

In order to determine the location and identity of these two Tulpehocken churches, we must consider some later statements of Boehm. According to his statistics of the year 1743, the older congregation built a new church in that year. Of this congregation Boehm reported in 1744, that it had received four acres as a gift and, as Boehm puts it, "they built upon it a tolerably large, beautiful and well-built frame church". The other Tulpehocken congregation had, as Boehm states in 1744, "some years ago bought 100 acres of land and built a small church upon it, but it is now altogether too small".

Comparing with these statements of Boehm the deeds of the two Tulpehocken churches we find that the Host Church in Tulpehocken township, Berks County, holds deeds for four acres of land, which correspond with the four acres of the older church, as mentioned by Boehm. On March 25, 1754, George Kantner granted to Valentine Unruh and John Mayer two acres, which in a declaration of trust, these two men acknowledged to have been deeded to them "in trust to the intent only, that we or such or so many of us as shall be and continue of the community and in religious fellowship with the said congregation and remain members of the Dutch Calvinist Church aforesaid". On March 26, 1754, John Riegel and his wife Catherine Elisabeth deeded to Valentine Unruh and John Mayer, two acres of land adjoining John Riegel's land in Tulpehocken township, the consideration being twenty shillings. This was sufficient to cover the lawyer's fees.

Trinity Tulpehocken Church, three miles east of Myerstown and one and a half mile west of Stouchsburg, just across the county line, in Lebanon County, holds a deed which shows that on December 10, 1745, Caspar Wister and his wife Catherine sold to Valentine Hergelrood, Adam Diffenbach, Francis Wenrich, Jonas Lerue, Henry Bassler and Bartholomew Sheffer, all of Tulpehocken, one hundred acres of land, in consideration of the sum of forty pounds of lawful money to them paid, situated on Tulpehocken creek, in Tulpehocken township. This is evidently the land of the second Tulpehocken church mentioned by Boehm.[88]

This division was considered at first by Boehm a temporary arrangement. He advised the Tulpehocken people to unite in building a central church large enough to accommodate all. For a while, it seems, his arguments prevailed. However, he could not stem the tide for any length of time. New settlements had been begun west of the Tulpehocken on the Quitopahilla and Swatara, and the people living there demanded religious services. As early as March 1, 1737,[89] Conrad Tempelman had taken up 200 acres of land in Lebanon township. On this farm, which was located "four miles south-east of Lebanon, at a place called Tempelman's Hill", he resided to the end of his life, and from there as a center he ministered to the neighboring congregations.

In 1740, Boehm proposed to the Classis of Amsterdam to organize Tulpehocken with Quitopahilla and Swatara (congregations reported to be of considerable strength) into a regular charge, and asked Classis to send them a minister. Meanwhile he advised those at Quitopahilla to unite temporarily with the western part of the Tulpehocken congregation. They accepted the advice and hence, in March, 1740, Boehm could report to the Classis: "They at Quitopahilla joined the congregation at Tulpehocken the more readily, because the latter will have to be served at two places, on account of its wide extent and rapid growth. One of these places will be nearer to them to go to church to, and may be counted instead of Quitopahilla, because it extends in that direction and is already in use".

On February 11, 1740, Boehm visited Tulpehocken and secured from the elders the pledge that the congregation would pay fifteen pounds and fifty bushels of oats towards a minister's salary. Swatara promised, on the 14th of February, five pounds and ten bushels of oats for the same purpose.

[88] The "Early History of the Tulpehocken Church, 1727-1747," was presented in full in a series of articles by the writer in the *Reformed Church Messenger* of June 26, July 10 and July 17, 1902.
[89] See Wm. Egle, *History of Lebanon County*, p. 8.

In April, 1741, Rieger tried to take the Tulpehocken churches away from Boehm, but, owing to some ill-considered remarks which he made in the presence of several of the elders, he did not succeed.

In 1743, Tupehocken, like other Reformed congregations, felt the influence of the union movement of Count Zinzendorf. As one of the missionaries of the movement, Jacob Lischy, came to Tulpehocken and offered to preach for the people. But, when they discovered that he was connected with Zinzendorf, they sent him away.

In 1743, Tulpehocken, like other Reformed congregations, tified Boehm that they had written to the Consistory of Zweibruecken, and that they had been promised a pastor. Meanwhile, they assured Boehm, they would be loyal to him until the new minister should arrive. He appeared in December, 1744. It was the Rev. Casper Ludwig Schnorr. On March 15, 1745, he informed the Classis[90] that he had accepted Lancaster, but was reserving twelve Sundays in a year for Tulpehocken and the neighboring congregations. But his ministry was cut short by his offensive conduct. In April, 1746, Schnorr entered his last baptism into the church record at Lancaster. Shortly afterwards he went to the State of New York.

The 25th of September, 1746, was a memorable day in the history of the congregation. On that day Schlatter, Weiss and Boehm were in "the wooden church" at Tulpehocken. Schlatter preached to an audience of more than six hundred people, and administered the communion to 101 communicants. After the service the people pledged themselves to give fifty pounds to a minister's salary.[91] Schlatter made out a call, and in answer to that call the Coetus of 1748 appointed the Rev. Dominicus Bartholomaeus to go to Tulpehocken as the first settled pastor.

PHILADELPHIA REFORMED CHURCH.

There was a third congregation to which Boehm began preaching in the year 1727. It was the Philadelphia congregation. It is a fact which deserves special emphasis that Boehm preached in Philadelphia before the arrival of Weiss in Sep-

---

[90] The original letter is in the Classical Archives at Amsterdam.
[91] See *Schlatter's Life and Travels*, by Dr. Henry Harbaugh, p. 134.

tember, 1727. In his report of 1744 Boehm makes these significant statements: "As regards the congregation at Philadelphia, Mr. Weiss took also that out of my hands on his arrival, by the above mentioned opponents, for I had then already preached there a few times at their request". This proves that the congregation at Philadelphia in some form was in existence before Weiss organized it in the fall of 1727. Boehm had probably not yet attempted a regular oraganization. If that had taken place he would no doubt have mentioned it.

On the Sunday following his arrival, September 24, 1727, Weiss celebrated the first communion service at Philadelphia. That is the first fixed date in the history of the congregation. Before the close of the year the following elders were installed at Philadelphia by Weiss: Peter Lecolie, John William Roehrig, Hendrik Weller and George Peter Hillegass. It was while pastor at Philadelphia that Weiss published in 1729 the first Reformed book printed in Pennsylvania. It was directed against the New Born, a sect which had been founded about 1718 at Oley, Berks County, by Matthias Baumann. To counteract the influence of these "most terrible of all men, who without hesitation declare themselves equal to God and greater than our Saviour" (as Boehm calls them), Weiss wrote his little book, whose title may be rendered as follows in English: "The Minister traveling about in the American Wilderness among people of different nationalities and religions, and frequently attacked; portrayed and presented in a dialogue with a citizen and a New Born. Treating of different subjects, but especially of the new birth. Prepared and to the advancement of the honor of Jesus composed from his own experience by George Michael Weiss, Philadelphia, printed by Andrew Bradford, 1729"; 12 mo, V pp. introduction, 29 pp. text.[92] In this little book Weiss refutes ably the principal heresies of the New Born.

The ministry of Weiss at Philadelphia was rendered difficult by the poverty of his people, who were unable to pay him a sufficient salary. To secure more means he ad-

---

[92] The only known copy of the original was discovered by the writer in the Congressional Library at Washington. Its German text, together with an English translation, is printed in *Penn Germania*, Vol. I, pp. 338-361.

vertised nine times in the "American Weekly Mercury", printed at Philadelphia, beginning with February 10, 1730, offering to teach students Logic, Natural Philosophy, Metaphysics, etc., the instruction to be given in the house of widow Sprogel, in Second Street.

When Weiss left the congregation in May, 1730, it was without a pastor for several months until John Peter Miller arrived on August 29, 1730. He became Weiss' successor for about a year, till the fall of 1731, when he was succeeded by Rev. John Bartholomew Rieger. A letter, written from Philadelphia, November 22, 1731, shows that Rieger was pastor of the congregation at that time.

From the time of Rieger we have the first statement of the approximate membership of the congregation. Dr. John Jacob Diemer, a prominent member of the congregation, wrote November 22, 1731, to the Synods: "In trying to collect the salary of our minister we have found in the three congregations, Philadelphia, Germantown and Skippack, not quite two hundred families, but we have not been able to raise more than thirty-eight pounds for our minister's salary".[93]

It was during the ministry of Rieger that the "Reiff Case" came to a climax, in April, 1734. As a result of this, Rieger withdrew and went to Amwell, N. J. Then forty-two members of the congregation appealed to Boehm on April 20, 1734, to help them in their unfortunate situation. After repeated oral and written requests Boehm went to Philadelphia on July 15, 1734, and preached a sermon of admonition to the congregation. It was so effective that the congregation concluded to accept the Church Order drawn up by Boehm and in force in his other congregations. Four weeks later, on August 18, 1734, a new consistory was installed and an agreement was entered into with the other congregations that Boehm should preach at Philadelphia once a month. In November, 1734, the Reformed and Lutherans in Philadelphia rented jointly an old butcher shop, "in Arch Street, near the Quaker burying grounds".[94] It was fitted up with benches and regular ser-

---

[93] The original is in the archives at The Hague, 74, I, 36.
[94] Thus located in the old church record of the congregation. The statement was made by Rev. Michael Schlatter.

DER
IN DER AMERICANI-
SCHEN WILDNUSZ
Unter Menschen von verschiedenen
Nationen und Religionen
Hin und wieder herum Wandelte
Und verschiedentlich Angefochtene
PREDIGER,
Abgemahlet und vorgestellet
In einem Gespraech mit Einem
Politico und Neugebornen,
Verschiedene Stuck insonderheit
Die Neugeburt betreffende,
Verfertiget, und zu Besorderung der Ehr
JESU
Selbst aus eigener Erfahrung an das
Licht gebracht

Von Georg Michael Weiss V. D. M.

Zu PHILADELPHIA:
Gedruckt bey *Andrew Bradford*, 1729.

THE BOOK OF WEISS AGAINST THE NEWBORN, 1729
The first book published by a Reformed Minister in Pennsylvania

vices were held in it till 1747. Boehm remained pastor of the congregation till the close of the year 1746, when Rev. Michael Schlatter succeeded him.

On December 21, 1746, Boehm installed Schlatter as pastor of the Philadelphia congregation and on the 15th of February, 1747, as pastor of the Germantown congregation. Boehm agreed, however, to keep on preaching at Philadelphia for six months longer, so as to enable Schlatter to continue his journeys through the country, visiting Reformed congregations.

OLEY REFORMED CHURCH.

In 1736, Boehm added another congregation to his extensive parish. It was Oley, in Berks County. German settlers from the State of New York had begun to settle in the Oley valley as early as 1712. The first Reformed services in Oley were held by Rev. George Michael Weiss, probably in 1729. It was at Oley that Weiss came in contact with the New Born, and his book against them was printed in 1729. Sometime afterwards actual congregational life manifested itself there, for on April 13, 1734, John Lesher, a Calvinist, conveyed by deed 132 perches of land to Gabriel Boyer and Casper Griesemer, in trust for the society of Christian people inhabiting Oley.[95] Upon this lot a small meeting house is said to have been built in 1735. In 1736, the congregation came under the control of Boehm. Upon the earnest request of the people Boehm visited Oley on May 4, 1736, and held the Lord's Supper there, at which time thirty-nine communicants were present. At the time of his second visit, November 17, 1736, forty members took part in the communion. It was at this time that Boehm installed four elders and two deacons elected by the congregation and himself was accepted by them as their pastor to visit them twice a year, during the week, to administer communion and baptize children.

Shortly afterwards young Goetschy came into the Oley region and succeeded in persuading a part of the congregation to adhere to him. At the time of his third visit, in the spring of 1737, Boehm found the congregation in a state of confusion. Hence he retired and left the field to Goetschy, who

---

[95] See *Pennsylvania German*, Vol. III, p. 119.

preached at Oley probably from 1737-1739. In 1740 Rev. P. H. Dorsius seems to have supplied the congregation occasionally. On February 5, 1740, the elders and members at Oley promised ten pounds and twenty bushels of oats towards a minister's salary. After that Oley disappears from view for a number of years. On September 23, 1746, Rev. Michael Schlatter met Frederick Casimir Mueller at Oley, who was ministering to "ten or twelve small congregations in or about Oley".[96] Schlatter offered to write to Holland to secure Mueller's ordination, if he would agree to abstain meanwhile from administering the sacraments. Mueller made the promise but broke it again the following Sunday. Hence Schlatter lost all interest in him. How long Mueller served Oley we are unable to say, but on April 9, 1755, John Lesher of Oley appeared before the Coetus at Lancaster and requested that Oley might be supplied by a minister of the Coetus. In the following year it was again given up, because they had again accepted one of the vagrant ministers.

PROVIDENCE REFORMED CHURCH.

In his statistics of the year 1743, Boehm refers to a newly gathered congregation in Providence township, where on April 4, 1743, thirty-two members communed. This congregation is now represented by St. Luke's Reformed Church at Trappe, Providence Township, Montgomery County. On May 3, 1744, another communion service was held "for the newly gathered congregation in Providence, in a barn". At this time 63 members participated in the communion. In connection with this service Boehm remarks that the first communion service in Providence was held November 5, 1743, when nineteen communicants were present. But as the communicant list of 1743 makes no reference to such a service on November 5th, and moreover the same list shows that there was an earlier service on April 4th, so that the service on November 5th could not have been the first, it is natural to conclude that the date, November 5, 1743, is due to a slip of the pen for November 5, 1742. The small number of communicants also argues for

---

[96] See Schlatter's "Private Diary," printed in *Journal of Presbyterian Historical Society*, Vol. III, p. 119.

the year 1742. From these considerations it appears as fairly certain that September 5, 1742, ought to be accepted as the first date in the history of the Providence church.

On October 18, 1746, Rev. Michael Schlatter preached at Providence in a barn, to a poor congregation.[97] Forty-two men obligated themselves to raise a salary of fifteen pounds annually and also some grain. In the spring of 1747, Schlatter reports, a church was built at Providence.[98] Boehm remained pastor of the congregation till 1748. By the Coetus of 1748, held September 28-30, 1748, at Philadelphia, Rev. John Philip Leydich was assigned to Falkner Swamp and Providence. He was installed as pastor of these congregations by Boehm on October 16, 1748.

BOEHM'S REFORMED CHURCH.

The last congregation to be organized by Boehm bears his name to the present day. It is Boehm's Reformed Church at Blue Bell, Whitpain Township, Montgomery County. When Boehm felt that old age was coming upon him and that he would not be able to make extended tours to distant congregations, he determined to found a congregation in the immediate neighborhood of his home in Whitpain township.

When Schlatter visited Boehm at his home October 20, 1746, the latter made use of this opportunity to lay his plans for the future before Schlatter, for on November 25, 1746, Boehm reported the results of this conference to the Synods of Holland. Boehm then informed Schlatter that he would like to give up Falkner Swamp and Philadelphia, as the work was becoming too difficult for him, and he proposed, in case Schlatter would consent, to organize a new congregation in Whitpain Township, about midway between Germantown and Old Goshenhoppen, about twelve miles from each of these places. To this congregation the members of the upper Whitemarsh and of the lower Skippack could attach themselves. Besides, many people of Reformed antecedents, but not attached to any church, were

---

[97] See *Schlatter's Life and Travels*, p. 139.
[98] Schlatter really refers, in December, 1746, to the church at Providence, which "is to be built in spring." This intention was no doubt carried out. See *Journal of Presb. Hist. Soc.*, Vol. III, p. 165.

living in his immediate vicinity. Schlatter agreed to this proposal and promised to mention it favorably in his report to Holland.

As a result Schlatter came to Boehm's home on February 3, 1747, to organize the new congregation. As it was a cold day but few members were present. Nevertheless, they proceeded with the organization of the congregation. Three elders were elected and signatures for the pastor's salary were secured. They amounted to only six pounds and three shillings. Schlatter declared the amount too small and refused at first to proceed with the organization. Then a characteristic incident occurred, fortunately preserved to us by Boehm himself: "I pitied (he says) the souls who were sad about this [refusal of Schlatter], for although they were few, yet they were dear and eager for salvation. I asked him [Schlatter] to report them, and I offered to serve them for fifteen pounds [annually]. Then his Reverence continued and organized the congregation fully. I pledged myself to conduct divine services for them regularly every two weeks, which I do heartily, and, if I am at home and have no other religious services elsewhere, I preach for them every Sunday". Schlatter reports in his diary, that by February, 1747, they had built a small stone church.[99] On February 18, 1747, John Lewis of the township of Whitpain, yeoman, sold to the Rev. John Philip Boehm, minister, Michael Clime, Arnold Ruttersham and Andrew Acker, churchwardens, a parcel of land containing one acre, for and in consideration of the sum of four pounds ten shillings. The deed recites that this land was sold "in trust nevertheless for the use of ye said congregation of the High Dutch Reformed Church, formed by the Christian Synod held at Dortrecht in Holland in the years 1618 and 1619 (so that the said congregation shall hold, follow and adhere to the principles of the Heidelberg Catechism and in subordination to the Reverend Classis at Amsterdam and for no other use, intent or purpose whatsoever, and further that the Tested Church Wardens of the said congregation from time to time for ever after shall be careful to uphold and maintain the above recited principles and that no church wardens shall have power

---

[99] See *Schlatter's Life and Travels*, p. 150.

to alter or make void anything that has been done or established before them or this present year, 1748, to the only proper use and behoof of the said congregation, their heirs and successors for ever". The deed was recorded May 10, 1748.

There were two other congregations in which Boehm was interested, although they never appear in his letters.

EGYPT REFORMED CHURCH.

The first of these was Egypt in Lehigh County. On page 15 of the old church record of the Egypt Church is the following entry: "On July 27, 1734, a son was born to Peter Traxel and was baptized by Rev. Mr. Boehm on September 23, 1734. Witnesses: Nicolaus Kern and his wife Maria Margaretha. Name of the child: David". This baptism implies most likely a visit of Boehm to Egypt, and if so, it was no doubt to preach there. Another child of Peter Traxel was baptized October 26, 1736, by John Henry Goetschy. In connection with that entry Peter Traxel is called "Censor of the Reformed congregation here". There is, therefore, no doubt that there was a Reformed congregation at Egypt in 1736, when Goetschy visited it to baptize a child. His baptism implies that he was pastor in Egypt in 1736. On the title page of the New Goshenhoppen record, written by Goetschy about 1736, Egypt is distinctly mentioned as one of his congregations. If the baptism of Goetschy in 1736 implies his pastorate at that time, it makes it highly probable that the same inference must be made from Boehm's baptism in 1734. We may therefore suppose that the Reformed people at Egypt gave Boehm an invitation to visit them, with which he complied on September 23, 1734.

Boehm was succeeded by Goetschy. The title page of the Egypt record is dated by Goetschy March 22, 1739, and a later baptism was performed by him on June 27, 1739. Hence Goetschy's ministry at Egypt extended from 1736-1739. On September 23, 1740, Rev. Peter Henry Dorsius (called Inspector Torschius in the record) baptized three children of the Egypt congregation at Saucon.[100]

Another visit of Boehm at Egypt was made July 28, 1741,

---

[100] See *Pennsylvania Archives, Sixth Series*, Vol. VI, p. 6, where the Egypt record is printed in full, Vol. VI, pp. 5-13.

when he baptized five children according to the record. In September, 1742, John Conrad Wirtz (Wuertz) began preaching at Egypt. His baptisms extend from September 17, 1742, to November 15, 1743.[101] After the latter date the congregation was vacant. In June 1747, Michael Schlatter visited Egypt and neighboring congregations. He writes in his diary: "From Wednesday to Saturday, the 24th, 25th, and 26th [of June] I visited the congregations in Manatawny, Magunschy, Egypt, and at the Lehigh, a circuit of forty-five miles, and came near to Bethlehem, a meeting place of the Moravians". Schlatter proposed to organize Heidelberg, Egypt and Jordan into a charge, and he reports that they had promised to contribute forty-two pounds, or 280 Dutch guilders, for the support of a minister. At the first meeting of the Coetus, in September, 1747, Egypt was represented by its elder, Abraham Wotring. On November 8, 1748, Schlatter received a call for a minister from Egypt and Heidelberg. A copy of this document was sent to Holland by Schlatter.[102] It is dated November 5, 1748, and is signed by Daniel Burger, Ulrich Musslie, Abraham Wotring, Jacob Kohler, Michel Hoffmann, John Nic. Schneider, John Weber and John Drachsel. On March 29, 1749,[103] Schlatter received letters from Macungy and Egypt asking him to administer the Lord's Supper for them. Upon Schlatter's request Boehm undertook to visit them. The visit was made on April 28, 1749, when Boehm administered the

---

[101] It has been supposed that the entries of Wirtz extended to December 21, 1744 (see C. R. Roberts, *History of the Egypt Church*, Allentown, 1908, p. 10), but a careful examination of the record by the writer shows that the two entries of 1744 were made by the same hand, which entered the earliest baptism in 1734. It was not Boehm. The handwriting is *certainly* not his. It was probably Mr. Traxel himself. It is the same hand that entered the baptism of Mr. Dorsius, performed in 1740, and the baptisms of Mr. Boehm in 1741. None of these were made by the pastors themselves. The Egypt record was probably bought and given to the congregation by young Goetschy. The Great Swamp record and the Berne record, begun by Goetschy, have the same shape and make as the Egypt record.

[102] Now in the archives at The Hague, 74, I, 51.

[103] By an oversight Dr. Harbaugh, in his *Life of Schlatter*, p. 188, omitted the month. It was not January 29th, but March 29th, 1749, as a comparison with the German edition in Fresenius, *Pastoral Sammlungen*, Frankfort, 1752, p. 298, shows.

communion. It was the last public service at which Boehm officiated before his death.

COVENTRY REFORMED CHURCH.

There is still another congregation of which Boehm was pastor, although he never refers to that fact in his letters, nor has any historian ever mentioned it. From the diaries of several Moravian missionaries it appears that Boehm was elected pastor of the Reformed church in Coventry township, Chester County, in 1746.

The Coventry congregation (now Brownback's in Chester County) called Jacob Lischy as its first pastor April 10, 1743. He drew up a constitution which was signed by thirty-six members on May 19, 1743. Lischy served the congregation till 1745, when other Moravian missionaries, laboring under the union movement of Zinzendorf, took his place. But their work at Coventry was not without opposition. In December, 1744, Jacob Lischy reported to Spangenberg: "Mr. Boehm also began to slander me and turned the congregation at the Schuylkill against me. He brought it so far that they opened the church for him, but closed it against me. I noted the time when he had appointed a sermon there. I then appeared with about ten elders from Conestoga. When he heard this he rode to the justice of the peace, upon whose land the church was located, and secured his written permission to preach in the church. But I was not frightened by that. I listened to his sermon, and, when he had pronounced the benediction, I stepped up before him and asked him whether he could prove his printed lies and slanders against me. He was confused and unable to do so, and thus was put to shame before the whole congregation".[104] It may well be doubted whether Lischy reported the exact facts about this incident. There was nothing in what Boehm had written about Lischy but what could be fully substantiated. But as a result of this incident Lischy claims that Boehm withdrew. This is borne out by the diaries of Lischy and Rauch for the year 1745, which report re-

---

[104] See Report of Lischy to Spangenberg, dated December 8, 1744. It was published by the writer in the *Reformed Church Review*, Fourth Series, Vol. IX, (1905), pp. 517-534, especially p. 529f.

peatedly sermons by them in the church at Coventry. But in 1746 Boehm renewed his efforts to dislodge the Moravians from Coventry. In this second attempt he was successful. Although Henry Rauch continued his visits to Coventry in 1746, he felt discouraged about the situation. Thus on June 21, 1746, he reports in his diary: "To day I visited Coventry. I found that it looks bad here and that there is nothing more for us to do. I do not know a single soul that is not hostile and my doctrine does not suit them. Most of them have returned to Boehm and the rest are ashamed of us, because we are despised". In his summary report for the year 1746 Rauch has this to say about Coventry:

"Coventry has for a long time lain heavily upon my heart, as I have already complained to Synod regarding the sad and wretched condition of the poor souls at this place. . . . For that reason it was difficult for me to preach there. Now I have heard that they have accepted Boehm. It will probably be well for me to leave it to Boehm altogether. One more sermon is yet announced for me there". This sermon was preached November 9, 1746. In connection with it Rauch notes: "Mr. Boehm also preached to-day, not far from here. He wants to prevent me in this way from winning the souls away from him again".

Another missionary who preached at Coventry and mentions Boehm in his diary is Leonard Schnell. Under date of October 16, 1746, he writes: "I made my way across the Schuylkill and intended to preach in the Coventry church. But, since they lately accepted Rev. Boehm as their teacher to preach to them for a salary, they refused to let the Herrnhuters preach in their church, after the Gospel had been preached to them free of charge for three years." How long Boehm served Coventry cannot be determined. Schlatter apparently never visited it.

These then are the congregations in whose organization and maintenance Boehm was directly interested. Arranged in their chronological order they are as follows: In 1725 he founded Falkner Swamp, Skippack and Whitemarsh; in 1727 Conestoga, the older Tulpehocken congregation and Philadelphia; in 1734 probably Egypt; in 1735 Cocalico; in 1736 Oley; in 1738 the second Tulpehocken congregation; in 1742 Providence; in 1746 Coventry and in 1747 Whitpain. These are thirteen congregations to which Boehm ministered, and of which certainly eleven and perhaps twelve were founded by his labors. This is indeed a fine record, unequalled by any other Reformed minister of his time.[104a]

[104a] It may be well to place on record the various monographs and articles that have appeared, regarding these churches of Boehm. FALKNER SWAMP: Dotterer, *Historical Notes relating to the Pennsylvania Reformed Church,* Philadelphia, 1900, pp. 86-89, 106-109; G. W. Roth, *History of Falkner Swamp Reformed Church,* New Hanover, Montgomery Co., Pa., 1904. SKIPPACK: Dotterer, *Skippack Reformed Church* in Lansdale Reporter of 1886, see *Historical Notes, Montgomery County,* pp. 117-124 (see above, p. 61); J. Y. Heckler, *History of Lower Salford Township,* Harleysville, 1888, pp. 413-426. WHITEMARSH: Dotterer, *Whitemarsh Reformed Congregation in the Holland Archives,* paper read before the Hist. Soc. of Montg. Co., Sept. 23, 1897. CONESTOGA: D. W. Gerhard, *History of the New Holland Charge,* New Holland, 1877; Dubbs, *Earliest Reformed Church in Lancaster County,* paper read before the Lancaster County Hist. Soc. Vol. V, No. 1, Lancaster, 1900, also articles mentioned above, p. 65. COCALICO: D. C. Tobias, *History of the Bethany Charge,* Lancaster County, Lititz, 1881. TULPEHOCKEN: See articles referred to above, p. 69. PHILADELPHIA: David van Horne, *History of the Reformed Church in Philadelphia,* Philadelphia, 1876; Hinke, *Early History of the First Reformed Church, Philadelphia,* in Journal of the Presby. Hist. Soc., Vol. II, pp. 292-309. OLEY: Owing to lack of material no satisfactory history of the Oley Church exists, but see Montgomery, *History of Berks County.* PROVIDENCE: Messinger, *Trappe Reformed Church, Providence,* in Pennsylvania German, Vol. IX, pp. 255-261. WHITPAIN: Jones Detwiler, *History of Boehm's Church* in *Sesqui-Centennial of Boehm's Reformed Church,* Norristown, 1891, pp. 56-105. EGYPT: Ben Trexler, *Skizzen aus dem Lecha Thale,* Allentown, 1886, pp. 8-26; C. R. Roberts, *History of the Egypt Church,* Allentown, 1908; *Anniversary History of Lehigh County,* Vol. I, Allentown, 1914, pp. 1021-26. COVENTRY: Fluck, J. L., *History of the Reformed Churches in Chester County,* Norristown, 1892, pp. 16-31.

CHAPTER VI.

BOEHM'S OPPOSITION TO THE UNION MOVEMENT OF COUNT ZINZENDORF.

The year 1742 was made memorable in the ecclesiastical history of the Germans in Pennsylvania by the arrival and consequent activity of Count Zinzendorf. The object of his coming was to rally all the Germans in the Province around their common belief in Jesus Christ as their personal Saviour, and to unite them into a kind of federated church, in which each group, without giving up its peculiar denominational differences, might learn to live and labor together in a higher unity of the spirit. The movement was therefore called by him "The Congregation of God in the Spirit". It was no doubt a beautiful ideal, but, as experience proved, incapable of realization. Moreover, it should not be overlooked, in estimating the nature of the opposition, that the Germans were not properly prepared to receive the movement favorably. There was no authoritative explanation on the part of Zinzendorf as to what the movement meant. On the other hand, the Germans had been warned beforehand that the coming of Zinzendorf boded no good for their churches. It was therefore natural that they should look upon it as an attempt of proselyting for the Moravian Church.[105] If the Moravian

---

[105] Two statements of men not hostile to the movement may be quoted to illustrate the popular feeling. On February 16, 1747, Conrad Weiser wrote to Rev. Mr. Brunnholtz, of Philadelphia: "The Count gave himself out to be a Lutheran minister at the first conference. He was the director and originator of these conferences, which cannot be denied by any honest person who was present. What were his intentions did not become evident at that time, except what was stated in the invitation issued by Henry Antes. But a brother and delegate from Ephrata told me in confidence that the Count had a large sack, into which he wanted to put all sects and separatists and then govern himself alone." John Adam Gruber, of Germantown, makes the following report: "One of their workers said without reserve to a friend one of these days: People should just wait, their aim was to overthrow

COUNT NICHOLAS LUDWIG VON ZINZENDORF

leaders were sincere in their purpose of rendering a real spiritual service to the sheperdless German congregations, the opposition of the Germans was no less sincere, because they honestly believed it to be destructive of their denominational existence.

In order to appreciate the magnitude of the undertaking, we shall take a survey of the German population of Pennsylvania about the year 1740.

There were first of all the "church people", comprising the Lutherans and the Reformed. According to a careful count the number of Reformed congregations in Pennsylvania in 1740 was at least twenty-six. Estimating each congregation as consisting of about one hundred communicant members (which is quite liberal), the total number of Reformed communicants for 1740 would be about 2600. The baptized membership was about three times as numerous, or 7800, in round figures 8000. Those who were Reformed by descent and training, but had not connected themselves with any church, were probably as many again. We are thus brought to a total of 16,000 Reformed people for the year 1740. This is about half of what Schlatter reports for 1750, when he estimated the Reformed membership as about 30,000.

The Lutheran congregations in 1740 were approximately just as numerous as the Reformed. A map of Pennsylvania, published at the Sesquicentennial of the Lutheran Ministerium of Pennsylvania in 1898, enumerates and locates 27 Lutheran congregations, as having been founded in Pennsylvania before the year 1740. The total number of Lutheran church members in 1740 was probably about the same as that of the Reformed people. Taking a round number of 15,000 for each

all sects, one the Reformed from which he came, the other the Lutheran, etc. Bro. Ludwig [Zinzendorf] preached publicly that he wanted to re-establish the old Lutheran church, and he spoke of himself and his Lutherans: 'We Evangelicals,' which appeared very strange to other people who were present and heard it." See *Heinrich Melchior Muehlenberg, Selbstbiographie,* p. 231 f; Fresenius, *Bewaehrte Nachrichten,* Vol. III, p. 188. Christopher Saur writes from Germantown, November 16, 1742: "It is well known that the Count brought about a convention of all parties. It was, without doubt, his intention to make one party, namely his own, out of them." See Fresenius, l. c., p. 788f.

denomination, we have a grand total of 30,000 "church people" in Pennsylvania in 1740.

GERMAN SECTS IN PENNSYLVANIA.

The German "sect people" may be roughly estimated as about 10,000. By "sects" the early Germans meant those who did not belong to the two legally recognized branches of the Protestant Church in Germany, the Lutheran and the Reformed.

The earliest of these "sects" to come to Pennsylvania were the Mennonites. Their first colony was brought over under the auspices of Francis Daniel Pastorius. They came with the ship "Concord", which landed at Philadelphia, after a long but safe voyage, on October 6, 1683. They settled Germantown, now a part of Philadelphia. From Germantown they spread to Skippack, which was founded by them in 1702. A second Mennonite immigration took place in 1710. These were Swiss Mennonites, who in 1712 purchased 10,000 acres of land along the Pequea creek in Conestoga township, Lancaster County. Large accessions to this colony arrived in 1717 and 1719. Jonathan Dickinson remarked in 1719: "We are daily expecting ships from London which bring over Palatines, in number about six or seven thousand. We have a parcel who came out about five years ago, who purchased land about sixty miles west of Philadelphia and prove quiet and industrious". In 1742 there were about six thousand Mennonites in the province.[106]

In their doctrines the Mennonites resembled the Quakers. Their founder had been Menno Simons, from Friesland, born in 1492, died in 1557. They refused the oath and military service. They preached the separation of church and state and freedom of conscience. They practised adult baptism only and insisted on simplicity of dress as well as of life in general.

Another sect which sought refuge in Pennsylvania were the Dunkers. Their founder was Alexander Mack, who organized the first Dunker congregation in 1708 at Schwarzenau,

---

[106] This figure is given in a letter of C. Saur, the well-known German printer, of Germantown, dated November 16, 1742, printed in Fresenius, *Bewaehrte Nachricten,* Vol. III, p. 790.

Westphalia. As their name indicates they insisted on (trine) immersion. Like the Mennonites they rejected infant baptism. They refused to take the oath, engage in military service, hold public offices and settle their quarrels by lawsuits. They were believers in the simple life. The first colony of twenty Dunkers, under their leader Peter Becker, arrived in Philadelphia in 1719. Others followed soon afterwards. Their main settlements were at Germantown, Coventry, Falkner Swamp and Conestoga. The organization of these Dunkers into regular congregations in 1723 and 1724, undoubtedly influenced the Reformed people in 1725 to follow their example. One of the most influential Dunkers was Christopher Saur, a printer, living in Germantown, who since 1739 issued a German newspaper which was read very widely.

In 1728, Conrad Beissel, who had been selected as one of the leaders of the Conestoga Dunkers, separated from the parent body, because he had become convinced that Saturday was the proper day to be observed as the Christian Sabbath. His followers were called Seventh Day Dunkers, or Sabbatarians. In 1735, they founded Ephrata on the Cocalico. It was a cloister in which communism and a celibate life were practised. About 1745, a press was installed at Ephrata, from which a host of mystical books were issued. Music was also cultivated. Their life was austere and ascetic, with obedience as the chief duty of the inmates. Men and women lived in separate buildings, some of which are still standing. The members were distinguished by a special monastic dress, the men had even adopted the tonsure.

Another religious body which sought shelter from persecution in Pennsylvania were the Schwenkfelders. They had been founded by a contemporary of Luther, Casper Schwenkfeld. Zinzendorf gave them temporary shelter on his lands in Saxony. In May, 1734, forty families, numbering one hundred and eighty souls, emigrated to Pennsylvania, under the leadership of a Moravian, George Boehnisch. They reached Philadelphia September 12, 1734, in the ship St. Andrew, John Stedman, captain. They settled along the Skippack and Perkiomen rivers, chiefly near Goshenhoppen, in Montgomery County. Their first minister was George Weiss, who died in 1740. One of their prominent members was Christopher

Wiegner, who settled near Skippack.[107]

Besides these four main bodies of the "sect people", which had regular, congregational organizations, there were other smaller groups, which settled in Pennsylvania in scattered communities.[108]

Among these smaller groups the "Hermits of the Wissahickon" were the earliest to come to Pennsylvania. Their first colony, consisting of forty men, reached Philadelphia in 1694. The main leaders were John Kelpius, Bernhard Koester, John Seelig and Daniel Falkner. They were mystics who engaged in all kinds of theosophical speculations. In 1742, Rev. H. M. Muehlenberg, the patriarch of the Lutheran Church, met one of them, "Herr Selig", living in the vicinity of Roxborough, "after the manner of an anchorite, instructing children". After the death of Kelpius in 1708, Conrad Matthai acted as the last leader of the Hermits on the Ridge till his death in 1748.

Another of these smaller "sects" were the "Newborn", with whom both Weiss and Boehm among the Reformed leaders came in contact. They were founded about 1718 at Oley, Berks County, by Matthias Baumann, who had come from Lambsheim in the Palatinate, where he had been awakened in 1701. They believed in the new birth, which involved, according to their teaching, an inner illumination of the spirit, by which both the Scriptures, as well as the sacraments, were made superfluous. It also implied sinlessness, which made the ministry and teaching useless. After Baumann's death in 1727, Martin Schenkel continued as leader of the sect. Henry Antes came in contact with them when he began preaching at Oley in 1736. Bishop Spangenberg is reported to have argued with them and silenced them. After that they disappear.

Another even smaller group called themselves the "Inspired". They believed, like the Newborn, in the "inner

---

[107] See H. W. Kriebel, *The Schwenkfelders in Pennsylvania*, Lancaster, 1904.

[108] For the German sects in Pennsylvania, see also Reichel, *Early History of the Church of the United Brethren, commonly called Moravian*, Nazareth, 1888, pp. 35-53; and especially Prof. Albert B. Faust, *The German Element in the United States*, New York, 1909, Vol. I, pp. 111-148.

light". They had spread in western Germany between 1710-1720, when Eberhard Ludwig Gruber and John Frederick Rock joined them in the Wetterau district and became their principal leaders. A son of the former, John Adam Gruber, came to Pennsylvania. He settled in Germantown, where he exerted considerable influence. His "Extensive Report", covering the religious conditions in Pennsylvania between 1732-1742, published in Germany, in Fresenius, "Bewährte Nachrichten von Herrnhutischen Sachen" Vol. III, is an important historical document, because it contains the testimony of an eye-witness.

Another group, scattered through various settlements, called themselves the "Separatists". They were persons who had formerly been Reformed, Lutherans or Mennonites, but now had withdrawn from all religious associations, either because they regarded "the religions" as too worldly and filled with sinners, with whom they did not care to associate, or because they had become indifferent to all religion. John Eckstein and John G. Stiefel are called "Separatists" in contemporaneous documents.

The last religious body of Germans to settle in Pennsylvania before 1742 were the Moravians. The name (against which they themselves have always protested) implied that the last survivors of the Moravian and Bohemian Hussites united with the Renewed Church of the Brethren (or Unitas Fratrum), when it was organized in 1727 at Herrnhut, the domain of Zinzendorf in Saxony. Zinzendorf himself was the leader in the new movement. In 1735, one of the Moravian refugees David Nitschmann, secured Episcopal ordination from the two last remaining bishops of the ancient church of the (Hussite) Brethren, Daniel Jablonski, court preacher of the king of Prussia, and Christian Sitkovius of Lissa, who was at the same time superintendent of the Reformed congregations of Poland. In 1737, Zinzendorf himself was consecrated bishop by Jablonski and Nitschmann, after he had received ordination as a Lutheran minister in December, 1734, at Tuebingen.

As the Saxon government was hostile to the new movement, ordering the Schwenkfelders to leave Herrnhut in 1733, and decreeing banishment from Saxony on the Count in 1736, it seemed well to look for another place of refuge. As a result land was secured in Holland and in America. In 1734, Rev. Augustus G. Spangenberg secured from Governor Oglethorpe of Georgia a tract of 550 acres, on the site of the present city of Savannah. A company of nine men, led by Spangenberg, arrived in Georgia in April, 1735. Twenty additional colonists, under Bishop David Nitschmann, came in the following year. But when they were called to arms during the war with Spain, they left Georgia in 1738 and 1739. The last party traveled in Whitefield's company to Pennsylvania, where they arrived in April, 1740. There they settled on 500 acres, which Bishop Nitschmann bought from Wm. Allen of Philadelphia, at the confluence of the Manakasy Creek and the Lehigh River, and, on December 25, 1741, the new settlement was named Bethlehem. Shortly afterwards another tract of 5000 acres, now part of Upper Nazareth township, was purchased from Mr. Whitefield. Bethlehem soon became the center of an extensive missionary activity.[109]

Such were the religious forces among the Germans in Pennsylvania when Count Zinzendorf arrived in December, 1741. The common opinion that they were without any religious services is entirely wrong. Considering the Reformed people alone, we have seen in previous chapters that from 1720-1740 they were served by at least five ordained ministers. Boehm especially had done a most valuable and successful pioneer work. His field covered virtually the whole district from Philadelphia to the Blue Mountains and from the Susquehanna to the Delaware. Besides him a number of other, regularly ordained pastors ministered to the Reformed people. Rev. George Michael Weiss had preached in Pennsylvania from 1727-1730, Rev. John Peter Miller, from 1730-1734, Rev. John Bartholomew Rieger, from 1731-1734 and from 1739-1743, Rev. Peter Henry Dorsius, from 1737-1743. Moreover numerous laymen had done their best to supply the spiritual needs of the people, like John Conrad Tempelman in the Conestoga valley, John Jacob Hock at Lancaster, John Bechtel at Germantown, John Henry Goetschy throughout the present Montgomery, Berks and Lehigh counties, William Straub in

---

[109] See the elaborate and thorough *History of Bethlehem, Pennsylvania, 1741-1892*, by Bishop J. M. Levering, Bethlehem, 1903.

Skippack and Indian Creek, and John Conrad Wirtz in Egypt and Saucon. In many of the congregations there were also lay readers and schoolmasters, who read sermons whenever the regular preachers were absent. But in spite of all these agencies the situation left much to be desired, nor was there any co-operation among the various leaders, but partly even suspicion and antagonism. Indeed the unchurched elements were constantly increasing, so that Rev. A. G. Spangenberg could write from his personal observation: "Many thousands of these people care so little about religion, that it has become proverbial to say of a man who does not concern himself about God and His Word: He has the Pennsylvania religion".[110]

VISIT OF ZINZENDORF TO PENNSYLVANIA.

There were two preliminary events which led up to the coming of Zinzendorf in 1741. The first was the sojourn of Rev. A. G. Spangenberg in Pennsylvania from 1736-1739. His object was to visit the Schwenkfelders and to become acquainted with the condition of the Germans and the Indians in the province. In his reports which he sent to Herrnhut he emphasized the spiritual destitution of the Germans and the need of the Indians. As a result Christian Henry Rauch was sent in 1740 to begin missionary work among the Indians in the State of New York. Through the same letters of Spangenberg, Zinzendorf first felt the call to minister to the destitute Germans in Pennsylvania.[111]

A second cause was the visit of George Whitefield, the great Calvinistic Methodist preacher, in Pennsylvania in 1740. Seeing the religious destitution of the Germans and being unable to preach to them in their own language, he wrote to Zinzendorf, requesting him to send missionaries to the Germans. In answer to this request Andrew Eschenbach was sent in 1740 to continue the work of Spangenberg, who had returned to Europe. Eschenbach arrived in October, 1740, and

---

[110] See *Leben des Herrn Nicolaus Ludwig Grafen und Herrn von Zinzendorf,* beschrieben von August Gottlieb Spangenberg, [1774], p. 1380.

[111] See J. Th. Hamilton, *History of the Moravian Church* (American Church History Series, Vol. VIII), p. 445; Reichel, *Early History,* p. 92.

immediately went to Oley to preach to the Germans in that neighborhood.

The purpose of Zinzendorf's coming to Pennsylvania is set forth by him in an address which he delivered in August, 1741, at Herrendyk in Holland. In it he said: "I have been destined by God to preach the word of the blood and death of Jesus, not with over-refinement, but with the power of God, without regard to what will happen to me. This has been my mission before I knew the Brethren. I am and shall indeed remain connected with the Brethren, who have taken up in their heart our Gospel of Jesus Christ and have called me and other brethren to the service of the Congregation, but I shall not thereby separate myself from the Lutheran Church, for a witness of Christ can live and stay in this religion. Nevertheless, I cannot restrict myself in my witness to one religion, for the whole earth is the Lord's and all souls are his, and I am a debtor to all."[112]

On November 29, 1741, (o. st.) Count Zinzendorf, his daughter, Countess Benigna, a young girl of seventeen years, and five companions arrived in Philadelphia, where a house had been rented for them on Second, near the corner of Race Street. His arrival excited considerable interest. In a few days Governor Thomas sent him a letter of welcome, in which he expressed his satisfaction with his plan of preaching to the Germans in the province. After a short stay in Philadelphia, Zinzendorf went to Germantown on December 7th. "On the following morning he visited in passing several friends, especially John Bechtel. He told him that he would like to see his workshop. Bechtel, being by trade a wood-turner, did not know at first that Zinzendorf meant his church, in which he had preached for many years. Finally, when he understood him, he took him in. Zinzendorf asked him how many people could be accommodated in this newly built church. He answered: "About a thousand". Then Zinzendorf replied that he could see he would have much to do on his return. But, although he preached there frequently, there were never that many people in it. He had also sent word to Bechtel twice from

---

[112] See Reichel, *Early History*, p. 93f.

Philadelphia that he would like to become his chaplain".[113]

On December 8th, Zinzendorf and his party started out for Christopher Wiegner's home in Skippack, and from there, on the following day, he went to Falkner Swamp, where he visited Henry Antes, who had been recommended to him very highly by Spangenberg. Antes accompanied the party to the Forks of the Delaware. On the way, according to the testimony of John Gruber,[114] Zinzendorf discussed with Antes the advisability of calling a conference of all German church people and sects. Finally the lot was used to decide the question. It was in the affirmative. The further question when it should be held was decided by lot "the sooner the better". Zinzendorf then commissioned Antes to send out a circular letter to the leaders of all parties to invite them to a conference to be held on the first of January, 1742, o. st., in Germantown. In the words of the call the conference was to meet "in order to treat peaceably concerning the most important articles of faith, in order to ascertain how closely we can approach each other in fundamental points, and in other matters that do not subvert the ground of salvation, to bear with one another in charity, that thus all judging and condemning among the above mentioned souls might be abated and prevented". The circular calling the conference was issued by Antes, December 15, 1741 (o. st).

Meanwhile Zinzendorf had gone to the Forks of the Delaware[115] and on Christmas eve (n. st.)[114a] named the new settlement there Bethlehem. On his way back to Philadelphia he stopped at Oley, where he preached in the house of John Bertolet. Then he made a detour to Conestoga, where he paid the Seventh Day Dunkers at Ephrata a brief visit. On December 19th, the Count and his party returned to Germantown, where he preached on the following day (Sunday, December 20, o. st.), in the German Reformed Church from I Tim. 3:16. This was

[113] See Adam Gruber's "Report" in Fresenius, *Bewaehrte Nachrichten*, Vol. III, p. 137.

[114] Fresenius, l. c., Vol. III, p. 138.

[114a] People found much fault with Zinzendorf, because he always used the "new style" calendar, which differed from the "old style" by eleven days. The former was not legally adopted in the British Empire till 1752.

[115] The itinerary of Zinzendorf is given in Reichel, *Memorials of the Moravian Church*, Vol. I, pp. 175-187.

his first appearance in an American pulpit. Five other sermons from the same text were preached by Zinzendorf in the Reformed church on the succeeding Sundays.

PENNSYLVANIA SYNODS.

In response to the call issued by Henry Antes, the first conference or "Pennsylvania Synod" met in the house of Theobalt Endt in Germantown. As Antes was well known and well liked in the whole province, there was a large attendance. Every German denomination was represented. There were Lutherans, Reformed, Mennonites, Dunkers, Sabbatarians, Schwenkfelders, Separatists, Mystics and Moravians. The only ones, however, who were regularly chosen to represent their denomination were four delegates from the Seventh Day Dunkers or Sabbatarians of Ephrata, the rest came in their private capacity. More than fifty persons handed in their names, although, according to the statement of Zinzendorf, about one hundred were present. The following were the most prominent members of the conference:[116]

Lutheran: Conrad Weiser.

Reformed: Henry Antes, John Bechtel, John Leinbach of Oley, and Christopher Meng of Germantown.

Mennonite: John de Tuerck of Oley.

Dunkers: Joseph Mueller, Andrew Frey, Abraham du Bois and G. A. Martin.

Sabbatarians: Prior Onesimus (Israel Eckerling), John Hildebrand and H. Kalkloeser.

Schwenkfelder: Christopher Wiegner.

Separatists: J. A. Gruber, Theobald Endt, Conrad Matthaei.

Hermit: J. G. Stiefel.

Moravians: de Thurnstein (Count Zinzendorf), John Jacob Mueller, secretary of the conference. Bishop David Nitschmann, Andrew Eschenbach, John C. Pyrlaeus, Gottlieb Buettner, Christian Henry Rauch and others.

Samuel Guldin, a Reformed minister, living in retirement at Roxboro, was also present for one day.

Henry Antes presided and opened the meeting by stating

[116] See Reichel, *Early History*, p. 98.

once more its purpose, which was not to dispute, but to bring to an end the mutual misunderstandings, suspicion and criticism among the various religious communions. It was a noble purpose, but impossible of attainment. It had hardly been stated when one of the Separatists, a tailor named Schierwagen, presented a paper in which he criticised Zinzendorf's sermons, especially what he considered its uncharitable expressions.[117] Zinzendorf is reported to have replied rather sharply. This brought the hermit, Conrad Matthaei, to the defense of the tailor, but he also is said to have been severely reprimanded by Zinzendorf. The latter may not have regarded his answer as such, but the result was that "Many good people went away sad and refused to come again".

As there were not only those present who desired a closer union, but also others who had conscientious scruples about too intimate a connection, the subject of union was discussed on the second day. The conclusion was then reached that, according to the declaration of Christ (John 17: 10-23), a closer fellowship of believers was not a sign of sinful attachment to any creature. The true communion of saints it was said, "is the Congregation of God in the Spirit throughout the whole world, constituting that spiritual body whose Head is Christ. But they also constitute the communion of saints, who agree in all essential points of doctrine, though outwardly belonging to different denominations. And thirdly, those small societies or congregations are a communion of saints who form a closer and more intimate connection among themselves in order that their ministers, as they who must give an account, may be enabled to watch the better over their souls".

On Epiphany, January 6, 1742, Zinzendorf was in Skippack, where he preached again in the house of Christopher Wiegner. A number of Schwenkfelders were present to greet their former patron. But, when Zinzendorf insisted that they co-operate with him in the union synods, they refused. He claimed to be the divinely appointed reformer of the Schwenkfelders, who had a right to their loyalty and co-operation. This they denied emphatically and refused to have hence-

---

[117] See Fresenius, *Nachrichten*, Vol. III, p. 148.

forth anything more to do with him.[118]

A similar conference was held with the Mennonites in Martin Kolb's house at Skippack, on January 13th. But it failed to shake their resolution to keep aloof from the union synods.

The second Synod was held January 14th and 15th, in the house of George Huebner at Falkner Swamp. Zinzendorf was elected presiding officer, or "Syndicus", as the minutes call him. But there were already indications that the conferences were not meeting with favor among the Germans. From Germantown none was present except John Bechtel. Most of the sect people had withdrawn. A few Dunkers and some delegates from the Ephrata cloister were still present. But this was their last appearance. The representatives of the Dunkers were warned that if they continued their associations with these meetings, they would no longer be recognized by their brethren as one of them. One of the decisions of the conference, expressing probably better the convictions of Zinzendorf than of most of the other attendants, was:

"The proper object of this assembly of all evangelical denominations is, that henceforth a poor inquirer for the way of life may not be directed in twelve different ways, but only in one, let him ask whom he will. But if any one should take a fancy to him who directed him in the way, and should wish to travel on the same according to his method, he has full liberty to do so, provided he be as yet in no connection with any religious society".

The third Synod met at Oley, February 10-12, o. st., in the house of John de Turk. At this time the Seventh Day Dunkers of Ephrata declared orally and through letters that they could no longer participate in the meetings. After their delegates had read their confession of faith, which expressed disagreement on the subject of marriage as well as on Baptism and the Lord's Supper, they withdrew, but not without having called forth the severe condemnation of the president. After their departure, the people of Oley, Lutherans, Reformed, Mennonites and others, who had been gathered through the preaching

---

[118] See Fresenius, l. c., p. 153; Kriebel, *The Schwenkfelders in Pennsylvania*, p. 113f.

of Eschenbach, were organized into a congregation. And, in order not to appear as proselyting these people, they were recognized as an undenominational congregation. Eschenbach, who was to continue as their pastor, was then ordained by David Nitschmann, assisted by Zinzendorf and Anthony Seiffert, a Moravian minister. At the same time three other Brethren were ordained, namely Christian Henry Rauch, who had acted as missionary among the Indians near Esopus, N. Y., Gottlob Buettner, destined to be missionary among the Six Nations, and John Christopher Pyrlaeus, whom Zinzendorf had appointed as his assistant in Philadelphia.

The most interesting act at this Synod was the baptism of three Mohican Indians, who had been converted through the teaching of Rauch. The assembly met, February 22, n. st., in the barn of Mr. de Turk, the three candidates were placed in the midst and with prayer were devoted to Jesus as his property. Then Rauch baptized them, after the Moravian custom "into the wounds of Jesus", with the names Abraham, Isaac and Jacob. The solemn act was concluded with the singing of a hymn, during which Zinzendorf and the other ministers laid their hands upon them.

Another important act which took place at this synod was the more complete organization of the movement. Of five men appointed by lot three were elected trustees of the synod, namely Andrew Frey, a Dunker, Gottfried Haberecht and Anthony Seiffert of Bethlehem. These three trustees were instructed by synod to elect two worthy men to superintend the Congregation of God in the Spirit. It was to be their duty to prevent, as far as lay in their power, this union from being again dissolved. It is doubtful whether this plan was really carried out, but the immediate result was that the few Mennonites and Schwenkfelders, who as private individuals had still attended the synods, now withdrew altogether. The Dunkers appointed their own annual conferences, which are still maintained and the Ephrata people declared in public print their opposition to the whole movement. Hence the next synod, which they had planned to hold at Ephrata, was convened at Germantown.

The fourth Synod met March 10-12th, o. st., at Germantown, in the house of Mr. Ashmead, to which Zinzendorf and his household had removed from Philadelphia. When Zinzendorf found that all the German sectarians had withdrawn, leaving only the Reformed, Lutherans and Moravians present, he proposed that the meetings be discontinued, as they had failed to realize their purpose, but the other members of the synod voted to continue. During the course of this synod Zinzendorf defined his position towards the Lutherans and Reformed churches and gave reasons why their united activity was desirable. He stated that he regarded the Lutheran Church in some respects preferable to the old Moravian, and open to all apostolic graces, if only its ministers would be valiant, single-minded, well-grounded in doctrine and would act with divine wisdom. He also declared that it was a great question whether a servant of Christ, who separated himself from the Lutheran Church, had gained anything by joining another sect.

Regarding the Reformed Church he referred to the first part of the published proceedings of the Synod of Berne of 1532, saying that the chief points of doctrine were there set forth according to the truth, in such a manner that a servant of Christ in that Church might, under the shield of his denominational creed, proclaim the pure Gospel. If, therefore, he said, these two churches would unite and hold their spiritual treasure in common, they might form a real apostolic church, and gradually absorb all smaller sects, whereupon the Moravian Church, seeing her dear brothers in one house, would be their faithful sister.

The fifth synod was held at Germantown, in the German Reformed Church, on April 6-9, 1742. The minutes reveal the attitude of the leaders to the religious condition in Pennsylvania. They state: "Pennsylvania is a complete Babel. The first to be accomplished is to liberate its prisoners, which cannot be done according to common rules: apostolic powers are required".

During the meetings of this synod a new catechism was read for the Reformed congregations. Its title may be rendered in English: "A Short Catechism for some Congregations of Jesus of the Reformed Religion, which hold to the old Synod of Berne. Published by John Bechtel, Minister of the Word of God. Philadelphia, printed by Benjamin Franklin, 1742".

From this title it has always been inferred that Bechtel

was the author of this catechism. But he was merely the editor. Zinzendorf himself was the author. This is clearly stated in the Bethlehem Diary. Under date July 11/22, 1742, we read: "Afterwards Bro. Andrew Eschenbach and Gottlob Buettner read from the catechism for the Reformed congregations in Pennsylvania, which Bro. Ludwig [Zinzendorf] wrote and Bro. John Bechtel edited". It is also acknowledged by Moravian historians. George Neisser in his "Annals of Moravian Settlement in Georgia and Pennsylvania", says under date March 11, 1742: "Bro. Ludwig preached in Philadelphia from the Gospel for the day. . . . He also completed a catechism entitled Kurzer Catechismus für etliche Gemeinen aus der reformirten Religion".[119] The catechism is full of practical Christianity and fervent in spirit, but it lacks method, and it can hardly be called a Reformed catechism, because, as Boehm remarks: "There is in it from beginning to end not a word of the articles of our Christian faith. Nor is there in it a word about Holy Baptism or Holy Communion, no word about the holy commandments of God and no word about the most holy prayer, which our Saviour has taught us to pray". As Saur refused to print this catechism, because it had Bechtel's name on it,[120] it was printed by Benjamin Franklin in Roman characters. An edition in German type was issued probably in Germany, although it retained the imprint "Philadelphia, 1742". An English edition appeared in the same year, "printed by Isaiah Warner, almost opposite to Charles Brockden's in Chestnut Street". A Swedish translation, made by Olaf Malander, was issued by the Franklin press in 1743.[121]

Immediately after the synod, on Sunday, April 11th, o. st.,[122] in the evening prayer meeting, Bishop David Nitsch-

---

[119] Reichel, *Memorials*, p. 181. John Adam Gruber, of Germantown, was also familiar with the fact that Bechtel had merely edited this catechism, see Fresenius, *Nachrichten*, Vol. III, pp. 176, 189.

[120] See Levering, *Bethlehem*, p. 90, note 4.

[121] See the facsimilies of the title pages in Dr. Dubbs' *Reformed Church in Pennsylvania*, p. 120.

[122] On April 22nd, new style, not April 18, 1742, as given by Dr. Harbaugh, *Fathers*, Vol. I, p. 317. See Levering, *Bethlehem*, p. 96; Reichel, *Early History*, p. 115; Reichel, *Memorials*, p. 183; Fresenius, *Nachrichten*, Vol. III, p. 183.

mann assisted by Zinzendorf ordained John Bechtel pastor of the Reformed congregation at Germantown and appointed him also as inspector over all the Reformed congregations in Pennsylvania, a position which he was not fitted to fill by training and temperament. Adam Gruber reports that Zinzendorf wrote to Boehm informing him of this appointment, "asking him not to regard it as strange that Bechtel had been made inspector over the Reformed ministers, and urging him to submit to him. Boehm is said to have given him a sharp answer".[123]

The sixth synod was held again at Germantown, in Lorentz Schweitzer's house, May 5-7, 1742. It was but poorly attended. The synods were evidently held too frequently, and as a result even those people who at first had taken an interest became tired and stayed away. Nothing of importance was transacted, but a plan was discussed to give the Lutheran churches belonging to the Union more coherence by a new catechism and a church-order. Adam Gruber states in his "Extensive Report" that "he (Zinzendorf) intended to have a new Lutheran catechism printed, just as he had published a Reformed catechism, according to the Berne Synod, under Bechtel's name".[124] This intention was, however, never carried out. At the same meeting Antes was ordered to preach at Oley, while Eschenbach was sent to Conestoga. This was done by Antes, after he had asked for and received a call from the people at Oley. He preached for them every second Sunday for some time. "He said now publicly that he was a Reformed member and regretted that he had ever left them".[125]

The seventh synod met June 2 and 3, 1742, at Philadelphia, in Mr. Evans' house. It was more largely attended than some of the earlier meetings, because fifty-six Moravian colonists, who had arrived in Philadelphia May 28th, on the ship "Catharine", attended in a body. They made a request to be received into connection with the Congregation of God in the Spirit. Whereupon not only they, but also all those who were to constitute the church at Bethlehem—one hundred and twenty in all—were admitted. Thereby the control of the synods

---

[123] Fresenius, *Nachrichten*, Vol. III, p. 193.
[124] Fresenius, l. c., p. 189.
[125] Fresenius, l. c., p. 187.

passed entirely into the hands of the Moravians, as they outnumbered by far all others. Henry Antes welcomed them in the name of the synod with the statement that "the undenominational Synod of Pennsylvania acknowledges the old Moravian Church just arrived, as a true Church of the Lord; that their ministers especially will be considered their brethren and fellow-servants; that as regards the internal arrangement of their Church, the Synod, according to its fundamental rules, will not interfere in any way, deeming this, as well as any other church independent and inviolable".

On the second day the synod stated its views as to the religious condition of the various religious bodies in the province in nine paragraphs. It resolved to convene in future regularly in a quarterly conference of ministerial workers, which should be open to all those who had remained faithful to the decisions of the first conference, acknowledged the divinity of Christ, did not believe in reprobation and promised not to abuse the confidence of the synod. Finally, Henry Antes was instructed to prepare a circular, in the name of the synod, in which all the children of God should be invited to join the Congregation of God in the Spirit.

This was the last of the monthly Union Synods. They had begun auspiciously, but as the influence of Zinzendorf and his Moravian assistants became more predominant, one after another of the denominations withdrew, leaving at last the Moravians in complete control. As far as the Reformed Church was concerned a distinct effort was made by the last Synod to create a division and to take the Reformed people away from the control and the supervision of the Church of Holland, on the plea that the latter was teaching an unscriptural doctrine of predestination. This is evident from the warning that was addressed to the Reformed people:[126]

"Because all those preachers who come from the Church of Holland are bound in their conscience to teach that God does not wish to save all people, the entire Reformed Church in Pennsylvania is hereby warned in the most solemn manner: We will prove before an assembly of them all, that whoever does not bring this doctrine with him to America and advocate

[126] See *Buedingische Sammlung*, Vol. II, p. 812f.

it here, is not acknowledged by them as a true teacher; but that whoever brings this doctrine with him, is absolutely necessitated to contradict the Apostles and Prophets. Inasmuch as we can call our own countrymen to witness that in Germany we did not believe this bold, adventurous doctrine, let each consider for himself whether he will learn it here; or for the sake of any man's self-interest, whether he will help in deceiving the Amsterdam Classis, which imagines that it is taught as a fundamental doctrine; or whether all those who approve of the twelve articles of the Synod of Berne, will openly acknowledge their adherence to this basis, and see to it that the office of the ministry in this country is conducted in agreement with it. Their well-known faithful Bechtel, who has now for fifteen years preached the Gospel for them in all simplicity, Henry Antes, Peter Miller[126a] and the former book-keeper of Basel, John Brandmueller, offer to take all sincere souls under their tenderest care, without designing in so doing in the least to stand in the way of other servants of Christ, who will unite with them to this end. As soon as we know the mind of any on this point, we shall appoint a general assembly to compare views in regard to a Christian ecclesiastical organization".

This appeal addressed to the Reformed congregations failed to move them. It remained for itinerant missionaries, sent out during the following years, to win adherents. It was through them that the Reformed Church was threatened with a serious division, and it was against them that Boehm launched his strongest attack.

With the close of the synods the activity of Zinzendorf among the Germans was practically at an end. On May 30th, he preached his farewell sermon in the Reformed church at Germantown, in the course of which "he praised and recommended Bechtel to them very highly, in his presence, and said that he (Bechtel) would soon have more than one hundred members, who would be organized into a congregation".[127] In accordance with this purpose Bechtel issued an invitation to all the Reformed people in Germantown and neighborhood to assem-

---

[126a] This Peter Miller was a shoemaker from Germantown, who died in November, 1753. He is mentioned repeatedly in the minutes of the Pennsylvania Synods.
[127] See Fresenius, l. c., p. 191.

MARKET PLACE AT GERMANTOWN, NOW MARKET SQUARE
1. Moravian School, 1742   2. Market House   3. Reformed Church, built 1733

(*By Courtesy of Dr. Naaman H. Keyser*)

ble in the Reformed church on Monday following Pentecost (June 7, 1742, o. st.). At that meeting he asked all those who wanted to be regarded as members of the congregation and hold to the Berne Synod, to put down their names. "Whereupon (as is related) 17 or 18 persons answered in the affirmative and signed their names".

In Philadelphia, where Zinzendorf had been preaching to the Lutherans, in the meeting house on Arch Street, held by them in common with the Reformed, he preached his farewell sermon on June 6th, after which he left with them his assistant, Rev. John C. Pyrlaeus. Zinzendorf had also preached in Tulpehocken, and before he left Pennsylvania he installed there John Philip Meurer as the Lutheran minister.

The activity of Count Zinzendorf in Pennsylvania called forth intense opposition from different parties. The Separatists were the first to attack him. The Ephrata community issued a broadside, containing a "Short Report of the Causes why the Ephrata Community has entered into an Undertaking with Count Zinzendorf and his people". This was followed in the year 1743 by three other pamphlets, written against the union movement by John Hildebrandt. Christopher Saur published in his paper, *Pennsylvanischer Geschichts-Schreiber,* numerous articles against Zinzendorf, which the latter answered in the *Pennsylvania Gazette.* John Adam Gruber, the separatist, published various pamphlets against the movement, in which he complained about "the untimely, arbitrary and premature convocation and convention of various parties and awakened souls, done under the name of Immanuel".

More important was the controversy in which Zinzendorf was involved with the leading Presbyterian ministers. Rev. Gilbert Tennent, Samuel Blair and others preached publicly against him, attacking him in terms which were by no means polite or charitable. A "Compendious Extract" was also published by them, in which Zinzendorf and his Pennsylvania Synods were severely criticized.

In Philadelphia matters came to a climax July 18, 1742, when Zinzendorf was absent on his first journey to the Indians. His assistant, John C. Pyrlaeus, was forcibly ejected from the meeting house, in which Lutherans and Reformed worshipped in common. In justification of their action they published "A

Protestation of the several Members of the Lutherian and Reformed Religions in the City of Philadelphia jointly concerned in the Lease of their Meeting House in Arch Street about the late Commotion which happened on Sunday the 18th of July, 1742". It was answered in the "Pennsylvania Gazette" of August 26, 1742, in a "Memorandum of the Rev. Lewis of Thürnstein", one of the minor titles which Zinzendorf used during his stay in Pennsylvania. In the issue of September 2, 1742, the people replied with "Remarks upon Count Zinzendorf's Memorandum". The result of this agitation was that Zinzendorf and his adherents withdrew, and he built at his own expense a new church at the corner of Race and Broad streets, known later as the Moravian church.

A confusion similar to that in Philadelphia was created in Tulpehocken by the preaching of the Moravian missionaries, first by Gottlob Buettner and later by Philip Meurer. As there was a reference in the Philadelphia "Protestation" to the troubles at Tulpehocken, it was answered, August 11, 1742, by the elders of the Evangelical (Moravian) Lutheran congregation of Tulpehocken in a pamphlet, entitled "The Confusion of Tulpehocken". Thus charges and counter-charges, with violent language indulged in by both sides, followed each other in rapid succession.

But the most elaborate and perhaps the most violent attack was made on Zinzendorf and his union movement by John Philip Boehm. Through the published minutes of the union synods the Reformed congregations were challenged to break their connection with the Classis of Amsterdam and unite in the union movement on the basis of the Synod of Berne. This was a challenge which Boehm could not ignore. To him the very existence of the Church was involved in remaining faithful to the Reformed standards of the past. The articles of the Synod of Berne meant nothing to him or to any other Reformed member.[128] He had probably never heard of them. The Canons of the Synod of Dort had to him most likely only an historical interest. He does not betray by a single word

---

[128] They are not contained in any of the numerous collections of Reformed confessions, such as Niemeyer's, Augusti's, Boeckel's, Vinke's, Heppe's, or Mess'.

that he ever read them. But he taught and preached the Heidelberg Catechism, and that creed he would not give up. Against it none of the objections of Zinzendorf could be raised,

Getreuer Warnungs
BRIEF
an die
Hochteutfche Evangelifch Reformirten
Gemeinden und alle deren Glieder,-in
PENSYLVANIEN,
Zur getreuen Warfchauung, vor denen Leuthen, welche unter dem nahmen von
HERRN-HUTHER
bekandt feyn.

Umb fich vor deren Seelverderblichen und Gewiffenverwüftenden Lehre zu hüthen und wohl vorzufehen, damit fie nicht
Durch den fchein ihres euferlichen fcheinheiligen Wefens, und felbft eingebildeten Gerechtigkeit und Heiligkeit, zu ihrer Seelen ewigen fchaden. mögen verführt werden.

Nach dem Exempel eines Ehrwürdigen
KIRCHEN RATHS von
Amfterdam
in *Holland.*

Und um, vor dem Allmachtigen Gott-tragender Pflicht und Schuldigkeit halben, gefchrieben von mir,
Joh: Ph: Böhm,
Hochteutfchen Reform: Prediger, der miranvertrauten Gemeinden in *Penfylvanien.*

Zu *Philadelphia:* Gedruckt bey A: BRADFORD. 1742.

TITLE PAGE OF BOEHM'S LETTER OF WARNING AGAINST THE MORAVIANS, 1742.

for it did not teach the doctrine of reprobation, so obnoxious to Zinzendorf and—to most Reformed people.

In order to guard his beloved Reformed Church against disruption and division, Boehm issued on August 23, 1742, a "True Letter of Warning addressed to the Reformed Congregations of Pennsylvania". In the preceding year two Dutch books, published against the Moravians by the Classis of Amsterdam, had been sent to him. Of these books he made faithful use, adopting from them also, unfortunately, their objectionable style, filled with vituperation and denunciation. It was the polemical language of the day.

The main part of the book (following p. 20) is chiefly historical. Boehm reviews in it the circumstances under which he first came in contact with Zinzendorf. It was during his visit to Philadelphia, December 25-27, 1741. At that time he learned of the intention of some Lutherans to have Zinzendorf preach in the union meeting house. As Boehm discouraged it, it did not take place. But on January 8, 1742, Zinzendorf wrote Boehm a letter inquiring whether he had any right to object to his preaching in the church, as the Lutheran elders had invited him. Boehm answered evasively. But on Sunday, January 10th, Zinzendorf preached in the meeting house for the first time to the Lutherans. As Zinzendorf introduced himself as a Lutheran minister, he received a call from the Lutheran congregation, which he accepted. To this act Boehm raised decided objection in his book, saying that he might indeed have been born and brought up in the Lutheran Church, but he could hardly call himself a Lutheran, after he had become a Moravian bishop.[126]

---

[129] The position of Zinzendorf was indeed peculiar. He had been ordained a Lutheran minister in 1734. In 1737 he was ordained a Moravian bishop, but regarded himself as still a member of the Lutheran Church. The Moravian Church was Lutheran in creed (it subscribed to the Augsburg Confession), but episcopal in form of government. See Levering, *Bethlehem*, p. 27. It was their subscription to the Lutheran creed which secured them toleration in Germany. Yet Zinzendorf considered the Moravian Church as an independent church. In his answer to Boehm, issued through George Neisser, he says: "It is certain that the Herrnhut Brethren until this hour, in all lands where they are found, stand indisputably upon the footing not of a merely tolerated church, but they stand rather as the oldest among the Protes-

Then Boehm reviews at length the various union synods. In connection with the first synod he expresses his surprise that Henry Antes participated in it. He refers touchingly to his former friendship with him and to the fact that he was one of the two men who with tears in their eyes urged the ministry of the Word upon him. He reminds Antes of his vows made at his confirmation, and calls upon him to return to "the truth of our Reformed religion".

Regarding the second synod, Boehm refutes the attempt made to show that the Mennonites approved of their organization by quoting from a Dutch book the declaration of one of the Mennonite ministers in Holland concerning the Moravians. He also condemned the use of the lot at the second synod. But his wrath was particularly roused by a reference to the "ministers of the Lutheran, Reformed and Tunker religion present at the conference". To this statement Boehm opposes the decree: "We Reformed members, standing under the Church Order, approved of and instituted by the Classis of Amsterdam, recognize no one as a member, much less as a minister of our Church, who contaminates himself with the Moravian soul destructive doctrine, until his total repentance of his serious lapse and return to our doctrine and Church, based upon God's Word".

In the third synod, Boehm objects to the statement that "Brother Christian Henry (Rauch) concluded to pour out the love of God and the Holy Ghost" and that he baptized the three Indian converts "in the death of Christ". He also finds fault that Zinzendorf called himself a Lutheran minister and yet associated with the Seventh Day Dunkers, who burned Luther's Catechism, that he had called their observance of Saturday as Sabbath "a respectable practice" and that he had taken part in their footwashing and love-feast, when he visited Ephrata.

In the minutes of the fourth synod, Boehm objects to the

tant churches." If Lutheran and Moravian churches were independent bodies, how was membership in both possible? In answer it might be said, that Zinzendorf before coming to America resigned his episcopal dignity, and hence fell back upon that of a Lutheran minister. However it may be explained, it was at this point that Zinzendorf exposed himself to attack.

statement "we claim the right which Jesus, according to John 17, has given to us over all the children of God in this land, whatever their condition may be, which right the laborers of the different religions have conceded to us at the first conference". Boehm denies that John 17 grants any rights or privileges to Zinzendorf, but contends that the rights spoken of are those of Christ himself.

In connection with the fifth synod, Boehm reviews at length the catechism published by Bechtel. Regarding its authorship he declares that Bechtel shot off only the bullet which Zinzendorf had cast. This catechism, Boehm declared, could not be regarded as Reformed, because it contained none of the recognized five points of catechetical material. It did not treat of the Apostolic Creed, the Lord's Prayer, the Commandments, the Lord's Supper and Baptism.

As regards the fifth synod, Boehm refuses absolutely to recognize the validity of Bechtel's ordination as that of a Reformed minister. A Moravian Bishop, he claims, cannot ordain a Reformed minister,[130] much less appoint him as inspector over all the rest.

In connection with the last synod, Boehm censures the arbitrary manner in which Zinzendorf changed long established sacred customs, as when he baptized a child by pouring water into its bosom. He also criticizes his arbitrary assumption of power, as when he announced the deposition of the Lutheran minister at Tulpehocken, Mr. Stoever.[131]

The book of Boehm was published in parts which appeared weekly. He began in June and finished the publication in August, 1742. There can be no question that it exerted considerable influence among the Reformed and Lutheran congregations and put them everywhere on guard against the operations of the Moravian missionaries. As Boehm was compelled to sell his book, he found that many poor people

---

[130] Lischy's ordination (also conferred by a Moravian bishop) was indeed recognized by the Reformed Coetus. He was not re-ordained. But before he was recognized as a Reformed minister, he had to submit a written confession of faith, which was approved, and then he was admitted by vote as a Reformed minister and member of the Coetus.

[131] That Zinzendorf attempted to depose Stoever is also stated by Gruber, see Fresenius, *Nachrichten*, Vol. III, p. 201.

were unable to buy it. He, therefore, issued in 1743 a four page broadside, in which he summarized his chief points, calling special attention to the missionary activities of the Reformed ministers in the union movement, Antes, Bechtel and Lischy.

Boehm was ably seconded in his attack by Rev. Samuel Guldin,[132] a Reformed minister from Switzerland, who had lived since 1710 in retirement at Roxboro, near Philadelphia. In 1743 Guldin published a book by Saur's press entitled: "Unpartisan Witness on the New Union of all Denominations in Pennsylvania, and also some other points." It consists of five parts, written in the course of the year 1742. In this book Guldin insists that there must be first union in Christ before there can be union with others. This spirit of union must come from above. It is not the work of men. It implies repentance and conversion. Only when thus drawn together by Christ and to Christ, can we be drawn to each other. The criticisms in the minutes of the union synods, he says, could not overcome the differences between the denominations, but rather intensified and aggravated them.

The book of Boehm was answered by Zinzendorf in a "Straightforward Account to the Public regarding the libellous Book of the Dutch Minister Johan Philip Boehm published by Andrew Bradford against the Herrnhuters. . . . Edited by George Neisser, from Sehlen, Moravia, schoolmaster at Bethlehem, Philadelphia, printed by B. Franklin, 1742." What is true of the so-called Bechtel catechism is likewise true of this book. George Neisser was not the author but only the editor. This is stated distinctly in the Bethlehem diary, under date August 9, 1742: "Bro. George Neisser was commissioned to edit a book, written (abgefasst) by Bro. Ludwig. Its print-

---

[132] Rev. Samuel Guldin was the earliest Reformed minister in Pennsylvania. He was born in Berne, Switzerland, in 1664. He entered the Latin school at Berne in 1679; became pastor at Stettlen, in the Canton of Berne, 1692-1696; assistant preacher in the Cathedral of Berne, 1696-1699; was deposed in 1699 because of pietism. Emigrated to Pennsylvania, arriving at Philadelphia, September 24, 1710. Lived in retirement at Roxboro, near Philadelphia. Preached occasionally in the Reformed Church at Germantown. He died in Philadelphia, December 31, 1745. See Dr. Good's *History of the Ref. Ch. in U. S., 1729-1792*, pp. 68-88.

ing has been entrusted to Bro. Henry Miller in Franklin's office and it has been sent to him." The title page does not claim for Neisser more than editorship and this was well known to his contemporaries.[133]

When Zinzendorf left Pennsylvania, December 31, 1742, to return to Europe, the main results of his activity in Pennsylvania were fourfold: First, numerous congregations had been organized at Bethlehem, Nazareth, Philadelphia, Hebron (at Lebanon), Heidelberg (in North Heidelberg township, Berks County), Lancaster and York. Second, provision had been made for systematic missionary work among the Indians. Third, schools had been established at Germantown, Frederick township, Oley and Heidelberg, and fourth, an extensive plan of itinerant missionary work had been put into operation. It was especially through the last method that the Congregation of God in the Spirit carried on its work during the following years, from 1743-1747.

[133] See Fresenius, *Nachrichten*, Vol. III, p. 677.

CHAPTER VII.

BOEHM'S OPPONENTS IN THE UNION MOVEMENT.

As Boehm came in contact with most of the Reformed ministers active in the union movement, their efforts should be reviewed in connection with his life. The principal Reformed missionaries who took part in the union movement of Zinzendorf were six, Antes, Bechtel, Lischy, Rauch, Brandmiller and Bruce.

HENRY ANTES.

The first, with whom probably the whole idea of the union synods originated, was Henry Antes. John Henry Antes[134] was born in the village of Freinsheim, in the Palatinate, July 11, 1701, and was baptized there July 17, 1701. His father was Philip Frederick Antes and his mother Anna Catharine. They had six children, of whom John Henry was the oldest. Frederick Antes and his family came to Pennsylvania in 1721. On February 20, 1723, Frederick Antes of Germantown bought of Hendrick Van Bebber 154 acres, situate in Philadelphia County, for which he paid £38.5.0, Pennsylvania currency. The land was part of the Manatawny tract, in what is now New Hanover township, Montgomery County. In 1728, Frederick Antes was one of the elders of the Falkner Swamp church, who petitioned the Classis of Amsterdam for the ordination of Boehm. In November, 1729, he was one of the three commissioners sent to New York, to be present at the ordination of Boehm in New York. According to the records

---

[134] For Frederick Antes and his son, Henry Antes, see the excellent articles of Mr. Dotterer in the *Perkiomen Region*. Frederick Antes, *Perkiomen Region*, Vol. II, pp. 60-61, 176-178; Henry Antes, l. c., pp. 106-108, 123-125, 145-147. On January 20, 1736, Mr. Boehm made an extract from his church record, relating to the marriage of Henry Antes and the baptisms of his children. This certificate is still in existence. It was translated and printed by Mr. Dotterer in his *Perkiomen Region*, Vol. I, p. 51f.

of the First Presbyterian Church of Philadelphia, Frederick Antes was married a second time, April 9, 1742, to Elizabeth Nayman. His will was made August 15, 1746, and was probated November 26, 1746.

His son, John Henry Antes, a millwright by trade, at an early date formed a partnership with William Dewees of Germantown. With him he engaged in the construction and running of a paper mill and grist mill on the Wissahickon. In the family of his partner Henry Antes found his wife. On February 2, 1726, he was married to Christina Elizabetha Dewees by his pastor, John Philip Boehm. In 1735 he is referred to as a resident of Frederick township. On September 2, 1735, he bought 175 acres of land in Frederick township. This became his permanent home and from it he was known as "the pious Reformed man of Frederick township".[135]

The year 1736 marked the beginning of Henry Antes' missionary activity. In a contemporaneous document, the old Moravian record of the Oley Church, now at Bethlehem, we find the following statement:

"In the year 1736, Henry Antes came to Oley and preached there with blessing. He found an entrance there and several were touched by the truth. The people expressed a great desire to hear his sermons, for which reason he visited this place faithfully. There were at that time all kinds of spirits in Oley, of which the Newborn were the dominant party. Dear Antes was not equal to them. He waited, therefore, for the time when the Lord himself would check them, which took place in the following manner: In the year 1737, our dear and reverend brother Spangenberg had come to Georgia and from there had traveled to Pennsylvania, which he reached in that year. He stayed for a little while at Skippack, where he heard of the work of the dear brother, Henry Antes. He then resolved to visit Oley and came there in the year 1737, accompanied by the sainted Wiegner.

"He is the first [Moravian] brother, who came to Oley and there he gave such testimony regarding the meritorious

---

[135] In a letter, dated March 15, 1743, Antes states that he had been in America twenty-two years. Hence he arrived in 1721. See Fresenius, *Nachrichten,* Vol. III, p. 745.

death of Christ, with such a demonstration of the Spirit, that the power of darkness received a severe blow. His first sermon was delivered in the house of Jonathan Herbein and the second in the house of Abraham Bertholet. He attacked the Newborn in his discourse from the words of I John 1:7, 8, 9. Through this address the spirit of the Newborn was so broken, that it could not gain strength again and is daily becoming weaker".

About the year 1737, an estrangement arose between Henry Antes and his pastor, John Philip Boehm. The exact cause is at present unknown. Boehm says in his "Letter of Warning" that Antes separated from the congregation "several years ago, because of altogether reprehensible reasons". John Adam Gruber declares that Antes, "who from the time of Spangenberg had been awakened, saw the decay of his Reformed party, and testified regarding it, for which reason he had to suffer sore trials from his brethren in the church and his teacher".[136] A third witness, John Antes, the son of Henry Antes, states in his autobiography that "Antes rebuked the stationed minister of this district for his unbecoming behaviour, on which account he felt so offended that he refused to baptize me".[137] It is, however, possible that Antes' association with Spangenberg brought about the ill-feeling between him and his pastor.

During the stay of Spangenberg in Pennsylvania (September, 1737-August, 1739) he gathered many like-minded persons around him and held with them weekly prayer meetings. After his return to Europe "some friends who through friendship with him had become better acquainted with each other and had expressed themselves more freely towards each other, met frequently, sometimes here sometimes there, in order to learn to know and comprehend God more fully. This continued with considerable blessing for two years".[137a] The headquarters of these meetings was the home of Christopher Wiegner at Skippack and the persons who met there and elsewhere in the neighborhood were known as the "Associated Brethren

---

[136] See Fresenius, *Nachrichten*, Vol. III, p. 135.

[137] Quoted by Mr. Dotterer in an article on John Antes, see *Perkiomen Region*, Vol. I, p. 92.

[137a] See Fresenius, *Nachrichten*, Vol. III, p. 121f.

of Skippack".[138]

When in the spring of 1740 Peter Boehler and a number of other Moravians came to Pennsylvania, Antes acted as guide to take them to what is now Nazareth in Northampton County, where they had contracted with Whitefield to erect a school for negroes on his land. Soon warm friendship arose between Antes and the Moravians, and "since Oley was lying upon his heart as his special field, he brought Brother Boehler to Oley and, as some say, Andrew Eschenbach, in the spring of 1740".[139] As Eschenbach did not arrive in Pennsylvania till October, 1740, the date "spring 1740" can refer only to Peter Boehler.

In the spring of 1740, Whitefield conducted his remarkable and memorable revival meetings in Pennsylvania, which brought him in contact with Henry Antes and the Germans in Skippack and Frederick township. Whitefield's companion and financial supporter, William Seward, has left the following account of the meetings at Skippack and Frederick in his diary:[140]

[138] Among the persons who were thus associated, may be mentioned: Henry Frey, John Kooken, George Merkel, Christian Weber, John Bonn, Jacob Wentz, Jost Schmidt, William Bossen, and Jost Becker, of Skippack; Henry Antes, William Frey, George Stiefel, Henry Holstein and Andrew Frey, of Frederick Township; Matthias Gemelen and Abraham Wagner, of Matetsche; John Bertolet, Francis Ritter and William Pott, of Oley; John Bechtel, John Adam Gruber, Blasius Mackinet and George Bensel, of Germantown. See Reichel, *Memorials,* p. 160. The Wiegner farm lies two miles south of Kulpsville.

[139] Quoted from the Oley church record, now at Bethlehem.

[140] See Seward's Journal, quoted by Mr. Dotterer, in his *Historical Notes,* p. 84. Whitefield's diary relates the same incidents as follows: "Thursday, April 24, 1740. Preached at Skippack, sixteen miles from Montgomery, where the Dutch People live. It was seemingly a very wilderness part of the country; but there were not less, I believe, than 2000 Hearers. Conviction seemed to fasten at the latter End of the Sermon. Travelling and preaching in the Sun again weakened me much, but by the Divine Assistance I took Horse, rode twelve miles, and preached in the Evening to about 3000 People at a Dutch Man's Plantation, who seemed to have drank deeply into the consolations of the Holy Spirit. We spent the evening in a most agreeable Manner. I never saw more Simplicity: surely, that House was a Bethel. The Dutch prayed and sung in their own Language, and then God enlarged my Heart to pray in ours."

"April 24, [1740]. Rose at five, wrote my Journal and dispatch'd several Letters to Georgia. Came to Christopher Wigner's Plantation in Skippack, where many Dutch people settled, and where the famous Mr. Spangenberg resided lately. It was surprizing to see such a Multitude of People gathered together in such a wilderness country, Thirty Miles distant from Philadelphia. Nothing but the mighty Power of God could effect this. Our Brother [Whitefield] was exceedingly carried out in his Sermon, to press poor Sinners to come to Christ by Faith, and claim all their Privileges, viz. not only Righteousness and Peace, but Joy in the Holy Ghost; and after he had done, our dear Friend, Peter Boehler, preach'd in Dutch to those who could not understand our Brother in English. Came to Henry Anti's Plantation in Frederick Township, Ten Miles farther in the Country, where was also a Multitude equally surprising with what we had in the Morning, and our Brother was equally carried out to press poor Sinners to know God, and Jesus Christ whom God hath sent.

"There was much melting under both Sermons, but my Heart was too hard, which I was drawn to complain to my dear Jesus, whose Blood and nothing less, can soften it, and forever blessed be his name, he heard my Prayers, and spoke Peace to my troubled Soul.

"At Night I was drawn to sing and pray with our Brethren in the Fields.

"Brother Whitefield was very weak in Body, but the Lord Jehovah was his Strength, and did indeed magnify the same in his Weakness, for I never heard him speak more clear and powerful.

"They were Germans where we dined and supp'd, and they pray'd and sung in Dutch, as we did in English, before and after Eating".

When Zinzendorf came to Pennsylvania, in December, 1741, Henry Antes conferred with him about the Union Synods, and on December 15, 1741, issued a call for a union synod, to be held on New Year's day 1742 (o. st.). Zinzendorf himself claimed later that the idea of such synods did not originate with him. He wrote: "I was neither the author nor advisor of these meetings,[141] which were called by Pennsylvanians who had become tired of their own ways. What the object of these meetings may have been, I am not able to determine. I should think that every deputy had his own instructions. What my ultimate object was, I know well enough, and have not for a moment endeavored to conceal. I wished to make use of this opportunity to enthrone the Lamb as the real Creator, Preserver, Redeemer and Sanctifier of the whole world, and at the same time to introduce, in theory and practice, the catholicity of the doctrine of His passion, as a universal theology for the German Pennsylvanians".[142]

Antes presided at the first Synod and took a prominent part in all the later synods. In the last synod he was commissioned to prepare a circular to the Germans asking them to join the Congregation of God in the Spirit. In the summer of 1742 Antes was again sent to Oley, after Eschenbach had been directed to go to Conestoga. Gruber reports that he received a written call from the people of Oley at this time, in which he was asked to preach for them every two weeks. After the year 1742 Antes withdrew from his missionary activity, but became active in the secular affairs of the Moravian settlements at Bethlehem and Nazareth.

When the fifteenth Pennsylvania Synod was held in his house in Frederick township, in March, 1745, he offered the use of his plantation and house to the Brethren as a boarding school for boys. The school was opened in June, 1745, and was maintained till 1750, when it was transferred to Oley. Upon the opening of the school, Antes and his family,—except

---

[141] This agrees with what Antes states in the call for the conference: "It has been under consideration for two years or more, whether it would not be possible to appoint a general assembly." To this statement Gruber remarks: "I have had for some years much intercourse with Henry Antes, as with my dear friend, but such a conference has never been mentioned, neither by him nor by any of the other friends in my presence, nor was there any desire of and urging for it. But Spangenberg mentioned it formerly in my presence, with whom I agreed and expressed the same wish that there might be harmony between the several well-inclined parties." See Fresenius, *Nachrichten*, Vol. III, p. 303f, note.

[142] See Zinzendorf's *Naturelle Reflexionen*, p. 194f, quoted by Reichel, *Early History*, p. 99.

THE TOMB OF HENRY ANTES

two of his sons who remained as pupils of the school,—moved to Bethlehem. There he had charge of the construction of mills, bridges, dams and houses for the Brethren. October 27, 1748, he was appointed General Business Manager for the Brethren, taking care of their extensive properties. In April 1750, Antes returned to his farm in Frederick township. His withdrawal was due to the introduction of white robes or surplices then worn by Moravian ministers at the celebration of the eucharist. Of this he disapproved as smacking of catholicism. Dr. Harbaugh quotes Antes as saying: "They introduced the mass-robes when they celebrated the communion." Henry Antes died July 20, 1755, and was buried on his own farm. His tombstone, still standing, bears a fitting German inscription, which may be rendered as follows in English:

> "Here rests
> Henry Antes:
> An Ornament of this Land;
> An upright, fearless
> Administrator of Justice
> And a faithful Servant
> Before the World's and God's People
> Fell asleep
> in Frederick-Town July 20
> 1755
> aged 54 years."

JOHN BECHTEL.

Closely associated with Antes in the Union Movement of Zinzendorf was John Bechtel. He has left behind an interesting autobiography, which deserves to be printed in full.[142a] He writes:

"I was born in the year 1690, on the 3rd of October, in

[142a] It was printed by Dr. Harbaugh, *Fathers of the Reformed Church*, Vol. I, pp. 312-316. We are able to make a number of corrections, on the basis of the original text, which is found in the "Bethlehem Diary."

Weinheim, at the "Bergstrasse",[143] in the Electoral Palatinate, to which place my parents had fled when the town of Franckenthal, where they had resided previously, had been burned by the French. My dear parents insisted from my earliest youth that I attend diligently church and school. In my ninth year my mother, and in my fourteenth year my father departed this world.

"In the year 1704, I came to Heidelberg as an apprentice to a woodturner, where, although I was with my blood relations, I was kept very strictly. Nevertheless, I was diligently kept to attendance upon church and the reading of the Bible, to which I had also a special inclination and as a result of which I felt many a good impulse in my heart. In the fall of 1709, I began to travel as a journeyman, whereby I came in contact with other journeymen and was compelled to mix with many a frivolous company. As a result I lost my pious simplicity and, I must confess it to my shame, that I became pretty reckless, so that I loved best to be with the wildest crowd. This continued for about three years, when my dear Saviour began to convict me in my heart in such a manner, that often in the gayest company I felt alarm; and his disciplinary grace wrought in me so mightily, that, when I returned home at night everything that I had done wrong during the day came up before me. Then I would often shed many tears and promise to do better, without realizing that I could not do this in my own strength, till at length, through the Saviour's grace, I remembered his words: 'Without me ye can do nothing'. Then I began with tears to pray that He might have mercy on me, and forgive me all my sins, and I vowed to change my life. I sought to withdraw more and more from my worldly companions, but I was often compelled to associate with them because of my trade.

"In 1714, I allowed my friends to persuade me to set up my trade in Heidelberg, and in 1715, I married my dear, sainted

---

[143] The "Bergstrasse" is the old Roman road which runs at the foot of the Odenwald, along the Rhine valley, beginning south of Darmstadt and running down to Heidelberg, a distance of 52 km. It passes through Weinheim.

wife,[143a] who in 1758, on February 7th, passed to her Saviour, here in Bethlehem. In our union, which lasted forty-three years, God gave us nine children, of whom five daughters are yet living. These had thirty-eight grandchildren, of whom seven passed to the Saviour, and sixteen great-grandchildren. It is my wish and prayer that they may all grow up for the dear Saviour and not one of them be lost.

"In 1717, I moved from Heidelberg to Franckenthal, where I resided nine years, until in 1726 I removed, with my wife and three children, to Pennsylvania. I lived nearly twenty years in Germantown. In 1738 I became acquainted with the dear Brother Joseph [Spangenberg], when he resided with Wiegner in Skippack, which place we went to visit once every four weeks. The sainted brother Antes, Stiefel, John Adam Gruber, myself and others from Germantown enjoyed many a blessed hour together. In 1742, when the dear departed Disciple [Count Zinzendorf] came to Pennsylvania, I became acquainted with him and other dear brethren. My heart felt at once a tender inclination towards them and I loved them sincerely. When I heard the dear Disciple [Zinzendorf] preach for the first time in the church in Germantown, I felt in my heart: 'Yes, this is the pure and true ground of salvation, Jesus Christ and His merits and sufferings. Other foundation can no man lay. Through His death alone life has been secured to us.'

"From that time on the [Moravian] Brethren were my dearest companions in my house; and when hatred and bitterness against the sainted Disciple and the Brethren began in the country, I also received my honest share, for my Reformed co-religionists in Germantown and vicinity,—whom I had served as preacher and whose Sunday services I had held for more than sixteen years [1727-1744], in accordance with a call from them, and its written confirmation from Heidelberg [Germany],—now began to give me considerable trouble, until

---

[143a] The name of Bechtel's wife was Maria Appolonia Marret, born May 14, 1691, at Heidelberg, to which city her parents had fled from Metz. She was survived by five daughters: (1) Mary Agneta Bechtel, born at Franckenthal, September 19, 1719, was married at Germantown, July 5, 1739, to Cornelius Weygandt. She died May 28, 1789. (2) Ann Margaret Bechtel, born at Franckenthal, September 13, 1721,

in the year 1744, on Sunday the 9th of February, they put me out altogether. The motto of the Congregation[144] for the day read:

> 'Jerusalem that is above,
> Is the mother of us all.
> There is in east and west,
> For those that are hard pressed,
> Still something that is good
> In our brotherhood'.

"But I did not know this motto, until I came to Bethlehem. Then it was certainly a true comfort to me. From that time I felt assured in my heart that I belonged to the [Moravian] Congregation. I asked the Saviour to grant me this favor of bringing me to the congregation. He heard my prayer and, after I had asked Brother Joseph [Spangenberg] and others for it, I secured permission, in the spring of 1746, to remove to the Congregation (at Bethlehem). This took place to my great joy on September 13th of that year. Now, I thought, I shall live for my dear Saviour alone, and, by His grace, I shall be content and so may He keep me until my end".

To this story of his life, as told by Bechtel himself, we may add a few additional facts taken from various sources.

His daughter Margaret, who in 1742 married the Indian missionary, Gottlob Buettner, describes in her autobiography how her father first met Count Zinzendorf:[145] "On his arrival at New York, the Count wrote to my father to meet him in

was married in 1742 to Rev. Gottlob Buettner, the Indian missionary. (3) Mary Susan Bechtel, born at Franckenthal, was married in May, 1748, to Rev. John Levering. (4) Maria Appolonia Bechtel, born at Germantown, June 12, 1733, was married to Christian Weber, at Bethlehem, and died December 27, 1808. (5) There was another daughter, concerning whom nothing is known. See J. W. Jordan, *John Bechtel*, Philadelphia, 1895, pp. 12-15.

[144] This motto was misunderstood by Dr. Harbaugh (Fathers, I, 315). The "Loosungen" were daily reading lessons of the Brethren Church, consisting of Scripture passages, verses of hymns and brief mottos. They are still printed annually. The sense, though expressed obscurely, seems to be that, though the heavenly Jerusalem is our ultimate home, meanwhile the (Moravian) Congregation furnishes the best place of refuge for the persecuted. This fitted Bechtel's case exactly.

[145] Quoted by Reichel, *Memorials*, p. 175, note *.

HISTORIC HOUSES IN GERMANTOWN
1. Theobald Endt House 2. John Bechtel House 3. Weygrandt House 4. Indian Queen Inn

(By Courtesy of Dr. Naaman H. Keyser)

Philadelphia. Through fear of incurring the displeasure of such of his friends as had been prejudiced against the Count, he hesitated to comply with his request. I urged him to go, I gave him no rest, and as my verbal persuasions were of no avail, I ran to the pasture, caught his riding-horse and brought it saddled and bridled to the door. This appeal father could not resist, and from regard to me he rode to town to see the remarkable man who impressed me deeply when I saw him next day at our house, and indelibly so, when not two weeks later I heard him for the first time proclaim the words of eternal life."

The activity of Bechtel in the Union Synods, his ordination on April 11, 1742 (o. st.) by Bishop David Nitschmann, and his ministry at Germantown have already been described in the last chapter.

In January, 1746, a number of people living in Germantown requested the Congregation at Bethlehem to open a boarding school for their children. The Union Synod, meeting at Bethlehem January 24-27, 1746, resolved: "We believe the time has come to open an institution for the children in Germantown and Philadelphia. We also accept the house of John Bechtel, which of his own free will he has offered to us publicly". When the school was opened, in September, 1746, Bechtel with his family removed to Bethlehem. There he served the "Brethren's Economy" for many years in his trade as turner. In December, 1776, he began to suffer from gallstones. He died April 16, 1777, in the evening at eleven o'clock and was buried in the old Moravian cemetery at Bethlehem on Sunday, April 20, 1777.

JACOB LISCHY.

More important even than the labors of Antes and Bechtel were the efforts of Jacob Lischy in behalf of the union movement. Indeed without his tireless journeyings, popular sermons and printed defenses the movement would have been a total failure, at least among the Reformed people.

Jacob Lischy was born at Muehlhausen, then in Switzerland, now in south-western Germany. His father, Jacob Lischy, was born in 1692 and died March 25, 1748. He married Anna Maria Kilian, January 17, 1718. Jacob, their oldest son, was born May 28, 1719.[146] A younger son, Paulus, was born November 23, 1721. Young Lischy was a linen weaver by trade.

In a pamphlet, published by him in 1748, Lischy gives the story of his youth. He was converted, he says, when fourteen years of age. In his 16th and 17th year he began to preach privately. When nineteen years of age he visited Marienborn, together with a candidate of theology from Basle. He liked it so well that he stayed there and at Herrnhaag, in the Wetterau, almost a whole year. Next he visited Herrnhut, the headquarters of the Moravian Church, and remained there three quarters of a year. When in the fall of 1741 a colony of emigrants was sent out to Pennsylvania, he was one of its

SIGNATURE OF JACOB LISCHY.

members. In February, 1742, the colonists were in London, where Spangenberg organized fifty-seven of them into a "Sea Congregation", with a chaplain, stewards, exhorters, servitors and nurses. They left London March 15, 1742, in the "Snow Catherine", which had been bought by the Moravians. They arrived in Philadelphia June 7, 1742. Twenty-nine of the passengers qualified in Philadelphia, by taking the oath of allegiance, on June 8th (or May 28, o. st.). Among them were Jacob Lischy and John Brandmiller, both of whom engaged later in work among the Reformed people.[147]

During the summer and fall of 1742, Lischy accompanied

---

[146] Although there are two Jacob Lischys mentioned in the church records at Muhlhausen, one born in 1716, the other in 1719, there can hardly be any question that it was the younger man that came to Pennsylvania. Lischy himself tells us that he was nineteen years when he came to Marienborn. There he stayed about a year and Herrnhut three-quarters of a year. Thus in the early spring of 1741 he was 22 years. This takes us back to 1719 as the year of his birth and identifies him with the younger Jacob Lischy.

[147] The story of the experiences of this colony is told at length by Bishop Levering, *Bethlehem*, pp. 108-116.

Zinzendorf on several journeys, one of them from July 24-August 2, 1742, was to the Delaware Indians, living beyond the Blue Mountains, west of the Delaware Water Gap. Later, Lischy reports, Zinzendorf "took me along when he traveled about through the country preaching, and tried to make me acquainted with the Reformed people. Thus he offered my services to the people in Berne township [Berks County], saying that I had already preached in Switzerland. Thus we came to Philadelphia and Bro. Ludwig [Zinzendorf] arranged that I should live with my father-in-law and from there should go out preaching, and make a beginning in the church at Germantown, which I did, and I preached before his departure also at Berne, where he recommended me. . . . At first I pursued the method of an itinerant preacher, preaching in houses and barns, wherever it was appointed and thus I made several trips through the country."[148] September 17, 1742, Lischy had married Mary, second daughter of John Stephen Benezet, merchant of Philadelphia. He was ordained in January, 1743, by Bishop David Nitschmann, assisted by Rev. Anthony Seiffert.

Shortly after his ordination Lischy settled at Cocalico, near Ephrata, from which place as a center he ministered to numerous Reformed congregations. In a report, submitted to Bishop Spangenberg in December, 1744, he reported about eighteen preaching places, where he had been ministering. They included the following: Heidelberg, Berne, Blue Mountains and Tulpehocken in Berks County; Hans Zimmerman's, Muddy Creek, two places in Cocalio township, Warwick, Donegal, Earl township and Kissel Hill in Lancaster County; Quitopahilla, Swatara and Muhlbach in the present Lebanon County, Coventry in Chester County, Goshenhoppen in Montgomery County and York in York County. Several of these congregations had given Lischy regular calls. Thus Coventry in Chester County called him April 10, 1743. On May 19, 1743, thirty-six members at Coventry signed a constitution drawn up by Lischy. At Muddy Creek four elders and more than forty members signed a call to Lischy on Thursday before Easter, 1743. In the constitution, entered by Lischy in the

[148] See Lischy's Report of December, 1744, printed in the *Reformed Church Review,* Fourth Series, Vol. IX (1905), p. 520.

Muddy Creek record occurs this significant statement: "The Holy Sacraments shall be believed by us and treated as is prescribed in the Heidelberg Catechism, without in the least adding thereto or detracting therefrom."

But the ministry of Lischy among the Reformed congregations was not without opposition. People began to suspect that he was not "echt reformirt." In order to defend his position he issued a pamphlet on March 1, 1743, entitled: "Jacob Lischy's a Reformed Minister's Declaration of his Intention, addressed to his Reformed Co-religionists." That Lischy was not the sole author of this pamphlet is evident from his report to Spangenberg, in which he states, referring to this declaration: "Brother Boehler assisted me very much and expressed my views thoroughly. Brother Antes assisted in getting the call into proper order. At the next conference it was decided that, after Brother Boehler had corrected the manuscript and had made a final copy of it, it should be printed. . . . After it was finished I distributed it wherever I preached. It had the desired effect, because it pleased everybody." The pleasure was, however, not of long duration. There was no denying that Lischy occupied an ambiguous position. In his eagerness to appear as a genuine Reformed preacher he even went so far as to deny his connection with his Moravian associates, which was severely condemned by the latter. Lischy himself pictures the situation very clearly in his report to Spangenberg. He writes:[149]

"How I felt at times I can hardly describe. I often thought of giving up the churches and preaching again in the houses, fields and woods, but the brethren would not permit this, as it would have caused a premature separation. They often dissuaded me from doing this, and I was told through Brother Boehler, that, if I did not try to hold the churches, my services would be no longer required, for they had resolved in the conferences that we should seek to sanctify the churches. Hence I gave full sway to my friends to keep and maintain the churches, which gave them the more courage to oppose and put to shame our adversaries. The latter, however, did not rest either, but furnished even stronger proof that I was really a

---

[149] See *Reformed Church Review*, Vol. IX (1905), p. 525.

full-fledged Herrnhuter and even the chief of them. They also called upon the Rev. Mr. Boehm to help them, who confirmed and strengthened them in their opinion by his book directed against me. Finally, when they attempted to call my ordination in question and my calls to the congregations, I was compelled to convene a large council of elders. I preached once more in my congregations and invited them to assemble on August 29, 1743, at Heidelberg, where of twelve or more congregations about fifty elders and deacons appeared." After preaching a sermon Lischy gave them a frank recital of his past life, explaining freely his connection with the Moravian Brethren in Germany, his coming to Pennsylvania, his ordination by Bishop Nitschmann and his efforts to serve them. Then he asked them whether, in view of his past record, they wished to renew their call to him. They were all ready to do so. This call, with a further statement, signed by eight elders, was printed as a broadside.

Lischy came into collision with Boehm at Tulpehocken and at Goshenhoppen. At the former place Lischy offered to preach, but before he could do so his connection with the Moravian Brethren was revealed and as a result he was refused permission. Even his offer not to oppose the ministry of Boehm could not gain him admission. At Goshenhoppen, Lischy preached in the spring of 1744. But, when Boehm remonstrated with the elders there, they expressed regret at having allowed him to come in. Boehm convinced them that Lischy was a Moravian by showing them his Moravian hymn book with his autograph in it.

In the fall of 1744, Lischy crossed the Susquehanna and went into York County. In the town of York he found a large Reformed church and "a still larger congregation of at least 300 souls". A call was sent to him, signed by two elders, George Meyer and Philip Rothrock, on August 12, 1744. After he had declined the call, it was renewed by the whole congregation May 24, 1745. This second call was accepted by Lischy and he preached his introductory sermon in York from Ezek. 2:1-7. But, before he was allowed to settle at York and Kreutz Creek as the regular pastor of these congregations, he had to pass through another trial, which was meant to determine his exact status. This time the Moravian authorities insisted upon finding out exactly where he stood. Hence, on March 20-21, 1745, a second church council of the Reformed congregations was held at Muddy Creek, attended by sixty elders of twelve different congregations. "Lischy was asked whether he was a Herrnhuter. At first he evaded the question, 'carrying the church around the village', as Henry Antes expressed it. Being more closely questioned by the other Reformed ministering brethren, C. H. Rauch, Bechtel and Antes, he publicly avowed that he was in connection with the Brethren at Bethlehem".[150] With this statement they were apparently satisfied for the time being.

In February, 1745, Rev. Christian Henry Rauch was associated with Lischy to assist him in preaching to the country congregations. A diary of Rauch from February 5-26, 1745, is still in existence, also diaries of Lischy from February 23-May 28, 1745, and again from August 13-September 8, 1745. Together they visited and preached at Muddy Creek, Berne, Heidelberg, Schwartzwald, Tulpehocken, Swatara, Quitopahilla, Donegal, Warwick, Nicolaus Kissel's (near Lancaster), Earl township, Coventry, Goshenhoppen, York, Kreutz Creek and Bermudian. As soon as Lischy had settled at York, his work as itinerant missionary was taken up by Rauch and Brandmiller.

The authorities at Bethlehem looked with increasing dissatisfaction upon the work of Lischy. But it was not till 1747 that he broke openly with them. On January 10, 1747, he sent a letter to Spangenberg, expressing his regret at not being able to be present at the Synod to be held in Bethlehem on January 15th. On April 22, 1747, Lischy came to Bethlehem with his wife for a visit. Three papers had been handed to him by Rauch, one of which he was asked to sign. The first declared that he wished to be regarded as a member of the Moravian Church, the second, that he wished to be a Reformed pastor under the Reformed Consistory of the Brethren, the third, that he wanted to be an independent Reformed minister. Lischy hesitated for a long time to make a decision. But a Synod, held at Germantown May 10-14, 1747, insisted upon it. A special conference was held with him May 25th, to help him to

[150] See Reichel, *Early History*, p. 191.

decide. No final conclusion was reached, however, until he met Schlatter on June 26, 1747, who agreed to write in his behalf to the synods of Holland. Then Lischy decided for the third alternative.

His case came up before the first meeting of the Reformed Coetus, in September, 1747, for investigation. At the second meeting, in September, 1748, he was asked to hand in his confession of faith, which he did October 26, 1748.[151] About the same time he wrote the "Second Declaration of his Intention", printed by Saur in 1748, by which he publicly defended his separation from the Moravian Church.

There is no more beautiful testimony to the unselfishness and generosity of Mr. Boehm than his reconciliation with Lischy and his touching reference to him in his last letters. In one of them, written November 21, 1748, Boehm refers to him as follows: "As for my part, I have good hope that he will be in future a faithful laborer in our true Church. May God, the only searcher of hearts, give him His blessing".

CHRISTIAN HENRY RAUCH.

Perhaps the ablest worker in the union movement of Zinzendorf was Christian Henry Rauch. From an autobiography, preserved in the Moravian archives at Bethlehem, we learn the main facts of his life.

He was born July 5, 1718, at Bernburg, in the County of Anhalt, Germany. Even in his tender youth he experienced the influence of God's Spirit upon his heart. He was awakened December 31, 1738, at Wolgast, Pomerania. He left there, in June, 1739, to visit the Moravian congregation at Marienborn, where he arrived August 2, 1739. He was received as a member of the congregation September 19, 1739. A letter, written by Spangenberg from Pennsylvania in November, 1737, caused several of the young men at Marienborn to dedicate themselves to the work of missions among the North American Indians. Among them was also Rauch. In this letter Spangenberg quoted the words of the Indian chief Shikel-

---

[151] A copy of this confession was sent to Holland. It is now at The Hague, 74, I, 51. An English translation was published by Dr. Good in the *Christian World* of December 17, 1898.

limy, which he addressed to Conrad Weiser on a trying journey to Onondaga. The Indian had said to him:[152] "My dear companion, thou hast hitherto encouraged us; wilt thou now quite give up? Remember that evil days are better than good days, for when we suffer much we do not sin; *sin will be driven out by suffering,* and God cannot extend His mercy to the former; but contrary-wise, when it goeth evil with us, God has compassion on us."

Through these remarkable words Rauch felt his call to be a missionary to the Indians. "On the 8th of November, 1739", he says, "I received the Word of the Lord to be the witness of His passion and death among the Indians in North America. On the 14th of November I was commissioned to this work, and on the 31st of December I began my journey from Marienborn to New York." On January 10, 1740, he reached Herrendyk in Holland, where he stayed ten weeks. He reached London April 5th and embarked for New York May 5th with Captain Bryant. He arrived safely at New York July 21st. On August 5th he spoke for the first time with two Mohicans, who invited him to visit them. On August 29th, he arrived at Shekomeko, his destination. As a welcome he was almost beaten by the Indians, who were all drunk and acted as maniacs. But he was not intimidated.[153] He set at once to work to learn their language with such good results that he was able to deliver the first sermon to them in their own tongue on Good Friday of 1741. In January, 1742, at the invitation of Zinzendorf, Rauch visited Philadelphia with the first three, converted Indians. In February they went to Oley to attend the third Union Synod. There Rauch was ordained, and, on the same day, February 22, 1742, the three Indians were baptized and named Abraham, Isaac and Jacob. A fourth Indian was baptized John, in April at Shekomeko, and five others, men as

---

[152] Quoted by Reichel, *Memorials,* p. 90, note.

[153] G. H. Loskiel in his *Geschichte der Mission der evangelischen Brueder unter den Indianern in Nordamerika.* Barby, 1789, p. 225f. (English edition, London, 1794, part II, p. 13), tells the story that Rauch, on his arrival went into the hut of the worst savage of the whole clan, Jschoop, seated himself at his side, told him of the Saviour, and then, saying that he was tired in consequence of the long journey, lay down at the fire and fell asleep. This single act of trust made a deep impression upon the Indian and won his confidence.

MONUMENT OF BUETTNER AND RAUCH AT SHEKOMEKO, N. Y., ERECTED 1859

well as women, in the presence of Zinzendorf and his party August 11, 1742. Rauch married Anna Robins on December 13, 1742, when Zinzendorf officiated. Together they continued the work among the Indians. In 1744 serious persecutions of the missionary began in Shekomeko, instigated by white people. December 15, 1744, the sheriff and three constables arrested Rauch and forbad him to continue his work among the Indians.[153a] As a result Rauch was recalled to Bethlehem. In February, 1745, he began his work among the Reformed congregations, assisting or rather supervising the work of Lischy. When Lischy retired beyond the Susquehanna and accepted a call to York, Rauch took up his itinerant preaching. Extensive diaries, covering his journeys from February 6-November 14, 1746, and from January 23-June 30, 1747, are still in existence, testifying to his whole-hearted devotion to his work. He supplied sixteen preaching places. In August, 1749, he accepted a call to the Moravian congregation at Warwick, now Lititz, in Lancaster county. He served this and neighboring congregations till 1753. Then he became pastor of the Moravian congregation at Salem, N. C., from 1755-1756. Towards the end of the latter year he went to Jamaica, to minister to the negroes on that island. In this work he continued till his death, which took place November 11, 1763. His work among the Reformed congregations was confined to the years 1745-1747.

JOHN BRANDMILLER.

Another itinerant minister visiting Reformed congregations under the auspices of the Congregation of God in the Spirit was John Brandmiller. The facts of his life are recorded briefly in his own autobiography, preserved in the achives at Bethlehem.

John Brandmiller (Brandmüller) was born at Basle, Switzerland, November 24, 1704. His father, of like name, was bookkeeper there. Young John was confirmed and went to communion for the first time in his thirteenth year. Shortly afterwards he was put under the care of an uncle to learn

---

[153a] In 1859, a monument was erected to Rauch and Buettner at Shekomeko, N. Y., by the Moravian Historical Society, to commemorate their labors. The monument was placed over the tomb of Buettner.

the printing business. Being of a restless disposition he ran away and went to Holland. There he engaged his services to a German baron, who intended to travel to Turkey, but at Treves the baron found a servant who suited him better and as a result young Brandmiller was dismissed. Then he made up his mind to return home. On the way, in Lorraine, he fell in with some Swiss officers, serving in the French army. They persuaded him to enlist as a soldier. After six weeks his company was stationed near a swamp, where many fell sick and died. Brandmiller also contracted the fever and came near death, but after some time recovered slowly. One day his captain handed him a letter from his father. After reading it he resolved to ask permission to come home. His father soon secured his release and he returned home, where he was received with open arms. Then he completed his apprenticeship as printer with his uncle. In March, 1735, he married Anna Maria Burkhard. Their union was blessed with three children, two of whom died in infancy. Having become acquainted with the Moravians, he moved to Marienborn and in the year 1739 to Herrnhaag. In 1741 he went with the "First Sea Congregation" to Pennsylvania, arriving in Philadelphia June 7, 1742. After a stay of six months he returned to Germany to fetch his wife, whom he had left in the Wetterau. He stayed at Herrnhaag, near Frankfort-on-the-Main, till the "Second Sea Congregation" was ready to leave in May, 1743. They sailed in the Moravian ship "Little Strength", leaving Cowes September 27th and arriving at New York November 26, 1743.

Brandmiller settled first at Bethlehem, acting there as steward or deacon of the congregation, till the spring of 1745, when he was sent out as an itinerant missionary to the Reformed people. On April 8, 1745, he left Bethlehem. He preached his first sermon at Nicolaus Kissel's, near Lancaster on April 12th. His circuit included Warwick, Kissel's, Donegal and Coventry. On April 28th, while crossing the Schuylkill in a canoe, it capsized, so that he nearly lost his life. On May 2nd (or May 13, n. st.) he was ordained in Philadelphia. In September, 1745, Brandmiller was sent to Swatara and Donegal to supply these and neighboring congregations. His diaries from September 1-24, 1745, and from October 26, 1745-January 11, 1746, describing his missionary activity, are still extant.

In January and February, 1747, and again in March and April, 1748, Brandmiller visited the Walloons at Esopus and New Paltz in the State of New York. From October 12-December 24, 1749, he made a visit with Leonard Schnell to the Germans in Virginia. In 1759 he removed with his wife to Friedensthal, where he served for eight and a half years as a reader. In 1768 he returned to Bethlehem. During the later part of his life Brandmiller acted repeatedly as printer of the Moravian Church. Thus between 1760-1763 he printed the *Harmony of the Gospels,* and a hymn book, translated into the language of the Delaware Indians, by the Rev. Bernard A. Grubé, and in 1767 *Tägliche Loosungen,* i.e., "The Daily Reading Lessons" of the Congregation.[154]

Brandmiller died at Bethlehem August 16, 1777, drowning accidentally in a mill-race. The diarist at Bethlehem states that the previous day had been hot and sultry. Brandmiller had complained about dizziness. He had been in the habit of going down to the water to bathe his face. While doing this he was overtaken by vertigo and fell into the water.

DAVID BRUCE.

The last of the Reformed itinerant preachers, of whom a diary has come down to us, is David Bruce.[155] He was born in Edinburgh, Scotland. He was a Scotch Presbyterian, a carpenter by trade, who joined the Moravians in England. When Zinzendorf came to America, in December, 1741, Bruce accompanied him. He became the first English speaking missionary of the Moravian Church in America. He married Judith, the oldest daughter of John Stephen Benezet, a prominent merchant in Philadelphia, July 10, 1742. (Jacob Lischy

---

[154] See *Pennsylvania Magazine of History and Biography,* Vol. VI, p. 249f. The "Harmony of the Gospels" was a manual used by the Moravian Church during passion week. They were printed at Friedensthal, to which place type had been sent from Europe.

[155] For Bruce's life see Levering, Bethlehem, p. 73, note; Reichel, *Memorials,* p. 24; Reincke, *Register of the Members of the Moravian Church,* p. 78; *Memorial of the Dedication of Monuments erected by the Moravian Hist. Soc.;* Philadelphia, 1860, pp. 161-168. The writer also used personal notes communicated by Dr. J. W. Jordan.

married another daughter). Bruce accompanied Zinzendorf on his first visit to the Indian country. He also assisted in the ministry at Bethlehem, Nazareth, Philadelphia and Dansbury (Stroudsburg), and in the Indian mission among the Delawares in Pennsylvania. In the beginning of 1743 he was in Philadelphia, where the Moravian parsonage, at the southeast corner of Race and Broad streets, constituted the headquarters for four or five itinerant evangelists and their families. Bruce took his turn regularly in preaching the Gospel in the city, and at a number of stations in the surrounding country. He was engaged in this work until the end of the year 1744, when he returned to Bethlehem. From there as a center he continued to itinerate sometimes among the Indians and again among English and German settlers in eastern Pennsylvania. From June to August, 1745, he itinerated among the Reformed congregations, chiefly in Lancaster County. But he preached also occasionally at Coventry in Chester County, at Tulpehocken, Swatara and Quitopahilla. A diary, describing this work, in somewhat awkward German, is still in existence. In 1746 he visited the English settlers, chiefly Scotch, in Lancaster and Bucks counties. In January, 1749, he was sent to the Indian mission at Wechquadnach, Dutchess County, New York. There he was quite successful as a missionary and was visited by Bishops Watteville and Cammerhoff. The former wrote of him: "In the last years of his life Brother Bruce found his proper sphere among the Indians." He died there after a short illness July 9, 1749, greatly mourned by the converts who were warmly attached to him. In 1859, the Moravian Historical Society erected a monument, jointly to his memory and that of Joseph Powell, who died in 1774, while laboring as evangelist among the white settlers of the Dutchess County, N. Y. The monument stands in what is now the town of Sharon, in Litchfield County, Connecticut. Bruce had one son who lived to maturity. His widow married later Dr. John F. Otto of Bethlehem.

It was through these and other missionaries that the Union Movement of Zinzendorf flourished from 1745-1748. But after the Reformed churches of Pennsylvania had been organized into a Coetus in 1747, and the Lutheran churches into a Ministerium in 1748, the twenty-seventh Pennsylvania

OPPONENTS IN UNION

Synod resolved itself into the First Synod of the Moravian Church in America, convened at Bethlehem in October, 1748.[155a]

[155a] For a study of the Union Movement of Count Zinzendorf the following printed *sources* may be consulted: (1) MORAVIAN: The Minutes of the Pennsylvania Synods, the first of which bears the following title: *Authentische Relation von dem Anlass, Fortgang und Schlusse der am 1sten und 2ten Januarii, Anno 1741/2, in Germantown gehaltenen Versammlung einiger Arbeiter Derer meisten Christlichen Religionen und vieler vor sich selbst Gott-dienenden Christen-Menschen in Pennsylvania;* Aufgesetzt in Germantown am Abend des 2ten obigen Monats. Philadelphia, Gedruckt und zu haben bey B. Franklin. The minutes of the first seven Union Synods were printed by Franklin in 1742, the rest, from 1745-1748, are in Ms. in the archives at Bethlehem. Zinzendorf, *Die Büdingische Sammlung einiger in die Kirchen Historie einschlagender sonderlich neuen Schriften.* 3 vols. Büdingen, 1742-1745; Zinzendorf, *Pennsylvanische Nachrichten vom Reiche Christi,* 1742; Zinzendorf, *Naturelle Reflexiones über allerhand Materien,* 1749; Spangenberg, A. G. *Leben des Herrn Nicolaus Ludwig, Grafen und Herren von Zinzendorf und Pottendorf,* 8 Theile in 3 Bände, Barby, 1772-1775. Also the Catechism edited by Bechtel and Zinzendorf's answer to Boehm's book, edited by Neisser, above referred to. (2) LUTHERAN: *Heinrich Melchior Mühlenberg, Selbstbiographie, 1711-1743,* herausgegeben von Dr. W. Germann, Allentown, 1881; *Hallesche Nachrichten,* new edition, 2 vols. Allentown, 1886-1895. (3) REFORMED: The writings of John Philip Boehm of the years 1742-1743; the booklet of Guldin, published in 1743, as well as the reports and pamphlets of Jacob Lischy, referred to above. (4) SECTARIAN: John Adam Gruber's *Ausführliche Nachricht,* etc., printed in John Philip Fresenius, *Bewährte Nachrichten von Herrnhutischen Sachen,* Vol. III, Frankfurt und Leipzig, 1748, pp. 97-236, with additional documents, pp. 237-872; see also the polemical tracts referred to above, p. 101f.

CHAPTER VIII.

BOEHM'S LAST LABORS.

The 7th of September, 1746, must have been a happy day in the life of Mr. Boehm. On that day there came to his home in Whitpain township the Rev. Michael Schlatter of St. Gall, Switzerland, who had been sent to Pennsylvania by the Synods of Holland to organize the Reformed congregations of the province into a permanent religious body, subordinate to the Church of Holland. Schlatter in his private diary describes his first meeting with Boehm as follows:[156]

"September 7th, I traveled to the plantation of Do. Boehm in Whitpain township. I found his Reverence busy in the field, but he went immediately with me to his house and showed me every possible kindness. He promised me also, after having heard my commission, to assist me with word and deed. This he is doing now in all sincerity, according to the best of his ability."

Thus the earnest prayers of Boehm, uttered incessantly for sixteen years had at last been answered, and his faith had been vindicated. Hence he wrote full of joy to the Classis: "Now we see that, after the Lord has made us to pass through such a severe trial, he will finally manifest His grace in answer to our continual prayers and will strongly incline the hearts of our devout Church Fathers to us, poor members of Christ. For you have now sent to us a man, brought from a great distance and with great sacrifices for the best interests only and the perfect establishment of our true Church." When Boehm notified the synods of Schlatter's arrival, under date December 12, 1746, he wrote in a similar strain: "Thereby my heart was made to rejoice greatly and especially do I give thanks unto the merciful God that He has finally, after much prayer and many sighs, listened graciously to me, poor burden-bearer, and allowed me to see such an effectual instrument and kind brother

[156] See *Journal of Presb. Hist. Soc.*, Vol. III, p. 107.

and fellow-worker in His holy service". Through Schlatter's coming Boehm realized that his long struggle and trying labors had not been in vain. The results of his labors were now made effective through a permanent organization.

As the congregations were too weak to support each separately a pastor, the first step which Schlatter took was to visit the various congregations in order to secure from each a pledge as to how much it was able to contribute to a minister's salary. On the basis of these pledges he united two or more neighboring congregations into separate pastoral charges, each of which was promised a pastor as soon as they could be secured from Europe. In this work of visitation Boehm assisted Schlatter faithfully. Boehm's attitude towards Schlatter's work is clearly seen in his report: "Do. Slatter entered upon this work with earnestness and soon traveled from place to place as much as time would permit. To some of these places I accompanied his Reverence". Thus, e.g., Boehm preceded Schlatter to Tulpehocken, "to gather the two congregations there together, on the 24th [of September], to preach a sermon preparatory to the Holy Supper, and to await my arrival there on the 25th". On that day the Lord's Supper was administered to 101 persons, while more than 600 persons, inside and outside the church, listened to Schlatter's sermon. The congregation had on that day the unusual experience of seeing three ministers in the pulpit at one time, "a circumstance which in all their lives they had not witnessed there before".[157]

Six years before, in 1740, Boehm had sent an elaborate report to Holland, in which he proposed to organize seventeen congregations into six charges. Meanwhile the number of Reformed settlers had largely increased. New congregations had come into existence. It was, therefore, necessary to group the churches together differently. Schlatter visited thirty-eight congregations in Pennsylvania, which he proposed to organize into thirteen charges. In this work of reorganization Schlatter frequently made use of the helpful advice which Boehm was able to give him.

After bringing together the congregations, the next work of Schlatter was to bring together the ministers. This was a

---

[157] See Harbaugh, *Life of Schlatter*, p. 134.

difficult task, as they had antagonized each other for years, and it was not easy for them to forget the past. But at last Schlatter's efforts were crowned with success. They accepted his invitation to meet at his home in Philadelphia. About this conference Schlatter reported to the synods:[158]

"October 12th, [1746], I had the satisfaction of having Dom. Boehm, Weiss and Rieger come to my house in Philadelphia, at my request. Dom. Dorsius would also undoubtedly have appeared, if his wife had not presented him with a child on the very day appointed for our conference. This was the first time that these three ministers, who for many years have been in this country, met together. The result of this brotherly conference was that not I but the all sufficient God completely united their hearts and souls in my presence, without any reservation or remaining difference and reconciled them, while they shed many tears of joy".

Articles of peace were drawn up and signed by the four men present. Unfortunately this interesting document has not been preserved. It probably never reached Holland. The feelings of Boehm at this conference are well expressed by him in his letter to the Classis, dated November 23, 1746. He writes: "It was indeed hard for me to stand in official and brotherly connection with men through whom I had to suffer so much affliction, to the injury of my health (as I have often complained with sadness to the godly Church Fathers, with ample proofs of my innocence). But, persuaded by Do. Slatter, there took place what Christ says Luke 17:4. Then I found myself also in duty bound to do what our dear Saviour commanded us to do. Thus it happened that all that is past was thrown into the fire of love".

No better evidence can be found of the absolute unselfishness and thorough consecration of Boehm in his work than his willingness to forgive his former enemies and to live and labor henceforth with them as his brethren. It was a severe test of his character as a true follower of Christ, but he came out of it triumphant.

The preliminary conference was followed, on September 29, 1747, by the definite organization of the Reformed churches

---

[158] See *Journal of Presb. Hist. Soc.*, Vol. III, p. 116.

MINUTES OF THE FIRST COETUS, SEPTEMBER 29, 1747,
WRITTEN BY BOEHM

and ministers. On that day four ministers (Schlatter, Boehm, Weiss and Rieger) and twenty-seven elders met in the old meeting house in Philadelphia and organized the Coetus (Convention) of the Reformed congregations of Pennsylvania. Mr. Boehm was present at this meeting with three elders, representing the congregations of Falkner Swamp, Providence and Whitpain. He does not appear as a prominent actor in the proceedings. There is but one action recorded of him at this meeting. He asked permission to use the money, which he had collected in New York, for the new church and congregation which had been started in Whitpain township. To this request Coetus assented with the condition, that of the forty-four pounds collected four pounds should be handed over to the people of Skippack, for whose benefit the money had originally been given.

Another fact, however, connected with the first meeting of the Coetus is worthy of record. We owe it to the care and thoughtfulness of Boehm that the minutes of this first meeting have been preserved. The original minutes, written by Schlatter,[159] have been lost. But Boehm made a copy of the original for his own use, which was found by Schlatter among Boehm's papers after his death and was sent by him to Holland.

A well deserved honor, perhaps the only one which he received in his ministerial career, was bestowed upon Mr. Boehm at the second meeting of the Coetus, held in Philadelphia, September 28-30, 1748. He was elected president of the Coetus. It was an important session, at which many far-reaching actions were taken. The influence of the president in shap-

---

[159] It has been stated repeatedly that Boehm was the secretary at the meeting of 1747. That this statement is incorrect appears from a letter of Schlatter to the Synods, dated April 6, 1750, in which he writes: "The enclosed transcript of the first Coetus minutes (taken from the protocol book of the Coetus reposing in my care, which is a folio book four fingers thick and into which the Acts of each Coetus were entered by my own hand) will show that my diary of 1747 and 1748, together with other writings relating to Mr. Lischi, were handed to Do. Boehm, he being at that time president, to send them to the Reverend Synods. After Do. Boehm had died about thirty miles away from his home, without leaving a will, I found this transcript after his death among his papers, it having been copied by his own hand and in his language."

ing action can be seen at every step.

In the first place, through Boehm's influence the doctrinal position of the Church was determined. As president he called attention to the fact that the Fathers in Holland expected the members of the Coetus to sign the Heidelberg Catechism and the Canons of the Synod of Dort. As a result a paper was drawn up to which all the ministers except Rieger, and one elder from each congregation, affixed their signatures, declaring their adherence to these creeds. That action fixed the position of the Coetus as a Calvinistic body.

Another important action was the adoption of a constitution. Here it was again the president, Mr. Boehm, who guided the action. He was successful in having the Coetus adopt the constitution which he had drawn up in 1728 for his congregations, and which had been ratified by the Classis of Amsterdam in 1729. Thus the instrument which held together the congregations of Boehm for twenty years, became now the bond of union by which all the Reformed churches were bound together into one religious body. It is indeed true that this constitution was largely a dead letter. In the existing records of the Coetus it is never afterwards referred to and each congregation continued to have its own congregational constitution. Moreover, only a few years later, in 1753, e.g., cases were decided in the Coetus according to the Church Order of the Synod of Dort. In 1754 copies of this Church Order were handed by Schlatter to each minister[160] and it is repeatedly referred to in later transactions of the Coetus. Nevertheless, as far as official and recorded action is concerned, the constitution of Boehm was the only constitution which the Coetus actually adopted, and to which the Fathers in Holland made no objection. It should also be noted that the Church Order of Boehm in its sixth article recognizes the Church Order of the Synod of Dort as valid and in force in Pennsylvania.

There were also a number of questions submitted to the Coetus, which emanated most likely from the president. They were questions with whose solution Boehm had been wrestling for many years. Now at last he found an opportunity of having them answered. The questions related mainly to the conduct

---

[160] See *Minutes of Coetus*, pp. 98, 116.

of the members of the churches. They were forbidden to take communion or to have their children baptized in any but their own churches, exceptions to be made only in special instances, with the knowledge and consent of their pastor. This was a question to which repeated reference is made in Boehm's letters. Another question had reference to the contributions to be made by the members. It was resolved that no one should be considered a member who did not contribute to the maintenance of the church. This too was a question which had given Boehm much trouble. This meeting of the Coetus, therefore, put the final stamp of approval upon Boehm's life and work. It accepted his doctrinal position, it adopted his constitution, it solved the problems with which he had struggled. It made him its leader and as president of the Coetus he died.

As president of the Coetus, Boehm was also instructed to have the minutes of the Coetus and the Constitution published. They were printed in 1748 by Gotthard Armbriester of Philadelphia, with an introduction written by Boehm. This pamphlet has become one of the scarcest of Philadelphia imprints, only two copies being known to be in existence.

Mr. Boehm had now come to the end of his long and useful career. His work had been completed. He had piloted the church safely from chaos to order, from strife to harmony. He was getting old and feeble and the state of his health compelled him to hand over his work to younger shoulders.

The first congregation which he surrendered was that of Philadelphia. In the postscript to his letter of November 23, 1746, he refers to the fact that he had promised Schlatter that he would hand the Philadelphia congregation over to him. It together with Germantown was to be constituted one charge with Schlatter as its pastor. On Sunday, December 7, 1746, Boehm made a public announcement of his own withdrawal and the installation of Schlatter as pastor of the congregation. The latter took place December 21st and Schlatter preached his introductory sermon in Philadelphia, on January 1, 1747, from Genesis 32:26. In order to give Schlatter an opportunity to complete his visitation of Reformed churches, Boehm consented to continue his monthly visits to Philadelphia for six months longer.

Two other congregations, which Boehm found increasingly difficult to supply were Falkner Swamp and Providence. With a view to being relieved of preaching at these places, he allowed Schlatter to combine them into one charge with the understanding of having them supplied by one of the new ministers, who was expected from Holland. On October 26, 1746, when Schlatter returned from his first journey, he stopped at Boehm's home over night. It was then that Boehm told him of his plans for the future. He proposed that, as there was no Reformed congregation between Old Goshenhoppen and Germantown, a distance of twenty-four miles, and as he lived almost in the center between these places, that a new congregation be organized near his home, in Whitpain township. Schlatter readily consented to that proposal and organized the new congregation for Boehm on February 3, 1747. It is called Witpen (Whitpain) in the early records. By February, 1747, a small stone church had been built, but as they were able to pay their pastor only ten pounds as salary, Schlatter proposed to connect it with Skippack, Indianfield and Tohickon. This intention was, however, never carried out. Having now a congregation near his home, Boehm was anxiously waiting for the arrival of a new minister, who might take over Falkner Swamp and Providence. He was, therefore, much rejoiced when, on August 17, 1748, Schlatter brought two new ministers to his home who had just arrived from Holland, Dominicus Bartholomaeus and John Jacob Hochreutner. Shortly after their arrival, Boehm reported to the Classis: "I would have liked to see one of them relieve me of my long journey to Falkner Swamp and Providence, for which there was some prospect, but it was represented to me, whether I would not prefer seeing the shepherdless congregations, which had no ministers, helped first of all, afterwards I might be relieved. I should not begrudge them this blessing and have a little patience." Such a touching appeal could not be disregarded by Boehm. He was at once willing to "continue working under the yoke which he had borne so long."

His hopes were, however, realized when, on September 15, 1748, Rev. John Philip Leydich arrived in Philadelphia. When Boehm heard of his arrival he went with an elder to Philadelphia to interview Schlatter. He begged him that Leydich be appointed as the regular pastor of Falkner Swamp and Providence, for, on account of his advancing age, 'he was no longer able to endure such wearisome journeys, as it is necessary to make, in order properly to serve this field." Schlatter promised to do all in his power to provide for these congregations. This promise was kept, for at the Coetus of 1748 Leydich was assigned to Falkner Swamp and Boehm was instructed to install him. This installation took place October 16, 1748. Coetus also commissioned Boehm to install Bartholomaeus at Tulpehocken, because Boehm had been for many years its faithful pastor. This commission was carried out October 23rd. Thus Boehm had successfully transferred his work upon younger shoulders and could now retire contentedly to his one remaining congregation. In December, 1748, Boehm sent his last letters to Holland, a long letter to a Classical deputy as well as the printed minutes of the Coetus to both the Classis and the Synods. These were his last communications to the Fathers in Holland.

SIGNATURE OF JOHN P. LEYDICH.

There is only one more official act of Boehm on record. March 29, 1749,[161] Schlatter received letters from Macungy and Egypt, requesting him to come up and administer the Lord's Supper to them. At the request of Schlatter, Boehm undertook to attend to the wants of these remote congregations. On April 28th, Boehm held the Lord's Supper at Egypt. On his way home, he stopped at the house of his oldest son in Hellertown. There he died unexpectedly and suddenly during the night of April 29th. His body was carried home and he was buried in the Church, now called after his name, in front of the pulpit under the altar. As no Reformed minister could be secured, a Mennonite preacher of Skippack, Martin Kolb,

[161] For this date see note 103.

preached the funeral sermon.[162] Having fought against the sects all his life, Boehm was at last buried by a sect preacher!

Schlatter heard of Boehm's death on May 2, 1749, when on a visit to Mr. Leydich at Falkner Swamp. Schlatter had intended to visit Mr. Weiss at Goshenhoppen, but through the death of Mr. Boehm he was compelled to cut short his journey and return to Philadelphia. On the 4th of May, Schlatter made copies of the writings previously placed in the hands of Mr. Boehm and sent them by way of England to the Synods of Holland and to the Classis of Amsterdam.

On May 7, 1749, Schlatter honored the memory of Boehm by a memorial sermon which he preached at Germantown, "not without deep emotion, on the death of Do. Boehm, the oldest of the German Reformed ministers in this country, who, during the space of many years, had to serve various congregations, and whose memory is blessed by many".

Long after Boehm's death a letter from the Classis of Amsterdam arrived for which he had asked very earnestly in his last communication to the Classis. It was a pity that he was not permitted to read it, but it would hardly have satisfied him, for to his definite requests only a very general answer had been returned.

When Schlatter was in Holland in 1751, he performed an act of justice. Upon his request, the Synod of South Holland, meeting at Leerdam, July 6-16, 1751, resolved to reimburse the widow of Boehm, at least to some extent, for the expenses which he had incurred in publishing the book against the Moravians in 1742. At the Coetus of 1752, it was resolved: "to pay the widow of Dom. Boehm in the name of the Synod, four pounds of this country's money".

Thus ends the record of a noble and unselfish life, a life spent in the service of the Reformed Church, which Boehm loved so much, and for which he was willing to make so many sacrifices. From the letters of Boehm, now published, his services to the Reformed Church are fully evident. They need only to be summarized here in conclusion.

In the first place Boehm may justly be called the *founder*

---

[162] See the extract from Saur's Paper, under date May 16, 1749, printed in the latter part of this book.

HOUSE OF PETER TROXELL AT EGYPT, BUILT IN 1744, IN WHICH BOEHM HELD HIS LAST COMMUNION

THE OLD "BOEHM HOMESTEAD" IN HELLERTOWN, IN WHICH JOHN PHILIP BOEHM DIED

of the Reformed Church in Pennsylvania. He was the first Reformed preacher in the province, who gathered his people around him for worship, beginning his work in 1720, long before Weiss, the next minister, arrived in 1727. He founded the first Reformed congregations in what is now Montgomery County in 1725. Later he extended the sphere of his activity to Conestoga and Tulpehocken and many other frontier districts. As we showed in an earlier chapter, Boehm was the pastor of thirteen congregations, of which he was instrumental in founding certainly eleven, probably twelve. His field covered practically all the territory from the Susquehanna to the Delaware and from Philadelphia to the Blue Mountains, a district which is now covered by eight counties. In this great field Boehm was an indefatigable missionary, supplying even the most distant congregations with preaching and the administration of the sacraments. In one of his letters, dated July 9, 1744, Boehm informed the synods that for eighteen years he had traveled every month 104 miles. To this must be added two more years till the arrival of Schlatter, and we have twenty years, in which Boehm traveled every year 1248 miles. We can, therefore, say that Boehm was the first among the traveling missionaries of the early Reformed Church, holding the great record of having traveled on horseback 24,960 miles, or sixty miles more than the equatorial circumference of the earth.

But Boehm was also the *preserver* of the Reformed Church in Pennsylvania. If it had not been for his faithful ministry of twenty years, the Reformed churches would, humanly speaking, have been scattered, as they were later dispersed in South Carolina, North Carolina and Virginia. Other men like Weiss, Rieger, and Goetschy came into the province for a few years, but then left again, unable to maintain themselves because of the meagre salary paid to the early ministers. Boehm himself, although he received annually not more than ten pounds (about 25 dollars), yet stuck to his post alone throughout all those years, never wavering in his confidence that God would ultimately send assistants to carry on his work. His faithful labors as a preacher were made effective by his organizing talent. This showed itself in the simple constitution, which he drew up at the beginning of his ministry and by which he held his congregations together. Although simple it was well adapted to the conditions then prevailing. It stood the test of practical experience. It would have worked even better, if it could have been introduced into all the congregations, as Boehm endeavored so earnestly to do. By his tact, patience and persistence Boehm successfully piloted his congregations through the long years of waiting, till finally Schlatter came and his work could be carried on to a successful completion.

Boehm was also the *defender* of his church. It was mainly through his efforts that the Reformed churches passed unscathed through the union movement of Count Zinzendorf. That was the estimate of his contemporaries. Thus Schlatter writes of Boehm in his private diary:[163]

"Do. John Philip Boehm appears to me to be a very upright man, to whom, according to common report, we are indebted to the fact that the Herrnhuters have not caused more confusion in many of the congregations. His Reverence has also the reputation of being faithful and punctual in his service, nor has he received much benefit from it, for no one is able to say, although I have asked more than thirty persons, that he receives annually more than ten pounds, Pennsylvania currency, from the four congregations which he serves. This does not include his perquisites for marriages, etc. Thus he had much labor and trouble."

Finally, by his elaborate and careful reports to Holland Boehm has become the *historian* of the early church. No other minister of the Reformed Church, in the period of the Coetus, approached him in the number and quality of the letters which he wrote. By these letters he has set himself unconsciously the most enduring monument. They are without question the most valuable inheritance which he has left beside his churches. They deserve to be published, for they are full of valuable information. Their very beauty testifies to his thorough education and love for order. They are logical in thought, well expressed and faultlessly written in their beautiful penmanship. By their publication he receives at last the recognition which he deserves, but which has long been denied

---

[163] See *Journal of Presb. Hist. Soc.*, Vol. III, p. 117.

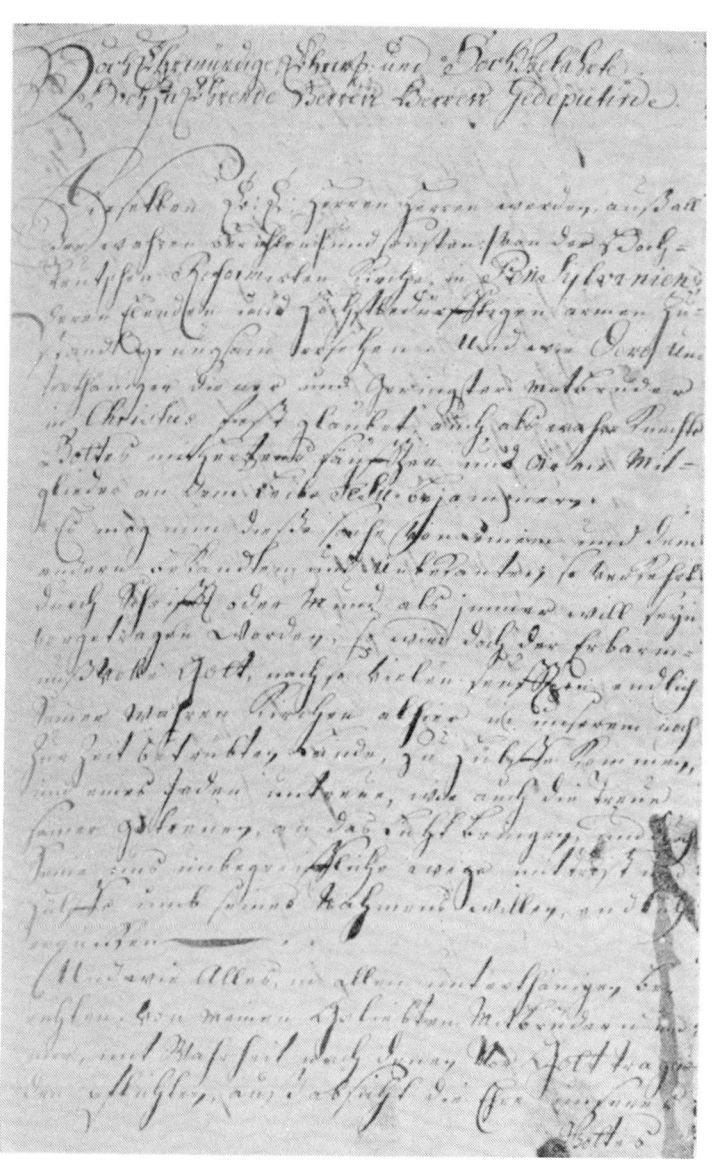

LETTER OF BOEHM, DATED JULY 9, 1744, SHOWING HIS
BEAUTIFUL PENMANSHIP

to him. Even Schlatter, who seems to have had a sincere regard for him, fails to give him just credit for the work he did. For, if we examine the diary of Schlatter for the purpose of discovering what work had been done before him, we are left under the impression that Schlatter himself organized practically all the congregations which he visited. While, with the ampler knowledge we now have, we know that all, or almost all, the congregations which Schlatter visited, were in existence before he came to Pennsylvania. Even during his lifetime Boehm was forced to complain that his work was overlooked. Thus, when Messrs. Bartholomaeus and Hochreutner came from England, he tells us, they brought with them half a sheet (eight pages) of an English print in which he "was not even deemed worthy enough to have his name mentioned,

SIGNATURE OF JOHN PHILIP BOEHM, TAKEN FROM A LETTER TO THE SYNODS.

but, referring to the shepherdless congregations, it was said: 'About the year 1720 they had one who was a layman'".

This neglect of Boehm's work has followed him through the later history of his Church. When Dr. Harbaugh gathered his materials for the "Fathers of the Reformed Church", he came upon the track of a large iron bound chest, in which all of Mr. Boehm's papers were said to have been preserved most carefully. Dr. Harbaugh finally came to the identical garret of a house on Third street, Philadelphia, where the chest had been stored for many years. But, alas, it was gone, and its papers had been burned twenty-five years before.[164] What a loss! What would we not give to see these papers! What a light they would have shed upon many a question which must now remain unanswered and obscure! And, because of the loss of these papers, Dr. Harbaugh was able to give of Mr.

---

[164] See Harbaugh's *Fathers*, Vol. I, p. 290.

Boehm's life and work but a brief and meagre sketch of sixteen pages.

Fortunately what was lost in Philadelphia has to some extent at least been recovered in Holland. Through these reports and letters, preserved in the archives of Holland, the importance of Mr. Boehm for the origin and early spread of the Reformed Church in Pennsylvania is fully seen and the value of his work has been made so apparent, that it can never again be forgotten.

CHAPTER IX.

BOEHM'S FAMILY AND DESCENDANTS.

We have seen in a preceding chapter that when Boehm came to Worms he was married to Anna Maria Stehler, and that during their stay in Worms their union was blessed with four children, two of whom died in infancy. The surviving children were Johanna Sabina, born May 2, 1709, and Anthony William, born April 27, 1714.

After leaving Worms Boehm's first wife died and he married again at Lambsheim, Anna Maria Scherer. The name of his father-in-law, Philip Sherer, is given in the deed, dated July 1, 1749, by which the children divided the estate and conveyed the plantation and homestead in Whitpain to the youngest son. While at Lambsheim and during the first ten years of his stay in Pennsylvania, four children were born to him. In a letter written to the Classis January 29, 1730, he refers to his "wife and six children, four of whom are yet of tender age". These children are mentioned in the deed of July 1, 1749, referred to above. They were: Anthony William, Johanna Sabina (Sevina), Anna Maria, Elizabeth, Maria Philippina and John Philip, Jr.

When Boehm came to Pennsylvania, he settled in Whitpain township, Philadelphia (now Montgomery) County. In 1734 he paid quit-rent on 200 acres of land in Whitpain township. This was no doubt the same tract, which he acquired by purchase September 9, 1736, from Rees Thomas, of Marion, gentleman, and Anthony Morris, of Philadelphia, brewer, and Phoebe, his wife. The deed locates this property as follows: "Whereas there is a certain Tract or Parcel of Land situate in the Township of Whitpain, Beginning at a Corner marked Post by Skippack Road, thence North West by the said Road one hundred and sixty Perches to a corner marked Post, thence North East by a Line of Marked Trees Dividing this from other part of a great tract whereof this is Part two hundred Perches to a Corner marked Post, thence South East by a

Line of Marked Trees dividing this from other part of the said great Tract one hundred and sixty Perches to a corner marked Hickory, thence South West by a Line of marked Trees dividing this from the Land of Evert In de Haven two hundred Perches [to] the Place of Beginning, containing two hundred acres part of a great Tract of Land reputed to contain 4500 acres formerly laid out for Richard Whitpain, citizen and Baker of London". The consideration was £165. 13s. 1d. The deed was recorded at Philadelphia, February 23, 1737. On this land Boehm built his home and here he lived to the end of his life. It was a valuable property, located in a desirable neighborhood, about fifteen miles from Philadelphia, provided with improvements, stock and implements, such as were found on the best plantations of the time. In temporal affairs Boehm was successful far beyond the average farmer of his day. This may have been due to some extent to the excellent management of his farm by his oldest son, Anthony William, in 1736 a young man of twenty-two years.

In order to set up his oldest son on land of his own, Boehm acquired additional property.[165] February 5, 1740, "The Honorables John Penn, Thomas Penn and Richard Penn, Esquires, the proprietors and governors in chief of the Province of Pennsylvania in and by a certain patent or grant under the hands of the said proprietaries and governors in chief, and the great seal of said province . . . did for them, the said proprietaries and governors, their heirs and successors, give grant and confirm unto the said John Philip Boehm a certain tract of land situate on Saucon Creek in the County of Bucks". This tract contained two hundred acres and allowance of six per cent. for roads. On May 16, 1743, the proprietaries granted to Boehm another tract, probably adjoining the first, containing 103 acres in Lower Saucon township. The eastern boundary of the two hundred acre tract is supposed to have been the Bethlehem Road, the southern boundary Water Street, now in the Borough of Hellertown. Under date September 30, 1747, John Philip Boehm and his wife Anna Maria, deeded the above two tracts to their oldest son Anthony

---

[165] See A. P. Horn, *Re-Union of Apple's Church and of the Boehm Family*, Hellertown, 1902, p. 91.

William, "in consideration of the natural love and affection which they have and do bear for and towards their oldest surviving son and heir apparent . . . for his better preferment in the world, and for divers other good causes them specially moving".

Rev. John Philip Boehm was naturalized April 10, 1741,[166] by the Supreme Court of Pennsylvania, with thirty other German Reformed and Lutheran people, several of whom were his parishioners. In his letter of July 25, 1741, to the Classis, he refers at length to this incident.

Mr. Boehm died without making a will. His widow, Anna Maria Boehm, renounced her right to administer the estate on May 6th, 1749, and on the same day letters of administration were granted to his youngest son, John Philip Boehm, Jr., of Whitpain township, on whose bond Michael Cleim, of Whitpain township, inn-holder, and Daniel Bouton of Philadelphia, baker, acted as surities. An inventory of his personal estate was made June 5, 1749, by John Jemison, Wm. Foulke and John Roberts. It was appraised at the respectable sum of £424. 10s. 7d. Among the items may be mentioned: Two Bibles, eight large books, three dozen small books, a riding horse, three working horses, a mare and colts, sheep and lambs, thirteen geese, seven stocks of bees and three negroe servants. There were also two "distills and two coolers", which could be found at that time on nearly every farm. In view of this inventory and his holdings of land Zinzendorf might well refer to him as "the rich plantation owner in Pennsylvania".[167] The inventory was exhibited in Court July 13, 1749. The administrator's account was settled February 27, 1755; the widow receiving her third, £130.0.0, and the five other heirs sums aggregating £218. 8s. 10d.

As stated, the Saucon lands passed into the possession of his oldest son, Anthony William, during the lifetime of Pastor Boehm. A settlement and adjustment of the whole estate was made between all the heirs on July 1, 1749. By this deed the

---

[166] See Pennsylvania Archives, Second Series, Vol. II, p. 352. The list is headed by John Philip Behm.

[167] In the book edited by Neisser, see Fresenius, *Nachrichten* Vol. III, p. 704.

daughters of Mr. Boehm conveyed to his youngest son, John Philip, Jr., the Whitpain farm with all its improvements and appurtenances. He, on his part, promised to maintain and support his grandfather, Philip Sherer, during his lifetime. This deed was recorded at Philadelphia January 4, 1751.

Anthony William Boehm[168] resided on one of the tracts, deeded to him by his father, in a house which is still standing in Hellertown. He acquired in addition three tracts in Upper Saucon township, the first containing 20½ acres, the second 38 acres and the third 68 acres 138 perches. Warrants were issued December 21, 1749, and on later dates. They were surveyed by surveyor, David Schultz, who delivered the surveys March 20, 1755. Patents were issued for them November 13, 1762. These three tracts, containing together 127 acres and 92 perches, are located in Upper Saucon township, Lehigh County. In 1761, Anthony Boehm was assessed £26.0.0, in Upper Saucon township. This shows that he had left Hellertown and removed to Upper Saucon township. It has been suggested that the fact of his wife, Hannah Phillis (Felicitas), inheriting a large tract of land in that vicinity, may have caused the removal. Anthony William Boehm died April 6, 1766. His grave has been discovered in a private cemetery on one of the above named tracts of land. Letters of administration were granted to his widow, Hannah P. Boehm, on May 10, 1766. His personal estate was inventoried at £133.12.7d. In the year 1767 his widow was assessed in Lower Saucon township for 40 acres clear land and 260 acres woodland. Anthony William and Phillis Boehm had one child, Philip Boehm, who became prominent in the War of the Revolution. In March, 1777, he was Lieutenant Colonel in Colonel Geiger's Battalion of the Northampton County militia. August 27, 1777, he was appointed paymaster of the militia of Northampton County. In 1780 he served as Coroner of the County.

Among the descendants of Anthony William Boehm, it is interesting to note that there are at least six ministers, two of

---

[168] For the brief sketches of Boehm's children constant use has been made of the material collected very carefully by Mr. Dotterer in his *Rev. John Philip Boehm*, Philadelphia, 1890, pp. 24-27; printed also as part of the *Sesqui-Centennial of Boehm's Reformed Church*, Norristown, 1891, pp. 29-55.

the Reformed and four of the Lutheran Church. The Reformed ministers are: Rev. Wilson F. More, now at Womeldorf, whose descent is: Anthony William (I), Philip (II), Anthony (III), Magdalene (IV), married James More, William More (V) and Rev. Wilson F. More (VI). The other Reformed minister is Rev. James A. Boehm, now (1915) at Sellersville, Pa. His descent is: Anthony William (I), Philip (II), Anthony (III), James M. (IV), Alfred J. (V), Rev. James A. Boehm (VI). The Lutheran ministers are: Rev. William Rath (1826-1889), whose descent is: Anthony William (I), Philip (II), Anthony (III), Susanna (IV), married Jacob Rath, Rev. William Rath (V), his brother Rev. Jacob B. Rath (V), and his son Rev. Myron B. Rath (VI). Another Lutheran minister descended from Anthony William Boehm is the Rev. Thomas C. Billheimer (V), son of Jesse Billheimer, married Juliann Boehm (IV), da. of Philip Boehm (III) s. of Philip Boehm (II) s. of Anthony William (I).

Johanna Sabina (usually called Sevina) Boehm, married Ludwig Bitting of Lower Milford township, now in Lehigh County. Ludwig Bitting was a son of Henry and Anna Catharine Bitting, who came from Freinsheim in the Palatinate with a passport, date April 24, 1723. Ludwig Bitting owned land in 1734 in Hanover township. In the same year he was naturalized. From 1736 to 1746 he was a member of the Great Swamp Reformed congregation. In 1749, and until his death, he lived in Lower Milford township. From 1758 to 1760 he represented Northampton County in the Assembly. He was born in 1703, he died about December 27, 1775. His will, dated September 25, 1771, gives his wife's name as Elizabeth, from which it may be inferred that he had married a second time. His children were: Ludwig Bitting, Henry Bitting, Anthony Bitting, Philip Bitting, Peter Bitting, also Anna Maria Bitting, who married Andreas Graeber, of New Goshenhoppen; Elizabeth Dorothea Bitting, who married Gabriel Klein, of New Goshenhoppen; Mary Catharine Bitting, who married John Klein; Christina Bitting, who married Franz Leidig, son of Rev. John Philip Leidig, of Frederick township.

Anna Maria Boehm, the second daughter of the Rev. J. P. Boehm, married Adam Moser, who in 1749 was living as a farmer in Philadelphia County. Nothing more seems to be known about him and his wife at the present time.

Elizabeth Boehm, the third daughter of the Rev. J. P. Boehm, married George Shamboh, weaver, of Upper Milford township, Bucks County. In 1740 a warrant for 230 acres of land in this township was issued to George Shamboh.

Maria Philippina Boehm, the youngest daughter of Rev. J. P. Boehm, married Cornelius Dewees, cooper, son of William Dewees, Boehm's most prominent elder at Whitemarsh. On July 26, 1745, Cornelius Dewees, of Whitemarsh township, bought thirty acres on the Skippack road for £108. On the first of January, 1751, Cornelius Dewees and his wife lived in Gloucester County, West New Jersey.

John Philip Boehm, the youngest son of Pastor Boehm, was married August 2, 1753, by the pastor of the German Reformed Church of Philadelphia to Anna Maria Yost (born May 1, 1734), daughter of Jacob and Elizabeth Yost, of Whitpain township. Their children were: (1) Elizabeth Boehm, born in September, 1757, buried November 24, 1765; (2) Philip Boehm, born July 28, 1761, buried November 1, 1765; (3) Daniel Boehm, born March 14, 1764, died November 28, 1765; (4) Mary Boehm, born in 1765, married May 25, 1784, to William Peltz; (5) Philip Boehm, born August 13, 1766; (6) Jacob Boehm, born October 29, 1768, buried July 16, 1773; (7) Daniel Boehm, born March 1, 1771, married December 2, 1792, to Catherine Peltz, daughter of William Peltz; (8) Elizabeth Boehm, born in March, 1778, buried October 30, 1788.

John Philip Boehm, as stated above, according to the settlement made between the heirs, July 1, 1749, became possessor of the farm and home in Whitpain township. February 6, 1759, he sold to Jacob Kurr 150 acres of this farm. About the year 1760 he moved to Philadelphia, where he engaged in mercantile business. He became a member of the German Reformed Church there and was at once made an officer of the congregation. In 1760 he was a deacon, in 1771 he was elected an elder. He held office till 1783. On June 6, 1777, he was appointed a Justice of the Peace for the County of Philadelphia. In 1778 he lived in a house on the west side of Second Street, between Arch and Race streets. He owned other property in the same neighborhood. He made his will September 5, 1788. He died in Philadelphia and was buried in Franklin Square, part of which was then used as a cemetery of the Race Street Reformed Church, on the 17th of September, 1790. His son, Daniel Boehm, continued the business of his father. From 1791 to 1802, Daniel Boehm was a grocer and merchant at 96 North Second Street.

For other descendants of Boehm reference may be made to the sketch of Mr. Dotterer, "Rev. John Philip Boehm", Philadelphia, 1890; and to the Boehm Family in "Re-Union of Apple's Church and of the Boehm Family", Hellertown, 1902.[169]

---

[169] For other books, treating of Boehm's life and labors, see Henry Harbaugh, *Fathers of the Reformed Church*, Vol. I, Lancaster, 1857, pp. 275-291; J. H. Dubbs, *Historic Manual of the Reformed Church in the United States*, Lancaster, 1885, pp. 164-168, 194, 200; J. H. Dubbs, *History of the Reformed Church, German*, Vol. VIII of the American Church History Series, New York, 1895, pp. 247-250, 266-270, 281; J. I. Good, *Historical Handbook of the Reformed Church in the U. S.*, Philadelphia, 1897, pp. 51-55; J. I. Good, *Early Fathers of the Reformed Church*, Reading, (1897), pp. 20-30; J. I. Good, *History of the Reformed Church in the U. S., 1725-1792*, Reading, 1899, pp. 89-107, 120-133, 265-278, 363-370; H. J. Ruetenik *The Pioneers of the Reformed Church in the U. S. of America*, Cleveland, 1901, pp. 42-54; J. H. Dubbs, *The Reformed Church in Pennsylvania*, Lancaster, 1902, pp. 79-85, 90, 135-136, 149, 176-177; Wilson F. More, "A Sketch of Rev. John Philip Boehm", in *Proceedings of the Re-Union of Apple's Church and of the Boehm Family*, edited by Rev. A. P. Horn, Hellertown, 1902, pp. 71-80.

THE CORRESPONDENCE OF THE REV. JOHN PHILIP BOEHM :: CONTAINING THE LETTERS AND REPORTS OF MR. BOEHM SENT TO HOLLAND AND THE LETTERS FROM HOLLAND ADDRESSED TO HIM :: 1728-1748

TRANSLATED AND EDITED BY
PROF. WM. J. HINKE, PH. D.

THE CORRESPONDENCE OF
JOHN PHILIP BOEHM

[I. THE CONSISTORIES OF THE GERMAN REFORMED CHURCHES OF FALKNER SWAMP, SKIPPACK AND WHITEMARSH TO THE CLASSIS OF AMSTERDAM, JULY, 1728.[1]]

To the Reverend Classis of Amsterdam:—

We, the undersigned, Elders of the Christian Reformed Congregations at Falkner's Schwamp, Schip Bach and Wit Marche, situated in the Province of Pennsylvania, in America, under the crown of Great Britain, find ourselves, in the name of our congregations under absolute compulsion and obligation, to have recourse to your Reverend Body, to lay before you the need and perplexity of ourselves and our congregations, and to entreat you to honor us with your Christian help by means of an ecclesiastical resolution, which will tend to our rest and the upbuilding of Reformed worship in this far-off region of the world.

This is the situation: Finding ourselves in great perplexity, the congregations commissioned us to consult regarding our affairs with some of the Dutch Reformed ministers,

[1] The original of this petition is no longer in existence, but a Dutch translation of it was entered into one of the Consistorial Records of the Collegiate Reformed Church of New York City. The book is marked "Kerken Raad Boek," Vol. A, pp. 68-76. It was translated and published by the Rev. Dr. T. W. Chambers in the *Mercersburg Review*, Vol. XXIII (1876), pp. 529-541; later by Dr. E. T. Corwin in the *Ecclesiastical Records of the State of New York*, Vol. IV (1902), pp. 2425-2437; also by the writer in the *Journal of the Presbyterian Historical Society*, Vol. VI (1912), pp. 303-316. The present translation is made directly from the Record Book in New York, which the writer copied in December, 1915. It contains numerous corrections of the earlier translations.

who, we heard, were to be found in the neighboring provinces. The easiest way for us would have been to apply to Do. Frelinghuisen[2] in New Jersey, since he is about forty miles nearer to us than New York. But, having already to contend with some errorists dwelling among us, who maintain among other things, that one can judge from the outside of a man whether he is a Christian or not, and various other matters which we judge not to be in accordance with the Reformed Church; and hearing from several persons on our journey that Do. Frelinghuisen maintains the same, at least his disciples openly asserted it with free condemnation of their neighbors, and other things not conformed to the Word of God and to the order of the Dutch Reformed Church; and being further informed (which is a matter of public knowledge) that Do. Frelinghuisen has made and still makes use of the services of an English Dissenting Minister[3] in the churches of Raretans, who also intrudes into such Dutch congregations and assemblies, as, by means of simple folks, he can gain admission to, and is, with Do. Frelinghuisen, strongly attached to Pietistic and Labbadist[4] sentiments, against which we also among our-

[2] Theodore Jacob Frelinghuisen was the first minister of the Dutch Reformed Church in Central New Jersey. He was born 1691, in Wolfenbuettel, East Friesland; licensed in 1717; pastor at Emden, East Friesland, 1717-1719; came to America in 1720; pastor of the Dutch Reformed congregations at Raritan, New Brunswick, Six-Mile Run, Three-Mile Run, North Branch, 1720-47; died in 1747. For a sketch of the life of this great man see Corwin, *Manual of the Reformed Church in America*, 4th ed., 1902, pp. 472-476. He was a great revivalist, hence the very antithesis of Mr. Boehm, who distrusted him.

[3] This was probably Rev. Gilbert Tennent, who was ordained at New Brunswick, N. J., in 1726. He was the Presbyterian pastor there till 1744, when he removed to Philadelphia. Boehm knew him, of course, only by hearsay and therefore failed to appreciate his eminently useful work. See Webster, *History of the Presbyterian Church in America*, Philadelphia, 1857, pp. 387-397.

[4] The Labadists go back to Jean de Labadie (1610-1674). Born in the Catholic Church, but unable to effect any reforms, he joined the Reformed Church in 1650. In 1659 he became pastor in Geneva. From there he went to Holland, where, in 1669, he founded a separate religious sect, known as the Labadists. They emphasized the inner light and rejected baptism and the Sabbath. A Labadist colony was settled on Bohemia Manor in Maryland, see Sachse, *German Sectarians of Pennsylvania*, Vol. I (1899), pp. 57-70.

selves have to contend; we, therefore, discouraged from applying to Do. Frelinghuisen, resolved not to shun the trouble of going farther and repairing to New York, to consult the well-known Dutch ministers there, and Do. Vincentius Antonides of Long Island.

When we had spoken with them, they advised us to betake ourselves to the Reverend Classis of Amsterdam for Christian aid, and to lay bare to them our perplexing condition in all sincerity and in necessary detail, and to submit to the ecclesiastical resolution which they should communicate to us regarding this matter. This advice of the said ministers was gratefully accepted by our congregations. Hence, we take the liberty of appearing with this, our letter, before your Reverend Body, and lay before your Reverences our embarrassment.

In this widely extended region, Pennsylvania, where the first settlers bearing the name of Christians were *Quakers*, and whither men of all sorts of opinions have repaired, about eighteen years ago [1710] there came from time to time, here and there, widely separated from one another, some of the Reformed religion, from different parts of Germany and other places, as also some few from the neighboring provinces of New York and New Jersey, etc. These, having increased in number, in order not to fall into the errors of those among whom they dwelt, induced and encouraged each other to hold religious services on each Lord's Day, etc., according to the doctrine and Church Order of the Reformed Church, as far as it was known to them.

Indeed, as early as the year 1720,[5] there came over to us Johan Philips Boehm, who, according to his testimonials, had faithfully discharged his office as schoolmaster and precentor in Worms, a city of Germany, for about seven years in succession, and was compelled to emigrate by the persecutions of the Papists[6] on account of the Reformed religion. Shortly

---

[5] The original reads: *"Immers in den jaare 1720 tot ons overgekomen zynde Johan Philips Boehm,"* which should be translated as given above, *not* "at least as early as 1720," etc. This correction in the translation is important, for it fixes Boehm's arrival in America definitely as having taken place in 1720.

[6] There is little evidence that there were actual persecutions of the Reformed people in the Palatinate in the year 1720. What comes

after his arrival, some of the neighbors established a religious gathering, in which the said Johan Philips Boehm, as Reader, maintained the ministry of the Word, to the best of his ability and to the great satisfaction of the people, for five years [1720-1725] in succession, without receiving any compensation for it. Afterwards (since we were very desirous of enjoying the Seals of the Holy Covenant, which we had not been able to secure in this far-off region according to the custom of the Reformed Church, and for want of which some had resorted to Dissenters[7]) he was at various times urgently entreated by all the Reformed people residing here or in this vicinity, to take upon himself the office and service of a minister, which he steadfastly refused, yet meanwhile constantly persevered in maintaining to general edification the exercises of religious worship as a Reader.

But the Reformed people in this widely-extended region,

nearest to it is a statement in the *Ephrata Chronicle*, Engl. ed., p. 8: "About the same time (1715-1720) many persons were banished from the Palatinate for conscience sake, at Frensheim, *Lambsheim,* Mutterstadt, Frankenthal, Schriesheim, etc., the most of whom ended their lives in Pennsylvania." More general and indefinite are the statements in the *Berigt,* printed in Holland in 1731, in which it is said (p. 2): "Not long after the first settlement, many of the *oppressed* inhabitants of Germany and particularly of the Palatinate and in the district of Nassau, Waldek, Wittgenstein and Wetterau, emigrated to Pennsylvania." In 1731 a ship with *refugees* (vlugtlingen) from the Palatinate was lying in the harbor of Rotterdam. They were visited by members of the Synod of South Holland, held at Dort, in July, 1731.

A statement very similar to that of Boehm, is, however, found in the affidavit of the prosecuting members in the Reiff case. They state: "The said Deponents being duly sworn upon the Holy Evangelists of Almighty God do depose & say, that for above the space of ten years by gone, great numbers of the subjects of the emperor of Germany, professing the Potestant Religion, or as 'tis equally called the Reformed religion and *having suffered hardships* in their native country *upon the score of their religion,* came over into the province of Pennsylvania and settled themselves in sundry parts of the said province."

[7] Some of the Reformed people brought their children to the Presbyterian minister in Philadelphia, the Rev. Jedidiah Andrews. In a letter, dated October 14, 1730, Mr. Andrews writes: "They did use to come to me for baptism for their children, and many have joined with us in the other sacrament." Other Reformed people were married by the Presbyterian pastor. See *Journal of the Presbyterian Historical Society,* Vol. I, pp. 123-133.

having increased to the number of fifty men,[8] strongly urged upon him (since they were a poor people living far from all Reformed congregations) to assume the office of a minister among them in the fear of the Lord, although he was not authorized to do so by any Reformed Classis—which authorization we did not then know to be so absolutely required as we now understand. But he, recognizing the weighty importance of such an office, entreated them to excuse him, alleging also that he had a family to support by the labor of his hands. Nevertheless, they all continued from time to time to urge this on him and, on their own initiative, offered and promised their support by voluntary contributions, according to their ability, however small that might be. They also assured him that he could not justify before God his refusal of assuming so urgent a work, since this, their unanimous request, was considered by them to be as lawful a call as was ever made upon any one, and they thought that this was sufficient, because they were far away from any Classis.

Thus, Reverend Classis, we confess that we at last prevailed upon Johan Philips Boehm to take upon himself the ministry among us in this widely extended region, without any other salary than was voluntarily given him, and to conduct himself in his service in no other way than according to the doctrine and Church Order of the Reformed Church. To that end, that all might be done in an orderly manner, a draft of a Church Order was prepared by Johan Philips Boehm with the help of the consistories, to be maintained by us in harmony with the constitution of the Reformed Church. This was read before the whole congregation and subscribed by all individually. Thus divine service has been faithfully and zealously maintained by Johan Philips Boehm as minister, for the space of three years [1725-1728], with much edification in all three congregations.

[8] There is a glaring contrast between this modest figure and the statements in the *Berigt* of 1731: "Among them [the inhabitants of Pennsylvania] are Mennonites, Lutherans and Reformed, but at the present time the Reformed, holding to the old Reformed Confession, constitute more than half of the whole number, being about 15,000." Rieger estimated the number of Reformed members in 1731 as less than 3000.

But last fall some objection began to be made to the ministry of Do. Boehm,[9] because he has not received a regular ordination by the Church. This compelled our congregations to give further consideration to this matter. Now we, the undersigned members of the Consistories together with all the members of the congregations, appointed two of the most capable persons among us, as Commissioners, and sent them upon this important business to the Reformed churches in the neighboring,—but oh, how distant—provinces to seek advice of judicious ministers for our direction; namely, what should or could be done to uphold the lawfulness of Mr. Johan Philips Boehm in his ministry among us.

We hereby respectfully submit to your Reverend Assembly the weighty reasons of our wish, desire and longing in this matter.

Johan Philips Boehm has borne himself so judiciously in the discharge of his godly office, not only in reference to the doctrine of the Reformed Church, but also in reference to his life, that we have not the least complaint to make against him; but on the contrary are obliged heartily to love and honor him. Through this condition of affairs all offense and scandal is daily more and more removed and the pure doctrine of the Reformed religion in accordance with the Church Order of Holland and according to our ability, is from day to day, the longer the more, spread and confirmed among us, in this wild American region.

Our three congregations, which are yet small and poor, namely at Falkner Schwamp, Schip Bach and Wit Marshe, the largest of which consists of only twenty-four men, the second of about twenty, and the smallest of not more than fourteen, are spread out more than sixty English miles[10] from each other

---

[9] It is an evidence of fine tact on the part of Boehm that the person who was the source of all opposition and trouble is not mentioned, the Rev. George Michael Weiss.

[10] Boehm probably estimated the circuit he had to make in visiting his congregations. From Whitpain (his home) to Falkner Swamp was 20 miles, from Falkner Swamp to Skippack 12 miles, from Skippack to Whitemarsh 16 miles, according to Boehm's report of 1739. But the distance between Harleysville (Skippack) and the Wissahickon (De Wees' home) is more than 20 miles by straight air line.

and are distant full one hundred and seventy miles from New York.

Inasmuch as the so-called Quakers constitute the largest number of the civil magistrates among us, your Reverend Body cannot form any other opinion of us than that we are living among all sorts of errorists, as Independents, Puritans, Anabaptists, Newborn, Saturday-folks,[11] yea even the most horrible heretics, Socinians,[12] Pietists, etc., among whom dreadful errors prevail; indeed heinous blasphemies against our great God and Savior and their own exaltation over His Majesty; for they claim that they have essential divinity in themselves; that they cannot sin; that what they condemn or approve is God's own condemnation or approval. They believe that there is no other heaven or hell than what is here on earth; they even deny Divine Providence, and assert that nothing needs God's blessing, but that all products of the ground and all offspring of animals and of the human race, come simply from nature, without any care on the part of God, and that prayer also is useless. Indeed, we do not know of any blasphemous opinion which has not its defenders among one class or other of those among whom we are dispersed.

Good as the land is in which we live, equally sad and unfortunate is our condition respecting spiritual things, as you can easily see. It is for this reason that the simple-minded people are exposed to the greatest danger of contamination, and this all the more, because most of them are inexperienced

---

The return to Whitpain (Blue Bell) was about 12 miles. His whole circuit was therefore about 64 miles, or according to his figures exactly 60 miles.

[11] The sect of the Newborn was founded by Matthias Baumann, in Oley, Berks County, about 1718. See Sachse, *German Sectarians of Pennsylvania*, 1708-1742, pp. 73-78, 156-159. The Saturday folks are the Sabbatarians (Siebentäger) or Seventh Day Dunkers of the Ephrata community. For a description of the religious condition among the German settlers in Pennsylvania, from 1700-1740, see above, pp. 84-8.

[12] By Socinians Boehm means probably some form of Unitarianism. Of course he had only a hearsay knowledge of these dreaded sects. This is shown by his curious climax, "Pietists." Of Pietism as an integral part of Reformed Church history, he apparently knew nothing. See Good, *History of the Reformed Church of Germany*, pp. 307-410. Zealous and earnest as Boehm was, he can hardly escape the charge of being somewhat narrow.

and poor, living great distances from each other. Therefore, we felt ourselves all the more under obligation without delay to set up a pure religious worship and to maintain it by every agency possible, in accordance with the Word of God; in order that neither we nor our children nor so many simple-minded souls, in whom there is still a longing for the true doctrine of the Holy Gospel, may be lost forever in this soul-destroying whirlpool of apostasy; but that they should work out each other's salvation with fear and trembling.

May your Reverend Body also be kind enough to notice that as the most unassuming sects (as they seem to be) among which we live, seek to captivate the simple-minded under a Pharisaic cloak of hypocrisy, so they are also very persistent in all kinds of allurements. Thus they show themselves willing to support the poor, provided they will come over to them. They also pretend among them that they cannot enjoy the ministry of the Word elsewhere. Meanwhile, they never cease their abuse of all Protestant ministers who have a fixed salary, insinuating that they aim for money only. Now, inasmuch as most of us are ignorant and poor and daily subjected to solicitation from outsiders, it was absolutely impossible for us to secure a minister with a definite salary, and this all the more, because at the time when Mr. Boehm undertook the service we were entirely without the necessary means. Unless we were willing, therefore, to abandon the innocent lambs, these poor people, as a prey to the constant attacks of ravening wolves in sheep's clothing, there seemed to be no other feasible way than that the aforesaid Boehm, who was known among us as a man of more than ordinary knowledge in the sound doctrine of the truth, of praiseworthy life and of exemplary zeal in resisting these errors and in warning the ignorant against them, who was also provided with laudatory testimonials from Germany, where for several years, as a member of the Reformed Church, he had been a schoolmaster and who was here engaged in agriculture,—there seemed, we say, no other way than that the said Boehm should be most urgently requested to assume the ministerial office among us, out of love for the work, without a fixed salary; yet under promise that we should see what voluntary contributions (which, however, could not be but small) we could collect for him from any who had means. Such then has been our course, partly to escape the slander of the sects, but chiefly because we could not help ourselves in any other way.

When, in the meantime, we heard and learned from the said ministers that, according to the Church Order of the Reformed Church, no one, whoever he might be, could be recognized as a lawful minister except after previous examination and approval by a Classis belonging to the Reformed Church; and that we, although in a case of extreme necessity and in ignorance of the proper manner of installing a minister in a Reformed Church, had erred in appointing J. P. Boehm as our minister; we felt greatly grieved in our hearts over our wrong action regarding him. As a result, following the advice of the said ministers (who declared that they could do nothing further therein) we now present our case, with all readiness and most submissively, to the Reverend Classis of Amsterdam, with humble prayer and most earnest request in Christ's name, that in view of all we have stated above, our great misstep may be overlooked and that the Reverend Classis may aid us with such acts as will tend to redress and settlement in this important matter and in our perplexed condition.

We also beseech the Reverend Classis kindly to consider the evil consequences which would ensue, if all that has been done amongst us should be declared null and void,—the ministry of Do. Boehm as called by us to be the teacher of the three said congregations, and his administration of the Seals of the Covenant in general and of Holy Baptism in particular,[13]—more than two hundred children having been baptized

---

[13] The circumstances were similar to those of Rev. John Casper Frymuth (Fryenmoet), a Dutch Reformed minister in the Minisink region, now Monroe County. In 1741 he induced Rev. George William Mancius, who had organized the Dutch churches on the Delaware in 1737, to ordain him. As many found fault with this ordination, application was made to the Classis of Amsterdam that he might be legally ordained. Classis granted permission in May, 1744. He was re-ordained by Mancius, December 16, 1744 (see *Eccl. Records of N. Y.*, IV, 2863f). On June 6, 1746, the Classis of Amsterdam decided that his previous baptisms were invalid and had to be repeated (l. c., p. 2910). According to a letter of Bishop Cammerhoff, dated August 13, 1747, some submitted to have their children re-baptized; others demanded their money back, because, according to his own confession, they had not received the value of their money. See Reichel, *Early History of the Church of the United Brethren (Unitas Fratrum)*, 1888, p. 32.

by him, besides various others who, through his zeal, have come over to us from the sects which despise baptism. How great a division would it create in our congregations, and how would it open the mouth of the errorists to deride us! Indeed, it is certainly to be feared that the exercise of the Reformed religion among so many foes would be sadly injured, and that which has hitherto been done to edification amid so many difficulties and in our weakness would be nullified; that our congregations in their very start would be ruined, and that many ignorant people would be sadly led astray into various errors.

However, notwithstanding all this (which we ask the Reverend Classis to take to heart), Mr. Boehm declares with us through this letter sent to you that he is willing and ready to submit fully to your Classical resolution, if the Classis deem it necessary for him to leave his ministerial office (which he did not in the least seek of himself, but which burden was pressed upon him by all unanimously) and to return to his secular calling and confine himself to the service of a Reader, to which he was called. By his acts he has only sought to satisfy his conscience, the more so because the love of the people has daily increased from the beginning of his service till now, and the congregations themselves have also grown from day to day. But, perhaps, if God should spare Mr. Boehm to us a little longer, he might be the instrumentality of bringing us to such a condition, that upon his death we might be able to call a minister from Holland. But we fear that if he should be compelled to give up his ministry now, we would fall into a much worse condition than we were in before, as we, Reformed believers, are few and poor and widely scattered in this wild and distant region of the world.

Nevertheless, we submit the whole question to the wisdom as well as to the pious and salutary resolution of the Reverend Classis of Amsterdam. And we request your Reverences most submissively, with persistent prayer, that your answer may be sent to us by the first opportunity.

But, inasmuch as we have made mention in this letter of the Church Order established by us, we feel bound to forward a copy of the same to your Reverences, in order that the Reverend Classis may see more clearly our mode of governing the Church. The following are our CHURCH ORDINANCES, drawn up formerly but recently revised, including submission to the Reverend Classis of Amsterdam:

[CHURCH ORDINANCES OF MR. BOEHM'S CONGREGATIONS.]

1. That the members of Consistories who are now in service in all the three villages shall be recognized and remain in office for their appointed term. Then all the members of the congregations (as has been done hitherto), with the minister and the members of the consistories, shall choose new members for the consistories. But, at the same time, all the members of the congregations, shall transfer, each to his own consistory, all power and right thereafter from year to year to elect officers by majority vote of the consistories themselves; since through the increase and spread of the congregations it is not practicable for all the members to meet just for this purpose.

The persons chosen shall be announced for three Sundays, each in his congregation, to see if any one makes any lawful objection; and if not, they shall be ordained after the third announcement. And if it should happen (as we hope it will not) that one or more of the consistorial persons should behave disorderly or create strife and division in the congregations, he or they shall be warned in time by the other members to discontinue such conduct, and if they do not comply, they shall be removed from their offices and others shall be chosen in their stead, from those who were last in service, and be regularly ordained and then serve. The same course shall be followed in case any one dies in office.

2. When an Elder or Deacon goes out of office, he may be exempt from service for two years and may then again be chosen; or even earlier, if it be deemed necessary by the Consistory then in office.

3. The Elders, Deacons and all the members of the three villages asknowledge and desire to retain for their minister, Mr. Johan Philips Boehm, who hitherto has performed his service among them acceptably and with fidelity, according to the doctrine of the Reformed Church.

4. The Minister, Elders, Deacons and the whole congregation shall fix the times when and the places where, on the Lord's Day and on others days, divine service shall be held.

5. The rite of Baptism shall always be administered, without fee, at the close of the divine service. Beside the

parents, there shall be witnesses at the baptism, and this edifying custom shall not be altered lightly. The witnesses must be sound in doctrine and blameless in life.

6. The Holy Supper shall be administered twice a year at each place where public worship is maintained. No one shall be admitted thereto, unless upon confession before the Consistory, and evidence of a godly life, or upon proper testimonials from other congregations, according to the Church Order of the Synod of Dort, of the years 1618 and 1619. All the members shall constantly, as far as able, attend worship and be present at the preparatory sermon. Those who neglect this shall be admonished by the Consistory, as they shall deem necessary. The parents shall diligently instruct the children in the Reformed religion, and to that end, shall carefully provide for their hearing God's Word, in the preaching and in catechization, so that the youth also may come to the Lord's table. All the members of the three congregations shall have the privilege to commune in any one of the churches, no lawful hindrance existing, so long as they have a minister in common.

7. The bread and wine for the Lord's Supper shall always be furnished and paid by the Deacons out of the alms that have been gathered, and they shall carefully reckon it up in the account.

The members of the Consistory, whether Elders or Deacons, to whom the church treasury and property are entrusted, shall annually render a good account of their administration before the congregation, and for this purpose shall keep a true record of receipts and expenditures. And the account, when approved, shall be signed by the minister in the name of all as satisfactory.

8. In order to meet all the necessities of the Church, the Deacons shall always collect the alms at the close of each service.

9. If any member, whether male or female, shall go astray into immorality or other sins, such shall be put under censure by the Consistory, until they promise and give evidence of amendment.

10. The office and duty of the Minister shall be to preach the doctrine of the Reformed Church in purity, according to

the Word of God; to administer the Seals of the Covenant at the proper time and place; to hold strictly to the Confession of Faith of the Reformed Church;[14] to expound the Heidelberg Catechism in regular order; to catechize (the children) and, in conjunction with the Elders, to exercise discipline. He shall not, without necessity, omit to hold services at the prescribed times and places, namely at Falkner Schwamp, Schip Bach and Wit Marche.

11. A Consistory meeting shall be held at least once every half year and the minister shall record all ecclesiastical proceedings in a book.

12. And if he should be inclined to leave, either because he has been called elsewhere or for other lawful reasons, he shall as soon as practicable give the congregations notice, so that they may not be left embarrassed, but may be enabled in time to secure another suitable man. The minister shall also in all other things deport himself as a true servant of Christ, under Him the Great Shepherd of the sheep.

13. The Minister, Elders and Deacons shall maintain a careful oversight over the congregation. They shall appear, at the appointed time and place to hold consistory meetings, and shall not omit the same without sufficient cause. They shall faithfully observe the foregoing rules, each in his respective office, to the best of his ability. Whoever knows of any offense, committed by any member of the Consistory or Church, shall feel bound in conscience to make it known, not through malice or hatred, but to prevent scandal. The accused shall not demand the name of his accuser, nor obstinately deny his faults, if proved, nor wickedly continue therein; such as do so shall not be regarded as members of the congregation, until they promise and show amendment of life.

And if any one bring any charge against the doctrines or life of the Minister or any member of the Consistory, or

---

[14] The Belgic Confession, framed by Guido de Bres, of Brabant, and others, about the year 1561, in French, is meant. It was adopted by the Synod of Dort in 1619. An abridgment, made by Festus Hommius, was recognized by the Synod of Middleburg in 1581. The shorter form is given by Augusti, *Corpus Librorum Symbolicorum,* Lipsiæ 1846, pp. 170-197; the longer in Niemeyer, *Collectio Confessionum,* Lipsiæ 1840, pp. 360-389.

against any other member, such person shall refrain from any disgraceful and slanderous words, and not seek private revenge, but refer the matter to the Consistory, which shall be bound to use all diligence to remove such scandal.

14. And as we hope that the Reverend Classis will, as speedily as possible, favor and sustain our Christian efforts, in our sad condition,—so we bind ourselves to lay all calls hereafter, for future ministers, before your Reverend Body, and await your decision; and further, to conduct ourselves with our present Minister according to such directions as you may deem useful for our congregations, according to the Dutch Reformed Church Order. Also the newly-elected members of the Consistory, before entering upon their office, shall annually subscribe all this, when you have approved it that they may the better perform these promises which we make for ourselves and our successors. And in order that everyone may strictly conform to the Dutch Reformed Church Order, according to his office and station, these proposed ordinances, with such amendments as you may suggest, shall annually be read before the congregation, at each new election or ordination of Consistory.

A written Confession of Faith,[15] prepared and signed by Do. Johan Philips Boehm, accompanies this letter.

We now have nothing more to write than to express our heartfelt prayer to God that what we have thus undertaken to do in his fear, may be received favorably by you. We have also offered many petitions, that through God's mercies we may receive your wished-for help, and fervent desires for a good result, which we shall always gratefully recognize as proceeding from the kind Providence of a gracious God over us, for the upbuilding and sustaining of His Church against the manifold errors and evils which are round about us.

To this end, as for the well-being of God's House in general, may our gracious heavenly Father, in the Lord Jesus, and through the Holy Spirit, abundantly bless your

---

[15] This important document is no longer in existence.

beloved persons, families and holy service. Such is the hearty wish and prayer,

> Reverend Fathers and Brethren in Christ, of your humble petitioning servants, brethren, yea children in the Lord, the Consistories of the three Reformed congregations at Falkner Schwamp, Schip Bach and Wit Marche.[16]

Pennsylvania,
July, 1728.

In the name of all
(Signed by each with his own hand)

WILLIAM DE WEES,[17]
ISACK DILBECK,
GEORG PHILIP TOTTERER,
FREDERICK ANTES,
JOH^s. MEYER,
JAC. MEYER,
GABRIEL SCHUILER,
JOH. BERKENBEIL,

SEBASTIAN REIFSNYDER,
LUDWICH KNAUWS,
LAURENS BINGEMAN,
JOH^s. REVENSTOCK,
GEORG KLAUER,
LEONHARD SPERR,
JOH. STEPHAN ULRICH,
JOH^s. LE FEVRE.

[16] Although signed by Boehm's elders, the letter was certainly written by Boehm. One of the earmarks of Boehm's letters is the form of his name. He always wrote it Johan Philips (Philippus) Boehm. But the form and contents of the letter also point to Boehm as author.

[17] Of these men De Wees, Dilbeck, Knaus and Rebenstock were members at Whitemarsh; John Meyer, Schuiler, Bingeman, Sperr, Stephan and Le Fevre belonged to Skippack; Dotterer, Antes, Jacob Meyer, Berkenbeil, Reifsnyder and Klauer belonged to Falkner Swamp.

Georg Philip Dotterer, the ancestor of the late Henry S. Dotterer, was in Pennsylvania as early as 1722. He settled in that year in Frederick Township, Montgomery County, where he bought a farm of 250 acres. He died November 6, 1741, and was survived by his wife and six children. See H. S. Dotterer, *The Dotterer Family*, Philadelphia, 1903.

[II. THE REFORMED MINISTERS OF NEW YORK TO THE CLASSIS OF AMSTERDAM, AUGUST 15, 1728.[18]]

NEW YORK, August 15, 1728.

Reverend, Godly and Most Learned Sirs,
  The Reverend Classis of Amsterdam.
Highly Esteemed Fathers and Brethren in Jesus Christ:—

When Mr. Johan Philips Boehm and William De Wees came before us on May 16, 1728, as Commissioners of the Reformed Christian Consistory of Falkner's Schwamp, Schipback and Wit Marche, and laid their case before us; on mature consideration, we found it of such a character, and of so much importance, that we advised them to present it, in all its details, to the Reverend Classis of Amsterdam, and cheerfully to submit to your official decision thereon. Otherwise we did not dare to think or hope that the Reverend Classis would even consider the case. We knew also that you would come to no other conclusion than what you would consider best for the honor of God and the welfare of their congregations. They have accordingly, within a few days past, sent us the enclosed papers,[18a] with the request that we would forward the same to your reverend body, and add a letter of our own in testimony of the foregoing. We hereby do this with our hearty good-wishes.

Reverend, Godly, and Very Learned Sirs,
  Your humble servants and fellow laborers in the Lord,
    G. DU BOIS,
    V. ANTONIDES,
    HENRICUS BOEL.

[III. THE CLASSIS OF AMSTERDAM TO THE GERMAN CHURCHES IN PENNSYLVANIA, NOVEMBER 28, 1728.[19]]

NOVEMBER 28, 1728.

Very Worthy and Much Beloved Brethren in the Lord:—

On the reading of your communication, sent to us by way of New York, under date of July, 1728, our Classis was deeply moved with sympathy at your distressed and lamentable condition, and at the same time felt that the reasonable complaints, which you poured into

---

[18] Copy of original in Liber A, Records of Collegiate Church of New York, p. 76. Printed first in *Mercersburg Review*, Vol. XXIII (1876), p. 541f; also in *Ecclesiastical Records of N. Y.*, Vol. IV, p. 2438f.

[18a] This refers to the preceding petition of July, 1728. See above, pp. 155-169.

[19] Copy of original letter in *Classical Letterbook*, Vol. XXIX, p. 33; first printed in *Mercersburg Review*, Vol. XXIII, p. 542; also in *Ecclesiastical Records of N. Y.*, Vol. IV, p. 2441f.

her bosom, had sufficient justification. Be assured that the Classis takes your cause to heart, and according to her ability, will endeavor to devise and accomplish what may serve for the attainment of your wishes, and the improvement of your condition.

The principal matter, about which you request our judgment and assistance, appears so important to our Classis, that she will take it into careful consideration, in order to send you her matured judgment upon the subject at the next opportunity.

Meanwhile, Worthy Brethren, you will have need of patience, courage and prudence. Do not grow weary under your trials. Quit yourselves like men and be strong. Make use of such facilities as are at hand. Neglect not the assembling of yourselves together, although you have to meet amid malicious adversaries. But be steadfast and immovable in the work of the Lord, knowing that your labor is not in vain in the Lord. Are you not zealous in a good cause? By it, the glory of God and the interests of the Kingdom of Jesus will be advanced. Search His Word constantly. Let your desires mount up before His throne in earnest supplications. Cast your troubles on the Lord. Rest in His wisdom, power, mercy and fidelity, as the One who knows, and is able and willing to deliver all who put their trust in Him. The good work He has begun among you, He is able also to finish; and He does not let the work of His hands fail. He has often shown that He plants and preserves His Church in spite of all opposition. Therefore, Brethren, be of good courage, and let not your hands hang down. Wait on the Lord, and He shall strengthen your heart.

May He who can do far more abundantly, above all that we are able to ask or think, hear you in your day of trouble. May He give you light for darkness, and endue you with wisdom, courage and fidelity, that you may persevere in your good work begun, with steadfast purpose of heart. May He cause you to experience in His own good time the desired results of all your efforts. May He fulfill all your desires.

This is all we have to say at present. Expect more particular advice at the next opportunity. We remain with brotherly greetings,
Respected and Much Beloved Brethren,
Your servants and sympathizing brethren in Christ,
CORN. HOUTHOFF,
Ecc. Amst. et Dep. ad res exteras, p.t. Praeses.
JOHN BAKKER,
Ecc. Amst. et Dep. ad res exteras, p.t. Scriba.

[Address]
To the Worthy, Godly and Esteemed Brethren, N.N.N.N., Members of the Consistories of the Reformed Churches in Pennsylvania, especially of Falkner's Schwamp, Schipback and Wit Marche.

[IV. THE CLASSIS OF AMSTERDAM TO THE REFORMED
MINISTERS OF NEW YORK, DECEMBER 1, 1728.[20]]

DECEMBER 1, 1728.

Worthy Sirs and Brethren:—

The document accompanying this (of November 28, 1728), is to the brethren in Pennsylvania. With their sad condition the Classis has great sympathy. The principal matter, which excites the greatest anxiety, is considered by the Classis too important to give an opinion on hastily. Therefore, all the circumstances of the case will be considered carefully by the Deputies, that the case may be ready for decision at the next meeting of the Classis, and those brethren will be informed of the resolution of the Classis as soon as possible.

Meanwhile, we have informed the brethren in Pennsylvania, that our Classis has accepted their complaints, and is ready to assist them by counsel and deeds. At the same time, they are exhorted to make use of the means of grace such as are ready at hand, until more favorable circumstances occur, to which end the Classis will use every endeavor.

The address, by reason of the omission of the same in the letters of those brethren, can only be expressed in a general way. We therefore request that you will forward our letter to them, enclosed in this, as soon as possible.

As for the rest, the Deputies desire that everything in the churches of New Netherland may be done in a regular manner. We say this, especially because complaints are sent up, in regard to the refusal (in certain places) to receive ordinary church-certificates. It will be agreeable to our Classis that every one act in this matter, not according to personal feelings, but according to the common Church-Order. The Classis thinks that as to the accepting of certificates, it is safer to follow the usual order of the church, than that church interests should be controlled by personal considerations.

Herewith, etc., etc.

[V. THE CLASSIS OF AMSTERDAM TO THE BRETHREN IN
PENNSYLVANIA, JUNE 20, 1729.[21]]

JUNE 20, 1729.

Reverend Sirs and Much Beloved Brethren:—

In fulfillment of our promise, in the letter sent you last year, and which we hope has reached you, we have now the pleasure to com-

---

[20] Copy of original letter in *Classical Letterbook,* Vol. XXIX, p. 34; first printed in *Ecclesiastical Records of N. Y.,* Vol. IV, p. 2443f.

[21] Copy of original letter in *Classical Letterbook,* Vol. XXIX, p. 37; first printed in *Mercersburg Review,* Vol. XXIII, p. 546f; also in *Eccl. Records of N. Y.,* Vol. IV, pp. 2468-71. A German translation of this letter, in the handwriting of Boehm himself, is in the archives at Bethlehem.

municate to you the resolutions, which the Reverend Classis of Amsterdam, after mature deliberation, has adopted, in reference to the condition of the Church-Government among you, and the transactions which have already taken place. Our resolutions in substance are as follows:

1. The Classis declares itself to be able to handle this case without reference to the Christian Synod.

2. The Classis finds in the acts of the Pennsylvanians all the inherent elements of a legal call, although all the usual formalities have not been complied with.

3. On such grounds the Classis decides that all the acts of the said Boehm, his teachings, and even his baptisms and his administration of the Lord's Supper, as well as his reception of members, must be recognized as legal.

4. In order to provide, however, what has hitherto been lacking, the said Boehm must now be ordained to the Sacred Ministry, according to ecclesiastical usage.

5. That this ordination may most properly and speedily be performed by one of the ministers of New York, who is authorized to do the same, nomine Classis.

6. That this ordination shall not be performed, however, before that the said Boehm has declared before the ministers of New York, that he accepts the Heidelberg Catechism and all the other Formulas of Unity, and that he will direct his ministry in accordance therewith, and that he submits to the "Church-Order" of the Synod of Dort.

7. Furthermore:—The Church-Rules which have been sent to us by the Brethren in Pennsylvania are found to be useful and edifying, and the Reverend Classis has no objection to allowing the brethren the use of the same for the government of their church.

8. And although the Reverend Classis, under the circumstances, approves this call for Domine Boehm, they desire that this way of making a call shall not occur again. They, therefore, accept the proposition of the Pennsylvania brethren, that, hereafter, when a new minister is needed among them, the Classis is to send them a competent and properly qualified pastor.

Thus you may perceive that the Classis is of the opinion, that inasmuch as the Pennsylvania brethren so earnestly and unanimously desire Domine Boehm to continue as their pastor, and that this call, originating as it did, out of the very heart of the congregation, must be considered as valid. Consequently all that he has heretofore done as their pastor must be considered legal; inasmuch as, in the new planting of the church and in a region so distant, the usual formalities for securing an ordination were not at hand.

Nevertheless, the Classis now expects that care will be taken by the brethren, that Domine Boehm be ordained to the Sacred Ministry, according to the plan proposed, by one (or more) of the ministers at New York, who are requested and authorized by our Classis to perform this act. Thus the work of the ministry may be carried on among you, according to the established Church-Order, and thus the Congregation of the Lord be edified and built up. We also cheerfully engage, on our part, to assist you at every opportunity, with our counsels and deeds, especially when another minister may be required among you.

For the rest, Worthy Brethren, we bow our knees to the God and Father of our Lord Jesus Christ, that you may be filled with all wisdom and spiritual understanding, and strengthened with all might, that Jesus Christ may dwell in your hearts by faith, and you may be rooted and grounded in His love. May He bless the ministry of your pastor with all kinds of fruit desired. May He crown your church with abundance of life, light and spirit. May His all-sufficient grace adorn, confirm, enlarge and perfect her, and make her a praise in all the earth.

Finally, Brethren, rejoice. Be perfect, be of good comfort, be of one mind, live in peace, and the God of love and peace shall be with you. Such is the desire,
Worthy Sirs and Beloved Brethren,
Of your friendly and well-wishing brethren,
The Classis of Amsterdam,
In the name of all,
J. BAKKER,
Dep. Cl. ad res exteras, p. t., Scriba.

Addressed: To the Reverend, Godly and Beloved Brethren of the Reformed Churches in Pennsylvania.

[VI. THE CLASSIS OF AMSTERDAM TO MR. JOHN PHILIP BOEHM. JUNE 20, 1729.[22]]

JUNE 20, 1729.

Reverend Sir and Highly Esteemed Brother:—
Inasmuch as the worthy brethren in Pennsylvania are desirous of having the lawful services of a pastor, and have chosen you for the ministrations of the Holy Gospel, and have therein encountered much opposition from others; and have, accordingly, poured out their complaints and fears into the bosom of the Classis of Amsterdam, with request for counsel, help and guidance in this business: the said Classis has maturely considered, in the fear of the Lord, all that has been presented before it, and has taken the following action:

[See the letter of June 20, 1729, directed to the German churches in Pennsylvania, for the eight articles of this action.]

* * * * * * * *

From these articles you will learn that the call to the work of the ministry, made upon you by the brethren of Pennsylvania, is recognized as legal, because the church itself desired your services, and

---

[22] Copy of original letter in *Classical Letterbook*, Vol. XXIX, p. 38; first printed in *Mercersburg Review*, Vol. XXIII, p. 547f; also in *Eccl. Records of N. Y.*, Vol. IV, pp. 2471-73.

the ministry of the Word was so necessary there. Therefore you did well to gratify the strong desire of the brethren in this matter. But now the Classis expects you carefully to follow what she requires, as expressed in these [eight] articles, both in reference to the Formulas of Unity, and in reference to your ordination by one of the ministers of New York. Each of these steps is in the highest degree useful and necessary, both for yourself and the church. Thereby you will also the more certainly avoid the criticisms of outsiders.

So then, dear brother, since you have undertaken the work of the ministry among the brethren, in the name of the Lord, He wishes all things to be done decently and orderly in His Church. Fulfill, therefore, our expectations in this matter, that also your boldness in the exercise of your ministrations may be the greater. Such a course will also tend to our happiness and satisfaction. You will, therefore, consult with the brethren how you may best obey the requirements of the Classis; and you will also be guided by the opinions of the New York ministers, even if they should think it necessary to summon you to proceed to New York, to receive at their hands the ordination required.

Furthermore, Reverend Brother, we most heartily wish that all desirable blessings may come down upon you personally and upon your work. May the Father of Lights enlighten you with His Spirit, which is the spirit of wisdom and of revelation, in the knowledge of Him, that you may also enlighten others. May the God of might gird you with all strength, that like a hero by the bed of Solomon, you may be ready and armed against an alarm in the night. May the God of all grace adorn you with every holy adornment, make you an example to the flock, in walk and faith, in love and purity.

In a word, may the Lord make your ministry glorious and successful, and deign in His own good time, to make you shine, in His kingdom as a teacher who has turned many to righteousness.

Reverend and Highly Esteemed Brother, we remain,
 Your cordial and loving brethren,
  The Classis of Amsterdam,
   In the name of all,

    J. BAKKER,
   Dep. Cl. ad res exteras, p. t. Scriba.

Addressed: To the Rev., Godly and Learned Mr. J. P. Boehm, Minister of the Holy Gospel in Pennsylvania.

P. S. We also request that you will please maintain correspondence with the Classis of Amsterdam.

[VII. THE CLASSIS OF AMSTERDAM TO THE MINISTERS AT NEW YORK. JUNE 20, 1729.[22]]

JUNE 20, 1729.

Very Reverend Sirs, Much Beloved and Highly Esteemed Brethren:—

While we take the liberty of requesting your services in sending the enclosed documents to Pennsylvania, we cannot, nor do we desire to hide from you, the action which the Classis has taken, concerning the condition of the churches in Pennsylvania, in connection with the complaints received, as follows:

[For the eight points, see the letter of this same date, written to the German churches in Pennsylvania.]

*   *   *   *   *   *   *   *   *

Reverend Sirs, we therefore take the liberty to request you, in the most friendly way, to put the last touch to the call of Domine Boehm, in order that he may be ordained to the Sacred Ministry, according to the directions of the above-mentioned articles. We understand well that there are ministers living nearer Pennsylvania than yourselves; but we have learned from the letter of the brethren [in Pennsylvania], that they did not wish to deal with those gentlemen in reference to this business of theirs; and that they had already consulted with you about everything. We feel, therefore, the greater freedom in entrusting our commission to you. This we do with all kindliness. Nor do we doubt but that you yourselves appreciate the necessity of this ordination, that our Church-Order may be maintained.

We leave to you the liberty of deciding as to the place where this ordination is to be accomplished: whether one of you shall go to Pennsylvania; or whether Domine Boehm shall be summoned to meet you midway between (New York and Pennsylvania), where he may meet with one of you gentlemen; or whether you should request him to come to New York; or whether some other plan should be adopted.

We also request that when you forward these documents to Pennsylvania, that you inform the brethren there, when and where this ordination, nomine Classis, is to take place; and we expect to hear, in due time, that this, our commission has been fulfilled.

Herewith, wishing the Lord's most gracious blessing upon you, upon your families and holy ministrations, we remain, with all esteem,

Reverend Sirs and Beloved Colleagues,
    Your servants, etc., etc.,
      The Classis of Amsterdam,
        In the name of all,
          J. BAKKER,
           Dep. ad. res exteras, p. t. Scriba.

AMSTERDAM, June 20, 1729.

Addressed: To the Rev., Godly and Learned, the Ministers of the Dutch Church of Jesus Christ in New York.

[22] Copy of original in *Classical Letterbook*, Vol. XXIX, p. 39; first printed in *Mercersburg Review*. Vol. XXIII, pp. 544-547; also in *Eccl. Records of N. Y.*, Vol. IV, p. 2473f.

[VIII. ORDINATION OF MR. JOHN PHILIP BOEHM IN NEW YORK ON SUNDAY, NOVEMBER 23, 1729.[24]]

RECAPITULATION AND PROCEEDINGS AT NEW YORK, NOVEMBER 18-25, 1729.

The Reverend Consistories of the three German Reformed Congregations at Falckner Swamp, Schipback and Witmarse, having advised with Revs. Gualterus Du Bois and Henricus Boel of New York, and Rev. Vincentius Antonides of Long Island, concerning their call to Johan Philips Boehm to be their minister, wrote to the Classis of Amsterdam, in order to obtain ecclesiastical assistance against the criticisms made regarding that call, laying for that purpose their whole perplexed condition, etc., before them in July, 1728.

Thereupon the Reverend Classis at first replied, under date of December 1, 1728, expressing their sympathy with their sad condition; receiving their complaints in order to help them at the first opportunity; and admonishing them to make use of such means of grace as were at hand.

Subsequently, on June 20, 1729, the Reverend Classis wrote again to Do. Boehm and to his consistories and to the ministers who had, for this purpose, corresponded with them. The brethren in Pennsylvania, having been invited and appearing fully authorized by the three consistories to finish all in a churchly manner, the letters (of the Classis) were opened and read. They were substantially as follows:

That the Reverend Classis, after mature deliberation, was of the opinion that the call, having originated within the congregation itself, must be regarded as valid, because of the unusual desire of the brethren in Pennsylvania for Do. Boehm, and that his work done by him as minister must be considered as legal, on account of the lack of the ordinary means of securing an ordination in a newly planted church in so distant a region; and also, because the ministry of the Word was so necessary, that Do. Boehm for this reason did well in complying with the urgent desire of the brethren. That the Reverend Classis was further of the opinion that Do. Boehm should now be ordained to the sacred ministry, according to the Church Order, this being demanded to avoid all further criticism, and that the ordination be performed by one of the ministers who had been in correspondence with them. Therefore, the Reverend Classis had authorized them to carry out the same in their name and to complete the appointment of Do. Boehm, with permission to do it at New York or elsewhere.

That is was the further resolution of the Reverend Classis, that

---

[24] The original is in Liber A, pp. 86-89, of the records of the Collegiate Reformed Church in New York. A copy was sent to Amsterdam and is now there in the "Pennsylvania Portfolio." Another copy was made by Boehm and sent by him to the Synods, now at The Hague, 74, I, 35. First printed in the *Mercersburg Review*, Vol. XXIII, pp. 549-553; also in *Ecclesiastical Records of N. Y.*, Vol. IV, pp. 2478-2484; *Journal of Presb. Hist. Soc.*, Vol. VI, pp. 317-321.

Do. Boehm, before the ordination take place, shall declare to the ministers who have carried on the correspondence that he accepts the Heidelberg Catechism and all the Formulas of Unity to regulate his ministry strictly in accordance with them; that he declares his readiness to submit to the Church Order of the Synod of Dort; that he promises to strive, by the grace of God, thus to fulfill all the duties of the holy ministry, whereunto the Reverend Classis wishes most cordially the divine blessing upon his person and work; and finally that he gives the assurance to maintain correspondence with the Reverend Classis.

That the Reverend Classis further resolved that the brethren of the consistories of the above-mentioned three congregations, shall obligate themselves, each in his official capacity, and their successors from time to time, to adhere to the prescribed articles, together with the congregations and Do. Boehm; that the Reverend Classis finds the church ordinances submitted to them useful and edifying and has no difficulty in allowing the use of them in the government of the church; that, although under the circumstances the Reverend Classis approves the call to Do. Boehm, yet they expect that nothing similar will again occur in the future. For this reason they accept the proposition of the Brethren in Pennsylvania that when hereafter a new minister will be needed, they shall send them one that is competent and duly qualified; that the brethren in Pennsylvania must see to it, that, according to the proposed arrangement, Do. Boehm be ordained by one of the ministers in correspondence with them, who are requested and qualified by the Classis to do this act; and that they submissively accept the kind offer of the Reverend Classis to render them counsel and help in all circumstances, even when a new minister is required.

It was also unanimously resolved and agreed to, according to the Church Order, that the ruling elders and deacons of the three congregations, after they have made known the letters of the Reverend Classis and have secured the ordination of Do. Boehm should, at the first opportunity, each in his own congregation, as well as others, who are similarly inclined, kindly request and urge a new voluntary subscription, according to their ability, for the payment of Do. Boehm's yearly salary, at such a time as the consistories may find best for its payment; that the ruling elders and deacons shall also, from time to time as may be convenient, use their utmost endeavors to collect from subscribers what each has promised for the support of Do. Boehm and to pay Do. Boehm his exact salary, at the appointed time.

That also, for this reason, the Church Order as sent by the brethren in Pennsylvania to the Reverend Classis, and by them approved and now enlarged by the above mentioned points, shall be signed by the newly elected members of the consistories before they enter upon their offices, for the better performance of their duties, namely to adhere strictly to the Heidelberg Catechism and all the Formulas of Unity and the Church Order of the Synod of Dort. And in order that every one in his office or station, may obey as far as possible the foregoing articles, these ordinances, as now revised by the

Reverend Classis of Amsterdam, shall be read in public, at every election or installation of a new consistory.

IN VIEW THEN OF ALL THE FOREGOING,

We, the undersigned elders, authorized by the Ruling Consistories of the three above mentioned German Reformed Congregations of Falkner Swamp, Schipbach and Witmarche, together with Do. Johann Philips Boehm, hereby declare:

That the commission, dated in Pennsylvania, November 4, 1729, authorized us, in the name of all, to ratify by our subscription, all that the Reverend Classis of Amsterdam has directed for the ordination and maintenance of Do. Boehm in the holy ministry among us, for the benefit of the three congregations, and whatever other action is taken and decided on, with us, according to the Church Order, by the ministers or the ministerium of New York in correspondence with us, and to keep the same always in full force in our congregations.

We, therefore, who are upon this commission declare that we have carefully considered all the foregoing, article by article, in accordance with the advice of the corresponding ministers or ministerium of New York, and that we ratify and adopt it all, for ourselves and our successors, and we promise submissively to obey it, each in his respective office, and by God's grace to maintain the same inviolably.

In testimony whereof, we hereby subscribe the same with our hands, as Commissioners at New York, November 18, 1729.

FRIDRICH ANTES,
Commissioner of Falkner's Schwamp.
GABRIEL SCHUELER,
Commissioner of SchipBach.
WILLEM DE WEES,
Commissioner of Witmarse.

So also in testimony of all this, I, Do. Johann Philips Boehm, do solemnly declare that whatever therein concerns me, I will, with God's help, perform to the best of my ability, subscribing my name thereto, at New York, November 18, 1729.

JOHANN PHILIPS BOEHM.

Be it, therefore, known to all hereby, that the above mentioned matter, declared by the Reverend Classis itself to be very important, and committed by them to the consulting ministers, Domines Du Bois, Antonides and Boel, to be carried out; also our letter to the Reverend Classis and their reply to us; and the foregoing action of the brethren in Pennsylvania, with all the details, were distinctly read, after prayer, in the presence of the brethren from Pennsylvania, and of Do. Boehm, to the Reverend Consistory of the Dutch Reformed Congregation, in their meeting in New York, on November 20, 1729.

And that thereupon, that Consistory unanimously resolved, that the said ministers had herein acted with strict regularity, as correspondents, according to Church Rules; and that inasmuch as the Reverend Classis had been pleased to entrust them with such authority, namely, the ordaining of Domine Boehm, on said condition, that they were under obligation to do the same:

Therefore, notwithstanding that they, with the entire Consistory, by definite resolution, stipulate that nothing of the kind shall ever be undertaken or performed hereafter, without an express order from the Classis:— still, upon the authority now conferred, the business must be formally consummated by them in the presence of this church, and in the face of any opposition.

Be it known then, that this ordination was thus performed by Domine Henricus Boel, and the consecration by the laying on of the hands by Domine Gualtherus Du Bois, in the presence of said Consistory, publicly, in the Dutch Reformed Church in New York, on Sunday afternoon, November 23, 1729. And that thereupon, the forenamed Consistory gave order to make a minute in reference to the same, in testimony of the truth thereof, which should be confirmed, as is proper, by the seal of the Church,—as is hereby done, at New York, November 25, 1729, by me,

In the Name and by the Authority of the Reverend Consistory.

HENRICUS BOEL,

L. S. *p. t. Praeses.*

N. B. The substance of the foregoing act with Do. Boehm and his [friends] on the eighteenth of November, and of what was done in the Consistory on the twentieth do., was for confirmation of the same, read publicly from the pulpit to the congregation by Do. Boel, beginning thus:

Beloved in the Lord,

In order that the Solemn Service, unusual here, which we are about to perform, wholly apart from any seeking of our own, at the command of the Classis of Amsterdam, and under the oversight of the Reverend Consistory of this congregation, may, under the blessing of the Lord, be to edification, and not be misunderstood: Be it known to you, &c, &c.

[IX. RECONCILIATION BETWEEN DO. J. P. BOEHM AND DO. G. M. WEISS, EFFECTED NOVEMBER, 24, 1729, AT NEW YORK.[25]]

When Do. Johan Philips Boehm, under the persistent pressure of the three High German Reformed congregations at Falkner's Swamp, Schipbach and Wit Marshe, in the year 1725, had assumed the minis-

---

[25] The original is in Liber A, pp. 89-90, of the records of the Collegiate Reformed Church in New York. A copy was sent to Amsterdam and is now in the Pennsylvania Portfolio. Printed first in the *Mercersburg Review*, Vol. XXIII, pp. 554-557; also in *Eccl. Records of N. Y.*, Vol. IV, pp. 2484-2487; and in *Journal of Presby. Hist. Soc.*, Vol. VI, pp. 321-324.

terial office over them, without ordination, notwithstanding the usual custom of the church, there arose in the year 1727 a complaint regarding this. Some in the congregation at Schipbach were led to withdraw from the ministry of Do. Boehm and to accept as their regular pastor, Mr. Georg Michael Weis, who had come over from Germany [in 1727] and was recognized by them as a regularly ordained preacher, inasmuch as he had been installed as pastor by the High German Reformed congregation in the city of Philadelphia and also at Germantown.

Thereupon some estrangement arose between Do. Johan Philips Boehm and Do. Georg Michael Weis. Meanwhile, however, the Reverend Classis of Amsterdam approved of the entire ministerial work of Do. Boehm, done before his ordination, on account of the unusual desire of the three congregations for him; and the Reverend Assembly [Classis] saw fit to authorize the Revs. Gualtherus Du Bois and Henricus Boel of New York and Vincentius Antonides of Long Island, whom they [the German churches] had used to correspond with the Reverend Classis, to consummate, in their name, the ordination of Do. Boehm, according to ecclesiastical usage, to silence all criticism. This was done with the full knowledge and approbation of the Reverend Consistory of the Dutch Reformed Church at New York, and under their oversight, publicly in the presence of the congregation, on November 23, 1729, and in the presence of Do. Weis, who had come to New York, at that time.

Therefore We, Georg Michael Weis and Johan Philips Boehm, together with the Commissioners of the above named three congregations of Do. Boehm, upon the peace-loving good counsel of the three Reverend Ministers, the correspondents, have jointly and heartily come to this firm conclusion and obligated ourselves to keep it, as we hereby do, namely,

That the Reverend Classis of Amsterdam has done well in this case, and the Reverend Ministers, the correspondents, have done well according to their bounden duty, in executing the orders of the Reverend Classis and consummating ecclesiastically the ordination of Do. Boehm.

That, out of Christian love for the peace and tranquility of the churches, we have assured each other solemnly, with fraternal giving of the hand to each other, that we heartily forgive each other for whatever offense we may have given and promise to forget it without ever bringing up again any of our differences.

That Do. Weis recognizes Do. Boehm as the lawful, ordained and regular minister of the three aforesaid Reformed congregations. That Do. Weis will altogether give up Schipbach and will declare to the congregation that he leaves it and the other two congregations to Do. Boehm as their only lawful minister, that he may pursue his work peacefully in the said three churches.

That henceforth there shall be a brotherly friendship between Do. Boehm and his churches and Do. Weis. That they will act as servants of the Lord towards each other, Do. Weis for the honor of Do. Boehm's ministry and Do. Boehm for the honor of Do. Weis' ministry in Philadelphia and Germantown.

That whatever other Reformed congregations, besides the three of Do. Boehm and the two of Do. Weis, shall desire Do. Boehm or Do. Weis or both by turns for their minister, both shall therein render brotherly aid.

That Do. Weis declares his heartfelt desire to become subordinate to the Reverend Classis of Amsterdam and requests the ministers who are corresponding, to inform the Reverend Classis to that effect. He testifies that he is ready and willing to comply with their ecclesiastical orders when sent over to him. Also that Do. Weis obligates himself to endeavor to bring his churches in Philadelphia and Germantown into the same subordination. Furthermore, that Do. Weis and Do. Boehm bind themselves, if other congregations should desire either of them for minister not to consent thereto, unless they, by their consistory or consistories subordinate themselves to the Reverend Classis, in order that ministers, consistories and congregations may maintain conformity therein, as is becoming in the Church.

That also the Reverend Classis shall humbly be asked whether any aid in money can be obtained from Holland as a voluntary contribution for the very needy congregations in Pennsylvania; and that, whatever monies have already been collected in behalf of the congregations of Do. Weis in Philadelphia and Germantown, the Reverend Classis be pleased if possible, to forward the same to them.

Furthermore, Do. Boehm with the commissioners of the three aforesaid congregations and Do. Weis together requested that they might hold and maintain, at every occasion which may occur, correspondence with the three ministers, Du Bois, Antonides and Boel, that they may conduct themselves to the best advantage of the churches. To which the three ministers gave their ready consent in hope of God's blessing and with His help.

Finally, that of all this, proper notice shall be given by Do. Boehm and his [officers] and by Do. Weis and his [officers], in order to forestall any opposition.

Thus agreed to, in the city of New York, November 24, 1729.

(Signed by each severally):

Commissioners of the three congregations:

FRIETRICH ANTES,	GEORG MICHAEL WEISS,
GABRIEL O. SCHULER'S mark,	*Minister at Philadelphia and*
WILLEM DEWEES.	*Germantown.*
	JOHAN PHILIPS BOEHM,
	Minister of the three congregations,
	Falkner Schwam, Schipbach and Witmarch.

We, the undersigned, upon the request of the ministers and commissioners, declare that the foregoing was thus enacted in our presence, as witnesses,

G. Du Bois,
V. Antonides,
Henricus Boel.
November 20, 1729.

The Commissioners from the High German Reformed Christian Churches of Falkner's Schwamp, Schipback and Wit Marshe, in Pennsylvania, with their Domine, Johan Philips Boehm, were admitted to a hearing in our Consistory. Their correspondent, Domine Vincentius Antonides of Long Island was also present, besides Domines Gualterus Du Bois and Henricus Boel, our Ministers.

After invoking the name of the Lord, the particular business about their churches was introduced. This related to their letters to the Reverend Classis of Amsterdam, and the replies of their Reverences to the same; also as to what had further been done in this country in this matter.

Thereupon it was resolved unanimously, in order to guard so unusual and remarkable proceedings from discredit, that this whole business with the Acts of our (New York) Consistory on the matter, and the accomplishment of the same, should be recorded in full in a certain Act-Book of the Church. This was done in the Dutch language.

[X. MR. BOEHM TO THE CLASSIS OF AMSTERDAM, JANUARY 29, 1730.[26]]

Very Reverend Classis:—

The very gracious letter of your Reverend Assembly, dated June 20, 1729, addressed to the humblest and the least of your fellow-brethren, together with the enclosed letter, addressed to my elders and brethren in the Lord, I duly received on November 4th of the same year. In it I found, with the greatest astonishment of a joyful heart, the glorious wonders and remarkable providence of the great God, in dealing so mercifully with the small body of believers in this, yet wild, country; in inclining so strongly the hearts of the Very Reverend Assembly toward us poor and miserable men and in appointing you so graciously to be a mother to our newly-planted, still very feeble and weak, but true Church of God, a mother in

---

[26] The original letter of Boehm, in German, is preserved in the archives of the Amsterdam Classis, in the Pennsylvania Portfolio. It was first printed by the writer in the *Journal of the Presb. Hist. Soc.,* Vol. VII, pp. 24-28.

whose lap we can enjoy comfort and protection, for Jesus' sake. And oh, that I were able to praise God sufficiently for this! Hence your most submissive and humble fellow-servant in Christ offers to your Reverend Assembly a dutiful and graceful heart, wishing for you, on behalf of himself and the congregations entrusted to him, the infinite love of the great God, and the unfading crown of eternal glory as your gracious reward. As regards himself he prays, with his whole heart, that the Prince of Peace, for the sake of his name, may graciously fulfil every wish, sent by your Reverend Assembly to your most humble fellow-servant in Christ, and that he may so equip his poor and feeble servant as to enable him, with his gracious assistance, to perform his service in such a way that he may help in extending his kingdom and hereafter may appear in his presence without fear.

Now, Most Reverend Classis, the service in the Gospel of Jesus Christ has been fully laid upon me and bound upon my soul through the ordination which took place in New York, in accordance with your august decision, so that, unless I want to hear hereafter the terrible judgment, I cannot withdraw my hand, so long as God gives me life. For this reason I implore God, with my whole heart, night and day, that, for the sake of His name He will graciously sustain me under my burden, in true and sincere perseverance in His service. For, as your Reverend Assembly may sufficiently infer, from all attending circumstances, my burden is almost unbearable, inasmuch as my days, and accordingly also the powers of my body, are declining,[27] so that I am no longer able to work hard throughout the whole week and on the Lord's days, etc., be at my several [preaching] places, which are far apart from each other, in order to attend to the duties of my office. Yet, the most important thing must have the preference.[28] Moreover, I had very little means when God brought me into this desolate country, so that I was hardly able to secure bread for myself and for my family, until I could, with God's blessing, obtain the

[27] This statement is surprising, as Boehm was not yet forty-seven years of age in 1730, when he wrote this letter. It implies perhaps that he had a weak constitution.

[28] Boehm means evidently his labor for the support of his family, when he writes of "the most important thing."

same from the soil. When I had labored long enough upon my land,[29] which I had secured with borrowed money whose interest I had to pay, and thought of making a beginning in paying off my debts, then it was God's way to select me, according to His providence, as His servant in the Gospel of His Son. From this service I could not consider myself released, as has been sufficiently made known to the Reverend Classis, because of the strong desire and the persistent pleading of the poor, scattered sheep of Jesus Christ, which had no shepherd; hence I had finally to submit to this yoke.

In this service I have now labored for four and a half years to my utmost ability, and (as I can truthfully say) I have received during all this time as my salary for my great trouble and neglect [of my farm] less than forty pounds rather than more. Yet I dare not say anything, because of the many sects which revile a minister most shamefully for receiving a salary; and, because of the great poverty, in which, at present, most of our people are living, I cannot admonish them, if I do not wish to scatter them again, but must patiently allow it to continue.

This has often caused me to shed tears in the solitude, when I was on my long and difficult journeys, because I could hardly see how I could get through, for I have a wife and six children,[30] four of them are yet of tender age, while my debts are still increasing, for I must attend to the duties of my office and neglect my work [on the farm]. This is the reason why I am unable to raise the interest, and as a result may lose my land again.

Therefore, your needy and poor fellow-servant of Jesus Christ appeals humbly and submissively to the Reverend Classis with the most earnest prayer, that you will remember him in Christian mercy and according to brotherly love, and cheer him with a small contribution. The God of all mercy will reward you richly, in body and soul, according to His grace.

Most Reverend Classis, I now live in unwavering hope, that, after Almighty God had caused us so wonderfully to seek the way to the confirmation in my office, (in spite of the

---

[29] For the land acquired by Boehm see p. 145f.
[30] For the family of Boehm, see Chapter IX of his Life.

opposition which He permitted to be made against the service forced upon me, which I discharged in the fear of God) and after enabling us to find it, through His fatherly guidance, in your Reverend Classis, now our congregations will daily grow and increase, under the grace of our almighty protector and through the watchful care of His faithful servants, although the mischievous spirit does not yet desist from attacking us.

I shall not fail obediently to report our condition to the Reverend Classis from year to year, according to your command, which will be done this time by your reverend correspondents, the ministers of New York.

Commending your reverend and precious persons, together with all your families and holy service, to the infinite love of Jesus, and myself to the true love originating from Him and to your favorable Christian remembrance, I remain, as long as I live,

Most Reverend Classis, Your submissive and obedient servant and humble fellow-worker in Jesus Christ,

JOHAN PHILIPS BOEHM,
Minister of the three Reformed Congregations at Falckner Schwam, Schipbach and Weitmarche.

Pennsylvania, in America, in
the County of Philadelphia,
January 29, 1730.

[XI. MR. BOEHM AND HIS CONSISTORIES TO THE CLASSIS OF AMSTERDAM, JANUARY 29, 1730.[21]]

Very Reverend Classis:—

The favorable answer, sent by your Reverences to your submissive and obedient servants, dated December 1, 1728, has been duly received by us, to our great joy, from the reverend ministers of New York and Long Island, shortly after its arrival. We have seen therein that our humble request, submitted to the Reverend Classis, has met with a kind reception,

[21] The original of this letter, in German, is at Amsterdam, Pennsylvania Portfolio.

that our just claims, which we had spread before you, were approved and taken to heart, and that we were assured of your support in our sad condition. The decision of the main point of our request was postponed, because of its importance, to the next opportune time. Meanwhile we were admonished not to be vexed by our trials, but to conduct ourselves as men and to make use of the means at hand among us; not to give up our [religious] meetings in spite of all opposition to this work of the Lord. We were assured that our labor would not be in vain in the Lord, because our zeal was spent in a good cause, through which the glory of God and the Kingdom of Jesus could be promoted. We were further admonished to seek guidance in the Word of God, to let many prayers ascend to the throne of God, and in our tribulations put all our trust in His mercy and faithfulness, for He can and will aid all those who have faith in Him and do not give up the work of His hands, as He has proved many times that it is He who plants His Church and preserves her in every persecution. We were also exhorted not to let our hands drop down, but to wait for the Lord and be strong in Him that He might make us strong.

These words made our troubled hearts rejoice again, inasmuch as we could clearly see in them the gracious and helping hand of our dear heavenly Father.

To strengthen our weak members the letters were read as soon as possible after their receipt, before all the three congregations, with the utmost urgent exhortation to all our members for Jesus' sake to remain steadfast and to adhere firmly to the Church Order, established by us in the fear of the Lord, with a sure confidence in the inestimable grace of the merciful God, which He had displayed, as it were, before our eyes. Thus we might see how we could be the happiest of men in our undertaking, having already shown us how He inclined the hearts of His faithful servants towards us, so that, for the glory of Jesus, they willingly offered themselves to promote to the best of their ability, the further cultivation of this spiritual vineyard of the great God, altogether newly-planted in this desolate place.

It seemed, however, as if some of our members, here and there, were very cold and indifferent, because of the notion suggested to them, that, because our minister was unordained, and as we had begun the work on our own initiative, it could therefore not be accepted as Reformed worship.

This continued until the Reverend Classis favored us most graciously with a godly, ecclesiastical decree, by which all our doubts and anxiety were removed, yea all disgraceful slanders against the service of our minister, performed among us in the fear of God, were entirely suppressed. For this grace we give thanks to our God, we praise and bless His holy name here in time and hereafter in eternity.

The letter, which was written by the Reverend Classis on June 20, 1729, was received by us through a special messenger from the Reverend Ministers of New York on November 4th of the same year. It contained the ecclesiastical resolution, passed by the Reverend Classis, consisting of eight articles regarding our church affairs in this country and the [ministerial] acts, already performed among us. It also contained a humble prayer to God, the Father of our Lord Jesus Christ, in behalf of us as members of the body of Jesus, that we might be filled with all wisdom and spiritual knowledge, that we might be strengthened by His strength, so that Jesus through faith might dwell in our hearts and we be rooted and built up in His love. It also implored the divine blessing upon the ministry of our beloved pastor with many desired fruits, that our congregations be crowned with much light, life and spirit, that through God's all-sufficient favor they be adorned, confirmed, increased, made perfect and prepared for His praise on this earth. It concluded with exhortation, comfort, admonition and benediction.

We could not receive this letter without tears, because of our surprise and heart-thrilling joy, considering that the Reverend Classis had so graciously listened to the prayers of us poor people, living in such a remote desert, where we hitherto seemed to be quite forsaken and without help in this world, and that you, so graciously and with such holy zeal for the Kingdom of Jesus Christ, have taken up our cause, that it might be planted among us and through us poor members in this desolate place. This great favor, which we have received from the merciful God through His ministers, we consider ourselves in duty bound humbly to recognize with continual thanksgiving, lying upon our knees before His holy throne. Nor shall we cease praying before His throne, that He, the rich and sufficient recompenser, may in His fatherly mercy richly endow you with all spiritual and bodily blessings and thus reward, here in time and hereafter in eternity, the help extended and the labor devoted to us for Jesus' sake.

Very Reverend Classis, we deem it unnecessary to report at length, how everything has been finished and carried out by the reverend ministers of New York, whom your Reverences had qualified to act in your name, (with whose orders we duly and obediently complied), how the whole rite [of ordination] was conferred upon our minister in New York, in the presence of the three delegates from our midst, because the Reverend Classis will find all this clearly and at sufficient length in the submissive report, made by your correspondents, the ministers of New York.[32]

Very Reverend Classis! Beside our humble and dutiful expression of gratitude for all that we have received, we take the liberty humbly to set forth to your Reverences our poverty, in the assured confidence that you will not take this ill of your children, so lovingly adopted by you, who are still so feeble and unable to help themselves. Especially since your Reverences have taken us so willingly under your protection and have assured us of your counsel and help.

Hence, Most Reverend Classis, our very humble petition is this: The foundation of our true worship, according to the Reformed religion and doctrine, has been laid in this desolate region by the Reverend Classis, and this first of all in our three congregations. Our Church Order [constitution] has been approved and ordained as useful and lawful, in accordance with which we shall, with the help of God, always live, as also in accordance with the Church Order of the Synod of Dort. Our minister, whom we had chosen, and whose ordination we had requested so humbly of the Reverend Classis, has already been ordained in accordance with your august decision. Thus God's spiritual vineyard is fully planted. For this may the name of the great God ever be praised.

Now we need most urgently for each congregation a house of God, or a fixed place of assembly and also a dwelling for

---

[32] See next letter, pp. 192-197.

our minister. To wander here and there, from one house or barn to another is too troublesome and also detrimental to the divine service, because of the ignorance of some persons in whose houses it is held, nor can one person be expected to allow the services to be held always in his house. Of ourselves we are unable to begin, much less to carry out, even the least, because almost all of us are newcomers in this poverty-stricken land and are burdened with our own debts. For even the small amount which each member subscribed and promised for the support of our minister, cannot be collected, although in the congregation at Falckner Schwam it amounts only to 8 lbs. 17sh., at Schipbach 5 lbs., 5sh., and at Weitmarsche 4 lbs. —sh., in all only 18 lbs. 2sh. But with many even this remains unpaid, because of poverty, so that he [the minister], like all of us, must patiently support himself by the labor of his hands. With this paltry contribution he is not even able to hire a servant to do his work, that he might attend to the duties of his office only.

With firm reliance upon God, the Father of all mercy and upon Christ His Son our spiritual ruler and king, we poor members address ourselves to the Reverend Classis as to the faithful servants of God, and to all true members of the body of Christ, with the urgent request to cheer us with a Christian and charitable contribution from the abundance with which the merciful Father has blessed them. We ask you to consider that this request is not made for our profit, but for the glory of God and the praise of the name of Jesus. We live in the sure hope that the same God for whose glory alone we ask it, will with His spirit strongly remind and convince the hearts of all those who know and love Him, that such aid will not be lost, but will be a sacrifice pleasing to Him, for which a believing soul will be rewarded a thousand fold here in time and yonder in eternity.

We, therefore, humbly ask the Reverend Classis to send whatever the Lord will graciously communicate to us, through our fellow-believers, to the reverend ministers of New York and to appoint the same to act as our supervisors, in the name of the Reverend Classis, whose good counsel we promise obediently to follow. We also pledge ourselves and promise herewith and by virtue of this, as we have done hitherto, and as has been established by the reverend corresponding ministers, to obey in all religious matters every ecclesiastical resolution of the Reverend Classis.

Herewith we faithfully commend your Reverences, as our exalted patrons, your precious persons, families and sacred services to the powerful hand of our dear heavenly Father, and ourselves, with renewed expressions of gratitude and a repetition of our most humble request, to your gracious protection and love. Praying for an early, favorable and gratifying answer, we are and remain,

>Very Reverend Classis of Amsterdam, our Very Reverend Brethren and Fathers in Christ. Your humblest and least servants, fellow-brethren and children in the Lord,

>>JOHAN PHILIPS BOEHM,
>>*Pastor of the above mentioned three congregations at Falckner Schwam, Schipbach and Weitmars.*

Pennsylvania, in America,
January 29, 1730.

[Falkner Swamp:]
FRIDRICH ANTES, BASTIAN REIFFSCHNEIDER,[34]
HANS WOLFFMILLER,

[Skippack:]   [Whitemarsh:]
HANS MEYER,[33]   WILLEM DEWEES,[37]
GABRIEL O. SCHULER's mark,[35]   JOHANNES X REBENSTOCK,
LAENERT SPAER,   ISACK DILBACK,
LORENTZ BINGEMAN.[36]   LUDWIG KNAUSS,[38]

Elders and Deacons of the three above mentioned congregations.

[33] The farm of Hans Meyer adjoined in 1735 that of Mr. Boehm, see Heckler, *History of Lower Salford Township*, p. 4.

[34] In 1734, Sebastian Reifschneider paid quit-rent on 100 acres in Hanover Township, Philadelphia County; see Rupp, *Thirty Thousand Names*, p. 474.

[35] Gabriel Schueler settled in Skippack at least as early as 1718 (see p. 25). In 1734 he obtained patents for four adjoining tracts, of about 425 acres, in Lower Salford Township. In July, 1728, he was one of the leaders who petitioned the Classis for Boehm's ordination. In November of 1728, he was one of the three delegates present in

[XII. THE NEW YORK MINISTERS TO THE CLASSIS OF AMSTERDAM REGARDING THE ORDINATION OF MR. BOEHM IN NEW YORK, APRIL 21, 1730.[39]]

NEW YORK, April 21, 1730.

Reverend, Devout and Very Learned Gentlemen.
Reverend Classis of Amsterdam.
Very Reverend Sirs, Fathers and Brethren in Christ Jesus:—

Your Reverences' esteemed letters of December 1, 1728, and June 20, 1729, sent to us by the Rev. Mr. Bakker, came to hand, together with the enclosed letters to Do. Boehm and to the Brethren in Pennsylvania, which we forwarded to them.

In obedient compliance with your Reverences' letter of qualification, wherewith you have been pleased to honor us in this affair, we have taken up and publicly carried out your directions, which, as we hope, you will learn to your entire satisfaction from the enclosed authentic document No. A[40] (to which is attached Do. Boehm's own sig-

---

New York at Boehm's ordination. In 1735, he assisted Boehm in the purchase of the Skippack church land (see p. 60). When the Old Goshenhoppen Reformed Church was built in 1744, Gabriel Schuler and wife donated the pulpit. In 1770, he was a resident of Frederick Township. He and his wife Catherine, Margaret Shuler, Elizabeth Shuler, John Shuler and William Shuler are buried in the burying grounds which belonged to Reiff's Church. See Heckler, *History of Lower Salford Township,* pp. 183-186.

[36] In 1730, Jacob Reiff sold 100 acres of his farm on the Little Branch of the Skippack to Lawrence Bingeman, who, however, lived only three years on this tract, when he died. See Heckler, l. c., p. 113. On May 10, 1728, Lorentz Bingeman signed a petition of the inhabitants near Falkner Swamp and Goshenhoppen, addressed to Governor Gordon. See Nead, *The Pennsylvania-German in the Settlement of Maryland,* Lancaster, 1914, p. 41.

[37] About William De Wees, John Rebenstock and Isaac Dilbeck, see pp. 21-24.

[38] Ludwig Knauss (Knoss) was married to Anna Margaretha Görlach in Germany. He lived at Tiltelsheim in the Wetterau, where his son, Sebastian Henry, was born October 6, 1714. He emigrated with his family to Pennsylvania in 1723. In 1734, he paid quit-rent on 100 acres in Whitemarsh Township. See Rupp, *Thirty Thousand Names,* p. 478. His son married Anna Catharine Transue on January 1, 1741. After his marriage the son settled at Macungie where he became one of the founders of the Moravian congregation at Emaus. See Reincke, *Register of Members of the Moravian Church,* p. 109.

[39] The original is in the Amsterdam archives, Pennsylvania Portfolio.

[40] Printed above pp. 177-180.

nature, as well as those of the brethren commissioned from Pennsylvania, and also an authentic copy of the acts of the Reverend Consistory of the Dutch Reformed Congregation in New York). The Reverend Consistory, together with the Brethren from Pennsylvania thought it best to send this to your Reverences, it being a Classical matter, together with the necessary report, in accordance with your Reverences' orders, all of which has had the full approval of all well-meaning persons here.

It is true that Do. Weiss had become the head of the opponents of Do. Boehm, and, since your letter regarding this had become known, had undertaken in more than one manner to write to us against Do. Boehm, in such a way as if we had taken sides. But we answered the complaints, one by one, in various letters, so that finally his Reverence, of his own accord, came himself to the ordination of Do. Boehm, and, after we had heard and answered everything in the presence of Do. Boehm and his delegates, he was present at the public ordination of Do. Boehm. He also confessed to us his sorrow about that which he and his adherents had undertaken against it and expressed his readiness to give Christian satisfaction and make a complete reconciliation. But, having seen our conduct in church affairs, he expressly requested us three ministers, just as Do. Boehm and his delegates asked for their own respective congregations, that we should promise him also to be and remain his correspondents.

Against this we presented our objections at length, namely that we had our hands more and more full of work in our own churches.

That we also incur many expenses through outside correspondence, by reason of postage, paying for lodging or entertainment day after day from morning till evening in our own homes (having been very rarely elsewhere) and that frequently many commissioners come at the same time, who,—because of their lack of acquaintance with New York, or other good opportunity, or because they cannot collect any money among the widely scattered inhabitants, or through poverty (as is mostly the case with new congregations in a foreign country) are unable to pay their expenses,—come frequently at a time most inopportune for us and ask that, because of their miserable condition or their great distance from home, we might help them as speedily as possible, while their church affairs, about which they ask our assistance, have often never been reviewed, are without parallel, very difficult, much involved and contain far reaching possibilities. That it causes us much trouble and thought, to secure the necessary information regarding all these things, and frequent consultations, in order to obtain if possible the correct impression of the affair and what is necessary to be done or not to be done, so that we can give good churchly advice to those that are perplexed. That, being compelled to be busy with outside affairs till late at night, and tired with these things, we must take up at night and at unseasonable hours the study for our own pulpits and thereby lose our own rest, as also through our solicitude (being unused to this work and having no brotherly Classical counsel at hand), to settle everything to the best advantage for the Low Dutch Reformed Churches here, or at least to escape unjust and harsh censure, such as we have already experienced.

Further, that we must continue to regard the outside correspendence as too hard for us, because your Reverences yourselves, although well supplied with good counsel, regarded the Pennsylvania affair as too important to decide it off hand, and yet meanwhile the commissioners of the distant churches give us no rest, but implore us in person and through letters to set them right in one way or another and, because there is danger in delay, to give them a decision for the tranquility of their churches.

That we are also conscious that we have not aimed for independence from your Reverences in anything, but have written in every case with the express condition of dutiful submission to your Reverences, as your most loyal servants, which we have shown in this as at every other opportunity throughout all these years in our holy service, and have always testified to our strictest adherence to your Reverences and have also endeavored, wherever it was possible, to unite the outside churches with us and to get them to maintain more and more the best harmony against schismatic churches and their elders, and, where new obstacles arise, to provide against them always in future authorizations of calls through new articles, which seem best to us for the tranquility (of the churches). Thus far, however, it has had this result in this country, that those who received their promotion neither through a call from the commissioners of your Reverend Assembly, nor through the approval of the Reverend Classis of Amsterdam, nor desire to obtain it in this country, have been opposed by us wherever possible, inasmuch as we wish to help none except they offer submission to your Reverences. Thereby we come into collision with their adherents, who endeavor, in order to further their own aims, to get the correspondence away from us and into their own hands and thereby alienate the congregations gradually from your Reverences. That thus far seems to be our reward on earth for all our expenses, endeavors, exertions and discouragements through new difficulties and for all our help, by which we desire to advance the true welfare of the Church.

Further that we, especially since the Raretan affair, live here in continual apprehension, whether, having given advice at the request of the perplexed, your Reverences will stand by us or by our opponents and their elders. Having consulted with each other regarding this, we agreed to ask your Reverences for an order, that, in case we were asked for advice, counsel and help, we should not make any efforts in affairs outside of our churches, but should keep away from all outside affairs. Thus we hoped to be freed in future from all expensive efforts as well as from malicious expressions against us. About which, God knows, we had such a bad quarrel, but if we had not, and had left the doings of Do. Frelinghuisen and his elders go on unchallenged, most if not all the German churches here would have been miserably divided. Now, although it might be better in New York, yet the congregation here has been kept in a better state of peace than almost all the rest.

For these reasons we declared to both Do. Boehm and Do. Weis, that having ordained Do. Boehm upon the orders of your Reverences, and both of them being present and ready to be reconciled, that we would assist them in this, but, inasmuch as our efforts and expenses, made here for the well-being of the Low Dutch churches only, and in order to maintain the ecclesiastical authority of your Reverences, were apparently sustained so poorly, we confessed that we were tired to make further exertions and would rather wait to find out whether your Reverences were convinced that we or our opponents were standing up for your Reverences and therefore for the true well-being of the churches here.

Yet both Do. Boehm and Do. Weis persisted, for the sake of mutual reconciliation, upon their request that we should promise them our correspondence and consider the fact how one-sided people would regard us in our sincerity for the Church and hence for your Reverences. That Do. Boehm and his people had addressed all their letters to your Reverences and upon this condition, which we, following our custom, had accepted in all our counsels and letters, namely with submission to your Reverences' decision, and not otherwise in any case. That they did not wish their own desires to be reported to your Reverences as their own, and that, in compliance with your Reverences' resolution regarding the ordination, the answer had been sent to us, without mentioning our names, in the capacity of their correspondents, and that thus they could ask all the more easily for the continuation of that which they thought had been of such benefit to them and to the congregations of the Lord and which had been favored by your Reverences. Do. Weis declared in addition that his Reverence also had concluded from our letters to Pennsylvania, regarding this matter, and from reports current there and at Raretans, regarding the differences pending there, as well as from the conversations with us regarding these things, that it was very necessary for the peace and well-being of the churches, for himself to enjoy our correspondence also, which he urged upon us, in order to secure a complete reconciliation and thus to promote more successfully the real well-being of the churches.

Thus, Reverend Gentlemen, against our intentions, we were forced to promise them again our correspondence; but not otherwise than with full submission to your Reverences. Wherefore we submit herewith to you in document, marked No. B., according to mutual agreement, a faithful copy of the articles of reconciliation, made by them voluntarily, and their submission to your Reverences, with humble request that you will grant your favorable approval and assistance to whatever you may consider, for good reasons, as right and proper. Of this document No. B, as well as of No. A, we gave to both, upon their request, authentic copies, in order that each might conduct himself accordingly in his field.[40a]

Meanwhile we leave and respectfully commend everything to your Reverences' sanctified wisdom and compassionate care for our churches, with dutiful request to let us know what has been approved by your Reverences and what not, in order that we can conform to it as much as possible, so that, if God spares our lives in the holy service, your Reverences may see more and more in this affair as in other cases our continued disinclination from supposed independence, and from all intercourse with the congregations for the sake of personal motives. Now, whether or not we shall hear from you at length the complaints brought in against us (as you sent them to Do. Frelinghuisen for him to answer) we shall lay bare the case of such complainant and our conduct therein in such a manner that your Reverences will be able to judge whether we or he disturbs the church and whether he encourages division for the sake of filthy gain and whether we on the contrary do not work for the common interests of the Church and in order to comply with good conscience with the Church Order. Thus we hope for a brotherly interpretation of our words and a churchly defense of ourselves against the apparently wrong undertakings of our opponents.

Enclosed are also the letters of Do. Boehm and his consistories, sent to us with the request to forward them. From Do. Weis no letter addressed to your Reverences, such as we advised him, has come to hand. We are uncertain as to the cause. From Do. Boehm and his [consistories] we received letters this spring, that the seceders there [at Skippack] had not yet been induced to peace, although both Do. Boehm and Weis had worked toward that end. Yet, that in time they seemed gradually to settle down to quietness and a general reconciliation. Hence the supposition is that Do. Weis is perhaps waiting with his letter to your Reverences, until he has brought his churches also into the promised subordination to your Reverences.

We beg your pardon that we have written more at length. It was in hope that our conduct might become clear to your Reverences, so that you might learn if it was according to the thoughts your esteemed letters, regarding the Raretan affair, expressed to our surprise rather elaborately. About this we wrote a short letter to your Reverences in January, 1728, but have not received an answer to it thus far.

We ask again submissively that you will not understand us in any other way than in accordance with what is really our aim, namely to oppose, with the help of God, the harmful schismatics and their elders (whatever wrong or misinterpretation we may suffer on their account) to the largest possible advantage of the Church. Thus our firm adherence to your Reverences will appear in every possible way, in order that, wherever we can, we may promote the honor of God and serve His Church to your Reverences' full satisfaction.

[40a] Document, No. B, is printed above, pp. 180-183.

Expecting your Reverences' favorable replies and protection, we remain with the most tender affection of our hearts and the most fervent wish to God, the Father of all grace, for the most prosperous outcome of all efforts for the upbuilding of Zion's fallen walls and for all blessings upon your reverend persons, families and most important church offices. We, who subscribe ourselves with all true reverence and respectful submission,

    Very Reverend Gentlemen, Highly Esteemed Fathers
     and Brethren in our Lord Jesus Christ,
    Your Reverences'
    Most submissive servants and troubled brethren
     in the Lord,
  G. Du Bois.[a]   V. Antonides.[a]
    Henricus Boel.[a]

[a] Gualtherus Du Bois was born at Streefkerk, Holland, in 1671; licensed by the Classis of Amsterdam, April 5, 1695; ordained by said Classis June 1, 1699; came to New York in 1699; pastor of Dutch (Collegiate) Reformed Church, New York, 1699-1751; died October 9, 1751. He was an able man, an excellent preacher, kind in spirit and catholic in his attitude to other churches, a pillar of strength for the Reformed Church of New York. He was greatly interested in the German Reformed churches of Pennsylvania. He assisted Boehm in many ways and welcomed Schlatter in 1746. See Corwin, *Manual of the Reformed Church in America*, 4th ed., pp. 438-442.

[a] Vincentius Antonides, born in 1670; pastor at Bergen in Friesland, Holland, 169.-1705; came to America in 1705; pastor at Bushwick, Flatbush, Flatlands, Brooklyn, New Utrecht, Gravesend, 1705-1744, also at Jamaica, 1705-1741; died July 18, 1744. He passed through many severe trials and troubles, but preserved throughout a kind and charitable spirit. See Corwin, l. c., p. 298f.

[a] Henricus Boel, born at Amsterdam in 1692; matriculated in Leyden University, September 17, 1712; pastor at New York, 1713-1754; died June 27, 1754. He was more of a controversialist than his colleague, opposing violently the revivalistic methods of Frelinghuisen, at Raritan, N. J. See Corwin, l. c., p. 329.

[XIII. MR. BOEHM TO THE CLASSIS OF AMSTERDAM, NOVEMBER 12, 1730.[44]]

Very Reverend Classis:—

All that the Consistory of the congregation of Schipbach has submissively reported to the Reverend Ministers of New York concerning the conduct of Mr. George Michael Weis, is shown in the enclosed letter, marked A, to which we received an answer, dated July 17, 1730, that at present no opportunity existed for sending the same to the Reverend Classis, and that they did not know of such an opportunity, but would let the matter rest until next spring. That such a report was necessary and obligatory appears from the agreement sent to the Reverend Classis by the Reverend Ministers at New York. In utter disregard of the Reverend Classis and of the ministers of New York, this agreement was broken by Mr. Weis and thus the harmful division in this congregation has been maintained up to the present time. The reasons why the Reverend Ministers desire that the Reverend Classis take notice of the actions of Mr. Weis are seen in the enclosed letter, marked B. That this Mr. Weis has been the first disturber and enemy of the divine service here, begun in the fear of the Lord, will be sufficiently evident from the copies of the enclosed letters, marked [C and] D, which, written in the original by his own hand, were laid before the Reverend Ministers of New York and are still in my possession. Moreover the enclosed paper, marked E, shows what other arbitrary things he attempted on his arrival in this country.

But now he has again forsaken our former fellow-members, whom he led away from good order, and, although he promised to return to them, there are few who believe that he will ever be seen in this wild country, if his plans and those of his companion, Jacob Reiff,[45] miscarry.

---

[44] The original letter, in German, is in the Amsterdam archives.

[45] Jacob Reiff was the youngest son of John George Reiff and of his wife, Anna Maria. He was born November 15, 1698. The first reference to him in Pennsylvania is on July 2, 1723, when he is mentioned in the diary of Gerhart Clemens, of Skippack. See Heckler, *History of Lower Salford Township*, p. 98. On December 1, 1727, Jacob Reiff, of Skippack, yeoman, bought three tracts of land, contain-

Meanwhile no peace can yet be expected, for there arrived this fall another man, named Miller,[46] whose father is pastor in the Electoral Palatinate, under the inspectorate of Kaiserslautern. He likewise avails himself of the liberty of this country, and so far has been preaching to the seceders at Schipbach, as the enclosed letter, marked F, shows. He promised them, as also the people in Philadelphia and Germantown, to take the place of Mr. Weis until the latter returns. In order to carry this out successfully, he betook himself to the Presbyterians in Philadelphia[47] (because he is unordained), that he might be ordained by them. This he told me himself in my house on October 19th, saying that, in the preceding week, he had handed to them his confession of faith concerning the points they had asked of him, and expressing the hope that the affair [of the ordination] would be concluded in the following week, which, as far as I know, has not yet taken place.

I warned him in a friendly way and advised him to go to the Reverend Ministers of New York and endeavor to have his ordination take place in accordance with the Church Order of the Reformed Church, whereby it would stand a better test before the world. To this he replied, that such a course was far too circuitous for him, and if he could gain his end by a shorter way he would take it, as there was no great difference. Moreover, he said, he would like to know who had given authority to the Classis of Amsterdam to rule over the Church in this country. He thought the King of England was more important than the Classis of Holland. Then I answered, that it was asking too much who had given her the authority, and that I did not care anything about that, but that I believed, if

---

ing 546 acres. The plantation on which he himself lived was located near the south-eastern corner of the present Lower Salford Township, near the Skippack Creek. This was the property upon which the Reformed church was erected. See Heckler, l. c., p. 99; also p. 111. A series of articles on "Jacob Reiff of Salford" was published by Mr. Dotterer in the *Schwenksville Item*, beginning September 4, 1885. See *Historical Notes of Montgomery County*, a book of clippings of Mr. Dotterer's articles in the library of the Pennsylvania Historical Society, pp. 105-113.

[46] This is John Peter Miller. For a sketch of his life, see p. 44ff.

[47] See letter of the Rev. Jedidiah Andrews, and Miller's own account of his ordination, pp 45-46.

the Classis had no such authority she would not have taken us under her care and supervision, that I for one was subject to her and would always be glad to act under her direction, etc. Then I received this fine reprimand: "There is such a glorious liberty in this country that the people themselves are free to elect, accept and also dismiss their preachers. It is not right to attempt to deprive them of this liberty and subject them to a Classis, which can then force upon them such ministers as she desires. Christians have liberty and are in this world under no head, Christ alone is their head in heaven".

He also remarked, that the people had called me only temporarily, until they could get another minister. I showed him my call. He said there was nothing in it, that they had called me for life. Then I answered him: The Reverend Classis had recognized it as a lawful call, if he were wiser than the Classis, he would have to take it up with her. I furthermore reminded him, that I also regarded Christ as the head of the Church, yet I believed that Christ ruled his Church on earth through agents, wherefore I would rather be under supervisors, divinely appointed, in order to preserve good order in the Church of Christ, than stand up in my own freedom. On this point he did not agree with me.

Meanwhile I must again attend to the duties of my office with a sad heart, and must see the congregation at Schipbach divided, which was becoming united again, and also see the danger of division extended to other churches.

Nevertheless, hoping that the Almighty will grant much grace through your Reverences, as through his faithful servants, I shall not cease earnestly to pray to him, from the bottom of my heart.

In transmitting to the Reverend Classis the blasphemies which the new Baptist sect, or "Tumplers" [Dunkers],[48] as

---

[48] The name "Dunker" is derived from the German verb "tunken," to immerse. They themselves use the name German Baptist Brethren. On December 25, 1723, the first "Brethren" congregation was organized in Pennsylvania by the trine immersion of six members in the Wissahickon Creek. They, together with seventeen members baptized in Europe, formed the first congregation at Germantown. In the fall of 1724 two other congregations were organized, one in Coventry Township, with nine members and the other in the Cones-

they call themselves, have made public through print, I wish to submit to your serious consideration the question, whether it is not the all too great liberty in this country, which causes such daring insolence. By this pernicious sect an appalling number of people has been misled and even married couples here and there have been separated when one party went over to them. The two chief heretics, who have been expelled from every other place, and who are the authors of the two pamphlets,⁴⁹ live in this country, where they engage in their blasphemous business, especially at Canastocka and at Falkner Schwam. They observe Saturday [as Sabbath] and do all

toga Township, with twelve members. The leader of the last was Conrad Beissel. In March, 1728, an awakening took place at Falkner Swamp, during which eleven persons were baptized. But a still more important event occurred in the same year. Conrad Beissel began to teach in public addresses that the Jewish Sabbath was the proper day to be observed. This led to a division of the Dunkers, and the formation of a new organization, the Seventh Day Dunkers or Sabbatarians. In December, 1728, Beissel was rebaptized, and then he rebaptized his followers. The efforts of Alexander Mack, the founder of the Dunkers, who arrived in 1729 with the last part of the Schwarzenau community, proved unavailing to heal the division. The statement of Boehm, that an "appalling number" of people had been won by them, must be received with considerable allowance. The total membership of the four Dunker congregations in 1725 was sixty-five members, yet their influence upon the organization of Reformed congregations is undeniable. For their missionary activity in 1724 see the *Ephrata Chronicle*, Engl. ed., Chap. IV. For a good history of the Dunkers see Falkenstein, *The German Baptist Brethren or Dunkers*, Lancaster, 1900.

⁴⁹ The first of these pamphlets was written by Michael Wohlfahrt, in 1729, in defense of the Seventh Day. The title page of the English edition is reproduced in Sachse's *German Sectarians*, Vol. I, p. 152. The second pamphlet was published in 1730 by Conrad Beissel, on matrimony. The *Ephrata Chronicle* (Engl. ed., p. 58) refers to it as the "Ehebüchlein." The two books were laid before the Classis of Amsterdam on June 4, 1731. They were handed to a committee to report on them. On September 3, 1731, the committee reported. "Regarding the two books from Pennsylvania, the committee reports that one of them is a dissertation on the Sabbath, wherein the writer contends that Saturday should be more properly observed as such than Sunday. As to the other book report will be made at the next meeting of Classis." On October 1, 1731, Do. Alstein reports that "the second book treats of marriage, it is not worthy of further notice."

kinds of work on Sunday, without shame. If some one takes them to account for this they say: Saturday was instituted by God himself, hence it is their Sabbath; but Sunday was appointed by the Pope and hence it is idolatry.

The blasphemous sect, which calls itself the "Newborn",[50] has almost been silenced, for its author, named Matheis Baumann, has been removed by God. A few of his adherents can still be found, and also a few who did not quite agree with him. The worst of them, named Martin Schenkel,[51] utters such blasphemous words against our Saviour (as one can hear from many people), that the ears of a true Christian tingle and his heart must weep, when hearing them. It is a great pity that there is no punishment in this country for such blasphemers. Indeed nothing else can be expected than that the just God, since no one punishes the profaning of His honor, will unawares inflict His judgment. But these men have no longer a large following.

However, the above mentioned *Tumplers,* although they are divided and hold conflicting opinions, mainly about the Sabbath or seventh day, have a large following everywhere, which is the result of nothing else but this great liberty. Yet nothing can be expected more certainly than their collapse, for their kingdom is altogether divided.

Meanwhile it is to be feared, that, if they are not checked,

---

[50] The New Born held public disputations at market times in Philadelphia, "where also Baumann once offered, in order to prove that his doctrine was from God to walk across the Delaware River." See *Ephrata Chronicle,* Engl. ed., p. 17. For the New Born, see p. 86.

[51] In 1719, one hundred acres were patented to George Martin Schenkel at Oley, south of Pleasantville, at a place still known as Schenkel's Hill. He was naturalized in 1729. See Rupp, *Thirty Thousand Names,* p. 434. In 1734, Martin Schenkel paid quit-rent on 100 acres at Oley. See Rupp, l. c. p. 475. He died shortly afterwards. His widow, Magdalena Schenkel, died prior to 1763, when her will was probated. It was dated July 6, 1751. She bequeathed to Martin Schenkel, Jr., 175 pounds, to Sarah Yoder 20 pounds, to Magdalena Aplen 20 pounds. Sarah Schenkel, in 1746, married John Yoder, the son of Johannes Yoder, who, after the death of Matthias Baumann, in 1727, was one of the leaders of the New Born. The *Ephrata Chronicle* (Engl. ed., p. 18) mentions Kühlenwein and Jotter as prominent successors of Baumann. (Communicated by Rev. John B. Stoudt, of Northampton, Pa.)

many poor people will be misled by them and threatened with great danger to their souls, for they are constantly traveling about through the whole country and are trying to enlist [in their ranks] as many as they possibly can. We hear all the time, frequently with great astonishment, of such or such a one who has gone over to them, even of Reformed people, which compels me to make a humble report concerning it. This is done in the hope that the merciful God will enable a Reverend Classis to find a way of checking these and other like dangerous errors. Nothing can be done here, everything passes, because of this liberty.

Very Reverend Classis! In the above-mentioned Canastocka[52] are found a large number of Reformed people, dispersed over a space well nigh twenty miles, who in the beginning of my ministry, on several occasions, urgently requested me to hold divine services and administer the Holy Communion to them. Hence I undertook the journey (for it is between fifty to sixty miles from my dwelling place) and administered the communion, at which occasion about sixty persons were present. Whereupon Mr. Weis, under date of October 2, 1727, wrote a letter to them (see enclosure marked D), with the oral statement that I would soon be stripped of my office. Shortly afterwards he went there himself and celebrated the Lord's Supper there with some who had crossed the ocean with him. By persuading these poor people that my work could not be approved in the Reformed Church, he soon scattered them. But subsequently, when they found that all this was only talk on his part, and that I had been ordained in New York by the Reformed ministers there, by order of the Reverend Classis, and that, by virtue of my legitimate call, all my acts, performed previous to my ordination, had been approved, they greatly regretted that they had allowed themselves thus to be imposed upon. They sent again a member of the congregation to me with the request not to hold this against them, but to come to them again. To this I consented, with

[52] Conestoga Township was erected in 1718. It included all the land west of the Octorara Creek to the Conestoga Creek; northward it seems to have extended as far as the present limits of Lancaster County. In 1718 the assessment list shows about seventy German taxpayers.

the proviso that I would do nothing contrary to my duty and the Church Order.

Thus a great many members of the congregation assembled on May 30, 1730, who requested me to tell them how my affair had terminated and what the condition of my three congregations was at present. I explained it clearly to them. Whereupon a heartfelt joy manifested itself in the whole congregation and the wish was expressed that the merciful God would also look upon this congregation with His eyes of mercy and bring it under the care of faithful servants of Christ. Not doubting God's grace, they begged me to arrange and transact everything in accordance with the Church Order, established by the Reverend Classis, and to lay the report thereof before the Reverend Classis. They also agreed unanimously to adopt explicitly the rule, that, if the Reverend Classis would accept them as her children and brethren, they would in future recognize none as their regular minister, unless he had been previously examined and approved by the Reverend Classis, or by its authorized delegates, as a true Reformed minister for this congregation. I aimed particularly for the adoption of this rule, because of the many heretics, found in this country and especially in this Canastocka, and because we are never sure what kind of ministers will now and then come into this free land, who will try, under a show of respectability to sneak into the Church of Christ, whereby irreparable harm may be done.

The same action was taken in another small congregation of about fifteen families, with the same humble request to the Reverend Classis. It is situated about ten miles from here.[53] The place has as yet no definite name, but is called, after the river on which it lies, Bergjamen [Perkiomen].

[53] What congregation this was is not entirely clear, but indications point to Old Goshenhoppen. The Old Goshenhoppen Church was about twelve miles from Boehm's home and the only church up the Perkiomen valley, which suits the description. The meeting place in 1730 may have been at a farmer's house closer to Whitpain than the church was located in 1744. In 1732 a warrant was secured for land in Upper Salford Township, Montgomery County, half a mile northeast of Salford Station, upon which in 1744 the first church was built.

The original petition, with the signatures of the four elders and two deacons at Canastoka, has already been transmitted by me to the Reverend Ministers at New York.[54] The other [from Perkiomen] I do not have at present in hand, but it is still in the hands of the congregation.

I, therefore, recommend most humbly, upon their own earnest desire, these two congregations to the Reverend Classis with the urgent request, for Jesus' sake, to take them under your highly esteemed supervision and to gladden them with a favorable answer and an admonition to true loyalty.

Another distant congregation[55] is also desirous of being brought into good order and I shall not fail to do all I can to bring the same under the blessed supervision of the Reverend Classis, for which purpose I have agreed to go to them on November 23rd next. I hope the Reverend Classis will not regard this as wrong.

With respect to the Reformed people of Philadelphia, I have been compelled to hear repeatedly, with a sad heart, from several of them the reply, (when I recommended the good work to them): "We are here in a free country and the Classis of Holland has no right to give us any orders". This statement, however, has been prompted, as I believe, by the persuasion of Mr. Weis alone, which is now continued by Mr. Miller. By it also the seceders at Schipbach have so long maintained the division there. It is surprising, how Mr. Weis, together with his companion, J. Reiff, dares to collect money in Holland for those in Philadelphia and for those whom he caused to secede in Schipbach. For we cannot believe that the Reverend Classis, without previous investigation as to how their donations will be used for the honor of Jesus Christ, will permit this to be done, in view of the fact, that such gifts could hardly be entrusted to such men, who recognize none as their head, but want to be their own masters.[56]

If Mr. Weis and Jacob Reiff should succeed in carrying

[54] This petition has not been preserved.
[55] This refers to the Reformed congregation at Tulpehocken, where Boehm administered the first communion on October 18, 1727, to thirty-two members. See p. 277.
[56] These fears of Boehm were fully justified, as is shown by later developments. See the history of the "Reiff Case," pp. 39-44.

out their plans, before they have submitted themselves to the Reverend Classis and the Church Order instituted by her, it would utterly thwart any attempt to bring the congregations here under a uniform order and the supervision of the Reverend Classis. Hence we could never hope for a harmonious Reformed Church in this country. For if they are so stubborn in their destitute condition, worse would follow if they needed no longer any help, which might become a permanent scandal.

All of which I submit to the godly consideration of the Reverend Classis, for if such harmful intruders could be checked, a beautiful harmony under one church order would soon be established in every place.

Herewith, Reverend Classis, your very humble and lowly fellow-servant prostrates himself at the feet of your Reverences, the faithful servants of God and administrators of our true Church, with the submissive and urgent request not to withhold your help, because of all this, from him and the dear congregations entrusted to him, but lovingly, for Jesus' sake, to take care of us, poor members of Christ.

Your humble servant also recalls to your Reverences the most submissive request made on January 29, 1730, in behalf of himself and his three congregations, and transmitted to you by the Reverend Ministers of New York.

We furthermore implore the Reverend Classis to take into your serious and highly esteemed consideration what could be done, by the proper authorities, with regard to the excessive liberty in this country, so harmful to the true Church, of which Mr. Weis and Mr. Miller have thus far made use, as also against the pernicious sects, which have been driven from all parts of the world into this free country.

Hoping that our gracious God will bless your plans and powerfully direct whatever redounds to His honor and the peace of His Church, commending Your Reverences, your precious persons, together with all your families and holy services, to the all-embracing protection of God and the grace of His Word, and comforting myself with your gracious and

Christian favor,

     I remain as long as I live,
     VERY REVEREND CLASSIS,
  Your most submissive, most obedient and most humble fellow-servant in Christ,
     JOHAN PHILIPS BOEHM,
   Pastor of the three Reformed Congregations at Falkner Schwam, Schipbach and Weitmarsche.

Pennsylvania, November 12, 1730.

P. S.

 Inasmuch as many things happen in this country, which, if they were all reported, might weary the Reverend Classis, though such report might often be of service, I desire the honor to have one of the Reverend Brethren, if he will take the trouble to do so, send me his address for this purpose, without hesitation.   BOEHM.

 [This letter of Mr. Boehm was accompanied by the following enclosures:]

ENCLOSURE A.

[LETTER OF MR. BOEHM AND THE CONSISTORY OF SKIPPACK TO THE REFORMED MINISTERS OF NEW YORK AND LONG ISLAND, MAY 17, 1730.]

Reverend, Learned and Godly Sirs, Gualtherus Du Bois, Henricus Boel and Vincentius Antonides:—

 Your Reverences succeeded of late, in the month of November, 1729, through extraordinary diligence and labor, to bring about an amicable adjustment between Do. George Michael Weis and Do. Boehm, the purport of which your Reverences will be able to perceive from the written agreement in your hands.

 But with sad hearts we must now report to your Reverences that Mr. Weis soon afterwards preached here under the pretext of delivering his farewell sermon, but he did not make the least reference to it in his sermon, much less did he read the agreement, though on our part we heartily requested it, but willingly allowed our adversaries to forbid him doing it. Shortly afterwards he preached again, then stayed away for some time until now, on the 30th of April, he returned at the request of the seceders, and held the preparatory service and on May 1st celebrated the Lord's Supper. He likewise preached on May 7th, being Ascension day, and again to-day. They are all called farewell-services. Moreover after these sermons and at other occasions he baptized children and married people. He thus revealed what intentions he had in mind during all this time. Through all this our poor congregation, which has been completely split by him, has been kept thus far in such harmful division and strife.

Moreover he is now setting further mischief on foot, for he has resolved to cross the ocean, with the avowed intention of going to Holland, to receive the money which, he claims, has been collected there in answer to his letter. He intends to put this out at interest, so that he can live on it. Then he is going to return. Through this the poor, seceding members, who have been driven into rebellion through him, will still further be hardened.

Now we believe nothing is more certain than this, that he and Jacob Reiff, who is going with him and who first introduced him into our congregation and helped him to create the harmful mischief, will endeavor to obstruct everything that we have done. For, as we learn, another testimonial,[57] such

---

[57] When Weiss and Reiff left Philadelphia, in May, 1730, Reiff was given the following power of attorney:

"Whereas our pastor, Mr. Weiss, has resolved, with his companion, Jacob Reiff, to make a journey to England and Rotterdam, for the purpose of receiving the collections, which have been made there and are intended for the erection of a church in this country, Jacob Reiff is hereby authorized to attend to all matters, in order that Mr. Weiss may be immediately dispatched with them [the collections] and start on his return to Pennsylvania. Thus we commit everything to him, [trusting] upon his good conscience and give him full authority. Witnessed with our hands. Done at Philadelphia, May 19, 1730.

"We herewith also express the desire that Jacob Reiff shall so arrange it, that in case Mr. Weiss will not or cannot return to this country, he, that is Reiff, shall forthwith bring with him a minister from Heidelberg and provide him with the most needful things. For, in case the collected moneys are no longer on hand, we consider it unnecessary for Mr. Weiss to proceed farther, but desire him to place the letters in the care of Jacob Reiff for delivery at their proper

as was sent formerly to your Reverences, has been handed to him, signed by many people, with which, as we hear it openly asserted, he intends to appear before the Reverend Classis. It is, no doubt, like the former filled with nothing but falsehoods.

Meanwhile this exceedingly unfortunate affair, which has separated the nearest blood-relatives, and has thrown them into fierce animosity against one another, will be kept up in this poor congregation; for everybody went to communion without order, so that we had to feel ashamed before others, neither will the harmful evil leave the other congregations untouched, since two of those who ought to have answered for their deeds, went over to him [Mr. Weis], nor can we see how Mr. Weis will justify his conduct before honorable men, much less before the great Judge. Besides he has arranged everything here, how matters are to be conducted until his return.

We, therefore, pray your Reverences graciously to assist us with your good counsel, for we Reformed people must certainly feel much ashamed because of the division caused by Mr. Weis. That he was the cause of it, and was always bent on mischief, is, we think, proved by his own conduct.

For to sign such a covenant with his own hand, before such reverend men, who for the glory of Jesus labored so zealously to restore everything to good order, and then to break the same in such a disgraceful manner,—such conduct is not only devoid of honor, but far removed from godliness, nor is it worthy of a minister to set such an example.

But we leave the further judgment of this to your Rev-
addresses, and himself request answers thereto.

"We all the elders of the two congregations at Philadelphia and Schibach.

[Philadelphia:]
J. DIEMER, D. M. P.,
PIETER LECOLIE,
JOHAN WILM ROERIG,
HENRICH WELLER,
GEORG PETER HILLENGASS,
HANS MICHEL FROELICH,
MICHEL HILLENGASS.

[Skippack:]
WENDEL KEIBER,
DEOBALT JUNG,
CHRISTOFFEL SCHMITT,
GERHART (G. I. H.) IN DE HAVEN,
GEORG REIF,
GEORG PHILIP DODDER."

A copy of this petition, made by Reiff and submitted to the Court of Chancery, is in the Harbaugh Collection of Mss. It was printed in the *Reformed Quarterly Review*, 1893, (Vol. XL), p. 58.

14

erences, praying that you will take it to heart, in accordance with your godliness.

We are and ever remain Your Reverences', our most honored Sirs', submissive and obedient servants,

J. P. BOEHM, *minister*.

Pennsylvania at Schipbach,
in our Consistory, May 17, 1730.

Elders { JOHN MEYER,
{ CHRISTIAN NEUSCHWANGER,[58]

Deacons { LORENTZ BINGEMANN,
{ PETER STEPHAN.

P. S.—The congregation of Germantown has been abandoned by Mr. Weis for some time.

ENCLOSURE B.

[LETTER OF THE NEW YORK MINISTERS TO MR. BOEHM AND HIS CONSISTORIES, JULY 17, 1730.]

EXTRACT FROM A LETTER OF THE REVEREND MINISTERS OF NEW YORK, GUALTHERUS DU BOIS, HENRICUS BOEL AND VINCENTIUS ANTONIDES, DATED JULY 17, 1730, ADDRESSED TO THE PASTOR AND CONSISTORIES OF THE THREE REFORMED CONGREGATIONS AT FALCKNER SCHWAM, SCHIPBACH AND WEITMARSCHE, IN PENNSYLVANIA.

Meanwhile it surprizes us very much and gives us great grief that we have learned from your letter, dated May 17th, how the sad division has been kept up unchanged, and has even been increased, not only through the seceders, but even through Do. Weis, contrary to the covenant so solemnly and dutifully made between you and Do. Weis. . . .

Let us, therefore, know from time to time, without reserve, how things are going and for what reasons and how Do. Weis has left the congregation of Germantown and also whether this congregation has accepted Do. Boehm as their

---

[58] Christian Neuschwanger signed the oath of allegiance at Philadelphia, August 24, 1728. In 1734, Bastian Reifschneider paid quit-rent on 100 acres of land in Hanover township. See Rupp, *Thirty Thousand Names*, p. 474.

minister and on what terms, that we may see whether it is done according to the agreement made with subordination to the Reverend Classis, in order that everything may be brought into good order.

It surprizes us in the highest degree that Do. Weis, notwithstanding his earnest request for correspondence with us on every occasion that might arise, and our promise to do so with submission to the Reverend Classis, is again proceeding on the old footing, neither communicating with us, nor even writing a letter to the Reverend Classis. At his departure he wrote last May a letter to Do. Boel alone, requesting him if money should be sent over from Holland for the congregation of Do. Weis (while Do. Weis, according to his letter, was going to England and Holland to gather in the money collected there), to receive the same and to hand it over to the authorized representatives of Do. Weis in Philadelphia. This he did without mentioning a word in his letter of the differences that had arisen or even referring to Do. Du Bois and Do. Antonides.

Hence we desire that the Reverend Classis be informed of the things since undertaken by him with the seceders.

[ENCLOSURE C].
[COPY OF A LETTER OF MR. WEISS TO MR. BOEHM, NOVEMBER 28, 1727].

Address: To deliver to Mr. Boehm.

S. T.—Especially Honored Sir and Friend:—

Inasmuch as God is not a God of disorder but of order and as He, therefore, demands that in the Christian Church everything be accomplished in accordance with Apostolic order; but, whereas it is well known that in many cases the gentleman [Boehm] has acted contrary to this order, since without inquiry and permission from the clergy, and taking into consideration only the fact that this is a free country, he has undertaken such an important office only and solely at the instigation of the people, although he was not examined as to his qualification by such men as are able to pass judgment, much less submitted to an ordination, having all the time dissuaded the people from writing for a clergyman, not to speak of his neglect to teach the catechism for the benefit of the young and old and of his admitting children to the Lord's Supper for the first time, without giving them any information or instruction on the subject of salvation,—and also, when I first came to this country, giving me such a reception that I can come to no other conclusion than that he aims at nothing else than his own, vain honor and advantage, not to mention for the present many other things,—

Now therefore, according to the decision of a Reverend Ministerium and by virtue of the authority which I possess in this matter as a regularly ordained servant of Christ, the gentleman is herewith summoned and requested to come to Philadelphia, and appear in the residence [manse] of the minister of the Presbyterian church, for the purpose of being examined in one or another of these things.

Wherewith, commending him to the divine favor, I remain the gentleman's   Devoted,

                                   G. M. WEIS, V. D. M.

Philadelphia,
November 28, 1727.

ENCLOSURE D.

COPY OF A LETTER OF MR. GEORGE MICHAEL WEIS, WRITTEN TO MR. SCHWAB,[59] OF CANASTOCKA, OCTOBER 2, 1727.

S. T.[60]—*Dear Friend:*—

If any persons at Canastocka feel disposed, for the strengthening of their faith, to partake of the Holy Communion, after preceding preparatory service, I should be informed at a favorable opportunity and at an early date, since I am staying sometimes in Philadelphia and sometimes outside in the country districts, so that I may know how to shape my course accordingly. To this end I should like to have a definite

---

[59] Hans George Schwab reached Philadelphia, September 18, 1727, on the same ship as Mr. Weiss. He settled in the Conestoga Valley. December 4, 1734, he secured a warrant for 150 acres of land on Mill Creek in Earl township.

[60] S. T., stands for Salutem Tibi, *i.e.*, "greeting to thee."

time appointed and to be informed of it, that is, at what time and place the service could properly be held, also how and by what conveyance I could come up, since I do not know the way and am still a stranger in this country.

The Lord's Supper was celebrated by me lately in Philadelphia,[61] at the request of the people, and I shall shortly administer the same at Goschenhoppen, above Schipbach, in which locality also many newcomers from the ships are found.

I am not a little surprised that Mr. Boehm allows himself to be used as a minister, indeed that he usurps such privileges and authority as do by no means belong to him, nor have been accorded to him by the clergy, as I have learned, to my satisfaction, from the ministers here, but that he assumed so important an office merely at the instigation of the people, while he cannot boast either of an external or of an internal call. For, where is the sufficient insight and knowledge, where is the true zeal for increasing the glory of God and for extending the kingdom of Christ, if a man looks out mostly for his own interests and allows himself to be betrayed into passion against one who had no evil thought in his heart? Who has examined this man, whether he possesses the qualifications for such an important office? Who has laid hands upon him, while it is said of teachers of the Word of God: "Examine them before letting them teach; hands should not rashly be laid upon them" [I Tim. 3:10; 5:22]. It might indeed be objected, (as in fact it has been done) that the people had most insistently requested and begged him to accept. The answer to this is: That, considered by itself, this was a good popular impulse, but the people surely cannot call any one save him who has been examined and ordained by the clergy and has thus been recognized as one duly qualified. To this it might be objected: There

---

[61] The Minutes of the Presbyterian Synod of Philadelphia (see Records, Vol. I, p. 87), show that September 24, 1727, was a Sunday. The following Sunday was therefore October 1, 1727. This letter to Mr. Schwab was consequently written on *Monday*, October 2, 1727. As it is likely that the first communion service in Philadelphia was celebrated on a Sunday, and as his reference "lately" (ohnlängst) implies the lapse of a number of days, September 24, 1727, may well be regarded as the *first fixed date* in the history of the Philadelphia congregation.

was no opportunity for this in this country, as there is no German ministerium. Be it then known that the English ministers ought to have been consulted, who would certainly have been willing to render assistance by word and deed, and would even have exerted themselves to have a good minister sent over from Germany. If this had not turned out as desired, Mr. Boehm might have led the people with reading and prayer or even with devotional exposition of Scripture, but he should not have administered the sacraments nor officiated at marriages, for which he did not have the least justification, inasmuch as he who wants to be a good Reformed minister ought to observe the laws which should govern a Reformed minister. Otherwise, we must look upon his work as something of his own contrivance, entirely different from the Reformed Church. Wherefore I cannot conscientiously recognize Mr. Boehm as a Reformed teacher and preacher, until he submits to an examination and is ordained in Apostolic manner, which he will never be able to do.

I am writing this for the information of every one. The pastor of this place[62] will see what is to be done in this case, especially since he was informed that he [Boehm] studied a little and was ordained by a Reverend Consistory.

These are my thoughts regarding the work of Mr. Boehm, which, from love of truth, I was compelled to make known publicly, so that every one may act accordingly. With a wish for your well-being, I remain,

Devotedly Yours,
G. M. WEIS, V. D. M.

Philadelphia,
October 2, 1727.

ENCLOSURE E.

[COMPLAINTS OF MR. BOEHM AGAINST MR. WEISS, NOVEMBER, 1730.]

1. Mr. Weis intruded into my three congregations, partly by cunning, partly by force, with the aid of some opponents,

---

[62] This reference is probably to the Presbyterian minister in Philadelphia, the Rev. Jedidiah Andrews, who from 1698-1747 was pastor of the old Buttonwood Presbyterian Church.

for at Weitmarsche word was sent to an elder that he [Weiss] would preach there on the next Sunday, if a horse were sent to bring him over from Philadelphia. This was done by the elder, because he knew that I had been to see Weis in Philadelphia,[63] and he supposed that we had agreed upon such an arrangement, and that it was done with good intention. But when the congregation assembled and learned that Mr. Weis had not said a word about this matter to me or to any of the elders of the congregation, an ugly tumult arose, which increased all the more because it was an arbitrary and irregular action and moreover because Mr. Weis administered holy baptism to seven children who were present, although he had not been called by this congregation.

At Schipbach and in Falckner Schwam he announced through the Lutheran minister. Mr. Henckel,[64] now deceased (who had slandered me publicly), that he would come there and preach, which he did without my knowledge or that of the Consistory.

2. He preached at branch station, called Goschenhoppen, about ten miles from Falckner Schwam; the last time, on October 12, 1727, he celebrated the Lord's Supper, without knowing the people, admitting among others two men from Falckner Schwam, who ought to have been taken to account because of their vicious lives.

3. He went into the house of a member of the Weit-

---

[63] In a series of advertisements, which appeared in the *American Weekly Mercury,* from February 3—April 9, 1730, Weiss offered to teach "Logick, Natural Philosophy, Metaphysicks, etc.," to all willing to learn. The place of teaching was to be "at the Widow Sproegel's," in Second Street. As Weiss was a single man in 1730, it is natural to infer that this was his lodging place. Widow Sproegel was the sister of Ludwig Christian Sproegel, who died in Philadelphia, June 5, 1727.

[64] This was the Rev. Anthony Jacob Henckel, who arrived in Pennsylvania as early as 1717. In 1718, he and his son-in-law, Valentine Geiger, bought land in New Hanover, from John Henry Sproegel, the agent of the Frankford Land Company. In 1728, Henckel fell from his horse, was carried into a neighboring house, where he dictated his will, August 17, 1728. Letters of administration were granted September 14, 1728. See the *Henkel Memorial,* edited by Rev. Dr. A. Stapleton, First Series, No. 1 (1910), pp. 8-13.

marsche congregation and baptized a child there without my knowledge.

4. At the above-mentioned Goschenhoppen, on the same 12th of October, and later on the 19th at Schipbach, that is in the very place to which I had been regularly called, and also on the 26th in Philadelphia, in these three public assemblies, he spoke of me by name and declared me to be an incompetent preacher, whom he did not regard as fit to administer the holy sacraments.

5. Without my knowledge he united in marriage two persons, whose banns I had published three times at their request, one day before the appointed time, that is on February 27, 1727.[65] N. B., The woman, according to evidence in my hands was already married to another man, wherefore I would have taken the necessary steps.

6. When he was in Schipbach on February 11, 1728, and preached there, he brought with him Peter and Michael Hillegass[66] and Michael Schmidt[67] from Philadelphia, who persuaded the people with the utmost efforts to give me up and subscribe an annual salary for Mr. Weis. This was done by many whose names are also found on my voluntary subscription list, whereby the small amount that had been signed for my labor (namely five pounds annually) was almost entirely taken away from me, and I have been compelled since then to serve this

[65] This date must be February 27, 1727-28.

[66] Michel Hillegas was born in 1696. The date of his arrival in Pennsylvania is not known. He was naturalized in April, 1749. He died October 30, 1749, and was buried in Christ's Church (Episcopal) Burial Ground, Fifth and Arch Streets, Philadelphia. His grave bears the following inscription: "In Memory of Michael Hillegas, who departed this life October 30, 1749, aged 53 years." Letters of administration were granted, November 7, 1749, to Margaretha Hillegas, his widow, and to Mich'l Hillegas, son of the deceased. Register of Wills office, Philadelphia, *Book of Administration*, Vol. F, p. 290. Their son, Michael Hillegas, Jr., born in Philadelphia, April 22, 1729, was the first treasurer of the United States, 1775-1789. See *Michael Hillegas and his Descendants*, by Emma St. Clair Whitney, Pottsville, 1891, pp. 7, 8.

[67] Rupp's *Thirty Thousand Names* has only one Michael Schmidt between 1727-1730. He signed the oath of allegiance September 30, 1727. He is, therefore, probably identical with the person here mentioned.

congregation without any salary.

7. On March 10, 1728, a week before his usual time, on my regular Sunday, which, according to report he had purposely so appointed beforehand, he came again with the above-mentioned two Hillegass brothers, Michael Schmidt, and several others, who here and there have been his adherents. Then there arose such a scandalous tumult before a large number of people who had gathered together of all kinds of sects and religions to hear something new from him, that it was a great disgrace to our Reformed religion. These men from Philadelphia, whom he had around him, absolutely denied my right to preach with all sorts of outrageous words against me, and forcibly expelled us from our usual meeting place (a private house, namely that of Jacob Reiff, because we had no church there). And when we tried to speak with Mr. Weis in a friendly way, one of the Hillegass brothers of Philadelphia cried out to Weis: He ought not to do us the honor of speaking with us, for we were all plainly a set of cattle. Thus I have been compelled hitherto to conduct my services here and there with my elders and the members who remained faithful to me and the Church Order, subscribed by them.

8. On June 22, 1729[68], he took possession of the church which had been erected at Schipbach, although my elders had started it, because Jacob Reiff and his brothers contend that the land belongs to them and that they have advanced most of the money, and as the highest creditors appropriated it. He preached in it till his departure, thus keeping up the harmful division in this congregation. Finally

9. Mr. Weis celebrated the Lord's Supper, without previous preparation, at a place named Oly,[69] (where the sect calling

---

[68] This date, June 22, 1729, marks the dedication of the first Reformed Church in Pennsylvania.

[69] This is the first reference to the Reformed people at Oley, for, of course, the visit of Weiss to Oley implies the presence of Reformed people there. For the early history of the Oley Reformed Church, see p. 73f. The first white settler at Oley is said to have been Johannes Keim, who settled in Oley in 1708 or 1709. In the fall of 1709, John LeDee and some others, "having obtained leave to look out for Lands above Perquicominck, chose a place called Oley, about 50 Miles distant from Philadelphia, and settled thereon, but without any agreement or survey." Isaac DeTurck, who is said to have been a

itself the "Newborn" originated) and baptized at the same time several children, among whom (as is reported) were also Indian children,[70] who, as unbelievers, go about like wild animals, without a knowledge of God or His Word. Of which he boasted with his own mouth before Mr. Peter Zenger,[71] sexton of the Reformed Church in New York, as the latter himself declared, etc., etc.

brother of Mrs. Keim, and who was originally a member of the Kocherthal colony, which settled at Newburgh, N. Y., in 1709, came to Oley in 1711. In April, 1712, John LeDee, with Isaac DeTurck and John Frederickfields (all Germans), "by further leave granted them, procured the surveyor (p. J. L. order) to lay out to John LeDee 300 acres, to Isaac DeTurck 300 acres, to John Frederickfields 500 acres, for which they agree to pay 10 pounds p. hundred." A patent for 300 acres was issued to Isaac DeTurck, on May 28, 1712. See *Pennsylvania Archives,* II Series, Vol. XIX, pp. 517, 524. The Yoder brothers, Johannes and Jost, Reformed people from Switzerland, soon joined the little group. Matthias Baumann, the founder of the "Newborn," must have settled at Oley before 1718, because a letter of Mrs. Maria DeTurck, dated May 14, 1718, clearly reveals his influence. In 1734, 34 settlers owned land in Oley township. (Communicated in part by Rev. John B. Stoudt).

[70] Mr. Weiss seems to have been much interested in Indians. While at Burnetsfield, New York, he wrote a book on Indians, in 1741, comprising 96 pages, in 8 vo., of which he sent a copy to the Classis of Amsterdam. Unfortunately it has not been preserved there, nor is any other copy known to be in existence. See *Eccl. Records of N. Y.,* Vol. IV, pp. 2760, 2778f.

[71] Peter Zenger is a man who became famous in the struggle for the freedom of the press in America. He was born in Germany in 1697. As a boy of 13 years he came with his mother, Johanna Zenger, a younger brother and a sister, to New York in the first large colony of Palatines, who reached New York in June, 1710, with Governor Robert Hunter. Peter Zenger was apprenticed to William Bradford, the printer, on October 26, 1711, for eight years. In 1726, Zenger started in the printing business for himself. In 1730, he became organist in the Dutch Reformed Church in New York (see *Eccl. Records of N. Y.,* Vol. IV, pp. 2398, 2495). In 1733, he started the *New York Weekly Journal.* In 1735 he was tried for publishing a false, scandalous and seditious libel. He was brilliantly defended by his counsel, Andrew Hamilton. His case became famous, because it established the freedom of the press in this country, and the principle that in cases of libel the jury are the judges both of the law and the facts. He died July 28, 1746. See *John Peter Zenger, His Press, His Trial and a Bibliography of Zenger Imprints,* by Livingstone Rutherford, New York, 1904.

ENCLOSURE F.

[COPY OF A LETTER OF MR. BOEHM AND THE CONSISTORY OF SKIPPACK TO THE REFORMED MINISTERS OF NEW YORK, NOVEMBER 5, 1730.]

Very Reverend, Very Learned and Devout Gentlemen.
Gualtherus Du Bois, Henricus Boel and Vincentius Antonides:—

In duty bound we herewith report submissively to your Reverences that whatever we reported to you under date May 17, 1730, concerning the harmful division, caused in our congregation by Mr. George Michael Weis and continued by him until his departure from here, contrary to all order and the solemn covenant made with him, all this has hitherto been kept up by Mr. Miller, who came to this country this fall. Coming into this country as an unordained minister and willing to be ordained by the Presbyterians in Philadelphia (as we hear), we have no other prospect before us but a continuous division in our poor congregation. Our hope for a good and God-pleasing harmony, established in brotherly love, which we expected to be able to report with rejoicing, after the departure of Mr. Weis, has been entirely taken away from us through the above-mentioned Mr. Miller. Hence we are unable to forecast what will become, in course of time, of our so sadly divided congregation. We are not able to help ourselves, because every one breaks in and makes use of the liberty in this country, to do whatever he desires. Yet we are heartily willing obediently to live in unchangeable subjection and submission to the Church Order, established among us by the Reverend Classis, and to their ecclesiastical ordinances which may in future be issued. Our condition grieves our hearts all the more, because our former members, with whom, in the beginning of our religious services, we had lived, as members of Christ's body, united in love in one congregation, have been led astray into such destructive separation and hatred by men who want to call themselves teachers of our true Church, yet despise the Reverend Classis as well as your Reverences.

We humbly pray your Reverences, as our highly esteemed patrons, who have exerted themselves with so much labor for our edification (which God may reward graciously), not to feel wearied because of us, innocent people, but graciously to represent us before the Reverend Classis with your influential intercessory letters, that we may learn how this disgraceful affair may be terminated.

We doubt not that the Reverend Classis, according to the wisdom which God vouchsafes to His faithful servants, will be able to find a way by which we, adopted by them as their children for Jesus' sake, may hereafter be preserved in peace, be relieved of our grief and again be built up into the Church of Christ.

Commending Your Reverences, our most esteemed Sirs, to the gracious protection of God, we remain,

Your most obedient and most devoted fellow-brethren in the Lord,

JOH. PH. BOEHM, pastor.

Schipbach, November 5, 1730.

Elders and Deacons
{
JOHN MEYER,[72]
CHRISTIAN NEUSCHWANGER,
LORENTZ BINGEMANN,
PETER STEPHAN.
}

[XIV. THE CLASSIS OF AMSTERDAM TO THE REV. JOHN PHILIP BOEHM, DECEMBER 5, 1730.[73]]

Reverend Sir and Beloved Brother:—

From your letter of January 29th, 1730, we learned that the letters of the Reverend Classis of Amsterdam, to the Consistory, as well as to yourself, were duly received, and that they tended to revive you, because the Classis takes such a hearty interest in the welfare of the churches in Pennsylvania.

We not only thank you for your kind wishes towards us, but we express our sympathy with you in your poverty. Especially do we do

---

[72] John Meyer (Mayer) was one of the seventy-five signers of a petition addressed by the people of the neighborhood of Falkner Swamp and Goshenhoppen to Governor Gordon, on April 29, 1728, asking for protection against invading Indians. See Rupp, *Thirty Thousand Names*, p. 470.

[73] A copy of the original is in the *Classical Letterbook*, Vol. XXIX, p. 65. It was first printed in the *Eccl. Records of N. Y.*, Vol. IV, p. 2521f.

this, because we are informed,—and to which we refer in no obscure terms to your Consistory,—that schisms and divisions still exist among you, and that many discontented ones—especially in the church of Schipbach—still stand aloof, dissatisfied with your service, and unwilling to acknowledge you as their pastor and teacher.

This grieves our very souls, because we well know that thereby the edification of the church will be greatly hindered, as well as the increase of the congregation. Therefore we have written in a fatherly and brotherly manner to the discontented in Schipbach, earnestly beseeching and admonishing them to reconciliation and unity. We hope God will so impress this upon their consciences that we may soon learn of the desired result; and that they have acknowledged yourself and ministry, and have received you as bishop of their souls.

Among other things we have proposed, as a means towards peace, that you and the Reverend Mr. Weis,—whom we find inclined to peace and promotion of our object,—exchange pulpits occasionally; you preaching in Philadelphia, and Mr. Weis in Schipbach. He might thus influence your congregation to peace. The congregation also, on observing your unity and friendship would be convinced of its necessity among themselves.

It is therefore our fatherly and brotherly advice and admonition to you to agree to this measure, and to arrange it with Rev. Mr. Weis—who has heartily agreed to it himself—and then to exercise all friendliness, gentleness and peaceableness, as becomes a servant of Jesus Christ, in order to quiet excited feelings, and to win the people by love. We have a well grounded hope that if you thus co-operate, with gentleness, that we shall see blessed results to our proposal and admonition. Thus not only the churches in the wilderness will be built up and edified, but you in your needy condition will be encouraged; for if peace is effected—for which we pray God—of course, some profit to your temporal condition will result. We have understood that there are some well-to-do members in the congregation at Schipbach, and that there is a building for divine service. Besides when peace is effected there will be more hope of assistance from other places. We shall be encouraged at hearing that our pious endeavors have been blessed. We hope for this from the All-Sufficient One, who has begun to plant His Church in that wilderness. May He cause His Church and congregations to increase to the honor of His adorable name, to the extension of the Kingdom of Jesus, and the salvation of many souls. May He strengthen you with His spirit, make your ministry fruitful, and unite your minds in the fear of His name and command His blessing upon all that is yours. With this wish, we remain, etc.,

J. BAKKER,
Dep. Cl. ad. res exteras.

P. S. We request that we may be informed in due time of the result of our counsel of peace; and that you will please to maintain the agreeable correspondence with the Reverend Classis of Amsterdam.

[XV THE CLASSIS OF AMSTERDAM TO THE OVERSEERS OF THE THREE GERMAN CHURCHES IN PENNSYLVANIA, DECEMBER 5, 1730.[74]]

To the Overseers of the three Congregations of Falckner Schwam, Schipbach and Weitmarsh.

DEAR BRETHREN:—

It appears to us from your communication of January 29, 1730, that the letters of the Reverend Classis came to your hands, and gave you joy; especially the last, concerning the ordination of Rev. Mr. Boehm, which we understand has taken place; and that some discontented ones were thereupon satisfied, and have recognized Rev. Mr. Boehm as their lawful pastor.

But, meanwhile, we are not ignorant of the fact that schisms and contentions still exist. This distresses us, because the churches are thereby threatened with great danger, and the planting and upbuilding of the churches are thereby greatly hindered.

Men and women, we admonish you to brotherly unanimity, and to the use of every gentle measure with the discontented, in order to secure mutual peace; that you co-operate with your pastors to destroy all alienation and discord, and the evils resulting therefrom; and that you sacredly maintain the Church Order which you have adopted; that the breach may be healed and the congregation be edified.

To this end, we have written not only to Rev. Mr. Boehm, but also to the discontented in Schipbach. Through this, we expect, with God's blessing, this desirable result. Thus, when peace is restored among the brethren, we believe that Rev. Mr. Boehm will be not a little strengthened, in his poverty, and animated anew; and that the church in Schipbach will rejoice in the exercise of public worship.

We will never withdraw ourselves, but will gladly come to the aid of your churches, not only with fraternal and fatherly counsel, but as far as possible also with deeds. Rev. Mr. Weis has already proof of this; for he has been provided with certain charitable gifts for the building of a church in Philadelphia.

The greatest inducements for continuing such charities towards you are, unanimity among yourselves, peaceableness, love for the church order and for the extension of the Savior's Kingdom among you. May God give you the spirit of charity.

Worthy Sirs and Beloved Brethren, etc.,

J. BAKKER,
Dep. Cl. ad res exteras.

Amsterdam,
December 5, 1730.

[74] A copy of the original letter is in the *Classical Letterbook*, Vol. XXIX, p. 64; first printed in *Eccl. Records of N. Y.*, Vol. IV, p. 2523f.

[XVI. THE CLASSIS OF AMSTERDAM TO THE CHURCH OF SKIPPACK, DECEMBER 5, 1730.[75]]

To the Friends and Elders of the Church of Schipbach.
MUCH BELOVED BRETHREN :—

Your letter of May 10, 1730, we have not only received, but carefully considered. We have learned therefrom your objections against the appointment and ordination of the Rev. Mr. Boehm as lawful minister and pastor in Pennsylvania; and especially that you would not like to accept and acknowledge him as a shepherd of Jesus Christ in the church at Schipbach, under pretext that he has succeeded in securing his ordination and confirmation, as regular shepherd and teacher, with the knowledge of only a few; and without the knowledge, and even in opposition to a majority of the church at Schipbach.

It grieves us brethren, to the soul, to see so injurious a schism and such discord in a newly organized church, whereby its growth must be greatly hindered, if not, except for proper interposition, entirely destroyed. It goes to our hearts. Oh! that you would take to heart the welfare of God's Church. Love for Zion and for the peace of the brethren, moves us to communicate to you our fatherly and brotherly admonitions. Receive then, brethren, we beseech you, in God's name and with a peace-loving heart, what we now send you, that all may tend to the restoration and confirmation of peace, to the edification of the church and to the salvation of many souls.

From the beginning, we declare that nothing rejoiced us more than the prospect of a possibility of peace. Were it within our power we would procure you a pastor and teacher who would be agreeable and acceptable to all, and who would build you up in doctrine and walk of life. But you know as well as ourselves, that this is beyond our ability; since you providentially dwell in a land where the means of grace—the dispensers of God's mysteries, are still unplentiful. In such places, therefore, one must be content with such means as God, in His good pleasure, grants in answer to prayer.

The Reverend Classis having taken into earnest consideration, and in the fear of the Lord, your remonstrance, and the earnest requests made by your delegates, is of the opinion:

That the Rev. Mr. Boehm ought to be recognized as the lawful shepherd and teacher in Pennsylvania, because by order of Classis, (upon the representation of the Rev. Mr. Boehm and certain ones in the churches of Pennsylvania, who earnestly desired it) he was confirmed and properly ordained thereto by the ministers in New York, who were requested to do this, if he submitted to the conditions prescribed to him by this Classis; and also, because, in connection therewith, reconciliation was effected between Rev. Messrs. Weis and

---

[75] A copy of the original is in the *Letterbook of the Classis,* Vol. XXIX, p. 61; first printed in *Eccl. Records of N. Y.,* Vol. IV, pp. 2525-2528.

Boehm, and each was allotted to a separate church by mutual agreement.

Beloved Brethren, your dissatisfaction with this act, and your representation that the request of Mr. Boehm and a few others took place without your knowledge, and that the ordination does not meet with your approval, cannot induce Classis to make null the solemn ordination of Rev. Mr. Boehm. The Classis is of opinion, therefore, that this ordination must stand. We hope this will not displease you, for how could so solemn an act be made void without desecration of God's name? Although the request for, and the ordination itself, took place without your knowledge, yet it did take place with the knowledge, and at the request, of some in the Church and in the Consistory. Inasmuch as the Reverend Classis recognizes Mr. Boehm as a lawfully ordained pastor, it is our earnest request that you not only be reconciled in a fraternal and Christian manner with Rev. Mr. Boehm, but that you accept and recognize him as your shepherd and the overseer of your church; that you lovingly listen to his teachings and Christian admonitions; that you receive from him the sacred seals of the covenant, maintaining and cherishing the communion of saints; that you may be the better built up in faith and in the hope of salvation.

If any among you think that it was a great misdeed that they were overlooked, and therefore refuse to submit themselves to peaceful counsels, then let the peaceably disposed labor with these brethren with all gentleness, to convince them; and to this end, the actual ordination which took place in New York will be a powerful argument.

And since a sacred reconciliation was effected between Rev. Messrs. Weis and Boehm, so that they sometimes now, in a spirit of fraternal unity, exchange pulpits; therefore let the Rev. Mr. Weis at such times, urge the discontented to peace, according to his own peaceable disposition, and promise thus to act as opportunity may offer. By such exchange and efforts, the churches will be impressed by the unity of faith.

Dear brethren, we pray you to consider that love is the basis of our admonition; that charity is the principal duty and adornment of the Christian; that love and unity among the brethren constitute the great strength of the Church of God, by which she it built up and established; that it ever behooves Christian brethren to forgive any wrong that has been done. We say, therefore, with Paul, "Put on, therefore, as the elect of God, holy and beloved, bowels of mercy, kindness, humbleness of mind, meekness, long-suffering; forbearing one another and forgiving one another, if any man have a quarrel against any; even as Christ forgave you, so also do ye. And above all things, put on charity, which is the bond of perfectness; and let the peace of God rule in your hearts; to the which also ye are called, in one body."

Please also to remember that you live in a country where the church has but a feeble beginning, where it has been but just planted, where, although the harvest is great, the laborers are few. It is only by God's grace that the light of the Gospel beams upon you at all, and that you have any opportunities to hear the truth. Do not show that you have received this grace of God in vain. Let it be seen that your hearts are filled with love for Gospel truth, that you seek the increase of God's Church, the extension of the Gospel, the promotion of the knowledge of the doctrine of truth, and the salvation of your souls. This will appear, if you use the means which God gives you, although they be not exactly according to your liking. Is it not better to hear the Word of God from the mouth of a minister, even though he be despised by some; even though he had been guilty of some error, rather than miss the ministration of the Word altogether? If you refuse to accept Rev. Mr. Boehm, how shall the Church be edified by the public declaration of God's Word, when the number of ministers in those regions is so small? Convince us, therefore, brethren, by peaceful conduct that you truly hunger and thirst after righteousness.

We pray you to consider that through disaffection the pious are grieved, the godless rejoice, and God's name is blasphemed among the unbelieving. But we beseech you, brethren, to labor with us to prevent this, and to this end listen to our brotherly admonitions. We expect this, with God's gracious blessing, because you count it a favor that the Reverend Classis takes to heart your affairs, and the condition of the churches in Pennsylvania. You also express your gratitude for this, and especially because you praise the Classis for seeking to advance the best interests of the Church. The greatest proof to us of this, your gratitude, as declared, will be your acceptance of this Christian counsel of the Reverend Classis. Thus will the breach be restored, offences avoided, the piety and edification of the churches promoted.

We add, finally, that you may learn from Rev. Mr. Weis and your delegate, how we are seeking to edify and quicken the churches in Pennsylvania, not only with loving counsels but also with loving gifts. In conclusion, we hope and pray that the God of love and peace may bind you together in love and peace and reverence for His name. May He cause the churches in Pennsylvania, as well as in the Netherlands to flourish, and may He command His divine blessing on you all.

In hope that we may be revived by an answer from you, announcing peace, we remain,

Worthy Sirs and Beloved Brethren, etc.

J. BAKKER,
Dep. Cl. ad res exteras.

Amsterdam,
December 5, 1730.

[XVII. THE CLASSIS OF AMSTERDAM TO THE MINISTERS OF NEW YORK, DECEMBER, 1730.[76]]

Reverend, Godly and Very Learned Gentlemen, Much Beloved Brethren in Christ:—

Your esteemed letter of April 21, 1730, enclosing also letters from Rev. Boehm and his Consistory, together with writings to Rev. Boehm, came duly to hand. We learned therefrom not only that our letters of December 1, 1728, and of June 20, 1729, were received by you, and that the letters enclosed were sent to Rev. Boehm and the brethren in Pennsylvania by your care; but also, to our great joy, that the ordination of Rev. Boehm had taken place, and that a reconciliation had been effected between him and Weis. We thank the good God that it pleased Him to bring this business to such a desirable end, by influencing their minds to peace, and by so blessing our endeavors.

We cannot neglect to commend your efforts in this matter, and to express our satisfaction therewith. The advice and direction of Classis were completely, and very exactly, executed by you, and with the greatest prudence and wisdom. We consider ourselves under great obligations to you for your charity and labor, as well as for your great care against congregationalism. This, you rightly judge, produces very injurious results. We pray God to remember your labor of love, and to crown you with his richest blessing, to the welfare and establishment of Zion.

We are not surprised, Worthy Brethren, that you are not pleased with so much troublesome correspondence, and that for the reasons given, you would gladly be excused. We well understand that repeated requests, especially of parties in dispute, are costly and difficult, giving you much perplexity, and frequently leaving dissatisfaction in those who are not suited. But we are still more rejoiced, and we acknowledge it with gratitude, that you have allowed yourselves to be convinced, notwithstanding the difficulties, as to the duty to continue said correspondence, and that thereby you console yourselves for the hard labor. Your conclusion gives us much satisfaction, Reverend Sirs, and we earnestly request you to persevere therein. We think it, therefore, unnecessary, to advance any new reasons, for we are convinced by your communication that you will not shirk the duty. We are sure you appreciate, as well as ourselves, the necessity and advantage therefrom to the Church of God. For whither could perplexed people and those in need of counsel, turn in a land where ministers of experience are few. How could schisms, with the offenses and disputes resulting therefrom, be avoided, except by the aid of men who have their senses exercised in the Word of God, and

---

[76] A copy of the original is in the *Letterbook of Classis,* Vol. XXIX, p. 58; first printed in *Eccl. Records of N. Y.,* Vol. IV, pp. 2528-2532.

in the government of the Church? We trust that God may prevent your ever sorrowing that you have taken this task upon yourselves. May He pour out upon you the spirit of wisdom. May He make you strong and of good courage, always abounding in the work of the Lord. May your counsels ever be successful, that the peace and prosperity of the Church may continue under your hands, according to the good pleasure of the Lord.

But agreeable as is your conduct, as well as the reconciliation affected between the Rev. Messrs. Weis and Boehm, we are grieved at the complaints of those who yet remain dissatisfied, and refuse to acknowledge Rev. Boehm as a lawful minister. They have written to us concerning this, seeking to invalidate the ordination that has been performed, on the pretence that all was done without their knowledge, and even in spite of them.

So far, however, is the Classis from agreeing to any such thing, that it ratifies that ordination as having been legally done, and declares your action right. The dissatisfied have also been particularly informed, with admonitions added, and earnest prayers, to recognize Rev. Boehm as their lawful pastor and teacher, and to confirm and approve the compact entered into by Revs. Weis and Boehm. We trust that our counsel of love, re-enforced by yours as speedily as possible, may have, under God's blessing, the desired result. We have also most kindly admonished Rev. Boehm and his adherents, to co-operate most gently, in order to win the dissatisfied ones by love.

Rev. Weis, with a delegate [Reiff], from the church of Schipbach, has been here to collect means to build a church in Philadelphia. This has enabled us to become well acquainted with him and to converse with him particularly about the dispute yet remaining. We testify to his praise that we found him gentle, modest and inclined to peace. He and his companion have faithfully promised their earnest co-operation, to seek to induce the dissatisfied to accept the resolution of Classis, and Rev. Boehm, as their lawful pastor. We have also proposed that Revs. Weis and Boehm should exchange pulpits, that the former might the better be enabled to quiet excited feelings; and the congregations, being convinced of the friendship of the pastors, might be moved to similar unanimity. Rev. Weis having consented to this, we have proposed the same to the Rev. Boehm.

We have favored the object of Rev. Weis as far as we could. His undertaking has been by no means fruitless. He has not only received gifts from the Synod of North Holland, but will receive them from that of South Holland, which has adopted the church of Philadelphia as recommended. The Consistory and Diaconate of Amsterdam have also done their part. He has even received permission from the Burgomasters of Amsterdam, to collect funds in the city at large. We have certainly shown ourselves willing to help the churches of Pennsylvania with both counsels and deeds. We trust this will be a blessed means, among other things, to convince the churches of Pennsylvania of our enthusiasm in their behalf, and move them to peace and concord. We will be very happy, as well as heartily thankful, to understand that all breaches are healed, and the churches united.

May the King of Zion make the church of your locality and the neighboring regions, as well as ours, to blossom as the rose. May He bestow upon her the glory of Lebanon, and the beauty of Carmel and Sharon. May He enable us to behold the beauty of the Lord and the glory of our God. May the All-Sufficient One bestow upon you abundantly an overflowing measure of His Spirit, and spare you long as blessed instruments in His hands to build up Zion's fallen walls, and to strengthen them. May He also crown your families, as well as your churches, with His gracious blessing, and at last give you the reward belonging to the faithful.

Such are our sincere wishes, as we subscribe ourselves. with esteem,
  The Classis of Amsterdam,
   In the name of all,
          Peter Elzevir,
    Ecc. Amst. Dep. ad res exteras, h. t. Praeses.
          John Vischer,
    Ecc. Amst. Dep. ad res exteras, h. t. Scriba.

Amsterdam,
 December, 1730.

P. S. Worthy Sirs:—Classis has resolved, in token of their appreciation of the trouble taken in the maintenance of our wholesome correspondence, and to enable you to have more light on cases as they occur, to send you a copy of the Minutes of the Synod of North Holland. These are for your personal use, and that of your churches in America, and others with whom you correspond. If this is not disagreeable to you, we will continue to do the same.

[XVIII. THE CLASSIS OF AMSTERDAM TO THE REV. MR. BOEHM, OCTOBER 19, 1731.[77]]

To the Rev. Mr. Boehm in Pennsylvania.
 Reverend Sir and Brother:—
 Your letter, together with those two little books sent to us, have been considered in Classis. You complain of Rev. Mr. Weis. We are sorry that discord and dispute have arisen, but we trust that Rev. Mr. Weis, who had not yet returned when you wrote that letter, but arrived afterwards, has conducted himself according to the instructions given him by the Reverend Classis, and that the discord and disputes have turned into mutual peace and love. For we do pray and ad-

---

[77] A copy of the original is in the *Letterbook of Classis*, Vol. XXIX, p. 88.

monish you, even as we also write to Rev. Mr. Weis, that you pursue peace and put on charity, which is the bond of perfectness and that you unitedly seek to advance the work of the Lord, with all unanimity, watchfulness and fidelity.

We take it for granted that the Rev. Mr. Weis has already arrived in Pennsylvania. The Classis expects from each of you a letter to inform us further of the condition of affairs. Then, having learned everything from each of you, we may deliberate accordingly, even as matters shall then appear to us. Meanwhile we do not conceal from you, that it seems strange that we have not yet received a single letter from Rev. Mr. Weis since his departure hence. We have no report yet whether he has arrived in Pennsylvania or not, and has taken over the funds which he received here. The Reverend Classis requests that you will inform us concerning this at the earliest opportunity.

As regards those two German books, which were sent to us with your letter, they were found to be so foolish as to deserve no consideration whatever. We do not think they will make any impression upon men of intelligence and judgment, and therefore we feel sure that the positions taken therein will crumble and disappear very soon, of their own accord.

But of more importance is the proposition which you make regarding the congregations in Canastoka and elsewhere, which would gladly subject themselves under the Classis of Amsterdam and request that the Reverend Classis empower you to visit these churches, etc., and that we send information thereof to those churches. This matter does not appear a bad one to Classis, and it will gladly contribute anything, which may be conducive to the welfare and edification of those congregations. But the Classis expects that those congregations will first appear themselves and make such a proposition, so that their object and request may be clearly manifest. Meantime the Classis thinks that you should consult about this matter further with Rev. Mr. Weis, and we request that you both then send us further information thereof, whereby these matters may be further decided.

This is what we have to write for the present. Wishing that the God of all grace grant you peace, charity and every desired blessing in the work of the ministry, and that the Lord may make it fruitful to the ingathering and upbuilding of many souls and to the extension of the Kingdom of Jesus, we remain, etc.,

J. BAKKER,
Dep. Cl. ad res exteras.

[XIX. THE SYNODICAL DEPUTIES TO THE REV. JOHN PHILIP BOEHM, DECEMBER 1, 1731.[78]]

Reverend, Pious and Much Beloved Brother in Christ, Philippus Boehm.
Dear Sir:—

The two Christian Synods of South Holland and North Holland have charged us, their Deputies, to inquire carefully into the state of the churches in Pennsylvania, in order that they might have information concerning all that might tend towards the growth of the vineyard of Christ and the upbuilding of the congregations among the High German churches there. We have received requests from Do. Weitsius [Weiss] and the elder Ryff for some charitable gifts for the building of some churches there and that we might give counsel for the establishment of a well ordered church organization.

We also have received a letter from Philadelphia and Schibbach, dated May 10, 1730, in which the writers, as elders and members of the congregation of Philadelphia and Schibbach, make complaints regarding your Reverence, that you have not studied, that you know no principles of theology and have not been lawfully ordained as minister. Further than that we have no accurate report, neither about the condition of the church, the church services, the number of the members, nor of the means at hand for the building of churches, nor of the support given to ministers and schoolmasters, nor of many other necessary things. We have written a lengthy letter to the Reverend Consistory of Philadelphia, which we ask you also to read and that you will give us a report beside the one they will be pleased to send us. Especially that your Reverence will defend yourself and make answer to the above mentioned accusations. We are also told that you have already left the province of Pennsylvania. But, if this letter will reach you, be pleased to write us as speedily as possible and report to us all that you consider necessary to convey a knowledge of the land and Church of Pennsylvania to our Christian Synods, also all that may serve to acquaint us truthfully with your affairs and the quarrel with Do. Weitsius. We advise and request your Reverence to seek peace with all men, especially with those who are sharers of the same precious faith.

Wishing further that the God of truth and peace will lead your Reverence into all truth and will guide you more and more by His Spirit and make you a zealous instrument in the work of the ministry, to the perfecting of the saints and to the edification of the body of Jesus Christ, we remain with all love in the Lord Jesus,

Your Reverence's
Ever Ready and Well-wishing
Friends and Brethren,
The Deputies of the Synods of South and
North Holland,
In the name and by order of all signed

Gouda, the 1st of   JACOBUS VAN OSTADE,[79]
December, 1731.   *Synodi Zuid Holl. Deputatus.*

[78] A copy of the original is in the archives at The Hague, 74, I, 3.

P. S. Please send your letter to Amsterdam, and address it to the Rev. Mr. Johannes Visscher, Minister of the Word of God at Amsterdam.

[XX. THE REFORMED CHURCH OF PHILADELPHIA TO MR. BOEHM, APRIL 20, 1734.[80]]

PHILADA., April 20, 1734.

Much Esteemed Mr. Boehm:—

We, the undersigned German Reformed co-religionists, find ourselves obliged, in the present state of our congregational and church affairs, to submit our need and our affairs to you as a member and minister of the Reformed Church, asking you for your good counsel and praying you to render us actual help.

It is not unknown to Mr. Boehm that four years ago [1730] the Rev. Mr. Weiss and Jacob Reiff, at some expense to our congregation, went from here to Holland and Germany, in order to collect there towards the building of some churches in this wilderness, since we, poor German inhabitants, are ourselves unable to do this. As a result some charitable gifts were collected, as Do. Boehm knows and himself received letters from Holland concerning it.[81] At the return of the said Rev. Mr. Weiss, who came back before Jacob Reiff, we learned from him that he had received 2140 florins, Dutch currency, from the kind Classes of Holland, for which he had given receipt and that they had moreover promised that another considerable sum should follow, after these 2140 florins had first been well spent for the intended purpose. But he, Mr. Weiss, had given said sum of 2140 fl. to the said J. Reiff.

At his departure from here[82] Mr. Weiss left a written statement,

[79] As Rev. Jacobus van Ostade was the first of the Synodical Deputies to correspond with the Reformed Churches of Pennsylvania, he deserves a brief notice. He was born at Haarlem, March 8, 1677, son of Hendrick van Ostade, a merchant. In 1693, he entered the University of Utrecht; became pastor at Wiermgerwaard in 1700; at Ilpendam, in 1707; at Parmerend in 1708, and at Gouda in 1716. While pastor there he began the correspondence with Pennsylvania in 1731. He died at Gouda July 18, 1745. He wrote a number of theological books. See *Biographisch Woordenboek der Nederlanden*, 14th Part, Haarlem, 1867.

[80] A copy of the original was sent by Boehm to the Synods. It is preserved in the archives at The Hague, 74, I, 26.

[81] The letters sent to Boehm from Holland were: (1) a letter of the Classical Deputy, J. Bakker, dated October 19, 1731; (2) a letter of the Synodical Deputy, Jacobus Van Ostade, dated December 1, 1731. For these letters, see above, pp. 228-230.

[82] Weiss must have left Philadelphia in September, 1731, for on September 22, 1731, a letter of recommendation was given him by the

which mentioned this sum. But when two years ago [1732] said Jacob Reiff also returned,[83] he denied having received such a sum and acknowledged to have received not more than 750 fl., appealing for the truth of it to the presence of Do. Weiss. Whereupon he was cited before Court[84] by the elders and was compelled to give bond. Meanwhile Rev. Mr. Weiss had been requested both by letter and by messenger to appear [before Court] in this matter. But he was never willing to come. Thus the case is still unsettled, for neither Jacob Reiff will give an account of his commission, nor will the elders account to the congregation for the alms and for the merchandise which they received from Reiff out of the church-money, (which they denied at first under oath) and thus clear themselves.

We also know that the Hollanders have written twice[85] and demanded to know how the collected money had been used, etc., yet we have never seen anything of the one nor of the other letter, and are therefore unable to say anything, except that we regret having been deceived in this matter.

Nevertheless, it seems to us unpardonable, both towards the Hollanders, because of their charitable gifts, as well as towards our descendants, that the case should rest here and that those who have the money now should be allowed to retain it for their own profit, and that the congregation, to which it had been given to be used for the glory of God, should be deprived of it. Therefore we desire to ask Mr. Boehm what he thinks of the affair and whether it would be advisable to report the case to the Reformed Classis of New York,[86] as

elders at Philadelphia, in which it is stated that Weiss had resolved to leave Philadelphia and go to Albany, N. Y. A copy of this letter was entered by Weiss into the church record at Catskill, N. Y., where he became pastor in February, 1732.

[83] Reiff returned in the summer of 1732, for in June, 1732, he was at Cowes, England. See *Reformed Quarterly Review*, 1893, Vol. XL, pp. 58-66, especially p. 65.

[84] For the suit of the Philadelphia Elders against Reiff before the Court of Chancery, see p. 43f.

[85] Three letters from the authorities in Holland to the Philadelphia congregation are on file: (1) Letter of the Synodical Deputy, J. van Ostade, dated December 1, 1731; (2) letter of Deputy van Ostade, dated July 2, 1732; (3) letter of Deputy van Ostade, dated January 11, 1733.

[86] There was, in 1734, no Reformed Classis of New York. The organization of the Reformed churches of New York, New Jersey and Pennsylvania was not discussed till April, 1738. Then the draft of a constitution was prepared, but the actual organization of the Dutch Reformed Coetus did not take place till September 8-10, 1747, at New York, see *Acts and Proceedings of the General Synod of the Reformed Protestant Dutch Church in North America*, Vol. I, New York, 1859, pp. ix-xiii.

to our Reformed associates in the faith, either to compel Mr. Weiss, by virtue of their authority, to come to this place, since the whole case depends upon him, or to manifest their Christian love to us by writing in our behalf to the Classes and Synods of Holland, to find out to whom and how much money they really paid, so that it may be reported to the courts here and that at the same time they [the courts] may be petitioned to require the restitution of the money from the party found guilty. To this end we hereby kindly and duly request you to assist us with a good recommendation at New York; for we have heard that you are under that Classis and under the protection of the Hollanders, to whom we would likewise willingly submit ourselves. Indeed, it does not seem to us contrary to propriety, that, since we ask help and assistance from the Hollanders as our fellow-believers, we should also stand under their Church Order and protection. Our three or four elders,[87] together with Jacob Reiff, who are opposed to this, partly because of bitter hatred of you personally, partly because of other reasons, do not support us in this matter, but we want to be free and independent of them, otherwise we desire to live in peace.

We hope also that the Hollanders will not take it amiss, that we desire such a statement and explanation, because we are all plain tradesmen and working people, who do not understand ecclesiastical affairs, but nevertheless desire a better condition of the churches in this country and city. Wherefore we also desire, after we have first secured a church building, that in course of time we may also be supplied with an efficient minister. The qualities which our present minister Mr. R. [Rieger] possesses are not able to accomplish anything with such plain people as are in this country, as may be well known to Mr. Boehm.

In the meantime we live in the certain hope that you will fraternally comply with our petition, for which we feel, according to our Christian duty, to be under great obligation to you.

We are herewith Yours, etc.,

Bernhard Sigmundt
Stephan Greiff
Joh. Ullrich Gaull
Joh. Jörg Baltz
Johannes Jork X
Hans Jörg Kremer
Lorentz Kuntz
Johannes Scherer
Jacob Uttre
Abraham Kintzing
Wendel Brechbiel

Joh. Jacob Orner
Heinrich Schösler
Daniel Steinmetz
Frantz Stiettelfreindt
Reichert Vetter
Ullrich Oellen
Andreas Klemmer
Joh. Jörg Senck
Rutolf Wiellecken
Joh. Jacob Neuzehöltzer
Johann Adam Klamber

[87] The lawfully elected elders in 1733, were, according to the sworn statement of Reiff: Peter Licolie, Johann Wilhelm Röhrig, Hendrik Weller and Georg Peter Hillegas, see *Reformed Quarterly Review*, Vol. XL (1893), p. 60.

Johann Michel Dill
Conrat Sattler
Johann Caspar Ullrich
Jacob Zetel
Zacharias Schuckert
Elias Strecker
Johannes Schmiet
Gerhard Cafferoth X
Hans Jörg Strohhauer
Peter Heut XX

Johann Michel Feder
Jacob Müller
Lorentz Hartmann
Rudolf Messerschmidt
Johann Engelbert Lock
Valentin Beyer
Joh. Niclas Ewig
Jacob Walter
Caspar Heyderich
Hans Adam Ribertus.[88]

That the above copy corresponds verbatim with the original, which is in my hands, I hereby testify with my signature.

JOHANN PHILIPS BOEHM.

[XXI. MR. BOEHM AND THE PHILADELPHIA CONSISTORY TO DEPUTY VELINGIUS, OCTOBER 28, 1734.[89]]

Right and Very Reverend, Pious and Very Learned Sir:—
Your pious letter of December 2, 1733,[90] to the Reverend Mr. J. Bartholomew Rieger and other members of the Con-

[88] The majority of these forty-two members arrived between 1727-1733. The time of their arrival, according to Rupp's *Thirty Thousand Names*, was as follows: Rudolf Wiellecken, September 21, 1727; Reichert Vetter (Fetter), August 19, 1729; Bernhard Sigmund, Johannes Scherer, August 29, 1730, in the same ship with Peter Müller, the later monk at Ephrata; Rudolf Messerschmid, September 5, 1730; Michael Feder, Johann Engelbert Lock (Lack), September 11, 1731; Wendel Brechbill, Joh. Georg Kremer, August 11, 1732; Valentine Beyer, Johann Georg Baltz, Nicolaus Ewig, Lorentz Hartman, Lorentz Kuntz, Johann Jacob Neuzehöltzer (Neihältzer), Conrad Sattler, Johannes Schmit, September 19, 1732. These eight persons, who arrived with others on the ship "Johnson," were evidently another Reformed colony; Jacob Walter, September 26, 1732; Joh. Georg Senck, October 11, 1732; Hans Georg Strohhauer, August 17, 1733; Joh. Ulrich Gaul, August 27, 1733; Joh. Michael Dill, September 29, 1733. Besides, Abraham Kintzing was naturalized in 1730; Johann Casper Ulrich, in 1734.

[89] A Dutch translation of this letter is preserved at The Hague, 74, I, 17.

[90] A letter of Deputy Velingius to Mr. Rieger, dated December 28, 1733 (no doubt identical with the one referred to here), is on file in the archives at The Hague, 74, I, 12.

sistory of the German Reformed Congregation at Philadelphia in Pennsylvania, only reached us on October 12, 1734. We learned from it that the letter, written in this place on March 4, 1733, and signed by Mr. John Barthol. Rieger and two other members of the Consistory,[91] was laid before the Christian Synods of North and South Holland in the months of July and August, 1733, together with another letter from Canastocka, dated February 13, 1733.[92]

In the first place we must give you most obediently an insight into the condition into which we have gotten since that time. The persons who represented us at that time were mostly self-made elders, irresponsible, and in the whole affair, as the congregation has clearly discovered, sought nothing else than together with Jacob Reiff, to lay their hands on the [collected] money, which is sufficiently evident at present. For Jacob Reiff had bought merchandise abroad with the money collected [in Holland], which goods, (for what reasons we know not) were seized and held in England,[93] and to this day not a penny has been handed over by Jacob Reiff, which greatly distressed these people. Having at a certain time a suspicion that Reiff intended to leave the country, they went and had him arrested for the collected money, without having from anybody obtained proper authority for it, neither knowing precisely the amount of the collected funds, nor how much he had received. The result was a quarrel and turmoil, by which the congregation made a wonderful discovery, for as they gathered one by one and perhaps 30 men were assembled, then Reiff said plainly before us all: "Doctor Diemer, Peter and Michael Hillegass are church-robbers, they steal the bread out of the mouths of the Reformed people in Philadelphia, of their

[91] This letter is also preserved at The Hague, 74, I, 15.

[92] The essential parts of this important letter of John Conrad Tempelman are printed above, pp. 62-64.

[93] In his answer to the Court of Chancery, Mr. Reiff explained that, "the master of the ship being unwilling to advance any money for the duty or customs of the goods so shipped for the use of the said congregation as aforesaid, he left them in the custody of the Collector of his Majesty's Customs at Cowes, on the Isle of Wight (where the said ship went to clear) as this defendant is informed of Mr. John Hope, a merchant there." *See Reformed Quarterly Review*, Vol. XL (1893), pp. 60-66.

children and children's children. I admit that I am a church-thief [kerkendief], but they are church-thieves as well as I. If they had not written to me, I would not have done it". Then he showed a letter which they had sent to him to Holland, which, after taking the authority from Do. Weiss (which he had received from the whole congregation) and transferring it to Jacob Reiff, read as follows: "Jacob Reiff shall take the collected money, buy merchandise with it and ship it to them. For his profits he is to have six per cent. and on his return to this country the money which he spent shall be refunded to him". This letter, which certainly ten of us read, was signed by seven men (who had usurped the eldership) with their own hands. They wrote further in their letter to Reiff, that he should do so at their risk and whatever might come of it they would guarantee him against loss with all their possessions, of which, beside them not a member of the whole congregation knew anything. From this no other conclusion can be drawn but that they did it merely for their own profit. Reiff then claimed that, according to their instructions, he had sent the goods over to them, the receipt of which they roundly deny. Through this quarrel no other prospect appeared to be in sight than the entire dissolution of the congregation, as already everything was on the point of disbanding.

Whereupon the congregation met again and came to the inevitable resolution to depose these men for these and other, sufficiently grave causes and to elect others, by a majority of votes, who would faithfully serve the congregation and remain united. This action was all the more legitimate, inasmuch as John Jacob Diemer, the physician,[94] never was an elder and

[94] John Jacob Diemer, of the city of Philadelphia, "Practitioner in Physick and Surgery," bought on March 16, 1733, a plantation containing 161 acres in Providence, from Richard Jones, of Providence, and Martha, his wife, for £153, of lawful money. The same parties bought, on the same date, a certain piece of land in Providence, containing 67 acres for £64. He was naturalized in 1734, see *Pa. Archives*, 2nd Series, Vol. VII, p. 116. On January, 1747, John Diemer was captain of one of the four companies raised in the province of Pennsylvania; see *Pennsylvania Archives*, First Series, Vol. I, pp. 724, 738. The Pennsylvania companies and their captains are enumerated in a letter of Samuel Perry, dated October 26, 1747. See *Colonial Records*, Vol. V, p. 134f. Dr. Diemer died in the beginning of November, 1757.

never could have been recognized as such on account of his openly shameful, scandalous and dishonorable manner of life, and even to day is immersed in a notoriously godless life. He was also the leader of the others by means of his artful and deceitful pen. Peter Hillegass too was never recognized as an elder by the people, but elevated himself to that office and acted with them, so that they belonged to the same class as Jacob Reiff, who also allowed himself to be greeted as elder in Holland and yet had never been recognized as such by these congregations. They then elected us as elders and deacons of the church, in the presence of Mr. John Barth. Rieger, who at that time served this congregation as minister, as the enclosed letter of April 2, 1734,[95] shows.

When Mr. Rieger had left this congregation, thinking perhaps that because of his absence we would not know what to do and we would have to unite again with the deposed persons, with whom he was in harmony, which the congregation, however, regarded as extremely harmful because of the evident deception which they had practiced,—then another plan was thought of, and they resolved unanimously (in order to prevent the entire ruin of the congregation) humbly to ask aid and assistance of Mr. John Philip Boehm, minister at Falkner Schwam, Schip Bach and Weitmarge, who is a lawfully ordained minister, (regarding which one may refer to the Acts of the Classis of Amsterdam concerning Pennsylvania). This was done immediately by means of a letter, dated April 20, 1734,[96] signed by forty-two persons and conveyed to him by two of our members.

Although by reason of the great and difficult labors of his ministry, his Reverence had sufficient reasons to excuse himself, nevertheless he took it to heart and resolved, after having con-

---

On November 17, 1757, his wife, Rachel Diemer, requested that her son, James, might be admitted to administer the estate of her husband. Letters of administration were granted to James Diemer, September 17, 1757 (see *Book of Administration,* Vol. G, p. 104). The estate of Dr. Diemer was divided April 15, 1760, between his widow and four children. (Taken in part from the *Dotterer Mss.,* in the Historical Society of Pennsylvania.)

[95] Given as a postscript to this letter, see p. 249.
[96] Printed above, pp. 231-234.

sidered it for a while and having taken counsel concerning it, to visit us. Whereupon, after several preceding written and oral requests, he came to us on July 15, 1734, and upon our written request he preached a sermon of admonition to our congregation on the 21st, whereupon the whole congregation, (excepting some who sympathized with the above-mentioned opposition-party) resolved and agreed, "inasmuch as this congregation has already suffered so much adversity, because it has existed hitherto without any fixed church-order, and every one did as he pleased, that therefore we submit to the Church Order, approved by the Reverend Classis of Amsterdam and established in Do. Boehm's three congregations, since after careful investigation we found it to be drawn up in accordance with God's Holy Word, that we hold fast to the Heidelberg Catechism and accept all the formulas of unity of the Christian Synod of Dort and introduce no other doctrine than our true Reformed teaching, which conforms to the Word of God and comprises the fundamentals of all good church discipline".

Immediately thereafter Do. Boehm, by an unlimited authority, signed by 36 members of the congregation, recognized us six chosen elders and deacons, and authorized us to act together, with earnestness and to the utmost of our ability, according to our conscience, as we could answer for it before God, to the glory of God and to the advancement and promotion of the common interest. Hence, four weeks later, on August 18th, we were installed in our offices by Do. Boehm, by virtue of the Church Order and in accordance with the resolution of the congregation, and we entered with the three congregations of Falkner Schwam, Schip Bach and Weitmarge into a covenant and brotherly union, and signed the same in the name of our congregation with our own hands. Thereupon we celebrated the Lord's Supper on December 15, 1734,[96a] with heartfelt joy. We now live in hope toward God that in a short time all the congregations in Pennsylvania will unite with us in a brotherly union under one and the same Church Order, whereby we can look forward to the largest growth of our true Church in this country. For this has caused hitherto the

---

[96a] The date is December 15, 1734, not September 15, as has been stated. The original reads: "op den 15 x br."

greatest injury that young ministers were unwilling to recognize any obligation to act according to certain standards in their ministry, but entered even Do. Boehm's congregation and caused division among the members, so that several times much scandal resulted and Do. Boehm had to suffer very much, yea even the sects made the Reformed people the object of their ridicule. This was indeed the chief reason why our congregation was threatened with total dissolution, as every one imagined that his own free will was the best. But this is now made impossible through the good church ordinances, to which all the members must be obedient. Thus we hope that through this union in our true worship the pious object of the Christian Synods will be attained.

To reply further to your Reverences, according to our ability and duty, we notice that the Christian Synod looks with sorrow upon our pitiful condition, and we are grateful to God Most High, that He by His grace causes the hearts of those to be compassionate, who have been a tender nurse to our true Church, which is still standing upon a weak foundation and unable to help herself. The decline of true religion is indeed deplorable in this country, and whence does it come but from a lack of faithful and orthodox ministers? The three ministers who arrived here at different times have introduced dissension and division even in the three regularly established conregations of Do. Boehm, and in addition, by their freethinking, have plunged the simple people into doubt with regard to the true Reformed religion, so that through these and other quarrels the number of those who since that time have gone over to the "Tumplers" [Dunkers], Seventh-day people, Mennonites and others is so large that it cannot be stated without tears in one's eyes, and who knows how many there are yet in this widely-extended country, who are unknown to us. The good God have mercy upon His own and preserve them from such like men.

The faithless conduct of Jacob Reiff is indeed abominable, but from what is stated above the Christian Synods can infer what was the chief cause of it. And we believe it is just as well as it is, than if their scheme, which they had made with Jacob Reiff had succeeded. For if they had received their share, they would surely have quarrelled among themselves.

Moreover, we deem it very fortunate for our churches if the Christian Synod still has in hand the itemized account of the money collected, mentioned in your godly letter of the above date, which these people have asked for.

We can report little favorable news of Do. Weiss, for as far as we know up to the present time he is unwilling to declare himself against Reiff, either in writing or by word of mouth.

That the above-mentioned letters from here to the Christian Synods have not given sufficient information, so that the money gathered by the Christian Synod could be sent over, can easily be traced to its cause, for in muddy water the bottom cannot be seen as easily as in clear water, hence the former is preferred by deceitful people.

We notice further that in the same letter a full yearly salary is demanded for ministers and schoolteachers, and as we have seen from the letter of Dr. Wilhelmi, minister at Rotterdam, written on June 20, 1734,[97] to the Consistory here, 6 preachers and 12 schoolmasters are to be appointed, which according to the letter of his Reverence would amount yearly to 660 pounds of sterling. We are terrified by the temerity of such a bold request. In order to bring its unreasonableness more clearly to light, our minister, who has the best knowledge of these affairs, has drawn up a dutiful specification of the places [of worship] and of the communicants, which we have examined together, and which we recognize, in view of the duty imposed upon us, as a dutiful and truthful account,[98] and we believe that four ministers would be able to perform the work properly to the further growth of our churches in this country, (whereof we shall transmit a submissive yearly report) if they would take to heart the obligation laid upon them.

As regards the request for 12 schoolmasters, we know not what to do with it. It is indeed true that it is very useful to have at every separate [preaching] place a man who can serve the people on the Lord's Day, whenever the minister is absent. But we are of the opinion that there is no place, but the good

[97] For a brief sketch of the life of Dr. John Wilhelmi (or Wilhelmius), see above, p. 39, note 49. The letter mentioned here by Boehm has not been preserved.

[98] This has reference to the report of Boehm, printed below, pp. 250-257.

Lord has there such a man who is capable of doing that, and who does not have to make a living by that alone, but is willing to take up the work for a voluntary gift, and if there is a school to be carried on, he can take from each who sends his children to him a proper fee. As to the appointment of general schoolmasters in this widely extended country, [we wish to say that] we do not know of a single locality where within a radius of 3 English miles 20 children of our faith could be gathered together, excepting at Philadelphia and Germantown, where this is a great need, as there the people live close together; as for the rest [of the country] no other measure can be thought of than that here and there the nearest neighbors together engage and pay a man, as many are already doing, in order to have their children instructed.

Thus we are,—because the Christian Synod is willing to quicken and help us poor and feeble fellow-members of Christ, their fellow-believers, with a Christian donation,—heartily content with whatever wise resolution the Christian Synod will deem practical and necessary in view of the accompanying, dutiful specification. And our souls rejoice that the Christian Synod, with a Christian and charitable heart is graciously pleased to provide not merely for individual poor persons or particular localities and consistories, but in general for the true Reformed worship in Pennsylvania and for the welfare of all of us. For we are not desirous that our fellow-members of the body of Christ should be set back on our account, since we just as gladly behold their increase and growth in the true service of the Master, as our own, in the assured confidence that the good Lord, according to His riches, will grant us aid as each one of us has need.

The congregation at Germantown has indeed undertaken to build a church, and is pretty well advanced with it,[99] but they

---

[99] This statement shows that the Reformed church building at Germantown was in process of construction in the year 1734. This is corroborated by a letter, written and signed by two elders and sixteen members at Germantown, on July 14, 1744, in which they state: "About ten years ago, four members of our congregation did their utmost, according to the best of their ability, to build a church for the congregation, hoping that thus the congregation could hold regular religious services, and that what these men had expended of their small

have contracted a debt for it, so that they are not much farther advanced than if they had just begun, for the money taken up by collections cannot amount to much in this poor country, according to our opinion. However, the church stands on a plot definitely purchased and is very conveniently located, almost in the center of the place.[100]

Further, it is not surprising that Peter Miller has not taken part in any of the matters, communicated to the Christian Synod by [the congregation in] Canastoka on February 13, 1733, inasmuch as he, from the beginning when he came to this country, was busy with what is stated in the specification.[101]

With reference to the members of the Reformed [Church] reported to you, as being 15,000 to 16,000,[102] we look upon that report with horror and are exceedingly surprised at such impudence, which could report, without a feeling of shame, such a scandalous falsehood to the Christian Synod. It is indeed true that there are very many Germans in this country, but if they could all be counted, which however, is impossible to do so easily, the total would not by far reach that number. But most of them are Mennonites. There are also more Lutheran

---

means for the building, would be paid back by the congregation, if they only had a minister, which, however, after the completion of the church, was not done, because they lacked a minister, although some years ago the Rev. Mr. Rieger served them for a short time." The four members were John Bechtel, Christopher Meng, Jacob Bauman and George Bensel, see note 107, p. 250.

[100] It is now the Market Square Presbyterian Church, at Germantown.

[101] See below, p. 254.

[102] That is not what Rieger wrote on March 4, 1733. His actual words were: "As regards the number of the members of the Reformed Church in Pennsylvania, we answer that we think that there must be altogether 15,000 to 16,000 *Germans*, but these people live scattered over more than 300 or 400 miles [of territory] and have no churches. We had thus far but two regularly called ministers, who cannot possibly be everywhere, hence *it is impossible to ascertain the actual number of members.*" In an earlier letter, written by Rieger, November 22, 1731, he estimates the members of the Reformed church as "hardly three thousand." There is a great confusion in the different estimates between the number of Germans, that of baptized Reformed members and that of communicant members.

LETTER OF 1734 243

than Reformed people. All "Tumplers" [Dunkers] are Germans, with whom the whole land is filled, also the Seventh-day people [Seevendaagers] and more sects besides. There is also a large number who live here and there and keep themselves altogether aloof from everybody, since they can see no means by which our church can be established in this country, among whom the Lord will preserve His own until His time comes. Hence we expect, if through God's grace we shall have obtained Christian support, many of these will come forward. But where is now the large number [of Reformed]? To us and Do. Boehm no more are known than are indicated in the accompanying specification.[108] Nevertheless, we shall not deny, but humbly

---

[108] The first estimate of the number of Reformed people in Pennsylvania occurs in the minutes of the Synod of South Holland, held at Breda, July 4-14, 1730. Rev. John Wilhelmius, of Rotterdam, then president of Synod, submitted a report in which he stated that "there are already 15,000 old Reformed confessors of the Palatinate [in Pennsylvania]. They are increasing every year, as for instance only a few weeks ago 600 left Rotterdam on three ships for that land." In the following year, at the Synod of South Holland, held at Dort, July 3-13, 1731, the Deputies of Synod reported that "they had conferred with the Rev. George Michael Weitzius [Weiss], minister of Philadelphia, and his elder, come over to Holland, regarding the churches of Pennsylvania, and that they had learned from them as well as from letters and reports sent over to them, that the Reformed Church of Pennsylvania consists of 30,000 baptized persons, among whom are 15,000 members that should be served." A similar statement is found in the first printed report of the Reformed Church of Pennsylvania, printed by the Synodical Deputies and submitted to the Synod of Dort in 1731. There it is stated: "There are Mennonites, Lutherans and Reformed, the last of whom being about the half of all, so that there may well be 15,000 Reformed members, holding to the old Reformed Confession." These estimates, which go back to the letters and reports of Weiss are certainly much too high. They are in striking contrast to other, much lower, estimates. In the accompanying report (p. 250), Boehm gives the actual number of communicants for the year 1734 in eight congregations as 386. The average membership was 48 or 50 in round numbers. Besides, Boehm mentions five other congregations, whose members are not estimated, namely Oley, Saucon, Macungie, Maxatawny and Great Swamp. No reference is made by Boehm to Old Goshenhoppen, Lancaster, Cocalico, Muddy Creek, Zeltenreich, White Oak and Egypt, all of which were in existence in 1734, as we know from other sources. Here are 20 congregations, which, if we estimate each at fifty members, would

call to mind that the communion services are indeed more numerously attended at one time than another, on account of bad weather and distant places, yet we believe that the number will prove to be not much more nor less than it is at the present time.

The Christian Synod desires to know the localities where churches could be built. The same is indicated as far as practicable in the specification. It also wishes to know who shall make their plans and how high the cost of the churches will be. Whereat we answer humbly to the Christian Synod: We are in duty bound to care as much as possible for our congregation, for her growth to the honor of God, for the salvation of our souls and those of our descendants,—and we request a Christian donation only for the Church of Christ and not for ourselves to gain temporal profit, how then can we say what we wish to have, we would rather leave it to the Christian Synod's pious philanthropy and will be heartily satified with what they, out of love, will bestow upon us and deem necessary, for the advancement of the Kingdom of Jesus, and we shall adapt ourselves to the charitable gifts which may be granted unto us and to what shall be set apart for each locality. We do not want to waste or throw away anything, but shall endeavor to preserve a good conscience before Almighty God in this matter, and, in order to prevent any evil suspicion, we desire to submit humbly to the Christian Synod our voluntary proposition, namely:

There dwells here in Philadelphia the honorable Mr. Thomas Lawrence,[104] a Hollander by birth, a wholesale mer-

---

give us an approximate membership of 1,000. But it must not be overlooked that the actual communicants in a given year are but a part of the total communicant membership. If we suppose that 75 per cent. of the membership actually communed, we would get a total of about 1,300 communicant members for the year 1734. The baptized members would be approximately three times as numerous, or about 4,000. The total number of adherents and others, Reformed by descent and training, might easily be again as numerous, or 8,000 in all. At another place (see p. 83), we figured out the total number of Reformed people as 16,000 for the year 1740, while Schlatter, for 1750, gives about 30,000. In other words, the Reformed membership seems to have doubled itself in each decade.

[104] Thomas Lawrence was born September 4, 1689, at New York.

chant, a judge and at present Mayor of Philadelphia and a lover of the true religion. Of him our minister, at our request, asked counsel and begged him to take upon himself the trouble for our church in this affair, if it should be necessary. He in turn met him at once willingly and amicably, that he granted his request immediately, that, whenever the Christian Synod or Classis of Holland should entrust funds for the German Reformed congregations in Pennsylvania into the hands of Theodore Hodshon, merchant in Amsterdam, then he as his correspondent would pay that money, sent as draft to Pennsylvania. Besides he assured him of all aid and counsel wherewith he might be able to serve our congregations. Moreover a Christian Synod and Reverend Classis may well rely upon the good name of this man. And, in order to show clearly and submissively that we wish to exercise every possible care in this matter, we voluntarily request that Mr. Lawrence be asked to let nothing come into our hands until it has been plainly shown to him that it will be used faithfully for the purpose for which it is given, which his Honor will not refuse, if it be asked of him.

May the Christian Synod entertain no doubt whatever that we shall hold to the doctrine of the Heidelberg Catechism and to the Confession of the Palatinate Church as agreeing with the rule of God's Word. But as regards the Church Order, the same will be found to be in nowise in conflict with that of Heidelberg, but for the rest it has been made to harmonize, as far as necessary, with the situation of our land and of our churches. It has also been sent over to the Reverend Classis of Amsterdam by the Reverend Correspondents, the ministers of New York and Long Island, and is to be found with the consistories in Pennsylvania.

As regards the information which the Christian Synod de-

He settled in 1720, in Philadelphia, where he entered into the mercantile business. In 1730 he was partner of Edward Shippen. He resided in Water St. He was Mayor of Philadelphia in 1727, 1728, 1734, 1749, 1753, and held that office at the time of his death in 1754. He became member of the Provincial Council, May 10, 1728. He was for some time Presiding Judge of the County Court. He died April 20, 1754, and was buried in Christ Church yard. See C. I. Keith, *Provincial Councillors of Pennsylvania*, Philadelphia, 1883, pp. 430-433.

sires concerning Mr. Boehm, from whom the Christian Synod received no reply to their letter sent to him on December 1, 1731, [it should be stated that] he did not receive the same until July 17, 1732, and it grieved him that the due reply had not come before the Christian Synod up to December 2, 1733. But he expects that it has now arrived, and if not, the Christtian Synod will find included in this letter all that it then desired.

Finally what concerns Arnold Hassert,[105] we have noticed in the gracious letter of the Christian Synod, written on December 1, 1731, to the Consistory at Philadelphia, that this Hassert was recommended and praised to the Christian Synod as a member of our Reformed Church and that everything might be properly handed over to him to be done;—this is again a brazen and impudent act to report such notorious lies to the Christian Synod, for this Arnold Hassert came to this country many years ago and become known as a Mennonite. Then he was many years here, no one knows what; at present he is among the Quakers. He is a man in whom we have not the least confidence. We cannot think otherwise than that, in order to carry out the scheme of Reiff, assistants were sought who were regarded as best qualified for it. But thanks be unto

---

[105] Arent Hassert was a prominent merchant of Philadelphia. On February 25, 1726, the Council of the Province considered a bill "for better enabling Arent Hassert, Ulrick Hageman and others therein named to trade and hold lands, etc." It was read, considered, and with some amendments returned to the House, cf. *Colonial Records,* Vol. III, p. 248. From August 5-26, 1731, Arent Hassert, advertised in the *American Weekly Mercury,* "large Holland pressing papers, several sorts of Boulting Cloth and Madder, lately imported from Holland and divers sorts of English goods, to be sold very reasonably." An advertisement of Dr. Hendrick van Bebber, which appeared in the *Pennsylvania Gazette,* under date May 4, 1732, states that Arent Hassert was then living in Laetitia Court, Philadelphia. He was naturalized September 25-27, 1740. Arent Hassert signed his will January 15, 1756, with a codicil added September 14, 1756. (Register of Wills office, Philadelphia, Book K, p. 511.) It was probated March 14, 1757, hence he died in the early part of March. See Diary of David Schultze in *Perkiomen Region,* Vol. III, p. 91. He had a daughter Elizabeth and a son, Arent Hassert, Jr. The latter's will was signed November 19, 1765, mentioning as his heirs his wife, Catherine, and his son, Jacob. It was probated January 14, 1766, at Philadelphia.

God that it failed and may He graciously guard against it in future.

In order to commend it to the deliberation of the Christian Synod we shall not withhold the fact that there are great differences in this country in the erection of churches and parsonages and what belongs thereto. For here in the city of Philadelphia there are indeed plots still for sale, but they are very expensive, for some time ago we were about to buy a plot, half an acre in size, which was to cost 187 pounds of our money, but we turned back again, as we were unable to raise so much, although it is still for sale to day; also lumber and stones must all be bought and mechanics are very high in their charges here. Hence these things [the building of churches] can be more easily accomplished at such places where lumber and stones can be had without expense. All this is now very expensive in Germantown also. Nor can a minister live as cheaply in the city as in the country, where he can keep cattle and the like for his support. Wherefore we humbly ask that the Christian Synod be pleased to take all this into its full deliberation, according to its wisdom, in order to make the distribution [of their gifts] proportionate, whereby all discontent will be removed and its instructions will be obediently followed.

As regards the ministers, the principal need which must be cared for is to provide them a living. Nevertheless we should be ashamed to be *always* troubling the Christian Synod and our fellow-believers for this, for although for the present we are poor, small in number and unable to do anything, yet we hope that the good Lord, since it would contribute to the glory of His holy name, will graciously cause us to increase, in order to be enabled to do more in future days. Meanwhile we are willing, (to which also our brethren will consent) to distribute as well as we can, in view of the poverty of many, and then to send humbly and submissively a detailed yearly account of whatever the Christian Synod may be pleased to bestow upon the communicants according to their godly consideration of our small number and our still existing poverty.

Further, Reverend Sir, we cannot refrain from making known to the Christian Synod, that Jacob Reiff and his adherents make a great distinction between the Christian Synod and the Reverend Classis of Amsterdam, [claiming] that they are in antagonism to each other and that the Christian Synod would assist no one who would have anything to do with the Reverend Classis of Amsterdam, whereby they have sought to create all manner of division in the congregation and have kept also many people and even our own congregation for a long time from good order. Now, however, we understand this better, since we have seen that it was only meant to keep the waters stirred up with the object of being better able to deceive.

We now come to the certain conclusion that through the brotherly union and adoption of one, well established, Church Order in our whole country, whereby a proper order among ministers, a brotherly love, obedience and unity, under good church discipline, among the members is created, the godly intention of the Christian Synod (whose purpose aims at nothing less than to enlarge the Kingdom of Christ in which rule unity and love) will be satisfactorily realized, in view of the fact that thus we shall be worthier of it, than if, as such wicked people would gladly see, we were living in the fires of continual dissension.

And what could be thought of as better for our true Church in Pennsylvania, than that we have the reverend corresponding ministers of New York as such faithful friends, as they have indeed shown themselves to be hitherto, for how could we be able to meet trouble, if in every case we should have to wait for months and years for counsel, for we dwell here in a land rich in sects, in which all kinds of happenings take place. But now, on the contrary, if necessity demands, we can obtain question and answer every week, so that we firmly believe, if such were not the case, a Christian Synod would rather help us to secure it than be displeased with it, since it serves to promote the honor of God.

Thus, Reverend Sir, being in this work in the proper spirit, we humbly ask a Christian Synod that whatever be sent hither, letters and particularly the itemized account of the donations received by Reiff, and what we shall do about them, be sent to Philadelphia in care of Mr. Thomas Lawrence, since the malicious spirit [of our opponents] is so cunning that, if the address were to the Consistory of Philadelphia, the letters would not be sure of reaching us.

Very Reverend Sir, we further ask humbly and without wishing to dictate, that the Christian Synod, be graciously pleased to request Mr. Thomas Lawrence that (especially with regard to the Reiff affair) he may give us his aid, in all godly justice, since his Excellency, being very willing to aid us, can secure great advantage to all of us.

In conclusion, we beg you, Very Reverend Sir, to look upon us, your obedient servants, and upon our very needy condition in this land, in Christian pity and brotherly love, and to excuse us, together with all our fellow-brethren in Pennsylvania, before the Christian Synod, wherein we may have done something amiss, against our will, so that we may soon be refreshed in our extreme need.

We shall always pray God, with humility of heart and fervent prayers from the bottom of our hearts, that He, as the God of grace and the rich rewarder of all kind deeds, will bless here below the temporal possessions of each one and hereafter will crown you with the crown of righteousness. Commending the Christian Synod, all families and the sacred service [of the Gospel] to God and the Word of His Grace, we remain,

Very Reverend Sir, your most obedient, submissive and humble fellow servants and brethren in the Lord Jesus,

The minister and elders of the German Reformed Congregation in Philadelphia,

JOHANN PHILIPS BOEHM, Pastor.

CASPER ULRICH, elder.   JACOB UTTRE, elder.
STEPHEN GREIF, elder.   ULLRICH OELLEN, elder.
ZACHARIAS SCHUCKERD, deacon. JACOB ORNER, deacon,

Pennsylvania, October 28, 1734.

Copia.

To Jacob Uttre, Caspard Ullrich, Stephen Greiff, Ullrich Oellen, Zacharias Schuckert, Abraham Kintzing.

I attest that the congregation, established here, has this day elected the above-named men as elders and deacons of the congregation by a majority of votes.

JOH. BARTH. RIEGER.

Philadelphia, April 2, 1734.

[XXII. FIRST REPORT OF MR. BOEHM TO THE SYNODS OF NORTH AND SOUTH HOLLAND, OCTOBER 28, 1734.[106]]

Truthful and Dutiful Specification of the High German Reformed Congregations in Pennsylvania, showing also how many communicants were present at the last Lord's Supper in each congregation, drawn up as follows by the undersigned:

Congregations:	Communicants:
At Falkner Schwam were found, September 22, 1734	63
At Schip Bach were found, September 29, 1734	41
At Weitmarge were found, October 6, 1734	22
At Philadelphia were found, September 15, 1734	88
At Germantown were found (according to the statement of two elders, namely Minck and Bentzel)[107] in September, 1734	30
At Cannastocka were found, May 31, 1730	75
At Dulpen Hacken were found, June 28, 1728	27
At Goschenhoppen, according to the statement of several members, about	40

It ought to be stated that certainly one half of the communicants of these congregations arrived here not long ago, are poor people, and partly servants.

Further report from Pennsylvania, regarding the above mentioned eight congregations, including beside them several places, which need to be provided for as much as possible. These are: Oly and also Sacon, in whose neighborhood are Makuntschy, Maxadani and Great Swamp, where, notwithstanding their being scattered very far apart, yet a considerable number of people can come together. As the population increases other congregations may be organized. For the pres-

---

[106] The original German report is no longer in existence, but a Dutch translation is in the archives at The Hague, 74, I, 18.

[107] On November 8, 1732, Henry Frederick, of Germantown, and Anna Barbara, his wife, conveyed by deed one-eighth of an acre of land to John Bechtel, turner; Christopher Meng (called Minck by Boehm), mason; Jacob Bauman, carpenter, and George Bensel, yeoman (the same as Bentzel), for fifteen pounds, in trust for the Reformed congregation. The land is described as "beginning at a stone set for a corner by the Germantown market place, being also the corner of Nicolas De la Plaine's land." Recorder of Deeds office, Philadelphia, Book I, Vol. 8, p. 327.

ent, however, although with much effort, they can suitably be served by four ministers in the following manner:

1. By one minister, Philadelphia and Germantown, which are 6 English miles apart; and as Germantown is a very advantageous place, if the congregation there would fraternally unite with that of Weitmarge (since they are very weak and but 4 English miles apart, and most of the people are going to live at Germantown), the same might very properly change its location [to Germantown], about which I, as the regular pastor at Weitmarge have already spoken to the elders there, who agree with me in acknowledging this to be beneficial and serviceable, and in case any order were given in the matter they would be willing to obey. By means of such a union they would also be in a better condition in due time to support a pastor themselves.

2. By the second minister, Falkner Schwam and Schipbach, which are about 12 English miles apart; and if he would conduct services at each of these places once every 3 weeks, he might between times, and on one Sunday, according to opportunity, preach at Oly,[108] and whenever it may be necessary.

3. By the third minister, Cannastocka [Conestoga] and Dulpehacken [Tulpehocken]. And, whereas Cannastocka[109] is

[108] Reformed settlers began to arrive at Oley as early as 1712. They had originally been part of the Kocherthal colony, which reached New York in December, 1708. Although Kocherthal was a Lutheran minister, yet the Minutes of the English Board of Trade, under date April 26, 1708, show, that of the 41 original emigrants 26 were Calvinists and 15 Lutherans (see Jacobs, *German Emigration to America, 1709-1740*, Lancaster 1899, p. 47). In June, 1708, fourteen other Palatines joined Kocherthal's company (*Col. Hist. of N. Y.*, V, 44), and with these (55 persons in all) he landed in New York (see list in *Col. Hist. of N. Y.*, V, 52f). They were settled at Quasaick, now a part of Newburgh, on the Hudson. In May, 1709, Kocherthal complained that 19 of the Germans had become "pietists." (*Doc. Hist. of N. Y.*, III, 544). These were most likely the Reformed (Huguenot) contingent. They left New York State in 1712 and went to Pennsylvania. Some of them settled at Oley, among others Isaac de Turk and Mary Weimar, whom he had married, the rest went to Lancaster County, among whom was Isaac Lefevre and Daniel Ferree.

[109] The first Reformed Church in the Conestoga valley is identical with Heller's Reformed Church in Upper Leacock township, Lancaster County, see p. 64.

spread over a great extent of territory (almost if not more than 70 miles from Philadelphia) and has very many Reformed people, if they had a faithful pastor of their own, they might then be united [into one charge], so that the pastor could conduct services at two or three places, as might be deemed advisable, and besides have services every 4 weeks at Dulpehacken,[110] which is about 18 miles distant. Now this was the condition of Cannastocka and Dulpenhacken at the period above mentioned, when at their request I administered the Lord's Supper to them, and Cannastocka accepted and subscribed to our Church Order; and although they were scattered by Peter Miller, yet I hope, with the help of God, to restore them to their former condition.

4. A fourth minister would greatly be needed at Goschoppen [Goshenhoppen], about 36 miles from Philadelphia.[111] He might conduct services there every 3 weeks, and use the rest of the time to feed the poor sheep at the end of the wilderness, in the above-mentioned Sacon,[112] Makundschi [Macungie],[113]

---

[110] For the early history of the Tulpehocken Reformed Church, see p. 66ff. The existence of a church building at Tulpehocken in 1727 is vouched for by a petition which, in September, 1727, was addressed by the "Inhabitants of the North West parts of the Township of Oley, Tulpehocken and parts adjacent," to the Court at Philadelphia, praying that "a high road be laid out, beginning at the Lutheran Meeting House at Tulpehocken and to end in the High road at the Quaker Meeting House near George Boone's Mill in Oley."

[111] According to Gordon's *Gazetteer of Pennsylvania,* printed in 1832 (see Dotterer, *Perkiomen Region,* Vol. I, p. 14), New Goshenhoppen is situated 37 miles northwest of Philadelphia. This shows that Boehm referred to the New Goshenhoppen church in 1734.

[112] This is the first reference to the Saucon Reformed Church, situated in Lower Saucon township, Northampton County. Between 1736-1739, Henry Goetschy preached at Saucon. In 1739, Mr. Boehm writes of Saucon Creek as "a somewhat out-of-the-way place, but many Reformed people live there." On September 23, 1740, three children, whose parents were members at Egypt, were baptized by "Inspector Peter Heinrich Torschius in the Sakum church." This was the Rev. P. H. Dorsius, of Neshaminy, Bucks County. He probably continued visiting Saucon till he left for Holland in May, 1743. In 1747 John Conrad Wirtz was serving "Saccony." See *Schlatter's Life and Travels,* p. 162.

[113] Macungie is a district in the western part of Lehigh County, now divided into Upper and Lower Macungie townships. The first

Maxadani [Maxatawny][114] and Grooten Schwam [Great Swamp],[115] who thirst for the hearing of God's Word, as the dry earth for water. Many people from these regions have already been to see me in great sadness and complained of the

organization of the Reformed people in this region probably took place at the "Ziegel Church," in what is now Weissenberg township. The Constitution of the congregation is dated "Macunchy, July 6, 1750." According to Rev. Wm. Helffrich, for many years pastor of the congregation, the old church record, now unfortunately burnt, contained baptisms up to the fourth decade of the 18th century. The first church was built in 1749. See Helffrich, *Geschichte verschiedener Gemeinden in Lecha und Berks Counties,* Allentown, 1891, p. 6f. Another early Reformed congregation in the Macungie region is Western Salisbury, near Emaus, whose first church building was erected in 1741. It is possibly older than the Ziegel Church. See *History of Western Salisbury Church,* [Allentown], 1911, p. 9; *Skizzen aus dem Lecha Thale,* Allentown, 1880-1886, p. 72.

[114] Maxatawny is a township in the eastern part of Berks County. Mr. Goetschy preached at Maxatawny before 1739. In 1739, Boehm says that a minister might serve Maxatawny in connection with Oley, "which is at a distance of ten miles." This implies clearly an organization.

The first Reformed services were held in Maxatawny, most likely in the house of Jacob Levan, at what is now called Eaglepoint. From the balcony of that house Zinzendorf preached in 1742, and Michael Schlatter on June 28, 1747. Jacob Levan, Sr., gave five acres and 106 perches of land for a meeting house at Maxatawny. Upon this land a church is said to have been built in 1755, under the pastorate of Frederick Casimir Mueller. In 1759, the congregation divided. Many of the members formed in that year a new congregation and built a new church, two miles further south, at Bower's, in Maxatawny township. See Rev. John B. Stoudt on the "Maxatawny Reformed Congregation," in the *Centennial History of Kutztown,* 1915, pp. 76-86.

[115] This is the first reference to the Great Swamp Church in Lower Milford township, Lehigh County. A very interesting reference to this congregation, unnoticed thus far, occurs in a letter of Rev. Boltzius, Ebenezer, Georgia, to Dr. G. A. Franke, of Halle. Under date of December 12, 1734, he writes: "In the above mentioned Great Swamp there is also a small Reformed congregation, which has its own preacher." (See *Heinrich Melchior Mühlenberg's Selbstbiographie,* Allentown, p. 213.) This preacher can have been none else than Rev. John Peter Miller, who entered baptisms into the New Goshenhoppen record till July 28, 1734. From 1736-1739, John Henry Goetschy served this congregation. He opened the oldest church record of the congregation on April 26, 1736.

lamentable state of their souls. There were also some, who being able to make the journey, have come at various times to commune in the congregation entrusted to me at **Falkner Schwam**, a distance of certainly 25 to 30 English miles, and brought children for baptism, which journey, however, is impossible for old persons and weak or pregnant women, so that it is not to be wondered at (especially when one remembers that there are children who for lack of a minister cannot be brought to baptism until they are several years of age) that my heart breaks and my eyes are full of tears about this condition. But I cannot accomplish this work alone, for my years are beginning to accumulate, and my poor body is also getting feeble, since I must not only make long journeys and preach, but also because the poor people are not able to support me, I must support my large family with hard, manual labor.

It is indeed true that three young ministers have been here, namely **Mr. George Michael Weis, Mr. Peter Miller, and Mr. Barthol. Rieger**, coming from the Palatinate, but for what they have done here I wish that God may forgive them, because, after they had disturbed the congregations for a long time, even those entrusted to my care, they again left and abandoned the sheep misled by their shepherds. Nevertheless one of them is still in this country, namely, Peter Miller. When **this man could not bring the people over to his opinion, he** quitted the ministry altogether, and he is now an oil-miller.[116] But what he was after, and thought of persuading the people to do, is plainly to be seen from this, overlooking everything else: about two years ago he went with one of his elders, whom he had installed in the congregation at Goschenhakken [Goshenhoppen], into the house of a Seventh Day "Tumpler" [Dunker], and there they allowed themselves to be called brethren and to have their feet washed by him; and this is the truth, whereupon followed his complete apostasy.[117]

[116] This is most likely the meaning of the Dutch term "Olypersser." It was first suggested by the late Prof. J. H. Dubbs, in his *Reformed Church in Pennsylvania*, p. 96, note 93. It agrees with Miller's own statement. See next note.

[117] It is of interest to put alongside of this statement of Mr. Boehm, Miller's own account, written on December 5, 1790, to a friend: "In August, 1730, I arrived in Philadelphia, and was there at the end

I have now for about eight years, ministered in my poverty to my three congregations entrusted to me at Falkner Schwam, Schipbach and Weitmarge, according to our Church Order. To them has been added three months ago the congregation at Philadelphia, which has entered on all points into a firm and complete agreement with me. To this Church Order none of the three young ministers would submit, but sought to live according to their own ideas, and Miller, in my presence called the Heidelberg Catechism a work of men, adding that Chris-

---

of the said year, upon order of the Scotch Synod, ordained in the old Presbyterian meeting house, by three eminent ministers, Tenant, Andrew and Boyd. Having officiated among the Germans several years I quitted the ministry, and returned to private life. About that time our small State was in its infancy. I never had an inclination to join it, because of the contempt and reproach which lay on the same; but my inward Conductor, brought me to that critical dilemma, either to be a member of this institution or to consent to my own condemnation, when also I was forced to choose the first. In my company had been the schoolmaster, three elderlings (Conrad Weiser one), five families and some single persons, which had raised such a fermentation in that church, that a persecution might have followed, had the magistrate consented with the generality. We have been incorporated with said congregation in May, 1735, by holy Baptism: When we were conducted to the water, I did not much differ from a poor criminal under sentence of death. Whoever [!] the Lord our God did strengthen me, when I came into the water and then in a solemn manner renounced my life with all its prerogatives without reservation and I found by experience in subsequent times, that all this was put into the divine records, for God never failed in his promise to assist me in time of need. At that time the solitary brethren and sisters lived dispersed in the wilderness of Conestoga, each for himself, as Heremits, and I following that same way, did set up my Hermitage in Dulpehakin at the foot of a mountain, on a limped spring, the house is still extant there with an old orchard. There did I lay the foundation of the solitary life, but the melancholy temptations which did trouble me every day, did prognosticate to me misery and affliction: Whoever [!] I had not lived there half a year, when a great change happened: for a camp was laid out for all solitary persons at the very spot where Ephrata stands and where at that time the President [Conrad Beissel] lived with some heremits. And now, when all heremits were called in, I also quitted my solitude and exchanged the same for the monastic life, which was judged to be more inservient to Sanctification than the life of a hermit, where many under a pretence of holiness did nothing but nourish their own selfishness." See Hazard's *Register*, Vol. XVI, p. 254f.

tians were a free people, and had no need on earth of a head, that Christ in heaven was their only head, and that he would not allow himself to be subjected to a human yoke, etc. Meanwhile the dissensions which have hitherto prevailed have been, by God's grace, mostly overcome, and the united congregations and members live in peace. Those few who in spite of every admonition, will not as yet unite in love, according to the rule of God's Sacred Word, we leave to their well-deserved judgment.

Thus writes, according to truth, upon his inevitable responsibility before the judgment-seat of God, he who esteems himself the least of all the servants of Jesus Christ, and unworthy of the Sacred Gospel, and testifies to it by his own signature, October 18, 1734.

Joh. Philips Boehm,
Reformed Minister in Pennsylvania.

The foregoing statistics, and the additional submissive report and proposals, made with due deference, are recognized by us, according to our bounden duty, as useful and tending to promote the interests of the true Church in Pennsylvania, and we agree with them in every respect. Moreover, we, the present ruling elders and deacons of the three congregations at Falkner Schwam, Schip Bach and Weitmarge, recognize and honor the Rev. Johan Philips Boehm, as a minister properly ordained by the Rev. Messrs. Gualtherus Du Bois, Henricus Boel and Vincentius Antonides, ministers at New York and Long Island, which was done by order of the Reverend Classis of Amsterdam (to which Reverend Classis we sent a submissive petition concerning it). This ordination took place in the presence of three of us, as elders delegated for this purpose. We also recognize him as our pastor, regularly called as the faithful shepherd of our souls, who has hitherto administered his office, under the greatest trials, in such a manner that we cannot complain in the least about any neglect on his part. We wish that the good Lord may graciously preserve him among us for many years in the same fidelity and zeal, to the best interests of His Church.

This we sign with our own hands, and dutifully testify to

LETTER OF 1734

it in Pennsylvania.

Done in our
Consistory at
Falkner Schwam,
October 20, 1734.
{ Gosen Thonis, elder.
Sebastian Reiffschneider, elder.[118]
Sigmundus Schmidts, elder
Johannes Herb, elder.
Johann Heinrich Schmidt, deacon.
Johannes Drinktdenhengst, deacon.

Done in our
Consistory at
Schipbach,
October 27, 1734.
{ Johan Ulric Stephen, elder.[119]
Jacob Arent, Sr., elder.
Philip Heink (!) Söller, elder.
Christian Leeman, elder.
Johannes Dintenmeyer, deacon.
Adam Kind, deacon.

Done in our
Consistory at
Weitmarge,
October 28, 1734.
{ William de Wees, elder.[120]
Christoffel Ottinger, elder.
Ludwig Knaus, deacon.
Johan Michael Gleim, deacon.[120a]

[118] Through the list of taxables published in Rupp, *Thirty Thousand Names,* pp. 470-478, it is possible to locate the homes of several of these men. Sebastian Reifschneider was paying quit-rent, in 1734, on 100 acres in Hanover township, Johannes Herb in Frederick township, (acres not given), J. Heinrich Schmidt, in Frederick township, on 80 acres.

[119] Ulrich Steffen paid quit-rent in 1734 on 50 acres in Salford township; Christian Lehman on 100 acres, also in Salford township; Jacob Arent qualified in Philadelphia, September 27, 1727. He was naturalized in 1734. See *Pa. Archives,* 2nd Series, Vol. VII, p. 116.

[120] William De Wees paid quit-rent in 1734 in Cresheim township on 150 acres; Christopher Ottinger, in Springfield township on 85 acres; Ludwig Knaus, in Whitemarsh township, on 100 acres.

[120a] John Michael Gleim qualified in Philadelphia August 17, 1731. In 1747, Michael Cleim became one of the trustees of the Whitpain church land. In May, 1749, Michael Cleim, innholder in Whitpain township, acted as one of the bondsmen for John Philip Boehm, Jr.

[XXIII. MR. BOEHM AND HIS CONSISTORIES TO THE CLASSIS OF AMSTERDAM, MARCH 10, 1738.][121]

Very Reverend Classis, Reverend and Devout Church Fathers:—

Your humble servants and children have hitherto been unable to refrain from dutifully describing the Church of Jesus as it exists here in temporal poverty. But since we have transmitted the submissive report and non-authoritative opinion, required of us by the Christian Synods, in the month of October, 1734,[122] through the Reverend Ministers in New York; also the submissive report to the Reverend Classis on November 29, 1735, through Captain Stettmann;[123] and the last submissive letter to the Reverend Classis, dated February 26, 1737, and sent through Captain Stettmann of this place; besides those letters which we sent very submissively, (with the knowledge of the Reverend Classis) to the Christian Synods,—we have not received during this whole time, in our so lamentable condition, a single word for our information and comfort, neither from the Christian Synods, nor from the Reverend Classis, as our devout Church Fathers. This has produced the greatest sorrow in our souls, for we do not know how to help ourselves, and we doubt, not so much that our submissive reports were not duly received as that your kind answers were withheld from us. For we cannot believe it possible that our devout Church Fathers should not have deemed their humble and obedient children worthy of a comforting answer in view of their urgent complaints and their truthful and dutiful reports.

---

[121] The original of this letter is in the archives of the Classis of Amsterdam.

[122] The letters of Boehm, written November 25, 1735, and February 26, 1737, apparently never reached their destination, for the Classical Minutes make no reference to them.

[123] In Rupp's *Thirty Thousand Names of Immigrants*, Captain John Stedman appears repeatedly. On September 11, 1731, John Stedman, Master, arrived in Philadelphia from Rotterdam, with the ship "Pennsylvania Merchant"; September 11, 1732, with the same ship; September 18, 1733, again with the same ship; September 12, 1734, with the ship "Saint Andrew"; September 26, 1737, with the same ship; October 27, 1738, with the same ship. On October 2, 1741, Charles Stedman, Master, arrived at Philadelphia from Rotterdam with the same ship, "St. Andrew."

Because it does not concern us so much as the great work of the great God, in the building up of the body of Christ. But we would ask the Reverend Classis with due deference, whether there are perhaps valid reasons.

We beg of you most humbly to gladden us soon with your comforting answer, for the condition in this country is still the same. Concerning the money collected by Weis and Reiff we have as yet nothing in hand. But we ask not to let the innocent sheep suffer on this account. If the receipts, given by them concerning it, together with a power of attorney were sent over to a man, designated by you according of your pleasure, as we suggested in our last submissive letter, then something could soon be done, but without them it will hardly be possible to obtain anything from them by legal process, for they have both sworn against one another. Now, if our devout Church Fathers should be pleased to send these to us, we would hope to secure it soon.

Last fall Do. Dorsius[124] arrived here as the regular minis-

[124] A few details may be added to the sketch given on p. 54ff of his life. April 5, 1734, he matriculated at the University of Groningen, Holland, and on September 17, 1736, at Leyden University, signing his name: "Petrus Henricus Dorsius, Meursanus, 25 [years], T. [Theologus]." Rev. Dr. John Wilhelmius, of Rotterdam, secured him for service in Pennsylvania. March 1, 1735, he wrote as follows to the Dutch Reformed congregation at Neshaminy, Bucks County: "I was much pleased from your letter, sent to me October 30, 1734, that you approve of the selection of this young man, not quite 26 years old and still unmarried. He has already studied much and understands the learned languages, Latin, Greek and Hebrew, so well that he is giving instruction in them to others. He is also far advanced in theology, and needs but little more training in the university. He is a pious young man, who is burning with the desire to preach the name of Jesus in the New World. I have asked him to sign a paper, by which he obligates himself, that, after his studies have been completed, he will go to you and accept your call." After being licensed and ordained in 1737, Dorsius sailed for America. He arrived at Philadelphia, September 26, 1737. He was pastor of the congregations of North and South Hampton, Bucks County, 1737-1743. He visited Holland, May, 1743—January, 1744, when he returned to Pennsylvania. He was again pastor of his former charges, 1744-1748. In the latter year he returned to Holland, where he served several congregations. He died about 1757. In that year his widow is referred to in the Coetus Minutes.

ter of the Low Dutch congregation at Jamine [Neshaminy] in Bucks County. With him there came another, named Van Basten,[125] who however is not yet ordained. He, therefore, travels about in the country, preaching here and there. He says that he has been sent here from Holland, but thus far he has not caused us any pleasure at all.

Very Reverend Classis, we repeat all the humble petitions of our previous submissive letters and again ask urgently and submissively that you will act as our representatives before the Christian Synods, presenting us as their obedient and submissive children, and that you will soon gladden us with a favorable answer. For we cannot help ourselves in our poverty and hence no growth of our true Church takes place.

With the firm hope, resting upon the Reverend Classis, that we shall soon be quickened by your God-pleasing love to us needy members,

We commend the Very Reverend Classis, as our devout Church Fathers, your reverend persons, all your families and holy service to the all-powerful protection and divine grace of the almighty and loving God, and remain unalterably,

Very Reverend Classis,
    Your submissive and obedient children and
                      fellow-members of Christ,
          JOHAN PHILIPS BOEHM, minister.

County of Philadelphia
in Pennsylvania,
March 10, 1738.

At Falkner Schwam { B. Reiffschneider, elder.
                        { J. B. Arent, elder.

At Schip Bach { J. U. Stephan, elder.
              { J. Arent, elder.

[125] According to Rupp's *List*, p. 109, "Joh. Herm. von Basten, Candidatus S. Th." arrived at Philadelphia, September 26, 1737 (or October 5, new style), with the ship "Saint Andrew," John Stedman, Master. Dorsius accompanied him, although his name does not appear in Rupp's list. In December, 1739, van Basten preached at Poughkeepsie, in 1739-1740 at Jamaica, Success, Oyster Bay and Newton. See Corwin, *Manual of the Reformed Church in America*, 4th ed., p. 807.

At Weitmarge { William de Wees, elder.
Ludwig Knaus, deacon.

At Philadelphia { Casper Ulrich, elder.
Jacob Walter,[126] [deacon].

[XXIV. THE CLASSIS OF AMSTERDAM TO MR. BOEHM, UNDATED, BUT WRITTEN IN JANUARY 1739.[127]

1739.

To Mr. John Philip Boehm.
Reverend Sir:—

The very poor condition of your church and yourself has become known to us through outsiders as well as through yourself, and aid has been requested by several to relieve your poverty. Your condition greatly grieves us and we are not disinclined to seek such help for you as we can, as opportunity offers and when circumstances favor it. But there is one thing, Reverend Sir, which somewhat detracts from our inclination in this matter and that is that there are certain rumors to your disadvantage, which have reached our ears, both by letter[128] and by word of mouth. It is said, that, not possessing much learning yourself, and not being particularly anxious to obtain it, you spend the whole week in manual toil and on the Sabbath you just read and mumble something from a postil [sermon-book], which conduct is not a little offensive. Hence you have been mocked by the Quakers and you have very few hearers. Now it is true that such reports do influence us, but it is also true that we do not wish to condemn you immediately because of this; for if accusations alone were sufficient, who would be innocent?

These things, however, give us a great concern about you; and even as we take the liberty in brotherly affection to remind you of them, we also earnestly request you to say nothing about them to

---

[126] A Jacob Walter, perhaps identical with this deacon, arrived in Philadelphia, September 26, 1732.

[127] A copy of the original is in the *Classical Letterbook,* Vol. XXIX, p. 253. The date appears from the minutes of the Classis. Under date January 13, 1739, the deputies were requested to write to Do. Boehm, asking him to clear himself of certain charges, contained in a letter brought in against him by Do. Wilhelmius, minister at Rotterdam.

[128] This was evidently the letter, sent by the opponents of Boehm, in the fall of 1738, to Dr. Wilhelmius, to which Boehm makes reference in the postscript of his letter of March 16, 1739, see below, p. 267.

others, but only make sure of your defense by sufficient testimonials. from trustworthy members of your church.

Thus will we become better acquainted with all the facts of the case and will be thereby guided in our measures and decisions.

Our prayer is that the Lord may fully sanctify us and preserve blameless our whole spirit, soul and body unto the coming of our Lord Jesus Christ. Yea, the Lord sanctify us and you by the truth, by His holy Word, which alone leads to salvation.

God be with you continually,
We are and remain,

JOHN PLANTINUS,
Praeses.
C. VAN DEN BOGAERDE,
Scriba.

P. S. You will also please be careful to guard with all earnestness against all manner of errorists and so also against the Moravians, who spread themselves everywhere even in foreign lands. They hold many doctrines contrary to the fundamentals of our pure Reformed Church.

[XXV. MR. BOEHM TO THE CLASSIS OF AMSTERDAM, MARCH 16, 1739.[129]]

Very Reverend Classis, Reverend and Devout Church Fathers:—

I desire to report, duly and submissively, to the Reverend Classis that his Reverence, Mr. Peter Henry Dorsius, minister at Jamine [Neshaminy] in Bucks County, here in Pennsylvania, in the month of November, 1738, sent his regards to me through a messenger and asked me to come to see him as soon as I had an opportunity of doing so, as it was very necessary for him to speak with me. Whereupon immediately, on the 28th of that month, I went to him. Then his Reverence showed me his letters from the two Christian Synods of North and South Holland, in which I saw that these Christian Synods had appointed his Reverence as their Commissioner and inspector[130]

---

[129] The original German letter of Boehm is in the Classical archives at Amsterdam.

[130] The title "inspector" was assumed by Dorsius, in his letters to Boehm (see p. 271), without authority from Holland. It was an office unknown to the constitution of the Dutch Church. Hence the Synods could not have appointed him to such an office.

over the German churches in Pennsylvania. Then his Reverence requested me to make a report, which I was ready to do, out of due respect for the Christian Synods, upon no other condition than that his Reverence give me a written request, in his own handwriting. Whereupon his Reverence wrote the same, as is shown by the accompanying copy, marked A.

Thereupon I used my utmost endeavor to advance the work of the Lord and placed the report into the hands of his Reverence, at his home, on February 26th, [1739], signed by 31 officiating elders and deacons of six preaching places, namely: Philadelphia, Falkner Schwam, Oly, Schip Bach, Weitmarge and Dolpihacken [Tulpehocken].

Very Reverend Classis, it is not difficult to understand how my heart was troubled in these affairs. For I sent a letter, dated November 26, 1735, through Casper Ulrich[131] an elder at Philadelphia, who himself made a trip to Germany at that time. Later on I sent a letter, dated February 26, 1737, and again on March 10 and 11, 1738.[132] These last two letters I handed to said Mr. Ulrich, who assures me that he sent them over every time through Captain Stättmann. Therein I reported submissively, according to my ability as formerly, everything which was required of me and what I considered necessary. But since the 19th of October, 1731, I have not received an answer from the Reverend Classis and a comfort in my deplorable and sad condition. Wherefore I had fears that either my submissive reports or otherwise your gracious answers had gone astray. But since his Reverence, Mr. Dorsius, at his first arrival in Philadelphia, in the fall of 1737, assured me that now all in Holland were united to assist in putting the Reformed Church in Pennsylvania into a good condition and in maintaining her therein, and since I myself then saw these letters from the two Christian Synods, I could not think otherwise but that the Reverend Classis had employed sufficient

---

[131] Casper Ulrich was naturalized in 1734. (See *Pa. Archives*, 2nd Series, Vol. VII, p. 116.) He signed his will November 22, 1751. It was probated December 10, 1751. He left his property to his wife, Eva, a son, Philip, and a daughter, who was the widow of Thomas Rutter. See Register of Wills office, Philadelphia, *Will Book*, I, p. 451.

[132] None of these letters, except the last, ever reached the authorities in Holland. They are not referred to in the Classical Minutes.

diligence to advance the best interests of the Church of Christ. I, therefore, considered myself in duty bound to help in the work of the Lord, according to my ability. For I have suffered many external and internal afflictions since our true worship has been established in this country through God's holy providence and grace and I, poor servant of Christ, had to be the first burden-bearer, as is sufficiently known to the Reverend Classis. But now the ice is broken and this only is wanting, to see the different posts manned by good watchmen who will continue to work, seek the lost and observe faithfully whatever else the Reverend Church Fathers, as God's servants, shall ordain for the extension of the Church of Christ.

His Reverence, Mr. Dorsius, whom the Christian Synods have now been pleased to appoint as superintendent of our true Church in Pennsylvania, shows indeed a real zeal faithfully to do all he can for the Church of Jesus in this country. To this end God has blessed him with wisdom. May the God of all strength further increase in his Reverence this zeal and wisdom, so that, as a true instrument [in God's hand], he may serve our true Church untiringly, with manly steadfastness, to the praise of God and the increase of the Kingdom of our Redeemer. I have no doubt, but firmly believe, that thereby, with the help of the Lord, the Church of Christ in this country will soon be brought to a glorious increase and beautiful prosperity.

Very Reverend Classis, since his Reverence, Mr. Dorsius, is not yet sufficiently acquainted with all the conditions here, I have given him a provisional division of the German preaching places, showing how they may be served most conveniently in six charges. With reference to my congregation at Weitmarge,[133] I proposed to him to unite it with Germandon, for Weitmarge is a very small congregation and on account of its location no growth can be expected. Moreover, Weitmarge is only four English miles from Germandon, and the largest part [of the members] hardly half that distance and sixteen miles from Schip Bach, and I would be satisfied to retain Schip Bach and Falkner Schwam alone, which afford enough work for a minister.

[133] For the history of Whitemarsh, see p. 58f.

This, Reverend Classis, I did not do because I underestimate the duties which I owe to this congregation, but for the sake of the comfort and welfare of ministers and congregations, nor will I leave Weitmarge until the Reverend Church Fathers approve and order it.

I shall now take the liberty to make a brief statement with regard to the place bought at Schip Bach, because I fear, as stated above, that my submissive reports did not reach their destination.

It is the most convenient place for congregational services at Schip Bach, where we can have in one plot everything that a congregation needs. There are 150 acres of land, of which about 60 are under cultivation. A well-built house and a barn are on it, which buildings may have cost 100 pounds. An orchard has also been planted.

I, together with the elders of the congregation, bought this place, in the month of August, 1735, at public auction, for 220 pounds.[134] The conditions were that we pay 50 pounds in the following fall, namely November 16, 1736, and then annually 15 pounds together with the interest on the remaining capital. But when the time came I could not get anything from the poor people, but the time was at hand. Then by necessity I traveled with an elder to New York. There they made many excuses on account of their own debts. However, we received, through the instrumentality of the Reverend Ministers of New York and Long Island, 44 pounds from liberal hearts. I suppose they have notified the Reverend Classis about this. In addition they contributed a little for my household, since I have no salary and my poor condition is well known to them.

When I came home again, conditions were so bad that I had to add from my own money what was wanting, of which five Pounds have not been returned to me up to date. I hoped to receive some collections at Philadelphia and elsewhere. I tried first Philadelphia, but did not get more than about eight Pounds. But the ridicule and derision, to which I had to listen from outsiders, hurt me very much. I was, therefore,

---

[134] For this transaction, see the history of the Skippack church, p. 60.

compelled to desist. In the country I could not do anything, the people are altogether too poor. Hence we were hardly able to raise the interest, for the time that had passed, wherefore we were obliged to lease the place for ten pounds annually, with the provision that we are to be permitted to hold services in the barn every four weeks, for we have no other place where we could do it. Thus we have at present still 170 pounds to pay, nor do I know how we can retain the place any longer without help. But now land becomes so scarce and expensive, that at Schip Bach one can hardly buy 100 acres of woodland for 100 pounds.

Now, as this burden is resting upon me and two of my brethren,[135] since we are responsible for it, I heartily long for kind help, without which it will be impossible for us to retain the place.

Very Reverend Classis, I have not received any benefit from it, but only trouble and annoyance and in addition expenses. For thus far I have lived on my own place with debts and must support myself and my family with the work of my hands. I cannot say that I have an annual income of 10 pounds for my troublesome labor and service, and the Reverend Classis knows how long I have worked in my service.

Very Reverend Classis, your most submissive, humblest and lowliest fellow-servant, who in spite of all will not allow any zeal and faithfulness to be lacking in his service of the Lord, as long as he lives and God gives him strength, prays for God's sake that, because of your abundant resources, you will remember your needy servant of Christ with your gracious intercession, and render him happy with a fitting answer as to what he shall do in the aforesaid affair. The rewarder of all good deeds will bless you manifold for it in body and soul.

To Him, our good God and Heavenly Father, and to the Word of Grace I devoutly commend

The Very Reverend Classis, your reverend persons with all

---

[135] These two brethren were, according to the deed (see p. 60), Gabriel Shuler and Ulrich Stephen. For Gabriel Schueler (Shuler) see p. 25. John Ulrich Stephen appears as John Stephen Ulrich in the petition of July, 1728, see p. 169. He resided in Salford township, see Rupp, *Thirty Thousand Names*, p. 476.

your families and holy service,

VERY REVEREND CLASSIS,

Your most humble and obedient servant and lowliest fellow-brother in Christ,

JOHAN PH. BOEHM,

Minister of the Congregations of Falkner Schwam, Schipbach and Weitmarge.

Witpen Township, Philadelphia County,
Pennsylvania, March 16, 1739.

Postscript.

Very Reverend Classis:—

After finishing my submissive letter I was informed by a member of the congregation at Philadelphia that last fall another very antagonistic letter[136] was written by some persons at Philadelphia, who, since the congregation has come under our Church Order, constantly strive to divide it and throw it into confusion. It was sent by one of them to the Christian Synods. They had signed this letter as elders and deacons of the Reformed congregation at Philadelphia. However, an investigation would again show that this is a dishonorable falsehood. Its motive is simply this, because they (as they have been named to me) are almost all such men, who, according to articles ten and fourteen of our Church Order cannot be counted as members of the congregation, much less could they be admitted to the Lord's Supper, until they promise and show amendment of life. Hence they rave thus. They will not admit that anyone has a right to speak to them about their wicked life, but they want to play the master.

Concerning the said letter, a member of the congregation told me that a Lutheran, against whom they had not guarded themselves, had told him that he had been in the room, had heard the reading and had seen the signing of the letter and had understood from it that they had most thoroughly denounced Boehm and his work, and that, if the Christian Synods should send any gifts to the congregation, they should direct them to their address.

[136] See above, p. 261, and note 128, p. 261. The elders of Boehm defended him against these accusations on May 3, 1741, see below, pp. 311-317.

In opposition to this I affirm, on my oath, that the congregation at Philadelphia though poor, is yet in a good, orderly and peaceful condition. I have served this congregation as its accepted minister since the month of August, 1734, in accordance with our Church Order. I have held divine service there one Sunday each month. When I administered the Lord's Supper there on the 10th of September, 1738, there were 75 communicants present. I do not intend to leave this good congregation, until, through the gracious providence of God and through the Reverend Church Fathers, they have been supplied with their own minister. Then I shall willingly leave the congregation to him, according to the agreement I entered into with the congregation at the beginning. I heartily wish that the good Lord may graciously send one soon, as it is very hard for me to supply so much, for I am getting old and my body is becoming weaker.

I also wish that the elders might be required to testify concerning this. They would be obliged to say, that they could not make an estimate that I had received more than ten pounds for all my hard work during all this time, partly on account of the poverty of the people, partly because of the trouble-makers, who would have liked to see me proceed with harshness with the result that the congregation would have been destroyed. I was, therefore, obliged to act very carefully and cautiously, in order to keep the united members together.

Now, if the Reverend Classis should receive such a letter, its truthfulness can be tested by the signatures of the people, for the names of the members of the consistory, at present in office, who were installed by me according to the Church Order, are as follows:

Casper Ulrich,
Nicolaus Ewig,[137]
Bernard Sigmund,
John Wendel Brechbill,
} Elders.

---

[137] Nicolaus Ewig, from Wachterstach, Germany, qualified in Philadelphia September 19, 1732. In April, 1734, he signed the call of Boehm, extended to him by the Philadelphia congregation. He died in Philadelphia, March 29, 1748, aged seventy-three years. (Taken from *Church Record of First Reformed Church*, Philadelphia.)

Jacob Walter,
John Gebhard.[138] } Deacons.

To add this for the information of the Reverend of the Reverend Classis, I regard as serviceable and as my duty.
March 18, 1739.   BOEHM.

[XXVI. MR. BOEHM TO THE CLASSIS OF AMSTERDAM, MARCH 26, 1740.[139]]

Very Reverend Classis, Reverend and Devout Church Fathers:—

Your most devoted servant rendered and sent a very submissive report to the Reverend Classis on March 16, 1739. But since it is to be feared that it has not reached its destination, I again enclose a copy of it and submissively direct your attention to all that is contained therein.

I also consider myself in duty bound to give the Reverend Classis a full and true account of all that was reported therein and what further happened until now. This is contained in accompanying copies, marked A, B, C, D, [E], and also in the enclosed summary of the pledges of each congregation towards a contribution for the ministers' salaries and lastly in the additional report.

The Reverend Classis is surely not unfamiliar with what the Christian Synods are said to have resolved concerning the sending of necessary ministers to this country. Hence I felt the greatest anxiety lest the reports, which I had handed to Inspector Dorsius (and with which I trust he observed all necessary care) had been lost by accident or in some other way and thus through loss of time the work of the Lord might suffer a disastrous check. Besides considering it my duty, I also sent the duplicates, in order that, if they were not received at both places, they might reach the Reverend Church Fathers at least in one place and give them a clear insight into our condition here.

---

[138] All these names, except the last, are found attached to the call, given to Boehm by the Philadelphia congregation on April 20, 1734, see p. 233f.

[139] The original German letter is in the Classical Archives.

The condition of our true church and the ways of the people are so well known to me that my eyes will be awake in solicitude and my heart will not cease sighing to God for His gracious help, for what could be considered greater than to preserve dear souls from destruction and torment. But if it should continue long that the people would have to be without ministers, having renounced now disorder and having promised to wait, what disorder would Satan not try to stir up again through the sects, and even through those, who among themselves are to be found as the most wicked men, that have ever practiced it? The disorder would be worse than it ever was before.

All good manner [of procedure] is employed by his Reverence, Inspector Dorsius. His Reverence handles affairs in so friendly and careful a manner, that my heart rejoices over it. Yet the ill manners of some proud and stubborn people, caused by the prevailing liberty, have already made him very indignant. However, it is only necessary to give them no audience and to silence the audacious Reiff. Then soon all would change, for there are only a few of them and Reiff is always the instigator. Yet they always try, when they put out a lying report, to make their number appear large through signatures, as they did on March 23rd last, when they signed a letter in Reiff's Church and, as is reported, had all the servants and boys sign it. What their object was in doing it, is unknown to me.

Very Reverend Classis, it pleased the Christian Synods to give a power of attorney to Inspector Dorsius and Dr. Diemer,[140] with regard to the money collected by Do. Weiss and Reiff. But thus far I have not noticed that any important steps in this case were taken. However, I know that Reiff only laughs at it. It is very sad that the poor congregations are in such misery, as has been stated repeatedly and that the money, given out of love to them, should remain so long in the hands of such wicked men, who have practiced usury with it thus far, while great help could be gained from it. With it we could retain the beautiful and useful place at Schip Bach, but if it

---

[140] The authorization, given to Dorsius and Diemer to prosecute Reiff, was contained in a letter of Deputy Ernst E. Probsting, dated May 3, 1739. It is mentioned in a letter of Diemer, dater November 18, 1742. The latter is in The Hague Archives, 74, I, 38.

lasts long, I and my brethren cannot keep it any more, for they now want the capital, of which since 1735 annually fifteen pounds should have been paid. But we had enough to do to pay the interest. Now, if they are in earnest, as we fear, then we shall be unavoidably compelled to sell the place again, for the obedient part of the congregation is small and poor. This would be a great loss to the congregation.

Concerning Dr. Diemer, I am very much surprized, yet I have no right to speak [complain]. For I cannot believe that the affair will go as it ought. Time will show, as I believe. Something may also be learned from a perusal of the reports from Pennsylvania, in which everything is truthfully recorded. I shall hope for the best and herewith repeat my former petitions.

Commending the Very Reverend Classis together with all their families and holy services to God and the Word of His grace.

I continue to remain as long as I live,

VERY REVEREND CLASSIS,
Your submissive and obedient servant and humblest fellow brother in Jesus, JOHAN PH. BOEHM.
Minister of the Congregations of Falckner Schwam, Schip Bach and Weitmarge.
Pennsylvania, Philadelphia County,
Witpen Township, March 26, 1740.

[As stated above, this letter was accompanied by the following enclosure:]

ENCLOSURE A.

[REV. P. H. DORSIUS TO MR. BOEHM, NOVEMBER 28, 1738.]

Do. J. P. Boehm, minister at Schipbach etc., is requested by me the subscriber, as deputy and inspector of the Pennsylvania German Reformed churches, to give a report of the following:

(1) How many German Reformed congregations are there in Pennsylvania, and how far are they from each other?

(2) How many elders, deacons and communicants are there in each of his congregations and how many congregations are served by him?

(3) How is each congregation supplied with schoolmasters and precentors?

P. H. DORSIUS.

Bucks County,
November 28, 1738.

ENCLOSURE B.

[REPORT OF MR. BOEHM TO THE CLASSIS OF AMSTERDAM, JANUARY 14, 1739.[141]]

After his Reverence, Mr. P. H. Dorsius, minister at Jamine [Neshaminy] in Bucks County, Pennsylvania, had shown to me, the undersigned, on the 28th of November, 1738, in his house at Jamine [Neshaminy], the letters sent to his Reverence by the two Christian Synods of North and South Holland, and after he had read to me that the two Christian Synods, for the sake of convenience, had authorized and ordained him as inspector of the Pennsylvania Reformed congregations, his Reverence requested me to give a report on the following questions:

1. How many German Reformed congregations are there in Pennsylvania and how far are they from each other?

2. How many elders, deacons and communicants are there in each congregation and how many are served by me?

3. How each congregation is supplied with schoolmasters and precentors?

Therefore I have considered myself under obligation to give his Reverence a dutiful specification and to make a full report concerning all other questions.

[I. CONGREGATIONS.]

As far as I know the congregations of the High German Reformed people in Pennsylvania[142] are these:

[1]. Falkner Schwam. In this congregation there are always four elders and two deacons. The Lord's Supper is administered twice a year. The communicants on September 17, 1738 [numbered] .... 89.

[141] A copy of this report was sent to the Synods also, now at The Hague, 74, I, 27.

[142] For the history of these congregations, see above, pp. 58-81.

[2]. Schip Bach. (About twelve English miles from Falkner Schwam). In this congregation the same custom [as to elders and deacons] prevails and it is treated like the last [as to the Lord's Supper]. There communed on September 24, 1738 ....36.

[3]. Weitmarge. About sixteen English miles from Schip Bach. This Weitmarge [Whitemarsh] is not more than four English miles from Germandon. Most of the people live still nearer and are about ten miles from Philadelphia. These three congregations are served by Boehm as their regular minister. In this congregation there are only two elders and two deacons, on account of the small number of members, but as to the rest [the Lord's Supper] the same custom prevails as in the above congregations. There communed on September 3, 1738 ....29.

N. B. With regard to the congregation at Schip Bach it ought to be mentioned, that it is so weak because for a considerable time one after another has maintained the confusion caused by Do. Weis in the year 1728, which Henry Goetschi still continues at this time. He preaches to the followers of Reiff, however few there may be of them, as if he were a regular minister. Still another, by the name of John William Straub, has undertaken to officiate as minister in all things, through which a considerable number of people have been drawn away from the congregation. Otherwise it would be again as strong.

[4]. Philadelphia. (It is served by Boehm. It is six English miles from Germandon.) This congregation accepted, in the month of July, 1734, the constitution, which is among the Pennsylvania documents of the Very Reverend Classis of Amsterdam, and which is in use here [in Pennsylvania]. The congregation has thus far been served by John Philip Boehm, whom they accepted as their regular pastor. He holds services in this congregation every four weeks. On September 10, 1738, the communicants present were......................75.

[5]. Germandon. With this congregation I have had no personal relations, nor have I any exact knowledge about its condition because, although it was often proposed to them, they were never willing to submit to any Church Order. Yet this much is known to me, because I asked two of the elders, Minch

[Meng][143] and Benzel,[144] that in the month of September, 1734, about thirty communicants were present. Since then John Bechtel has preached for them and has undertaken to administer the sacraments. Then they also allowed the old Gulde [Guldin][145] to preach in their church. Now the Lutherans also make use of it, and thus the Reformed people there are at present in a rather poor condition.

[6]. Cannastocka [Conestoga]. This place is very far away, a distance of more than seventy miles from Philadelphia. The Reformed people there have in fact organized themselves into three congregations. The first which was started I call the Hill Church.[146] It lies in the center. I served this congregation in agreement with their call (which was to visit them twice a year) on October 15, 1727. As this was the first time that a [Reformed] communion service was ever celebrated in Cannastocka, there were present fifty-nine communicants. But these visits were made only a few times. Then Do. Weis slandered me in this congregation by a very abusive letter (which I have in my possession).[147] He thereby misled them and drew the congregation to himself. But soon afterwards he left them again. Whereupon Miller went there to carry on the work of Weis. At that time Miller drew also Dolpihacken [Tulpehocken] to himself. I warned them afterwards often against this false spirit, but the misguided and simple-minded

---

[143] John Christopher Meng, from Mannheim, Germany, arrived in Philadelphia, August 24, 1728. By trade he was a mason. In 1734, he paid quit-rent on 15 acres of land in Germantown. His home above Chelton Ave., Germantown, is the building lately occupied by Mr. Oliver Jester as a tin shop. See Dr. Keyser's description of the house in *Old Historic Germantown* (Proceedings of Pa. German Society, Vol. XV (1904), p. 24f.

[144] John George Benzel (Bentzel) was naturalized in 1730 (see Rupp, *Thirty Thousand Names,* p. 435). In 1734 he owned and paid quit-rent on 15 acres of land in Germantown (see Rupp, l. c., p. 473). His house, which stands on the north corner of Upsal and Main Streets, Germantown, was built by him in 1727. In 1788, it was purchased by Michael Billmeyer, a Germantown printer. See Keyser, l. c., p. 32.

[145] For Rev. Samuel Guldin, the earliest Reformed minister in Pennsylvania, see note 132, p. 107.

[146] This church is identical with Heller's Church in Upper Leacock township, Lancaster County. For its history, see pp. 62-65.

[147] Printed above, pp. 212-214.

people clung to him, until finally the deception, with regard to which I had so faithfully warned them, came to light and this Miller publicly went over to the evil sect of the Seventh Day "Tumplers" [Dunkers] and was baptized in Dunker fashion at Cannastocka in the month of April, 1735.[148] He took with him about 10 families, Reformed and Lutheran, from the congregation at Dolpihacken, who did as he did.[149]

This caused a great alarm among the congregations. Those who were kept by God sent therefore messengers and letters to me and once more asked for help, which I did not dare to refuse. I went to them again, and there were, on May 11, 1735, in the said first congregation or Hill Church, at Cannastocka, communicants ....92.

On the same journey I administered the Lord's Supper, at their own request, in the second congregation (the name of the place is Cocollica [Cocalico]),[150] which had been gathered previously. There were present, as communicants........60.

But as regards the third congregation in Cannastocka, which has been gathered in the new town called Lancaster,[151] I have

[148] Miller himself stated repeatedly that this baptism took place in May, 1735. See *Ephrata Chronicle,* Engl. Transl., p. 73; also Miller's letter of December 5, 1790, quoted above, note 117, p. 254f.

[149] Another account of Miller's conversion was given by Boehm in his book, "Faithful Warning," published in 1742, see below, p. 353f.

[150] Cocalico, so named after the Cocalico Creek, is now Bethany, at Ephrata, Lancaster County.

[151] The first reference to the Reformed congregation in Lancaster, is found in a letter of Conrad Tempelman, written on February 13, 1733, to the Synods of Holland. It is printed in part, p. 62ff. In it the number of members is given as thirty. The congregation must have originated between 1730-1732. Its elders in 1733 were John Jacob Hook and Andrew Halsbrun. The first church record of the congregation was opened in 1736. It presents the following historical statement regarding the first church building and the first pastor: "Now as regards the building of our church, the beginning was made in the year 1736, and by the help of God it was so far completed that on the 20th of June, or upon the festival of Holy Whitsuntide, we held divine services in it for the first time. The teacher, preacher and pastor, called to this office of God, was the reverend and truly pious John Jacob Hock. Guided by God's Spirit, he chose as his introduction [reading lesson] the words in the prophecy of Isaiah, in the 35th chapter, and the first verse: 'The wilderness and the solitary places shall be glad for them! And the desert shall rejoice and blossom as the

no information, for up to this time they have acted according to their own pleasure. They have never cared for church order, but thus far have allowed themselves to be served by irregular men. However, I hear that it is a pretty strong congregation.

These three places in Cannastocka are situated as follows:

Lancaster $\begin{cases} \text{southward;} \\ \text{six miles to} \end{cases}$ Hill Church $\begin{cases} \text{six English} \\ \text{miles to} \end{cases}$ Cocollica

[7]. Dolpihacken. From Cannastocka it is about eighteen English miles to Dolpihacken. Served by Boehm. This place is probably nearly as far from Philadelphia as Cannastocka. Both are situated towards northwest. It is a pretty large place, and the congregation there has also contemplated a division. But it seems to me to be more advisable to have a meeting place in the center, as it was in the beginning. With this plan the majority agree, even those who live at the greatest distance from the center. Then the minister could supply the neighboring places, where already many people live, and where still more are gathering, at the times appointed to serve them, as it might be arranged later.

Some years ago it seemed that Cannastocka and Dolpihacken could be served with difficulty, but if necessary by one

---

rose.' The text itself [of the sermon] was the latter clause of the 4th verse of the 103rd Psalm: 'Who crowneth thee with loving kindness and tender mercies.' And we joined with each other in singing the 84th Psalm. As regards the election of the first elders of the church, John Henry Bassler, Felix Müller, John Gorner, and Peter Dörr, were elected by the congregation and declared duly qualified. It was resolved at the same time that two should withdraw annually and that again other two should be elected in their places; accordingly at the expiration of the first year, John Henry Bassler and Peter Dörr retired and Peter Balspach and Frederick Strubel were elected in their places; which order it is now our intention to follow as long as the good God in His grace shall keep us together. We hope also that those who shall come after us, into whose hands this book shall fall, will continue to do the same, in order that the praise and honor and glory of God may be advanced day by day, the longer the more. Amen. The first deacons elected were John Käller and John Stephen Rammerstberger." See *History of the First Reformed Church*, Lancaster, Pa., by W. Stuart Cramer, 1904, pp. 8-12. John Jacob Hock served the congregation from June, 1736, to October, 1737. In April, 1739, John Bartholomew Rieger became pastor of the congregation. He served it till February, 1743.

minister. But since then both have spread to such an extent that it is impossible for one minister to serve them as they should be. For this Dolpihacken has much increased since Miller has become such a disgrace. I travel thither, according to their request, twice a year and administer the Lord's Supper. On October 19th and 22nd last year [1738], there were present as communicants at two places[152] .... 134.

N. B. When I administered the Lord's Supper there for the first time, in the month of October, 1727, at the same time as at Cannastocka, there were only 32 communicants. In this congregation there are, in accordance with our Church Order, four elders and two deacons. Two elders and one deacon go out of office regularly every year and just as many come in, the same as in all the congregations which I serve.

[8]. Goschenhoppen. Of this congregation I know little, for it never wanted to be under our Church Order, but desired to be its own master. When Do. Weis, as stated above, came into the country and caused great confusion, they faithfully adhered to him. When he traveled to Holland, in order to obtain the well known money collected there, they immediately clung to Miller,[153] who, assisted by another person,[154] continued to serve Goschenhoppen. Besides, they kept, by their services, the congregation at Schip Bach in a state of continuous restlessness and ill-feeling, which had been begun by Weis. All my requests, entreaties and warnings were in vain. After these men had failed, they arbitrarily made Henry Goetschi their pretended minister, when he was hardly eighteen years of age and but half a year before had received the Lord's Supper for the first time from Do. Rieger at Germandon.[155] Goetschi at once

[152] For the two Tulpehocken churches in 1738, see p. 68.

[153] Peter Miller made 69 baptismal entries in the New Goshenhoppen record, extending from June, 1731, to July, 1734. See *Perkiomen Region*, Vol. III, p. 94f.

[154] This other person may have been John William Straub. See Boehm's remarks in connection with Skippack, above p. 273.

[155] Boehm probably misunderstood the situation. In November, 1736, Goetschy received the Lord's Supper in the Reformed Church of Germantown from the hands of Rev. J. B. Rieger, and he joined the congregation at the same time as a member. In 1744, when in difficulty in New Jersey, Goetschy requested and received a certificate from the Germantown church, stating that fact. This certificate is printed

undertook to administer the Lord's Supper, and to baptize, to install elders and to marry people. In short he did what belongs to the office of a regular minister. Goschenhoppen still has him at present as its preacher, and permits him to keep up and carry on this disorder from Goschenhoppen as a center, not only at Schip Bach, but at other places also.[156] He has done this, for instance, at Oly, where he misled the congregation, which was established by me at their request, and he now serves them also. At Dolpihacken he attempted to do the same through three uncalled-for visits, but he was refused. Yet he does not discontinue such improper actions.

Meanwhile this Goschenhoppen is a congregation or a place where a faithful shepherd and minister is greatly needed, through whose wise administration a flourishing congregation ought soon to be established. There are also several congregations near Goschenhoppen which should be provided for, as Great Swamp and Sackon Krik [Saucon Creek]. These, although they can be served by the minister of Goschenhoppen with the administration of the sacraments and sometimes with a sermon, yet need to be provided with good readers, who have the ability to catechize, especially at Sackon-Krik, because it is a somewhat out-of-the-way place and many Reformed people live there.

[9]. Oly. This place has been in such a condition since I am in this country (which is now eighteen years)[157] that it is astonishing to hear about the many sects among them. The worst were those who called themselves "The New Born". Without hesitation they declared themselves to be equal to God and greater than our Saviour; they pretended to be free

in Dr Good's *History*, p. 185. It does not state that this was the first communion service he had ever attended, nor was it probably intended to imply this.

[156] Goetschy enumerates the following eleven preaching places on the title page of the New Goshenhoppen record, which was probably written in 1736: Skippack, Old Goshenhoppen, New Goshenhoppen, Great Swamp, Saucon, Egypt, Maxatawny, Moselem, Oley, Berne and Tulpehocken.

[157] In the *Minutes of Coetus*, p. 10, the word "about" was inserted before "eighteen years," by mistake. The German sentence reads plainly: "*Welches nun 18 Jahre.*"

(from sin), and more such things, which it would be too much to relate in detail. However, after God had removed such shameless blasphemers of His name, the true Christians met and desired to establish, by the help of God, a congregation according to our true Reformed doctrine. They therefore applied to me for help and assistance (of which I have proof). Whereupon I went there and found with heart-felt joy, after a careful investigation, a goodly number of very eager souls, firm in our Reformed doctrines. Then I began the Lord's work among them. I called the congregation together and made them acquainted, according to the best of my ability, with our Church Order. The congregation then elected four elders and two deacons, whom I installed, according to the Church Order, and in accordance with the desire of the congregation, on November 17, 1736. The congregation then accepted me to visit them twice a year (during the week) to administer the Lord's Supper and to baptize their children. When everything had been duly constituted, after a preparatory service, I administered the Lord's Supper, and the communicants present numbered .... 40.

But scarcely had this been done, when Henry Goetschi came and acted as above mentioned in the description of Goschenhoppen. Some who had long been separated from the Reformed church and had had intercourse with the above mentioned sects, as the New Born, used Goetschi in order to create confusion in the newly organized congregation. To make a beginning they offered that, if the congregation would accept this Goetschi, they would again come back to the Reformed Church and be helpful in all things. This pleased Goetschi, who pretended to have lately been recognized and ordained in Philadelphia[158] as a regular minister. He immediately preached in my place, and directly after the services baptized a child before the congregation. When later on I called the elders to account concerning this disorder, they excused themselves by saying, they had not asked him to do so; they had thought that he was ordained, as he told them, and he also acted as if I were satisfied with the arrangement. But the

---

[158] The Presbytery of Philadelphia examined Goetschy in 1737, but did not ordain him. See sketch of his life, p. 52f.

consistory was thereby divided, because some of the elders and deacons had not at all consented to let him preach unless having previously spoken to me about it, and since they now heard the contrary they were all at variance. But those who were led astray let everything pass, and Goetschi therefore continued, and has acted up to this time as if he were an ordained minister. At present I do not know how things are there, but this much I know, that a part of the elders and deacons whom I installed have until now withdrawn from the work. Nor have I been there since, because there has been such a confusion through Goetschi that I could not bring forth any fruit. But said instigators soon withdrew again, and aided little towards the building up of the congregation.

From all this it may be seen how necessary it is that a very faithful pastor be appointed to this congregation, that he may seek the lost and bring back those who have gone into error, so that even there the body of Christ may grow through His grace. The minister of this congregation can supply also the place which is called Gaguschi [Cacusi],[159] where (as I hear) likewise a considerable congregation has gathered. This place is about seven or eight miles from the center in Oly. Goetschi has also presumed for some time to serve this congregation with all the means of grace. A minister might also at the same time serve Maxadani [Maxatawny], which is at a distance of ten miles.

These places above mentioned are the nine main congregations with their subordinate preaching places, consisting of High German Reformed people, in Pennsylvania, as far as they are known to me, together with the statement how far they are apart from each other and whatever other information was required. But whatever God will permit to grow in the future and what members he will gather, when the number of inhabitants increases, is known to Him only. However, I think that six ministers would be sufficient to serve these congregations.

[159] Cacusi, so named after the Cacoosing Creek, is now St. John's or Hain's Church, near Wernersville, Berks County. The oldest church record of the congregation calls it the "Congregation in Heidelberg." It is located in Lower Heidelberg Township, Berks County. In January, 1739, a little log church had been built there, see below, p. 281.

[II. CHURCH BUILDINGS.]

Now concerning the church buildings in all these congregations, there have been erected the following (as far as I know):

Germandon.   A well built, pretty large stone church.

Cannastocka.   The Hill congregation has a small log church. The congregation at Lancaster has also one of logs. The congregation at Cocollica has also one of logs.

Dolpihacken.   There they laid out a cemetery, but not in the center, and erected on it a small building of logs, but not servicable for public worship.

Goschenhoppen.   As I heard from people that live there, they built a pretty large church at that place, which will be sufficient for them for some time, but it is poorly made of wood.

Schip Bach.   A log church was also built there ten years ago, when Do. Weis caused trouble in this congregation. But Jacob Reiff caused the lot on which the church stands to be transferred to his name, and still refuses admission to the properly organized congregation. One irregular minister after another has permitted himself to be used by Reiff and his followers to keep up the trouble in the congregation. This is the place which Goetschi quite irregularly still serves, to the great hindrance of a union in the congregation. For this reason the regular congregation was obliged to buy a lot at Schip Bach, which is at a very convenient place. But I fear that on account of the poverty of the members, unless God sends some help by His grace, the lot will be lost again on account of the debt still resting upon it. That would be the greatest loss to the congregation, since it would be difficult to obtain another lot.

At Falckner Schwam, Weitmarge, Oly, and Philadelphia and also at their subordinate preaching places, there is as yet nothing. Services are held with great inconvenience in houses and barns. Except at Gaguschi (Cacusi) near Oly, where as I hear, they have built a little log church for their use.

[III. SCHOOLMASTERS AND PRECENTORS.]

Now concerning the last point, how the congregations are supplied with schoolmasters and precentors, there is, as far as I know, nobody with a fixed position. My congregation at Falckner Schwam is well supplied. The name of the schoolmaster is John Reiffschneider.[160] There is also a schoolmaster at Philadelphia, his name is John Berger,[161] who is known to Do. Dorsius. But no one can make a living by it. The reason is, that no school in the country can bring enough children together for one to make a living by it (except at Philadelphia and Germandon, where the people live close together). Moreover the congregations have not the means and are not able at the time being to raise money enough to support anybody. There is as yet in the whole country no dwelling either for minister or for schoolmaster. Singing up to this time had to be conducted as best we could.

This is what I have been able to report according to the above mentioned request of Do. Dorsius. Nor do I believe that I can be accused (if the report be investigated) of having done anything useless against my better knowledge. But I have done all to the glory of God and the upbuilding of His true Church in this country.

JOHAN PHILIPS BOEHM,
High German Reformed Minister in Pennsylvania.
Pennsylvania, January 14, 1739.

The above report, which was made according to the request of his Reverence, Mr. P. H. Dorsius, minister at Jamine [Neshaminy], by his Reverence, Mr. John Ph. Boehm, our beloved teacher and faithful pastor, we, as the present members of the consistories, have heard read from beginning to end and have well understood.

---

[160] John Reiffschneider was no doubt a relative, probably a son of Sebastian Reiffschneider, who appears first in 1730 as one of the elders at Falkner Swamp.

[161] John Berger was still schoolmaster and precentor in Philadelphia in 1747, when, on April 6, 1747, he was given four pounds by the consistory for his pains and trouble. In an advertisement, inserted in Saur's paper of January 16, 1749, he still calls himself the Reformed schoolmaster in Philadelphia. Schlatter refers to him in his private diary, see *Journal of Presb. Hist. Soc.,* Vol. III, p. 168.

Now, as we think that everything in the same is thoroughly truthful, we can also officially attest (each consistory for its own congregation) that everything which concerns the same and is stated above is, according to the best of our knowledge, in reality so, as we do hereby:

Elders and Deacons of the congregation at Philadelphia, attest January 28, 1739.
{ Caspar Ulrich, elder.
Niclas Ewig, elder.
Bernhard Sigmund, elder.
John Wendel Brechbiehl, elder.
Jacob Walter, deacon.
John Gebhard, deacon. }

Elders and Deacons of the congregation at Falckner Schwam, attest February 4, 1739.
{ Bastian Reifschneider, elder.
Jacob Krausen, elder.
John Tricktenhengst, elder.
John Dunkel, elder.
Andrew Weis, deacon.
John Diet. Bucher, deacon. }

Elders and Deacons of the congregation at Oly, attest February 5, 1739.
{ Sebastian Gref, elder.[162]
John Frederick Leibi, deacon.
Henry Werner, deacon. }

Of the congregation at Schip Bach, attest February 11, 1739.
{ Jacob Arnet, elder.
Andrew Oberbeck, elder.
Ulrich Stefen, elder.
Adam Meyrer, elder.[163]
John Wuehrmann, deacon.
Jacob Beyer, deacon. }

[162] Sebastian Gref (Graaf) paid quit-rent on 100 acres in Oley Township, in 1734, see Rupp, l. c., p. 475.

[163] In 1734, Hans Adam Mauerer (same as Meyrer) paid quit-rent on 100 acres in Salford township; at the same time Hans Weyerman (same as Wuehrmann) paid quit-rent on 50 acres in Salford township, Rupp, l. c., p. 476. In 1728, "Hans Wörman" was one of the signers of a petition from the inhabitants of Falkner Swamp and Goshenhoppen, addressed to Governor Patrick Gordon. The name has hitherto not been recognized (Rupp, l. c., p. 470 omits it). But it is the sixth name in the second column of the signers of the petition, reproduced in facsimile in Vol. XXII of the Proceedings of the Pennsylvania-German Society. See D. W. Nead, *The Pennsylvania-German Settlement of Maryland*, Lancaster, 1914, facing p. 40. There are

Of the congregation at Weitmarge, attest February 18, 1739.
{ Willem de Wees, elder.
Christopher Ottinger, elder.
Ludwig Knaus, deacon.
Philip Scherer, deacon.[164]

Of the congregation at Dolpihacken, attest February 22, 1739.
{ Jacob Itzberger, elder.
Barthel. Schaefer, elder.
Andrew Aulenbacher, elder.
John Haak, elder.
Jacob Wilhelm, deacon.
John Knoll, deacon.

ENCLOSURE C.
[REV. P. H. DORSIUS TO MR. BOEHM, DECEMBER 6, 1739.]

Do. John Phil. Boehm, minister at Schip Bach, etc., is kindly requested by me, the undersigned commissioner of the two Netherland Synods, both of North and South Holland, to inquire among the High German churches of Pennsylvania, what each family is willing to contribute towards the support of a minister within the congregation or to a yearly salary, in order that the friendly request of the Reverend Christian Synods be complied with, which are greatly interested in the advancement of our Christian Reformed religion in Pennsylvania, and which have offered assistance to that end, provided that every congregation submit to their wise counsel; to which must be added, that they expect that all the Reformed congregations, out of respect to the Reverend Christian Synods, will refuse to hear the unordained ministers and hirelings, and refuse to accept them for the administration of the holy sacraments, etc., among whom are included the young Goetschy and Van Basten, who while students presume to do everything that belongs to a regular minister; in which matter the Christian Synods are very anxious to know where and how they were ordained and how they can appropriate to themselves the name of candidates, otherwise they must expect the displeasure of the Christian Synods and the consequences thereof.

P. H. DORSIUS,
Done in Bucks County, *Minister in Bucks County.*
December 6, 1739.

several other names of Reformed people which have not been recognized in this list: Gerhart de Heffe, the 25th name, is Gerhart In de Haven; Lorenz Bingeman, 1st name in second column; Conrad Reiff, 20th name in second column; Edward In de Havor (In de Haven), 21st name in third column.

[164] This is very likely Boehm's father-in-law, whose name was Philip Scherer.

ENCLOSURE D.

[CERTIFIED PLEDGES OF THE REFORMED CONGREGATIONS TOWARDS MINISTERS' SALARIES, FEBRUARY-MARCH, 1740.]

Do. John Philip Boehm, minister at Schip Bach and of the congregations here in Pennsylvania, which are mentioned below, has shown to us the friendly request of his Reverence, Mr. P. H. Dorsius, desiring to find out from the High German Reformed churches of Pennsylvania, what each family would contribute, without fail, to the annual salary and for the support of a minister in its congregation, so that the friendly request of the Christian Synods of South and North Holland might be heeded, since they have been greatly interested in the advancement of our Christian Reformed worship in Pennsylvania and have offered their assistance, provided that each congregation submit to their wise counsel, to which must be added that the Christian Synods expect all Reformed congregations, out of respect to the Christian Synods, to refuse to hear the unordained ministers and hirelings, and not to allow them to administer the holy sacraments, etc.

Therefore, we humble ourselves before the loving God, our heavenly Father, and praise His name, who graciously reveals at last to us, poor members of Christ, the gracious help, for which we have so long yearned and prayed in this country, where the danger to souls is so great, and He shows us how He intends to carry on His work by His faithful servants for our and our descendants' salvation of soul and eternal good.

Therefore, we poor members of Christ and true fellow-believers place ourselves under the fatherly protection of the Reverend Christian Synods as our devout Church Fathers, and commend ourselves to your sanctified care. We shall incessantly pray to God that He may pour out on you all spiritual and temporal blessings and bless your holy service.

We also promise herewith, out of obedient respect, to obey all the above mentioned requirements, humbly asking the Very Reverend Christian Synods to forgive the mistakes which we committed in this respect by reason of our necessity and simplicity.

But since it would be impossible and almost hurtful to allow the congregations, which are not yet supplied with regular ministers, to remain for a long time without receiving the Holy Sacraments, as there are innumerable men to lead them astray, therefore Do. John Philip Boehm has offered, if God spares his life and his bodily strength permits him to do so, to administer the sacraments to the unsupplied congregations, according to his ability. We acknowledge this as a grace of God, for we have no reason to make the least objection to his life, doctrine and conduct, and we shall heartily pray the kind God to support him by His power. Without his offer we could not have demanded of him to take this burden upon himself, because of the widely extended country, for he has enough work in the congregations entrusted to him and elsewhere throughout the country.

We also have the joyful hope that all the measures whatsoever that are to the glory of God and the advancement of the Church of Christ, undertaken by his Reverence, Mr. P. H. Dorsius, minister in Bucks County, whom the two Christian Synods have appointed inspector over this great work, will be devised in accordance with the wisdom given to him by God. He has sufficiently shown his sincere zeal in this work of the Lord; only we are heartily sorry that he is unwell and pray God that He will graciously strengthen and preserve him.

Concerning the statement what each family could contribute, without fail, to the annual salary, we must remark that in this moneyless country we are in a very poor and needy condition. The reasons are that almost all come to Pennsylvania on account of poverty and want of bodily food at other places.[165] There are still many of the first immigrants who have barely extricated themselves out of their debts; many are yet deep in debt; besides there is at present still a large number of those who have not paid for their ocean voyage and had to begin with debts. Moreover, there are also many who have not yet finished the years for which they bound themselves out as servants.[166] They must serve sectarians here and

---

[165] The principal causes for emigration from Germany were then as now, economic. Religious considerations, except in the case of the sects, played but a very subordinate part.

[166] The subject of "Redemptioners" and "Indentured Servants"

there, they themselves possessing less than nothing, yet, according to their certificates they are members of our true Church, Reformed according to the Word of God.

Wherefore we, as elders and deacons now in service in the Reformed congregations mentioned below, do hereby pledge ourselves, after careful investigation and mature deliberation, that it may be certain and the congregations be obliged to pay it annually, as soon as regular ministers are sent to them by the Christian Synods. We hereby dutifully attest this, with the approval of the congregations, each for his own congregation.

[CONGREGATIONAL PLEDGES.]

[1]. The congregation at FALCKNER SCHWAM pledges itself to contribute to the annual salary of the minister, surely and without fail:

Ten pounds of this country's money and
Twenty bushels of oats,
which we hereby attest:

The Congregation at Falckner Schwam, January 6, 1740.
{
John Tricktenhengst, elder.
John Dunkel, elder.
Frederick Reymer, elder.[167]
Jacob Kraus, elder.
John Dieter Bucher, deacon.
Adam Raeder, deacon.
}

in Pennsylvania has recently been investigated by Frank R. Diffenderfer in his book, *The German Immigration into Pennsylvania*, Lancaster, 1900; Part II, The Redemptioners, pp. 141-317; See also Geiser, *Redemptioners and Indentured Servants in Pennsylvania*, New Haven, 1901.

[167] Frederick Reymer (Reimer) arrived in Philadelphia in the ship "Thistle," and signed the declaration of allegiance August 29, 1730. On January 22, 1731, he bought of Henry Pannebacker and his wife, Eve, 100 acres of land in Frederick township. August 6, 1736, he bought of Joseph Groff and Barbara, his wife, 41 acres, 106½ perches, originally, also a part of the Pannebacker tract. Frederick Reimer made his will May 9, 1755, naming his wife, Elizabeth Reimer, and his son, John Peter Reimer, executors. The will was probated February 11, 1758. One of his daughters, Elizabeth Reimer, who married Francis Shunk, of Providence township, became the grandmother of Governor Francis R. Shunk. See Dotterer, *Perkiomen Region*, Vol. I, p. 103.

[2]. On January 13, 1740, Do. John Philip Boehm, our minister, presented to us in our regular congregation at Schip Bach all that is stated above. The congregation accepted everything with deep respect for the Very Reverend Christian Synods. But with regard to the contribution towards a fixed annual salary of a minister we state that the congregation is very weak and small, because the young Goetschi and another man, by the name of John William Straub, have assumed the ministerial office as unordained hirelings and have taken away two parts of this congregation and thus far have kept up the division. Therefore, we cannot promise a fixed sum. But, if the disorder could be removed and the congregation by the grace of God be reunited, then the members of the congregation are willing to stand in line with the congregation at Falckner Schwam, which, like ourselves, has Do. Boehm as its minister.

This we, the elders [and deacons] now in office attest hereby:

The Congregation at Schip Bach, date as above.	Ulrich Steffen, elder. Jacob Arnet, elder. Andrew Oberbeck, elder. Henry Wuehrmann, deacon. Hans Adam Meyrer, elder.

[3]. The Reformed congregation in Oly was first established in the year 1736, on May 4th, by the Rev. John Philip Boehm, upon our urgent request. The Lord's Supper was celebrated immediately and there were present thirty-nine communicants. At the second time, on November 17, 1736, forty were present. But when he administered the same the third time, the congregation was in a state of confusion, caused by the young Goetchi, who had sought adherents, and by some who had fallen away from the true religion and by others. Thus the congregation has been in a deplorable condition since then. But we, the elders now in office and members of the congregation pledge ourselves that the congregation in Oly shall contribute:

Ten pounds of this country's currency and
Twenty bushels of oats.

Hoping that the congregation, under the good administration of his Reverence, Inspector Dorsius, and by the admonition of the Rev. Mr. Boehm, will change for the better and unite in a Christian spirit, we sign this with our hand:

Oly, February 5, 1740.
{ Sebastian Gref, elder.
Frederick Leibi, deacon.
Henry Werner, deacon.
Isaac Levan, member.[168]
Jan de Bois, member.

[4]. The congregation of Maxadani [Maxatawny] will contribute, without fail, to the annual salary of a Reformed minister:

Four pounds of this country's currency, which we, the elders now in office in this congregation attest:

February 7, 1740.
{ Daniel Levan, elder.[169]
Peter Leibi, elder.

[5]. The Reformed congregation at Dolpihachen [Tulpehocken] promises to pay annually towards a minister's salary:

Fifteen pounds of this country's currency and
Fifty bushels of oats,

which we, the elders now in office attest by order of the congregation:

February 11, 1740.
{ Henry Meyer, elder.
Jacob Wilhelm, elder.
Andrew Aulenbach, elder.
John Haag, deacon.
John Fohrer, deacon.

---

[168] Isaac Levan, one of the sons of Daniel Levan, set out for Pennsylvania in 1715. He located in Exeter township near Reading. In 1730, Isaac Levan, resident of what is now Berks County, was naturalized. In 1734, he paid quit-rent on 230 acres of land in Oley Township. See Rupp, *Names,* p. 475. He died in 1758. See Stapleton, *Memorials of the Huguenots in America,* p. 68f.

[169] This is no doubt Daniel Levan, the emigrant, a son of Daniel Levan and his wife Marie Beau, Huguenots from Piccardy, France. They fled to Amsterdam, where they became members of the Huguenot Church there, and where one of their sons, Abraham, was baptized September 20, 1698. In 1715, four of the sons of Daniel, the refugee, set out for Pennsylvania, namely, Abraham, Isaac, Jacob and Joseph. Their brother Daniel followed in 1727. They settled in Berks County. See Stapleton, *Memorials,* p. 68f.

[6]. The Reformed congregation at Schwatare[170] [Swatara] promises to contribute annually to a minister's fixed salary:

Five pounds of this country's currency and
Ten bushels of oats,

which we, the elders and members of the congregation at the present time attest, with its approval:

Schwatare,
February 14, 1740.
{ Martin Kapp, deacon.
George Meyer, member.
John Philip Hautz, member.[171]
Daniel Schue, member.[172]

[7]. The Reformed congregation at Cocollica [Cocalico] promises to contribute annually to a minister's fixed salary:

Six pounds of this country's currency and
Twenty bushels of oats,

which we, the present elders and members of the congregation hereby attest with their consent:

Cocollica in Cannastocka,
February 15, 1740.
{ Jacob Weis, deacon.
Andrew Holtzbaum, deacon.

[8]. Canastocka. The Reformed congregation of the

---

[170] The original Swatara Church stood halfway between Fredericksburg and Jonestown, near the line of the former South Mountain Railroad, in Swatara Township, Lebanon County. About 1765, the congregation divided, one-half going to Stumpstown (now Fredericksburg) and forming there what is now St. John's Church, of Fredericksburg, the other going to Jonestown and forming there a congregation of the same name, St. John's Church, at Jonestown. The latter belongs now to the Swatara charge, the former to the Bethel charge, in Lebanon Classis. See E. Grumbine, *Two Dead and Lost Churches on the Swatara*, 1901. (Paper read before Lebanon Co. Hist. Soc., Vol. I, No. 14.)

[171] Philip Hautz and Anna Margareth, his wife, brought a son to Rev. Conrad Tempelman for baptism, December 16, 1740. His name was Philip Lorentz. Another son, Christopher, was baptized by Tempelman, January 23, 1753. Entered in *Swatara Church Record*.

[172] A daughter of Daniel Schuy and Anna Maria, his wife, named Barbara, was baptized by Rev. C. Tempelman, June 25, 1741. Another daughter, named Catharine Elizabeth, was baptized June 8, 1747. Entered in *Swatara Church Record*. Daniel Schuey died 1777, leaving nine children. See Stapleton, *Memorials*, p. 122.

Berg Kirch [Hill Church] promises to contribute annually to a minister's fixed salary, if one is sent to them by the Christian Synods:

Eight pounds of this country's currency and
Twenty-five bushels of oats,
which we hereby attest:

February 16, 1740.
{ Lorentz Herchelroth, elder.
Michael Albert, elder.
Michael Weidler, elder.[173]
John Leyn, elder.[174]

[9]. The High German Reformed Congregation in Lancaster, Canastocka, resolved to contribute:

Fifteen pounds of this country's currency,
towards the annual support of a Reformed minister. For the confirmation and unfailing contribution of the above named sum, we subscribe our names in good faith and with firm determination:

February 17, 1740.
{ Jost Frenler, elder.
Niclaus Treber, elder.
John de Huff, elder.

[10]. The High German Reformed congregation in Philadelphia promises as a yearly contribution towards the fixed salary of its minister:

Ten pounds of this country's currency,

---

[173] Michael Weidler was born September 14, 1705, at Kirchart, in the Palatinate. A warrant for 185 acres of land, lying on Conestoga Creek was issued to him January 19, 1733. On February 11, 1743, two acres of land, adjoining Jacob Heller's land, "Whereon the meeting house now stands," was deeded to "John Line and Michael Widler, by Philip Scot, of Leacock township, for the use of the Presbiterian Congregation of the said Church in Leacock aforesaid." At the meeting of Coetus in 1747, Weidler represented the charge of Rev. J. B. Rieger. He died July 23, 1770, and was buried in the cemetery adjoining Heller's Church.

[174] On October 23, 1735, a warrant for 100 acres of land in Leacock township, "adjoining John Line's land," was issued to Jacob Heller. John Lein was one of the trustees of the Heller Church property (see last note). In 1748, he represented his congregation at the Coetus.

which we, the elders in office, attest:

Philadelphia,
February 24, 1740.
{ John Wendel Brechbiehl, elder.
John Michael Diel,[175] elder.
Valentin Beyer, elder.
John Gebhardt, deacon.
John Jacob Maag,[176] deacon.

[11]. The congregation at Weitmarge [Whitemarsh] consists of very few families and is willing to belong to the congregation at Germandon. If the latter should be supplied with a regular minister by the Reverend Church Fathers, then Weitmarge is willing to contribute its share towards his support, to which we, the elders long in office, hereby subscribe our names:

Weitmarge,
March 16, 1740.
{ William de Wees, elder.
Christopher Ottinger, elder.
Philip Scherrer, deacon.

[12]. The Reformed congregation at Germandon [Germantown] has been for a considerable time in a miserable condition, on account of all kinds of sectarians, of whom some arose even among ourselves who wanted to be ministers. Therefore, many members, together with ourselves, stay away entirely from the congregational meetings. But we hope that, by the grace of God and the help of the Reverend and Devout Church Fathers in Holland, this congregation may soon be put into a good and God-pleasing condition. For this we shall incessantly pray to our Heavenly Father, in order that the salvation of our and our descendants' souls may be accomplished. Hence we

---

[175] John Michael Diel qualified in Philadelphia, September 29, 1733. In August, 1748, he was sexton of the Philadelphia Reformed Church.

[176] John Jacob Maag qualified at Philadelphia, August 30, 1737. In 1747, he was one of the elders of the Philadelphia congregation and treasurer for the new church building. He signed his will May 5, 1767. It was probated May 20, 1767. It contained this provision: "I also give unto the needy or poor housekeepers belonging to the Dutch Reformed congregation five pounds to be divided among said poor by my executors as they think fit and that in one year after my decease." His other beneficiaries were his wife, Catherine, and his son-in-law, George Button.

are of the opinion that if, by a good and wholesome ordinance, this congregation at Germandon and that of Weitmarge would be united,

Ten pounds of this country's currency,
would annually and without fail be contributed towards the salary of a minister, which we at Germandon hereby conscientiously attest:

Germandon, { John Niclas Rauch.
March 18, 1740. { Jacob Baumann,[177]

[13]. From the copy made by the hand of Henry Goetschi.

In accordance with the above ecclesiastical arrangement, the congregation in New Goschenhoppen promises:

Ten pounds.   { Herman Fischer,
   Elders.   { George Steinmann,
                  { Casper Holtzhauser,
                  { Andrew Greber.

The congregation in Great Swamp:

Five pounds.   { Felix Brunner,
   Elders.   { Michael Eberhard,
                  { Christian Willauer,[178]
                  { Jacob Wetzel.

The congregation at Saucon Creek:

Five pounds.   { George Best,
   Elders.   { Frantz Blum,
                  { Frederick Scholl,
                  { Tobias Baal.

[177] Jacob Bauman qualified at Philadelphia October 2, 1727. In 1734 he paid quit-rent on eight acres of land in Germantown. See Rupp, *Names*, p. 473. He was one of the four trustees of the Germantown church. See note 107.

[178] Christian Willauer was born 1706. February 22, 1734, he obtained a warrant for 150 acres of land "between New Cowesohoppin and the Great Swamp." January 1, 1734, his son, John Adam, was baptized by Rev. John Peter Miller. In 1757, he was a member of the Great Swamp Church, under Rev. G. W. Weiss.

The above copies, marked A, B, C and D have been carefully examined and found to be exact transcripts of the true originals. These originals are signed as follows: A and C with the signature of his Reverence, Inspector Dorsius; B and D with the signatures of the elders and deacons now in office in the congregations mentioned above (except Goschenhoppen, Great Swamp and Saucon Creek; these are copies made from the copies of young Goetschi). This we hereby attest:

At Falckner Schwam,
March 30, 1740.
{ FREDERICK REYMER, elder.
JOHN TRICKENHENGST, elder.
ADAM RADER, deacon.

SUMMARY

of that which each High German Reformed congregation here in Pennsylvania[179] pledged itself to contribute unfailingly to

---

[179] Although Boehm included in the following list most of the Reformed congregations in existence in Pennsylvania in 1740, his list is by no means complete. It will serve a useful purpose if we present a list of all the Reformed congregations, known to us at present, which were in existence in 1740, together with the year of their organization. Those years that are marked with an asterisk (*) are only approximate. In those cases the first year when they are actually mentioned in still existing records has been chosen. We arrange them according to counties and the latter in chronological order:

I. In Montgomery County: (1) Falkner Swamp, 1725; (2) Skippack, 1725; (3) Whitemarsh, 1725; (4) New Goshenhoppen, 1727; (5) Old Goshenhoppen, *1730.

II. In Lancaster County: (1) Hill Church, Conestoga, 1725; (2) Lancaster, *1733; (3) Cocalico, *1733; (4) Muddy, Creek, *1733; (5) Seltenreich, Earltownship, *1733; (6) White Oaks, *1733.

III. In Philadelphia County: (1) First Church, Philadelphia, 1727; (2) Germantown, 1727.

IV. In Berks County: (1) Tulpehocken, Host Church, 1727; (2) Oley, *1734; (3) Berne, *1736; (4) Maxatawny, *1736; (5) Moselem, *1738; (6) Cacusi, 1738.

V. Lehigh County: (1) Egypt, *1734; Great Swamp, 1734; (3) Heidelberg, *1740.

VI. Northampton County: (1) Saucon, *1734.

VII. Lebanon County: (1) Tulpehocken, Trinity Church, 1738; (2) Swatara, *1739; (3) Quittopahilla, *1739.

This list shows that by the year 1740, *at least twenty-six* congregations were in existence, of which Boehm mentions seventeen in the above list. But the younger Tulpehocken Church mentioned elsewhere (see p. 398), must be added as the eighteenth congregation.

the annual salary of a minister, promised by the then officiating elders and deacons with their own hands (in case ministers are sent to them by the Very Reverend Synods of Holland), including an additional report.

			Pounds of Pa. Currency	Bushels of Oats
1 {	The congregation in Falckner Schwam, January 6, 1740...		10	20
	" "	at Schip Bach, January 13, 1740........	10	20
	" "	in Oly, February 5, 1740	10	20
2 {	" "	in Maxadani, February 7, 1740	4	
	" "	in Gaguschi, pledged nothing	..	..
	" "	in Dolpihacken, February 11, 1740......	15	50
3 {	" "	at Schwatare, February 14, 1740.......	5	10
	" "	in Quitebehele, united with Dolpihacken	..	..
	" "	in Canastocka, called Cocolica, Feb. 15.	6	20
4 {	" "	at the Hill Church, February 16, 1740..	8	25
	" "	in Lancaster, February 17, 1740........	15	
	" "	in Philadelphia, February 24, 1740.....	10	
5 {	" "	at Germandon, March 16, 1740 }	10	
	" "	at Weitmarge, March 18, 1740 }		
	" "	at New Goschenhoppen	10	
6 {	" "	at Great Swamp	5	
	" "	at Saconkrik	5	
		Total	123	165

ADDITIONAL REPORT.

1. Concerning the congregation at Gaguschi [Cacusi]. I was there on the 8th of February [1740] and spoke with Jacob Rieser, who showed me the way to N. Riehm,[180] a deacon, with whom I stayed over night. Next morning he went with me to John Kirschner. I explained to them the affair as well as I could. But I noticed more distrust than zeal for this good and beneficial cause. When I finally desired to know their will and opinion, they answered that they would consider the case among themselves and come to me to Dolpihacken on

---

[180] The letter N. is used in German to indicate a name unknown to the writer. The Berne church record (a neighboring church) mentions a Martin Riem, whose son, John George, was baptized February 20, 1749. His sponsor was John George Riem.

the 10th and 11th [of February] and sign the paper. But, although I waited for them beyond the appointed time, they did not come.

2. Concerning the congregation Quitebehele[181] [Quitopahilla], we considered the case, and since this congregation is still very weak, and only one man, by the name of John Blum[182] (a very able man for a reader) lives about eight miles from Dolpihacken, but all the others live nearer to that place, we found it advisable to wait until in time more people live there, and till then save the trouble and expense of a minister. They, therefore, joined the congregation at Dolpihacken the more readily, because Dolpihacken will have to be served at two places, on account of its wide extent and rapid growth. One of the places will be nearer to them to go to church to, and may be counted instead of Quitebehelen, because it extends in that direction and is already in use.

3. Concerning the congregation of Germandon. When at one time I wanted to speak to them about it, I found little attention. His Reverence, Mr. Dorsius, knows the conditions there as well as I. Yet I firmly hope to God that some time it will be better. Then the weak congregation at Weitmarge can be united with it, as it has shown all the time a willingness to do so, and it can hardly be arranged in any other way.

4. Concerning the congregation of Goschenhoppen, I know not what to say. I have been there three times, yet I have not been able to do anything, although I entreated them very urgently not to cast aside the grace of God, now so clearly visible. When I went to them the third time, they (namely

---

[181] The Quittopahilla church, so named from the Quittopahilla Creek, a tributary to the Swatara, is today represented by the Hill Church, near Annville, about three and a half miles west of Lebanon. This is the first reference to the congregation that has come to light.

[182] John Blum arrived in Philadelphia, September 4, 1728. He took out a warrant for 100 acres of land in Lebanon township, December 19, 1737. The land was patented to him March 17, 1741. His will was dated January 5, 1759. It was probated at Lancaster, November 13, 1759. (Communicated by Dr. S. P. Heilman.) He was repeatedly visited by Moravian missionaries. Thus Rev. Leonhard Schnell, under date June 25, 1746, writes in his diary: "Today I went over the Quitopehill and appointed a sermon at Peter Kucher's. I visited N. Blum, a dear old grey man, who is preacher there."

the elders) held a meeting on the 23rd of February, and a part of them promised me at last to come on the 26th or the 27th, in order to sign the paper. I also heard that the people in Great Swamp [Gross Schwam] and those at Saconkrik were not at fault. However, I did not see any of them.

POSTSCRIPT. Since the Inspector, Mr. Dorsius, could not go to Germandon, I went there on March 18th, 1740, accompanied by an elder from Weitmarge, by the name of Christopher Ottinger. We two, and two other members there, deliberated, as is found at the end of the paper marked D. I firmly hope to God that when the [proposed] arrangement has once been made, and they are supplied with a regular minister, it will soon be one of the most beautiful congregations, for ten miles in circumference all must attend services there. The church there is a beautiful, well built stone church. It is also quite large, but they still owe 140 pounds to four men,[183] as Mr. Baumann, whose name is signed above, told me.

J. P. BOEHM.

ENCLOSURE E.

[PROVISIONAL REPARTITION OF THE REFORMED CONGREGATIONS IN PENNSYLVANIA, 1740.]

Provisional repartition of the churches of the High German Reformed people in Pennsylvania, and how these churches may be combined and served in the most convenient and useful way by six ministers, according to the testimony of the elders and deacons of most of the places, as contained in the above report, which was required of me:

I. For one minister Philadelphia and Germandon; he might live most conveniently at [Philadelphia].

II. Falckner Schwam and Schip Bach, to which also Weitmarge belongs. These are the three congregations of Boehm, for which he was ordained by the Very Reverend Classis of Amsterdam through the Reverend Ministers at New York, on November 23, 1729. Weitmarge, because it is only

---

[183] These four men are mentioned in the deed, see note 107.

four miles, and partly half that distance from Germandon and sixteen miles from Schip Bach, may with greater convenience be joined to Germandon, whose people might there attend church services. Do. Boehm and the elders at Weitmarge are willing to consent to this (if such a union should please our Reverend Church Fathers) and Do. Boehm desires to retain Falckner Schwam and Schip Bach as his remaining two congregations. The parsonage can most suitably be located at Schip Bach, if the church lot, which was bought there, can be retained. Therefore he prays very earnestly for greatly needed help, so that it can be kept by the congregation.

III. Canastocka, in which there are three [preaching] places. The minister could live most conveniently near the Hill Church, from which he would have to go six miles in opposite directions.

IV. Dolpihacken, where probably a place could be found in the center, where everything can be located together. The subordinate preaching points here are: Quitebehelen and Schwadare, both, according to report, seven or eight miles farther up. They are reported to be pretty strong congregations, but consisting mostly of poor people, who cannot help themselves at all.

V. Oly. There the same condition prevails, and perhaps a suitable place may still be found, from which Gaguschi and Maxadani may be served.

VI. Goschenhoppen. As in the last two congregations, a place might here also be found for a minister's dwelling house, which would not be too-inconvenient in order to supply Great Swamp [Grossen Schwam] and Saconkrik [Saucon Creek] from it.

[XXVII. THE CLASSIS OF AMSTERDAM TO REV. JOHN PHILIP BOEHM, APRIL 1, 1740.[184]]

To Rev. John Philips Boehm.
Reverend Sir and Esteemed Brother:—
The Reverend Classis of Amsterdam duly received your last letter of March 13th, 1739. It gave them much satisfaction that you

[184] A copy of the original letter is the *Classical Letterbook*, Vol. XXIX, p. 274.

were so zealously diligent in seeking to edify the churches in your vicinity and to promote their general welfare. May the Lord grant blessed results to your labors, and incite you to greater watchfulness and to yet more earnest efforts in the ministry of the Gospel.

It was peculiarly agreeable to the Classis that you did not withdraw yourself, but that you showed your willingness to give explanations to the Rev. Mr. Dorsius, upon his written request, to the questions put by him to you, concerning the condition of those churches of which you have the oversight. We perused with great pleasure and joy the accurate account which you prepared of your churches, a copy of which you also sent us. This gives us the light we needed, to enable us to understand the exact condition of the churches in Pennsylvania. Therefore in the name of our Classis, we commend you for your careful investigation and earnest efforts in this matter. We now earnestly request you, and fraternally admonish you that you persevere in this course; and in unison with Mr. Dorsius,—to whom you give praise, to our gratification—to co-operate in everything, which may be of great service for the upbuilding and extension of the kingdom of Jesus among you.

We also want to assure you that all letters sent to us by you before 1739, were duly answered during the same year. No doubt by this time the answers have reached you. Never will we delay to answer, by the first opportunity, any letter which comes from you.

It was not without our being painfully affected, that we learned how much you were oppressed with various difficulties, under the heavy burdens of the ministry. We want to help you in all these things and shall endeavor to do so. To this end we will bring your request before the next Synod of North Holland, which is held in the year 1740, that you may receive some aid, to enable you to keep the church-ground from being forfeited, to the great injury of the congregation. We are not without hope that our endeavor thereto will not be altogether fruitless. We will also most gladly give you some personal aid and encouragement, for we greatly commiserate your straitened circumstances. Therefore our Classis has resolved that its churches should try to collect some money to send to you for your support.

And now what you wrote in your postscript, that some evil-minded persons in Philadelphia had written to us to your disadvantage: On this subject the Classis has already spoken, and from which you can perceive how much we seek to guard against all injustice, or lack of Christian caution, by a hasty judgement, without thorough investigation, and also hearing from yourself.

Further, Worthy Brother, it is the prayer of our souls that the Great Shepherd of the sheep may endow you richly, enabling you to gather the lambs of the flock into the spiritual fold, and to care for them with wisdom, and guide them by exemplary doctrine and deportment. May consolation and strength from above be granted you abundantly, to the glory of the Savior's name, which must forever become glorious among all churches. We are with all cordiality, etc., etc.

JOHN PLATINUS, *Praeses.*
TIBERIUS REYTSMA, *Scriba.*

Amsterdam,
April 1, 1740.

P. S. Enclosed, find a book by Rev. Mr. Kulenkamp, from the worthy Consistory of Amsterdam, for the service of yourself and other ministers in Pennsylvania. Meanwhile the Classis sends you for your support, in your poverty, the sum of . . . [185] [fl. 309].

[XXVIII. MR. BOEHM TO THE CLASSIS OF AMSTERDAM, APRIL 4, 1740.[186]]

Very Reverend Classis, Reverend and Devout Church Fathers:—

I had serious doubts about sending the enclosed copy (of a letter) to the Reverend Classis, believing that on its account I might be regarded with displeasure. Yet I thought it indispensably necessary, in whatever aspect I considered it, to let the Very Reverend and Devout Church Fathers see it, for they in their exalted wisdom will know what to do with it, in order that your poor fellow-servant may be guarded against further trouble.

This letter caused constant mischief, and was the continual support of the wicked associates of Jacob Reiff since the time of its arrival in this country. (Do. Weis brought it along from Holland.) The Christian Synods in their letters to his Reverence, Mr. Dorsius, have sufficiently declared their displeasure with the unordained preachers and hirelings.

About eight years ago I was shown this letter (of which the enclosed is a copy) from a distance, with the statement, that they did not concern themselves much about me and my Church Order, and that they knew what power and liberty they had.

Now, although I tried hard during all this time, yet I

---

[185] The amount is not stated in the copy of the letter in the letter-book of Classis, but the Minutes of Classis give it as fl. 309 ($123.60).

[186] The original German letter of Boehm is in the Classical Archives.

could not obtain the letter, until a few weeks ago. It came by accident out of their hands into mine.

Now I believe firmly that this letter was cunningly forged,[187] for

1st. A long time ago I heard from the lips of Reiff himself that he had received the same from Do. Wilhelmi in the Dutch language and that he had it translated into the German language in Holland.

2nd. The signature is written by the very hand of the translator, while the name of the translator is not mentioned. This ought to be entirely different.

3rd. The letter consists of six sheets, which have been sewed together with a blue silk ribbon and sealed. I cannot believe that it is Do. Wilhelmi's seal, for I have the seal on two letters in three forms, none of which is like it.

4th. In these letters Do. Wilhelmi wrote me, after I had notified him that they did such things in the name of his Reverence (which they did as the letter shows) and he assured me, if such was done in his name, it was done without his knowledge and approval. His letter is dated June 30, 1736.

5th. The so-called "Report and Instructions concerning Pennsylvania," drawn up by ten commissioners and printed by order of the Christian Synods (probably in 1731),[188] is almost uniform with the regulations of the enclosed letter. But nothing is mentioned (in the Report) about that which is contained in the beginning of the letter, with regard to the power and liberty which the letter grants to the people of this country and to the exercises of which it urges them. The letter likewise does not say to whom money had been given in Holland. The printed pamphlet, however, mentions that a considerable sum of money had been placed into the hands of Do. Weis in

---

[187] The whole letter was not forged. That would have been too difficult an undertaking, but a few sections were inserted, as indicated below.

[188] This "Report" has the distinction of being the first printed account of the Reformed Church of Pennsylvania. It was printed by the Synodical Deputies. The similarity of the report to the latter part of Wilhelmi's letter proves that Doctor Wilhelmi was the author of this "Report" of 1731. It was submitted to the Synod of South Holland, meeting July 3-13, 1731, at Dort.

Holland.

Hence no one would be a more fitting person to lead the poor, misguided people back upon the right way and bring about unity, love and a God-pleasing order, by exposing such cunning and fraud, than his Reverence, Do. Wilhelmi, whom God would graciously reward for it. This would certainly be the case, because many have passed away without being reconciled, and many have gone over to the sects on account of the trouble and disharmony occasioned by this letter, so that my heart often bled and sighed to God. I should be very glad if I had a letter regarding it in my hands (for if it gets into the hands of Reiff's adherents it will be hidden). Then, with the help of God, I would soon gather my sheep and perform my work among my congregations with a double joy and my bitter sorrow would soon be sweetened.

But as long as this letter has been here my work has been rendered useless among many. The slanderers and liars found it a weapon against me and I had to put up with a small compensation for all my difficult and wearisome toil and labor, and thus lose my food for the support of my body. But the most painful result was that I had to see my labor made fruitless with many, because of this letter, and had to behold more harm in all the congregations of the whole country than I could bring about growth.

The Reverend Classis can, therefore, clearly see that it is not my fault that our true church in this country did not grow. For Henry Goetschi has shown this letter everywhere and thereby caused me much persecution, until he learned differently from his Reverence, Inspector Dorsius. Then he heartily repented and asked my forgiveness in the presence of his Reverence, which I granted him with all my heart. I also wish him success and intercede for him with God and our Reverend Church Fathers. He obediently submitted to the decision of the Reverend Christian Synods and desisted immediately. May God give him blessing and grace that he may become an efficient instrument to edify others.

I also made this suggestion to his Reverence, Inspector Dorsius, to propose to the Christian Synods, in sending the desired ministers, to ordain each for his particular place. For some places are more acceptable than others and the people also differ. I think that thereby future quarrels could be entirely avoided, and all would have to be content. May God give His gracious blessing upon his work for the salvation of many.

Your obedient servant commends herewith the Very Reverend Classis, your reverend persons, with all your families and holy service, to the dear heavenly Father and to the Word of His grace, and himself to your blessed and affectionate care and he remains,

VERY REVEREND CLASSIS,
Your most submissive and obedient servant,

JOH. PH. BOEHM,
Minister at Falckner Schwam, Schip Bach and Weitmarge.
Witpen Township,
Philadelphia County,
Pennsylvania, April 4, 1740.

[ENCLOSURE A.]

[LETTER OF THE REV. DR. JOHN WILHELMIUS OF ROTTERDAM TO THE REFORMED BRETHREN IN PENNSYLVANIA, DECEMBER 31, 1730.]

Grace and Peace be to the Brethren, who are partakers of the heavenly calling, and love the Lord Jesus unceasingly.

I thank my God that He has deemed me worthy to speak in behalf of your church before the churches of the Netherlands, and that with such a good result that they have accepted your church to show their liberality towards it and to assist it with counsels and deeds. I feel one with you in spirit to such an extent, that I always make mention of you in my prayers and implore God to preserve your church, to edify, bless and strengthen it to the end that, as the church of the Palatinate has been the mother church of that of the Netherlands, so also their descendants may be the glory of Christ, a means of praise on earth and a place of refuge, where those that are persecuted in Europe for the sake of the truth, will find a secure shelter in course of time. Nothing will give me so much joy as to hear good reports of you and as often as I shall have opportunity to render you any service. It is offered to you by me heartily and fraternally.

Because of this love for you, I am much grieved over the disturbances which have arisen among you by reason of the ordination of Philip Boehm, since I fear that from this little spark, kindled by the devil among you, such a fire of discord and division will be kindled among the confessors of the truth, that it cannot be quenched, that the professors of our faith will be scattered and the hope for the building up of the Church of Christ will be lost, unless it be extinguished in time.

I have transmitted both of your letters of complaint, one to the Classis of Amsterdam and the other to that of Rotterdam, and, since the Classis of Amsterdam had already deliberated upon this matter, and had more knowledge of it than our own Classis [of Rotterdam], I sent the letter first to the Classis of Amsterdam, in order that I might learn what it would do in your just cause. For I thought, in case your affair should turn out as desired, its resolution might then be communicated to the Classis of Rotterdam, and we could in that case also adopt it.

Since, however, I learn from Messrs. Weiss and Reiff that the first Classis [that of Amsterdam] insists upon its former resolution and that Boehm is to be confirmed in his office, I have transmitted your letter, on November 21st, to the Classis of Rotterdam, which, after having read it, found it to be of such importance, that ten commissioners were appointed, three from our Classis, three from the Classis of Delft and four Deputies of the Synod [of South Holland], to investigate the affair most carefully and report to the Classis, and also communicate to you its advice, that you may make use of it. But, as this cannot be done before the next meeting of the Classis at Easter, I could not meanwhile remain quiet and allow Mr. Weiss to return empty handed, without communicating to you my own personal thoughts about this affair and submitting them to your consideration.

They are to this effect: That you should accept the counsel of the Classis of Amsterdam, in order to preserve by this means the harmony and peace of the church, until God, through the death of Mr. Boehm or through other means, brings about a change. By doing this, you will be able to keep and retain the favor, good will and assistance of this conspicuous Classis, all the more because this Classis received letters from commissioners of your church, which asked for Boehm, whose ordination took place as a result of it. He, moreover, cannot be expelled from his office without scandal and disgrace.

Nevertheless, in case this advice be not acceptable to you,[189] and your hearts cannot unite with him [Boehm], nor be promoted, edified and comforted by his ministry, and your church be exposed to ridicule and contempt, as you write in your letter, and as I heard from the two delegates, I give it as my personal opinion, that, in order to remove present and future quarrels, you have the divine right, given to

---

[189] The four paragraphs that follow were likely inserted into the German translation. They are absolutely contradictory to what precedes and follows. No minister under the Dutch Synods could have given such advice, which aimed at the ex-communication of the elders at Skippack and the deposition of Boehm. The very insistence on the supposed "divine right" of the congregation betrays its origin.

you by God in Christ Jesus, which you may, can and must use to elect, on your own responsibility, a minister in accordance with the Word of God and the Church Order.

For your nation, which is living in a free land, is a perfectly free church, dependent upon none, which has in herself the right to govern herself, to form an ecclesiastical government, to elect such elders as she pleases, if only it be done according to the Word of God. Being independent of every church in the world, whichever it may be, you can accept and follow advice or decline to do so. While it is entirely different with the churches in New Netherland [New York], which have been organized by the Church of Holland.

Inasmuch as this is so, the congregation of Schippach, Schwam and neighboring places has the *divine right* herself to elect a minister, whom she may find fit for that position, and it is my opinion that this procedure should be followed: The consistory should assemble and investigate the conduct of the men, who in the name of the whole congregation wrote to the Classis of Amsterdam, asking for Boehm, and when it shall appear that therein they did not act truthfully, or that they themselves were deceived, the consistory must bring them to a confession of their guilt and punish them by excluding them from the table of the Lord and its communion, inasmuch as they were the cause of the disturbance. They should treat Do. Boehm also in the same manner, and, if it be found that he deceived these men in their simple-mindedness by his cunning and his artifices, I advise that these things be recorded properly and sent over to the Classis of Amsterdam, so that you may be justified and the Classis be assured that its resolution was based on deceptive tales.

After this has thus been done, the consistory may notify the congregation, that all the male members meet at a specified time to vote one by one for the election of a minister, acting according to the Church Order of the Palatinate, then proceed to the ordination. And, to the end that all this be done orderly, the advice and guidance of the nearest, regular minister, that can be secured from Staten Island or Bucks County, should be requested, in order that he may be present and preside over the transaction.

However, my dear Brethren, my concern extends not only to the present disturbance, but also to all other disagreements, which in future may arise among you and which are certain to arise, because Satan will set everything to work, in order to frustrate the building up of the Church of God and subvert it, which will be easy for him to accomplish as long as your church has not formally been organized and you have not established a fixed order among you, according to which you will know how to regulate your affairs in the future. Inasmuch as it is too tedious to secure advice and counsel for each and every occurrence from the European churches and their advice, moreover, is too uncertain, because our Church does not know all the circumstances of affairs and the condition of your nation, it is much more convenient for you to deliberate upon your own affairs, for they are best understood by yourselves.

In what manner your nation can best be brought to a well-ordered church-government is a question of much thought, concern and wisdom, regarding which I have meditated often and asked God for enlightenment. After much consideration the following manner appears to me to be the most convenient and I submit it to your consideration:[190]

FIRST. The Consistory of Schip Bach must send a circular letter to all men, who were members of the church, throughout the whole country, and request them to send some of their people to a general conference, in order to consult regarding the advancement of the Church of God in this colony. This conference should consist of twenty-four men, who have authority to establish a provisional Church Order, and report their conclusions to the people who have sent them, which, after necessary changes have been made, shall be adopted in the following meeting, so that they and their descendants may obligate themselves to it [by subscription].

SECOND. This conference should then

A. Divide the whole country into five parishes and fix certain limits, so that each member and family may know to what parish they henceforth belong, and in future no disputes may arise regarding this.

B. Each parish must have a church, to which those shall belong, who live within its boundaries.

C. Each church must have a pastor and a schoolmaster, who shall also be the precentor, so that five churches, five pastors and schoolmasters must be provided.

D. Each church must have its consistory, consisting of the minister, four elders and four deacons.

E. All business must be transacted in this consistory by majority votes.

Regulation regarding Ministers.

They must have all the requisite qualifications in accordance with the Palatinate Church Order. They must do all that the Church Order prescribes.

Regulation regarding Elders.

It must also be in harmony with the Church Order and the Formulas [of the Reformed Church]. Each must serve two years.

Regulation regarding Deacons.

It must be their duty to take up the collection, count the collected money in church, after the services in the presence of all the deacons;

---

[190] The similarity between this constitution and the one printed in the "Report" of 1731 are so striking that they must go back to the same author. As Dr. Wilhelmi elaborates these regulations in this letter before they were printed he must be the author of them.

record day and date and how much it was, keep the money and not expend it, unless by order of the Consistory.

REGULATION REGARDING EACH CONSISTORY.

1. Each Consistory must consist of the minister, elders and deacons.

2. Each minister must preside over the meeting, present matters, announce the decision according to the majority of votes, and open and close the meeting with prayer.

3. Each member must have a determining vote, and the president a double vote, in case of a tie.

4. The time of meeting must be according to opportunity for each church, at least four times a year, before the Lord's Supper, to consider whether church discipline should be applied to the members.

5. Besides the ordinary or regular meetings, the president shall also call a special meeting, upon the request of a member of the consistory.

6. The members of the consistory must be changed every year in such a way that two of the four elders retire, in whose place two others shall be elected.

7. The matters which shall be transacted by each consistory are: (1) Complaints must be heard, in case there are any, which may be raised by members of the consistory, one against the other; (2) The conduct of the congregation must be investigated, those that are in error and give offense must be proceeded against and church discipline must be exercised according to the Church Order; (3) They must deliberate about the alms, where and how they are to be applied, keep a record of it and submit once a year a financial statement, publicly in church, to all those that may be present.

8. Each Consistory must keep a minute book, in which to record all important matters that have been transacted. The minutes must be read and signed, at each session, by the president.

9. All the resolutions of the Consistory, taken by majority of votes, must stand, even if some one protest against them.

10. Church Discipline must be exercised according to the Church Order of the Palatinate.

REGULATION REGARDING AN UPPER CONSISTORY [OR CLASSIS].

Inasmuch as the Church Order of the Palatinate agrees fundamentally with the Presbyterian government of Geneva and of the Netherlands, I am of the opinion that all the members of the consistories should have one power and authority. But, while this authority is wielded in the Palatinate by Inspectors and Superintendents, who must bring all matters before the Prince, I believe that [in Pennsylvania] it could be done more appropriately by an Upper Consistory [Classis], for whose government the following regulations may be made:

1. This Upper Consistory must consist of delegates from each

of the five consistories, namely a minister, elder and deacon of each, and thus it will include fifteen persons.

2. This assembly must be held once a year during the summer.

3. The place of meeting should be in the center of the country, so that delegates can come together more conveniently from all sides.

4. This assembly, being in session, should elect, by majority of votes, a president and secretary. It should be opened and closed with a public sermon, to be preached by the ministers in turns.

5. All that is transacted must be determined by majority of votes, at which occasion each member shall have one vote, but the president, in case of a tie, a double vote. All resolutions are to be entered by the secretary into a minute book, and must be copied by each consistory, to preserve them in the churches, for the advantage and use of each consistory.

6. The duty of this Upper Consistory must be:

A. To read what was transacted in the preceding year.

B. Each Consistory must read from its minute book all that occurred and was recorded in its midst during the whole year.

C. The condition of the Church in the whole colony must be supervised, and the question must be considered where new churches can be established, owing to the expansion of the Church.

D. Ultimate and final decisions must be given in all cases which may be brought by each consistory through appeals before the assembly.

E. Supervision must be exercised over the money which may be collected in Europe or in its own midst for the use of the churches.

F. Annual correspondence must be maintained with the churches of the Netherlands, the growth and increase of the churches must be made known, counsel and advice, when necessary, should be sought, and resolutions should be taken regarding it.

G. This assembly shall represent the whole church of this colony and shall treat with higher and lower authorities in Pennsylvania, according to opportunity or the demands of the situation.

Regulation regarding the Means of Subsistence, or the salary, and the question of the expenses of the divine service and the support of the churches, the schools, the consistories and the church buildings.

Inasmuch as the service of God and the salvation of our eternal and immortal souls are the most important work, which God demands of us, and for whose sake we are in this world, it has come to pass that God put the obligation upon his ancient people, that each property owner should annually give a tenth part of all his income for the service of the temple and the support of the ministers, besides the offering of the firstlings and other things more. And, although this law is now abrogated, nevertheless all Christians are under the necessary obligation that each one must contribute his share for the maintenance of the divine service, the churches and the schools, to educate therein our dearest possessions and to promote our happiness. How large the share is to be, which each one should contribute, is not defined in the

Word of God [New Testament], but there is a general feeling and opinion, not only among Christians but also among many heathen, that one should sanctify the tenth part of one's annual income for this purpose. For this reason it would not be unreasonable for each Reformed member in the colony to set aside and contribute the tenth part of his produce.

But, in consideration of the fact that this could not be done, without appreciable hardship, during the first stage in the growth of the colony, I am of the opinion that each one that is baptized should contribute annually one English shilling. This appears to me (not wishing to anticipate a better plan) a convenient and sufficient means for the necessary support of the divine service. For, supposing that there are twenty thousand baptized members, young and old, and that each one contributes a shilling, it would amount annually to one thousand pounds sterling. Now, if each minister receives annually fifty pounds and each schoolmaster annually fifteen pounds, it would amount annually to three hundred and twenty five pounds, so that there would remain six hundred and seventy five pounds, with which the following items could be paid: (1) The meeting of the Great Consistory, which will cause annually some expenses, together with the traveling expenses and the entertainment of the members while in session, which may last from eight to fourteen days; (2) the support of the widows and the surviving children of the deceased ministers, who cannot and must not be neglected, nor die from want; (3) above all two young men must be selected by the Upper Consistory and educated with this money for the ministry of the Church. To this end they must be sent to higher schools in America or even in Europe, in order that the churches may always be supplied with pastors from their own people and the inhabitants of Palatinate extraction may enjoy the honor and respect as well as the advantages of this service, to which they furnish the necessary sums; (4) the candidates, who have no appointments; (5) With this money a school of higher learning could also be established, consisting of four professors, one of whom could teach the Latin and Greek languages, the second the Hebrew and Oriental languages, the third Church History and Philosophy and the fourth Sacred Theology. In this manner you would have everything in your own organization necessary for your support, maintenance and prestige.

The method to be followed for the collection and expenditure of monies might be regulated as follows:

1. That each family shall bring its shilling at the communion service at Easter to the Consistory of its own parish.

2. That each Consistory shall transmit the money thus received to the Upper Consistory, held once a year.

3. That each minister shall receive his salary there, by giving a receipt and also the salary of his schoolmaster, which is to be handed over to the latter at the minister's return, upon getting a receipt from him.

4. That an account of the receipt and expenditure of the money, together with the balance on hand, shall be communicated to each Consistory, so that a report and explanation can be made to each congregation, by which it will appear how the money has been well administered.

Besides these dues no other fees or so called jura stolae [dues of the cloth] shall be paid, as baptismal and wedding fees or still others.

The symbols of bread and wine shall be paid for out of the alms.

In consideration of the fact that thus payment is made by each member, rich and poor, contributing alike, I am of the opinion, that it should be left to the free choice of the rich to give more occasionally. It may be freely expected of them that at this or that opportunity they will give a larger sum for the service of the churches, the work of the deacons or to the general treasury.

Inasmuch as this is such a reasonable, just, easy and fair constitution, by which the divine service can be established, I trust that none, who entertains any reverence of God or love for the divine service, any sincere desire for the salvation of his soul and true concern for his descendants, will withdraw from his duty, especially when one considers the advantages that will be enjoyed thereby, namely

A. The Church of Pennsylvania will not be dependent upon any one, existing by itself and not needing any one's approval.

B. The Church in Pennsylvania will thereby grow in influence and authority above all other sects, because they will learn that the whole body of the churches is now united and joined together for each other's help and assistance.

C. She will be ordered and governed by her own means and will have her own fellow-countrymen for her shepherds and supervisors, who will stand under the supervision of her own Consistory and will thus shepherd the congregations with wisdom and intelligence.

D. When such a deacons' treasury and also a general treasury has once been established, people of means, when they have made a successful business venture, or are about to die without children, will set apart and make provision to donate a part of their property to such a treasury, or bequeath it through a legacy.

E. The European churches will be more ready and willing to contribute their charitable gifts more liberally, when they learn that they will be used and administered by the whole nation and when they receive information how and for what purpose they will be used.

Furthermore I believe that in each Consistory a special book should be kept, in which to record the baptized persons, those that have been married and buried as well as the members who make their confession of faith, so that the people may know at all times how strong they are and what their condition is.

REGULATION REGARDING THE ELECTION AND ORDINATION OF MINISTERS.

The first church which has already been formed and has its own Consistory has also the power to elect its minister and can have him installed by another regular minister, who may be requested to do so.

The second church as well as all the other churches have the same right and they may act in this matter as follows: The minister that has been elected can be examined by and in the presence of the first Consistory, which has a regular minister, and, after preceding proclamation, can be ordained by the latter.

The same method may be followed in other churches, or else each Consistory may address a letter to the Consistory of the Palatinate, requesting that a minister be sent from the Palatinate, who has been ordained by the imposition of hands and commissioned for such a church.

Behold, my dearest and most valued friends in Christ Jesus our Lord, these are my own thoughts, which I have formulated for myself, and which I ask you to receive as a token of my love and care, which I have for your welfare.

Consider them, meditate upon them and follow them, or not, according to the condition of affairs. I shall be pleased to learn what the ten commissioners that have been appointed will do, which I shall communicate to you in course of time. Meanwhile I hope that God will grant you wisdom to direct this great work aright, so that all of Europe may rejoice when it hears that the condition of your churches is flourishing and that thereby the way has been prepared that Jesus, the King, will be preached to the wild heathens, who have never heard of him before. This is a great work, which will require at first much labor and trouble, but for which the Lord will give enlightenment, if it is undertaken prayerfully and with a holy zeal.

Concluding herewith, I remain, with all the attachment of my heart,

My Noble Sirs' well wishing
Servant in the Lord Jesus,

JOHANNES WILHELMIUS,
Doctor of Sacred Theology and Minister
of the Congregation at Rotterdam.

Rotterdam,
December 31, 1730.

[XXIX. DEFENSE OF MR. BOEHM BY HIS CONSISTORIES, MAY 3, 1741.[191]]

Very Reverend Classis, Devout Church Fathers:—

With deep deference to the Reverend Classis, your obedient children and fellow-believers of our holy and true Reformed

[191] The original German letter of Boehm is in the Classical Archives.

doctrine cannot refrain from first of all giving expression to our gratitude for the kind gift bestowed by the Reverend Classis upon our beloved and faithful teacher and pastor. We wish that the Lord Jesus may recompense every kind and benevolent benefactor and be his eternal reward. For thus far it has not been in our power to support him and his household as is proper, in order that he might be able to devote himself entirely to his [pastoral] service. Notwithstanding this, we sincerely declare, upon our official responsibility, that Do. Boehm has not neglected anything of that which we had agreed upon, when we called him to our congregation in Philadelphia (namely to hold services here on one Sunday in every month). Although our congregation consists largely of poor day laborers and fresh immigrants, many of whom still owe their passage money, who could contribute little or nothing, yet he has been patient with all and we have not observed in the least that, on that account, he became neglectful of his official duties, or that he despised or frowned upon any one who could not as yet give him anything for his hard labors and long trips, which he has to make from one place to another. On the contrary, Mr. Boehm has tried to earn a living for himself and his family on the farm where he lives, in addition to his hard pastoral work. From this we can only infer that it is his greatest pleasure to serve faithfully the congregations of Christ, of which he is the founder[192] and which he gathered everywhere in this country; and to preserve them in our true Reformed doctrine, according to his ability, until it please God to send more help, for which he and all of us have heartily prayed. We certainly believe, because we are convinced of his indefatigable zeal in his work and his active love for the truth of the Gospel, that, as long as God spares his life and he enjoys strength of body, he will not leave off, even if the trials which he has to endure should last still longer. Why, then, should we not be heartily grateful to our merciful God, especially the majority of the members in our true church here (who are not able to contribute anything towards a minister's salary), that He has given us such a steadfast and faithful shepherd and teacher, who discharges the duties of his office in our pure Reformed doctrine, according

---

[192] For Boehm as the founder of Churches see pp. 58-81.

to the pure truth of the Gospel of Jesus Christ? He has not contaminated himself with sects or any heretical doctrine, nor has he ever swerved from the true doctrine which we have learned in our Heidelberg Catechism, of which we are witnesses. Of this we have many a sad example here (as is well known to the Classis) in the case of other ministers. But no one can truthfully say this of our minister, Mr. John Philip Boehm. For this God be praised for ever! The same strong God preserve him furthermore to the end of his life, by His grace, in His Word, which is the truth, for the salvation of himself and of all our souls. May He recompense him richly with His eternal reward of grace.

Now, Very Reverend Classis, we have learned from a letter, by the Reverend Classis in the year 1739 to Mr. Boehm, but not received by him until December 15, 1740, that some reports detrimental to Mr. Boehm had come to the knowledge of the Reverend Classis, both by word of mouth and by letter, namely, it was charged that Mr. Boehm had no education and that he was not desirous of obtaining one, that he worked during the whole week and on Sunday he read from a sermon book and talked at random; that in addition he led an offensive life, on account of which he was derided by the Quakers.

In regard to the first charge, that our minister has no education, we answer no more than this, that we have heard all [Reformed ministers] preach who have come here, to none of whom would we give preference as far as we understand the exposition of the holy Gospel of Jesus Christ as the Word of God. We are well satisfied with the teaching of our minister, which we believe to be unadulterated and according to God's holy Word. With regard to the charge that he does not strive to grow in wisdom and knowledge of divine things, we have quite different indications.

2. He is charged with working during the whole week. We cannot refute this charge. The reason for it has been stated above. But this is certainly nothing dishonorable and no one has had cause to be offended by it. We believe that there are some who would have liked to see him burden the congregation with a sufficient salary to support his family, so that they might have a reason, because of their inability to pay it, to leave the congregation disgruntled. But he con-

sidered it an unpardonable sin to bring about such a result and thereby cause the ruin of the congregation, gathered by him, rather than a disgrace to suffer and labor with his congregation and barely eke out a living. Every one who suffers for Jesus' sake may form his own opinion in this matter.

But with regard to the charge that, by reason of this, he reads on Sunday something from a sermon book and only talks at random, we declare that we have never heard him do this, but as often as we have heard him, we have always found that God had graciously given him enough to edify us, so that we do not believe that ever any one went home without being gratified, except those, whom, according to their opinion, he had attacked too severely because of their errors, false teaching in this land and other vices. We cannot sufficiently express our surprise that there can be such people, who so shamelessly and devoid of all love, report to the Reverend Classis such base falsehoods; and above all charge our minister with an offensive conduct, in order to put him under suspicion by the Reverend Classis.

Now, Very Reverend Classis, we heartily desire that these people be called to account for it and be required to state wherein his offensive conduct consists. We are convinced that they cannot prove and substantiate a single point.

We at any rate, who attend to our office with the greatest care, can freely declare, on our vow and conscience as before God and sign it with our own hands, that we have not noticed any vices in him, which could cause any one to take the least offense. We heartily wish that we could conscientiously affirm the same of those who report such untruths and who are not unkown to us, but unfortunately they lack much to our great regret. Hence, Very Reverend Classis, we heartily wish that these men (who have no other object but always to hinder our work of divine worship and delay the time that we shall receive help), were as well known to the Reverend Church Fathers as they are to us. Then they would find no hearing any more, for as long as they are heard there is no doubt that the old enemy will not cease to hinder us at all times, by his cunning and through them as his instruments, in the work of God, which was begun in this country for the welfare of our poor souls. Finally we know nothing of the derision of the Quakers.

Now, Very Reverend Classis, concerning the church collections, received in Holland by Do. Weis and Jacob Reiff, we were told that we could not receive the least help until this money was put to the right use. If this be so, then may it move God's pity, that the poor, innocent congregations which cannot help themselves, shall suffer for these faithless men. Nor can we have confidence in Diemer's faithfulness (commissioner in this matter with Do. Dorsius), for we know and some members of our congregation have seen in a letter,[198] written to Reiff in Holland, that Diemer and six others with him are just as much to blame for the loss and deception as Reiff, of which the Reverend Classis has already been informed. Who then can imagine that one will go against the other? May God forgive him whose fault it is that Diemer received this commission. In the meantime we must see that Reiff trades with and gets interest from this money, while the poor congregations might have been partly helped with it. This grieves us very much. Yet we hope that in course of time there will be an end of this. If it had been deemed expedient to entrust this case to our minister alone, we believe, we would already have seen a different outsome.

The Very Reverend Classis, however, will have obtained a clear insight into the condition and circumstances of all our churches in Pennsylvania from the truthful reports of the years 1739 and 1740, all of which were received by the Reverend Classis. The zealous, devout and solicitous Church Fathers will surely show their holy interest in our poor Church of Christ, in their true fellow-believers, in our pure doctrine and in our faithful pastor, for which we herewith humbly pray, for Jesus' sake, so that the days of our sadness may be shortened as much as possible and simple souls may be kept from falling into folly.

In such undoubted hope to the kind and loving God, and with the heartfelt wish and prayer for His heavenly blessing upon the Very Reverend Classis, all our Church Fathers, your persons, all your families and holy service, we commend ourselves to your fatherly care.

We are and remain,
VERY REVEREND CLASSIS,

[198] For this letter written to Reiff while in Holland by seven of the Philadelphia members, see Boehm's letter of October 28, 1734, p. 236:

Your submissive fellow-members and children in the Lord,

Philadelphia,
January 25, 1741.

Of the High German
Reformed Congregation
in Philadelphia.

{ John Michael Diel, elder.
Valentin Beyer, elder.
Rudolf Wielecken, elder.
John Henry Klemmer, elder.
  (his H I K mark)
Jacob Maag, deacon.
John Ludwig Seipel, deacon. }

The above was sent to us by our brethren in Philadelphia and we have heard it read distinctly. Accordingly our brethren's words are in all things likewise our own and we attest and sign the same with them, according to our duty, with our own hands:

Of the congregation
  at Schip Bach,
  February, 1741.

{ Jacob Arnet, elder.
Ulrich Steffen, elder.
Andrew Oberbeck, elder.
  (his A. O. mark)
Henry Wuehrmann, deacon. }

Of the congregation at
  Weitmarge, March, 1741.

{ William de Wees, elder.
Philip Scherrer, deacon. }

Of the Reformed congregation
  at Falckner Schwam,
  March, 1741.

{ John Druckdenhengst, elder.
John Dunkel, elder.
Frederick Reymer, elder.
  his
Jacob X Krausen, elder.
  mark
John Dieter Bucher, elder.
Adam Raeder, deacon. }

Of the Reformed congregation
  at Dolpihacken,
  May 3, 1741.

{ John George Peruh,
Martin Schel,
John Fohrer. }

We, the undersigned, having heard that Do. Dorsius and Jacob Diemer had been given a power of attorney concerning the collection-money, received by Jacob Reiff and Do. Weis in Holland for the Pennsylvania churches in order to obtain the same by the laws of this country, and being unable to notice any progress in this case, went to Mr. Dorsius and asked him how this case stood. His Reverence answered among other things, that he could not do anything in this affair, the Governor had it in his hand. Then we went to the Governor and asked him whether he had the affair in hand, whereupon the Governor answered that he knew nothing of it, that it might possibly be in the hands of the Secretary. Then we went to the Secretary, Mr. Pitters[194] [Peters], and asked him whether he had the case concerning said money in hand. He answered in the affirmative and immediately read the case to us. From it we saw that the case should justly have had a better representative. When we asked the reasons why there was no progress, he said that it had not yet been handed to an attorney. And thus the case stands yet to-day, as far as we know, which we hereby attest.

I testify to everything stated above,
  WENDEL BRECHBIEHL, former church elder.

I testify to that which Mr. Dorsius said,
  VALENTIN BEYER, active elder.

I testify to that which Mr. Dorsius said,
  JACOB WALTER, deacon.

I testify to everything stated above,
  JACOB MAAG, active elder.

This is enclosed by us, whose names are signed above, so that the Reverend Classis of Amsterdam may see what is done here with the collection money. This was written in March, 1741.

---

[194] This was the Rev. Richard Peters, born about 1704, son of Ralph Peter, town clerk of Liverpool. He took orders as deacon in 1730, as priest in 1731, at Chelsea. He married December 25, 1734, Miss Stanley. He came to Pennsylvania in 1735. He became assistant to the Rev. Archibald Cummings, rector of Christ Church, Philadelphia. After the death of the latter his friends failed to secure his appointment as rector. He became Secretary of the Province and Clerk of Council, being appointed February 14, 1743. In 1749 he became a member of the Provincial Council. In 1762 he resigned his clerkship and was then elected, December 6, 1762, rector of Christ Church. He resigned his rectorship September 23, 1775. He died July 10, 1776. See Keith, *Provincial Councillors of Pennsylvania*, pp. 235-241.

[XXX. MR. BOEHM TO THE CLASSIS OF AMSTERDAM, JULY 25, 1741.[195]]

Very Reverend, Very Learned and Devout Gentlemen, Deputies of the Classis of Amsterdam:—

The following letters, sent to me by your Reverences, were received by me, namely:

1. A letter written by the reverend gentlemen, Messrs. John Plantinus and Bogarten, Deputies of the Classis in 1739,[196] in which it is stated that the Reverend Classis has learned of our lamentable condition, from others as well as from ourselves, and that the Classis sympathizes with us and will try to help us. Moreover, the cause is given why the inclination of the Classis was withdrawn for a time, namely on account of accusations against me. Therefore the Classis desires me to produce testimony by reputable members of the congregation, in my defense.

Finally, I am admonished to watch against all kinds of sectarians and also against the Moravians. To this end the Pastoral Letter, written by the Reverend Classis, was sent to me, etc.

2. The letter of the reverend gentlemen, Messrs. John Plantinus and Tyberius Reytsma, Deputies of the Classis, dated April 1, 1740,[197] from which I learn that the Reverend Classis received my submissive letter of March 13, 1739,[198] and that my submissive reports, contained therein, had been received with high favor, and it had been regarded with high pleasure that I was willing to comply with the written request of his Reverence, Do. Dorsius, in reporting to him the condition of the congregations entrusted to me. I was, moreover, admonished to continue henceforth in harmony and union with his Reverence, Mr. Dorsius, to extend the kingdom of Jesus. For this praise I am thankful to the Reverend Classis. I was also notified that the Reverend Classis had graciously answered all my letters of 1739, and the hope was expressed that I had re-

---

[195] The German original is in the Classical Archives.

[196] Printed above, pp. 261-262.

[197] Also printed above, pp. 298-300.

[198] Boehm's letter of March 16, 1739, with postscript dated March 18, 1739, must be meant. See above, p. 262ff. It is the only letter of March, 1739, which arrived in Holland.

ceived them, and that the Reverend Classis has taken to heart my miserable condition. The Reverend Classis also promises graciously to attend to my request concerning the church property [at Skippack], at the coming Christian Synod of North Holland of the year 1740. It would be a great loss to the congregation if it were to lose the property, but the Classis entertains good hope.

Finally, in a postscript: "Enclosed a book of the Rev. Mr. Kulenkamp,[199] sent at the request of the Reverend Consistory at Amsterdam, for your use and for the reverend ministers in Pennsylvania. Meanwhile the Reverend Classis sends to your support in your poverty the sum of —— florins,[200] mentioned in the other letter," of which the draft is wanting.

3. A letter by the Rev. Mr. Tyberius Reytsma, Deputy of the Classis, dated August 3, 1740,[201] in which was enclosed a draft to the amount of £46.5.3, New York currency. This sum was collected by the churches belonging to the Reverend Classis of Amsterdam, in order to cheer me. I was informed that a package with two letters, written to me in the name of the Reverend Classis, had been sent to the Rev. Mr. Boel, minister at New York, from whom I might obtain them, giving also an order that he might receive the money for me. It was further stated that the Reverend Deputies of the Classis had received my last letters and had given them to the translator. It was also promised that a gracious answer would be given to them at the first opportunity, and that I would be informed what the Christian Synod of North Holland had transacted and resolved for the welfare and spread of our churches in Pennsylvania.

4. Another letter by the Rev. Mr. Tyberius Reytsma, Deputy of the Classis of Amsterdam, dated August 31, 1740,

---

[199] A copy of this rare book is in the possession of the Rev. Dr. J. I. Good. It is the main source from which Boehm drew his information about the Moravians, which he used in his book published against them in 1742.

[200] The exact amount of florins is omitted in the original. The minutes of the Classis state that it was fl. 309, or $123.60.

[201] The letters of the Classical Deputies, dated August 3 and August 31, 1740, are no longer in existence. No copies were entered into the Classical letter-book.

in which was enclosed a second draft, for use in case the first had been lost. In this letter I was assured that the letter sent by Do. Wilhelmi[202] should be investigated at my earnest request. The hope was expressed that the contribution, sent by the Reverend Classis to comfort me in my burdensome service, might tend to keep me in the service of the Church of Christ.

In consideration of all this, I have regarded it as my duty not to fail in duly answering again and in handing in a further submissive report:

1. I return thanks unto God, the Father of all mercy, from the depth of my heart, and will not cease to praise His name, that He rules so powerfully the hearts of our devout Church Fathers and inclines them toward us poor church members. Yea, I shall continually call upon Him, because He will at last permit me to see the growth of His churches here, so that His name may be glorified more and more among us to His praise and the salvation of many souls.

I have left it to all my fellow-brethren and elders (as it was required by the Reverend Classis), to defend me,[203] according to their conscience and in conformity with their duty against the many harsh calumnies and untruths of malevolent people.

For the admonition of my devout Church Fathers I return, next to God, the great Ruler, to you most humble thanks. I hope that you will never hear anything else said about me truthfully but that I have labored, to the best of my ability, in the work entrusted to me, and I hope, through the grace of God, to continue therein until the end. I cannot prevent slanders, but I rejoice that the Lord knoweth my heart and that He will not suffer the innocence of any of His people to be hidden.

2. It causes me the greatest pleasure that the Reverend Classis was so much pleased with my true and dutiful report concerning the condition of our churches here. But what [trouble] it has caused me here, the Reverend Classis can learn from the enclosed, marked A. For after I had handed in the

---

[202] For this letter of Wilhelmi, see above, pp. 303-311.
[203] For this letter of defense, dated March 3, 1741, see above, pp. 311-317.

report to his Reverence, Mr. Dorsius, and the letters were sent off, I came to his Reverence and asked him whether the report had been sent over, his Reverence answered: No, he had it in his trunk, but he had written to the Christian Synods in regard to those things, etc. I did not like this, for I had been riding through the country about 300 miles in the severest winter season. We had some words between us; however, nothing unseemly. Among other things his Reverence remarked, the affair had been entrusted to him and he knew what to do. He had kept the report for his own safety. To which I answered: "To me it does not seem well that the light which makes clear the whole condition of our congregations to our devout Church Fathers, who manifest such a holy concern for our churches, should be seen by your Reverence only and kept in your trunk, and not be brought to those who desire to see it; for it seems to me that the report, together with your additional report, should have been sent to them," etc.[204]

I was, therefore, glad that I did what I did, and I hope that the report will come to your notice in this way. However, the words of his Reverence (which he uttered at another occasion) caused me serious thoughts, namely, that the affair had been given over and entrusted to him by the two Christian Synods, and that no one else's letters (from whatever source they might come) would be considered, but they would be laid aside, except what he would write would be accepted, etc. I do not know whether his Reverence has later on transmitted the report in the original. That may be as it will, for I always make two copies of such important documents and have them also signed personally, so that in case of attack I am safeguarded.

In the meantime some men from Goschenhoppen came to me and asked whether the reports had been sent away by his Reverence, Mr. Dorsius. I answered that his Reverence had told me they were still in his trunk, but his Reverence had

---

[204] Mr. Boehm had good reason to complain, for as he had expected, at the North Holland Synod of 1740, Dorsius received all the credit and commendation for the "accurate" report he had sent over. That it was Boehm's report he had failed to state.

written, in his own words, about them to Holland. When his Reverence visited these people, as is shown in the above-mentioned enclosure, marked A, they asked him also. He answered in the affirmative, whereupon these people asked, whom they should believe, Boehm said no, and his Reverence yes? Then he began immediately to scold in such terms as is stated in the enclosure and other unnecessary talk.

Now, since his Reverence has not only injured me, although I was entirely innocent and did not mean any harm, but also the respect of my devout Church Fathers, according to whose orders I received holy ordination from the Reverend Ministers of New York, in your name, and was installed in the holy service, therefore I consider it unpardonable to remain silent about it, but I handed my letter, in February, 1740, to the Rev. Mr. Boel, minister in New York, when I lately received my letters from him. I also handed to him the defense of my brethren, the elders then in office, enclosed herewith, marked B.

But, since I am uncertain whether the letters will arrive and whether his Reverence, Mr. Dorsius, will accuse me before my devout Church Fathers, or perhaps has already done so (for my bitterest enemies, as Diemer and the Hillegass brothers, are generally in his company when he comes to Philadelphia), and I can hardly believe that his Reverence is ignorant of the slanders against me, which have also been sent to Holland, I, therefore, deemed it necessary to give, very submissively, a true report of how it happened and also my defense against it. In all this my devout Church Fathers can see how I must suffer, almost beyond measure. But on this account no one shall take away my courage and prevent me from working in the vineyard of the Lord, as far as it is entrusted to me, and as long as my strength permits, whereunto God may grant me grace, according to His mercy. If, however, his Reverence should not be satisfied, then he must bring authentic proof how I wronged him, for my joy and hope with regard to him was very great and I thought assuredly his deeds would correspond to his words, but now a great additional burden and affliction has been caused by him. For the derision that followed his words, as given in the testimonial [Enclosure A], directed both against himself and me, by men of all kinds of opinions, of whom many were present, cannot be described. However, I shall bear it with patience and leave it to my devout Church Fathers and their wise judgment.

Regarding the statement that the Reverend Classis answered graciously all my letters of the year 1739 and hopes that the answers were received by me, I want to say that thus far I have seen nothing dated 1739, save the letter mentioned in the beginning [under No. 1], which had remained behind (according to the postscript of his Reverence, Mr. Reytsma) and was enclosed with these letters. Therefore I ask respectfully to let me know whether the Reverend Classis sent me something else besides this, through whom it was sent and to whom it was addressed, so that I may be able to inquire.

The book of the Rev. Mr. Kulenkamp, together with the Pastoral Letter of the Reverend Consistory of Amsterdam against the heretical teachings of the Moravians, I received, together with the other letters, from the Rev. Mr. Boel in New York, on December 16, 1740. I am heartily grateful for this book and the letter, which I regard as an invaluable jewel. It is necessary to use them here, for not only these (which have not much influence as yet), but countless other errors are found here. May the grace of Jesus Christ be further with this reverend and devout man, strengthen him and reward him eternally for his faithful work, which defends powerfully the glory of God and His holy Word.

3. Regarding the third letter. For the draft enclosed therein, I received the money soon after presenting the same, from Mr. David Clarkson in New York, his Reverence, Mr. Boel accompanying me thither. For it I return hearty and humble thanks to the Reverend Classis, as well as for its care. May the good Lord bless likewise every benefactor for it, here temporally and hereafter eternally.

I am now expecting with yearning desire the promised answer[205] to my last submissive letters. May the gracious God

---

[205] This promised answer was apparently never given. The Classical letter-book has no letters addressed to Boehm in 1741 and 1742. The next letter of Classis addressed to Boehm was dated May 9, 1743. It answered Boehm's letter of 1742. See p. 372f.

soon grant us the joy of hearing that good resolutions have been agreed upon for His Church here. We heartily long for it, so that His honor may be great in this country also, and the Gospel of His beloved Son may be propogated and spread among us more and more.

4. Concerning the fourth letter. It would be useful, if anything perchance be found regarding Do. Wilhelmi's letter, to make it known to all the congregations here, for the party of Reiff and several other parties similar to it, depend upon it to this day and do whatever they desire. For, when Goetschi left Schip Bach, the party of Reiff immediately accepted another man in his place for the church which is built on the property of Reiff. His name is John William Straub, who was schoolmaster in the Electoral Palatinate, in the village of Gronau. There he committed adultery and was, therefore, deposed and then he came to this country. Notwithstanding this, the party of Reiff uses as its minister this shameless man, who besides is a drunkard. He preaches for them, administers the Lord's Supper, baptizes their children and officiates at marriages. Thus this congregation, divided through Weis in the year 1728, and kept in division and discord through Miller, Rieger and Goetchi in succession, is at present continued in the same condition by this infamous man, all of which I am compelled to witness with great grief of soul, because as yet no protection from the secular government is granted to us by the good Lord for our church and its order. This would perhaps be one of the most essential elements for the promotion of the whole work of God, if it could be brought about by our devout Church Fathers, through the gracious help of God.

When about a year ago I met Mr. Dorsius, I complained to him of these things and asked him to assist me in the effort to determine whether such vile people could not be restrained from doing such things. But his Reverence declined with the following words: "We live here in such a country that I cannot do anything against it." This evil and all the disgraceful things of the self-willed and ignorant people have no other source than the letter sent by Do. Wilhelmi, which says distinctly that in this country one need not consult anybody in regard to church affairs, but every one is at liberty to do as he pleases. It seems to me that my sending over [a copy of] this letter accounts largely for the ill-will which his Reverence, Mr. Dorsius bears me. For, after I had secured this letter from Mr. Goetschi, after many efforts, and it became known to Mr. Dorsius, Goetschi came directly to me, brought me greetings and implored me to give him the letter again, under all kinds of pretexts. He also said that the Inspector, Mr. Dorsius, deemed it advisable to return the letter to the people, otherwise trouble might arise. But I thought that they were trying to make the letter disappear. I declined, therefore, in a friendly way and retained the letter. Now, whether his Reverence, Mr. Dorsius, is also of the opinion that every one in this country may do as he pleases, I leave to men endowed with wisdom to find out. For his Reverence ordained this young Goetschi, who caused so much harm here with the assistance of disorderly people and by the arbitrary transgression of our Reformed Church Order and customs. This ordination took place, after he had left Goschenhoppen and had lived half a mile from his Reverence and studied under him for one year, on the 7th of April last [1741], with the assistance of Do. Frühlinghausen of Randany [Raritan] and of another man, whose name I have not been able to find out as yet. But, as far as I have heard, he is said to have been one of the Tennents,[206] who are of the Weitfield followers, otherwise called Presbyterians. I shall try to obtain certainty. This Goetschi, as reported in my last submissive letter, asked indeed for my forgiveness, in the presence of Mr. Dorsius, of all the wrongs committed against me, and promised to live according to order. This occurred on the 21st of February, 1740. But what he did soon afterwards (and it can hardly be thought that he did it without the knowledge of his Reverence, Mr.

---

[206] In his report of 1744 (see p. 419) Boehm confirms this statement here that it was one of Tennents who assisted in Goetschy's ordination. As Frelinghuisen was associated in his revivalistic work, with Gilbert Tennent, Presbyterian pastor at New Brunswick, N. J. (See *Eccl. Records of N. Y.*, Vol. IV, pp. 2557, 2569, 2587), he was most likely the third minister in this transaction. When this ordination was reported to Holland the Fathers refused to recognize it as valid, and before he was received into the Cœtus of New York, Goetschy had to submit to an examination and reordination, which took place in September, 1748. See *Acts of Dutch Reformed Church*, Vol. I, p. XXIIIf.

Dorsius) may be seen from the enclosure marked C. He likewise made two oral offers to my regular congregation in Oly (according to their testimony), whereby this congregation also was separated and divided.

Mr. Bartholomew Rieger also did the same, who on account of his former offense would not have been accepted as minister at Amwell[207] [N. J.], if he had not given me full satisfaction, on account of his scandalous conduct, shown in breaking into my congregations; and if my own letter had not shown that such [satisfaction] had taken place. He complied with this condition, as appears from the enclosed copy, marked D. Notwithstanding this, he has not been ashamed to act against his pledge and promise in the congregation at Dolpihacken, without speaking to me about it beforehand.[208] He also (like

---

[207] After having been pastor of the Reformed congregations of Philadelphia, Germantown and Skippack, 1731-1734, Rieger became pastor at Amwell, N. J., now the Presbyterian Church at Ringoes, Hunterdon County, N. J. See Chambers, *Germans in New Jersey*, p. 105f. There he stayed, probably till 1738. In 1739 he moved to Lancaster, where he baptized the first child on April 22, 1739. His ministry at Lancaster extended from April, 1739, till February, 1743.

[208] In corroboration of this complaint, Boehm added the following signed statement from two Tulpehocken members:

"Mr. Barth. Rieger, whom the people in Canestocka, in the new city, had hired for two years as their preacher, and whose time was up, at the request of several obnoxious persons, came to Tolbenhacken in the month of April, 1741, and preached there in one of the congregations. Among all kinds of expressions used by him, Mr. Rieger, in the presence of Simon Schirmann, a former elder, were these: 'What do you think if you were in a city in which were a pious and godly Lutheran preacher and an ungodly Reformed preacher, with whom would you go to the Lord's Supper? Would you not rather go to the Lutheran preacher than to the Reformed'? Whereupon Schirmann answered: 'I would dislike doing that. I would rather go to none than to a preacher of another religion.' But Rieger said he would do that and not feel any scruples of conscience about it. Whereupon George Meyer replied: 'I don't know about that, Mr. Rieger, I have once sworn by the bloody banner of Jesus to live and die in my Reformed religion, and I would regard it as perjury and apostasy. I could never do it.' Whereupon Rieger said to this G. Meyer: 'I would not go with you at all, because you are a sinner.' What consequences will result from such talk for the growth of our Reformed churches, especially when the one who engages in it pretends to be a teacher, we leave to every well-grounded Reformed member. That

Goetschi) has done considerable harm to this congregation, whereby the communion was noticeably decreased. Meanwhile I attended to my work in spite of all this, because these things were carried on behind my back and it was also desired of me, and I went there again at the appointed time. However, it caused a harmful rupture in the congregation. But thus far they have seen neither Goetschi nor his Reverence, Mr. Dorsius.

The intention of Mr. George Michael Weis may be learnt from the accompanying copy, marked F. This account he made at the time mentioned therein and he, together with his accomplice, J. Reiff, had the supposed elders of the party of J. Reiff, inexperienced men, come together and told them the Reverend Classis desired an account of the collection-money, so that the money which was still in Holland might also be sent. For this purpose he and Reiff had made up the account and they [the elders] had to sign it only. Then [he said] he would soon send it over to Holland and the money still there would soon arrive. If it had not been for one man, who was present and experienced in such things, they would have secured the signatures, for these people had already the pen in hand. But that man frustrated their plan. They, however, took copies of the account, but returned to Mr. Weis the original written by his own hand. (That was a mistake.) At that time I knew of it, but could secure no evidence of it, because they all belonged to the party of Reiff. I have now obtained the copy through the man who preserved it, who has become my friend. He is a truthful man, who told me everything that took place, which would be too much to relate.

However, I shall mention this: When Mr. Weis spoke to them about the account, that the people in Holland had

the above-mentioned conversation took place as stated, we testify upon our conscience and by the signatures of our hands.
"Given at Dolbenhacken,
   "May 3, 1741.
            "I testify to this,
               "SIMON SCHIRMAN.
            "I testify to this,
               "GEORGE UNRUH, elder."

asked for it, he said, the Reverend Classis had written to him, the letter was in Philadelphia and he was sorry he had forgotten it, for otherwise he would have showed it to them.[209] Reiff heard this, said nothing, but commissioned a man to go to Philadelphia and ask for the letter in the name of Weis and bring it to him, Reiff. The man succeeded and did as he was told. When Reiff read the letter, it was found therein (as three men told me) that Weis should think the matter over and straighten out the affair of the collection-money, for Reiff could not be forced, since he, Weis, was the recipient of the money and, therefore, had to answer for it. Then Reiff laughed and said to the people: "See here is the proof that I owe you nothing, you must try to get it from Weis and whatever Weis can prove that I owe him, for that I shall answer and make it all right with him." It is this upon which Reiff depends, for Weis does not have one single syllable stating that Reiff received money from him. Meanwhile Reiff kept this letter and still has it in his possession. Moreover, I learned that Reiff used the following expressions: "As much as the account shows so much have I spent, whether they sign it or not, I do not care, and, if it comes to a test, I want to know who is to pay the money spent lavishly and the expenses." Is that seeking the welfare of the Church of Christ and faithful service? Let every member of the Church and every pious soul, who in faith loves Jesus and His Word, judge. This account is also proof of cunning unfaithfulness. For, in addition to the unnecessary squandering of money, Weis asks 50 pounds for his labor and trouble. In addition the N. B.[210] ought to be noted. Furthermore, the victuals mentioned under item one are not specified, how much, nor is it stated what Reiff demands for his labor and trouble. It seems that this has been kept back, so that in case a surplus be left, it might be used to strike an even balance.

Reverend Gentlemen, I should be sorry if I knew that by my submissive letter I was causing you vexation and trouble, but I cannot help it. It seems to me that I must give, in all

---

[209] For this letter of the Classis to Mr. Weiss, dated October 1, 1736, see *Eccl. Records of N. Y.*, Vol. IV, p. 2676.

[210] N. B. stands for *Nota Bene*, equivalent to our "postscript."

humility, to my devout Church Fathers a true report of all things which to my mind are helpful to our true Church. I, therefore, cannot omit to give you a further report of present events as follows:

Our Proprietor, Mr. Thomas Penn,[211] was told by a Reformed man, named Jacob Sigel[212] (to whom the Proprietor is well inclined), that all religions and sects were supplied with churches and meeting houses in Philadelphia, and we Reformed people only had to meet in a hired place,[213] and more-

[211] Thomas Penn (1702-75), son of William Penn, succeeded in 1714 to one-fourth of the proprietorship of Pennsylvania. In 1732 he went to Philadelphia where he assumed the direction of the colony until the arrival of this elder brother, John, in 1734. After his brother's return to England, Thomas remained in the colony, where he presided at Council meetings. In 1740 he held a great conference with the Indians. In 1747, upon the death of his elder brother, he inherited the latter's half interest. Then he returned to England to take charge of his interests. They were eventually purchased by the Crown. See *New International Encyclopedia.*

[212] Jacob Siegel qualified in Philadelphia September 27, 1727. His will was signed August 14, 1751. It was probated April 27, 1752. His beneficiaries were his widow, Susannah Siegel; his son, Benjamin, and his daughter, Catherine. See Register of Wills Office, Philadelphia, *Will Book*, I, p. 508.

[213] The first meeting place of the Reformed people in Philadelphia deserves a more extended notice. In 1747, Rev. Michael Schlatter wrote in the church record of the congregation the following statement regarding it: "Thus far the congregation has worshipped in a small old house, built of boards, from November, 1734, together with the Lutheran congregation, at first every other Sunday, later, when the Evangelicals [Lutherans] had built a stone church in the year 1744, they occupied it alone and paid annually to Mr. William Allen the sum of four pounds . . . for said house on Arch Street, near the Quaker burying ground." Count Zinzendorf gives an account of it in the *Büdingische Sammlung*, Vol. III, p. 579: "The German Lutherans in Philadelphia had indeed an old barn fitted up for their services, and in order to save money they had left to the Reformed people every fourth Sunday for a proportionate sum." Rev. H. M. Mühlenberg (*Selbstbiographie*, p. 128) calls it "an old butcher shop, which Lutherans and Reformed had rented together for worship." The elders of the Philadelphia congregation speak of it (*Weekly Mercury*, September 2, 1742) as "an old rotten house which may soon fall to pieces." The oldest Lutheran church record (preserved in the Historical Society of Pennsylvania) contains an account of repairs

over, our contract was only for one more year and then we would again be at a loss where to go. Would not his Honor be so kind as to supply us with a place? Whereupon his Honor answered: "Until now nobody has asked me seriously about this matter. Have you indeed a minister?" Sigel answered in the affirmative. His Honor inquired after my name, which Sigel told him. Fortunately his secretary, Mr. Pitters [Peters], who is my friend was present. He said he knew me very well. Then his Honor told Sigel to bring me and another man of the congregation to him. He would consider the matter and let us know. Then Caspar Ulrich, a former elder, took an extra horse and called for me on the following day. Now when I, together with Caspar Ulrich and Sigel, came into the presence of his Honor, on the 2nd of June last, his Honor was very friendly and said, he had given orders to his general surveyor to show us a lot; if we liked it, we should have it directly. The lot was shown to us immediately. It is a place within the city limits, 150 feet wide and 300 feet long. It adjoins one of the main streets with its narrow end. It is certainly worth 200 pounds (Pennsylvania currency).[214] His Honor offered to allow us at the other

made to this house in July, 1735, as follows:

For boards	£2	15	0
To the carter for hauling	0	3	0
For hauling lime	0	3	9
To the carpenter	1	13	0
For shingles	0	2	6
For 17½ lbs. of nails, from Strohhauer	0	14	7
For 12 lbs. of more nails	0	10	0
For a piece of wood	0	1	0
For whitewashing the schoolhouse	0	1	0
For carrying the benches into the other house	0	1	0
For beer and rum during the work	0	8	8
For locksmith's work	0	7	10
Total	£7	1	5
One half of this	£3	10	8½

The division into two parts shows that the Lutherans paid one-half of the costs, the Reformed the other half.

[214] On June 18, 1741, Mr. Boehm and Jacob Siegel purchased this lot, now in the northeast corner of Franklin Square, of John Penn, Proprietary, in trust for and for the use of the German Reformed

narrow end a small street, running through the whole square, so that we could enter our cemetery from all sides. When we returned to his Honor, he asked us how we liked the place. We answered: "Very well, but the place would be too expensive for us, for we had a poor congregation, as his Honor knew perhaps." We inquired what his Honor would ask for the lot. His Honor was thinking about it. However, we did not let him name the price, but said: His Honor should treat us as a kind Lord, for we did not seek our own profit, but divine service and we were not inclined to bargain with his Honor, but if possible would accept his terms. Then his Honor said in a very friendly manner: "I shall not sell you this lot as I sell other lots. Give me 50 pounds sterling and annually 5 shillings rent, but under the condition that the lot will always be used by your congregation and for divine service, otherwise the lot remains my property."

Now, since we saw the kind disposition of his Honor, we thanked him humbly. His Honor further told us, if he could be of further assistance to us in our undertaking, we should apply to him. Then the lot was surveyed. But now the poor

congregation in Philadelphia as a burying ground. The price was £50, and five shillings yearly as quit-rent. See D. Van Horne, *History of the Reformed Church in Philadelphia*, 1876, p. 20. The lot was located "between Sixth and Seventh Streets, bounded northward by Vine Street, eastward and westward by vacancies and southward by the ends of Sassafras Street lots; containing in length north and south 306 feet and in breadth east and west 150 feet." The congregation proceeded at once to use it as a burial place. An examination made in 1835 showed that the oldest tombstone then visible was dated December 14, 1742. Unfortunately Thomas Penn failed to consult the original maps of Philadelphia, drawn by William Penn, who had laid out this land as a part of a public square, hence difficulties arose. The burying ground was gradually enlarged by successive purchases till, in 1797, the whole enclosure extended 630 feet, north and south, by 250 feet, east and west. These encroachments attracted the attention of the city authorities in 1797. The City of Philadelphia then brought suit to recover possession of the ground in question. In 1836, the Supreme Court of Pennsylvania decided that the Proprietary Grant of part of Franklin Square in 1741 to a religious corporation for burial purposes was void. (See Commonwealth vs. Altburger et al., I Wharton, 469.) An injustice was, however, done the congregation, because it was never properly compensated for the loss of its valuable property, which had been bought in good faith.

congregation cannot pay anything. However, I shall see to it, that his Honor will be patient with us for a time and I shall offer him to pay the interest of the debt, so that, if after a given time his Honor is not paid and the lot cannot remain for divine service,[215] according to the stipulated condition, we shall not make money on it, but will return it to his Honor, in order to gain time for further deliberation. My purpose in this case will be made known to his Honor. To me it seems inadvisable to allow the control over these things to come into the hands of these poor and inexperienced people. Therefore, I think that when any donation has been voted or will be voted to the church here, including that which is contributed by charitable gifts, it should be transferred by deed to our devout Church Fathers as their property. This would insure, in the first place, better authority for obtaining the absolutely necessary protection of the government for our Church and its ordinances. Secondly, ministers would not have so much vexation from the people, if they had no voice in the matter. For if the people rule, every vagabond may cause factions and all kinds of mischief and we can never expect peace. This can be guarded against if no minister can reside on your property except one who has been properly ordained and appointed by you. I shall report obediently to my devout Church Fathers the further progress of this affair, before the departure of his Honor, and at the first opportunity which I can find.

Finally and lastly, Reverend Gentlemen, I deem it necessary to report to you that no other opinion prevails here in Pennsylvania than that we shall have, according to all indications, a royal government here in a short time. To this end our governor, his Excellency Mr. George Thomas,[215a] works

---

[215] This lot was never used for a church, but only for a cemetery. On March 12, 1741, the church lot on Race Street below Fourth was purchased for the congregation by Peter Wager. It was 49½ feet wide on Race Street and 204 feet deep. See Van Horne, l. c., p. 20; also Recorder of Deeds Office, Philadelphia, *Book D,* Vol. IV, pp. 112-114.

[215a] George Thomas was a planter from Antigua. He was appointed Deputy Governor in the summer of 1737, but was detained in London till the following year, assuming the duties of his office in

most strenuously. Against it all sects, Quakers, Dunkers, Mennonites and all others put forth all their efforts. However, it seems that the Protestants will win. On October 1, 1740, there was a great tumult in Philadelphia,²¹⁶ as it was election

August, 1738. In 1739, serious contentions arose between the Governor and the Assembly. The latter refused to vote money for military preparations and the Governor in return refused to sign the bills passed by the Assembly. In 1741, a reconciliation was effected between them. On May 5, 1747, the Governor informed the Assembly of the death of the eldest of the Proprietors, John Penn, and, at the same time, he announced his intention of resigning, which was received with sincere regret. He was capable and industrious, but too zealous for the interests of the proprietaries and the crown. This brought him into conflict with the strong Quaker element in the colony. "His considerate forbearance towards the Quakers, during the latter part of his administration was rewarded by the esteem of the people and the confidence of the legislature." See W. C. Armor, *Lives of the Governors of Pennsylvania*, Philadelphia, 1872, pp. 141-145.

²¹⁶ The newspapers of the day contain no notices of this election riot, but two years later the election was accompanied by serious rioting, accounts of which appeared in the newspapers. October 7, 1742, the *Pennsylvania Gazette* gave the following description of the riot on October 1, 1742: "In this city, when the People of City and County were assembled in the Market Place and had just begun the choice of Inspectors, a Body of Sailors, supposed to be about 70 or 80, collected from several ships in the Harbour, appeared at the Foot of Market Street, arm'd with Clubs, and huzzaing march'd up in a tumultuous manner towards the People. As they were mostly strangers, and had no kind of Right to intermeddle with the Election, and some ill Consequence was apprehended if they should be suffer'd to mix with their Clubs among the Inhabitants, some of the Magistrates and some other Persons of Note met them and endeavor'd to prevail with them to return peaceably to their ships, but without effect. For they fell on with their Clubs, and Knocking down Magistrates, Constables and all others who oppos'd 'em, fought their way up to the Court House and clear'd the Place of Election, the People retiring into the Market House and Second Street in a kind of a maze at such unexpected and unusual Treatment. After the Sailors had triumph'd a while before the Court House, they march'd off, and the People, without pursuing them, continued and finished their Election of Inspectors, which was no sooner done but the Sailors returning more numerous and furious than at first, fell upon the people a second time, and knocked down all that came a-near, several were carried off for dead, and the Confusion and terror was inexpressible. But the Inhabitants, losing at length all Patience, furnished themselves with sticks from the neighboring wood-piles, and turned upon the Sailors,

day for a new assembly, through which the governor tried to bring about his purpose. But he did not succeed. The Protestant country people were so prejudiced by the Quakers and other sects, which told them of all kinds of hardships that would follow, that they, therefore, clung to the old liberty and the old assembly. A large part of them were persuaded by these arguments and gave the Quakers a plurality of 128 votes against the new assembly, the party of the governor. His Excellency was very angry about it, especially with the Germans.

Our Proprietor, Mr. Thomas Penn, agrees with our Governor, also a few prominent Quakers. I hope on the next election day it will be different. Meanwhile all efforts are put forth to make it a success, for the German people will now be naturalized in a different way than formerly, namely, by order of the King and Parliament.[217] They must take an oath which was given to me in High German, in order to explain it to the people of Protestant faith. It is enclosed, marked G. May Almighty God give thereunto His grace. For then I hope to see the Gospel of Jesus Christ succeed in this country. Those who can be naturalized, according to the order of King and Parliament, must have lived seven consecutive years in Pennsylvania. They must be of the Protestant religion, and must produce a certificate from their minister that they have received the Holy Communion not more than three months before. If this is found to be true, they are accepted, otherwise not. They must take an oath on these points. On the 10th of

---

who immediately fled to their ships, and hid themselves, from whence they were drag'd out one by one, and before night near 50 of them were committed to Prison. A good Watch was Kept that Night to prevent any new tumult, and the city has ever since been quiet."

[217] The first naturalization under the new law took place September 25-27, 1740, when 74 persons were naturalized by the Supreme Court in Philadelphia. Among them were quite a number of Reformed people. Among others: John Bartholomew Rieger, John William Straub (cf., p. 54), Jacob Arent, of Skippack; John Wendel Brechbill, Jacob Walter, John Michael Dill and Jacob Uttre, of Philadelphia; Adam Reder, of Falkner Swamp; Leonard Knopp, of Goshenhoppen, and the Lutheran minister, John Philip Streeter, who preached in the Alsace Church near Reading. See *Pa. Archives*, 2nd Series, Vol. II, pp. 347-349.

April of this year more than 200 were in Philadelphia, in the Supreme Court. They thought it was just as before, but they were all rejected, except those who were properly qualified and had their certificates. These numbered 28, Reformed and Lutherans.[218] The Quakers may also be naturalized, but not much was said about them, for there are hardly any here except natives. But I understand that they also must take an oath to find out whether some are foreigners, but I am not quite certain.[219] I also asked the Secretary of the Governor at that time, whether the certificates of unordained ministers were valid, for I complained a little about this. Then I received this answer: *"The Law states that the people must have received the communion, but of whom the law does not say. Therefore, they could do nothing in this matter"*. But I think if once the one thing is changed, the other will follow.

Reverend Gentlemen, if God should so order it that the government should come into the hands of our beloved king, then I think (I have already heard a great deal about it), that it will come about as in England, and also here in Maryland, that all the inhabitants of the country, whoever they may be, must pay an annual church-tax, out of which the Protestant ministers are paid,[220] towards which the Right Reverend Bishop of London would soon work, for his Reverence has thus far

---

[218] The description of this naturalization is so detailed that we can infer at once that Boehm was personally present. This is borne out by the record. On April 10-11, 1741, thirty-one persons were naturalized by the Supreme Court, of whom John Philip Behm is the first in the list. Besides him there were at least three Reformed people of Skippack, who were naturalized at the same time. They were: Andreas Overbeck, Christian Leaman [Lehman] and Ulrick Stephen. See *Pa. Archives,* 2nd Series, Vol. II, p. 352.

[219] The records of the Court show that the Quakers and others, who had conscientious scruples about taking an oath, were permitted to make a simple affirmation. Even some Reformed people were among them, like Abraham Kintzing, of Philadelphia (see p. 233f) and George Bensell, of Germantown. See *Pa. Archives,* 2nd Series, Vol. II, pp. 349-351.

[220] This was a curious delusion of Mr. Boehm, for, if Pennsylvania had become a royal colony, like Virginia, the Episcopal Church would have become the Established Church, to which all Protestants alike would have been compelled to pay tribute, in addition to paying their own ministers.

sent annually the sum of 60 pounds sterling to each of his ministers. This would be unnecessary later on. Then would be the time to provide for our Church in this country and we would aim for more than six ministers, for since the time the [last] report was sent 3 or 4 more [preaching] places have come into existence far away in the wilderness,[221] where the sheep assemble having no shepherd. There was an adequate reason for this outcome of the affair, for in Pennsylvania one may count three or more Germans of all kinds to one Englishman, hence most of the tax would be paid by them.

I shall pay close attention to the outcome of this affair and I shall not fail to report submissively to you, as soon as possible. I do not doubt that our devout Church Fathers will be able to accomplish a great deal through the wisdom given to them by God, and will know how to plan for our good.

So far as the collection-money, received by Mr. Weis and Jacob Reiff, is concerned, everything is quiet. Of his Reverence, Mr. Dorsius, I do not hear that he concerns himself about it or makes any efforts, and Diemer, who very strangely was recommended for this work, can only be a harmful commissioner, because he himself is involved, as has heretofore been reported sufficiently. He will have a poor desire to have the case ended.

I was several times at the place where the letters are, which the Christian Synod wrote to his Excellency, the Governor.[222] I learned from them that the two gentlemen might have fought bravely with the sword [evidence] which they had in hand. However, the case is as stated above. Nevertheless, because it pleased the Christian Synods to commission others for this work, but did not trust me, I must keep quiet. Yet I

---

[221] It is to be regretted that Boehm does not mention these new preaching places. They are probably to be found in Lancaster and Lehigh Counties, where a number of churches were in existence, which were not included in Boehm's report of 1740. See note 179, p. 294.

[222] On April 15, 1739, Rev. E. E. Probsting, Deputy of the Synod, wrote to James Logan, Governor of Pennsylvania. See *Reformed Quarterly Review*, Vol. XL (1893), p. 67f. When Logan answered this letter, December 13, 1739, he stated that on account of ill-health he had retired from office, but he promised to make an investigation. *Minutes of Synodical Deputies*, under date June 7-8, 1740.

am heartily sorry. For the poor congregations can in no case help themselves. May the good Lord grant that it may soon come to a decision. My congregation at Schip Bach is in the same situation as reported before. The congregation at Falckner Schwam is likewise very poor, though harmonious. The place where we worshipped until now has been sold. Whereupon the elders were compelled to make other arrangements. They, therefore, bought next to this place three quarters of an acre for church and cemetery, hoping that, if God grant us help, we might be able to retain it.[223] We succeeded so far that on the 21st of last June we were able to hold our services for the first time under a roof. However, they still owe the largest part of the cost. Thus poverty is everywhere. May God help us.

Now, Reverend Gentlemen and dearly beloved Patrons, for the time I have reported everything which I consider useful and necessary, in all truthfulness and love for the work of our God, and I now commend myself with all the congregations of Jesus here to your Christian love and kind remembrance, wishing heartily that the Lord Jesus may richly bless your work for His true Church and that He may increase your joy over His salvation. Yea I wish from the bottom of my heart that the Almighty God and Father of our Lord Jesus Christ in His immeasurable love may graciously watch over all our devout Church Fathers, their persons, their whole families and holy service for the glory of His holy name and your eternal salvation.

I am and hope to remain unalterably my devout and highly esteemed Church Fathers' submissive and obedient servant and the least of the fellow-servants of Jesus.

JOHANN PHILIPS BOEHM,
High German Reformed Minister in Pennsylvania.
Witpen Township, Philadelphia County,
Pennsylvania, July 25, 1741.

[223] The original deed of the Falkner Swamp church property has not yet been found. This passage fixes the date for the erection of the first church building. It was 1741. On June 21, 1741, services were held for the first time in this building. In his report of 1744, Boehm refers to it as "a well-built frame church, which may last a long time, but they owe nearly sixty pounds on it." See p. 413.

ENCLOSURE A.

[STATEMENT ABOUT THE VISIT OF DORSIUS IN GOSHEN-HOPPEN, OCTOBER 20, 1740.]

When Mr. Dorsius, minister at Schamine [Neshaminy] was at Goschenhoppen on the 24th of September, 1740,[224] and baptized children, in his anger against our minister, Mr. Boehm, he burst out, without any reserve, in the following expressions among many others: "If Boehm says that I have not sent the letters which he wrote regarding the church to Holland, he lies like a scoundrel", and this he repeated several times.

Further: Boehm counts no more in Holland than this boy (pointing to a little boy) and he must know that he has to learn of me, for he is no ordained minister. He is only placed here provisionally, and if he cannot keep his mouth shut, then I'll make him. And more like that.

This is herewith duly attested.

    Ulrich Steffen, elder of the congregation at Schip-Bach.

    Martin Hildebeutel, of Old Goschenhoppen.

    Jacob Frack, of Old Goschenhoppen.

The above words, namely: "Boehm does not count more in Holland than that boy", etc., and similar expressions, I heard from his own lips, to which I herewith duly testify.

    Andreas Oberbeck, elder of the Reformed congregation at Schip Bach.

Schip Bach and Old Goschenhoppen,
    October 20, 1740.

That this copy is an exact duplicate of the original shown to us, we herewith duly testify.

    Frederick Reimer, elder of the Reformed congregation in Falckner Schwam.

    Ulrich Steffen, elder of the Reformed congregation at Schip Bach.

---

[224] The presence of Dorsius and Goetschy at Goshenhoppen on September 24, 1740, is corroborated by the church record, which shows that eight children were baptized on that day. See *Perkiomen Region*, Vol. III, p. 112.) The entries are in the handwriting of Goetschy. The next letter (see p. 339) shows that "Goetschy read the baptismal formula, while Dorsius baptized the children."

ENCLOSURE B.

[DEFENSE OF MR. BOEHM BY HIS ELDERS, NOVEMBER 30, 1740.]

The Rev. John Philip Boehm has shown to us, the members of his consistories, now actually in service in the three congregations entrusted to him at Falckner Schwam, Schip Bach and Weitmarge, a certificate signed by reputable men, in which we read that our minister and pastor was covered, in the congregation at New Goschenhoppen, in the presence of a great multitude of people with unbearable, abusive and scandalous terms by his Reverence, Mr. Dorsius, minister at Schamine.

We believe that thereby the name of God was desecrated, because his Reverence, Mr. Dorsius, tries to make void and exposes to the mockery of unprincipled people the holy ordination, which our faithful pastor, who has now for 15 years worked among us under such a heavy burden, received from the Reverend Classis of Amsterdam through the reverend corresponding ministers at New York. Thus his Reverence assists in bringing about the further demoralization of these people. His Reverence visited the congregations of Sackon [Saucon] and New Goschenhoppen on his return home from Minising.[225] As far as we know he did not visit any others in the backwoods. At that time his Reverence had the young Goetschi preach the sermon and read the baptismal formula, while he baptized the children.[226] Afterwards all that is stated above took place. It is impossible for us to let the case rest here, because his Reverence has not only treated our beloved minister so unkindly, but he also attacked thereby the respect due to reverend men and devout Church Fathers, who established our pure divine worship in this country, by despising the holy ordination, granted to him in the fear of God and because of oppo-

---

[225] This Minising was probably the Dutch Reformed Church at Minisink, now Nominack at Montague, Sussex County, N. J., which was founded in 1737, according to Dr. Corwin. See his *Manual*, 4th ed., p. 990. This congregation was first supplied by Rev. George William Mancius, the Dutch Reformed pastor at Kingston, N. Y., later by Rev. John Caspar Frymuth. See Corwin, l. c., pp. 481, 598.

[226] See note 224, p. 338.

sition to him. We hope, therefore, that his Reverence, Mr. Dorsius, will be requested to reveal the reasons for his unbecoming conduct towards our minister. These, as far as we know, are not of such weight that he can rely on them, they may even be used against him. Hence our official duty compels us to testify duly and truthfully that we are not able to make the least complaint against the life, doctrine and conduct of our minister and his maintenance of order in his congregations, according to our constitution established by the Classis of Amsterdam. But we are fully satisfied and well pleased with him and we have heard nothing else from all our predecessors, since he served the above mentioned congregations. We therefore duly testify to this and sign it with our own hands that, until this day we have heard nothing of our pastor, Mr. Boehm, save that which is good and laudable, with the only exception of the remarks of his Reverence, Mr. Dorsius.

Of the congregation in Falckner Schwam, November 10, 1740.
- John Dunkel, elder.
- John Tricktenhengst, elder.
- Frederick Reimer, elder.
- Jacob X Krausen, elder. (his mark)
- John Dietrich Bucher, deacon.
- Adam Röder, deacon.

Of the congregation at Schip Bach. November 11, 1740.
- John Adam Meirer, elder.
- Andrew (O. B.) Oberbeck, elder. (his mark)
- Jacob Arnet, elder.
- Henry Wurmahn, deacon.

Of the congregation at Weitmarge, December 5, 1740.
- Christopher Ottinger, elder.
- William de Wees, elder.
- Philip Scherrer, deacon.

Having read the above letter of defense, signed with the autograph signatures of the members of Do. Boehm's congregations, now actually in office, and having well considered the same, we, the members of the consistory of the Philadelphia congregation, now actually in office, likewise sign it now. We especially feel it our duty to do so, since Mr. Boehm in the year 1734, in the month of August,[227] took our distress to heart, for the sake of Jesus, while before that time one after another had proved a hireling and left our congregation, so that it had fallen into decay and seemed to be dead. But the forsaken flock appealed with piteous pleadings to Mr. Boehm and he has now served us for more than six years, according to the best of his ability, and he has used all diligence, in order to preserve this congregation, until the good Lord sends further help. Nor do we believe that he will forsake us as long as God spares his life. Like our brethren in the other congregations we have nothing to complain of in regard to his life, doctrine and conversation, but we are well pleased and attached to him in love and peace. To this we herewith duly testify with our signatures, however with grief because of the abuse he suffered, for we have never heard the least unkind word against his Reverence, Mr. Dorsius, from the lips of Mr. Boehm.

Of the High German Reformed congregation in Philadelphia, November 30, 1740.

Valentine Beyer, elder.
John Michael Diel, elder.
Rudolf Wiellecken, elder.
his
Henry (H K) Klemmer, elder.
mark
Jacob Maag, deacon.
John Ludwig Seibel, deacon.

The above is a verbatim duplicate of the original.

BOEHM.

[227] This date fixes the beginning of Boehm's ministry at Philadelphia as August, 1734. On the basis of Boehm's report of 1739 (see p. 273), July, 1734, was formerly taken as the date, but in reality Boehm states in that report only the date when the congregation accepted his constitution. On August 18, 1734, the elders were installed, see p. 238.

ENCLOSURE C.

[LETTER OF THE TULPEHOCKEN CONSISTORY TO MR. BOEHM, APRIL 20, 1740.]

Reverend and Dear Pastor:—

After we had received your letter of March 9, 1740, stating that you would come to us, in order to administer the Lord's Supper, we desire to inform you that Mr. Goetschius also sent us a letter[228] that he and the Inspector [Dorsius] would come in May and administer the Lord's Supper. Therefore we do not know what to do.

Herewith we commend you to the protection of the Most High, and remain,

Your loving parishioners,
HENRY MEYER, elder.
JACOB WILHELM.

Tolbenhacken,
    April 20, 1740.

---

[228] In the archives of the Amsterdam Classis is an earlier letter of the Tulpehocken elders, which describes this visit of Goetschy. It is as follows:

"Account of that which took place at Tulpehocken, how Mr. Goetschi came to us here, preached and administered the sacrament of baptism. All of us members heard that a preacher was staying with Goetschi, and some of the elders went to see Goetschi to ask how it was with the young man [probably Van Basten, see p. 260], whether he was able to serve a congregation and whether we could have him or not. He said that we could have him, but he was not yet fully qualified to preside over a congregation. Then one man, named Henrich Ludwig Schwartz, asked him, namely Goetschi, whether he would come to us several times and preach for us till the young man was fully qualified to serve the congregation. But the congregation had not authorized him, namely Schwartz, to ask for that but only for the young man. Then he [Goetschi] answered, if the congregation was satisfied, he would come. Then he came, preached and baptized children, but without asking permission of the elders.

"To this we herewith testify.
"Dolpehacken,
    "February 11, 1740.

"HENRICH MEIER,
"VALENTINE HERCHELROTH,
"HENRICH BASSLER,
"BARTHEL SCHAEFFER,
"HENRICH ZELLER."

This copy is the exact duplicate of the original which is in my hands.   BOEHM.

ENCLOSURE D.

[STATEMENT OF REV. JOHN B. RIEGER, FEBRUARY 27, 1735.]

I sincerely regret that unlawfully and without the consent of Do. Boehm, lawful pastor of Weitmarge, Schippack and Falckner Schwam, I conducted services in his congregation at Schippack, which is diametrically opposed to the Church Order of the Dutch Reformed Church (which order I confess agrees more than any other with the teaching of Christ, the practice of the apostles and the ancient customs of the Church) and which I promised the Rev. Mr. Boel, minister in New York and the Rev. Mr. Antonides, minister on Long Island, last year not to do again. I ask Do. Boehm and his consistory for their brotherly forgiveness and to bury under a Christian amnesty all that may ever have passed between him and me, and to give me thereon the hand of brotherly fellowship, of reconciliation and love. What has happened shall not happen again. The fire of youth, passion and so forth can do much. I further promise to do in the future everything in my power in the interest of Do. Boehm and his congregation, and when there is an opportunity to speak well of him to his opponents. Nor shall I fail to do and to say what shall recommend and reconcile him to them.

Do. Boehm need the less doubt my word, because, in the presence of their Reverences, Messrs. Du Bois and Boel, ministers at New York, I promised to subordinate myself and my congregations to the Classis of Amsterdam, to be willingly and entirely subject to its discipline and, should I, in one thing or another give offense, also to its censure; pledging myself, as proof of my subordination to the Reverend Classis of Amsterdam, to send a written agreement, before the 14th of April next, if I am living and enjoy health, to the correspondents, Messrs. Du Bois, Antonides and Boel, and if I neglect the same, or have not then furnished it, without giving sufficient reasons to the satisfaction of Messrs. Du Bois, Antonides and Boel, that in that case Do. Boehm and his consistory may continue their action against me and may prosecute me by correspondence and by every other ecclesiastical and lawful manner, customary in such cases. All this was sacredly promised without cunning and guile and signed for its proper observance, in New York, on February 27, 1735.

JOHN BARTH. RIEGER,
Minister at Amwel.

The above statement was shown to us by Do. Rieger. It appears to us as satisfactory, and we hope that Do. Boehm and his consistory (unless they have important reasons to the contrary) will accept it as an evidence of reconciliation.

This was witnessed and signed by us, at the request of Do. Rieger, at the place and date as stated above.

G. Du Bois,
Henricus Boel.

I herewith attest that the two preceding statements agree verbatim with the true originals, signed with autograph signatures. Pennsylvania, July 20, 1741. Boehm.

ENCLOSURE E.

[LETTER OF REV. G. M. WEIS TO MR. C. ULRICH OF PHILADELPHIA, JUNE 20, 1741.]

To Caspar Ulrich at Philadelphia.
Burnetsfield, in the County of Albany,

June 20, 1741.

Dear Sir and Friend:—

Last year I received a letter from the Reverend Classis of Amsterdam concerning the ecclesiastical affairs in Pennsylvania, all of which were recommended to me with the assurance that the Classis would help me with advice and as far as possible with deeds. They gave as their opinion that I should again be received as minister among you in Pennsylvania and be reinstated in my former office (as may be seen more fully from the extract of the Classical letter[229]

---

[229] A copy of this Classical letter, dated June, 1739, is preserved in the *Classical Letter Book*, Vol. XXIX, p. 257. In it the Classical Deputies write: "We have learned of your good intentions and watchfulness for the best interest of the church in Pennsylvania, not only from your letters, but we have also received information from a person who left Philadelphia October 20th of last year [1738]. He said indeed that he had heard nothing of your intention to return to Philadelphia, and he added that if you should again undertake to preach there it seemed to him improbable that the undertaking would bear fruit, and in proof of this he gave such reasons that we would rather keep silent about them than mention them, so as not to hurt your humility. Therefore, we are induced all the more to declare to you that if you can again receive another appointment to the ministerial office, under circumstances agreeable to yourselves, it will be agreeable to us." See *Eccl. Records of N. Y.*, Vol. IV, p. 2734. Weiss probably misunderstood this Classical letter, for the advice seems to be to accept a call elsewhere than Philadelphia.

lately sent to Philadelphia). Therefore, I desired, out of obedience to said Classis, to make this known to you, my dear friends at Philadelphia and at other places, so that you might not be ignorant of it, and have time for deliberation concerning this affair, in order that the work of the Lord begun among you may at last have a happy issue, which every one earnestly looks for.

May the Great God grant that all may tend to the glory of His holy name! May He produce in the hearts of men true Christian love. This is my hearty wish. Commending yourself and your family to the protection of God, I remain with friendly greetings,

My esteemed friend's devoted servant,

GEORGE MICHAEL WEIS,
p. t. minister of the Reformed Congregation of Burnetsfield.

That this copy agrees verbatim with the original autograph, I herewith attest,
July 20, 1741.

BOEHM,
Minister in Pennsylvania.

ENCLOSURE F.

[ACCOUNT OF THE COLLECTION MONEY DRAWN UP BY WEISS, MAY 8, 1738.]

SCHIP BACH, May 8, 1738.

Account drawn up with J. Reiff concerning the collection money, which he received in my presence in Holland at Rotterdam, Harlem and Amsterdam, of which the following disposition was made:

RECEIPTS according to the Collection
   Book sum total..............2104 Holland guilders

EXPENDITURES: Of this sum was paid for necessary expenditures and other purposes:
1. For the voyage from Philadelphia to London
   without food taken along...............18 pounds
2. For board in London during one month, together
   with duty for me and Jacob Reiff......5£ 7sh. 6d.
3. For passage from London to Rotterdam for
   each ....15sh. sterl.
   1 chini [guinea?] for the bed and 3sh. for board.
4. Expenses for half a year's stay in Holland and
   necessary journeys[230] ....700 Holland guilders

---

[230] This statement is important, because it fixes the length of Mr. Weiss' stay in Holland. He first appeared in Holland in August, 1730. Hence he left in February, 1731. See p. 41.

5. At Rotterdam, shortly before my return to London, Jacob Reiff gave me..250 Holland guilders Of these I paid the passage to London from Rotterdam, since Jacob Reiff remained in Holland, 12sh., a chini for the bed, 6sh. for board. The passage from London to Maryland 8£, without food, which I took along. The journey from Maryland to Philadelphia by land and sea 3£ 12 sh. 1d. For board in London 16sh.

In addition for my trouble and labor for the year 50 pounds.

N. B.—Jacob Reiff declares that he paid me for clothing and a few books......110 guilders and 14 stuivers.

Note: When pounds and shillings are mentioned sterling money is meant.

ENCLOSURE G.

THE FORM OF THE DECLARATION OF ALLEGIANCE.

I, N. N., do hereby publicly promise (swear) and announce that I will be faithful to his Majesty, King George II. I also confess truly and under oath that with all my heart I hate, despise and deny as an ungodly, heretical doctrine and idea, that princes or rulers, by an excommunication of the Pope, or by any other authority or permission from Rome, may be deprived of their dignity and deposed or murdered, be this by their subjects or others.

I likewise declare (swear), that no foreign prince, ruler, prelate, state or potentate, whoever he may be, neither has any right, authority or power, nor should have any power, right and authority to rule and command in ecclesiastical and spiritual affairs throughout the whole kingdom of Great Britain and all the countries and dominions belonging to the same.

THE EFFECT OR CONTENTS OF THE OATH OF ALLEGIANCE.

I, N. N., do hereby solemnly and sincerely and faithfully declare (swear) that his Majesty, King George II, is the true and rightful king and possessor of the crown and the kingdom of Great Britain and all the countries and dominions belonging to the same.

And I do also faithfully declare (swear) it as my belief that the person who during the reign of the last king, James, pretended to be Prince of Wales and also after the death of said king took upon himself the title James VIII, King of Scotland and James III, King of Great Britain, has no right whatever to the crown of the kingdom of Great Britain and the countries belonging to the same, and I hereby renounce all homage and obedience to him. On the other hand, I do solemnly promise that I will be faithful and obedient to his Majesty, the present King George II, and his rightful heirs, and that I will strive to faithfully disclose and report all secret alliances and treacherous plots of which I may learn, which may be made both against his high person, crown and government, as against his rightful succession; and I do sincerely and faithfully promise and pledge myself that with heart and hand, property and life, I will defend his Majesty's title and government against all those that pretend to be Prince of Wales, both in regard to said James and all other pretenders whoever they may be, as such is confirmed by an act of Parliament, called: "An Act showing the rights and liberties of subjects and establishing the succession to the crown of the last Queen Anne and her natural heirs of the Protestant religion"; and further in another act, called: "An Act of further limitation of the crown and better insurance of the rights and liberties of the subjects, willed and confirmed by the late Queen Anne in want of natural heirs, to be succeeded by the Princess Sophia, Electress and widowed Duchess of Hanover, and her natural heirs of the Protestant religion."

All these things I do sincerely and honestly declare, yea promise and testify that my opinions are according to my words and the general sense and meaning of them, without ambiguous words or secretly containing a subterfuge and reserve of whatever it may be, and I make this declaration (oath), denial and promise heartily, willingly and faithfully, upon my Christian faith.

[XXXI. BOEHM'S BOOK AGAINST THE MORAVIANS, AUGUST 23, 1742.[231]]

Faithful Letter
of Warning
addressed to
The High German Evangelical Reformed
Congregations and all their Members in
Pennsylvania
For their faithful Warning against the People who
are known as Herrn Huters
That they may take care and guard themselves
against their Doctrine, destructive of soul
and subversive of conscience and hence
that they may not be led astray to the eternal
loss of their souls, by the
appearance of their external hypocritical conduct,
and their fancied righteousness and holiness.
After the example of the Reverend Consistory
of Amsterdam in Holland
By reason of the duty and obligation
imposed upon him by Almighty God
Written by me
JOH. PH. BOEHM,
*High German Reformed Minister of the
Congregations entrusted to me in Pennsylvania.*
Philadelphia, printed by A. Bradford, 1742.

[231] It is hardly necessary to state that the editor does not share Boehm's feelings towards the Moravians. He cherishes rather a sincere regard and admiration for their splendid missionary work in behalf of Christ's Kingdom throughout the world. These documents relating to the union movement are published simply as historical documents, to show conditions as they were then and what the feelings of the chief actors were. It is to be regretted that Boehm indulged in the same coarse abuse which was then the prevailing style in theological polemics. The two books sent to him from Holland abound in the same sort of language. We omit as irrelevant all merely controversial sections and confine ourselves to a few historical paragraphs of his book, which give first-hand information about events, in which Boehm took part personally. No one can or should doubt that Boehm was an honest man, and when he tells about events which he knew from personal observation, his statements must be accepted as representing

LETTER OF 1742

[The first part of Boehm's book is taken up with a presentation of the chief contents of two books sent to him from Holland. The first was entitled: "Pastoral and Paternal Letter addressed to the flourishing Reformed Congregation of this city, meant for the discovery and exposure of the dangerous errors of the people known as Herrn Huthers. Written by the Ministers and Elders of the Consistory of Amsterdam.

"Amsterdam, printed by Adrian Wor and Heirs, under the Elms, MDCCXXXVIII".

The second and much more elaborate book, sent to Boehm from Holland, was written in answer to an anonymous reply to the "Pastoral Letter", and was intended as a further exposure of the supposed heresies of the Moravians, by its author, the Rev. Gerhard Kulenkamp, pastor at Amsterdam. Its prolix title may be translated as follows:

"The Corrupt Mysticism, Spiritism and Enthusiasm of the so-called Herrn Huthers laid bare. Out of their High German Hymn Book and their other writings most clearly exposed and their agreement with the corrupt mystics and spiritists in Germany and the Shakers in England demonstrated as a renewed faithful warning against these people and as a full defense of the Pastoral and Paternal Letter of the Reverend Consistory of Amsterdam. Now added as a reply to the faithless accusation of a certain anonymous writing. Published upon the earnest request and at the order of the Reverend Consistory and out of love for the truth which is according to godliness, by Gerhardus Kulenkamp, Minister at Amsterdam.

Amsterdam, printed by Adrian Wor and Heirs under the Elms, MDCCXXXIX".[231a]

The first twenty pages of Boehm's Book are taken up with an analysis of the chief contents of these two Dutch books.

---

the event as he saw it. Only one known copy of this book of Boehm has survived, which is now in possession of the Rev. Dr. J. I. Good. It is a small octavo, containing IV, and 96 pages of closely printed text. A partial reprint of the book was issued in Germany in 1748 by the Rev. John Philip Fresenius, in his *Bewährte Nachrichten von Herrnhutischen Sachen,* Frankfurt, 1748, Vol. III, pp. 562-677.

[231a] A facsimile of the title page of this rare book was published by the writer in the *Journal of the Presbyterian Hist. Soc.,* Vol. VII, facing p. 353.

On p. 21 he continues as follows:]

What has happened here of late,—my dear and beloved Brethren and Sisters in Jesus, faithful members of the congregations entrusted to me (yea all those who will read this in the fear of the Lord),—I shall faithfully report to you, in view of my duty and the obligation resting upon me because of my office which I hold among you, in accordance with the best of my knowledge and the truth which is pleasing to God, so that I may not leave you in ignorance and without warning.

Probably most of you know that Count Zinzendorf, together with the people accompanying him, namely the above mentioned Herrnhuters whose leader he is, arrived at the end of last year in Philadelphia, the capital of Pennsylvania. There the Evangelical Lutherans,—because this Count of Zinzendorf calls himself a Lutheran,—adhered to him (at first only a part of them) at the instigation of some, whose character is well known, (who will reveal themselves later on) and thus it came to pass that the Count was invited to preach for them.

Then it happened that, on Christmas day last past, the 25th of December, 1741, I went to Philadelphia and conducted my usual service with the Reformed congregation, intending to hold another service on the 27th day of the month, which was Sunday. Inasmuch as I had spoken with a certain member of the Lutherans and he had agreed (because no Lutheran minister was present) to read a sermon and thus hold a regular Lutheran service for this congregation on the second Christmas day, that is Saturday,—as he had done repeatedly upon request, according to the best of his ability,—I resolved to attend together with all the elders of the Reformed congregation and other members, as was the usual custom.

When, with several elders and members of the Reformed congregation, I went that day to the meeting house, not knowing anything about what was going to take place, many people of both congregations stood in front of the house on the street, which presented a remarkable appearance, for they were walking one behind the other. When we came nearer we heard what was the cause of this concourse of people, namely Count Zinzendorf was going to preach, which had been arranged by some, but many did not want to allow it. We kept silent (because it did not concern us) until some of the Lutherans (among whom were elders, as I believe) asked, what I had to say to it. I answered:

"I believe I have more information about these things than many of you and hence I want to protest, so that none can say that the Reformed people (or myself) had consented to it, to have Count Zinzendorf [preach] at the time appointed for the Reformed. We Reformed people cannot prescribe to you Lutherans. If you do something against yourselves, we want to have no part in what may come of it".

As a result nothing came of it and the Count stayed away. But there was talk that the originators of this affair were much displeased with me, saying, Boehm has done this! Then word was passed that the Count would hold a meeting in his own house towards evening, which took place. A considerable number of people, of all persuasions (because it was something new) came together. Then he announced that in future he would preach in his house, which he did the following day, Sunday, the 27th of December.

After that he continued, as he had done several times before, to preach at Germantown, in the church built there for the High German Reformed congregation. What reports we have about the addresses delivered there, will be stated later.

Meanwhile, through the instigators of the affair in Philadelphia, to whom we referred above, it came so far among the Lutherans that Count Zinzendorf preached to them, at their appointed time in our common church. For this reason the Count wrote me the following letter, under date January 8, 1742, which reads verbatim as follows:

"To his Reverence, Mr. Jacob Boehm, Dutch Minister of several Pennsylvania Churches. At his plantation.

"My dear Mr. Boehm:—

"The officers of the Lutheran denomination, in which I was born and brought up, and on the basis of which I stand in the service of our Church, have requested me to preach in their church. I cannot well deny them this, because I accepted such invitations in many cities and places of the Lutheran religion in Germany, until within a few days of my departure for this country, and preached everywhere the Gospel willingly and in good order.

"But inasmuch as I know that you preach in the same

church, and I do not hold the doctrine of unconditional reprobation, a doctrine which in my religion is confessedly regarded as wholly and fundamentally erroneous;

"I have thought it proper to inquire of you, whether you have a right to make any objection to my preaching there, as I do not want to molest any one nor encroach upon his rights. While, on the other hand, I do not want to surrender any of the rights of the Evangelical elders. However, I have never yet ascended a pulpit in opposition to any one, who had a right to object. I find conditions such that I must make inquiry of Mr. Boehm. Afterwards I shall act as I find it proper before the Lord. I remain, Yours ready for service,

LUDWIG VON THURNSTEIN,
V.D.M. Eccl. Mor. EE.
Philadelphia, January 8/19, 1741/42."

The messenger had besides an open note reading as follows:

"A receipt is necessary, and if Rev. Mr. Boehm is not at home, it ought to be sent to him, so that a reply may, if possible, be secured before tomorrow evening.
Philadelphia, January, 8/19, 1741/42."
"The messenger will be paid here in Philadelphia".

That this appeared strange to me, I cannot deny. For, if the Count had not been trying to gain something, he would hardly have done me the honor of writing to such a humble man as myself, nor do I doubt that, if he had been aware that all the affairs of the Herrnhuters were known to me from the book, approved and printed in Amsterdam in 1739, he would have saved himself the trouble of writing. Hence I hesitated, nor did I find it necessary or advisable to answer so hurriedly. But, out of love for the messenger, who is a daylaborer from Philadelphia and needs his wages, I was ready and willing to give him a note acknowledging its correct receipt, which reads as follows:

"The letter sent to me by Count Zinzendorf, under date January 8, 1742, through Michael Hahn of Philadelphia, I have this day received, which is herewith certified to Mr. Hahn. But the immediate answer which was demanded therein to the question whether I had a right to raise an objection to Count Zinzendorf's preaching in the church, which both Evangelical congregations have in common, I am unable to give at this time for certain reasons. Meanwhile I adhere to the words, which I spoke to the Lutheran elders at Philadelphia on December 26, 1741, namely: I think that I have more information about these things than many of you. I therefore want to protest against any one saying that from the Reformed people (or from me) consent was given to Count Zinzendorf to preach in our place and time. We Reformed people cannot prescribe to you Lutherans. If you do something against your own interests we do not want to have part in the consequences that may result. To this I adhere, and remain of every sincere person a willing and devoted servant".

"JOHANN PH. BOEHM, *Reformed Minister*".

Now regarding this letter of Count Zinzendorf sent to me, I cannot believe that it was written from a sincere and good motive, but more likely in the hope of entrapping me in an ill-considered answer, which might be used to injure our Reformed churches and cause confusion among them, so that he might all the better gain his purpose.

[In the following pages (pp. 24-61) Boehm reviews and criticises at length the Minutes of the seven conferences, which were held under the auspices of the Union Movement, from January to June, 1742. These minutes, entitled *Authentische Relation*, etc., were printed by Franklin in 1742. As this criticism of Boehm is very lengthy, and contains little of historical information of permanent value, only two extracts from it will be presented. The first refers to an interesting incident preceding the conversion of Peter Miller to the Seventh Day Dunkers] :

On this third page the writer refers to a magistrate and the careful arrangement by which this person, together with others from every known religion in Pennsylvania, who could understand the German language, were induced to be present.

As to the identity of this magistrate I have heard from people who were present (but during the day only) that it was Conrad Weiser of Dolpihacken, who is said to be a justice.

If it is he, then let every Evangelical Christian think what hope there is that he will do something for the honor of the Gospel of Christ. For when Peter Miller, formerly a pretended Reformed minister in Dolpihacken, became a real disgrace to our Reformed churches when he went over to the Seventh Day Tumplers [Dunkers] and was baptized in Dunker fashion and with him several others,—this Conrad Weiser was one of them. He was a Lutheran[232] and at that time an elder of the Lutheran congregation in Dolpihacken.

Again, when the four Seventh Day Tumplers [Dunkers] namely Peter Miller (mentioned above), Michael Miller, Conrad Weiser and Gottfried Fidler, burnt the Reformed Heidelberg Catechism, the Lutheran Catechism, the Psalms of David, the Paradies Gärtlein [Garden of Paradise] and the Exercise of Godliness, in all 36 books, burning them in derision and disparagement in Gottfried Fidler's house, he was one of them. Nor is it known that since that time he has turned back to his Lutheran religion.[232a] Let each one among you, my be-

[232] The Lutheran membership of Conrad Weiser has recently been called in question (see Dubbs, *Reformed Church in Pennsylvania*, p. 97, note 96), but without sufficient reason. All contemporary writers are agreed that he was a Lutheran. This is the testimony of Boehm. He would certainly not have called him a Lutheran if he had been "the chief elder of the Tulpehocken Reformed Church," as has been claimed. Peter Miller, in the *Ephrata Chronicle* (p. 71), calls him an "elder of the Lutheran faith." Zinzendorf, in his reply to Boehm, expresses his surprize that Boehm referred to Weiser, since "he is not Reformed" (Fresenius, *Bewährte Nachrichten*, Vol. III, p. 710). Weiser took part in a Lutheran communion service (*Hallesche Nachrichten*, new ed., I, 362). Muehlenberg reports him to be a Lutheran: "At Tulpehocken, many years ago, some Lutherans, among whom was Mr. Weiser, had taken up a piece of land." Finally Weiser himself stated, according to Muehlenberg, that "he held all the principles of our Evangelical religion" (*Hallesche Nachrichten*, new ed., I, 449). The fact that Weiser acted as trustee of the Reformed Church at Reading (Miller, *History of the Reformed Church in Reading*, p. 17) proves nothing, for he was also a trustee of the Lutheran Church at Reading (Fry, *History of Trinity Lutheran Church, Reading*, 1894, p. 18). The attitude of Weiser at Tulpehocken and his association with Peter Miller is explained by Miller himself: "He was the teacher's main stay, for they were on intimate terms together." But friendship with Miller did not constitute membership in the Reformed Church. See also Schmauk, *History of the Lutheran Church in Pennsylvania*, p. 473.

[232a] The writer has in his possession the original of a letter of Conrad Weiser, dated September 3, 1743, by which he separated his connection with the Ephrata Community. It was translated and published in C. Z. Weiser, *Life of John Conrad Weiser*, 2nd ed., Reading, 1899, pp. 128-130.

loved, consider what this means and what supports the Count is putting under his building.

[The second extract deals with Henry Antes]:

I cannot sufficiently express my surprise regarding Henry Antes, who several years ago severed his connection with our Reformed congregation at Falkner Schwam, for altogether reprehensible reasons. I spoke with him several times about necessary matters and, in view of his statements, I always entertained strong hope that, through the mercy of God, he would again come back to the right path (which hope I cannot yet give up) although such well known and altogether objectionable things have taken and still take place. But I sigh to the gracious and merciful God, that He may take pity on him and all those who have gone astray through the spirit of error, for the sake of their dear and immortal souls. I shall leave it to every pious and orthodox Christian to have his own thoughts about that which Henry Antes has done and continues to do. For he was born under the clear light of the Gospel and received Holy Baptism, by which he entered into the covenant with God, which He made with believers.

Of this covenant he was put in remembrance, according to the Word of God, of which I have no doubt (for I knew his zealous and faithful pastor well), at his first participation in the Lord's Supper. At that time he must have promised, without doubt, before his pastor and the officers of the Church of Christ, yea in the presence of the righteous God, that he would remain faithful, till the end of his life, to our religion, which he once accepted and which is founded on the Word of the true and living God, and alone leads to salvation.

The vows which he made not to men but to God Almighty he has broken. And for several years he has gone about, through the spirit of error, among all kinds of heretical people and erroneous opinions. At present he allows himself to be used by the above mentioned Count Zinzendorf in his sect, being led about like a blind man with a stick.

Could one imagine that Henry Antes, who (as I willingly confess) has received more than many others, would so sin against his God and, leaving the truth, betake himself to such a soul-destroying doctrine?

Ah, in the future perhaps, when God's grace has enabled

him to see the depth of Satan, he will heartily humble himself and consider that the only searcher of hearts is not deceived by hypocrisy and sham piety (which has always ruled among all self-invented sects) for he sees the thoughts of the heart and nothing is hidden from him.

God knows well, regarding Henry Antes and myself, how both our hearts were once bound together in a cordial love for the divine truth in our Reformed doctrines. And he has not forgotten, I am sure, that he was one of those who by their tears induced me to take the yoke [of the ministry] upon my neck.[233] Nor have I on my part been able to forget this love, and shall never forget it, although I have been much grieved by him. And, when I think of him, I make mention of him in my prayers before God, asking Him to set him and all the erring ones right, by the light of His spirit.

But I would heartily and sincerely counsel him, if he will accept it for himself, because it concerns his immortal soul, not to delay too long with the honest examination of himself, and not to think that it is no longer necessary, otherwise it may be postponed to the end of his life, of which none knows how near it is.

[On p. 61 of his book, Boehm begins the review and criticism of another publication of Count Zinzendorf, issued in 1742, *Bruder Ludwig's Wahrer Bericht,* etc., of which the following extract refers to the Reformed Church of Germantown and to the meeting house in Philadelphia]:

Again, Count Zinzendorf writes: My heart has always felt at home in the Reformed Church, in Germantown. That I can honestly say. (Here he himself confesses that it is the Reformed church). Listen, my beloved, this he writes on February 20, 1742, that his heart always felt at home in the Reformed church in Germantown and he adds, "if there were only three souls there, he would sow [the seed of the Gospel] as much as he was able".

But what did he say three months later, on May 21st, when at the same place? He called the people of Germantown Sepa-

---

[233] The two men who, with tears in their eyes, persuaded Boehm to take up the work of the ministry, must have been his two most prominent elders, Henry Antes and William DeWees. See also p. 29.

ratists. Some want to add even more insulting terms, which he applied to them in his Christian and becoming zeal, so that it was a disgrace. And what did he say on the 30th of May in Philadelphia, when he scolded those of Germantown just as badly and even worse? And in his conversation there he tried to persuade his followers in Philadelphia that they should rent the meeting house alone, so that I might not preach in it any more but he alone, otherwise he would not preach to them any longer. He also offered that he would rather pay the fourth part of the rent, paid by the Reformed people, out of his own means.

Is that acting honorably by the Count, like a Christian? He pretends (falsely and blasphemously), as can be seen above, that Jesus has given him the right over all the children of God without distinction in this country. Whoever recognizes this as sincere, does not know how to make a distinction, and will at last be compelled to feel ashamed before himself, before God and before his fellow-men.

[On p. 71 of his book, Boehm returns once more to the minutes of the Union Conferences. In this part the sections referring to John Bechtel are of interest]:

"When the catechization according to the new (but as I shall show false) catechism was finished, then, after having read the autograph commission of the two antistites[234] of the united Evangelical churches of Germany and Great Poland, their vicar in America ordained our brother John Bechtel, thus far the faithful minister of the Evangelical Reformed church of this place, before the assembled congregation, as pastor of this church and commissioner of all the others who hold, in the chief doctrinal points to the Synod of Berne, in the name of

---

[234] The two men were: Daniel Ernst Jablonski, court preacher of the King of Prussia, and Christian Sitkovius, superintendent of the Reformed churches of Poland. These two men were at the same time bishops of the ancient Brethren Church of Moravia and Bohemia. On March 13, 1735, Bishop Jablonski, with the written concurrence of Bishop Sitkovius, conferred episcopal ordination upon David Nitschman. He is referred to above as "their vicar in America." The intention of this ordination was, without question, to create a Moravian bishop. Sitkovious could not transmit his authority over the churches of Poland, and hence Boehm was perfectly justified in questioning Bishop Nitschman's right to ordain *Reformed* ministers.

the Father, the Son and the Holy Ghost, and the two deacons, whom he appointed, were associated with him".

Behold, Beloved, how they write here about an autograph letter of the two authorized officials of the united Evangelical churches of Germany and Great Poland and of one appointed as their vicar in America, but who these authorized officials and their vicar appointed by them are is passed over in silence. (It is, according to report, the so-called Brethren Bishop, David Nitschmann, hence a Herrnhuter). . . .

Now with regard to John Bechtel one should think that he would feel ashamed to stand on the ground upon which his feet rest, if he has no higher thought. Inasmuch as he has tainted himself for some time with all kinds of heretical opinions and ran after them most sedulously. Thus he has been a despiser of the fundamentals of our Reformed doctrine and of the Heidelberg Catechism and an evident hypocrite, as is known to almost all men. And now he allows himself to be ordained by these enthusiasts as pastor of a Reformed church and as a commissioner of all the others [Reformed] in this country. This will never be recognized as valid by the learned men and overseers of our Reformed churches. For he cannot be counted as anything else but an enthusiast and, until his complete conversion and repentance of his grave error, he cannot be regarded as a member of our Reformed church, much less as a pastor of a Reformed congregation and for the time being as commissioner over all the others. Likewise all those who allow him to administer to them the sacraments cannot be admitted to the table of the Lord in a Reformed congregation, before their complete conversion and repentance.

Nevertheless these Herrnhuters want to give full legality to this affair by calling this John Bechtel "hitherto the faithful pastor of the Reformed church here". Regarding this I need not write much, but I must express my surprise (for he himself must be convinced of the falseness of this statement) that he allowed this to be done, without shame, to his own disgrace. For it is well known to most of the people in this country (who are German Protestants) that this is an absolute lie.

Nor can I note with sufficient astonishment that this John Bechtel himself makes use of such shameful untruths, calling himself a Reformed minister and proudly boasting of the publication of a pietistic book, under the name of a catechism, whose title reads verbatim as follows:

"A Short Catechism for some congregations of Jesus of the Reformed religion in Pennsylvania, who hold to the ancient Synod of Berne. Published by John Bechtel, Minister of the Word of God. Philadelphia, printed by Benjamin Franklin, 1742."

Is this not an empty bragging with his invalid ordination, which he received from these enthusiasts, by which his obnoxious pride can most clearly be seen. Behold, Beloved, what else is aimed at hereby but a division of our Reformed churches in Pennsylvania? For we have the Heidelberg Catechism, which is in use among us and which is embodied in our Church Order, approved and well established by the Reverend Classis of Amsterdam (to which the largest number of the Reformed congregations in Pennsylvania have long submitted). Hence we have no need of such a catechism, published by John Bechtel, a man who has gone over to the sect of the Herrnhuters and has become unfaithful to the Reformed churches. Yet it is perfectly clear that he only shot off the bullet which Count Zinzendorf had cast.

[Then follows a lengthy criticism of this catechism extending from p. 79-84, after which he continues as follows:]

This little book John Bechtel calls a catechism for some Reformed churches of the Reformed religion in Pennsylvania, which hold to the Synod of Berne. Yet there is in it from beginning to end not a word of the articles of our Christian faith (that is omitted because the Herrnhuters do not want to pray to God the Father, but only to the Saviour, as has been stated before). Nor is there in it a word about Holy Baptism or Holy Communion, no word about the holy commandments of God, and no word about the most holy prayer, which our Saviour has taught us to pray. How then, my beloved, yea I ask all Christians of whatever denomination they may be, how can this booklet justly be called a catechism for some congregations of Jesus by John Bechtel? And with the addition, for those who hold to the Synod of Berne! Who can be so simple as to believe that the Christian Synod of Berne would recognize this book as a catechism for the congregations of Jesus belonging to the Reformed religion. This is altogether evident, if one holds alongside of it the true Berne Catechism, approved by the authorities there and printed in Berne, in the government printing office in 1688. . . .

Hence John Bechtel will not succeed in persuading the sincere Evangelical Reformed members of our churches to recognize his ministerial office, to which he lays claim in the booklet published by him. I also entertain the hope that God will give grace to his people so that they will be able to recognize the hurtful and cunningly mixed-in poison in the food prepared for them, before they swallow it. For God has given so much wisdom, according to His Grace, to every honest Evangelical Christian, that he can distinguish between black and white, even if both are simply labelled: Color. But, because of this one word, the one will not be taken for the other, because the words black and white clearly distinguish the matter.

For this reason mark this, Beloved, whoever calls himself truthfully an Evangelical Reformed minister must necessarily have been ordained and installed by overseers of this religion who have the power to do this and not by enthusiasts. Judge yourselves, dear brethren, how can they ordain ministers for the Evangelical churches?

Now this John Bechtel, as has been stated above, was ordained by these enthusiasts as a Reformed pastor of the Evangelical Reformed church here (Germantown is meant) and for the time being as commissioner over all the others who in the chief doctrines, hold to the Synod of Berne.

Behold, Beloved, this cunning and impertinent malice of these enthusiasts, for such procedure is unheard of, how they seek to carry on their affairs by force to advance their Herrnhutish Saviour. From which it can be inferred what they would do if they had the power.

What is to be thought of this John Bechtel and all those who recognize and accept his work, and what ought to be done with them, has been intimated above.

This John Bechtel, in the first place, has been ordained (illegally, for they had no right to it), which needs no further proof, by such sectarians, who publicly through print have been declared before all the world to be enthusiasts and spiritists. Must he not be the same as they, and one of their teachers?

For,

In the second place, in Germantown, when the Herrnhuters held there their so-called love feast, he was present as a member and, as is reported, was the first to receive the bread. Must he, therefore, not be regarded as a Herrnhuter? Judge for yourselves, Beloved!

Nevertheless, he dared impertinently to administer the Lord's Supper to the Reformed people in Germantown, on the second Easter day, at which occasion a number of simple people, who formerly adhered to the Reformed religion, received it from him. Thus they followed him and apostatized from our Reformed Church.

By this instance it can be seen how cunningly and craftily they seek to captivate the poor people with their soul-destroying Herrnhutish ropes.

Thereupon he announced to all the Reformed people of Germantown and neighborhood, that they should assemble in the Reformed church there on Monday following Pentecost, which was done. At that time Bechtel proposed to them to organize the Reformed church in Germantown. To which end each one who wanted to be a member of the congregation and desired to hold to the Berne Synod (which is an unknown quanity to most people here) should put down his name. He was willing to be their ordained minister (in what manner and with what validity has been shown above) and would be ready to administer the sacraments in the Reformed manner, and would teach a catechism, the Heidelberg, or Basle or Berne Catechism, whichever they desired. Whereupon (as is related) about 17 or 18 persons answered in the affirmative and signed their names.

Behold, dear brethren, for what purpose John Bechtel allows himself to be used by the Herrnhuters and how willing he is to become a cunning and tempting recruiting officer for this Herrnhutish sect, and in all earnestness desires to assist in making our Reformed Church here in Pennsylvania Herrnhutish or Zinzendorfian, or at least in giving her that name and in making her suspected in all the world, as though she had completely gone over to this soul destroying and conscience wrecking doctrine,[235] had become unfaithful and had been captivated with Herrnhutish ropes. This with the result that all favor and love of our divinely blessed fellow-believers here and there and all their Christian help would be cut off from our Church in this country. This, if we were silent, would be spread throughout the world with loud boasting, according to their usual custom.

But in this he, a hypocrite,[236] who for years roamed about among all kinds of sects (which needs no further proof, but is well known to every one) will, as I hope to God, completely fail. For he received his share [of condemnation]—because of his conduct at the first Herrnhuter assembly, held on the first and second of January, 1742, in Germantown,—in the official protestation then issued. This protestation I will now insert here verbatim, in order that you, my dear congregations, may see how I discharged my duty as your regular pastor and all the elders then in office. The same reads as follows:

"Whereas we, the undersigned minister, elders and deacons of the High German Evangelical Reformed congregations here in Pennsylvania, have seen a so-called Authentic Relation, etc., which was drawn up regarding a meeting of all kinds of people, of every persuasion, which took place January 2, 1741/2, in the house of Theobald Ent in Germantown, and

"Whereas we have read in it on p. 7, that the writer of this Relation, with the grossest perversion (of the truth), expressed himself in these words: "When no one else was expected to appear, a brother of the Reformed religion prayed

---

[235] Boehm knew the doctrines of the Moravians largely through second-hand sources. He trusted too much in the judgment of the authorities in Holland, whose objectionable style he also adopted. That the doctrines of the Moravians are now thoroughly evangelical can be seen by a reference to the *Moravian Manual,* Bethlehem, 1901, pp. 85-91.

[236] There is no evidence that Bechtel or those Reformed members who sympathized with him were hypocrites. Boehm evidently could not understand how one's sympathies could pass beyond the narrow denominational lines. Bechtel was, according to all accounts, a sincere soul, to whom denominational creeds meant nothing, but faith in Jesus Christ as his Saviour everything.

very heartily," etc., and

"Whereas we know of no true, steadfast member of our Evangelical Reformed Church, who has tainted himself with this doctrine that is of ill-repute in Holland, Germany and all other places (of which we have a sufficiently thorough and reliable report), and can therefore not regard this in any other light than an endeavor to throw suspicion upon our Reformed Church in this country before all our fellow-believers in all places of the world, as though she was implicated in this affair,

"Therefore we, as officers of our congregations, cannot let this matter rest, but want to protest, vigorously and with every formality, against such an impertinent and cunning falsehood. And we protest constantly (against this as well as every future attempt), inasmuch as we cannot recognize as a brother in communion with us any one, whoever he may be, who separates himself from our Church or has already been separated, or will in future separate himself, and who professes his adherence to such an assembly and its doctrine, mixed with all kinds of opinions, until he shall fully return to the divine truth upon which our doctrine is founded. Whereunto we herewith testify and sign it with our own hands:

JOHANN PHILIP BOEHM, *Minister*.

"Elders and Deacons of the High German Reformed Congregations in Pennsylvania, mentioned below.

"In the months of February and March, 1742.

In Schippach:
Adam Meyrer, elder.
Jacob Arnct, elder.
Andrew Oberbeck, elder.
Henry Wuhrmann, deacon.

In Philadelphia:
Rudolf Weilecken, elder.
Henry Klemmer, elder.
Jacob Walter, elder.
Nicholas Ewig, elder.
John Ludwig Seipel, deacon.
Philip Burckhard, deacon.

In Falckner Schwamm:
John Dirck den Hengst, elder
John Dunckel, elder.
Frederick Reimer, elder.
John Jacob Kraus, elder.
John Ditrich Bucher, deacon.
Adam Roeder, deacon.

At Weitmarge:
William Deewees, elder.
Christopher Ottinger, elder.
Michael Cleim, deacon.
Philip Scherer, deacon.

In Tulpohokin:
Henry Meyer, elder.
Henry Zeller, elder.
George Unruh, elder.
Martin Schell, elder.
John Foehrer, deacon.
Peter Schell, deacon.

In Oly:
Sebastian Graef, elder.
Frederick Leibi, elder.
Henry Werner, deacon.

[There can be no question that Count Zinzendorf himself provoked a good deal of criticism by his own arbitrary and unprecedented actions, which clashed unpleasantly with ordinary custom. The following incident may serve as an example]:

On p. 112 they boast "All those who were present were deeply moved when on the second of June the child of a stocking weaver in Philadelphia, a Swiss, received baptism (administered by Count Zinzendorf). What caused this commotion can be learned from those who were present. I was told, that when they wanted to bare the head of the child, the Count said it was not necessary. For sins ought to be washed away from the heart. He told them to open the dress of the child in front. When that was done, he poured a considerable amount of water into the bosom of the child, and said: I baptize thee with the blood of Christ, in the name, etc. Let each one judge for himself whether it is found in Scripture that such things should be done and said, as the Count did and said. Another child was present, which, as is related, was more than a year old. This was too old for the Count to do to him the same as to the child just born. "He therefore laid his hands upon it, because it had passed the period of purest innocence, and he handed it over to baptism as a candidate, exorcised in future through faith". (This is again a newly invented method of the Count).

[A serious clash occurred on July 18, 1742, in the Lutheran and Reformed meeting house in Philadelphia. Boehm refers to it as follows:]

After they had falsely and untruthfully persuaded the Lutherans that they were true Lutherans, and had induced them to believe them, they accepted the Count and his representatives to preach for them. But, when they wanted to administer the Lord's Supper to them in the church, on Easter Monday of this year (which I curtly refused them, when

Pyrlaeus, one of his apostles asked me for it, because it was my time and place, in order that they might not glory over the Reformed) those of the Lutheran congregation, who never wanted to have anything to do with them, were brought to serious thought and realized with the others that fraud was practised on them and that their affair was nothing but pure deception. They, therefore, locked the door,[237] because they were found to be no Lutherans. This lock they (the Herrnhuters), together with some few who were attached to them, broke open with irons and tongs. The outcome of the affair, because the lockbreaker was bound over for court, has to be awaited. Now, what do you think of such people, Beloved? Judge for yourselves! Are they true Evangelical Christians? Are they shepherds coming in through the right door (which is nothing but a regular call and commission) to guard the best interests of the sheep?[237a]

---

[237] There is no evidence whatsoever that Boehm had anything to do with this change of the lock, or that he had suggested it, as has been stated recently. The Moravians naturally blamed the Reformed, because they appear to have entertained the delusion that all the Lutherans were on their side. When dissatisfaction broke out among the Lutherans they at once charged it to the Reformed members. In this they were certainly mistaken, as is evident from the account of Muehlenberg, printed below.

[237a] How intensely Boehm felt about this incident can be seen from a letter of Secretary Peters, who wrote, on January 15, 1743, to the proprietaries, informing them of this incident. He had not fathomed the true character of the triangular controversy. He had only mastered it so far that he knew that it was a fight between the followers of Zinzendorf, or the Moravians, and the Lutherans. Of the Reformed party he had apparently never heard and took Pastor Boehm for a Lutheran minister. But his graphic picture of Boehm probably approaches correctness. He wrote: "There is a great quarrel between ye Lutherans and Moravians, chiefly on account of principles. The Count's party increasing considerably, the Lutheran minister, Philip Boehm, could not bear it. The Lutheran meeting house is on a lot of Mr. Allen's, and by contract with the Lutherans, as I understand, ye Moravians were to use it every third Sunday. Philip Boehm wanted to hinder them from this contract, and finding no other method would do, one Sunday morning, as Christopher Pyrlaeus was performing Divine service, a party of Lutherans appeared at ye door. He took no notice. . . . . . Ye Lutherans then came on with violence, and drove him and the Moravians out of the meeting house,

[COMMOTION IN THE PHILADELPHIA MEETING HOUSE, JULY 18, 1742.]

[The same incident is described more at length in a report of John Adam Gruber, a resident of Germantown, which was published by the Rev. John Philip Fresenius, in his *Bewährte Nachrichten von Herrnhutischen Sachen*, Frankford, 1748, Vol. III, pp. 205-207]:

On July 18 [1742], it happened in Philadelphia, that,—after Mr. Pirleus, whom Mr. Ludwig [Zinzendorf] had installed as Lutheran preacher in his place, had preached several times in the church which the German Protestants use in common,—those Lutherans who did not adhere to him and Mr. Ludwig, did not suffer him to preach any more and, being stirred up as related above, they put a lock on the door. But Mr. Pirleus and his adherents, who refused to desist, broke the door open (some had said that it cost only ten pounds to do that) and when he [Pyrlæus] was in the pulpit and preached, the opponents came in and objected. They told him to leave, but when he did not comply, saying he had first to tell them something, they warned him again to leave or they would use force. But he was not willing to go. Then two of them took him by the arm and led him out. About this a great tumult arose, many hard words and also some pushes with the elbows were given. Then those inclined to the Herrnhuters ran to the magistrates and complained that the others had pulled out Mr. Pirleus by the hair (which was not true), while their people had been as patient as lambs. They also boasted everywhere about their sufferings for the sake of Christ. Both parties were bound over by the magistrate for court. An attempt was made to have the Herrnhuters and the others compose their differences peacefully, but they did not want to. When Mr. Ludwig [Zinzendorf] heard it, he hurried down from the Indians with some of his companions, accused the opponents violently, insisted on his rights, saying they had called him as their minister, he would assert his right and, if the court would not give him his right, he would bring the case before the Supreme Court, and, if he could not get his right there, he would bring it before Parliament in England. Now, he said, he would preach there himself and would see what they could do with

and locked ye doors. The Count got the Lutherans indicted for a riot. . . . . At the trial, ye Lutherans were acquitted. There is indeed a mortal aversion between Boehm's congregation and ye Count's people. . . . . I tried to soften and accommodate ye differences between ye two parties, and thought I had some influence on Boehm; but ye moment I mentioned it his eyes perfectly struck fire, and he declared with great passion he would as soon agree with ye devil as with ye Count. He is a hot, indiscreet man; and after expatiating on the Christianity of his temper, I left him with abundance of contempt." Quoted by Mr. Dotterer in his *Rev. John Philip Boehm*, Philadelphia, 1890, p. 15. The original is in the Pa. Hist. Soc.

him. But when he came with his people, the others were already in the church, one of them reading a sermon. He stopped when Mr. Ludwig entered, but he told him to finish. When he wanted to speak after the former had concluded a tumult arose, especially some of the women scolded him violently and threatened, if he would dare to stand up and speak, something bad would happen to him. They did not want him under any circumstances. Then he went away trembling, together with his adherents, saying he would preach there until he had built a new church, etc. Meanwhile he gave orders that his adherents should buy a place and build a new church, which was done and it was completed in a few months. This fight about lumber and stones continued till he left the country. Indeed it even increased, for his followers were sued about the cup and the church record, which were in the hands of one of his followers. A few days after his [Zinzendorf's] departure the suit was decided in court, by which his followers drew the short end.

[Rev. H. M. Muehlenberg in his Autobiography (p. 139f) also gives a detailed account of these events. He writes]:

The Count had at first passed himself off as a Lutheran minister and had induced the people to give him a written call, but without their signatures, as they assured me. After he had preached for the Lutherans several times in an old house, which they had rented in common with the Reformed congregation, the Lutherans became suspicious and scattered. Each one of the officers took what he could lay his hands on to keep it safely, e. g., one took the church record, another the collection bag, a third the alms-box, a fourth the cup, etc. Afterwards one of the deacons (Thomas Maier) put a lock on the meeting house. When on the following Sunday it was the turn of the Lutherans to have services, the Count sent his assistant, Mr. Pirleus, together with the people whom he had won over from the Lutherans, to the meeting house. They broke off the lock with a piece of iron, entered, sang and Mr. Pirleus ascended the pulpit to preach. The Lutherans and Reformed stood outside. Then a Lutheran elder went in and called upon Mr. Pirleus to leave the house with his people. Mr. Pirleus answered: "You are no Lutherans, you are going the wrong way." Then several Reformed men entered and pulled Mr. Pirleus out of the house. These unlawful actions on Sunday, the breaking of the lock, scolding, etc., gave of course much offense, so that the Governor took occasion to ask, why the Germans were beating their women? It became a great tumult. They pushed each other and stepped on each other. The women screamed, etc. There were many spectators. The Zinzendorfians brought the matter before Court, suing the Reformed and Lutherans. It has become a long drawn out affair and is still before the Court. That party which has the most votes, of those that rented the house will win. There are said to be many more Reformed and Lutherans than those that broke away and went over to the Zinzendorfian party. Consequently the Lutherans and Reformed had a right to the meeting house they had rented and the Zinzendorfians had no right to break off the lock. This tumult which I have just described took place on the 18th of July, 1742, old style. About two weeks later, when the Lutherans had begun their services with singing and reading, the Count with his people entered. The Lutheran officers warned him urgently to leave and not to disturb them. He then withdrew. Some time later they wanted to compose their differences peacefully. To that end some elders from the congregation at Philadelphia and some from the Providence congregation on the one part, and Mr. Peter Boehler on the part of the Count met, but they could not agree. Mr. Boehler submitted to them written articles of doubtful propriety. When among other things they held up to Mr. Boehler the wrong of breaking open the lock, he illustrated their right with a fitting comparison, namely "if pigs came before a locked barn and wanted to get in they would take hold of the door and lift it off its hinges with their snouts." Whereupon the elders answered him: "Then the pigs must also submit, if the owner of the barn comes and drives them out with a whip."

[Regarding this incident the Reformed and Lutheran congregations issued jointly the following official protest, which is inserted verbatim and literatim:]

A Protestation of the several Members of the Protestant Lutherian and Reformed Religions in the City of Philadelphia, jointly concerned in the Lease of their Meeting House in Arch Street, about the late Commotion which happened on Sunday, the 18th of July, 1742.

The members aforesaid have thought it absolutely necessary to acquaint their Fellow Citizens of the remainder Persuasions, or whom it may concern in general, that the said Commotion at the time and place aforesaid, can no ways be imputed to any tumultuous disposition of theirs; for they hereby freely appeal to every one that has been a liver in this province and especially to them that reside in this city of Philadelphia, whether they have not (ever since the first time they began to constitute a body in this place) always behaved calmly, peaceably, quiet and obedient to the civil Magistrates, and no ways disturbing neither the public peace nor that of any other persuasions either publickly or privately? Challenging by these presents every one (excepted only those that became of the late Proselytes to our present Adversaries the Moravians, as they are commonly called) to prove anything to the contrary against them.

Whence therefore this new and unexpected alarm? Whence all this rumor and commotion? Whence this importuning of our worthy magistrates, to protect every quiet and orderly behaving subject in their Religious Worship? Certainly and undoubtedly for none else but from these newcomers, who by their disturbing Genius, as they have set several places in Europe in great confusion, wherefore they have been cast out of divers places (as appears by undoubted and approved testimonies sent over to us from our churches in Europe) so they have acted the same in other places of this province, especially about Tulpehocken.

These Moravians, or rather missionaries of that society, pretend to adhere to certain articles of a Synod of Bern, of more antiquity and consequently, as they pretend, of better authority than our Confession of Augsburg and that of the Catechism of Heidelberg, pretending also the present existence of such an united Church in Germany and Poland (against all which we solemnly protest). In pursuance of this they are wont to metamorphize themselves into Lutherans, sometimes into Reformed, nay into all religions, by which means they get their proselytes, which they afterwards employ to subvert the constitution maintained by the rest, whilst they themselves keep behind the scenes: These new Proselytes are persuaded to be true orthodox from that Religion they were of, and thus deluded, become great zealots for the Reforming of their Fellow Brethren: As therefore to

The Species Facti

"There came at the time and place aforesaid, some of these deluded pretended Lutheran Proselytes aforesaid, asking from us (the authors of this protestation) the key of the Lock (which we had put on at the Door of our meeting, for to prevent the eating forth of this gangrene) intending to enforce upon us their preacher, who, we are told, hath been ordained by Count Zinzendorff (against which Preacher we also solemnly protest). The key therefore being refused, they concluded (at a venture as some said that it could stand them in not above Ten Pounds if they did wrong, whereby every one may perceive what such people would do if they had the Power) to force the door open, which accordingly they did, introducing their preacher who, as it were, was with some difficulty persuaded to it, but at last consented; which some of our people (because the chiefest part of the members were absent and would undoubtedly have prevented it, taking for an assault, sent one from amongst them to desire the preacher to leave the Oratory, because it was their House, and that he had no business there, etc. Which he refused, alledging he had something to say to them first; whereupon provoking discourses from both sides ensuing, some took hold of the preacher and led him out in the street, during which time there happened some pushes with elbows and scolding from both sides, but it came not to any blows, our people exhorting each other not to commit any hostilities, but to take recourse to our worthy Magistrates and their Protection, as becomes good Christians."

This our dear friends and neighbors is the true cause of the premises, whereby, to our great sorrow and affliction the Lord's Day was prophaned, and our Honourable Magistrates molested and importuned, to whose wise determination of the matter we have appealed by law with all due submission and Reverence; praying God Almighty for their preservation and his blessing of them and all their subjects, to the end that we may continue to lead a quiet, peaceful and Christian life under their Protection.

[The book of Boehm was signed:]
Witpen Township, Philadelphia County,
August 23, 1742.   JOH. PHIL. BOEHM,
Pastor of the High German, Evangelical Reformed Congregations in Pennsylvania.

[XXXII. MR. BOEHM TO THE CLASSIS OF AMSTERDAM, NOVEMBER 17, 1742.[238]]

Very Reverend Classis:—

Your most submissive and obedient servant (with all the congregations here) waits with a cordial longing for a gracious and comforting answer to the last submissive letters of January 25th and July 25, 1741. But, since we have thus far received no answer, we herewith respectfully repeat all our former, submissive petitions.

In the meantime I cannot forbear obediently to transmit the accompanying [booklet] to the Very Reverend Classis, since I consider it my duty. From it the Reverend Classis can learn all that has happened here thus far. I shall be heartily glad if my undertaking is not disapproved of by the Reverend Classis. Under the circumstances I could not act differently. For there was no time to seek further counsel, as the wolf at first carried on furiously, and him whom I should have sought near by, I could not find.[239] Hence I had to take up the [shepherd] staff in order to defend myself. Accordingly I acted in this manner, as the Reverend Classis can see. If your humble servant did wrong in anything, the good Lord will surely forgive him, for he knows that it was done heartily, out of sincere love for the Gospel of His beloved Son, and for the sake of the poor and simple souls, whom heretical spirits try to lead astray from the path of truth; and likewise on account of the Reverend Classis, under whose supervision I have the duties of a

---

[238] The German original of Boehm's letter is in the Classical archives.

[239] It is not clear to whom Boehm refers in this sentence. It could not be the Rev. P. H. Dorsius, for he was not on friendly terms with him in 1742. It may have been one of the Dutch Reformed ministers of New York.

shepherd and watchman. I have felt thus far that it was not in vain, for which I shall praise God for ever. It is true my family had to suffer to some extent on account of it, for each sheet cost forty shillings to set up in type, which I had to pay without help. But, as the Lord liveth, I could not have any but English letters (the German printer excused himself, he was not altogether just).[240] As a result, where there is one of our High Germans, who can read it, there are perhaps twenty who cannot read it. Thus far I have sold only a few towards covering my expenses, and I may have to wait several years until all my expenses are paid. If I could give it away, many might want it for their instruction, but I am unable to do this, as my income is still in the old condition and I heartily desire to see a different state of affairs here, which should be regulated according to the intention of the Reverend Fathers. May the merciful God, who is also almighty, help His poor, true believers in this country and touch the hearts of the richly blessed members of the body of Christ.

These enthusiasts and fanatics offer themselves everywhere in this country to preach and to install schoolmasters, and all this entirely free of charge, in order to draw to themselves and lead astray the poor and helpless people, who form the majority here. But the remonstrances have had this effect, with God's blessing, that every evangelical person just for this reason considers their doings all the more dangerous and understands them better, so that they have had as yet little success.

Your humble servant and the least of the fellow-workers of Christ petitions, therefore, the Reverend Classis, for a favorable and kind answer and for information what he should do in future, in order that you may encourage him with further instructions, the necessity for which appears from the accompanying report. In the meantime I shall not cease from defending and watching as long as God gives me grace and life and as He shall lead me.

[240] The German printer was Christopher Saur. As he did some printing for Count Zinzendorf in 1742, e. g., the Moravian hymn book, entitled *Hirten-Lieder,* he may have been unwilling at that time to print a book against Zinzendorf, although later he did not hesitate to express his dissent from Zinzendorf and his efforts.

I herewith commend the Reverend Classis, every person, together with all your families and holy service to God and the Word of His grace and myself to your pious and devout prayers before God and to your remembrance.

Your humble and obedient servant and the least fellow-brother in the Lord,

JOHANN PHILIPS BOEHM,
*High German Reformed Minister
at Falckner Schwam, Schip Bach and Weitmarge
and Philadelphia.*

Witpen Township,
  Philadelphia County,
  Pennsylvania, November 17, 1742.

P. S. After having finished this letter, I hear that Count Zinzendorf intends to leave here to return to Holland[241] and Germany. He leaves his false apostles here and promises to send more of them.

[XXXIII. CLASSIS OF AMSTERDAM TO MR. BOEHM, MAY 9, 1743.[242]]

To. Mr. Boehm.
  Reverend Sir and Colleague:—

We safely received your last letter of [November 17, 1742] and learned from it how you sought to advance the well-being of the congregations entrusted to your care, and with this in view have judged that you must make your observations upon some actions, opinions and errors, held and brought forward by the Count of Zinzendorf, the chief advocate of the Moravians in Pennsylvania, and to communicate these in print to your churches, to warn them and to guide them into the right way. The Reverend Classis praises your zeal in this matter, wishing that it may be granted unto you to minister to your congregations in the strength of the Lord, so that the Lord, according to the riches of His glory may strengthen them by His strength and by His Spirit, in the inward man, so that Christ may dwell in their hearts

---

[241] Zinzendorf left Philadelphia December 31, 1742, old style, or January 11, 1743 (n. st.). He sailed from New York January 20, and reached Dover, England, February 28, 1743. See Reichel, *Early History*, p. 139.

[242] A copy of this letter is found in the *Classical Letter Book*, Vol. XXIX, p. 356.

by faith, and they may be rooted and grounded in love, that they may fully comprehend with all saints what is the breadth and length and depth and height and know the love of Christ that passeth knowledge, so that they may be filled with all the fulness of God. Certainly such dispositions and labors embrace in themselves the most precious weal and the blessedness of the partakers of the Lord's favor. May these then ever be found in you and your members.

For the rest, the Classis does not find itself as yet thoroughly in a condition to write a satisfactory answer to your former letters of January 25, and July 25, 1741, concerning Mr. Dorsius and those who are his supporters, these come now through other reports. This is certain, he is no Inspector of the Church in your regions. If he conduct himself as such, he goes beyond his appointment. That which we request of you in respect to him and the Church in your region is, that you shall be pleased to inform us more precisely in the future, how the one or the other is doing or behaving himself, and whether the so-called Moravians do injury to your congregations, in what this consists, and what is done about it in your regions. We are inclined to serve you as far as lieth in us, with our counsel, as affairs and circumstances may require. And that this may tend to the well-being of you and yours is our wish. The Lord strengthen you in all things in body and soul, and His loving kindness be extended over you forever. Thus do we write in the name of the Reverend Classis, remaining

                    Reverend Sir and Colleague

                    (Signed as before)

Amsterdam, May 9, 1743.

[XXXIV. SECOND FAITHFUL WARNING OF MR. BOEHM, MAY 19, 1743.[243]]

SECOND FAITHFUL WARNING AND ADMONITION

to my very dear and esteemed Reformed fellow-believers, and to all others who love the Lord Jesus and to whom His holy Gospel and His holy sacraments are most precious. My wish for them is, that they, without exception, by the grace of Jesus Christ, the love of the heavenly Father and the powerful and effectual assistance of God, the Holy Spirit, may be kept from

---

[243] For this document use has been made of the copy which Boehm sent to the Synods, and which is now preserved in the archives at The Hague, 74, I, 32. It contains several marginal notes made by Boehm himself.

error and harm to their immortal souls. Amen.

All My Beloved!

With you, my fellow-believers, I wish to speak first of all, and may it be for the information of all other dear Christians.

Everywhere in Pennsylvania, it is plainly evident that some of our Reformed religion are so careless in watching and praying, as commanded by Christ, Mark 14:28, that the devil, who goeth about like a roaring lion, seeking whom he may devour, finds it easy to lead such souls astray, to the eternal loss of their souls and finally to devour them, because they are slack in true Christianity, but eager to run after strange and even false doctrines.

A year ago I published, in accordance with my duty and obligation, my FAITHFUL LETTER OF WARNING against the so-called Herrnhuters (who came to this country at the close of the year 1741) and against their doctrine, pernicious to the soul and destructive to the conscience. It consists of 6¼ sheets of small print. I also made known that it could be bought from *Casper Ullrich* and *Michael Hillegas* in Philadelphia, from *Jacob Baumann* in Germantown, from *Gabriel Schüler* and *Peter Speicker* in Schipbach, from *Henry Türinger* in Falckner Schwam, from *Isaac Levan* in Oley and from *George Unruh* in Dolpihacken. The letter contained throughout true information, as I had received it from Holland (approved by the great university of Leyden in Holland) and from other places. I am sure that every one who examines this letter properly and considers it thoughtfully will not only be able to recognize it as truth, on account of all the things the Moravians have done among us thus far, but also guard himself against their abominable doctrine, for the eternal welfare of his soul. But it seems that many were not disposed to pay the small amount necessary to secure this letter, and rather preferred to remain ignorant in this most important affair, for it concerns immortal souls. Hence some who are entirely ignorant have already allowed themselves to be led astray disgracefully. Such inconsiderate people, who so slightly regard and without conscience break their oath, which they swore to Almighty God at their first participation in the Lord's Supper, will find this not only unanswerable before God, but they are

Abermahlige treue Warnung und Vermahnung an meine sehr werthe und theuer geschätzte Reformirte Glaubens-verwandte, wie auch alle andere die den Herren JESUM lieb haben, sein Heil. Evangelium und seine Heil. Sacramenten in höchstem werth halten. Denen sambt und sonders wünsche ich, daß sie, durch die Gnade JESU CHRISTI, die Liebe seines Himmlischen Vatters, und den Kräfftig-würckenden beystandt Gottes des Heil. Geistes mögen bewahrt werden vor allem Irrthum und Schaden ihrer unsterblichen Seelen. *Amen.*

Alle sambt Geliebte.

BOEHM'S SECOND WARNING AGAINST MORAVIANS, 1743

also a disgrace to themselves and their relatives, who adhere firmly to the Reformed religion in other countries, wherever they are. For when they will learn that they have so inconsiderately accepted the pernicious and ruinous doctrine of the Herrnhuters (which is known everywhere in Germany and has been driven out almost everywhere) and have so disgracefully forsaken their Reformed religion, which is founded on the Word of God (for the sake of which divine truth our brethren in the faith in France and in other countries, have been persecuted) they will not only be heartily sorry for it, but also be ashamed.

This and the love to you, my dear brethren in the faith, and to your immortal souls, again impels me to send you with these few words my faithful warning and admonition, in order to inform you concerning that which I perhaps know better than you, so that no one may be able to excuse himself, neither before God nor before man, that he had been led astray without being warned.

For I daily hear how *Jacob Lischy, John Bechtel and Henry Antes,* together with their helpers are so zealously exerting themselves in order to put our Reformed religion entirely in the shade here in Pennsylvania and to bring all under the control of the Herrnhuters, and that by cunning tricks and false appearances they pretend to be Reformed ministers; *Jacob Lischy,* a Reformed and ordained minister from Switzerland, as he calls himself in his deceitful DECLARATION OF HIS OPINION,[244] published March 1, 1743, in which, however, he also shows distinctly, at the bottom of the 3rd page and at the top of the 4th page, that he belongs to the Herrnhuter congregation. It will turn out as in the case of *Peter Miller,* who was ordained by the Presbyterians in Philadelphia as an Evangelical minister, but what is he now? A Seventh Day Tumpler [Dunker]. John Bechtel (also pretends to be) a Reformed minister, for the above mentioned Lischy had ordained

---

[244] The German title of Lischy's pamphlet reads: *Jacob Lischy's Reformirten Predigers Declaration seines Sinnes an seine Reformirte Religions—Genossen in Pennsylvanien* [1743], 8 vo., 8 pp. For a facsimile of the title page see Dr. Dubbs' *Reformed Church in Pennsylvania,* p. 125.

him* which, however, took place in the meeting of the Herrnhuters in Germantown, in the month of April, 1742.) What a great and bragging title he adopted at his invalid ordination was shown clearly enough in my former LETTER, p. 77 and following.

Henry Antes likewise pretends to be a Reformed minister, but as yet I do not know who ordained him.[245] It was undoubtedly done in the same manner as in the case of John Bechtel, or he may boast of an immediate call, as he really seems to do, for I am told that he said to the assembled people at Oley, that he was without sin, for the Savior had taken possession of him, etc.

Now, dearest friends, what should be done with these three, Lischy, Bechtel and Antes, and how their intentions may be learnt, I shall tell you faithfully and truthfully, as far as I know, and I propose to stand by it.

Concerning *Jacob Lischy*. This spring he pretended at Dolpihacken, in the presence of two Reformed elders, to be a Reformed minister from Switzerland and assured them that he had nothing to do with Count Sinsendorf [Zinzendorf] and the teachings of the Herrnhuters, but that he had come to this country last summer on board of a merchant ship.[246] Indeed he convinced them by his smooth words, so that they appointed a time for a meeting in order to accept him, if their brethren would consent to it. But when they met, some of them knew better that he was a regular Herrnhuter, and they sent him away. He had also offered, (because I had been accepted by them to come to them once every six months in order to administer the Lord's Supper and Baptism) that he would not oppose me nor do these acts, but leave them to me; he only desired to be their preacher and preach for them. But, since they were told that in one home he had said, if only he had been in the church twice or three times, it would all be dif-

---

* People thought so because Bechtel said at one time that a Reformed minister had ordained him, for none was known who pretended to be such except Lischy. But it was Nitschmann. (Ms. note of Mr. Boehm.)

[245] Antes was never ordained, as far as we know.

[246] Lischy came to Pennsylvania with the "Snow Catharine," a ship owned by the Moravians, see above, p. 120.

ferent, they realized still more his subtle deceit.

I was also informed by a certain trustworthy man, that this Lischy is said to have sworn by the throne of God, in the presence of certain people at Gaguschi [Cacusi] in Bern township, that he had nothing to do with the doctrine of the Herrhuters.[247] As a result he was admitted into the Reformed church there, whereby much mischief has been caused among the members of that congregation. Again, Lischy preached in a private house in Bern township and said in his sermon: People should not worry, all men would be saved. None should be lost. Whereupon George Heen [Hain][248] there, at the above mentioned church, called him to account soon afterwards, demanding that he should prove this from the Scriptures. Only rogues and thieves talked in this manner. On account of this (the word thief) he was cited [before a justice] by a warrant of Conrad Weiser and bound over to the Court at Lancaster.

Again, in Oley he preached several times in the barn of Isaac Levan, pretending to be a Reformed minister from Switzerland and denying that he had anything to do with the doctrine of the Herrnhuters, but finally, after earnest question-

---

[247] It ought to be said, in justification of the Moravian authorities, that they thoroughly disapproved of the deceitful conduct of Lischy. This appears from numerous documents in the archives at Bethlehem, Pa.

[248] John George Hain (Höhn) appears first in Ulster County, N. Y. June 6, 1717, John, son of John George and Veronica Höhn, was baptized there in the Old Dutch Reformed Church. George Hain came to Lancaster (now Berks) County at any early date. January 21, 1735, a warrant for 400 acres of land, lying on a branch of Schoolkil, was issued to George Haine. Another warrant for 100 acres, lying near Goshen Hill, "adjoining to a tract whereon he is already settled," was issued to him March 21, 1735. A warrant for 200 acres on the Great Spring Creek in Tulpehocon Township, "adjoining to his Father, George Haynes, land," was granted to Peter Haynes on May 22, 1735. George Hain signed his will November 16, 1743. It was probated April 8, 1746. He mentions in it his wife, Veronica, and nine children, namely John Christian, John Peter, John George, John Adam, John Frederick, John Henry, John Casper, Sibilla, married to Jacob Freymeyer, and Elizabeth, married to William Fisher. In the inventory the tract of land on which the church stands (Cacusi or Hain's) is valued at ten pounds. He gave this church land.

ing, he confessed that he had taken part in the love feast with Count Zinzendorf. Whereupon these people in Oley did not desire to hear Lischy any more. Across the Schulkiel,[249] not far from Keyser's mill and also at Moderkrick [Muddy Creek], he likewise preached several times, and by his dissimulation brought the ignorant people so far that they were willing, as is reported, to accept him as their Reformed minister, etc. This is the fine Reformed minister, Jacob Lischy. For the present I shall not mention other things. This is sufficient.

Concerning the second *John Bechtel*, it is not necessary to write much, for he himself admits that he received his ordination (as stated above) from Jacob Lischy.* Now it is well known that every bird hatches his like. What an arch hypocrite this John Bechtel has been for several years is sufficiently known to many Germans in this country, and what will yet become of him time will show, nor dare it be concealed. He has already found fault with the Heidelberg Catechism, for he had promised to teach the same faithfully at Germantown, but already the following Sunday he reserved the privilege not to teach the 80th and 114th question . He claimed that they were not true, for the 114th question said one could not keep these commandments of God perfectly. That was not true, for those converted to God *could keep them perfectly, for they were no longer sinners*. He desired that they should sign a letter, in which he had set still more snares, but it was not done at that time.

Concerning the third, *Henry Antes*. Only a few weeks ago, when some one asked him: How can you call yourself Reformed? You go to the Herrnhuters and take part in their love-feasts. He answered: "Why, how strange you speak. Is that a reason that I should not be Reformed? I am Reformed; I am also a Lutheran; I am also a Mennonite. A Christian is everything", and so on. Now let every one think it over, what kind of a spirit must dwell in such a man, and let him judge for himself. Many other things could be said

---

[249] The congregation across the Schuylkill was Coventry, now Brownback's, which extended a call to Lischy to become its pastor on April 10, 1743.

* A mistake! For the Moravian brother, Bishop David Nitschmann did it. (Ms. note of Mr. Boehm.)

of Antes, if one wanted to speak of him at length.

Mark this, Beloved! At first when the Herrnhuters came to this country they pretended to be Lutherans. Now a number of them are Reformed. If this is true, it is also evident enough that such men are possessed by a false spirit of error and that they are false prophets, who everywhere seek to put on sheep's clothing, in order to deceive men and thereby lure them into their own net; and even if all this were not the case, this one thing alone is enough, that these three, Lischy, Bechtel and Antes, were present on the 11th, 12th and 13th of May, in Philadelphia, at the beautiful and joyful feast, which they call love-feast. They participated in it diligently, so that they are genuine Herrnhuters. Now, are they true Reformed ministers, as they falsely assert? Let each judge for himself.

I for my part consider them Moravians, who indisputably belong to these enthusiasts and fanatics. They are like the "strolling Jews", who went about and adjured them who had evil spirits by Jesus whom Paul preached, Acts 19:13. But the acts of these false apostles of the Herrnhuters are much more daring. For one of them, by the name of *Gottlob Bittner*[250] of Dolpihacken, adjured even the Lamb of God in his

---

[250] Gottlob Buettner was born in Silesia, December 29, 1716. He became acquainted with the Moravians at Marienborn, Herrnhaag and Herrnhut; came to America in October, 1741; was for a short time spiritual advisor of the single brethren in Bethlehem; preached to Lutherans at Tulpehocken and neighborhood and was finally appointed to labor among the Indians at Shekomeko, N. Y. In January, 1742, he visited this station to invite and accompany Rauch, the Indian missionary, to the Synod, which was to be held at Oley, Pa. They took with them three Indian converts, who were baptized at Oley, February 22, 1742. At the close of the Synod, Buettner was ordained by Nitschman and Zinzendorf. Soon afterwards he was sent out as pastor of the Lutheran congregation at Tulpehocken, but was recalled in September, 1742. On September 14, 1742, he was married to Margaret, third daughter of John Bechtel of Germantown. In October, he set out with his wife to Shekomeko. There Rauch and Buettner preached to the Indians in English and Dutch. Their work was opposed by unscrupulous white men, who would rather see the Indians drunk than converted. The law was invoked against the missionaries and they were finally compelled to give up their work. Before Buettner could leave, he fell sick of a pulmonary complaint, and died February 23, 1745. In 1859 a monument was erected to him and Rauch

prayer with these words: *"Thou Lamb of God, I adjure thee by thy sacred wounds, that thou wilt reveal the souls that shall be led to thee"*. This is terrible to listen to, let each judge for himself (it is credibly attested). In addition, they are running about of their own accord and do not come through a regular call, as through the right door into the sheepfold of Jesus Christ, but they climb up some other way; and those that do this are *thieves* and robbers, says Christ, who speaks the truth, John 10:1. And v.10 he says: "A thief cometh not, but for to steal, and to kill and to destroy".

Now, beloved brethren, if some of you have really been led astray by such false liars, I think that the reason for it was, because you did not know any better, and for this reason you may all the sooner be declared innocent, for you believed their smooth words and had intercourse with them, thinking that they had told you the truth, and that they were Reformed ministers. But since all their words are lies and since they seek only to lead you astray to the sect of the Herrnhuters[251] and away from your evangelical doctrines and to destroy your souls, therefore the promise you gave them is annulled by itself, to your greatest praise before God and all your fellow-believers.

Do not consider it advantageous that they always offer to preach free of charge to you. This is the unmistakable sign that they are false prophets, for the Lord ordained it that they who proclaim the Gospel should live by it. Read the 9th chapter of the first epistle of Paul to the Corinthians and consider especially verses 9 and 14. And read Galatians 6:6,7. Then you will easily perceive their cunning deceit, for their offer is against the doctrine and admonition of the apostle, and even

---

at Shekomeko by the Moravian Historical Society. See *Memorial of the Dedication of Monuments erected by the Moravian Hist. Soc.*, New York, 1860, pp. 134-143. A picture of the monument is inserted, facing p. 122.

[251] This was, of course, not the aim of Zinzendorf. That it was the ultimate result of the movement to carry those who participated in it over to the Moravian Church was due to the failure of the movement. When all the other denominations withdrew and organized their forces, there was nothing left to the Moravians but to organize along their own lines.

against the words of Christ himself, Matth. 10:10 and Luke 10:7, where a workman is regarded by him as worthy of his meat and hire. And a true servant of Christ in His Gospel, whose duty it is to attend to his service, has sufficient work. But he needs food and raiment. This does not come of itself, for God has not so ordered it, but according to His holy Word it shall come from those for whom they work, Gal. 6:6. No true evangelical Christian has refused to do this thus far. But it is plain why these enthusiasts and fanatics employ this means, so pleasing to ignorant people, namely in order that their cause may seem agreeable and sweet and people might be entangled all the better in their net, and that later on they might obtain not only a part of their possessions, but all of them for their sect and thereby make it rich and great. But I think they will not meet many fools, but many a cunning Pennsylvanian will lead them around by the nose for a while, and finally when it comes to the test, everybody will know how to take care of his property for himself and his family, and he will let go such sly foxes, as is right, etc.

Just for this reason Count Zinzendorf became so indignant at all who opposed him and his false doctrine here in this country. For in Canastoka he said that he had to hasten to Philadelphia, for the court was in session and *as sure as his name was Count Zinzendorf, four men would have to hang.* But a considerable time has passed since, and as yet nobody has been hung on his account.

Again, when the Count preached in Dolpihacken for the last time, he said in his sermon: *Thunder and lightning will strike all ministers who hinder souls from following the Lamb.* (This is credibly attested.) Behold, Beloved, can you conceive that such a man is a minister of the Gospel of Jesus Christ? Moreover, we can see from all the testimonies of the Holy Scriptures that he does not seek to lead the souls to the Lamb of God, Jesus Christ, but away from him into eternal perdition. These expressions are of such a nature that one would almost commit a sin by saying of such a daring man that he was a Christian. In addition, consider his two letters (which have appeared in print) one from London to Mr. Neumann in Germany, the other from Philadelphia to the Cooper Vende and his wife in

Germantown.[252] These two letters are known, hence it is unnecessary to say much about them. But the hairs of a Christian will stand on end when he thinks of their astounding contents.

Behold, dear fellow-believers, this Count Zinzendorf is the head and founder of the sect of the Herrnhuters, who has gathered together the wavering from all kinds of people. Those whom he finds suitable for his purpose he turns into all kinds of ministers. Thus he regarded Lischy, Bechtel and Antes adapted for the purpose of leading the Reformed people astray to his sect of Herrnhuters. They are now seeking to carry on the work of enlisting people in all earnestness and with the worst deception, as the things mentioned about them above clearly show.

Now, whom do you think you are following if you attach yourselves to these three, or to one of them, or to any of their kind, and allow yourselves to be led astray? Do you think that then you are a member of the Reformed church, and that you will be able to answer for it before Him, who shall judge all? I do not think so. But you will be regarded by yourselves as well as by all true evangelical Christians as Herrnhuters, whatever they may be, who have been declared in public print before all the world and with public approbation in Holland, to be enthusiasts and fanatics. Therefore I hope that you will be mindful of your vow, which you have sworn before God, and withdraw entirely from these false heretics to your souls' salvation and eternal welfare. If perhaps time hangs heavy upon you, because as yet we are not supplied with a sufficient number of Reformed ministers, still do not think that our God has forgotten us and that He will not hear us at last. But know that God does everything in His time and not as we desire it. This is in order to try His people. Let us look up in Christian patience to the Lord and to His fatherly care. Let us edify and admonish each other from the Word of God, according to our ability, in all order and piety, then will God at last come and provide for us with necessary and sufficient

---

[252] The letter of Zinzendorf to Frederick Vende, cooper of Germantown, is printed in Fresenius, *Nachrichten*, Vol. III, pp. 722-725. The letter to Mr. Neumann is also reprinted there, p. 729f.

means. Let us not act as the children of Israel in the wilderness, who, when Moses stayed away a long time, did not want to wait, but desired to have gods and made a golden calf. Beloved, read in Exodus the 32nd chapter and consider especially the last three verses, how this people fared on account of their sin.

Therefore, let my prayer find a hearing among you and do not act in this way, but be patient and wait for the help of the Lord, for that is a precious thing. Do not think that it is my fault that you have to wait so long for ministers, as I have been accused by some evil but foolish people here and there. But those who know, and there is a large number of them, how I have asked for more than 15 years for ministers, will be better able to speak of this. Likewise do not speak against our devout Church Fathers, as if it were in their power. They cannot force the matter, however much they desire it, but must leave this important work, which everybody does not understand, to the providence of God. Therefore, beware of this, for they are servants of God and he who touches them touches the apple of his eye. How much they desired to help us, I know better than many of you.

Now, Beloved, I shall not be surprised, if I must again endure mockery on account of this faithful letter of warning. But I do not expect it in the least of any true evangelical Christian, and for others I do not care. If the Herrnhuters have anything against it, they are at liberty, and no one can prevent them, from defending themselves, with their pen, before the whole world. I shall always welcome them, for I do not intend to enter into oral disputes with them or their friends. And if they desire to bring it before higher courts of judgment, I am willing to be judged where I am wrong. But one thing I do wish, that if perchance they in concert should again manufacture something, they should omit the unseemly, boasting and black lies and not insult so impertinently a poor, simple soul (as they have done George Neiser,[253] schoolmaster

---

[253] George Neisser was born April 11, 1715, at Sehlen, Moravia. He went to Georgia with the first Moravian colony in 1735; came to Pennsylvania in 1737, and was one of the original occupants of the first house in Bethlehem. He was also the first schoolmaster and postmaster of the town. In 1748 he was ordained and served in various congregations, lastly in Philadelphia, where he died in 1784. When

in Bethlehem) and publish it under his name. That is not nice. My humble advice to them is, that in future they save their useless, bragging and ugly lies. At some time they may come to another place, where people do not know so much of the Herrnhuters as in Pennsylvania, then they may be able to dispose of them.

Dear friends and fellow-believers, as also all men who love God and the sincere truth of His holy Word, herewith you have received that which I was unable to withhold from you, on account of a fervent love for you and your immortal souls. It is a statement of those things which I thought most necessary to make known to you, so that you may be on your guard. Let every one ponder it in his own heart and beware of eternal perdition, which is threatening. Pray to God that He may lead you by His Holy Spirit in the right way, according to His Word, that you may be a healthy member of the true Church, the body of Jesus Christ, that hereafter you, with your Head [Christ], may enter into eternal joy and the glory of the heavenly Father.

In the meantime I offer myself to serve, according to my limited ability, all who may desire it, as long as God will grant me grace, my physical strength will permit, and as often as time may allow. I heartily wish that the almighty and merciful God, by His Holy Spirit, may convert all that can be converted and strengthen His believers in their weakness, so that at last they may receive the crown, which is prepared for them who in true faith remain steadfast unto the end.

This is the wish of him who signs himself with hearty greetings to you all,

Your well-meaning and devoted,

JOHAN PH. BOEHM,
High German Reformed Minister in Pennsylvania.

Witpen Township,
  Philadelphia County,
    May 19, 1743.

Count Zinzendorf published a reply to Boehm's book, it was George Neisser who *edited* the book for him. This is distinctly stated on the title page: *Herausgegeben von Georg Neisser.* There is no claim of authorship by Neisser, as the readers of the book inferred wrongly. A reprint of the tract appeared in Germany by John Philip Fresenius in his *Bewährte Nachrichten,* Vol. III, pp. 677-715.

LETTER OF 1744

[XXXV. TULPEHOCKEN CONGREGATION TO MR. BOEHM, MARCH 27, 1744.[254]]

[Address:] This letter is to be delivered to the Rev. Mr. Boehm, Evangelical Reformed Minister at Schibach.

TOLBENHACKEN, March 27, 1744.

First of all, a friendly greeting from us, the elders of the two churches of the Reformed congregation of Tolbenhacken [Tulpehocken] to the Very Reverend and Learned Sir, the Rev. John Philip Boehm.

Your message sent to us has been transmitted orally by Peter Ruth. From it we learned that our letter, written to Holland several years ago, was not sent off by you. We have also heard that you intend writing again to Holland. Hence we ask you to excuse us from writing this time for the following reason: because, as you know, we wrote a year ago to Germany for a minister. Last fall we received an answer, promising for certain to send us a minister. We received two letters from Germany, from which we learned that the Upper Consistory of Zweibruecken[255] made known our desire to the Consistory at Heidelberg, also in Switzerland, in Hesse and in Holland. Last fall we wrote again and now have to wait until next fall for an answer. We hope it will not displease you that we have done this, for, in the first place, we have not left nor offended you, but rather treated you with respect even in Germany. Besides, we have never received a report or letter from Holland through you, that we should get a minister. Moreover, we had to do it for conscience sake, seeing that for lack of a faithful pastor many a poor soul has been led into error and is still daily being led astray. If you could have come more frequently, we believe that many things would not have happened. We, therefore ask your Reverence to be pleased to come to us as soon as possible and celebrate the Lord's Supper. We still place our confidence in you and shall stay with you until we have a minister. We again ask that you will send us a letter as soon as possible, to let us know when you will come, so that we can announce it to the congregation.

[254] The original German letter is in the archives at The Hague, 74, I, 39.

[255] On March 10, 1744, Rev. Caspar Schnorr appeared before the Synodical Deputies and reported that he had been called by the Consistory of Zweibruecken to be pastor at Tulpehocken. But, as he had no proper testimonials, the Deputies refused to aid him in his journey to Pennsylvania. He appeared before the Classis of Amsterdam, April 13, 1744, but met the same refusal there. Schnorr arrived in Pennsylvania in November, 1744. On March 15, 1745, he wrote to the Classis that he was serving Lancaster, but was also preaching at Tulpehocken once a month.

Commending ourselves and you to the protection of the Great God,

We remain our highly honored pastor's, Rev. Philip Boehm's faithful parishioners and brethren.

Elders. {
GEORGE UNRUH,
JACOB SCHOB,
WILHELM ALBERT,
VALENTIN HERCHELROTH,
ADAM STUMPF,
ADAM DIFFENBACH.
}

This letter came into my hands on April 21, 1744. It is enclosed in order that the Reverend Messrs. Deputies may see how eager these congregations are, and also why nothing was subscribed by them. When I was with them, according to their request, at the end of the month of April, I realized that in their desire for a minister they had promised more than they were able to keep, which is of course laudable, but afterwards is sad, when the means are wanting.

BOEHM.

[XXXVI. MR. BOEHM AND HIS CONSISTORIES TO THE SYNODS OF HOLLAND, MARCH 18, 1744.[256]]

Very Reverend Sirs of the Two Christian Synods of South and North Holland, Devout Church Fathers:—

We, your humble and obedient brethren in our most holy faith and fellow-members of the body of Jesus Christ, can hardly furnish this submissive (desired) report without heartfelt tears, for

The enclosure, marked A (as it is, open) was transmitted by his Reverence, Mr. Dorsius, minister at Schamine [Neshaminy], in Bucks County, who arrived here in Philadelphia, once more from Holland, on January 17, 1744, and was brought here [Philadelphia] by an elder, named Nicolas Ewig, on the 21st of the same month (after its contents were known to almost everybody in the city) to the house of Casper Ulrich[257]

---

[256] The German original in the archives at The Hague, 74, I, 30.

[257] Caspar Ulrich first appears in the Philadelphia congregation in April, 1734 (see p. 234). In the same year he was naturalized (see *Pa. Archives,* 2nd Series, Vol. VII, p. 116). He signed his will November 22, 1751. It was probated December 10, 1751. He left his property to his wife Eva, to a son Philip, and to a daughter, who was the widow of Thomas Rutter. See Register of Wills Office, Philadelphia, Will Book, I, p. 451.

(where our minister, Mr. Boehm, has lodged hitherto), with the direction to hand it to him on his arrival and that he should read it from the pulpit to the congregation the next morning, (upon which the common people almost passionately insisted). This, however, he did not do, since, in the first place, it did not appear therein that the Christian Synods had so ordered it, and it was, moreover, evident that it would only give occasion to some quarrelsome spirits for a new disturbance, but he quieted the congregation, and thereupon, in keeping with churchly custom, he consulted only with the elders of that and other congregations.

From this letter we learn that it had pleased the two Christian Synods of South and North Holland to receive some information from the mouth of Do. Dorsius, minister in Bucks County, regarding the condition of the churches in Pennsylvania, for which the two Christian Synods had waited hitherto in vain! This grieves us sincerely. But we hope that the Christian Synods will perceive sufficiently from the enclosures, marked B and C, who is really to blame for this, for those two submissive reports were at that time, at the request of his Reverence, Mr. Dorsius (who subscribed himself as one fully authorized by the two Christian Synods of South and North Holland and Inspector[258] of the Pennsylvania German Reformed churches, as the copy, which is added to the enclosure, marked B indicates) made ready with the utmost possible care and the greatest exertion of our minister, who in the midst of a severe winter traveled hither and thither throughout the

---

[258] When Dorsius came to America in 1737, it was through a private arrangement between himself and Rev. John Wilhelmius of Rotterdam, who acted as agent of the Neshaminy congregation in Bucks County. Before leaving Holland for Pennsylvania, Dorsius appeared before the Deputies of the Synods, June 11-14, 1737. They asked him to secure for them some information about the German churches in Pennsylvania, which Dorsius promised to do. There was, therefore, no official relation between Dorsius and the authorities in Holland. He had not been appointed to any office and he had no right whatever to claim the position of "inspector," as he did in his letter to Boehm (see p. 271). That Dorsius had been appointed inspector was definitely denied by the Classis in its letter to Boehm of May 9, 1743. See p. 373.

whole land[259] (without asking or receiving any compensation for it). Then, without any loss of time, they were taken by him in person, namely the enclosure, marked B, on February 26, 1739 and the enclosure, marked C, on March 18, 1740, to the home of his Reverence at Schamine [Neshaminy], a distance of about 12 miles, and placed into his [Dorsius'] hands. Everything contained therein was considered as carefully as possible, according to our duty, in part by our predecessors, in part by us, the elders now in service. Nor do we know how we could have considered it any better or discharged the duties resting upon us in the congregations of Christ more conscientiously than we did. We, therefore, send exact copies, which were found to agree verbatim with the genuine originals (which our minister caused us to sign in duplicate copies and of which he kept one for his own security.) These we send, most obediently and dutifully attested, to the two Christian Synods.

However, we must indicate submissively how the majority of our congregations increase perceptibly, under the blessing of God. Thus the dutiful statistics, drawn up by our pastor, Mr. Boehm, and enclosed under letter D, will furnish a visible proof to the Christian Synods that the report, that our congregations instead of increasing are decreasing was not given in good faith. This is also true of the statement that every congregation was standing by itself and that there was no harmony and union between them. This is refuted by the copy of our Church Order [constitution], enclosed under letter E. This Church Order has been observed since the organization of our congregations, according to its contents and in all its articles, as much as possible and we have lived according to it. Moreover, since all our elders before their ordination have hitherto subscribed to the same, we intend to continue it, in the fear of the Lord, without any change made by us, especially as it was drawn up with reference to the conditions of our widely extended country.

However, if the Christian Synods, for the welfare of our congregations and the improvement of order, deem it advisable

---

[259] In view of the great difficulties under which the report of Boehm had been prepared, and the detailed and accurate information which it contained, it ought to have received more careful attention in Holland.

to add anything thereto, we will heartily be willing and ready to render obedience.

Because of this Church Order, a true Christian and brotherly unity prevails in the congregations, mentioned in the statistics under letter D. Nevertheless, it has grieved us much and has caused us no small injury that there are still some, who have not acknowledged nor accepted this Church Order, who do not attend any of the churches mentioned in the statistics, nor are willing to recognize any order or any one as head over them. Of this condition unpardonable mischief-making has hitherto been the cause.

Although our congregations are now increasing, they consist almost entirely of poor people, who arrive ever year from all sorts of countries and of whom many are seen going about the country begging for their passage money. Yet they are precious souls and our fellow-members (according to their certificates, without which few of them come to us) of the body of Christ. And we are both willing and in duty bound to receive them kindly and lovingly into our congregations, although they can contribute nothing towards the maintenance of necessary things. Yet we confidently trust, that the Christian Synods, as devout Church Fathers and faithful nursing mothers of our true Church in almost all places of the world, will not look upon the number of people, but upon our (at present) still deficient ability, and have pity upon us.

Now our souls, sad before because we seemed to be entirely abandoned, have been gladdened, inasmuch as we have seen in your gracious letter that the Messrs. Deputies take much interest in the welfare of our churches and are willing to contribute as much as possible. This, we believe, would already have taken place, if a true and clear report and information had not been lacking. May God forgive him who has kept it back. For, since the founding of our churches here, there have been many people, who though they were of Reformed antecedents, kept aloof, because there were no Reformed church services here, and they joined no religion or sect, because they were of the opinion that our cause could not be maintained in this country, principally because of our inability to support ministers. They are now, within the last few years, scattered here and there, mostly among Mennonites (who may be in the majority), Tumplers [Dunkers], 7th Day as well as 8th Day Tumplers[260] and such like. Especially Count Zinzendorf (who arrived here at the end of December, 1741) and his brood of false apostles, brought along or made many converts here, some under the name of one religion, others under the name of another (of which the enclosure, marked F, namely the second printed "Faithful Letter of Warning", will give some information to the Christian Synods.) In this they succeeded because they came in sheep's clothing and with smooth hypocritical words offered their services to all people and for nothing. All this would surely have gone differently, if some assistance and help (especially in the sending of faithful ministers) had come from our richly blessed fellow-brethren.

As regards our established congregations, we thank the merciful God that He has so far preserved our fellow-members, that we can say of but few that they perjured themselves. We would also constantly and fervently pray to the Lord Jesus, as our true archbishop, that He will let His all-seeing eyes graciously keep watch over our congregations, as His little flock, entrusted to us.

Further, with regard to the request made by the Messrs. Deputies to Do. Dorsius, that his Reverence, together with his fellow-laborers and officers of the congregations here, would draw up an accurate account and short report, covering the entire condition of these congregations, and cause it to be signed by ministers and consistories, in order to send it over, with regard to this request we declare herewith, that regarding ministers, we know at present of none in the whole province of Pennsylvania, who is a regularly ordained Reformed minister among our High German churches, except Mr. John Philip Boehm, who with us and we with him send up many a sigh to God that He will graciously have mercy upon the poor sheep in this wilderness, scattered among so many sects, and

---

[260] By "Eighth Day Dunkers," Mr. Boehm means probably the original Dunkers or German Baptists, whose first colony came to Pennsylvania under the leadership of Peter Becker, in 1719. In 1723, their first congregation was organized in Germantown. The "Seventh Day Dunkers," under Conrad Beissel, separated from the original organization in 1728. In 1735 the Ephrata settlement was started by the adherents of Beissel, commonly called "Siebentäger," or Sabbatarians.

will send faithful laborers into His vineyard.

Together with our beloved and first minister in this country faithfully perservering in his service, we do jointly comply with what the Reverend Synods have requested, for the honor of God and the growth of our true Church here, in churchly obedience, with all sincerity of heart and according to our duty. But the fact that we do not entrust it to the Rev. Mr. Dorsius, we hope the Christian Synods will forgive us, in view of the substantial reasons adduced by us, and because we do it for the best interests of our churches, and [we ask] that they [the Synods] will not unfavorably regard what we take the liberty to send of our own accord, in submissive obedience, concerning our church affairs, to the Christian Synods.

Finally, as regards the union with the Scotch Presbyterian Synod,[261] we trust that the Reverend Christian Synods will not take it ill of us, that we humbly request to be permitted to abide by our Church Order, established from the beginning in our churches, incorporated in our church records and subscribed by all who have thus far been members of our consistories, as was mentioned above. And, whether the Christian Synods be pleased to add nothing or something for its improvement, which, as stated above, we shall recognize and accept with gratitude and obedient hearts, we ask the Christian Synods submissively to be pleased to confirm it furthermore for its better enforcement, since we hope confidently that (in that case) the congregations, still outside of its influence and in disorder and confusion, would at once unite with us, which would contribute to the long desired strengthening of our ecclesiastical communion.

The reasons which we have, to be kindly allowed to remain for ourselves, are: Almost none of our people, or at least very few of them understand the English language. Next, the Heidelberg Catechism, upon which our Church Order is based in articles 11 and 16, is the rule of our doctrine and in accordance with it all the German Reformed people have thus far been

---

[261] On the attempted union between the German churches of Pennsylvania and the Presbyterian Synod of Philadelphia, see the documents published by the Rev. Prof. J. I. Good, D. D., in the *Journal of the Presb. Hist. Soc.*, Vol. III, pp. 122-137.

confirmed in their [European] homes as well as in this country. Furthermore, we are pledged in article 6 of our Church Order to treat all new communicants, coming from the outside, according to the Church Order of the Synod of Dort of the years 1618 and 1619; and, according to article 16, we are bound to hold to all the Formulas of Unity and to the Synod of Dort. We know of no formulas [liturgies] which are used by the Presbyterians here,[262] either at Baptism or at the Holy Supper or at the consecration of marriages or at other occasions, and therefore such a change would be regarded by most people as a defection from our true religion, which would be very harmful to the growth of our congregations.

This then, Very Reverend Christian Synods, is what we, your obedient and humble children in the Lord, have to report submissively. We have now lived for a long time in a very poor and distressed condition and still recall the reckless and ungodly fraud[263] of Do. George Michael Weiss, who was formerly here, and of Jacob Reiff, still living among us, regarding the money collected in Holland for the churches here. Of this money, with which nearly all the congregations could have been assisted somewhat, thus far not a penny has been delivered, which the righteous God, we believe, will not leave unpunished. Meanwhile, the innocent sheep in all the congregations have had to suffer from it. Nor is there any prospect that anything will come of it (although Do. Dorsius and Doctor Jacob Diemer, of whose disposition we trust the Christian Synods have some knowledge, have received a power of attorney several years ago) unless it be put into different hands, for then the case can be pushed with a free conscience.

Meanwhile some of the poor, penniless congregations,

---

[262] The first official liturgy of the Presbyterian Church in the U. S. A., "for voluntary use," was issued in 1905, entitled *The Book of Common Worship*, Philadelphia, The Presbyterian Board of Publication and Sabbath School Work.

[263] The chief blame for the unfortunate "Reiff affair," involving about fl. 2100 collected in Holland, ought not to be put on Weiss, who never had charge of the money, but upon Reiff and the elders in Philadelphia, who directed his actions. They advised investing the money in merchandise. When this venture proved a total failure, none of the parties was willing to bear the loss, and as a result Reiff was unwilling to pay out the money.

whose worship had been held thus far in poor houses and barns, which was no longer possible because of the increase of members, could not help themselves in any other way but by undertaking themselves to build churches. For this purpose those who had the largest means contributed their share, but since those unable to give could not be asked to contribute anything, they were compelled to run into debt, upon which they must now pay interest. This cannot at all or with difficulty be paid from the alms that come in. At present we cannot state accurately how the matter stands in each locality, but it will be investigated as far as possible and be added hereunto, stating as it truly is.[264]

From this the Reverend Christian Synods can see that we are unable to provide, with our own means, dwelling houses for ministers and readers (of which houses there are as yet none at any place), which are indispensably necessary.

Hence, we prostrate ourselves as needy fellow believers before the Christian Synods, praying with humble hearts that the Reverend Christian Synods will pity us with Christian charitableness, and for Christ's sake support us with suitable contributions, when they see that it is indispensably necessary.

Especially do we ask the Reverend Christian Synods that, according to their fatherly care, they will graciously remember us first of all in this most necessary request, namely that the poor, widely scattered sheep of Christ in this land will be provided with faithful ministers and servants of the Gospel of Jesus Christ; for our pastor, who joins with us in this humble request and who has been with us faithfully for more than 18 years (without being a burden to any one, but having patience with us in our poverty) has now passed his 60th year[265] and is becoming physically incapable of enduring the constant travels round about in the country in all kinds of weather. Neither do we know how long God will leave us together. What would become of us afterwards if we had to part, especially in view of the many and dangerous sects around us, the Christian

---

[264] This refers to the longest and most exhaustive report which Boehm sent to Holland in July, 1744. See pp. 408-425.

[265] As Boehm was baptized October 25, 1683, he was most likely born in the same month.

Synods will kindly take into consideration.

The great and merciful God, as the abundant rewarder of all good, will richly reward it, because it is only sought and only done for the honor of His most holy name, the upbuilding and increase of the true members of the body of Jesus Christ in his true Church. We shall unceasingly pray before the throne of our true and merciful God, that He will graciously cause His hand of blessing, which is extended over our richly favored fellow-believers in the Netherlands, to reach to the end of the world, especially over their flourishing ecclestiastical organization. May He sanctify and bless the Reverend Christian Synods, as patrons of the true Church, in all their plans to the honor of His holy name and the eternal salvation of many precious souls.

We wish for the Reverend Christian Synods, for each of your godly persons, the eternally valid reward of grace and the crown of eternal blessedness, in return for your work in this service of the Lord.

Commending you, together with your families and holy service, to God and the Word of His grace, we remain,

The two Christian Synods' of South and North Holland

Humblest and most submissive brethren and children in the Lord, members of the consistories, now in service in the German Reformed churches in Pennsylvania, in whose name we sign,

Of the congregation at
Falckner Schwam,
February 26, 1744.

Johan Philips Boehm, minister.
John Druckdenhengst,[266] elder.
John Dunkel, elder.
Frederick Reymer, elder.
Jacob X Krausen, elder.
  mark
John Dieter Bucher, deacon.
Adam Räder, deacon.

---

[266] John Druckdenhengst, Johannes Dunkel and Jacob Kraus were naturalized at Philadelphia, September 24, 1741. See *Pennsylvania Archives*, 2nd Series, Vol. II, p. 353f.

Of the congregation at
Schipbach,
March 4, 1744.
{ Jacob Arnet,²⁶⁷ elder.
his
Andrew O Oberbeck, elder.
mark
Adam Meirer, elder.
Henry Wuehrman, deacon.

Of the congregation at
Weitmarge,
March 11, 1744.
{ Willem De Wees,²⁶⁸ elder.
Christopher Ottinger,²⁶⁹ elder.
Michael Kleim, deacon.
Philip Scherer, deacon.

Of the congregation at
Philadelphia,
March 18, 1744.
{ Rudolf Wiellecken, elder.
Jacob Walter, elder.
John Daniel Bouton,²⁷⁰ elder.
John Michael Diell,²⁷¹ elder.

[267] Jacob Arnet arrived in Philadelphia, September 27, 1727. He settled in Lower Salford Township, Philadelphia County. He was a weaver by trade. He signed his will January 15, 1751. It was probated December 22, 1753. See *Will Book,* K, p. 134, at Philadelphia.

[268] William De Wees, of Germantown, miller, signed his will November 22, 1744. It was probated July 13, 1745. He died March 3, 1745, and was buried in the Axe Burying Ground (Dotterer, *Historical Notes,* p. 25). The beneficiaries of his will were his wife Anna Christina; his sons, William, Cornelius, Philip and Garrett, and his daughters, Christina, Margaret and Mary. See *Will Book,* H, pp. 2-4, at Philadelphia. *The De Wees Family,* collected by Mrs. Philip E. La Munyan, Ellwood Roberts, Editor, Norristown, 1905.

[269] Christopher Ottinger, of Springfield Township, Philadelphia County, innholder, signed his will November 12, 1748. It was probated November 28, 1748. He left his property to his wife Eva; to his sons, Christopher, William and John, and to his daughters, Mary, Elizabeth, Catherine and Barbara. See *Will Book,* G, p. 351, at Philadelphia.

[270] John Daniel Bouton arrived in Philadelphia, August 27, 1739. He was naturalized April 14, 1747 (see *Pa. Archives,* 2d Series, Vol. II, p. 372). He was a baker by trade. On April 13, 1759, he made his will. It was proved November 24, 1762. His beneficiaries were his wife; his sons, George and Jacob; his daughter, Wilhelmina and the wife of his deceased son Frederick. See *Will Book,* M. p. 425. According to the church record he died November 14, 1762, aged seventy-one years, ten months and several days. On December 13, 1773, the widow of Daniel Bouton was buried, aged eighty-one years.

[271] John Michael Dill (Diel) qualified at Philadelphia, September 21, 1727, a member of the colony of Rev. G. M. Weiss. He was

[This letter was accompanied by the following enclosures:]

ENCLOSURE A.

[LETTER OF DEPUTY JOHN W. A MARCK TO THE REFORMED CONGREGATIONS IN PENNSYLVANIA, SEPTEMBER 20, 1743.]

To the Ministers and Members of the Consistories of the Reformed Congregations in Pennsylvania.
Very Reverend Sirs, Much Beloved Brethren in Christ:—

Grace and peace be to the Brethren together with faith and love in Christ Jesus.

It has pleased the two Christian Synods of South and North Holland to receive some light and information concerning the state of the churches in Pennsylvania from the mouth of Do. Dorsius, minister in Bucks County, Pennsylvania, lately come over from there, for which they had thus far waited in vain.

They would have preferred to have heard a more advantageous report, but they were sorry to learn that instead of improving they seemed to deteriorate, of which among other reasons the principal reason seemed to be the lack of ministers, the smallness of the salaries, and especially that every church existed by itself and that they had no fellowship among each other.

The Deputies take much interest in the welfare of your churches, and are willing to contribute to it as much as possible.

But, although Do. Dorsius has given them some information and in so far satisfied them, yet they are not yet so fully informed concerning it that they can give it real help.

For this reason they have requested Do. Dorsius that his Reverence, together with his fellow-laborers and the officers in the congregations of those regions, would draw up an accurate account and short report concerning the entire condition of their churches, cause it to be signed by the ministers and consistories, and hand the same over, the sooner the better, to his Reverence, that it may be sent back on the same ship with which his Reverence is now sailing to Pennsylvania. Its skipper expects to be back in the month of February, 1744, so that it can be deliberated upon in the month of March and following, and a report concerning it can be laid before the two Synods.

Especially do the Deputies wish to be informed, since they understand that there is a Scotch Presbyterian Synod, whether the High German and Low German [Dutch] congregations could not unite with it? And, if that cannot be done, whether another church organization

naturalized September 25-27, 1740, together with Jacob Walter and John Wendel Brechbill, two other Philadelphia elders.

could not be established, in order to maintain there good order? The Deputies are of the opinion that this is of utmost necessity, in order to prevent their total ruin and advance their best interests.

We trust that your Reverences, who are truly interested in the welfare of the Church of God, will comply with our legitimate request and gladly carry it out.

Commending your Reverences herewith to God and the Word of His grace, we remain with favorable inclination towards you,

Reverend Sirs, Much Beloved Brethren in Christ, Your Reverences' Devoted Servants and Fellow-Brethren, The Deputies of the Synods.

Signed in the name of all by me,
JOHN WILLIAM à MARCK,
Pastor Goudensis, Deputatorum h. t. Scriba.
THE HAGUE, September 20, 1743.

The above letter is the same which was sent by Mr. Dorsius, minister in Bucks County, Pennsylvania, on his return from Holland, thus open as it is, to our minister, Mr. John Philips Boehm, to Philadelphia, on January 21, 1744, which we attest,

JOHN DANIEL BOUTON, *Elder.*
JACOB WALTER, *Elder.*

ENCLOSURE B.

[This is identical with the report of Mr. Boehm, dated by him January 14, 1739, and by his consistories January 28-February 22, 1739, addressed to the Classis of Amsterdam. It was given as enclosure B. of Boehm's letter of March 26, 1740, sent to the Classis. It is printed p. 272ff. The catalogue number of the copy at The Hague is 74, 1, 24.]

ENCLOSURE C.

[This is identical with enclosure D. of Boehm's letter of March 26, 1740, addressed to the Classis. It is printed p. 285ff. The copy at The Hague is marked 74, I, 27.]

ENCLOSURE D.

[STATISTICS OF THE COMMUNICANTS OF THE REV. JOHN PHILIP BOEHM, FOR THE YEARS 1743-1744.[272]]

As a High German Reformed Minister I have celebrated the Lord's Supper in the following High German Reformed Congregations. The names of the congregations and the number of the communicants were as follows:

[272] The original in the archives at The Hague, 74, 1, 29.

		Men	Women	Total	New Communicants Boys	Girls
1743 Spring						
March 13	At Weitmarge	24	27	51	..	..
March 20	At Philadelphia	49	49	183	1	1
April 17	Ditto	48	37			
March 27	At Falckner Schwam...	71	60	236	5	8
April 24	Ditto	56	49			
April 3	At Schip Bach	18	18	36	1	..
April 4	At Providentz Township, in a newly gathered congregation[273]	19	13	32	..	..
May 6	At Tolpihacken, in the new church	65	59	253	1 2	3 3
May 8	Ditto, in the old church	66	63			
	Totals			791	10	15
In the Fall						
Sept. 11	At Falckner Schwam, called New Hanover Township	66	63	239	4	8
Oct. 9	Ditto	55	55			
Sept. 18	At Schip Bach, Salforth Township	16	19	35	..	1
Sept. 23	At Dolpihacken, in new church	38	57	126	4	3
Sept. 25	Ditto, in the old church N. B. In Tolpihacken the old church is now called the new, because the congregation there built this year a new church[274]	62	64			
Oct. 2	At Philadelphia	41	49	144	..	2
Oct. 29	Ditto	36	38		..	3
Oct. 23	At Weitmarge	23	24	47	..	1
	Totals			591		26

JOHANN PH. BOEHM.

[273] This congregation is now St. Luke's Reformed Church at Trappe, Providence Township, Montgomery County, Pa.

[274] The old Tulpehocken church is identical with what is now Host Church, in Tulpehocken Township, Berks County, Pa. The new Tulpehocken church is now Trinity Reformed Church, near Myerstown, Pa. See p. 68.

LETTER OF 1744

Communion Services in the High German Reformed Congregations, which have been held by me, the undersigned, in the spring of 1744.

1744		Communicants	Totals
March 25	At Falckner Schwam, on Easter	110	213
April 22	At the same place	103	
April 1	At Schip Bach		33
April 8	At Weitmarge		33
April 15	At Philadelphia	112	213
May 13	At the same place, on Pentecost	101	
April 27	At Dolpihacken, in old church	149	290
April 29	In the new church there	141	
April 24	In the newly organized congregation at Medenkrik [Muddy Creek],[275] about 12 miles from Oley. I held divine service for the first time in their newly built little church and administered the Lord's Supper; there communed		33
May 3	On Ascension Day, at the newly gathered congregation in Providence. At the first communion there, on November 5, 1743,[276] there were present 19 communicants; at this time there communed (in a barn)		63
	Total		878

JOHAN PHILIPS BOEHM,
High German Reformed Minister in Pennsylvania.

[275] The Muddy Creek Church is in East Cocalico Township, Lancaster County, about seven miles northeast of Ephrata. There probably was an earlier organization started by Peter Miller. But Lischy reorganized the congregation when he became its pastor in 1743. His first baptism there is dated March 30, 1743. In the old Lutheran Muddy Creek record baptisms of Peter Miller are recorded between 1730-1733.

[276] This date is probably a mistake for 1742. See p. 74.

ENCLOSURE E.

[CHURCH ORDER OR CONSTITUTION OF MR. BOEHM'S CONGREGATIONS, IMPROVED IN 1730.²⁷⁷]

ANNO 1730.

The following are our church ordinances, heretofore drawn up and now improved, with obedient submission to the Very Reverend Classis of Amsterdam, namely,

1. That the consistories which are now in service in the three congregations at Falckner Schwam, Schipbach and Weitmarsche shall be recognized and remain in office for their appointed term, when all the members of the congregations (as has been done heretofore), together with the minister and consistories, shall elect new members of the consistories.

But, at the same meeting, all the members of the congregations shall transfer, each to his own consistory, all power and right thereafter from year to year to elect officers by a majority vote of the consistories themselves, because with the growth and spread of the congregations it is not feasible to bring together all the members just for this purpose.

The persons elected to the consistory shall be announced, each in his own congregation, three Sundays, to ascertain whether any one has any lawful objection to offer, and, if not, they shall, after the third announcement, be installed in office.

And should it happen, which we do not expect of any one, that one or more of the members of the consistory should give offense by his conduct in any way whatsoever, or seek to create strife and division in the congregations, he shall be promptly admonished by the remaining members of the consistory to discontinue such conduct, and should any one not heed the admonition he shall then be removed from office, and another member from among the number last in service shall be elected by the minister and the remaining members of the consistory and be regularly installed; then he shall serve as if he had been continuously in office.

2. Should one who has retired from the office of elder or deacon be free two years he may thereafter be re-elected, or even sooner, should this be considered necessary by the con-

---

²⁷⁷ Original in Hague Archives, 74, I, 34.

sistory then in office.

3. The elders, deacons and members of the three above-mentioned congregations have recognized Do. Johann Philips Boehm as their regular minister, and desire that with the grace of God he may long continue in faithful service, according to the doctrine of the Reformed churches, as he has done hitherto.

N. B. Here it is to be observed that instead of the name of Johann Philips Boehm, who was the first minister of these three Reformed congregations in Pennsylvania, the name of the minister actually in these congregations shall be clearly announced.

4. The minister, elders and deacons and the entire congregation shall observe, both on the Lord's day and on other days, the time when and the place where divine service is appointed; yet they may change the same at pleasure.

5. The Sacrament of Baptism shall at all times be administered without fee after divine service. Beside the parents, witnesses shall be present at the baptism, and this well-established custom shall not be lightly changed. As witnesses at the baptism shall be chosen persons who have confessed the pure doctrine of the Gospel, and whose lives are blameless.

6. The Holy Supper shall be administered twice a year in every congregation in which divine worship is maintained. No one shall be admitted thereto unless upon confession before the consistory and evidence of a godly life, or proper testimonials from another Reformed congregation, in accordance with the Church Order of the Synod of Dort of 1618 and 1619.

All the members shall always appear at the preparatory sermon, and after the service shall come forward. In case they become careless in this matter they shall be spoken to by the consistory as may be found necessary.

The parents shall faithfully instruct the young in Reformed worship, and shall see to it that they give faithful attention to the hearing of the Word of God, both in preaching and in catechetical instruction, so that the youth may also be admitted to the Holy Communion.

All the members may commune in each of the three congregations, and to this there shall be no lawful objection so long as they have the same minister.

7. The bread and the wine for the Holy Communion shall always be bought and provided by the deacons out of the alms that have been collected, and afterward they shall give a faithful account of the same.

8. To meet this and other necessities of the church, the alms shall always be gathered by the deacons while the congregation leaves the church, or otherwise, as the consistory may direct.

9. The members of the consistory, whether they be elders or deacons, to whom is entrusted the church treasury or other property, shall annually render before the consistory an exact account of their stewardship. For this purpose they shall keep a faithful record of all receipts and expenditures, and when found correct the accounts shall be signed by the minister and an elder in behalf of all as approved.

10. Should a member of the congregation, male or female, fall into any sin, he shall be placed under the supervision of the consistory until he promise and give evidence of amendment of life.

11. It shall be the office and duty of the minister to preach the pure doctrine of the Reformed Church according to the Word of God, and to administer the holy Seals of the Covenant at their appointed time and place; always to adhere to the confession of faith of the Reformed churches and to the Heidelberg Catechism; to explain the same regularly and consecutively; to hold catechetical instruction, etc. He shall give special attention to church discipline and correct practice, together with those who have the oversight of the Congregation. He shall not omit to hold divine service at the appointed times and places, namely at Falckner Schwam, Schipbach and Weitmarsche.

12. At least once every half year the consistory shall hold a meeting, but the minister shall enter in a book all church matters.

13. Should it happen that he be inclined to remove, either being called elsewhere or for other weighty reasons, he shall give notice as soon as possible to the congregations, so that they may not be left embarrassed, but may in time secure another suitable man.

And, further, in all other things the minister shall conduct himself as a faithful servant of Christ, the Great Shepherd of the sheep.

14. The minister, together with the elders and deacons, shall exercise careful oversight over the congregation; shall attend to the time and place appointed to hold consistory meetings, and shall not absent themselves without weighty reasons.

They shall faithfully administer, according to their best ability, everything embraced in this church discipline, each according to his office; and if any one knows of any scandal concerning another, be that one an officer or any other member, he shall feel conscientiously bound to make known the same, not from envy or hatred, but to prevent all offense.

The accused party shall not be allowed to ask for the name of his accuser, nor shall he stubbornly deny the sin proved against him nor obstinately persist in the same. Those who thus act shall not be regarded as members of the congregation until they promise and show amendment of life.

And in case any one has anything to say against the doctrine or life of the minister, or of any other member of the consistory, or against any member, he shall abstain from all disgraceful and slanderous language, and shall not avenge himself, but shall make known the matter to the consistory and leave it in its hands. The same shall then be bound hereby to use all diligence to prevent scandal as much as possible.

15. The ruling elders and deacons of the congregation shall at all times faithfully see to it that in the most friendly way it be brought to the attention of every member of the congregation, and of every one else who shows a disposition to manifest his love in this way, to make a free-will offering to the minister's salary, and such contributions shall be received by the consistory, through a person appointed for the purpose, at the time most convenient to make the payment, and shall then be paid by this person at the appointed time to the minister on his fixed salary.

16. This Church Order, which was sent by us with obedient submission to the Very Reverend Classis of Amsterdam in the month of July, 1728, and which was approved by this very reverend assembly, is hereby enlarged and established. So also what was added by the very reverend ministers, Revs. Gualtherus Du Bois and Henricus Boel of New York and

Vincentius Antonides of Long Island, appointed for this purpose by the Very Reverend Classis of Amsterdam, and concurred in by the three delegated elders of the three congregations of Falckner Schwam, Schipbach and Weitmarsche, namely: Frederick Antes, Gabriel Schueler and William De Wees, under the date of November 18, 1729, shall be kept inviolate according to our best ability; in order that we may hold steadfastly to the Heidelberg Catechism, all the Formulas of Unity and the Synod of Dort; neither shall we nor our descendants be permitted to add anything thereto, to take anything therefrom, or to act contrary thereto, nor to receive or acknowledge any one as their regular minister before such a one, as well as every thing else, be submitted by the consistory of the three congregations to the Very Reverend Classis of Amsterdam or to their delegates and approved by the same; and at all times the answer received shall be final.

17. The preceding Church Order of our three congregations mentioned above shall be read publicly each year to the whole congregation at the time of the installation of new elders and deacons, and that they may adhere to them more firmly, the new elders and deacons, before they are installed, shall each year subscribe to it in their own hand writing, and shall then be properly installed in office in the presence of the congregation. As we hereby do.

[Signatures.]

That these preceding church ordinances of the three above said congregations agree verbatim with the original, inserted into our church record, and that the High German Reformed Congregation at Philadelphia accepted the same, according to the minutes of the church record, in the year 1734, and hence maintains Christian unity and fellowship with all the congregations living under this church order, and that all ministerial acts have been done in accordance with the same, this is attested by

JOHANN PHILIPS BOEHM, minister.
JOHANN DANIEL BOUTON, elder.
JACOB WALTER, elder.

Philadelphia,
March 18, 1744.

ENCLOSURE F.

[This is the *Second Faithful Warning*, issued by Mr. Boehm, May 19, 1743. It is printed above, see p. 373ff; and also the reference to it in the letter of March 18, 1744, see p. 390.]

[XXXVII. MR. BOEHM AND THE PHILADELPHIA CONSISTORY TO THE SYNODS OF HOLLAND, JULY 8, 1744.[278]]

Very Reverend Christian Synods:—

As we hope submissively, the Christian Synods will sufficiently learn from our obedient and dutiful report concerning the entire state of the churches in Pennsylvania, how in accordance with our duty we have complied with everything that the Christian Synods requested of us in the letter, dated September 20, 1743, sent to us by the Rev. Mr. Dorsius, and received by us on January 21, 1744. We lost no time, but, since we lacked an opportunity to send the report dutifully, it has, to our great regret, remained in our hands for such a long time.

We also consider our duty towards the Christian Synods to enclose a statement regarding the events that took place after the completion of our report. It is as follows:

After his Reverence, Mr. Dorsius, had preached at Germantown last Easter Sunday, May 13, 1744 (as mentioned at the end of the enclosed specification)[279] he likewise administered the communion at that place on April 22nd, at which occasion 44 men and 40 women communed. Now, we have nothing at all to say against this, since that congregation has not been willing to come under our Church Order and to enter into ecclesiastical communion with us. But we leave it to his Reverence, Mr. Dorsius, to answer for this. We think that, as a minister of the pure Gospel of Jesus Christ, he would have a glorious opportunity, by good admonitions, to effect good results among these people who evince such a quarrelsome

[278] The original of this letter is in the archives at The Hague, 74, I, 22.

[279] Identical with Boehm's report to the Synods, dated July 8, 1744. See p. 424.

spirit among themselves. For, according to the Gospel of Jesus, love, peace and harmony are to be planted among the brethren, and they are to be faithfully reminded that no strife must be maintained among the members of Christ.

But, on the contrary, some of us who were present had to see with a sad heart that not only this congregation by such service and administration of the Lord's Supper is maintained and confirmed in their hitherto disorderly condition, but even our congregation at Philadelphia, which has for some time continued in good order, has not been spared, for nine members of our congregation received communion from Rev. Mr. Dorsius at Germantown, some of whom have stayed away for a considerable time from our services, of which we have never been able to find out the reason. While some, because of their life and conduct, ought to have been disciplined according to our Church Order, others ought first to have been examined, because they have evidently much intercourse with the Moravians.

Such people were admitted by Rev. Mr. Dorsius to communion, without examining them why they had come from Philadelphia to Germantown, inasmuch as the Lord's Supper was administered [in Philadelphia] a week before and also, after previous announcement, three weeks later, according to our Church Order, as is shown in the enclosed specification.

This complaint is dutifully submitted to the Christian Synods, because Rev. Mr. Dorsius compelled us to do so, trusting humbly that the Christian Synods will give ear to our petitions for the peace and welfare of the Lord's congregations, and prevail upon his Reverence, Mr. Dorsius, that he offend no more the orderly congregations, (because, as we hear the congregation at Falckner Schwam makes the same sad complaint against him), for if such things should become customary (since no congregation, however good it may be, can be found without some obstinate members), a proper ecclesiastical household would become impossible, especially if the ministers, upon whom much depends in this respect, pay no attention to it.

As for the rest, we cannot say that his Reverence, Mr. Dorsius, cares much for the welfare and growth of our congregations, nor does he exert himself that the German Reformed

Church here, together with its minister, may be quickened in its poverty and weakness by long expected kind assistance. For, since the time (as stated in our previous, submissive report) that we received through his Reverence the esteemed letter of the Christian Synods (we declare officially) we have not heard one word from his Reverence, asking how the affair was proceeding or endeavoring to contribute well-meant counsels in behalf of this important and necessary undertaking. Hence we do not know how we are to regard the affair, as far as his Reverence is concerned. But, since we cannot expect any help and protection from the government, we shall trust to the grace of God and patiently wait for His gracious help, that with His assistance and through the Christian Synods, as our devout Church Fathers, this most necessary object [of an ecclesiastical organization] be attained.[279a]

Commending the Very Reverend Christian Synods, each one of your godly persons, together with your families and holy services, to God and the Word of His grace, we remain in all submission and ecclesiastical obedience,

The members of the Consistory now in office in the High German Reformed Congregation at Philadelphia.

      JOHN PHILIPS BOEHM, minister.
      JOHN DANIEL BOUTON, elder.
      JACOB WALTFR, elder.
      NICHOLAS X EWIG, elder.
      JOHN MICHAEL DIELL, elder.
      JOHN GAEBHART, deacon.

Philadelphia,
July 8, 1744.

[279a] The desirability of a regular ecclesiastical organization is clearly indicated in the letter of the Synodical Deputy, John William à Marck, under date September 20, 1743. See above, p. 396f.

[XXXVIII. REPORT OF MR. BOEHM TO THE SYNODS OF NORTH AND SOUTH HOLLAND, JULY 8, 1744.[280]]

A TRUE ACCOUNT
of the origin of the German Reformed congregations in Pennsylvania, with the required statistics of the communicants and their increase from time to time, to which has been added a further report of the condition of the congregations, made by the undersigned, as follows:

Formerly, when there were no Reformed services in this country, the Reformed people at Falckner Schwam, Schipbach and Weitmarsch came together and when they took communion it was with the Presbyterians in Philadelphia, up to the year 1725.[281]

But, because this appeared to some as not in accord with our Reformed Church, they stayed away and became much scattered, as wandering sheep having no shepherd, which was very distressing to observe.

Accordingly they resolved once more urgently to request me (J. P. Boehm), although for full five years I had declined to do so, that I would become their pastor. This was so touchingly represented to me by two of their number thereunto commissioned that our hearts melted together in tears, and in the name of all the people it was pressed upon my conscience whether I had the courage to answer for it at the last judgment, if I should leave them thus without help and allow so many souls to remain scattered among all kinds of sects, of which this country is filled. I thought indeed that it would be better for me if I could escape this yoke and support my family with my work and agriculture, but I was convinced by my conscience that I could not do otherwise. I allowed myself therefore to be persuaded to this work. With humbleness of heart I addressed myself to the Lord's work, and drew up with my brethren, as well as we could a Constitution of the church, so that all things might be done in good order. We divided the charge into the three congregations mentioned above, and when

---

[280] The original German report of Boehm is no longer in existence. But a Dutch translation of it is preserved in the archives at The Hague. Its catalogue number is 74, I, 33.

[281] For confirmation of this see p. 28.

the Constitution had been presented to and accepted by the whole people, I was regularly elected by each one of the congregations, and a formal call was extended to me by the elders. Whereupon I began the ministry of the Lord in His name. After I had preached a few times to my dear congregations, namely Falckner Schwam (which place is at present called New Hanover township), Schipbach and Weitmarsch, which had entrusted themselves to my ministry, we celebrated the Lord's Supper, and there communed for the first time on October 15, 1725, at Falckner Schwam 40 members; in November at Schipbach, 37 members; on December 23, at Weitmarsch, 24 members.

This was the first beginning.

These, our services, were continued in the best order for two years in such a manner that my heart rejoiced. Moreover, since that time again as many communicants arrived. At that time a congregation was also gathered in Canastocka [Conestoga], namely, the first (which I used to call Hill Church, the oldest of the three which are now associated together); also one at Tolpehacken (where now also two have come into existence, six miles apart). These two congregations at Canastocka and Tolpehacken likewise called me. They desired to be organized, which desire I granted, and began the work and ministry of the Gospel among them in conformity with our Church Order. Subsequently the Lord's Supper was celebrated among them and there communed on October 14, 1727, at Canastocka, 59 members; on October 18, 1727, at Tolpehacken, 32 members. (At both places for the first time).

Whereupon after that time Frederick Hillegas[282] arrived in this country with a companion. He also had two brothers, called Peter and Michael,[283] living at Philadelphia, but he him-

[282] John Frederick Hillegass was born November 24, 1685. He died January 6, 1765. In 1736, he was a member of the New Goshenhoppen Reformed congregation. His daughter, Elizabeth Barbara, was baptized there, June 4, 1732, by Rev. John Peter Miller. His wife, Elizabeth Barbara, died March 4, 1759. See *Perkiomen Region*, Vol. II, 170; III, 94.

[283] On March 18, 1755, letters of administration were granted to Michael Egge and Michael Deal, on the estate of Peter Hillegass. See *Book of Administration*, Vol. G, p. 16, at Philadelphia. On November

self lived at New Goschenhoppen. He brought with him the well known Mr. George Michael Weiss, a youthful preacher (who afterwards sailed for Holland with the likewise well known Jacob Reiff to collect money, of which, however, they have up to this date not yet rendered any account nor handed it over), whom they sought to force in a violent manner and in a shameful way into all my congregations here. Thus with this Weiss they were a hindrance to me and antagonized me, inasmuch as Weiss immediately began in a rude manner to belittle me with shameful letters which I have now in my possession. He ran around everywhere, tried to push me violently out of my office and preached in all my congregations, without first consulting me about it. His attacks became so rude that although very few adhered to him, and these only at the instigation of Hillegas and Doctor Diemer, I began to fear that our work, which we had carried on thus far in the name of the Lord, might thereby indeed be ruined.

Particularly did he throw into confusion the congregation at **Schipbach**, to which the bold and impertinent Jacob Reiff, who had created a party of his own, contributed materially his share. However heartily and frequently I have admonished with regard to this the congregation at Schipbach, which separated at that time, yet up to this day I have not been able to unite them again, because a party has been formed there, which has been kept continuously by one irregular minister after another in the fire of disorder. When Weiss went to Holland, Peter Miller preached there (who now for a long time has been a Seventh Day Dunker); after him came Bartholomew Rieger (whom I never considered, on account of certain evidence, to be different from or more sound in the Reformed doctrine than Miller). He preached there for some time. After that they accepted young Goetschi, who also follows at present the Moravian teachers (although he was ordained for Long Island by Do. Dorsius (who pretended to be inspector over the German and Dutch churches in this

7, 1749, letters of administration were granted to Margaretha Hillegas, widow of Michael Hillegas and to Michael Hillegas, son of the said deceased. Register of Wills Office, Philadelphia, *Book of Administration*, Vol. F, p. 290. See also note 66, p. 216.

country). After that they were served for some years by John William Straub, at one time schoolmaster in the Palatinate at Cronau (who was dismissed there for adultery). But these people, besides some others whom he had lured away from the congregation at Schipbach, have again deposed him because of his scandalous conduct (for in addition he is a great drunkard). But I still hope that when Reiff has once been taken to account for the collected money, he will have to give up the church which stands upon his property, wherein I have not yet been allowed to preach, being compelled to go with my little flock of organized people from one place to another, and get along with houses and barns. If aid should then be given to us in our helpless condition, everything would come right again, and it is possible that Schipbach might then become a fine congregation. But toward this I can contribute nothing, if it remains as it is now, for I have no power here, and we are without help from the secular authorities.

As regards the congregation at **Philadelphia**, Mr. Weiss also took that out of my hands on his arrival, aided by the above mentioned opponents; for I had then already preached there a few times at their desire. But when he returned from Holland, and had acted so unbecomingly about the collected money with Reiff, he suddenly departed before Reiff came back, which was a year later, and thus abandoned the congregation. Whereupon they allowed themselves to be served by the aforesaid adventurers, and last of all by Bartholomew Rieger, from whom they again withdrew when they saw how his affairs stood, but only when they were nearly ruined. After all these things they called me (the entire congregation, man for man, signed the call; there were 42 signatures, dated April 24, 1734,[284] of which I enclose a copy) and asked me that I might come to their rescue. It seemed to me indeed a very difficult matter to bring such a disorganized congregation into order. But I ventured to do so after they had requested me two or three times, and I began the Lord's work there also, restoring them to such a good condition that up to this time I served them, even as my first three congregations, once a

---

[284] For this document, whose actual date is April 20, 1734, see pp. 231-234.

month. Be it understood, this refers only to the religious services; for regarding the aforesaid collections I have no authority, but in this I did by their request what I could, which, however, until now has not had much result.

To **Tolpehacken,** on account of the great distance, I go but twice a year; during the remaining time the two congregations in that locality have religious services by means of sermons read to them. They remain in good order, and do not allow themselves to be in the least delighted with the false apostles of the Moravians (although these, especially Jacob Lischy, have frequently sought until now in an artful manner to steal in among them).[284a]

What further concerns the growth and increase of the several churches, it may be stated that in each of them as named herein, from the beginning to the present time, the Lord's Supper has been administered every half year, according to the Church Order. But the congregations were much disturbed up to the year 1734 by great disorders and continued personal attacks (nothwithstanding that I had received the sacred ordination of the Gospel ministry on November 23, 1729, from the Reformed ministers at New York, thereunto authorized by the Very Reverend Classis of Amsterdam, as appears from the enclosure No. 2).[285]

But the statistics presented herewith will show what progress the above mentioned congregations have made after the aforesaid year 1734 until now:

[284a] The identity of the two Tulpehocken churches can be established by the following facts: (1) In 1743, the older Tulpehocken congregation built a new church, in which Boehm celebrated the first communion on May 6, 1743 (see pp. 398, 416); (2) In his report of 1744 (see p. 416) Boehm states that this congregation, which recently erected "a tolerably large, beautiful and well-built frame church," owned four acres of land, which had been donated; (3) The other Tulpehocken congregation had bought 100 acres of land and had built a small church upon it (see p. 416); (4) The Host Church has deeds for four acres; Trinity Church, near Myerstown, has a deed for 100 acres. This establishes clearly that the Host Church is the older Tulpehocken.

[285] It is printed above, see pp. 177-180.

	COMMUNICANT MEMBERS			
	1734	1737	1740	1743
At Falckner Schwam,				
April 7	40			
April 3		37		
April 26			152	
March 26, 131; April 24, 105				236
N. B. As the communicants largely increased the Lord's Supper was held there twice each time.				
At Schipbach,				
April 14	53			
April 9		55		
April 6			39	
April 3 (Easter)				36
At Weitmarsch,				
April 21	24			
April 16		15		
April 13			59	
March 13				51
At Philadelphia,				
September 15	88			
March 1		91		
April 20 (Easter)			130	
March 20, 98; April 17, 85				183
At Tolpehacken,				
In May		103		
In May			119	
May 6, at one place 124 } May 8, at the other place 129.				253

My further humble report which I have to make to the Christian Synods concerning the present condition of each of these congregations in particular, with regard to different matters, is submitted in view of the duty and obligation I owe to you. Their condition, as far as known to me, is as follows:

The congregation at **Falckner Schwam** has erected a well-built frame church, which may last a long time, but they still owe nearly sixty pounds on it. They have as yet no dwelling house for either pastor or reader.

As regards the congregation at **Schipbach,** there is a frame church there, but Reiff had the cunning to have it placed on his land, and thus he and his party have it under their control and in their possession. On this account I and my little flock, who hold loyally to the Church Order, were compelled (because we had no fixed place where we could hold our services, and had to take refuge from place to place) to select a place for that purpose. We bought therefore a plantation of 150 acres for 220 pounds, but for lack of funds we sold 100 acres for 100 pounds and retained the 50 acres, upon which already before this a building stood, which is new, and was not erected for less than 100 pounds. It is suited in every way for a parsonage, and upon that piece of land a neat and suitable church and schoolhouse could be built, right along the road. Indeed, as regards location, standing in the midst, between the people's houses, it is more advantageous and better located than the one standing on Reiff's land. This plan could be carried out for as little money as Reiff would charge us for land and church. To this place our good-hearted Reformed brethren in New York and on Long Island, on the urgent request of the honorable Consistory there, have sent us 44 pounds. That amount and six pounds in addition were paid in, so that we are still 70 pounds behind in this. This place has now been rented with the condition that we always retain the liberty of holding services there. And from the rent the interest is paid. But because we were so discouraged and saw no help, my brethren did not have anything more to do with it, but wished to sell the land again or load the whole burden upon my neck. In order not to let this place go so lightly out of our hands, I pledged myself alone for it, and I have yet till next August 1st, more than a year's time in which to pay. Should it now please God to be gracious to us and incline the hearts of our Church Fathers in their liberality toward us, for which we poor people have long waited, we will forever be thankful to them for it.[286] Finally, I have not had until now a penny's profit from this place, neither have I looked for it, but live all the time, up to this date, in my own house. But because of my inability I do not see how I can longer retain this property, unless some one comes to my aid.

In the congregation at **Weitmarch**, we have as yet nothing at all (in the way of a church building), but during all this time we have held our religious services always at the house

---

[286] Not receiving any aid from Holland, Boehm was compelled to sell this property again, December 28, 1745. See p. 60.

of Elder William De Wees, without any unwillingness on his part or the least expectation of payment. The honest man cherishes the steadfast hope that God will yet furnish means (to build a church).[287]

At **Philadelphia** we had thus far, in common with the Lutherans, an old dilapidated butcher's house, at an annual rent of three pounds;[287a] finally this was raised to four pounds, which we must now pay alone, for the Lutherans have built a church there of 70 by 45 feet. From this, people, who have experience in building conclude that it could not have been erected for

---

[287] William De Wees died, before this hope was realized, March 3, 1745. See note 268, p. 395.

[287a] A contract with the Lutherans regarding this meeting house is found in the *Büdingische Sammlung*, 1744, Vol. III, p. 60, which reads, verbatim, as follows:

"Contract between the Reformed and Lutherans in Philadelphia concerning the church held in common by them.

"To day has been made an agreement between both the German congregations, as follows, viz.:

"The here German Congregation *Reformed* gives up to the German Lutheran Congregation one Part of the House, which has been hired of Mr. Hamilton, for the common use, and that with this Condition, that the said Lutheran Congregation shall pay three Pounds out of four, which is the whole yearly Rent due for the said House to Mr. Hamilton. The Reformed Congregation on the other side, for their fourth Part of the House, shall pay one Pound. Since this Lease doth last yet 19 months, therefore the said Reformed Congregation, will keep it in her own hands, that, if they should meet with a minister who would preach to them twice a month, They, the Lutheran Congregation, should be obliged to resign their third Part of the Meeting-House to them again without the least Hesitation or money.

"To the Confirmation and Assurance of this matter we made two writings of the same Tenor of which each party has one.

"Dated: Philadelphia, 1st of January 1740/1.
       "MATTHEW SCHUTZ,
       "JACOB FRIEDERIC KLEIN,
       "LEONARD HERMAN,
       "PHILIP CHRISTOPHER WARNER."

When Mr. Andrew Hamilton, Esq., died on August 4, 1741, the property passed into the hands of his son-in-law, Justice William Allen. The Reformed people worshipped in this building till December, 1747.

less than 1500 pounds,[288] which by their own means they could do as little as the Reformed. Nevertheless the walls and roof are actually finished, so that they must have received much assistance through collections; from whence we do not know. Likewise they have a stone church in Providence township, of 50 by 38 feet, which is complete in all respects; they now have four ministers. Regarding the circumstances of one of them, Mühlenberg by name, I learn that his people give him what they can, he receives this on account, and the remainder he receives from London, whence he was sent hither. I have no acquaintance with the others, but it appears that they prosper. It also looks as if this Church, in case we are left without aid, would be able to do us considerable injury, for some young men are known to me whom they have won.

I and the Reformed officers of Philadelphia addressed our Lord Proprietor over two years ago for a plot of ground. He consented and finally gave us one, although within the city, one acre in extent, for 50 pounds sterling, at a yearly ground rent of six shillings, from which he might have realized as much as 200 pounds, upon which we now since that time bury our dead; before we had to bury our dead in a negro slave cemetery. But what does this benefit us? The money for the land is now bearing interest, and the congregation can scarcely raise from the incoming alms the annual expenses of our meeting-house and this plot of ground.

Regarding the congregations at **Tolpehacken,** the one some years ago bought 100 acres of land and built a small church upon it (but which is now altogether too small, and, as I recollect, I have heard from them that they have a debt of about 30 pounds on land and church. The other congregation at Tolpehacken received as a gift a little piece of land consisting of four acres, and erected upon it a tolerably large, beautiful and well-built frame church.[289] I heard, when I was last with them, and for the first time held services in the church, and at the same time celebrated the Lord's Supper, that they owed

---

[288] The exact amount of the cost, according to the *Hallesche Nachrichten,* new ed. Vol. I, p. 151, was £1607, 14s. 9¼d.

[289] For the two Tulpehocken churches and their identification see pp. 68, 412.

as much as 60 pounds, although they did not yet have chairs or pews. Both these fine and very loyal congregations well deserve to be served and guided by a godly and faithful pastor. In the first congregation they have a faithful reader and schoolmaster, Francis Layenberger, who has been thus far a faithful watchman against the sects. I trust that, although his income is very meagre, he may yet be able to stay for a while. In the second congregation one of the elders is reader, and thus they continue their religious services in the fear of God, living in good hope that God will graciously help them.

Of **Canastocka** I cannot say much, since for a long time I have not conducted the services among them. For some time they accepted any one they could get, and now they have nobody. There are at present three congregations. In the new city of Lancaster they had last John Barth. Rieger, but because he had always had very much intercourse with all sorts of people and all sorts of sects, they took an aversion to him. Toward the end of last year Count Zinzendorf attended his church, of whom he made very much, and took him into his house. On the next Sunday his sermon (as I have heard in truth) was nothing but a glorifying and praising of the piety and doctrines of the Moravian brethren. It also happened that he (Rieger) and Zinzendorf were present at the house of a certain man, Jacob Baurle;[290] there the Count said he must hasten to Philadelphia, for court was now in session there, and as surely as his name was Count Zinzendorf he would see to it that four men should hang, and nothing could save them but the king's mercy. (This arose from the fact that Count Zinzendorf had made the Lutherans at Philadelphia believe that he was a Lutheran minister, whereupon they took this

[290] John Adam Gruber, a resident of Germantown, tells this incident, as follows, in his "Elaborate Report" in Fresenius, *Nachrichten*, Vol. III, p. 220: "When he [Zinzendorf] had preached in the new city at Canastoka, and at table, in the presence of Rev. Mr. Rieger and a man named Baierlin, spoke of the tumult in Philadelphia, Mr. Ludwig [Zinzendorf] struck with his hand upon his breast and said: 'As truly as I am and have been born a Count, I shall see to it that some (namely those who led Mr. Pirleus out of the church) will be exemplarily punished by the Court, and if I cannot get any satisfaction here I shall appeal to the King of England, that two or three of them be hung.'"

Count for their preacher). Afterwards he installed one of his creatures, named Pyrlaeus; then they discovered his cunning tricks, and thrust the same, with the aid of the Reformed (but I was not present) out of the meeting-house, which they had in common.

For these words a lawyer of Philadelphia caused Jacob Bauerle to be summoned by the court at Lancaster (I have this from the lawyer's own mouth). And now when Rieger, who was present, was also made to give testimony, he excused himself by saying, "he had not heard it". (I have heard this only recently from the above mentioned Jacob Bauerle's own mouth) which, added to other grievances, induced the people to get rid of him, which they could readily do, as he was engaged by them on certain conditions. Thereupon Rieger went away from here,[291] but his wife and children are still here. What has become of him I do not know, but it is said here that he has written to his brother from Leyden, in Holland.

The surrounding congregations, around or near Canastocka, have long ago taken up with a man, Conrad Tempelman by name (he is from Heidelberg) a tailor by trade, and have made the same their minister. I know him, for he was schoolmaster and reader in the Hill church when I served them at the beginning. Of the same I noticed at the time nothing wrong in his life or conduct, and since have heard of him nothing but what was praiseworthy, especially that he is very watchful against the sects, and that his congregations are very much united.

Regarding the congregation at **Goschenhoppen,** it has a suitable frame church upon a piece of land consisting of 50

---

[291] In 1743 Rieger went to Holland to study medicine. On March 22, 1744, he matriculated at Leyden. On October 7, 1743, the Clerk of the Classis of Amsterdam was instructed to write to Rieger and to ask him to give an account of the Church of Pennsylvania to the Classis. On November 5, 1743, Rieger appeared personally before the Classis and promised to send in a report regarding the Church in Pennsylvania. The report of Rieger was received April 13, 1744. Rieger returned to Pennsylvania about May, 1745. About Rieger's visit to Holland see *Ecclesiastical Records of N. Y.,* Vol. IV, pp. 2812, 2823, 2845.

acres, donated by some one[292] that all religions and sects
should have the privilege of building a church thereon, and I
lately learned from an elder of theirs that the church is paid
for. Two years ago four of them bought a plot. They intended
to hand it over to the congregation for a parsonage if they
were reimbursed for their outlay. How much it costs I do
not know. This congregation up to this time has claimed the
privilege accorded to them in the letter which Reiff had when
he returned from his collecting tour, and purported to be
written by his Reverence, Doctor Wilhelmi, of Rotterdam
(whereof a copy may be found among the Pennsylvania papers).
Hence they will not submit to any church order. And no matter how much I may admonish them, they remain of the same
mind. They had taken young Goetschi to be their pastor, but
when Do. Dorsius arrived he withdrew from them, went to
him, studied a year with him, and after this year he was
ordained as a minister for Long Island, in the month of April,
1741, by Mr. Dorsius, assisted by Do. Frelinghuysen of Raritan,
and still another (as I learned afterwards), Tennant by
name,[293] of whom it was said at that time that he was one of
the Whitfielders. Meanwhile, since Goetschi was no longer
with them, Do. Dorsius has several times administered the
Lord's Supper to this people before his journey to Holland.
As I learned on Tuesday after last Easter at Goschenhoppen
from a ruling elder, it is arranged that he shall again administer it to them in the month of May next coming. On this
Tuesday after Easter, when I happened to come to Goschenhoppen, I found this among them: On Good Friday they had
allowed the base deceiver, Jacob Lischy, to preach in their
church, who at the same time baptized two children. When I
represented to two elders, who were together on this Tuesday
after Easter, the impropriety of this act in the presence of

---

[292] The land for the New Goshenhoppen church was donated by
John Henry Sprogell, before the year 1729. Failing to get a deed
from him the congregation was compelled, in 1749, to buy the land
from his heirs. This appears from a survey made of the land by David
Schultze, in May, 1769.

[293] It was Gilbert Tennent, pastor of the Presbyterian Church
at New Brunswick, N. J., who was associated in his work with Frelinghuysen. See *Eccl. Records of N. Y.*, Vol. IV, pp. 2557, 2569, 2587f.

several people, in having permitted a Moravian to do such things, they answered me, that they themselves had held it up to him, but he had protested with an oath and called upon God to forsake him if he were a Moravian. He claimed to be a Reformed preacher from Switzerland. Then I showed them his Moravian hymn book, entitled "Shepherd Songs of Bethlehem, for the use of all who are poor and humble",[294] which before this was his own pocket hymn book, and had come into my hands in a wonderful but honorable way, in which he had written his name with his own hand; when they compared the letter which he had written to them with it and saw that it was his own hand-writing, they realized his wicked conduct; the more so because when they told him that I had this little book, he denied it was his, saying that he knew nothing of the book, that others could easily write his name in a book; he could not prevent that, and that for this reason he had long regarded me as a treacherous Boehm, of whom he had heard before in Holland, etc. Then they acted as if they were sorry. But one among them, Michael Radner, confessed that it was his fault alone that Lischy had come into the church. Whereupon I took my departure. The next day I spoke with another ruling elder, who was not present the day before. This one said to me with a sad heart, almost with tears; "But what shall we do? Mr. Dorsius has told us we should not think that we could get ministers from Holland. We should ourselves see to it what was to be done. The Hollanders had said: "What do the Pennsylvanians imagine themselves to be? They live in a free country, have nothing to pay to any royal court, yet want to give but 10 pounds in such a large congregation to a minister; then we cannot provide them with ministers", etc. Nevertheless, I admonished them to remain steadfast in prayer, and without being discouraged to wait upon God's

---

[294] The German title of this hymn book reads: *Hirten-Lieder von Bethlehem, enthaltend eine Kleine Sammlung evangelischer Lieder zum Gebrauch von Alles was arm ist, was Klein und gering ist,* Germantown. Christopher Saur, 1742, 12 mo., 128 pp., index 10 pp. It is a collection of three hundred and ninety-six hymns, which were printed by Christopher Saur for Count Zinzendorf soon after his arrival in Pennsylvania. See Seidensticker, *First Century of German Printing*, Philadelphia, 1893, p. 15.

favor. As for me, I felt assured that if our devout Church Fathers desired to admonish us and were displeased about anything, they would not thus rudely present it, but speak of it in an amicable and friendly manner, becoming to servants of God. But according to my expectations the affairs of our church would take quite a different turn under the providence of God and His guidance, etc. And thus we separated.

Lastly, the congregation at **Germantown.** This is in a sad state, as regards loyalty to our true Reformed doctrine. Yet many years ago they built a handsome stone church, on which there is quite a debt. But in spite of all our admonitions, warnings and prayers they constantly permitted every errorist to associate with them. For when Barth. Rieger, who, when he served Philadelphia, also preached for them occasionally, had left them, they allowed John Bechtel to preach constantly to them, whom I plainly enough described to them in my first and second Letter of Warning. Thus also old Samuel Guldi,[295] who according to his own statement, was minister in the three principal churches in Bern, Switzerland (whence he was dismissed on account of his pietism and came to this country), has often preached there. Meanwhile they also consented to have a sectarian crowd gather there every Sunday afternoon, of whom one had been before an Inspirationist, another a Pietist, Separatist, and whatever other kinds might be mentioned. These then assembled in the church, selected a passage of the Bible, and then disputed about it. But they allowed no one to compare Scripture with Scripture, but were of the opinion that every question could be decided by every one's conviction. The vulgar called these people Disputants, but they called themselves The Free Assembly. Nevertheless these antics soon amounted to nothing.

After this they let Count Zinzendorf and his Moravians take possession of the church, who preached there awhile, and the turner John Bechtel[296] was one of his worst proselyters. But since this Count Zinzendorf got into confusing quarrels and contentions with those Separatists, who came down on him

---

[295] For a sketch of Rev. Samuel Guldin see note 132, p. 107; also p. 274.

[296] For a sketch of the life and work of John Bechtel see pp. 115-119.

too hard, he left this congregation of Germantown to his brother, John Bechtel, went away and returned to Philadelphia. Then these thoughtless people permitted themselves to be led astray by this Bechtel through his hypocritical and smooth words, since he pretended that he would in the future adhere to the Reformed doctrine, and he brought it by means of his sectarian creatures so far among them that, on his promise henceforth to adhere to the Heidelberg Catechism in its purity in all its points, they engaged him on January 27, 1743, for a year, as their pastor, giving him a testimonial thereof in writing. But hardly a week afterwards he wanted a paper signed by four officers in the congregation, in which he excepted the eightieth and the one hundred and fourteenth questions. On being asked why, he replied: The eightieth question was unnecessary in this country and the one hundred and fourteenth (he said) was not true because those who were converted no longer committed sin, and not only could keep the commandments of God, but it was very easy for them to do so. Whereupon the largest part of the congregation opposed him all the more, but however they might try to induce him (to leave), he had their paper, and they had to get along with him that year.

During that year he meanwhile established himself firmly with his Moravians in the church. They built a gallery in it, bought an organ for 60 pounds and put it on the gallery, intending by means of these heavy expenses—since the Reformed were so far back in their payments and unable to pay—in this way to get this church under the control of the Moravians. For this purpose they also offered to furnish the money. But when the year agreed upon was up, on January 27, 1744, they obtained control of the church and got rid of Bechtel, whom they dismissed. But the costs of the alterations and the organ had to be refunded. How they were able to do this I cannot imagine.

Meanwhile if these people had a loyal disposition, upon which we could rely, and if that congregation would let itself be governed according to church order, it would be of great importance to offer assistance. But I have not yet been able to find the necessary requisites among them. For when they were now rid of Bechtel, on the next Sunday thereafter nearly all the Reformed people in the vicinity, from far and near, came together (most of the Weitmarsch people were also there) to consult in what manner the best and most suitable measures might be taken that this congregation be brought into a good condition. At this time (according to the testimony of the elder from Weitmarsch, William De Wees) not a single member was present who did not vote for this, to call me also at Germantown as their regular pastor, under the same conditions as mentioned in the enclosed letter C, on page 6, regarding the little Weitmarsch congregation,[297] that both these congregations be brought under our Church Order and be combined. But because one ought to deal very cautiously with such people, it happened that on February 20th last, as in passing I conversed with one, named Minck [Meng], at his house in Germantown about these matters. I gave him this as my resolution: That I was very glad that it had finally come so far, and that whenever they would come and place themselves under our ordinances and enter into our Christian communion, wherein already stood the Weitmarsch congregation, whose regular minister of God's Word I was, I would with all my heart and gladly serve them, and, until God would be pleased to send from elsewhere other aid, would help them, to the best of my ability, in conducting their religious services. And if they would agree to this then I would expect from the congregation, or from their elders in their name, a written certificate thereof, mentioning whatever they desired me to do. Whereupon I in return would likewise let them have my answer in my own writing. In answer to which this Minck replied, this shall be done; which, however, they did not carry out. And it seems that the thought to be in subjection to church order, when every one is not permitted to act in everything arbitrarily and according to his own pleasure, was not agreeable to some. These then, acting on their own authority, on March 11th, allowed a vagrant to preach in their church, a locksmith by trade, living at Raritan, but who, as if he were a country apostle, travels everywhere through the land to preach; and thus they acted simply on their own authority,

---

[297] This statement is found in Boehm's report of 1740, sent to the Classis, of which he enclosed a duplicate to the Synods in 1744. It is at The Hague, 74, I, 27. The passage is printed above, p. 296. See also p. 298, paragraph II.

without their four chosen elders knowing anything about it, much less appointing it or consenting to it, which I have learned from the mouth of some of these four men, and I also ascertained their displeasure at such proceedings. This act does not appear to be of a more encouraging nature than the previous acceptance of Bechtel; the more so as Bechtel when preaching towards the end of his year one Sunday morning announced at the conclusion of the service that in the afternoon just this locksmith (who was present) would preach, which also took place. From which one can readily judge that this man and Bechtel are about of the same sort and played together under the same cover. Finally, before Easter, they also went to Neshaminy and asked Do. Dorsius to preach for them, and hence on Easter Sunday he preached at Germantown.

Do. Dorsius has also promised the people at **New Goschenhoppen** to administer the Lord's Supper there on May 6th, and that on the 7th he would be at **Old Goschenhoppen**, situated about four miles from Schipbach, where the Lutheran and Reformed people wish to build a union church (whereby again some members will be drawn away from Schipbach, for until now this district had belonged to Schipbach) and on May 7th he will lay the cornerstone. On this occasion the Lutheran preacher (Andres[298] by name, and Do. Dorsius are each to preach a sermon. Do. Dorsius asked said Lutheran pastor to announce this from his pulpit for the benefit of his Lutheran congregation, which he did on April 8th. Afterwards I was told by some of my elders who were present that the Lutheran minister said distinctly: "Rev. Inspector Dorsius will administer the Lord's Supper on May 6th at New Goschenhoppen for the Reformed people, and on the 7th ditto at the laying of the corner-stone of the union church at Old Goschenhoppen, he as well as myself (the Lutheran Pastor) will preach the first sermon", which words a certain man, who had heard them, told me with astonishment in my home on the 16th of April.

[298] This was John Conrad Andreae, who, from 1743-1750, was pastor of the Lutheran congregation of Old Goshenhoppen, New Goshenhoppen and Indian Field. He died January 1, 1754, at Germantown. See *Hallesche Nachrichten*, new ed., Vol. I, p. 265f.

What all these things mean,—to foster the spirit of independence in congregations which with difficulty allow themselves to be brought under church order; and to make no attempt to lead them to something more edifying and wholesome, and what consequences this will cause in the future,—all this time alone will show.

April 20, 1744.   J. P. BOEHM.

P. S. On May 6th, Do. Dorsius administered the Lord's Supper at New Goshenhoppen; several persons from Falckner Schwam communed there without saying anything.

On May 7th, the corner-stone[299] of the above mentioned union church was to be laid; a considerable number of people were present, but the day was rainy. Do. Dorsius did not come. It was then postponed till Whit Monday, May 14th, old style. Do. Dorsius again did not come. But an elder of New Goschenhoppen was appointed to represent Do. Dorsius and thus the work was accomplished.

July 7, 1744.   BOEHM.

(On Sunday, July 8th, Do. Dorsius was at Canastocka).

[299] This cornerstone has a most interesting Latin inscription, which reads verbatim and literatim:

>   LIberaLItas pLebIs
>   LVtheranæ atqVe
>   reforMatæ has æDes
>   Vna eXstrVXIt.
>   I. C. ANDREÆ PAST. LVTH.

Translated literally it reads:

>   The liberality of the people
>   Lutheran and also
>   Reformed erected
>   Unitedly this temple.
>   I. C. Andreae, Lutheran Pastor.

The unique feature of this inscription is its use of capitals or larger letters, found throughout the first four lines. By these larger letters the date of the cornerstone laying is given, as can be seen from the following:

>   Line 1. LI + LI + LI 153
>   "   2. L + V + V   60
>   "   3. M + D 1500
>   "   4. V + X + V + XI   31
>   ----
>   Total 1744

It was most likely the Lutheran pastor who used this ingenious method to indicate the date of the cornerstone laying.

[XXXIX. MR. BOEHM TO THE DEPUTIES OF THE SYNODS, JULY 9, 1744.[300]]

Very Reverend Sirs, Very Learned and Much Honored Messrs. Deputies:—

The Reverend Gentlemen will learn from all the true reports (and otherwise) concerning the High German Reformed Church in Pennsylvania, its miserable and very needy and poor condition. And, as your humble servant and least fellow-brother in Christ firmly believes you, as true servants of God, will commiserate with hearty sighs us, poor members of the body of Christ.

This our cause may have been presented ever so wrongly by a known or unknown man, through writing or orally, yet the merciful God will finally, after much sighing, come to the rescue of His true Church in this as yet deplorable land of ours. He will bring to light the unfaithfulness of every one as well as the faithfulness of his faithful ones, and by His incomprehensible providence will finally refresh us with comfort and help, for His name's sake.

That everything in all our submissive reports, sent by my beloved fellow-brethren and by myself, was reported truthfully, in accordance with our duty as before God, purposing to seek the honor of our God and the welfare of our churches here, I, your obedient servant wish to assure you herewith before God, by virtue of the duties resting upon me. Your servant is likewise compelled to present humbly to your Reverences his own need and to commend himself to your Reverences' hallowed care, as men of God who can do much in this respect. For the almost unbearable toil and labor, which your poor fellow-servant has in the office which was pressed upon him, will be sufficiently evident to your Reverences from everything. It is now more than eighteen years that his travels, only to his regular [preaching] places, amounted to 104 English miles every month. In addition he had to perform the duties of his office and for this he received no fixed salary thus far, but he can affirm, without violating his con-

---

[300] The German original is in the archives at The Hague. The catalogue number is 74, I, 37.

science, that he does not believe, if he counts the years and the income, that he has received more than ten pounds yearly. (The perquisites for weddings are excluded). This is because of the inability of the generally poor people and our cause is not on a firm basis; and the numerous wicked sects, especially the Herrnhuters, would make excellent use of it to lead astray the simple souls, if one should ask a fixed and sufficient salary from such poor people. Therefore your servant has been patient in everything, from the beginning until now, so that our Church might grow; and he has eaten his own bread, which he has earned by the work of his hands, with the blessing of God, and has lived in his own simple cabin.

But since my best years, in regard to the body, have been devoted to this work, and now inability approaches, and I am not able to cease from my work with a good conscience, since I see no other help, I grow indeed timid. Yet I have the firm belief and the assured hope that the Lord our God will provide, and that He will now incline your kind hearts to the least of your servants and poor fellow-laborers and to his dear congregations, so that they may be supported in their need by your much availing intercession, for which he herewith beseeches you humbly for Jesus' sake.

Commending your Reverences, each of your reverend persons, families and holy service to God and the Word of His grace, I am and remain,

Your submissive servant and least
fellow-brother in the Lord Jesus,
JOHAN PHILIPS BOEHM,
Reformed Minister in Pennsylvania, in Philadelphia County, at Falckner Schwam, Schipbach and Weitmarsch.

Witpen Township,
  Philadelphia County,
    Pennsylvania, July 9, 1744.

P. S. Letters which you may desire to send, may be addressed in care of Mr. Caspar Ullrich, Baker in Philadelphia.

[XL. MR. BOEHM TO THE CLASSIS OF AMSTERDAM, NOVEMBER 23, 1746.[301]]

Very Reverend Classis, Much Esteemed and Devout Church Fathers:—

The Very Reverend Classis will have learned sufficiently from all our submissive reports, which have been made, in conjunction with my fellow-brethren and elders, not only the weakness of the Reformed congregations in this land, but also my unbearable labor, toil and sorrow which I had to undergo. Without doubt you felt compassion in your hearts for me, as I have borne all these things for a voluntary and but small remuneration, and as I have prayed incessantly to Almighty God to give us, according to His eternal love and mercy, such means as might help His true Church after such continued supplications.

Now we see that, after the dear Lord has made us to pass through such a severe trial, He will finally manifest His grace in answer to our continual prayers and will strongly incline the hearts of our devout Church Fathers to us, poor members of Christ. For you have now sent to us a man, brought from a great distance and with great sacrifices for the best interests only and the perfect establishment of our true Church, in order to supply the same with a sufficient number of faithful ministers, the name of the reverend gentleman being Michael Slatter.[302]

His Reverence arrived in Philadelphia on the 25th of August of this year. He visited me soon afterwards, on the 27th ditto, at my home, with two members of the congregation at Philadelphia. He showed me at that time first of all his instructions, dated The Hague, May 28, 1746, from the two Christian Synods of South and North Holland. He read the same to me word for word and then gave them into my hands for several days. I found them so emphatic that I could not have the least doubt that the Reverend Christian Synods know the fitness of Do. Slatter for this important un-

---

[301] The original German letter is at The Hague, 74, I, 43.

[302] Schlatter reached Philadelphia September 6, 1746 (or August 26th, o. st.). He visited Boehm immediately on the next day. See *Schlatter's Life,* p. 127.

dertaking, for his instructions are signed by six venerable men, as deputies of the Reverend Synods. All of this cannot be unknown to the Reverend Classis. I rejoiced heartily over it and felt bound by my conscience to comply with it obediently and to contribute to it, according to my ability, so that I might help to advance this work of the Lord.

Do. Slatter entered upon this work with earnestness and soon traveled from one place to another, as much as time would permit. To some of these places I accompanied his Reverence. How he succeeded at each place to which he traveled is laid before you at length in his report, already sent to the Reverend Christian Synods and the Reverend Classis of Amsterdam.[303]

Since the year 1740, that is six years ago, when I specified and grouped for the Reverend Classis all the places known to me, at the request of Do. Dorsius (which report I sent faithfully during the same year to the Reverend Classis),[304] the country has increased and changed very much. Hence it is necessary to group the congregations differently. Do. Slatter has carefully noted this and recognized its necessity because of the wolves, which have increased since that time and are still increasing, going about through the flock of Christ. Hence he has recognized it to be indispensably necessary that the divine services be held more frequently than I believed to be sufficient at that time. He is now arranging everything with a view to the best interests and the establishment of the Church. His Reverence is also pleased to use my humble advice in such matters.

What places or congregations his Reverence will further seek out and organize, will appear next spring, the Lord willing and we still living.

However, I consider it my submissive obligation and duty to report to the Reverend Classis what plans have been considered with regard to my congregations, which are subordinate to the Reverend Classis and which I have served hitherto

[303] The first report of Schlatter, dated December 15, 1746, was published by the writer in the *Journal of the Presb. Hist. Soc.*, Vol. III, pp. 105-121; 158-176.

[304] See pp. 272-284, and also pp. 285-298.

with great difficulty, but according to my ability, in conformity to the Church Order established by the Reverend Classis.

The poor but numerous and well organized congregation at Falckner Schwam is twenty miles from my home. I have served it 21 years once a month, but it becomes very burdensome to me to continue this any longer.

There is, however, a new congregation at Providentz,[305] about eight miles from the former, of which I have made mention before. It is indispensably necessary to organize it, hence Do. Slatter is willing to connect it with the congregation at Falckner Schwam and to organize a charge with these two congregations.

The congregation at Schipbach, as I have complained repeatedly to the Reverend Classis, has been so scattered by past divisions that, according to all appearance, there is no more hope of maintaining a congregation there. The few members of the upper part of this congregation can go conveniently to Old Goschenhoppen, where Do. Weis is the regular minister.

The congregation of Weitmarge, which at all times consisted of but few members, through the death of the aged, faithful elder, William De Wees, has come to a standstill[306] (because his house was at all times our church, but since his death it can be so no longer, nor is there any opportunity to worship elsewhere, much less are there the means to build a church). The lower part of the congregation has gone to Germantown, which will serve to strengthen the congregation there, in like manner as that at Old Goschenhoppen.

The congregation at Philadelphia, which submitted in the year 1734 to the Church Order, established by the Reverend Classis (as is well known to the Reverend Classis and which being carefully sent over, will be found among the Pennsylvania papers), I have served monthly, according to the Church Order, as their regular minister, accepted by them, and I have promised them to maintain this service until something else will be ordered by the Reverend Church Fathers in Holland,

---

[305] St. Luke's Reformed Church, at Trappe, Providence Township, Montgomery County.

[306] Boehm meant to say that it has been discontinued.

which has now been done by them through his Reverence, Mr. Slatter.

Now it is the intention of Do. Slatter to unite the congregation at Germandon with this congregation [at Philadelphia], in order to make it a charge for one minister.

The outcome of this arrangement would be that I would have to serve one of these places, for both were hitherto my dear congregations. The members of none of these two congregations are opposed to me, as the testimonials of my three and of other congregations, formerly demanded of me and sent over to you, as also our last submissive letters from Philadelphia, credibly testify. But since Do. Slatter is fully convinced of the great toil and labor, hitherto endured by me, and of my continual travels throughout the country, in all kinds of changing and rough weather in winter and summer, and as he sees that I have faithfully performed it, but through it have been brought to such a state, that according to my opinion I will not be able to continue this traveling much longer, through which the congregations that I might accept would lack regular services because of my disability, for this reason Do. Slatter considers both the congregations as well as myself, as I can feel my strength waning. The Reverend Classis can readily believe this, as I have now completed the 63rd year of my life.

He [Slatter], therefore counselled with me and asked for a proposal from me, so that I might be able to conclude my days in the service of the Lord, which I made as follows (as I would long ago have liked to do, but was unable to carry it out, because I was almost the only worker here):

Witpen township, where I live, lies almost midway between Germandon and the above mentioned Old Goschenhoppen, which are about 23 or 24 miles apart. Weitmarge and Schipbach being in a straight line. I now proposed that a regular congregation be established in this township, to which the members of Upper Weitmarge and those in the lower part of Schipbach and the country round about might attach themselves, which congregation I could serve from my home, even after I have become incapable of traveling.

Now, if the godly Church Fathers would turn the eyes of love upon the least of their fellow-servants (because it is only one congregation and not much can be expected from it), so that I might have the necessaries of life, I would gladly be exempt from other burdens, and be content with this, not because of indolence and laziness, but for the weighty reasons quoted above. It would then be a joy to me in my old age, because there are many living in this neighborhood, who, although they are of Reformed antecedents, yet have not joined any church nor have any interest in this work, to lead some of these into our true Church and to help in the salvation of their souls.

What has meanwhile taken place, upon the instigation of his Reverence, Do. Slatter, with reference to an organization[307] between Do. Weiss, Rieger and myself, which was sent by us three from Philadelphia to the Reverend Christian Synods and the Reverend Classis of Amsterdam has, we trust, come into your hands before this time. Do. Slatter did not rest until he had accomplished it.

It was indeed very hard for me to stand in official and brotherly connection with men through whom I had to suffer so much affliction, to the injury of my health (as I have often complained with sadness to the godly Church Fathers, with ample proofs of my innocence). But, persuaded by Do. Slatter, there took place what Christ says, Luke 17:4. Then I found myself also in duty bound to do what our Saviour commanded us to do. Thus it happened that all that is past was thrown into the fire of love. The true prince of love, Jesus, preserve the peace among his unworthy servants, Amen.

Now I feel assured that the Reverend Classis will be pleased with this and not put to the account of any one that which has happened.

However, I humbly ask the Reverend Classis to gladden the heart of the most submissive, humblest and least of your fellow-brethren with a gracious answer to our last letters from Pennsylvania, which, as Do. Slatter informed me, have reached you, and to which I would like to receive a personal answer. Meanwhile, in accordance with the counsel of his Reverence, Do. Slatter, I shall continue to serve, in my usual order and

---

[307] This refers to the preliminary conference held on October 12, 1746, in Schlatter's house in Philadelphia. See p. 134.

according to my ability, in all of the congregations to which I have ministered hitherto, until this matter has been decided.

And now, Very Reverend Classis, I shall live in submissive hope,—in consideration of the fact that I have faithfully spent my best years in the Lord's service and have had little temporal profit from it, but rather did not even spare my own property, for I took from it 26 pounds and 10 shillings for printing,[308] when I wrote against the ungodly Moravians, of which pamphlets I gave away more than I sold and hence will not get back half of the expenses, (especially since I have still many copies on hand) to the detriment of my family, which I could have supported better if I had been without this burden, and now I am no longer able to support them with manual labor,—I live in hope that you will graciously represent the case of your humblest fellow-servant, with your most powerful intercession, before the Reverend Christian Synods.

I, therefore, commend myself to the favor of the very reverend and devout Church Fathers, and to their most gracious care, asking the dear Lord, that He will graciously bless them in body and soul, here in time and yonder in eternity.

Commending the Very Reverend Classis, my devout Church Fathers, each of your persons, together with your families and holy service, to God and the Word of His grace,

I am and unalterably remain,
Very Reverend Classis,
Your submissive, obedient, humble and least fellow-brother in the Lord,

JOHAN PH. BOEHM,
Reformed Minister in Pennsylvania.

Witpen Township,
Philadelphia County, Pennsylvania,
November 23, 1746.

[POSTSCRIPT OF NOVEMBER 25, 1746.]

Very Reverend Classis:—

I consider it my duty to inform you also of that which I learned after November 22nd. When I came to Philadelphia

---

[308] This money was in part restored to Boehm's widow in 1752. See p. 140.

on the 23rd of November, to perform my official duties, I learned from an elder that they were very much perplexed concerning the congregation, believing that I would leave the congregation and give it to his Reverence, Mr. Slatter. For they were not sure that they could have Mr. Slatter as the regular minister of the congregation. Yet on account of their great love for his Reverence and having the firm hope that they would have a faithful and zealous minister in him, they wished to be sure of him.

Then I made this known to his Reverence, on account of my sincere love for this my dearly beloved congregation. His Reverence gave me the following answer:

"As yet I am the regular minister of no place in Pennsylvania, nor will it be necessary for me to accept a call until the time that my commission, which I have from the Christian Synods, has expired. For until that time no congregation shall have any expense or burden on my account, for I have no permission for this".

I myself can truthfully attest that his Reverence never asked anything wherever he has been in this country, and even where he was offered a compensation for his labor, he accepted nothing, and what is more, his Reverence preaches sometimes, on the three Sundays intervening between my preaching, both in Philadelphia and in Germantown (since he cannot travel in winter and therefore stays in Philadelphia) without pay, and the small perquisites on these days he forces upon me saying that until later they belonged to me and not to him and he would not take anything away from me, his brother. But, in order to quiet the congregation in Philadelphia, for which he also had a love, [he said] he would before his time accept a regular call, made with my consent, if the conditions on both sides were favorable, but with the provision, that in his absence (for next spring he might have to be absent for three months on account of his commission) I should not desert the congregation, but officiate in the same as heretofore, until he had finished his work. This I have promised his Reverence willingly and heartily, and by the help of God I expect to do so.

What may happen in the future time will show.

November 25, 1746.   J. PH. BOEHM.

[XLI. MR. SCHLATTER TO MR. BOEHM, NOVEMBER 29, 1746.[309]]

Very Reverend, Very Honorable Sir,
DEAREST BROTHER IN CHRIST JESUS:—

Yours of day before yesterday came to hand in good condition. The copy of the postscript is above correction and written in a truly brotherly spirit. I shall carefully enclose your reverend letter to the Classis of Amsterdam in mine and next week surrender them to the guidance of God and the tempestuous sea.

With regard to the time at which I am expected to be with you, because of the organization of the new congregation and the building of its church, I leave it to you to appoint either Tuesday, the 9th or Thursday, the 11th of December. Send a horse a day beforehand.[310]

Concerning the affairs of the Philadelphia congregation, about which I counselled with you, I deem it to be the shortest and surest way, after careful deliberation, that your Reverence, for my sake and that of the congregation, take the trouble to come Sunday the 7th of December to Philadelphia to preach, and, if you then think best, make the necessary announcement of the matter under consideration to the congregation, and with their consent and approval announce my name for the first time or introduce me, according to the custom of the church.

I would then do the same in the afternoon with the consistory, in order that it together with me may be installed two weeks hence by your Reverence, so that I can deliver my introductory sermon on New Year's day. By following such a course everything would be done before the Christmas festival.

I do not doubt that your Reverence will be pleased with this proposition. Hoping this, I take the liberty tomorrow to announce to the congregation that you will preach, God willing, the following Sunday in the morning and will make an important statement to them.

Meanwhile I have the pleasure to send my best regards to yourself and your worthy wife and also your dear son, of whom I hope that he is now fully recovered. Commending myself most respectfully to your continued friendship, I ask, with every respect, for the honor to be,

My most reverend and esteemed friend's and dearest fellow-

---

[309] Sent by Boehm to the Synods (see next letter, p. 437), now at The Hague, 74, II, 8.

[310] We cannot be sure that this visit of Schlatter to Whitpain was really made. There is no further evidence that he actually went there at that time. We know that the organization of the Whitpain congregation actually took place in February, 1747. See *Life of Schlatter*, p. 149f.

brother's devoted and most willing servant,

MICH. SLATTER.

Philadelphia, November 29, 1746.

[XLII. MR. BOEHM TO THE DEPUTIES OF THE SYNODS, DECEMBER 12, 1746.[311]]

Very Reverend, Very Learned and Devout Sirs, Deputies of the two Christian Synods of South and North Holland:—

His Reverence, Mr. Slatter, who was sent hither by the two Christian Synods, arrived here this fall with your instructions, dated 'sGraven-Haage, May 13, 1746.[311a] Thereby my heart was made to rejoice greatly and especially do I give thanks unto the merciful God that He has finally, after much prayer and many sighs, listened graciously to me, poor burden-bearer, and has allowed me to see such an effectual instrument and kind brother and fellow-worker in His holy service. May the Lord Jesus bless him further and preserve him in His grace, that he may be blessed all the days of his life, and afterwards may he shine like the brightness of heaven in the eternal kingdom of the joy of our God. Amen.

Very Reverend Sirs, his Reverence, Mr. Slatter, brought me refreshing tidings, among others that our last letters from Philadelphia, of the year 1744, came to the hands of the Christian Synods. He thought that later on a kind answer to me would follow, for which I have thus far waited painfully.

But your obedient servant and least fellow-worker can wait no longer to express his gratitude for the efforts showing a sanctified zeal for the true Church of Jesus in this as yet desolate land.

I, therefore, thank you with the most humble reverence, from the bottom of my heart, wishing your Reverences in the inmost of my soul, all rich and gracious blessings of body and

---

[311] The original German letter of Boehm is in the archives at The Hague, 74, I, 44.

[311a] The correct date of Schlatter's instruction is May 23, 1746, as appears from the copy preserved in the Minutes of the Deputies. See also Fresenius, *Pastoral Sammlungen*, Vol. XII, p. 221.

soul. May the merciful and gracious God and Father of our Lord Jesus Christ bless our Church Fathers who labor so faithfully in His work, each person, family and holy service, and may their reward of grace be the crown of glory in heaven. Amen.

Very Reverend Sirs, your servant is also willing to inform you, in due reverence, concerning some occurrences here, thinking that it is best, inasmuch as the united servants of God should know the same things, to send you true copies of all which has been reported in these present affairs to the Very Reverend Classis of Amsterdam. Thus your Reverences may see from that which was obediently sent to the Very Reverend Classis of Amsterdam on the 23rd and 24th of November, 1746, what your obedient servant asked for and what he again submissively asks from your Reverences.

You can also see from the enclosed original letter, dated November 29, 1746, what his Reverence, Mr. Slatter has asked of him.

Very Reverend Sirs, how can I do otherwise than comply with the request of his Reverence, Mr. Slatter, also out of respect to the Christian Synods and the Very Reverend Deputies, especially since it all tends to the glory of God and the upbuilding of our true churches here.

In the confident hope that your Reverences will look favorably upon the least of your fellow-servants, with eyes of love for Christ's sake, and expecting a kind and favorable answer also with respect to the above-mentioned affair, I close and commend your very reverend persons, families and holy service to God and the Word of His grace, and myself to your sanctified love and favor, remaining obediently,
  Very Reverend Sirs,
Your obedient and humble servant and the least fellow-servant
  of Jesus Christ,
      JOHAN PHILIPS BOEHM,
      Reformed Minister in Pennsylvania.
Witpen Township, Philadelphia County,
  Pennsylvania, December 12, 1746.

[XLIII. MR. BOEHM SENDING THE MINUTES OF THE COETUS OF 1748, NOVEMBER 21, 1748.[312]]

Very Reverend Christian Synods of North and South Holland and Very Reverend Classis of Amsterdam, Devout Church Fathers:—

To the Very Reverend Christian Synods and the Very Reverend Classis of Amsterdam your most submissive and humble fellow-servant sends herewith most obediently the minutes of the second Coetus of our Reformed churches in Pennsylvania, held on September 28, 1748, conformable to the unanimous resolution of the Reverend Coetus (as can be seen in the 11th article) in printed form.

From them the Reverend Christian Synods and the Reverend Classis of Amsterdam will see, it is hoped, that we thought of nothing else but to keep our still weak but true Church in this land in the pure doctrine, to govern it in peace and harmony, so that by its spread the name of God might be glorified and the kingdom of Jesus, our dearest and most perfect Saviour, be enlarged.

But with regard to Do. Rieger's excuse in article 3rd, concerning that which I consider as the chief and most necessary thing, in which special caution is required in this wretched country, so full of sects, we submit the same to the devout and most careful judgment of the Reverend Christian Synods and the Reverend Classis of Amsterdam, awaiting your kind reply and instruction regarding it.

As regards the signing of the minutes of the Reverend Coetus by his Reverence [Mr. Rieger] as secretary, this was impossible, as his residence is so far away from mine, for he resides in Cannastocka [Conestoga]. Moreover, I thought that, as he excused himself from accepting and subscribing to the above mentioned main point, he would hesitate to sign the entire minutes in which this point is incorporated, because he would thereby contradict himself, hence it was omitted.

In the meantime the Reverend Christian Synods and the Reverend Classis of Amsterdam may regard the minutes as entirely credible and sufficient, inasmuch as all the other

---

[312] Original German letter in the archives at The Hague, 74, I, 49.

reverend brethren and ministers who were present signed it with their own hands, as did also the elders whom they had with them and who are named in the minutes, not one of them having raised the least objection. I am ready to send over, on demand, the original which is kept here.

Meanwhile his Reverence, Do. Slatter, had gone to Lancaster, and preached there November 13th, and I [preached] for him in Philadelphia, where I stayed until the 16th, on account of the printing [of the minutes].

When Do. Slatter came home on the 15th, his Reverence said that he was commissioned to sign Do. Rieger's name as secretary, but it was too late, as the printer had completed his work.

Regarding Do. Weiss, neither he himself nor any of the elders of his three congregations, namely Old and New Goschenhoppen and Great Swamp, appeared. I do not know what was the reason.[313]

As to the case of Mr. Lischy, mentioned in article 4, he has reserved to himself the right to send his confession of faith to his Reverence, Do. Slatter. For my part, I have good hope that he will be in the future a faithful fellow-laborer in our true Church. May God, the only searcher of hearts, give him his blessing.

The heart-rending and most deplorable case of Do. Hochreutner, our dearly beloved and much esteemed brother, I shall not touch upon here, because Do. Slatter will describe it at length, he being better able to do so, having full knowledge of it. I content myself with saying that he lost his life by an unfortunate gun-shot in Do. Slatter's house in Philadelphia.[314]

---

[313] The copy of a letter of Weiss to Schlatter, dated December 12, 1748, is on file in the archives at The Hague, in which Weiss excuses his absence because of sickness.

[314] The tragic death of Rev. John Jacob Hochreutner was noticed in Saur's Paper, *Pennsylvanische Berichte,* under date November 16, 1748. He writes: "John Jacob Hochreutner, student of theology, born in St. Gall, Switzerland, was called as Reformed pastor to Pennsylvania. He arrived this fall at Philadelphia and was lately appointed pastor at Lancaster. When he was told that he would find a congregation of rough and insolent people, not at all broken in, he answered: 'I wish I were a woodchopper.' His congregation sent a horse for him to Philadelphia. He intended to travel to Lancaster in company with

It was assuredly a hard blow for our Reformed Church in Pennsylvania, and a still greater trial for the old and young members of the body of Jesus in our true Church. The ways of God are wonderful and always holy.

This is what I was ordered to send to the Reverend Christian Synods and the Reverend Classis of Amsterdam. I have done it according to my duty and the best of my ability.

Imploring our omnipotent, faithful God and heavenly Father upon my knees to preserve with His grace and blessing His true Church in this dangerous land against all wicked and false laborers, to support it by His omnipotence, and graciously to keep it by His providence, which is inscrutable, that it may be enlarged to the honor of His name. Amen.

To the same God who helps all those that trust in him and to the Word of His grace, your most submissive and humble fellow-servant in Christ Jesus commends the Reverend Christian Synods and the Reverend Classis of Amsterdam, as our godly Church Fathers, your devout persons, families and holy service. With heart and soul I wish you blessing, life and the eternal crown for your great toil and the Christian care and solicitude, which you show for our still feeble and dependent

the ordinary post on October 13th. But at the appointed hour he was found dead in his room, booted and spurred, the shotgun at his side. A shot had passed through the left breast and the bullet lay flat against the shoulder blade, near the skin. There was no suspicion that he intended to shoot himself. The ramrod was not entirely in its place, hence it is supposed that he wanted to pull out the rod or push it back. There was found on his person a written sermon, which he had intended to preach two days later. It had as its text the divine call to the young Samuel (I Sam. 3). Report has it that he had a good character, also a certain degree of piety and had made a good beginning in the Christian life."

Schlatter, in his *Journal*, states: "A gun which, when he was yet in the ship, he had loaded with a ball, which he now attempted to extract without having the necessary means to accomplish it, exploded in his hands, and pierced his body so that he lay dead in my room when my wife and maid-servant came in to inform him that an elder with a horse was ready at the door to take him away"! The sermon, which Schlatter found in his pocket, he had printed, "agreeably to the solicitations of many," under the appropriate title, "The Swan Song." It was translated and published by Dr. J. H. Dubbs in the *Reformed Quarterly Review* for July, 1886.

but true Reformed Church and all its faithful servants. We commend ourselves with our whole Church and faithful fellow-servants (next to God who is all in all) to the Reverend Christian Synods and the Reverend Classis of Amsterdam for their continued fatherly and Christian affection, care and solicitude.

Calling myself in all humility the most submissive, humble and obedient servant of the Reverend Christian Synods of North and South Holland and of the Reverend Classis of Amsterdam.

JOHANN PHILIPS BOEHM,
The first burden-bearer in all Pennsylvania, now merely pastor of the newly organized and still small congregation of Witpen in Philadelphia County, p. t. Coetus Praeses.
Witpen Township, Philadelphia County,
November 21, 1748.

[XLIV. MR. BOEHM TO A CLASSICAL COMMISSIONER, NOVEMBER 22, 1748.[315]]

Very Reverend and Very Learned, Devout and Much Honored Sir and Gracious Patron:—

From your Reverence I cannot conceal my hearty grief, because I was assured by Do. Schlatter almost two years ago, at the time of his arrival here, that our last letters from Pennsylvania had been received by the Reverend Church Fathers. Their answer would have been brought along by him [Schlatter], if his departure had not been so hurried, but it was promised that it would follow at the next opportunity. Thus far, however, I have seen nothing of it.[316] Hence, I fear that the old servant and his burdensome work in the service of the Lord, performed so laboriously, will at last be forgotten entirely. Nevertheless, I shall meanwhile co-operate faithfully,

---

[315] The original German letter of Boehm is in the Classical archives at Amsterdam.

[316] The letter, for which Boehm was waiting so patiently, must have come in the course of December, 1748, for it caused the next letter of Boehm.

and with the grace of God, as long as I am able, I shall not cease to show my faithfulness before God and my devout Church Fathers, until I am ordered to stop.

Herewith I transmit to the Very Reverend Classis of Amsterdam the things that have taken place in our Reformed churches. I did not know how to do it better than to entrust it to your Reverence, to send it to its proper place. I ask earnestly that your Reverence will deem your humble fellow-servant worthy to gladden him with a short, sealed letter.

Commending your Reverence and all the faithful servants of God, together with all their families and holy service to God and the Word of His grace, and myself to your affectionate and kind favor as also to your powerful intercession, I am,

Very Reverend Sir,
My much honored and highly esteemed Patron,
Your submissive and devoted,
JOH. PH. BOEHM.

Witpen, in Philadelphia County,
November 22, 1748.

[XLV. MR. BOEHM, TO A CLASSICAL COMMISSIONER, DECEMBER, 1748.[317]]

Very Reverend, Pious and Very Learned Sir:—

The letter sent by your Reverence to your most humble fellow-brother certainly exhausts all Christian love, favor and timely care.[317a] It emboldens me to submit to your Reverence privately and confidentially one or more questions and also to communicate to you several things, hoping that your Reverence will not take it amiss from your humble fellow-worker, and if he fails in anything pardon it and supply him with better information which he will receive with obedient submission, hence

(1). Inasmuch as I see at the end of Do. Slatter's in-

---

[317] This letter of Boehm is also in the Classical archives.

[317a] This letter from Amsterdam must have reached Pennsylvania after November 22, 1748, the date of the preceding letter of Boehm, for at that time it had not yet come to hand.

structions, that, after his Reverence has brought all the things committed to him in order, within the space of half a year, he shall hold a Coetus (N. B. his arrival here took place on August 27, 1746,) which he did at the end of the month of September, 1747, at which meeting he presided, according to instruction. After the lapse of a year a second Coetus was held. What transpired then can be seen in the Coetus Acts which were obediently sent over to you. Now, does Do. Slatter's commission still retain its authority? (This seems to be implied in Art. IV of the Coetus Protocol, referring to the transmission of Lischy's confession of faith, which contradicts the same [protocol art. III] and in several other items, especially in art. XII, where the same claim is made). Or shall everything relating to the administration of the Reformed churches in Pennsylvania be automatically transferred to the whole Coetus? That would be for the best interest of our churches and also the safest plan. For, if such an important matter be left in the power of one man only, things are often done with a bias and not in the right way. Moreover, such procedure is involved in his [Schlatter's] instructions, because, after the first Coetus and after handing in his report, he has the liberty to select as his congregation *one of those which were organized by him,* where he shall be installed and which he shall serve as long as it pleases his Reverence. Accordingly, his Reverence is like any other of his fellow-brethren.

Now, although I handed over and surrendered the principal congregation in Philadelphia to his Reverence, out of respect to the Reverend Christian Synods and out of love to his Reverence (yet with a certain reservation, as the enclosed copy of my testimonial from them[318] will show, which will also prove how I acted with this congregation when it was in need and how I managed it), nevertheless, I hope that his Reverence, Do. Slatter, will not be considered more than any other of his brethren, incorporated into the Reverend Coetus, and that he will be a regular pastor, otherwise it will not contribute to our peace in the future.

[318] This document has apparently not been preserved. At least it has not been found thus far.

(2). Inasmuch as Do. Rieger, according to the third item in the minutes of our Coetus refused to accept the most important and principal point, and as there are many other things which make it as clear as daylight that he is not sound and orthodox in our pure Reformed doctrine, must he still be president, because he was elected as the next one, and can he have seat and voice in our Coetus? Or should the Reverend Coetus, for just and sufficient reasons, elect another faithful and submissive fellow-brother for this position?

Likewise, what should be done with Do. Weiss, who, as I have learned for certain, received the invitation to the Coetus and yet neither he himself appeared nor did he send any of his elders,[319] for I learned of one of them that his Reverence had said nothing to any one concerning it? Especially because his Reverence has not complied with his duty, involved in the third point of the Coetus minutes, and has not signed this declaration.

(3). Regarding Mr. Lischy [I wish to say that] although, through his beautiful confession, made before the Coetus, he won my heart, so that, as the Lord liveth, I mean it well with him and rejoice over him in my soul, yet I cannot forbear mentioning to your Reverence how it was with him formerly. Because I had called him a Herrnhuter, he had offered at many places to prove me an evident liar, for he did not want to be anything else than a Reformed minister from Switzerland. When the people called him to account and convicted him [of falsehood], he said: 'I had called him a Herrnhuter, but he was no Herrnhuter, he was a Swiss, hence I was a liar,' etc. Again, at several places where the people did not want to trust him he swore saying that God might depart from him and the sun shine on him no more, if he were a Herrnhuter, and when he could deny it no longer he extricated himself with the above answer. But inasmuch as Lischy was an extreme and corrupt Zinzendorfian, my soul rejoices all the more over the great grace of God which he experienced and I do not deny that he has captivated my heart and I look indeed for his faithfulness and care in behalf of our Church, for he revealed to me on the 2nd of November last in Germantown, that Do.

---

[319] Weiss sent a letter of excuse to Schlatter. See note 313.

Rieger before the Coetus had tried to make an agreement with him, proposing that when they should come to the Coetus, they would endeavor to make an altogether new Church Order, so that a member who wanted his child baptized in infancy could have it baptized, and whoever wanted it first to grow up and reach years of discretion should be permitted to do so and if one wanted it to remain unbaptized, he might have it that way, for this was a land where it could be done, etc. This he [Lischy] told as a warning that we should be on our guard concerning Rieger. But I report all to you in confidence and with the hope that he [Lischy] is really sincere, although I cannot search men's hearts and cannot at present understand his possible motives. However, I am so simple-minded as to believe that in view of these facts it would be better (not in order to injure him but to test his sincerity still more) to proceed slowly with him until from those whom he serves in his Gospel ministry sufficient and official testimonials regarding him have been secured. All of which I submit to your Reverence's wise consideration and I shall look forward to further information.

Do. Slatter very hastily and urgently insisted last year at the first Coetus that Lischy should have a seat and that Coetus should write [to Holland] in his behalf, in order that he be recognized as a Reformed minister. But I was absolutely opposed to it and delayed action, all the more because I saw that several intelligent men disapproved of it very much together with me. As a result I caused considerable ill-feeling towards myself, but I did not mind that, because I never look for my own honor and profit, but I care only for the advantage and the best interests of our Church in this country as far as I am able with the grace of God.

The same thing took place this year in the Reverend Coetus, when a man, with the name of Wuertz,[320] applied to

---

[320] John Conrad Wirtz (Wuertz) was born November 30, 1706, in the Canton of Zurich, Switzerland. He left Zurich in October, 1734, together with the colony of Rev. Maurice Goetschy, whose daughter, Anna, he married. He arrived with the party in Philadelphia, May 29, 1735; became school teacher at Old Goshenhoppen, later he taught school for a Mennonite congregation in Conestoga Township. He began preaching about 1742. From September, 1742, to December,

us. He is also very likely known to you. When I, as president, asked him what his desire was, he submitted his case as follows: It was well known that he had served his congregations as a preacher for a long time, hence he desired to request the Reverend Coetus to assist him in securing his ordination as a minister. When I asked him to retire and then inquired of every one regarding him, not one member of the Coetus was in favor of taking up the case of such a man, who was well known to many of them, except Do. Slatter, who remained silent, but who during the previous year had worked with me in his behalf. But because I had learned long ago what a disorderly tramp [Landläufer] he had been, who administered the sacraments without permission and against all admonitions, I did not consent to Do. Slatter and prevented such action.[321] Among others one of the elders arose in the Coetus and said that there was a place up in the country, along the Susquehanna, where the people wanted him as their schoolmaster. There he might do well, but he insisted on being a preacher. Then he [Wuertz] was called in again and this place was proposed to him, but he answered very little. Do. Slatter, however, said, how can the man get there? He does not even have enough money for his traveling expenses and he asked whether the Coetus would be satisfied if he give him of the Reiff money five pounds as his traveling expenses. I refused to have anything to do with that. His Reverence had settled that affair, had taken the money and would himself have to give an account of it. This was also the opinion of most of the others, who said that they did not want to have

---

1743, he was pastor at Egypt; from 1745 to 1749 he was preaching at Saucon, Springfield and the Forks of the Delaware. September 27, 1750, he applied to the Presbyterian Synod of New York for admission. He was received as a probationer by the Presbytery of New Brunswick, September 3, 1751, and ordained by this Presbytery as pastor of Rockaway, N. J., June 5, 1752, which he served till 1761. He was dismissed by the Presbytery, October 21, 1761, to become the pastor of the Reformed Church at York. This he served from May, 1762, to September, 1763. He died at York, September 21, 1763. See Harbaugh, *Fathers*, Vol. I, pp. 388-394; Good, *History*, p. 253-255.

[321] The Presbyterians thought evidently better of Wuertz than Boehm, who was prejudiced against him and forgot that he had once been in the same plight.

anything to do or say with regard to that money. Nevertheless, Do. Slatter gave him that amount, although he did not think it was necessary to insert it as an item in the minutes, to which I assented for the sake of peace. As far as I am concerned, Reverend Sir, I have just reasons for refraining from having anything to do with that money or being in any way responsible for it. For this affair was concluded by Do. Slatter without me, by calling in only Do. Weis, and by settling with the insolent Reiff. It is enough that I have been so shamefully insulted because of it. But, for the sake of peace, I shall be silent about this affair, except when I shall be asked regarding it. Then I shall state the truth according to my conscience, as before God.

SIGNATURE OF WUERTZ FROM THE EGYPT RECORD

But in order to report a little more about the case of Wuertz, let me say that he came to this country with the old Goetschi,[322] who had been a minister in Switzerland, in the Canton of Zurich, and had left that country because of adultery. This man had a daughter, whom this Wuertz married across the sea. She had a child who died on the ocean, but he came to this country. Meanwhile he was accepted at Old Goschen-

[322] This is the Rev. Maurice Goetschy, who was born in 1686. On December 4, 1702, he matriculated in the Latin school at Zurich. In 1710, he entered the ministry, becoming, in 1712, assistant pastor at Bernegg, in the Rhine valley, and in 1720, pastor at Saletz. He was deposed in 1731. He left Zurich, with a colony of 400 emigrants in October 1734, which landed at Philadelphia, May 29, 1735. Rev. Maurice Goetchy died on the day following his landing. His funeral was held in the Presbyterian church in Philadelphia, according to a letter of his son, John Henry Goetschy, dated July 21, 1735.

hoppen to teach school. But they soon got tired of him and sent him away. Afterwards the Mennonites at Cannastocka [Conestoga] accepted him for the same work, but he was dismissed by them just as quickly, etc. Many other things may be passed over, because from these, which are true and known to all men, it can be sufficiently inferred how matters stand with him and that I am not unjustly opposed to him.

They try indeed to move me always with these words: 'He is a very poor man, out of pity for him we ought to help him to get a living. He is way up in the woods, far away from us, he can hardly do any damage'. But what does that mean? We must, I believe, consider the welfare of the congregations, which belong to our Church in Pennsylvania, although they be situated far away from us, and not regard them any the less worthy of a good and faithful teacher than those served by ourselves, so that our godly Church Fathers in time may see with hearty joy their great work prosper among all the scattered souls which hunger for the Word of God and that they may not have this experience, of seeing such persons have a seat in and preside over our Coetus.

It is indeed true that if able men could be secured in this country, the heavy traveling expenses [from Europe] could be saved, which would be a great joy to me. But that we should recommend persons who have no ability as suitable, I do not believe to be acceptable to the Reverend Christian Synods and the Reverend Classis of Amsterdam, nor should we be responsible for it. I believe that such people ought to be left alone, if we cannot help them soon with regular ministers, until such congregations see the prosperity and growth of other congregations, which have regular ministers and thereby become eager for a better condition than the one in which they are and also become willing to offer and promise a reliable salary. Then the dear Lord will find means to help them.

I cannot reveal to your Reverence with my poor pen the heartfelt joy which I experienced when I saw the two reverend brethren sent over to us, Messrs. Hochreutner and Bartholomie.[323] I would have liked to see one of them relieve me of my

---

[323] John Jacob Hochreutner was born April 27, 1721, at St. Gall, Switzerland. He received his education at St. Gall; was licensed there

LETTER OF 1748 449

long journey to Falkner Schwam and Providentz, for which there was some prospect, but it was represented to me whether I would not prefer seeing the shepherdless congregations, which had no ministers helped first of all, afterwards I might be relieved. I should not begrudge them this blessing and have a little patience. The dear Lord would perhaps soon send more help. Whereupon I willingly resolved (because I saw such an earnest desire for a regular minister, especially among the Tulpehocken congregations) to continue working under the yoke which I had borne so long. This continued for a short time when a dear man, my hearty and friendly fellow-brother, Mr. John Philip Leydich[324] arrived. Then it was found suitable and he was also willing to take my place. Hence at the Coetus of this present year, just as Do. Hochreutner accepted his call to Lancaster, Do. Bartholomie to Dolpihacken, so also Do. Leydich at the same time his call to Falckner Schwam and Provi-

---

December 16, 1743; commissioned for Pennsylvania November 15, 1747; was appointed as pastor at Lancaster, but shot himself accidentally October 14, 1748. His introductory sermon, which he intended to preach at Lancaster was published by Schlatter in 1748, as a quarto of 15 pages, printed by Johann Boehm at Philadelphia. For a reproduction of the title page see Dr. Dubbs' *Reformed Church in Pennsylvania*, p. 159.

John Dominicus Carolus Bartholomaeus was born December 13, 1723, at Heidelberg, of Catholic parents; was educated at Heidelberg and at Franecker, Holland; licensed September 4, 1747, by the Classis of Franecker; ordained and commissioned for Pennsylvania November 15, 1747; came to Pennsylvania, in company of Hochreutner; installed as pastor of Tulpehocken, October 16, 1748; officiated there 1748-1752; in the latter year he lost his mind; was for many years confined to a hospital in Philadelphia, where he died July 28, 1768.

[324] John Philip Leydich was born at Girkhausen, Westphalia, April 28, 1715, the son of the Rev. Leonhard L. Leydich; was commissioned by the Synod of South Holland in July, 1748; arrived at Philadelphia September 15, 1748; was installed as pastor of Falkner Swamp and Providence, October 16, 1748; officiated as pastor of Falkner Swamp, 1748-1765; at Providence, 1748-1784; at Vincent, 1753-1765; at Coventry, 1768-1784; at Upper Milford and Salisbury, 1766-1771; at Pottstown, 1770-1784. He died after a long and useful ministry, January 14, 1784, and was buried in what is known as Lydig's Burying Ground. For the inscription on his tomb-stone see Dotterer, *Perkiomen Region*, I, 54; for his history see Dotterer, *Historical Notes*, pp. 2f; 50f; 59f.

denz. Then I was commissioned by the Reverend Coetus to install Do. Leydich and Do. Bartholomie in their service at their several places. Do. Slatter assumed the duty to install Do. Hochreutner at Lancaster. I carried out my commission on the 16th of October at Falckner Schwam and on the 23rd of October at Dolpihacken. The commission of Do. Slatter was not carried out through the calamity [befalling Do. Hochreutner].

One other thing, Reverend Sir! When Do. Hochreutner and Do. Bartholomie arrived here by way of England they brought from there half a sheet of an English print,[325] which was shown to me, but was not given into my hands. In it I saw that the Reverend ministers of our true religion in London had very touchingly presented our needy condition and asked for charitable gifts, whereupon also (according to Mr. Slatter's statement to me) 90 guineas came in, of which they gave to each of the two brethren 30 guineas for their journey. The other 30 guineas they had kept back for a later occasion.

But I saw in it also that the old servant, who for more than 20 years has worked so laboriously and has suffered so severely and (because of the poverty existing among the sheep) almost at his own expense, surrendering to this work his best years which he owed to his own family, laboring thus to his own detriment in worldly things,—I saw that he was not even deemed worthy enough to have his name mentioned in it, but, referring to the sheperdless sheep, it was stated: "and about the year 1720, they had but one who was a layman".

Now, Reverend Sir! I do not seek any temporal honor, for I esteem it lightly. It is enough for me, if I have the praise of my master, Jesus Christ, who knows my heart. However, because I fear that I shall be forgotten in the distribution of the charitable gifts, which I need very much for the support of my family, since I have served so long and faithfully almost without any salary, I often feel sad, yet the Lord will provide and grant me my modest share. But I saw, alongside of the well recommended names of Do. Hochreutner and Do. Bartholomie, especially the name of Do. Slatter with

---

[325] No copy of this English, eight-page circular, has thus far come to light.

this remark, that all the charitable gifts could be safely sent to the Rev. Mr. Slatter (if I understood it correctly in my reading over it very rapidly). About this Do. Slatter expressed himself as follows: "Do you, my brother, not think that this should be a great joy to me, that I am thus highly commended and that all the charitable gifts shall be sent and entrusted to me"?

But, my Reverend Sir, allow me to pour out my heart to you in the confident assurance that you will receive it as well as your most humble fellow-servant means it from the bottom of his heart for the peace of the Church in the future and for the preservation of a God-pleasing harmony among the brethren of our most holy faith, and let me make known to you my sincere opinion, but with due deference.

Would it not be better in order to avoid all suspicion, discord and disagreement and to prevent and cut off every seduction of the brethren by the evil spirit (for if the least discord among ministers is noticed in this country, there is no end of slander among the sects and even the church members take offense at it, so that he whom it concerns experiences great annoyance in his congregations), if all the charitable gifts, which are to be given as salary or to the advancement of our still needy churches in this country, were consigned to the Coetus, which even the President, without the presence of a designated number of his fellow-brethren, could not open, by which all trouble could be forever avoided? For if this duty were imposed upon me, I would decline it and not aim for this, that my brethren would have to beg for that which had been contributed as charitable gifts for their pressing need. I am also of the conviction that in such a case one should not be interested nor have an exalted opinion of oneself. All of which I submit to your Reverence for your devout consideration, according to the wisdom and love granted to you by God and for our peace, such as is well-pleasing to God.

Now, I shall not conceal from your Reverence what has tended to our discord. When Do. Slatter was installed in the congregation at Philadelphia, I described to his Reverence how everything had proceeded so peacefully thus far, because I had conducted everything according to the Church Order, established among us, and I expressed the hope that his Reverence would continue in this established order, for his own peace and welfare. But I received this answer: "I have my own Church Order (that was the one of St. Gall) and is not everyone at liberty to make a Church Order. I told him that it would be an innovation, to which he answered, that he had been told orally in Holland, it was left to his own discretion. When he would come to this country he should be governed by the congregations and should find out what each congregation preferred. If one congregation wanted to have the Swiss order, it could have it, or another the Dutch order likewise so and if any congregation wanted the Palatinate order, he should let them have it. I answered him, that it was difficult for me to believe that, for that would not make our congregations in Pennsylvania real, intimate sisters, but only stepsisters, yet I was forced to believe it.

Meanwhile he [Schlatter] uses constantly his St. Gall Church Order, and, because in its formulas of baptism and communion as well as in the marriage formula and the installation of elders, it appears as strange and unusual to the people, I have often been asked with surprise and disapproval, why this was done, but I have never given much of an answer to this question. Hence it would be useful and very fine, if we were given the instruction to adhere only to all the formulas of unity, which are not only in the Palatinate Church Order (of which there are a few copies in this country) but also in almost all our Reformed hymn books, which I also signed with my own hand when I received the holy ordination in New York on November 23, 1729. Nor can I forget the duties which I then assumed, for the section referring to this reads as follows:

"Also in reference to the Church Order sent by the Pennsylvania brethren to the Reverend Classis, and by that body approved, and now enlarged, as above, that the newly chosen members of the consistory shall, from year to year, before entering upon their duties, for the surer performance of their engagements, subscribe all this,—namely to adhere strictly to the Heidelberg Catechism, the Formulas of Unity and the [Acts of the] Synod of Dort. And in order that every one, in his office or station, may obey as far as possible the foregoing rules, these church-ordinances as now revised by the Reverend

Classis of Amsterdam, shall publicly be read before the churches yearly, when a new consistory is chosen and ordained".

After the commissioned elders had signed this, I subscribed to it also, as follows:

"So also in testimony of all this, I, Do. Johann Philips Boehm, do solemnly declare that all that herein concerns me, I will, with God's help, perform to the best of my ability, subscribing my name hereto, at New York, November 18, 1729.

"JOHANN PHILIPS BOEHM".

From this I have no intention to depart in the least point, just as little as I shall refuse to show the most submissive obedience, if the Reverend Christian Synods and the Reverend Classis of Amsterdam, as our devout Church Fathers, shall add anything to it for the best interest of our true [Reformed] churches in Pennsylvania.

To this end I believe, without wishing to dictate, that it would be very useful and good if as many Palatinate Church Orders could be sent to this country as there are congregations, that they might always remain in the churches (or at least in the hands of each minister) and I doubt not that every congregation, if they cannot be sent as gifts, would without question pay for them.

If we were directed to these formulas of unity, it would have its good results and this undoubted dispute would be made impossible in the future, nor would it be necessary to speak of that which is past and thus rouse displeasure.

Your Reverence was pleased to write that the congregations are now offering larger salaries than formerly. This is true. But what is the cause? Your Reverence will consider that the former offer was made years ago, while at present some congregations, to which people have moved, have become again as strong as formerly and have now more means and are able to do more. Besides there are now congregations in places where there were none formerly. How I went to work at that time when Do. Dorsius asked me (because he was not able and made all kinds of excuses) I shall now relate to your Reverence.

I took this upon me even in the most severe winter season

and traveled (as can be seen in the "Specification",[326] to be found among the Pennsylvania papers) from one place to another, gathering almost everywhere the members of the congregations (of whom there were in many places not one fourth as many as there are now) and announced to them the pious intention of the Reverend Church Fathers, the only condition being that they wanted to know how much every congregation was willing and able to give to the fixed salary of a minister, and, if they wanted to have a regular minister in their congregation, they themselves should make an estimate. After having done this, they had to give, in my presence, to their elders and deacons full authority to sign this statement in their name, that it was their will and command and would surely be kept, which, in case of failure, could have been obtained through the help of the civil authorities, for, if it stands on such a footing, no congregation would allow a claim to be made. Thus the deacons learn to admonish the members (in accordance with Art. 15 of the constitution) especially those who are still being added to the congregations.

That I still have this in mind and aim for it, can be seen by your Reverence from the 7th item in the minutes of the Coetus, but I go still farther! It might happen that a minister would go away on a journey or die, in such a case the congregation is entitled to call another pastor. If at that time the congregation would not do the right thing and their minister would get a call to another place and leave them (which no one could take ill of him) they would be deprived of their minister. Before they would allow this to take place (especially if they liked their minister), they would rather do their best to keep him. Thus the best interests of our churches here could be secured by and by with love and without any odious compulsion. Moreover, if we proceeded cautiously through such a process, our pious Church Fathers could in a few years be relieved from the heavy burden of securing a gracious addition to our salaries, if not altogether at least partly and in time fully in the congregations now really in existence. And if, contrary to our expectation, obstinacy and wickedness manifested themselves, it would be natural that they would have to pay him

---

[326] See pp. 285-298.

who left them the arrears in his salary, to which they could be legally compelled through their [written] obligation. All of which I regarded formerly, according to my simple way of thinking, as very useful, and I still consider it so at this present time. But I wish, that, in order to labor still more and better in this work of the Lord, all serviceable information might be given to me, which, from the bottom of my heart, I shall always receive humbly but also gladly and willingly and act accordingly, and, even, if I were not the president, I would fraternally assist you and willingly serve you.

Now, Reverend Sir, let me not forget my own small congregation, newly organized, nor myself, but let me give you a simple recital as to why it was begun.

When Do. Slatter had come to this country and had made his visit to the country congregations, according to his commission, he stopped with me on his return.[327] Then I gave him to understand that I was afraid, that, in view of my years and the many fatigues which I had borne, I would not be able to stand it much longer, as I could well feel; hence I desired heartily, that my great burden, borne so long, might be lessened, for at the time I was almost incapacitated from work.

His Reverence asked me to make a proposition with regard to it. Then I explained to him, that, as he knew, Schipbach had scattered of itself and was no more, but that at Old Goschenhoppen, four miles above, a union church had been built with the Lutherans. From that place to Germantown was 24 miles, where no services were held. Almost in the center was my own home, and I knew that round about me Reformed people, desirous for their own true worship, were living.

Then I asked him, whether he did not regard it as advisable to establish a Reformed congregation in this district? Yet with this condition, that it should become one of the congregations standing under the supervision of the devout Church Fathers in Holland, so that it might not be abandoned after my death, otherwise it would not be worth while to organize it, in view of the few days of my life.

[327] This visit of Schlatter in Whitpain took place on October 20, 1746; see *Life of Schlatter,* p. 141.

But if he regarded it advisable and knew of a plan for it and if he thought that I would be supported in it, so that I could live according to my need, then I would like to be more quiet in my old age and would be satisfied with this, at first small, congregation and thus spend my life in the service of the Lord. Then his Reverence assured me, that I would not be abandoned, and that he would mention this case as favorably as possible in his report. He also found, that it was necessary and very advantageous to plant a congregation in this district, because of the great distance from other places, and he thought that in time means could be found to take care of this congregation after my death.[328] For the time would come when Philadelphia would want to have its own minister. Then, when Germantown also would get its minister, it could be so arranged that he could preach on certain Sundays to the congregation at Witpen, which is a distance of 10 miles on a good road. Thus it could be supplied after my death.

To this end he [Schlatter] came and preached on the 3rd of February, 1747, in my house[329] but it was cold and only few people assembled. However, we elected three elders. Do. Slatter then wrote down what each one was willing to give to the annual salary. It amounted to 6 pounds and 3 shillings. Do. Slatter declared this to be too little. A congregation ought to give at least 15 pounds, otherwise he could not report it as a congregation. I pitied the souls who were sad about this, for although they were few, yet they were dear and eager for salvation. I asked him to report them, and I offered to serve them for 15 pounds [annually]. Then his Reverence continued and organized the congregation fully. I pledged myself to conduct divine services regularly every two weeks, which I do heartily, and if I am at home and have no other religious service elsewhere, I preach for them every Sunday. I then advised my brethren in order to increase the salary somewhat,

---

[328] Schlatter himself supplied Witpen, after Boehm's death. Thus on November 1, 1750, he says: "I traveled sixteen miles from here to Witpen—a congregation which I am accustomed to visit once a month since the death of Do. Boehm—where, on this visit, I administered the Holy Supper to thirty-six members." See *Life of Schlatter*, p. 194.

[329] For the early history of the Witpen (now Boehm's) Church, see pp. 75-77.

since we have no poor [to take care of] in this country (for all the poor must be supported by the township to which they belong, according to the order of the government) to call our alms a contribution and use it for the salary of the minister, which they approved (Do. Slatter likewise) and resolved to act accordingly. During the last year it amounted to three pounds and some shillings.

If the strong congregations in this country were without debts on account of the building of the churches, this would be excellent help, and they would be able at many a place to contribute six times as much as now, which in time may be hoped for.

We at Witpen built meanwhile a little stone church on an acre of land, which was bought and well insured. On the inside the church is 30 feet long and 27 feet wide. According to agreement I can apply 40 pounds to this purpose, which money I had collected in New York as early as October, 1735, intended for a church lot for the now scattered congregation at Schipbach. But the church has cost in reality more than 70 pounds. It is well made, with durable walls and roof, door and shutters. It is still without windows and inside devoid of all neessary furniture, so that more than 50 pounds may well be needed. But we cannot help ourselves, as there are but few of us and without any means. Hence, we would rather go into the church as it is, as we have done throughout the whole summer, and sit on the bare floor or on logs of wood, rather than make debts, because if we did that I would have to suffer most. For to have debts of such a kind in a congregation, especially if there are poor people, is too hard a thing, as I have already experienced at Falckner Schwam and at almost all other places.

We can see this now especially at Philadelphia. There they began three years ago to build a church upon a very expensive but beautiful place, bought with borrowed money. As their pastor at the time I laid the cornerstone of this building.[330]

---

[330] This was a six-cornered church. With reference to it, Mr. Schlatter has made the following entry in the church record: "On the 6th of December [1747], that is, on the second Sunday of Advent, the writer of this, Michael Schlatter, pastor here, preached for the first time in the six-cornered stone church of the Reformed congregation on Race Street, from the words of David in Psalm 65:5, with

We intended to begin very modestly, because we had no means. Meanwhile Do. Slatter arrived and became their minister, as has already been related. He at once took up the work in an expensive manner and it will be an exceptionally beautiful church. But what is gained? They have debts on their place and borrowed money on interest, so that their actual debts, according to their own statement, amount to more than 600 pounds, although they themselves have contributed a considerable sum. Meanwhile the workmen (as is proper) want to be paid and now they must borrow more money on interest, if they do not want the workmen to handle them too severely. For the English people make short work in case of debts. They seize the people who have put them to work (these are twelve men, in part not well-to-do) and who are under bond, and throw them into prison very quickly.

Now they want to make Do. Slatter responsible for it, who had advised them to do so and had promised to write to Switzerland and everywhere else for contributions. But now they can see no evidence of an urgent appeal when they are deep in debt. This has caused his Reverence much worry and has given him much to contend with. As I know these people and am acquainted with their condition and manner of action, I cannot think otherwise than that there will be an exceedingly sad outcome,[331] unless they get vigorous help from outside and will thus be saved. Otherwise the result will not be good, which would grieve me in my soul, for the sake of his Reverence and my former, dear congregation. Therefore, I heartily invoke for myself, for my own as well as for all other con-

---

the divine grace and assistance. But the church was not yet plastered, and it had at the time neither gallery nor windows." In September, 1748, a Swedish traveler, Peter Kalm, visited Philadelphia. He gives the following description of this Reformed Church: "The German Reformed Church is built in the west, northwest part of the town, and looks like the church in the Ladugoord field near Stockholm. It is not yet finished, though for several years together the congregation has kept divine service in it." See Kalm's *Travels into North America*, Engl. Transl., Warrington, 1770, p. 41.

[331] The outcome was what Boehm feared, a quarrel. The financial difficulties, caused by the expensive church building, were one of the causes of the Schlatter-Steiner controversy. See Dr. Good's *History*, pp. 376-390.

gregations of our true Church in this country, the grace of our dear Lord and His compassionate blessing. Especially and above all proper care should be taken of the faithful shepherds, who otherwise must administer their office, at least for a while, in want of bodily food, because their sheep are at present still naked, yea some would not be able to endure it much longer.

May, therefore, the almighty and merciful God, who at last, after so much sighing and weeping, has heard those whom he knows, in so far at least that he turned the hearts of our devout Church Fathers to them, may He continue to do so, for they not only themselves, but by their powerful appeals also in our behalf among the pious and divinely blessed brethren of our faith, are able to accomplish the best results for us, their destitute Reformed children in Pennsylvania, which the Director of all pious hearts is now showing to His faithful servants and has made evident, by inclining them by His grace strongly, towards us. I shall constantly upon my knees, through humble prayer in thanksgiving and praise, implore the dear Lord, that, through the powerful operation of His Holy Spirit, He will continue to incline your hearts towards us. Consider moreover, that in all this holy work we have to do with Jesus, who is our only salvation, and who will accept that done unto His humblest brethren as done unto himself. We hope also, without any doubt and with firm faith, that the reward of all faithful servants of God, who labor diligently in this work of propagating the true Church of God, will be the eternal crown of glory in the blessed eternity, to the praise and honor of our God here and hereafter without ceasing.

Now, Reverend Sir, as I have referred above to the introduction of a number of innovations, in order that you may not think that I consider a harmful innovation something which is not such, I shall relate several to you, very simply, namely:

When Do. Slatter was hardly installed in Philadelphia, he did not even ask for the constitution and the church record which had been kept there thus far, for which reason I retained it in my hands, because I noticed that he was not willing to pay any regard to that which had been done, and for fear that some of the written agreements, embodied therein, might even be destroyed and also because I wanted to see what would be the outcome there. I determined to preserve it in some way, especially because the people in Philadelphia have thus far not given his Reverence a regular call. It would take too long to relate at length why this was omitted.

It was the order and custom in this congregation as in others to have four elders and two deacons in service, together with the minister, of whom every year two elders and one deacon passed out of service (if it was at all feasible) and two new elders and one deacon came in, according to the regulation of the constitution.

But his Reverence made the number at once twelve, of whom six were elders and six deacons, adding to those in office enough to make up that number. Then he installed them all anew, those who were in service as well as those newly elected. This he did in the Lutheran church, where his Reverence preached (I was present), using the following ceremony:

All of them had to stand in a row, he standing before them, reading (the installation service) and making a lengthy address to them. Then he laid his hands upon their heads, two and two at the same time, giving the one his right hand and to the other his left, etc. All of this was not in harmony with the formula in the Dutch Bible, to which I had been directed. Nor did I regard it as proper that the elders and deacons already in service were treated like the newcomers. That meant clearly to declare invalid and to despise the installation of the elders in office, which had been performed by me according to the formula in the Dutch Bible. However, as no one was present who thought about this matter, I kept quiet for the sake of peace, although I felt much grieved about it in my heart.

Moreover, (to pass by several other things) when Do. Leydich had accepted his call to Falkner Schwam and Providenz, after the Coetus had been held, where all present had obligated themselves (as can be seen in the minutes) to act according and adhere firmly to the Church Order (Do. Leydich was at that time staying in Germantown) Do. Slatter held the communion on October 9th, at Philadelphia. He asked Do. Leydich to assist him in it. The latter did not know the least about the order or the custom which had been followed in this country. Do. Slatter ordered him to hold up the cup with his outstretched arm during the reading of the liturgy while he did the same with the bread, holding it in one hand. Your Reverence can imagine what talk this caused among the people, for no Reformed member had ever seen a Reformed minister act in such a manner, except indeed the idolatrous masspriests, who lift up the monstrance in that way, when the people, who live in darkness, strike their breast.

Now, when Do. Leydich learned later on that this was here among us a strange innovation and a ceremony which none had ever seen and that he had been used to introduce it, I found him much displeased about this matter and very sad, when I installed him at Falckner Schwam on the 16th of October, as stated above. I also saw some elders there much dissatisfied. How I felt, especially because of the many strange remarks which I had to hear here and there about it, I leave to your Reverence to imagine.

Suppose even that there were places in this world where such things were customary, although we know of none, yet here in our true churches, which among the many confused sects are exposed to sufficient temptations through all kinds of strange ceremonies, such things ought to be carefully avoided and we should adhere to the usual order prescribed to us, which our sainted predecessors as regents of our pure Church introduced and which are, without question, modelled in harmony with the Word of God, and, in the fear of the Lord, we should continue with their constant observance.

1748, DECEMBER 2nd,

Mr. Lischy came to me to see me. He related that he had preached last Sunday at the Modenhrik [Muddy Creek], where there were two large, beautiful congregations. The people there were very zealous and steadfast in our Reformed religion and doctrine. He had supplied them thus far, but because of his manifold labors across the Susquehanna, among his own congregations, and because of the great distance, it was almost impossible for him to do so. They had, therefore, concluded to send two elders with him to his Reverence, Do. Leydich, at Falckner Schwam, who is 30 miles from Modenkrik, to learn whether Do. Leydich would take the trouble to visit them once a month on a weekday, in order that the congregations might be supplied until God would send more help. To this end they had been with Do. Leydich yesterday, who, after considering the question whether it was possible for him to do so, had consented. Furthermore, Do. Lischy related to me, that on his journey downwards he had been with Do. Rieger and other good friends at Lancaster, where he heard from several persons, that Do. Slatter, when he preached there on November 13th last, had insisted (as had been suggested to them of late) that they should give Mr. Rieger satisfaction regarding the things that had happened between Mr. Rieger and themselves.

Whereupon they demanded that they be shown anything in which they had offended him, and as long as that could not be done and as they themselves did not know of anything, there was no need of such an act. Moreover, they did not conceal from his Reverence that they would have nothing to do with Mr. Rieger, and, because he had intercourse with all kinds of sects, they could not regard him as a true Reformed man, much less as a Reformed minister and would not tolerate such a minister in their congregation. They would rather help themselves as well as they could, hoping that through the grace of God they would not be left helpless.

Further, Mr. Lischy related to me that he had spoken with Mr. Rieger in his home. He had told him that he had been present of late at the preaching services and the love feast of the Seventh Day Dunkers in their cloister. He had been touched with strange feelings. What good words they had spoken, what edifying discourses they had held, indeed what exceptionally pious people they were!

He also intended to put a child in this cloister to have it educated there. To that end he had to urge them very much until they consented to receive it. It was no easy matter, but finally he had received a letter from Peter Miller (this is the well known Miller, who long ago preached to the Reformed people in Pennsylvania and then went over to the Seventh Day Dunkers, was baptised in Dunker fashion and became such a disgrace). He [Rieger] gave Lischy the letter to read. In it Miller notified Rieger that he had resolved to receive his child into the cloister. A small room had already been gotten ready for it and some one had been appointed to have charge of the child. He could bring it when it suited him. He should bring only bedding along. The pleasure which Rieger showed made him [Lischy] think that he really took the child there this week. J. PH. BOEHM.

[XLVI. TITLE PAGE AND PREFACE TO THE CHURCH ORDER OF 1748.]

Church Order
of the Reformed Churches
in Pennsylvania
which
in the year 1725, was drawn up by D. Johan Philipp Boehm, then unanimously elected minister of the assembled members of the Reformed churches, read before the assembled members, considered as good and useful by all members and willingly accepted by them. After the election of the necessary elders and with their unanimous counsel handed for correction to the
Very Reverend and Very Learned Sirs,
The Corresponding Ministers of the Very Reverend Classis of
Amsterdam,
Gualterus Du Bois and Hericus Boel
of New York and
Vincentius Antonides of Long Island, who
transmitted it to the above named Very Reverend Classis of Amsterdam; recognized and permitted by the Reverend Assembly as good and lawful. Thereafter also established in the congregations then organized. Various Reformed congregations submitting to this Order have hitherto been governed in good peace.
But inasmuch as
the Coetus of the Reformed Churches in Pennsylvania, granted by the Very Reverend and Christian Synods of South and North Holland, at its last regular, annual session, held on September 28, 1748, in Philadelphia, recognized this Church Order, brought before it, as useful and salutary, the Coetus unanimously resolved to issue the same through public print for the profitable information of every member of the Reformed churches. To carry this resolution into effect, the whole Reverend Coetus entrusted it to
D. Johann Philipp Boehm, Minister at Falckner Schwam, Providenz and Witpen, p. t. Coetus Praeses.
Philadelphia, printed by Gotthard Armbriester, residing in Arch Street, 1748.

PREFACE.[332]

TO THE PIOUS AND BELOVED READER.

A lamp is not lighted and put under a bushel, but on a stand, and it shineth unto all that are in the house.

Thus speaketh the mouth of truth, our perfect Redeemer and Saviour, Jesus, Matthew, chapter V, verse 15.

As no kingdom or government can exist in this world, be it spiritual or temporal, without being directed by good and well regulated order, of which the Living Word tells us:

That God is a God of order and desires that everything be done orderly [1 Cor. 14:40].

Hence an order, instituted after the will of God, in spiritual as well as in temporal affairs, may justly be compared to a light.

Therefore, such a light and order, when once established, is not to be put under a bushel and remain hidden or obscured, but on a stand, to make it visible to all men, in order that such light may give light to all that are in the house, and that the same men, who are under such government and in such a congregation, where order ought to rule, may always see their obligation, remember their duties and be enabled, by the grace of God, to govern their life, conduct and conversation accordingly.

This is an indispensably necessary thing, since many a kingdom of this world has experienced much trouble and tribulation and even total destruction because of disorder and the wickedness and disregard of God's law, flowing from it, of which a terrible example is the city of Jerusalem, destroyed because of its great wickedness and disobedience. The same has been the experience of the Oriental churches in Asia, for which God, in His true, eternal love and grace, had set up on a stand the clear light of the Gospel of Jesus Christ, which,

---

[332] One copy of the Church Order is in the archives at The Hague, of which two photographic reproductions have been brought to this country. The other known copy is in the library of the Historical Society of Pennsylvania, 1300 Locust Street, Philadelphia.

BOEHM'S CONSTITUTION, PUBLISHED BY HIM IN 1748

however, refused to see with it, but through contempt and neglect left the way which our perfect Redeemer and Saviour had shown them with this light. Wherefore the just God, who, because of His righteousness, cannot leave persistent and obstinate sinners go unpunished, again overturned this clear light, so that now their descendants lie imprisoned in the darkness of the Mohammedan religion.

Now, dear people, it is sufficiently known to us all, why Pennsylvania was formerly a land in which no light of the Gospel of Jesus Christ was to be seen, until at last it pleased the merciful God to choose it, according to His eternal grace, in order to plant within it the Gospel of His Son; and hence he awakened men, granted them intelligence and wisdom to make provision that it be inhabited by Christian people. Thus it has had hitherto, by His blessing, such a growth, that it is wonderful to contemplate, and is still growing and increasing, under the blessing of God. This appears clearly from the time that the following Church Order was established to conduct our divine services orderly. For at that time it was of insignificant appearance, but now at this time it is much more favorably apparent what grace God has shown to us.

Especially since at the present time our merciful God has inclined the hearts of our devout Church Fathers in Holland, in the Very Reverend Christian Synods of South and North Holland and in the Very Reverend Classis of Amsterdam, to us and our destitute members, so that with a sanctified zeal they sought ways and means and found them at last, under the blessing of God (because it was not unknown to them, that I, as the first Reformed minister, ordained for the service of God in this country, was formerly alone, and in my weakness was unable to supply all because of the great extent of this country). For they sent us in the year 1746, at their own expense, the Rev. Michael Slatter, lately minister in St. Gall in Switzerland (who left everything there in order to help our churches here in Pennsylvania) as their commissioner. They furthermore, very liberally, offered to give us their assistance, according to the best of their ability, to help and support our Reformed churches here. He (Slatter) was also ordered to establish a regular, annual Coetus with the ministers now in this country, and with their assistance, which his Reverence faithfully carried out and it (the Coetus) had its first session in the year 1747, on September 29th.

Whereupon and until the second Coetus, held September 28, 1748, the Very Reverend Christian Synods sent us three ministers, namely Messrs. John Jacob Hochreutner, Dominicus Bartolomaeus and John Philip Leydich, without expense to our congregations, which three ministers took their seats in the second Coetus and, in the fear of God, assisted in the deliberations, according to the best of their ability, granted to them by God, regarding the well-being of our churches. They also accepted the congregations assigned to them by D. Slatter with the consent of the whole Reverend Coetus, namely: Mr. Hochreutner the congregation at Lancaster, Mr. Bartolomaei the two congregations in Dolpihacken and Mr. Leydich the congregation at Falckner Schwam. The last had been my dear congregation, entrusted to me for more than twenty-three years, but now, because of the approaching disability of my old age, when I can no longer venture to make long journeys, I gladly and willingly surrendered it, for the good of the congregation, to D. Leydich, together with the new congregation in Providenz.

As each one [of these ministers] saw the love and kind disposition to his person, of the congregations assigned to him, they accepted them in the name of God, with tears yet willingly, because they beheld therein the providence of the allwise God, and they promised to look after them as their spiritual shepherds, according to the ability, which God would graciously grant unto them.

For this we are bound to be exceedingly thankful, next to God, to our Very Reverend and Pious Church Fathers, and we feel under obligation to pray most humbly before God for every spiritual and bodily blessing to come upon them, for through them we expect, under God's blessing, a good progress and growth of our churches. We must confess that even in eternity we cannot thank God sufficiently for all we owe to Him.

But, in order that many people might not sin against our gracious God, out of ignorance, by despising His eternal love and provoking His wrath upon us (so that he might take away from us the clear light of the Gospel of His dear Son and punish us severely), it has been deemed good and useful, after full deliberation by the Reverend Coetus, to issue through public print this Church Order, established in the fear of God and formulated as much as possible in accordance with the condition of the province of Pennsylvania, together with all the transactions and resolutions of the Reverend Coetus, taken on the 28th of September, 1748, in brotherly love and unity, as in the presence of God. Thus each member of our Church can see it without hindrance and we hope that the sincere members of our churches, who are concerned for their own salvation, will not only recognize it, with the entire Reverend Coetus, as good and useful, but, as all the members of the Reverend Coetus do themselves, they will also submit to it with true and dutiful, churchly obedience, will seek to direct their life and conduct in accordance with it and through orderly and pious behaviour will humbly endeavor to secure God's further grace and blessing for their bodies and especially for their immortal souls.

Since then, my Beloved, the Reverend Coetus has honored me, their unworthy and lowly fellow-servant and co-laborer in the Gospel of Jesus Christ, to issue this work through public print, I wanted to spare no pains to do this work faithfully, according to my humble ability, and hence I have provided it with this brief and simple introduction, hoping that it will not displease any one who is a true member of Christ and a lover of His holy Gospel.

In this simplicity of my heart, and yet with sincere love to God and His Word, which is alone able to save, and seeking the increase of the Kingdom of Jesus Christ, to the eternal praise of the almighty Creator,

I wish each one who loves Jesus and with his whole heart is attached to the Gospel, all the blessings of God, profitable for body and soul, Amen.

I am the well-wisher of all good for body and soul to each one and

   Yours Ready for Every Service,

    JOHANN PHILIPP BOEHM, *p. t. Praeses.*

[XLVII. CLASSICAL DEPUTIES TO MR. BOEHM,
JUNE 2, 1749.[333]]

To the Reverend Mr. Boehm, Pastor at Witpen.
Reverend, Very Learned and Much Esteemed Brother:—

Although we have answered your esteemed letter as far as seemed necessary in our letter to the Reverend Coetus, we nevertheless desire to add this one as proof of our affection and esteem for you. We have been induced to this by your letter, in which you stated that you were grieved in not having received a letter from us in a long time, and that you feared, that the old servant with all his labors might be forgotten. Our silence was not caused by want of love and esteem for you, but we must practice brevity and cannot always answer all private letters, because we have very many foreign churches and church assemblies, both in the East Indies and in the West Indies. Our Classis corresponds not only with Pennsylvania and New Netherlands, but also with the brethren in Surinam, in Ceylon, in the Cape of Good Hope and at many other places.

That your Reverence still desires to proceed heartily in the work of the Lord pleases us very much. May the Great Shepherd sustain and help you, and enable you to perceive that your labors are pleasing to Him and are of profit and saving benefit to many souls. That you at present minister to the recently established and yet small church of Witpen, we trust is not against your inclination, or to your grief, although you seem to express yourself somewhat complainingly in regard to it.

May the Lord enlarge that church and edify it through your ministry and enable you to persevere with joy, in the cheerful expectation of the reward of grace to God's faithful servants.

Farewell, Worthy Brother. We commend you to God and the Word of His grace, remaining with brotherly affection and esteem.

Your obedient servants and brethren, the members of the Classis of Amsterdam,

In the name of all,
Martinus Schnetlage, Cl. Dep.
John Temminck, Cl. h. t. Dep.

Amsterdam, June 2, 1749.

[333] A copy of the original is in the *Classical Letter Book,* Vol. XXX, p. 157, No. 95.

APPENDIX

I

DOCUMENTS RELATING TO MR. BOEHM'S DEATH AND THE DISPOSITION OF HIS PROPERTY.

[XLVIII. NOTICES OF MR. BOEHM'S LAST LABORS AND DEATH, 1749.]

Extracts from Schlatter's Diary, pp. 188-190.

  1749. On the 29th [of March], I received letters from Magunschy and Egypt, with urgent request that I might come over and administer to them the Holy Supper. At this time Mr. Boehm, at my request, took it upon himself to attend to the wants of these remote congregations.

  On the 2nd [of May], I visited Mr. Leydich in Falkner Schwam, a distance of 49 miles from thence (Tulpehocken). His Reverence had just the day before returned from a visit to various congregations. On the way, I heard the unexpected news of the sudden death of Mr. Boehm, which occurred in the house of his oldest son, after his Reverence had yet on the previous day administered the Holy Supper in the Egypt congregation. Thus our small number of laborers in this great harvest was again made less by this stroke.

  On the 7th [of May], I preached at Germantown, not without emotion, a funeral sermon on the death of Mr. Boehm, the oldest of the High German Reformed ministers in this country, who for the space of many years had to serve various congregations, and whose memory is cherished by many as blessed.

[XLIX. OBITUARY NOTICE OF MR. BOEHM IN SAUR'S PAPER, MAY 16, 1749.]

Pennsylvanische Berichte, No. 108, May 16, 1749.

  On April 29th, during the night, the Rev. John Philip Boehm died, without previous sickness, for on the day before he held a preparatory service for the Lord's Supper. It so happened that no Reformed preacher could be had to preach his funeral sermon, hence they engaged Martin Kolb, a Mennonite minister, to preach the funeral sermon.[334] If such things become customary and common, without necessity compelling it, the envy and antagonism of parties will soon come to an end. How beautiful will it be at that time when there will be one shepherd and one flock. Till then patience!

[LEGAL PAPERS RELATING TO THE DISPOSITION OF MR. BOEHM'S PROPERTY.]

[L. THE WIDOW RENOUNCING HER RIGHT OF ADMINISTRATION, May 6, 1749.]

Anna Maria Boehm, widow & Relict of Jn°. Philip Boehm, Deced., Renounces her Right of Administration on the Estate of the Deced.

Witness her hand & seal this 6th May, 1749.

ANNA MARIA BOEHMIN.
[SEAL]

[LI. LETTERS OF ADMINISTRATION GRANTED TO JOHN PHILIP BOEHM, JR., MAY 6, 1749.]

[Book of Administration, Vol. F, p. 235, Register of Wills Office, Philadelphia.]

To John Philip Boehm of Whitpain Township, yeoman, son of John Philip Boehm, late of ye same place, Clerk, Deced., (Anna Maria, ye widow, having renounced) Greeting.

Memorandum, that Letters of Administration in common form were granted to John Philip Böhm, ye son, above named on the Estate of the said Deced.

Invent^y to be exhibited on or before the 6th day of June next and an acc^t on or before the 7th day of May anno 1750.

Given under the seal of this said office the 6th day of May, 1749.

WM. PLUMSTED, Reg^r. Genl.

The securities to the Bond of Administration were Michael Clime, Innkeeper of Whitpain Township and Daniel Bouton, Baker of the city of Philadelphia and County of Philadelphia.

---

[334] Martin Kolb and his brother Jacob came to Germantown as early as 1707 (C. H. Smith, *Mennonites in America,* Scottdale 1909, p. 145). About 1709, Martin Kolb moved to Skippack, on the Van Bebber tract. (Smith, 1. c., p. 119), where a Mennonite meeting house was erected in 1725. In 1734, Martin Kolb paid quitrent on 100 acres in Skippack township. See Rupp, *Names,* p. 475.

[LII. BOND OF ADMINISTRATOR, MAY 6, 1749.]

[No. 9, 1749, Register of Wills Office, Philadelphia].
[Endorsement]:

Adm^s Bond
John Philip Böame yeoman
on ye Estate of John Philip Böame, Clerk,
Dated May 6, 1749. Registration Book F, p. 235.

Know all Men by these presents that we John Philip Böhm of Whitpain Township, yeoman, son of John Philip Böhm, late of ye same place, Clerk, Deced; Michael Cleim of ye same place Innholder & Danl. Buttong of Philad^a., Baker, are held & firmly bound unto W.m. Plumsted, Reg^r. Genl. for ye Probate of Wills & granting Lr^s. of Admceon in & for ye Province of Pennsylv^a. In ye Sum of Two Thous^d. Pounds Lawfull Money of ye s^d. Province To be p^d. to the s^d. Reg^r. Genl. his certain attorney Excors admors or Ass^s. To ye wch Paym^t well & truly to be made & done. We bind ourselves our Heirs Exors & Admors joyntly & severally for & in the whole firmly by these presents.

Sealed wth. our Seals. Dat^d. the 6th Day of May anno 1749.

The condicon of this obl. is such that if the above bounden John Philip Bohm, yeoman, Admor of all & singular the Goods Chetls Rights & Credits wch were of John Philip Böhm Clerk Deced, (Anna Maria having renounced) do make or cause to be made a true & p'fect Inv^y. of all and singular the Goods Chetls Rights & Credits wch were of ye s^d. Dec'd, wch have or shall come to the hands possion or knowledge of ye s^d. John Philip ye son or in ye hands Possion or knowledge of any other pson or psons for him & ye same so made do exhi^t. or cause to be exh^d. into ye Reg^r. Genl. Office at Philad^a. at or before the 6th Day of June next ye same Goods Chetls rights & credits wch were of ye s^d. Decd. at ye time of his death or wch at any time after shall come to ye hands possion or knowledge of any other pson or psons for him do well & truly admer accord. to Law and further do make or cause to be made a true & just acc^t. Calculacon or reckon^g. of ye s^d. Admcon at or before ye 7th day of May anno 1750 and all ye rest & residue of ye s^d. Goods Chetls rights & credits wch shall be found rem^g upon ye s^d. adm^s. acc^t. the same being first exh^d. & allowed by ye Orphan Court of y^e [County] of Philad^a. shall deliver & pay to such pson or psons respectively as ye s^d. Court by its Decree or sentence shall limit & app^t. and if it shall hereafter appear y^t. any last Will or Testament was made by ye s^d. Deced. & ye Exor or Exors therein named do exhibit the same into ye s^d. office making Request to have it allowed & approved of accord-

ingly, if the s^d. John Philip Böhm being thereunto requested do render & deliver up ye s^d. Lrs of Admcon. Approbacon of such Testament being first had & made in ye s^d. office. Then this obl. to be void or else to be & remain in full force & vertue.
Sealed & [signed]

In the presence of
Pet^r. Hodgson

{ John Philip Böame
Michael Cleim
Daniel Bouton.

[LIII. INVENTORY OF MR. JOHN PHILIP BOEHM'S ESTATE, EXHIBITED JULY 13, 1749.]

[No. 9, 1749, Register of Wills Office, Philadelphia.]

A true Inventory of all and single the Goods and Chattels, Rits [Rights] and Credits of John Philip Bame in ye County of Philadelphia, Desesed. Appraised the fifth day of June, 1749.

And is in Manner as follows Appraised by us Underwritten William Foulke and John Roberts and John Jemison, viz.

	£	s.	d.
To his wearing Apperill	8	0	0
To his Riding Hors Saddal and Bridal & Whip	10	0	0
To Cash	4	19	0
Doe [Due] on Bond & Bils	29	5	0
Doe on Book	26	10	1
To 6 Table Cloths 8 pare pillow cases & three sheets fore Napkins five hand towels and Bolster three nets fore Baskets & some yarn	4	1	0
For 11 yards & 3 Quarters of Cloth	3	6	0
For 7 yards & 3 Quarters of Cloth	1	18	0
For 5 silver spoons	1	10	0
For Bed & Bedding	5	0	0
For Clock and Case	8	0	0
For 1 Comb & Looking Glass	0	3	0
For 3 slats	0	3	0
For 1 Cubbert & Lumber	1	0	0
For 3 Dasson [Dozen] small Books	1	0	0
For 8 large Books	1	0	0
For 2 Bibles	3	0	0
For 1 Vise & 1 Lock	0	14	0
For 1 Earthen jar and 1 hammer & hooks & stapels	0	3	0
For 2 puter Dishes 1 Bason 1 putor tankert & 1 mogg [mug]	1	2	0
For 1 putor tea pot	0	6	0
For 21 putor plates 5 putor dishes 3 putor por-			

angers & 1 putor mustard pot	2	18	0
For 2 Duson & a half of putor spoons & copper cettel	1	16	0
For 2 Iron Cettels & 2 Iron pots	1	5	0
For tongs & Gridiron Lossaback pot Hoeks frying pan 2 Leadals flesh fork	0	16	0
For 2 Candal Sticks and Lantran Choping Knife Mill Hook & Lamp	0	7	0
For 2 Leadals 1 scinner 1 grator Iron Mortar & pestal and Brass Lid	0	10	6
For 1 pare of stilards [stilyards] & Dripping pan & Littal Stove & Iron to Bake Cakes in	1	0	0
For 2 Box Irons & Heators	0	6	0
For 13 Gese [Geese]	0	13	0
For 1 sled 1 Iron plow & trees & Wheal Barrow 1 Iron Harrow	1	4	0
For 1 Waggon and Harnes & Old Cart & Old Harnes	10	0	0
For some Black Walnut Bords (in Mill) thrashing Mill & cutting box & knife	2	18	0
For some oats	0	5	0
For 7 stocks of Bees	1	15	0
For 1 old cutting knife & yoke & curry comb & hook	0	4	0
For 2 pitch forks 2 plows & Irons & two swingle trees	1	7	0
To sheep & lambs	5	10	0
To fore yearlings cow cinde [kind] and six cows and three calfs	24	16	0
To 3 working horses and 1 mare & colts	30	0	0
To 1 horse colt saddal & Bridal	10	0	0
To 3 Iron Hoppels 1 Appel Mill & Trough & 5 Iron Bolts	1	6	0
To 1 Mall 3 Iron Wegges [wedges] and Hold fast and 2 Grind stones	0	15	0
To 9 Agurs and 19 small carpenter Tools & 2 ads 5 old axes	2	2	0
To 2 cradals 7 old siths 3 siths sneads & 2 wooden scows & Iron Stump Rasor and Shingels	0	11	0
To 1 Sedar [cedar] tub & cegg & shecal [sickle] & Chane [chain] 27 hogs heads	2	5	0
To 14 sidor [cider] Hogsheds	2	10	0
[To] Iron Stove	3	0	0
To 8 Hogsheds Civars and one tub	0	10	0
To 2 Distills and two Coolers	40	0	0
To 3 tubs 1 Bocket 1 funal & old Brack and old Irons	0	11	6

To first koming [?] & 1 sheep scin 1 calf scin 3 Barels and Churn Wood and Lumber........	1	19	0
To 6 Troughs & 6 Weeding Hows, 2 Drilling Hows 2 spads 1 shofel 1 dung fork................	1	8	0
To 3 old guns....................................	2	0	0
To earthen pots & pans 6 stone bottals............	1	2	0
To 1 Tea Cattel & cossy [cozy] covers & 2 glasses 3 glass bottals	1	0	0
To 4 saws, 1 old tooling wheel 1 Table to 9 chears & stools	2	10	0
To sum wheate	1	4	0
To 1 Dow Trough Half Bushel & cegg and ax, Lamp & Ink stands	0	10	0
To old Irons	3	0	0
To one old Bed & Bedding	1	7	0
To 3 Littal wheels & 3 Hettochils [Hatchels] 6 schicals [sickles]	2	12	0
To 2 feather Beds & 1 chaf Bed & some feathers & Bed stead 2 small spits.....................	4	11	0
To some Raggs, some Baggs & some yarn 1 soling & lining to feathers	6	10	0
To 21 yards of Lining, some wool & Bascets & scals chese kag	3	0	0
To Linings old Chests to some Books therein....	5	4	0
To 1 Beme [beam] and some other small things 1 pare of Hinges & Iron Sledges...............	0	12	0
To 2 Beds and Bedsteads and Beding...........	6	10	0
To 1 padlock and Bed & beding	1	2	0
To open heded Barrals, Old Iron and Buckwheat and old Boxes	0	18	6
To Beaf & Beacon................................	0	10	0
To plane stocks, copper pot, scilet, Old Irons Cabuk [cabbage] knife & table..................	0	15	0
To 2 crosscut saws & some oake Bords, sith & Cradal Reak & Bee Hives....................	2	17	0
To knives and forks, old Nutt Trenchers, Sisors [scissors] & snufers	0	12	0
To pigg Iron and one saddal & some Leather & Bridal Bitt & Scrine	9	5	0
To 1 saddal pilow & saddal baggs & other Leather to 1 saddal	2	5	0
To 1 hogshed and some Rum & one hogshed with some molasses & hogshead of Sidor..........	2	7	0
To 1 cask of some shugar & 2 ceggs & half Barel & Vinegar & old Butter tubs................	0	15	0
To 1 Chest & Table.............................	0	2	0
To wheat and Rey in ye ground..................	20	0	0

To Oats, Indian Corn, Flax & Hemp in y⁰ ground.   8   0   0
To y⁰ three servants, 2 Boys and one Girl........ 30   0   0

Total some errors exc. £423 10   7

JOHN JEMISON,
WM. FOULKE,
JOHN ROBERTS.

Exhibited July 13, 1749.

[LIV. THE ACCOUNT OF JOHN PHILIP BOEHM, JR., ADMINISTRATOR OF HIS FATHER'S ESTATE, FEBRUARY 27, 1755.]

[No. 9, 1749, Register of Wills Office, Philadelphia.]

1749.

July 13th. The accom^t. charges himself Dr. with all and singular ye goods chattles rights and credits which were of ye s^d. Deced. as mentioned in an Inv^y. thereof Exhibited into & remaining in the Reg^r. Genl. Office at Phila^d & am^t. to £423.10.7.

By allowance for his several payments & Disbursm^{ts}. made as on the other side as per rec^{ts}. and am^t. to £75   1   9
By the Widows Thirds p^d......................£130   ..   ..

£205   1   9

By the Balance paid to ye five other Heirs of ye s^d. Deced, as by their Release for the same......£218   8   10

£423 10   7

Philad^a 27 Feb^r 1755.
Errors excepted
John Philip Bame, Adm^r.
account aff^d.

Accompt of the Estate late John Philip Behm Deced. Exhibi^d. 27th Febr. 1755.

Paid to the Creditors of my Father:

	£	s.	d.
To Gothart Armbrister	11	0	0
To John Theobold End..........................	3	3	6
To Christopher Sour............................	0	1	0
To Abraham Evans.............................	1	0	7
To John Deheaven	0	8	6
To Joseph Cadwalleder.........................	0	7	6
To Sebastian Miller............................	2	7	8

To William Dixsy	0	15	0
To Hananiah Pugh	0	10	6
To John White	0	5	10
To Judah Foulke	1	11	0
To Jacob Fisher	0	16	10
To John Robarts	0	13	6
To Jane Adams	0	14	0
To John Lewis	0	5	6
To George Kastner	0	2	6
To Sophia Maybury	4	16	10
To John Morris	0	7	0
To William Foulke	1	17	11
To Jacob Arnt and Gabriel Scheuler and Peter Spyker	3	3	0
To Edward Dehaven	0	8	3
To Peter Swortee	1	11	4
To Thomas Adams	0	6	0
To John ?	0	15	0
To Anthony Bame for Funeral Charges	4	10	0
	£41	18	9
By allowance for cash charges in the Inv^y. it being the property of ye Elders of Skipack meeting house & since paid to them	£31		
p^d. for ye Adm^r. & fit Inv^y		17	..
p^d. for making up ye acc^t. writing sundries	1	15	..
	£75	1	9
p^d. the widow thirds £130 Ballance p^d. to ye 5 other children & releases for ye same	[348.	8.	10]
	[Total £423.	10.	7]

[LV. DEED GIVEN BY THE DAUGHTERS OF JOHN PHILIP BOEHM TO HIS YOUNGEST SON, JOHN PHILIP BOEHM, JR., JULY 1, 1749.]

[Recorder of Deeds Office, Philadelphia, Vol. G, No. 12, p. 450, ff.]

THIS INDENTURE made the First Day of July in the year of our Lord One Thousand seven hundred and forty nine Between Adam Moser of the County of Philadelphia in the Province of Pennsylvania yeoman and Anna Maria his wife, Ludwig Bitting of Lower Milford Township in the County of Bucks in the said Province yeoman and Sevina his wife, George Shamboh of Upper Milford Township in the said County of Bucks Weaver and Elizabeth his wife and Cornelius Deweese of Gloucester County in West New Jersey Cooper and Maria Philipina his wife (They the said Anna Maria, Sevina, Elizabeth and Maria Philipina being the Daughters of Johann Philip Behm, late of Whitpen township in the said County of Philadelphia, yeoman deceased) of the one part and Johann Philip Behm of Whitpen township aforesaid, yeoman, the youngest son of the said first named Johann Philip Behm of the other Part.

Whereas the said Johann Philip Behm, the father, became in his life time lawfully possessed of Goods and Chattels and seized of and in Lands Tennements and Hereditaments situate in the said Province of Pennsylvania, viz. Two tracts of Land situate at or near Saucon Creek in the said County of Bucks containing together about Three hundred acres or thereabouts and one Plantation in Whitpain aforesaid containing two Hundred Acres or thereabouts And He the said Johann Philip Behm the Father in his Life time Portioned and Preferred his Eldest son Anthony William Behm by a Grant of the Saucon Lands aforesaid and Died Intestate, and administration of his Estate was committed unto his youngest son Johan Philip Behm, party hereto, the Widow having judicially renounced,

AND WHEREAS it is mutually agreed by and between the parties hereto that the said Johann Philip Boehm his son shall hold to him and his heirs for his part, the aforesaid Plantation in Whitpain and that he his Heirs Executors or Administrators shall maintain & support their Grandfather Philip Sherer with all necessaries during the Term of his natural Life, and that the said Adam Moser shall have and receive (over and besides what he hath already received of his said Father-in-law in his Life time in part of his said wife's Portion) the sum of One Hundred and sixty three Pounds three shillings for his and her part of her said Father's Estate And that the said George Shamboh shall have and receive (over and besides what he hath already Received of his said Father-in-Law in his Life time in part of his said Wife's Portion) the sum of One Hundred and thirty nine Pounds, ten shillings for his and her full part of their said Father's Estate And that the said Cornelius Deweese shall have and Receive (over and besides what he hath already Received of his said Father-in-Law in his Life time in part of his said wife's Portion) the sum of One Hundred and Twenty Nine Pounds thirteen Shillings for his and her full part of their said Father's Estate Each one whole share (including what they have heretofore Received respectively) amounting to One Hundred and Seventy Pounds a piece and that the said Ludwig Bitting shall have and Receive the whole sum of one hundred and seventy Pounds for his and his said wife's full part of their said Father's Estate he the said Ludwig having heretofore Received no part of his said Wife's Portion, Provided always and is hereby mutually agreed by and between the parties hereto each one of them the said Adam Moser, Ludwig Bitting, George Shamboh and Cornelius Deweese, their Heirs Executors and Administrators respectively shall well and truly bear the one full and equal fifth part (the whole in five equal parts to be divided) of all the just Debts of the said Johan Philip Behm the Father which he owed at the time of his Decease and shall well and truly pay or discount the same unto the said John Philip Behm the son his Executors, Administrators or Assigns, NOW THIS INDENTURE WITNESSETH that the said Adam Moser and Anna Maria his wife Ludwig Bitting and Sevina his wife, George Shamboh and Elizabeth his wife and Cornelius Deweese and Maria Philipina his wife for and in consideration of the several sums of money herein before particularly mentioned and unto them respectively well paid or secured to be paid by the said Johann Philip Behm at and before the sealing and Delivery hereof The Receipt of which security they do hereby acknowledge Have granted Remised Released and confirmed and by these Presents do grant Remise, Release and Confirm unto the said John Philip Behm the son (in the actual possession now being) and to his Heirs and Assigns all that the said Plantation or Tract of Land situate in Whitpain Township aforesaid containing Two hundred acres (which one Rees Thomas, Anthony Morris & Phoebe his wife by Indenture of the ninth Day of September 1736 Recorded at Philadelphia in Book F, Vol. 9, p. 250 sec^d. granted unto the said John Philip Behm the Father and to his Heirs and Assigns, Together also with all and singular the Rights Members Improvements Hereditam^{ts}, and appurtenances whatever thereunto belonging and also all and every of the Estate and Estates Parts and Purparts Use Possession Property Claim and Demand whatsoever of them the said Adam Moser and Anna Maria his wife, Ludwig Bitting and Sevina his wife, George Shamboh and Elizabeth his wife and Cornelius Dewees and Maria Philipina his wife, of in and to the said Whitpain Plantation and of in and to all and singular other the Lands Tennements and Hereditaments whatsoever of their said Father Johann Philip Behm in his Life time at the time of his Decease, To have and to hold the said Whitpain Plantation and all and singular other the parts Hereditaments and Premises hereby granted or mentioned to be granted with the appurtenances unto the said Johann Philip Behm the son his Heirs and Assigns To the only proper Use and Behoof of him the said John Philip Behm the son his Heirs and Assigns forever, Under the proportionable part of the yearly Quit Rent accruing for the same Premises to the Chief Lord of the Fee thereof And the said Adam Moser doth hereby Covenant for him and his heirs and for the said Anna Maria his wife and her heirs, the said Ludwig Bitting doth hereby covenant for him and his heirs and for the said Sevina his wife and her heirs, The said George Shamboh doth hereby covenant for him and his heirs and for the said Elizabeth his wife and her heirs, and the said Cornelius Deweese doth hereby covenant for him and his Heirs and for the said Maria Phillipina his wife and her Heirs, severally and respectively and not jointly to and with the said John Philip Behm the son his Heirs and Assigns That they the said Adam Moser and Anna Maria his wife and their Heirs respectively, the said

Ludwig Bitting and Sevina his wife and their heirs respectively, The said George Shamboh and Elizabeth his wife and their Heirs respectively and the said Cornelius Dewees and Maria Phillipina his wife and their heirs respectively, The said Lands purparts and premises hereby granted or mentioned to be granted with the appurtenances unto the said Johann Philip Behm the son his Heirs and Assigns against them the said Adam Moser & Anna Maria his wife, Ludwig Bitting & Sevina his wife, George Snamboh & Elizabeth his wife and Cornelius Dewees and Maria Phillipina nis wife & their Heirs respectively and against all and every other person and persons whatsoever lawfully claiming or to claim by from or under them or any of them respectively shall and will warrant and forever defend by these Presents And the said Adam Moser, Ludwig Bitting, George Shamboh and Cornelius Dewees severally and respectively and for their several and respective Heirs, Executors and Administrators do covenant, promise and grant to and with the said Jn. Philip Behm party hereto his Executors and Administrators by these presents, That each of them the said Adam Moser, Ludwig Bitting, George Shamboh and Cornelius Dewees shall and will well and truly pay or cause to be paid unto the said Johann Philip Behm party hereto his Executors Administrators or Assigns the one full and equal fifth part aforesaid of the whole amount of the just Debts of the said John Philip Behm the Father due at the time of his Decease and further also that it shall and may be lawful to and for the said Johann Philip Behm the son his Executors and Administrators to keep to his and their own use all and singular the goods Chattels and credits of the said Intestate without any account to be given for the same, The aforesaid One Hundred and Seventy Pounds a piece including each one's share of the Personal Estate of the said Intestate, as well as of the aforesaid Plantation at Whitpain and of all other his Lands and Tennements (The aforesaid Saucon Lands excepted).

In witness whereof the said Parties to these Presents have interchangeably set their Hands and Seals hereunto. Dated the Day and Year first above written.

Sealed and delivered by the above named Cornelius Deweese and Maria Philipina his wife. In the Presence of us
    GARRETT DEWEES
    FREDERICK BUTTON.

Sealed and delivered by the above named Adam Moser & Anna Maria his wife, Ludwig Bitting & Sevina his wife And George Shamboh & Elizabeth his wife in the Presence of us
    SEBASTIAN DRUCKEMULLER,
    JOHANN NICHOLAS STAEHLER.

ADAM MOSER (Seal)
ANNA MARIA MOSER (Seal)
LUDWIG BITTING (Seal)
SEVINA BITTING (Seal)
GEORGE SHAMBOH (Seal)
ELIZABETH X SHAMBOH (Seal)
    her mark
CORNELIUS X DEWEES (Seal)
    his mark
MARIA PHILLIPINA DEWEES (Seal)

Memorandum the sixteenth Day of August 1749 Personally appeared before Thomas Lawrence, Esqr. One of the Justices, etc., Frederick Button of the City of Philadelphia Baker and made Oath on the Holy Evangelists of Almighty God that he was present and did see the above named Cornelius Dewees and Maria Philipina his wife sign seal and as their Deed deliver the above written Indenture and that his this Appearers Name thereunto subscribed as witness of the same is of his own handwriting and that together with him one Garrett Dewees also signed as another witness of the same. In Witness whereof the said Thomas Lawrence have hereunto set my hand & Seal the Day and Year aforesaid.

THO^s. LAWRENCE (Seal)

Memorandum the sixteenth Day of August anno Domini 1749 Personally appeared before me Thomas Lawrence Esqr. Johann Nicholas Stähler of Upper Milford Township in the County of Bucks, yeoman and made oath on the Evangelists of Almighty God that he was present and did see the within named Adam Moser and Anna Maria his wife, Ludwig Bitting and Sevina his wife, George Shamboh & Elizabeth his wife, sign seal and as their Act and Deed deliver the within written Indenture and that his this Appearers Name thereunto subscribed as a Witness of the same is of his own Handwriting & that together with him one Sebastian Druckemüller also signed as another witness of the same. In witness whereof I have hereunto set my Hand and seal the Day and Year aforesaid.

THO^s. LAWRENCE (Seal)
Recorded 4th January 1750/51.

APPENDIX

II

GERMAN REFORMED CONGREGATIONS IN PENNSYLVANIA BEFORE THE YEAR 1750.

The following list, like the map which accompanies it, does not aim to enumerate churches, that is church buildings, but congregations which were in existence before the year 1750. They met in private houses or in churches then actually built. The exact spot of these meeting places is uncertain in many cases. It is, however, to be presumed that they were somewhere near the present churches, whose location is indicated on the map and in the following list. The congregations visited by Schlatter (41 in all) are indicated by an asterisk(*), those referred to by Boehm (24 in all) are marked by a dagger (†).

I. MONTGOMERY COUNTY.

1. *†Falkner Swamp, founded 1725, in New Hanover township, near Swamp village.
    Oct. 15, 1725, first communion, see Boehm's report of 1744, p. 409. The first church was built in 1741, see p. 337.

2. *†Skippack, founded 1725, at Harleysville, Lower Salford township.
    Nov. 1725, first communion, see Boehm's report of 1744, p. 409. The first church was dedicated June 22, 1729, see p. 217; discontinued in 1748, revived as Wentz's, Worcester township, in 1762.

3. *†Whitemarsh, founded 1725, in Whitemarsh township.
    Dec. 23, 1725, first communion, see Boehm's report of 1744, p. 409. The meeting place was the house of Wm. De Wees, see p. 415; disbanded in 1745, see p. 430.

4. *†New Goshenhoppen, founded 1727, near East Greenville, Upper Hanover township.
    Oct. 12, 1727, first communion, see Boehm's letter of Nov. 1730, p. 216. First church built before 1739, see p. 281.

5. *†Old Goshenhoppen, founded about 1730, near Salford Station, Upper Salford township.
Mentioned by Boehm, Nov. 1730, see p. 204; warrant for land secured 1732; first church built 1744, see p. 425.

6. *†Providence, founded 1742, St. Luke's at Trappe, Providence township.
Nov. 5, 1742, first communion, see Boehm's statistics of 1744, p. 399; first church built in 1747, see Schlatter's private diary in *Journal of Presb. Hist. Soc.*, III, 165.

7. *Indian Creek, founded about 1745, (called also Indian Field) Christ's, Indian Creek, near Telford, Franconia township.
Oct. 20, 1746, visited by Schlatter, see *Life,* p. 140, when he preached "in a wooden church".

8. *†Whitpain, founded 1747, Boehm's Church, at Blue Bell, Whitpain township.
Febr. 3, 1747, organized by Schlatter, see Boehm's letter of Dec. 1748, p. 456; church built in 1747, see *Life of Schlatter,* p. 150; also p. 456, above.

II. LANCASTER COUNTY.

9. †Hill Church, Conestoga, founded 1725, Salem, Heller's. Upper Leacock township.
Founded by Tempelman in 1725, see his letter, quoted above, p. 62; first church built before 1739, see p. 281.

10. *†Cocalico, founded about 1730, Bethany, near Ephrata.
Referring to a communion in May, 1735, Boehm states that it had been gathered previously, *i. e.,* during his pastorate, 1730-1731, see p. 275; first log church built before 1739, see p. 281.

11. *†Muddy Creek, founded about 1730, in East Cocalico township.
1730-1733, baptisms of Peter Miller, recorded in Lutheran Muddy Creek record. In April, 1744, Boehm refers to their "newly built little church," see p. 399.

12. *†Lancaster, founded between 1730-1732, First Reformed Church, Lancaster.
First mentioned by Tempelman, in letter of Febr. 13, 1733, see p. 64; first church built in 1736, see p. 275.

13. *Seltenreich, founded about 1732, near New Holland, Earl township.
Existence implied in Tempelman's letter; Sept. 8, 1732, a baptism by Tempelman of Susanna Bauman, da. of Henry and Catharine (Derr) Bauman, in Earl township, according to family Bible; first church built before 1744, see Lischy's report of Dec. 8, 1744, in *Reformed Church Review,* X, 1906, 94.

14. *Reyer's Church, founded about 1732, Zion's at Brickerville, Elizabeth township.
Existence implied in Tempelman's letter; entries by Tempelman in old church record (now lost) went back to 1735; first church built in 1735, according to record, see statement of Rev. D. C. Tobias in *Reformed Ch. Messenger,* of Oct. 14, 1874.

15. *Donegal, founded in 1743, Christ Church, Elizabethtown, Mount Joy township.
Organized by Lischy, June, 1743, according to Lischy's diary at Bethlehem; first church built in 1744, see report of Lischy in *Reformed Church Review,* X, 1906, 91.

16. Whiteoak, founded about 1747, Jerusalem Church, at Penryn, Penn township.
Sept. 21, 1747, date of deed for church land, see Tobias, *History of Bethany Charge,* p. 18; first church built about 1748.

17. Little Cocalico, founded about 1749, Swamp Church, near Blainsport, West Cocalico township.
Taufbuch beym Michael Amweg, begun July 20, 1749; first Church built 1755, see *Reformed Church Review,* XX, 1916, 37.

III. PHILADELPHIA COUNTY.

18. *†Philadelphia, founded 1727, First Reformed Church, Philadelphia.
First sermons in Philadelphia preached by Boehm, see p. 411; Sept. 24, 1727, first communion by Weiss, see p. 213; first meeting house rented in Nov., 1734, see p. 72; first church begun by Boehm in 1745, see p. 457.

19. *†Germantown, founded 1727, now Market Square Presbyterian Church.
Weiss was the first pastor in 1727, see p. 181; first church built in 1734, see p. 241.

IV. BERKS COUNTY.

20. *†Tulpehocken, founded 1727, Host Church, Tulpehocken township.
Oct. 18, 1727, first communion, see Boehm's report of 1744, p. 409; first services in Reed's Lutheran Church, see p. 67; first log church built in 1733, see p. 67; new church built in 1743, see p. 398.

21. *†Oley, founded about 1734, Salem, at Oley, in Oley township.
First sermon preached at Oley by Weiss in 1729; April 13, 1734, date of deed for church land, see p. 73; mentioned

by Boehm in his report of 1734, see p. 251; first church is said to have been built in 1735 (*Pa. German,* III, 119), but it is not mentioned by Boehm in 1739, see p. 281.

22. *†Maxatawny, founded about 1734, now St. John's at Kutztown. Kutztown.

    Mentioned by Boehm in 1734, see p. 253, by Goetschy in 1736; first meeting place in house of Jacob Levan, one mile N. E. of Kutztown; first church built about 1755, see *Centennial History of Kutztown,* p. 76; mentioned by Schlatter as Manatawny, see *Reformed Church Review,* XX, 1916, p. 85.

23. Bern, founded about 1736, in Bern township.

    Mentioned by Goetschy in 1736, in New Goshenhoppen record; a church was at Bern when Lischy began preaching there in 1743, see *Reformed Church Review,* IX, 532.

24. †Cacusi, founded about 1736, St. John's, or Hain's, near Wernersville.

    Mentioned by Goetschy in 1736; a church was built there before 1739, see p. 281.

25. Moselem, founded about 1736, now St. Peter's, in Richmond township.

    Mentioned by Goetschy in 1736; first meeting place possibly in Moselem Lutheran Church; in 1762, the Reformed erected a building on the west side of the Moselem creek, one mile southwest of the Lutheran church.

26. Blue Mountain Church, founded 1739, Zion's at Strausstown, Upper Tulpehocken township.

    Date of founding as given on cornerstone of new building. First mentioned by Lischy as at the Blue Mountains, in his report of Dec., 1744, see *Reformed Church Review,* IX, 1905, p. 533; date of warrant for church land, March 7, 1746; according to Montgomery, *History of Berks County,* 1886, p. 1095, the first church was built "nearly one hundred and fifty years ago," but that is no doubt too early.

27. Alsace, founded about 1740, Grace, Alsace, on the northeastern boundary of Reading.

    Visited by Leonard Schnell, a Moravian missionary, in October, 1746, according to his diary; by Muhlenberg, in June, 1747; a union church was built there between 1743-47, see *Hallesche Nachrichten,* new ed. Vol. I, p. 348; Vol. II, p. 188.

28. Hill Church, in Oley Hills, founded 1741, St. John's, Hill Church, Pike township.

    Founded as a union church, according to church record, in 1741; first church built in 1747, according to the record.

CONGREGATIONS IN 1750   485

29. Dunkel's, founded in 1744, New Jerusalem Church, Greenwich township, near Virginsville.
Year of organization given in proclamation, issued by the congregation in 1859; a church is said to have been built in the same year, 1744, on two acres of land, presented by Conrad Koch, see *Geschichte und Regeln der Neu Jerusalem Kirche*, Kutztown, 1896, pp. 12, 21. The receipt for the warrant of the church land is dated August 30, 1748.

30. Schwartzwald, founded about 1745, in Exeter township.
Visited by Lischy, April 8, 1745, according to his diary; visited by Muehlenberg in 1746, see *Hallesche Nachrichten*, new ed., Vol. I, p. 108; a church was built before 1746.

31. Belleman's, founded about 1746, in Centre township.
Warrant for church land dated May 14, 1746, according to Early, *History of the Churches of Berks County;* date of first church unknown.

32. *Little Lehigh, founded about 1748, now Longswamp, in Longswamp township.
First church begun in September, 1748, according to the church record; mentioned by Schlatter as Little Lehigh, see *Life*, p. 203.

V. LEHIGH COUNTY.

33. *†Egypt, founded about 1734, near Coplay, Whitehall township.
July 27, 1734, first baptism by Boehm, in church record; mentioned by Goetschy in 1736; the first log church was built in 1764, see Roberts, *History of Egypt Church*, 1908, p. 13.

34. *†Great Swamp, founded about 1734, one mile north of Spinnertown, in Lower Milford township.
First referred to Boehm in 1734, see p. 253; warrant for church land dated May 23, 1738, see Weiser, *Monograph*, p. 42; date of first log church not known.

35. *†Macungie, founded about 1734, Ziegel Church, Weisenberg township.
First mentioned by Boehm in his report of 1734, see p. 252; baptisms in the old church record went back to "the thirties," according to Helffrich, *Geschichte*, p. 6; mentioned as Magunchy by Schlatter, in June, 1747; a small church with tile (hence the name Ziegel) was dedicated by Philip J. Michael on July 20, 1750.

36. *Heidelberg, founded in 1740, near Saegersville, Heidelberg township.
Date of founding according to Helffrich, *Geschichte*, p. 33; first church built in 1744, according to same authority.

37. *Schmaltzgass, founded about 1740, New Jerusalem, Western Salisbury, near Emaus, in Salisbury township.
    First church built in 1741, according to the church record; the deed, dated Dec. 15, 1745, mentions the church and the first pastor, John William Straub, see *Skizzen aus dem Lecha-Thal*, Allentown, 1886, p. 72.

38. *Jordan, founded about 1744, in South Whitehall township.
    Warrant for land secured in 1744; union church built in 1745; mentioned by Schlatter in 1747, see *Life*, p. 163; the Reformed people separated and built their own church in 1752, on land presented by Lorenz Guth, see *Anniversary History of Lehigh County*, 1914, Vol. I, p. 884f.

39. *Allemaengel, founded about 1745, called also Lynn, now Ebenezer, at New Tripoli, Lynn township.
    First church built about 1745, according to Helffrich, *Geschichte*, p. 47; Moravian records report Wirtz at Allemaengel in 1748.

40. Weisenberg, founded about 1747, in N. E. corner of Weisenberg township.
    Date of founding according to Helffrich, *Geschichte*, p. 39; first church built in 1754.

41. Upper Milford, founded about 1750, near Old Zionville, Upper Milford township.
    Date of founding according to *Anniversary History of Lehigh County*, Vol. I, p. 790; oldest known burials in cemetery in 1753; first log church built about 1750.

VI. NORTHAMPTON COUNTY.

42. *†Saucon, founded about 1734, near Hellertown, Christ's, Lower Saucon township.
    Mentioned by Boehm in 1734, see p. 252; by Goetschy in 1736; the Saucon church is referred to in 1740 in the Egypt record.

43. *Forks of Delaware, founded about 1746, at Morgan Hill, near Easton, now First Church, Easton.
    Communion set is dated 1746, see Kieffer, *First Settlers of Forks of Delaware*, 1902, pl. facing p. 48; visited by Schlatter in June, 1747, see *Life*, p. 162. "The first church in which the Easton congregation worshipped, stood at the foot of Morgan's Hill, about a mile and a half from town, a little to the left of the old Philadelphia road. This building was dedicated to the service of God in 1758." See *Weekly Messenger* of Febr. 8, 1837, a statement made most likely by Rev. Thomas Pomp, from 1796-1850 pastor of the congregation.

44. *Indian Creek, founded about 1747, at Jost Dreisbach's mill, in Lehigh township.
Probably mentioned by Schlatter as "Great Lehigh," in 1747; according to the letter of Simon Dreisbach of Jan. 1773, the Indian Creek congregation was older than Indianland and the Mooretownship Church, see *Ref. Ch. Review,* XVIII, 1914, p. 214; continued in 1772 as Stone Church at Kreidersville.

45. Mooretownship Church, founded about 1750. The date 1723, frequently given, is unsupported by any contemporaneous evidence. Emanuel, Petersville.
According to Rev. J. C. Becker, who became pastor in 1811, there were three congregations in that neighborhood about 1750, namely, one each in Moor township, Indianland and Indian Creek, see Church Record of Stone Church, at Kreidersville.

46. Indianland, founded about 1750, St. Paul's, in Lehigh township.
Date of founding according to Rev. J. C. Becker, see preceding congregation; first church built in 1756, according to a document preserved in the church.

47. Plainfield, founded about 1750, St. Peter's, in Plainfield.
Warrant for church land dated Oct. 18, 1750, see *Pa. German,* Vol. X, p. 306; date of first church unknown.

VII. LEBANON COUNTY.

48. *†Tulpehocken, founded 1738, Trinity, Tulpehocken, near Myerstown.
Oct. 1738, first communion, see Boehm's report of 1739; p. 277; Schlatter mentions the two Tulpehocken churches in his diary, see *Life,* p. 135; in May 1743, Boehm refers to a church, see pp. 398, 416.

49. *†Swatara, founded about 1739, near Jonestown, now St. John's, at Jonestown, Swatara township.
First mentioned by Boehm in Febr. 1740, see p. 290; baptisms in church record also go back to 1740; a church was in existence in 1743, when Lischy began preaching there, see *Ref. Ch. Review,* X, 93.

50. *†Quitopahilla, founded about 1739, now Hill Church, near Annville.
First mentioned by Boehm in 1740, see p. 296; a union church was built in 1744, dedicated August 12, 1744, according to agreement in church record.

51. Millbach, founded about 1743, St. Paul's, Millbach.
First visited by Lischy in 1743, see his report of Dec.

1744, in *Ref. Ch. Review,* IX, 1905, p. 533; baptisms in church record go back to 1747; a stone church was built in 1751, see Dubbs, *Reformed Church in Pennsylvania,* p. 178f.

52. Kimmerling's, founded about 1745, St. Jacob's, Kimmerlings, in North Lebanon township.
The date 1745 is on an old flagon, belonging to the congregation; a stone church was built in 1752, see Schmauk, *The Early Churches in Lebanon County,* 1902 (Publ. of Lebanon County Hist. Soc., Vol. I, p. 369).

53. *Schaeffer's Church, founded about 1746, St. Paul's, Schaefferstown.
First mentioned by Schlatter in Oct. 1746, as served by Rieger, see Schlatter's private diary, in *Journal of Presbyt. Hist. Soc.,* Vol. III, p. 118.

54. Grubben Church, founded about 1747, in South Lebanon township, now extinct.
First mentioned in letter of Conrad Weiser, dated May 15, 1747, see Fresenius, *Nachrichten,* III, 828; deed for church land dated Jan. 7, 1755, see Klopp, *History of Tabor Church,* Lebanon, 1902, p. 8.

VIII. BUCKS COUNTY.

55. *Neshaminy, founded 1710, a Dutch Reformed congregation, under the Coetus of Pa., now the Dutch Ref. Church at Churchville.
Founded by Rev. Paulus Van Vlecq, May 20, 1710, see church record, printed in *Journal of Presbyt. Hist. Soc.,* I, 118-138; a stone church was built in 1746, see *Life of Schlatter,* p. 129.

56. *Tohickon, founded about 1743, St. Peter's, Tohickon.
Sept. 1, 1743, date of deed for church land; first church built about the same time.

57. *Springfield, founded about 1745, Trinity, Springfield, near Pleasant Valley P. O.
Visited by Schlatter June 29, 1747, see *Life,* p. 162.

IX. CHESTER COUNTY.

58. Coventry, founded in 1743, Brownback's, in Coventry township.
April 10, 1743, Lischy called as first pastor; a church was built in 1744, see Lischy's report of Dec. 1744, printed in *Ref. Church Review,* X, 92.

59. Vincent, founded in 1744, now the East Vincent Church.
Date of founding according to Fluck, *History of Reformed*

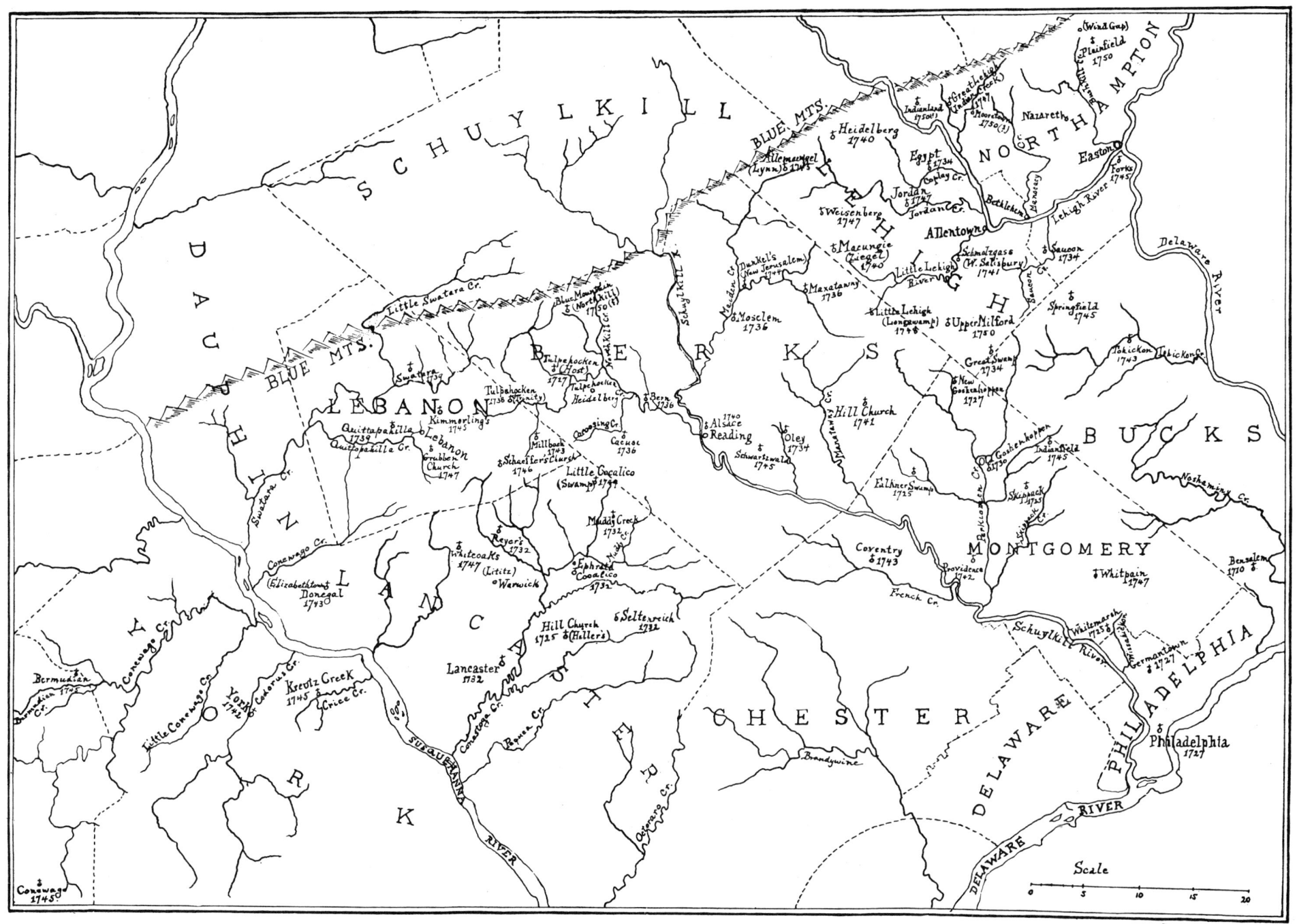

MAP OF PENNSYLVANIA, SHOWING THE LOCATION OF THE GERMAN REFORMED CHURCHES ORGANIZED BEFORE THE YEAR 1750.

Churches in Chester County, 1892, p. 32. The date seems to be inferred from the church record, begun in 1758, in which earlier baptisms, going back to 1744, are entered; first mentioned in *Coetus Minutes* in 1753, see p. 107; first church dedicated by Leydich, May 27, 1758, see Fluck, l. c., p. 33.

X. YORK COUNTY.

60. *York, founded in 1742, Trinity, First Church, York.
    Land donated in 1742, according to church record. Lischy called as first pastor, May 24, 1745; a church was in existence in 1744, according to Lischy's report, see *Ref. Church Review*, X, 97.

61. *Kreutz Creek, founded in 1745, near Hellam.
    May 23, 1745, Lischy preached his first sermon there, according to this diary; services were held in a schoolhouse. A church at "Crice Creek" is mentioned in the Bethlehem Diary, under date Oct. 20, 1747.

XI. ADAMS COUNTY.

62. *Bermudian, founded in 1745, now Mt. Olivet, near Bermudian P. O.
    Organized March 19, 1745, by Reformed and Lutherans, see *Hallesche Nachrichten*, new ed., I, 195; Lischy visited "Bramotsche" on that day, acording to his diary; first church dedicated April 15, 1754, see *Pa. German*, X, 457.

63. *Conewago, founded in 1745, Christ Church, near Littlestown.
    Visited by Lischy and Rauch in 1745 and 1746, according to their diaries; visited by Schlatter May 4, 1747, when he preached in a schoolhouse, see *Life*, p. 153. The warrant for the church land is dated September 10, 1750. A church is said to have been built before the year 1755. See Ault, *Historical Sketch*, p. 5.

INDEX

Acker, Andrew, 76.
Acts of Dutch Ref. Church, 232, 325.
Albert, Michael, 63, 291.
Albert, Wilhelm, 386.
Allebach, Christian, 60.
Allen, Wm., 88, 329, 415.
Allegiance, Declaration of, 346.
Amsterdam Archives, 37, 70, 172, 174, 176, 177, 183, 186, 192, 198, 220, 222, 223, 226, 228, 258, 261, 262, 269, 298, 300, 311, 318, 319, 323, 342, 370, 372, 441, 442, 468.
Amwell, N. J., 51, 326, 343.
Andreae, Rev. John C., 424, 425.
Andrews, Rev. Jedidiah, 27, 28, 32, 45, 46, 158, 199, 214.
Anniversary Hist. of Lehigh Co., 81.
Antes, Frederick, 35, 36, 61, 109, 110, 169, 179, 182, 191, 404.
Antes, Henry, 82, 86, 91, 92, 98, 99, 100, 105, 109-115, 124, 355, 356, 375, 376, 378, 379, 382.
Antes, John, 111.
Antonides, Rev. Vincentius, 33, 157, 170, 177, 183, 197, 207, 210, 211, 219, 256, 343.
Armbriester Gotthard, 137, 463.
Armor, *Lives of Governors of Pa.,* 333.
Arnet (Arent), Jacob, 257, 260, 283, 288, 316, 334, 340, 363, 395, 476.
Arnet, J. B., 260.
Associated Brethren, 111, 112.
Augusti, *Corpus,* 167.
Aulenbacher, Andrew, 284, 289.

Authentische Relation, 131, 353.
Aweeg, Gertruy, 25.
Aweeg, Jan, 25.
Aweeg, Margriet, 25.

Baal, Tobias, 293.
Bakker, John (Cl. Dep.), 171, 174, 175, 176.
Bakker, Rev. Jacobus, 35.
Balspach, Peter, 276.
Baltz, John George, 233, 234.
Barents, Anneken, 25.
Bartels, Sebastian, 25.
Bartholomaeus, Rev. Dom., 138, 143, 448, 449, 450, 466.
Bassler, Henry, 68, 276, 342.
Bauerle, Jacob, 417, 418.
Bauman, Jacob, 242, 250, 293, 297, 374.
Baumann, Matthias, 71, 86, 202, 218.
Bechtel, John, 88, 90, 92, 94, 98, 100, 106, 112, 115-119, 124, 242, 250, 357, 358, 360, 361, 375, 376, 378, 379, 382, 421, 422, 424.
Bechtel's Catechism, 96, 106, 107, 131, 359.
Becker, Jost, 112.
Becker, Peter (Dunker), 85, 390.
Beissel, Conrad, 47, 85, 201, 390.
Benezet, John Stephen, 121, 129.
Bensel, George, 112, 242, 250, 274, 335.
Berger, John, 282.
Berkenbeil, John, 61, 169.
Bermudian (Adams Co.), 124.
Bern (Berks Co.), 53, 121, 124, 278, 294, 377.

Berne Synod, 102, 361.
Bertholet, Abraham, 111.
Bertolet, John, 91, 112.
Best, George, 293.
Beyer, Jacob, 283.
Beyer, Valentine, 234, 292, 316, 317, 341.
Bethlehem, 88, 91.
Bethlehem Diary, 97, 115.
Bingaman, Lorentz, 36, 169, 191, 192, 210, 220, 284.
Biographisch Woordenboek, 39, 231.
Bitting, Ludwig, 149, 476, 477, 478, 479, 480.
Blair, Rev. Samuel, 101.
Bloemers, Marritye, 25.
Blum, Frantz, 293.
Blum, John, 296.
Boehler, Rev. Peter, 112, 113, 122, 368.
Boehm, Anna Marie (Scherer), 18, 146 147, 470.
Boehm, Anna Maria (Stehler), 8, 145.
Boehm, Anna Maria (daughter), 145, 149, 476, 477, 478, 479, 480.
Boehm, Anthony William, 8, 145, 146, 148, 476, 477.
Boehm, Clement Lewis, 3.
Boehm, Daniel, 151.
Boehm, Elizabeth, 145, 150, 477, 478, 479, 480.
Boehm, Franciscus Ludovicus, 8.
Boehm, Hannah Phillis, 148.
Boehm, Johanna Sabina, 8, 145, 149, 476, 477, 478, 479, 480.
Boehm, John Christopher, 8.
Boehm, John Daniel, 3, 4.
Boehm, John Philip, Jr., 145, 147, 148, 150, 470, 471, 475, 477, 478, 479, 480.
Boehm, Margartha, 3.
Boehm, Maria, 3.
Boehm, Maria Philippina, 145, 150, 477, 478, 479, 480.
Boehm, Philip Lewis, 1-6.
Boehm's Church; see Whitpain.

Boel, Rev. Henricus, 33, 170, 177, 180, 183, 197, 207, 210, 219, 256, 319, 322, 323, 343, 344.
Bon, Margriet, 25.
Bon, Peter, 24.
Bon, John, 112.
Book of Common Worship, 392.
Bossen, William, 112.
Bouton, Daniel, 147, 395, 397, 404, 407, 470, 471, 472.
Boyer, Gabriel, 73.
Boyd, Rev. Adam, 46.
Brandmiller, John, 100, 127.
Brechbill, John Wendel, 233, 234, 268, 283, 292, 316, 334, 396.
Bruce, David, 129, 130.
Bruner, Felix, 293.
Brunnholtz, Rev. Peter, 66, 82.
Bucher, Dieter, 283, 287, 316, 340, 363, 394.
Buedingische Sammlung, 99, 131, 329, 415.
Buettner, Rev. Gottlob, 92. 95, 97, 102, 118, 131.
Burnetfield, 344.
Burckhardt, Philip, 363.
Button, Frederick, 479.

Cacusi, 280, 281, 294, 295, 298, 377.
Cafferoth, Gerhard, 234.
Cammerhoff, Bishop, 130.
Catskill Ref. Ch., 30, 42.
Cent. Hist. of Kutztown, 253.
Cocalico, 65, 121, 275, 276, 281, 290, 294, 295.
Coetus Minutes, 61, 136, 278.
Collegiate Ref. Ch., N. Y., *Records,* 155, 170, 177, 180.
Colonial History of N. Y., 251.
Colonial Records of Pa., 27, 236, 246.
Conestoga (Canastocka), 31, 47, 48, 62-65, 79, 98, 114, 203, 205, 229, 235, 250, 251, 252, 274, 275, 277, 281, 290, 294, 295, 298, 409, 417, 418, 425.
Confession of Faith of Boehm, 168.

INDEX 493

Corwin, *Manual*, 22, 156, 197, 260, 339.
Coventry (Chester Co.), 78-80, 121, 124, 128, 130, 378.
Cramer, W. S., *History*, 276.

De Bois, John, 289.
De Huff, John, 291.
De Turk, Isaac, 217, 251.
De Turk, John, 92, 94.
De Wees, Cornelius, 23, 150, 477, 478, 479, 480.
De Wees, Christina Elizabeth, 110.
De Wees, Garret, 23, 479, 480.
De Wees, Gerrit Hendricks, 22.
De Wees, William, 22, 25, 33, 35, 36, 58, 59, 110, 169, 170, 179, 182, 191, 257, 261, 284, 292, 316, 340, 363, 395, 404, 415, 422, 430.
Diemer, Dr. John Jacob, 43, 50, 56, 72, 209, 235, 236, 270, 271, 315, 316, 322, 336, 392, 410.
Diffenbach, Adam, 68, 386.
Diffenderffer, *German Immigration*, 20, 287.
Dilbeck, Isaac, 21, 22, 25, 36, 169, 191.
Dill (Diel), John Michel, 234, 292, 316, 334, 341, 395, 407.
Dintenmeyer, Johannes, 257.
Doc. Hist. of N. Y., 251.
Dolpihacken; see Tulpehocken.
Donegal, 121, 124, 128.
Dörr, Peter, 276.
Dorsius, P. H., 53, 54-57, 74, 77, 88, 134, 259, 262, 264, 269, 270, 272, 282, 284, 285, 286, 288, 294, 296, 297, 299, 300, 302, 315, 317, 318, 321, 322, 324-327, 336, 338-340, 342, 370, 373, 386, 387-388, 390, 391, 392, 396, 397, 405, 406, 410, 419, 420, 424, 425, 429, 453.
Dotterer, George Philip, 61, 169, 209.
Dotterer, H. S., *Dotterer Family*, 169.
Dotterer, H. S., *Historical Notes*, 21, 22, 23, 24, 32, 61, 81, 112, 199, 449.
Dotterer, H. S., *Perkiomen Region*, 21, 26, 47, 109, 111, 246, 252, 277, 287, 338, 409, 449.
Dotterer, H. S., *Rev. J. P. Boehm*, 148, 366.
Dotterer, H. S., *Whitemarsh Cong.*, 81.
Dotterer, H. S., *Mss.*, 237.
Drinktenhengst, Johannes, 257, 283, 340, 363, 394.
Druckenmüller, Sebastian, 479, 480.
Du Bois, Rev. Gualtherus, 33, 170, 177, 183, 197, 207, 211, 219, 256, 343, 344.
Dubbs, J. H., *Earliest Ref. Ch.*, 81.
Dubbs, J. H., *Hist. of Ref. Ch.*, 151.
Dubbs, J. H., *Manual*, 151.
Dubbs, J. H., *Ref. Ch. in Pa.*, 22, 45, 97, 151, 254, 354, 375, 449.
Dunkel, John, 283, 316, 340, 363, 394.
Dunkers, 84, 85, 94, 95, 200, 239, 243, 390.
Dunkers, Seventh Day, 47, 50, 65, 85, 91, 94, 95, 105, 161, 201, 239, 243, 275, 354, 375, 390, 410, 462.

Earl Township, 121, 124.
Eberhard, Michael, 293.
Ecclesiastical Records of N. Y., 34, 57, 155, 163, 170, 174, 176, 177, 180, 218, 220, 222, 223, 226, 325, 328, 344, 418, 419.
Eschenbach, Andrew, 89, 92, 95, 97, 98, 112.
Eckstein, John (Separatist), 87.
Egle, *Hist. of Leb. Co.*, 69.
Egypt, 53, 77-79, 139, 278, 294, 469.
Endt, Theobald, 92, 362, 475.
Ephrata, 48, 64, 85, 94, 95, 101, 105.
Ephrata Chronicle, 67, 47, 158, 201, 202, 275, 354.
Ewig, John Niclas, 234, 268, 283, 363, 407.

Falkenstein, *Baptist Brethren,* 201.
Falkner, Daniel, 86.
Falkner, Rev. Justus, 24.
Falkner Swamp, 28, 29, 58, 61, 75, 109, 138, 139, 155, 160, 190, 215, 238, 250, 251, 254, 257, 260, 264, 272, 281, 282, 283, 294, 295, 297, 305, 316, 337, 340, 398, 399, 409, 413, 425, 430, 449, 450, 457, 460, 461, 466, 469.
Faust, Albert B., *German Element,* 86.
Feder, Johann Michel, 234.
Feree, Daniel, 251.
Fidler, Gottfried, 48, 354.
Fischer, Herman, 293.
Fluck, *History,* 81.
Fohrer, John, 289, 316, 364.
Frack, Jacob, 338.
Frederick, Henry, 250.
Frederickfields, John, 218.
Frederick Township, 114.
Frelinghuysen, Rev. Theo. J., 54, 156, 157, 194, 325, 419.
Frenler, Jost, 291.
Fresenius, *Nachrichten,* 66, 83, 84, 87, 91, 93, 94, 97, 98, 100, 106, 108, 110, 111, 114, 131, 147, 349, 354, 366, 382, 384, 417.
Fresenius, *Sammlungen,* 78, 436.
Frey, Andrew, 92, 95, 112.
Frey, Conrad, 21.
Frey, Henry, 21, 112.
Frey, William, 112.
Froelich, Hans Michel, 209.
Fry, *History,* 354.
Frymuth, Rev. J. C., 163, 339.

Gaguschi; see Cacusi.
Gaul, John Ulrich, 233, 234.
Gebbard, John, 269, 283, 292, 407.
Geiser, *Redemptioners,* 287.
Gemelen, Matthias, 112.
Gerckes, Antonie, 25.
Gerhard, *History,* 64, 81.
Germantown, 31, 45, 46, 50, 59, 72, 91, 96, 100, 121, 137, 140, 241, 247, 250, 251, 264, 273, 277, 281, 282, 292-298, 326, 351, 356, 357, 360, 378, 379, 405, 406, 421, 422, 430, 434, 460, 469.
Gleim, Johann Michael, 76, 147, 257, 363, 395, 470, 471, 472.
Goetschy, John Henry, 51, 52, 53, 54, 60, 73, 77, 88, 253, 273, 277, 279, 280, 288, 293, 302, 324, 325, 327, 338, 342, 410, 419, 447.
Goetschy, Rev. Maurice, 51, 447.
Göhr (Gehr), Johannes, 64.
Good, Rev. J. I., *Early Fathers,* 151.
Good, Rev. J. I., *History of Ref. Ch.,* 1725-1792, 41, 107, 151, 278, 446, 458.
Good, Rev. J. I., *Hist. of Ref. Ch. of Germany,* 161.
Good, Rev. J. I., *Hand Book,* 151.
Gordon, *Gazetteer,* 252.
Gorner, John, 276.
Goshenhoppen, 31, 47, 53, 56, 121, 123, 124, 140, 213, 215, 216, 250, 252, 278, 279, 281, 296, 298, 325, 338, 418, 419.
Goshenhoppen, New, 23, 47, 52, 53, 77, 252, 293, 294, 295, 329, 410, 424, 425, 439.
Goshenhoppen, Old, 52, 59, 60, 138, 204, 278, 294, 424, 425, 430, 431, 439, 447, 455.
Great Swamp, 52, 53, 250, 253, 278, 293, 294, 295, 297, 298, 439.
Greber, Andrew, 293.
Gref, Sebastian, 283, 289, 364.
Greiff, Stephan, 233, 249.
Griesemer, Caspar, 73.
Gruber, John Adam, 82, 87, 92, 98, 101, 111, 114, 117, 417.
Grumbine, *Two Dead Churches,* 290.
Guldin, Rev. Samuel, 92, 107, 274, 421.

Haak (Haag), John, 284, 289.
Haberecht, Gottfried, 95.
Hague Archives, 50, 57, 62, 72, 78,

INDEX

125, 230, 231, 232, 234, 250, 270, 272, 373, 397, 400, 405, 409, 423, 426, 428, 435, 436, 438, 464.
Hahn, Michael, 352.
Hain, John George, 377.
Hain's Church, 280.
Hallesche Nachrichten, new ed., 21, 354, 416, 424.
Halsbrun, Andries, 64.
Hamilton, Andrew, 415.
Hamilton, *History,* 89.
Harbaugh, *Fathers,* 97, 115, 118, 143, 151, 446.
Harbaugh, *Life of Schlatter,* 70, 75, 76, 78, 133, 252, 428, 435, 440, 455, 456, 469.
Hartman, Lorentz, 234.
Hassert, Arnold, 246.
Hautz, John Philip, 290.
Hazard's Register, 28, 45, 46, 255.
Heckler, *History,* 40, 59, 60, 81, 191, 192, 198.
Heidelberg (Berks Co.), 121, 123.
Heidelberg (Lehigh Co.), 78, 294.
Heidelberg Catechism, 35, 76, 103, 122, 135, 173, 178, 238, 245, 255, 313, 354, 358, 359, 361, 369, 378, 391, 404, 422.
Heidelberg Consistory, 30, 33.
Helffrich, *Geschichte,* 253.
Heller, Rudolf, 63.
Heller's Church, 64, 251, 274.
Henckel, Rev. Anthony J., 66, 215.
Hendricks, Marytye, 25.
Herb, Johannes, 257.
Herbein, Jonathan, 111.
Herchelroth, Lorentz, 291.
Herchelroth (Hergelrood), Valentine, 68, 343, 386.
Hermits of Wissahickon, 86.
Herrnhuters, 348, 352, 358, 374, 378, 380, 382, 427, 444.
Heut, Peter, 234.
Heyderich, Caspar, 234.
Hildebeutel, Martin, 338.
Hill Church (Conestoga), 64, 65, 274, 275, 276, 281, 291, 294, 295.
Hill Church (Lebanon Co.), 296.

Hillegas, Frederick, 30, 409.
Hillegas, George Peter, 30, 31, 32, 43, 71, 209, 216, 217, 233, 235, 237, 322, 409.
Hillegas, Michael, 30, 32, 43, 209, 216, 217, 235, 322, 374, 409, 410.
Hist. of Western Salisbury, 54, 253.
Hochreutner, Rev. J. J., 138, 143, 439, 448, 449, 450, 466.
Hock, John Jacob, 64, 88, 275.
Holstein, Henry, 112.
Holtzbaum, Andrew, 290.
Holtzhauser, Casper, 293.
Horn, *Re-Union,* 146, 151.
Host Church (Tulpehocken), 68.
Houthoff, Corn. (Cl. Dep.), 171.
Huebner, George, 94.
Huntersfield, N. Y., 41.

In de Haven (see Ten Heuven).
Indian Creek, 54, 60.
Indianfield, 138.
Indians, 31, 95, 105, 121, 125, 126, 127, 130, 218, 379.
Inspired, 86, 87.
Itzberger, Jacob, 284.

Jablonski, Rev. Daniel, 357.
Jacobs, *German Emigration,* 251.
Jordan, *John Bechtel,* 118.
Jordan (Lehigh Co.), 78.
Jork, Johannes, 233.
Journal of Presb. Hist. Soc., 24, 25, 26, 42, 54, 60, 74, 75, 81, 132, 134, 142, 155, 158, 177, 180, 183, 282, 349, 391, 429.
Jung, Deobalt, 209.

Käller, John, 276.
Kalm, *Travels,* 458.
Kantner, George, 68.
Kapp, Martin, 290.
Keiber, Wendel, 32, 209.
Keim, Johannes, 217.
Keith, *Provincial Councillors,* 245, 317.
Keith, William, Governor, 26, 43.

Kelpius, John, 86.
Kern, Nicolaus, 77.
Keyser, *Historic Germantown*, 58, 274.
Kind, Adam, 257.
Kintzing, Abraham, 233, 234, 249, 335.
Kirschner, John, 295.
Kissel Hill (Lanc. Co.), 121.
Kissel, Nicolaus, 124, 128.
Klamber, John Adam, 233.
Klauer, George, 61, 169.
Kleim; see Gleim.
Klemmer, Andreas, 233.
Klemmer, John Henry, 316, 341, 363.
Knauss, Ludwig, 36, 169, 191, 192, 257, 261, 284.
Knibbe, Rev. David, 54.
Knoll, John, 284.
Knopp, Leonard, 334.
Kocherthal, Rev. J., 251.
Koester, Bernhard, 86.
Kolb, Martin (Mennonite), 94, 139, 470.
Kooken, John, 112.
Kraus, Jacob, 283, 316, 340, 363, 394.
Kremer, John George, 233, 234.
Kreutz Creek, 123, 124.
Kriebel, *Schwenkfelders*, 86, 94.
Kuhlenwein (Newborn), 202.
Kuntz, Lorentz, 233, 234.

Labadists, 156.
La Munyon, *De Wees Family*, 395.
Lancaster, 64, 70, 275, 276, 291, 294, 295, 417, 439, 450, 462.
Lansdale Reporter, 61, 81.
Lawrence, Thomas, 244, 245, 248, 480.
Layenberger, Francis, 417.
Learned, *Pastorius*, 22.
Lecolie, Peter, 31, 71, 209, 233.
Le Dee, John, 218.
Leeman, Christian, 257, 335.
Lefevre, Isaac, 251.
Lefevre, John, 26, 169.

Leibi, John Fred, 283, 289, 364.
Leibi, Peter, 289.
Leinbach, John, 92.
Lesher, John, 73, 74.
Lerue, Jonas, 68.
Letter of Warning, 103, 104, 111, 348-365, 373-384, 390, 405, 421.
Levan, Daniel, 289.
Levan, Isaac, 289, 374, 377.
Levan, Jacob, 253.
Levering, Bishop, *Bethlehem*, 88, 97, 104, 120, 129.
Lewis, John, 76.
Leydich, Rev. J. H., 61, 75, 138, 139, 140, 449, 460, 461, 462, 466, 469.
Leyn, John, 64, 291.
Lischy, Jacob, 64, 70, 79, 106, 119-125, 375, 376, 379, 412, 419, 420, 439, 443, 444, 445, 461, 462, 463.
Lischy's *Declaration*, 122, 375.
Lischy's *Second Declaration*, 125.
Lock, John E., 234.
Logan, James, Governor, 336.
Loskiel, *Geschichte*, 126.
Lutherans, 83, 243, 242, 415, 417.

Maag, John Jacob, 292, 316, 317, 341.
Mack, Alex. (Dunker), 201.
Mackinet, Blasius, 112.
Macungy, 78, 139, 250, 252, 469.
Maier, Thomas (Lutheran), 367.
Manatawny, 109.
Mancius, Rev. Wm., 339.
Matthaei, Conrad (Hermit), 92, 93.
Maxatawny, 53, 78, 250, 253, 278, 280, 289, 294, 295, 298.
Mayer, John, 68.
Meels, Catrina, 25.
Meels, Hans Hendrik, 23, 25.
Meirer (Meurer), Adam, 283, 288, 340, 363, 395.
Members of Ref. Ch. (Number), 83, 242, 243, 250.
Memorial of Dedication, 129, 380.
Meng, John Christopher, 92, 242,

INDEX

250, 274, 423.
Mennonites, 84, 105, 139, 239, 243, 246, 389, 448.
Mercersburg Review, 155, 170, 172, 174, 176, 177.
Merkel, George, 112.
Messenger, Reformed, 8, 15, 65, 69.
Messerschmidt, Rudolf, 234.
Meurer, Rev. John Philip, 101, 102.
Meyer, George (Swatara), 290, 326.
Meyer, George (York), 123.
Meyer, Hans, 36; see also John.
Meyer, Henry (Tulp.), 289, 342, 364.
Meyer, Jacob (Falkner Swamp), 61, 169.
Meyer, John (Skippack), 169, 191, 310, 220.
Miller, Rev. John Peter, 44-48, 60, 63-65, 67, 72, 88, 199, 205, 206, 219, 242, 253, 254, 255, 274, 275, 277, 353, 354, 375, 410, 462.
Miller, Peter (Germant.), 100.
Miller, Henry (printer), 108.
Miller, Michael (Tulp.), 48, 354.
Miller, *History,* 354.
Minisink, 339.
Moravians, 87-88, 99, 372, 374, 376, 379, 380, 422.
Moravian Manual, 362.
Moselem, 53, 278, 294.
Montgomery, *Hist. of Berks Co.,* 81.
Moser, Adam, 149, 476-480.
Muddy Creek, 65, 121, 124, 294, 378, 399, 461.
Muehlenberg, Rev. H. M., 21, 86, 329, 354, 365, 367, 416.
Muehlenberg's *Selbstbiographie,* 66, 83, 131, 253, 329, 367.
Muehlbach, 121.
Mueller (Miller), Frederick Casimir, 74, 253.
Mueller, Felix, 276.
Mueller, Peter; see Miller.
Myers, Christian, Jr., 60.

Nead, *Germans in Md.,* 192, 283.
Neisser, George, 97, 104, 107, 108, 383, 384.
Neshaminy, 53, 54, 260, 262, 272, 387, 388.
Neuschwanger, Christian, 210, 220.
Neuzehölzer, John A., 233, 234.
Newborn, 71, 73, 86, 110, 161, 202, 278, 279.
New Castle, 22.
New Goshenhoppen; see Goshenhoppen, New.
New York Weekly Journal, 218.
Niemeyer, *Collectio,* 168.
Nitschmann, Bishop David, 87, 88, 92, 95, 97, 119, 121, 123, 357, 358, 376, 378, 379.

Oberbeck, Andrew, 283, 288, 316, 335, 338, 340, 363, 395.
Oellen, Ulrich, 233, 249.
Old Goshenhoppen; see Goshenhoppen, Old.
Oley, 31, 71, 73-74, 86, 91, 94, 98, 110, 114, 217, 250, 251, 278, 281, 283 288, 294, 295, 298, 377, 378, 379.
Orner, John Jacob, 233, 249.
Ottinger, Christopher, 257, 284, 292, 297, 340, 363, 395.

Palatinate Church Order, 453.
Pannebecker, Hendrik, 23.
Pannebecker, Frederick, 23.
Pastorius, Daniel, 21, 84.
Penn Germania, 71.
Penn, Thomas, 329, 334.
Pennsylvania Archives, 30, 49, 77, 147, 218, 236, 257, 263, 334, 335, 386, 394.
Pennsylvania Gazette, 101, 102, 246, 333.
Pennsylvania German, 73, 81.
Pennsylvania Magazine, 129.
Pennsylvania Synods, 92-106.
Pennypacker, *Life of H. Pannebecker,* 23.
Pennypacker, *Settlement of Ger-*

mantown, 21, 24.
Peruh, John George, 316.
Peters, Rev. Richard, 317, 365.
Philadelphia, 31, 41-46, 48, 50, 51, 70-73, 75, 101, 104, 137, 205, 211, 213, 216, 222, 230, 235, 247, 250, 251, 261, 265, 268, 273, 281, 283, 291, 294, 295, 297, 316, 326, 341, 350, 351, 357, 364, 366, 368, 398, 399, 404, 405, 411, 413, 415, 416, 428, 430, 431, 434, 435, 439, 443, 451, 459, 460.
Pietists, 161.
Polhemus, Rev. Theo., 22.
Pott, William, 112.
Powell, Joseph, 130.
Presbyterians, 27, 46, 52, 199, 212, 213, 214, 391, 396, 408, 446.
Presbytery of Phila., 53, 279.
Providence, 74, 75, 138, 398, 399, 430, 449, 460, 466.
Pyrlaeus, Rev. John C., 92, 95, 101, 365, 366, 367, 417, 418.

Quakers, 27, 157, 161, 246.
Quitapahilla, 69, 121, 124, 130, 294, 295, 296, 298.

Räder (Röder), Adam, 287, 294, 316, 340, 363, 394.
Radner, Michael, 420
Rammerstberger, John S., 276.
Raritan, N. J., 194, 423.
Rauch, Rev. C. H., 79-80, 92, 105, 124, 125-127, 379.
Rauch, John N., 293.
Rawle, *Equity in Pa.,* 43.
Rebenstock, John, 24, 25, 36, 169, 191.
Rebenstock, Sibilla, 25.
Records of Presb. Ch., 45, 52.
Recorder of Deeds Office, Phila., 250, 332, 476.
Redemptioners, 286, 287.
Ref. Ch. Record, 65.
Ref. Ch. Review, 31, 42, 79, 121, 122, 209, 232, 233, 235, 236, 440.
Register of Wills Office, Phila., 215, 216, 237, 246, 263, 287, 292, 329, 395, 409, 410, 470, 471, 472, 475.
Reichel, *Early History,* 86, 89, 90, 92, 97, 114, 124, 163, 372.
Reichel, *Memorials,* 91, 97, 112, 118.
Reiff, Hans Georg, 21, 32, 39, 198, 209.
Reiff, Jacob, 32, 37, 39, 40, 41-44, 53, 59, 192, 198, 205, 208, 217, 227, 230, 231, 232, 235, 236, 237, 239, 247, 248, 259, 270, 281, 300, 301, 302, 304, 315, 316, 324, 327, 328, 336, 345, 346, 392, 410, 411, 414, 419.
Reiffschneider, John, 282.
Reiffschneider, Sebastian, 36, 57, 61, 169, 191, 257, 260, 283.
Reimer (Reymer), Frederick, 287, 294, 316, 338, 340, 363, 394.
Reincke, *Register,* 129, 192.
Renberg, Dirck, 24.
Renberg, Gertruy, 25.
Renberg, Michael, 24.
Renberg, William, 24.
Report (Berigt) of 1731, 27, 41, 159, 243, 301, 306.
Ribertus, Hans Adam, 234.
Riegel, John, 68.
Rieger, Rev. J. B., 42, 47, 49, 50, 60, 70, 72, 88, 134, 135, 234, 235, 237, 242, 249, 254, 277, 326, 334, 343, 410, 411, 417, 418, 432, 438, 439, 444, 445, 462, 463.
Riehm, Martin, 295.
Ritter, Francis, 112.
Roberts, *History,* 78, 81.
Röhrig, J. W., 31, 41, 71, 209, 233.
Roth, *History,* 61, 81.
Ruetenik, *Pioneers,* 151.
Rupp's, *Names,* 30, 49, 191, 192, 202, 210, 216, 220, 257, 258, 260, 266, 274, 289, 293, 470.
Rutherford, *J. P. Zenger,* 218.
Ruttersham, Arnold, 76.

Sachse, *Sectarians,* 156, 161.

INDEX

Salisbury, Western, 54.
Sattler, Conrad, 234.
Saucon, 53, 77, 250, 252, 278, 293, 294, 295, 297, 298, 339.
Saur, Christopher, 83, 85, 371, 420, 475.
Saur's Paper, 66, 101, 140, 439, 469.
Schaeffer, Barthel, 284, 342.
Schell, Martin, 316, 364.
Schell, Peter, 364.
Schenkel, Martin (Newborn), 86, 202.
Scherer, Johannes, 233, 234.
Scherer, Philip, 148, 284, 292, 316, 340, 363, 395, 477.
Schipbouwer, Elisabeth, 25.
Schirmann, Simon, 326, 327.
Schlatter, Rev. Michael, 44, 73, 75, 78, 124, 132-135, 137, 138, 139, 140, 143, 244, 329, 428, 429, 430, 431, 432, 434, 436, 437, 439, 440, 441, 442, 443, 445, 450, 455, 456, 457, 458, 459, 465.
Schmauk, *History,* 24, 67, 354.
Schmidt, Christopher, 32, 209.
Schmidt, Joh. Heinr., 257.
Schmidt, Jost, 43, 112.
Schmidt, Michael, 32, 216, 217.
Schmidt, Sigmund, 257.
Schmiet, Johannes, 234.
Schnell, Rev. Leonard, 80, 129.
Schnorr, Caspar Ludwig, 70, 385.
Schob, Jacob, 286.
Schol, Elsye, 25.
Scholl, Fred., 293.
Schoolmasters, 240.
Schössler, Heinrich, 233.
Schuckert, Zacharias, 234, 249.
Schue, Daniel, 290.
Schuler (Schuiler), Gabriel, 25, 35, 36, 60, 169, 182, 191, 266, 374, 404, 476.
Schwab, Hans Georg, 31, 64, 212.
Schwartz, Ludwig, 342.
Schwartzwald, 124.
Schweitzer, Lorentz, 98.
Schwenkfelders, 85, 87, 93.

Sects in Pa., 84-88, 239.
Seidensticker, *German Printing,* 420.
Seiffert, Rev. Anthony, 95, 121.
Seipel, John L., 316, 341, 363.
Selig, John (Hermit), 86.
Selle, Maria, 25.
Seltenreich, 65, 294.
Senck, John G., 233, 234.
Separatists, 87, 421.
Servants, Indentured, 286.
Seward, William, 112.
Sesqui-Centennial of Boehm's Ch., 81, 148.
Shamboh, George, 150, 476-480.
Sheffer, Bartholomew, 68.
Shekomeko, 126.
Shikellimy, 126.
Singing, 282.
Sigel, Jacob, 43, 329, 330.
Sigmund, Bernhard, 233, 234, 268, 283.
Sitkovius, Bishop, 357.
Skippack, 21, 25, 26, 28, 29, 31, 32, 37, 40, 44, 46, 48, 50, 52, 54, 58, 59-61, 72, 112, 134, 155, 160, 190, 205, 207, 213, 215, 216, 217, 220, 222, 223, 227, 230, 238, 250, 251, 257, 260, 264, 265, 266, 270, 273, 277, 278, 281, 283, 288, 294, 295, 297, 305, 316, 319, 324, 326, 337, 340, 345, 398, 399, 408, 409, 410, 411, 413, 424, 430, 455, 476.
Smith, *Mennonites,* 470.
Socinians, 161.
Söller, Philip, 257.
Spaer, Lanert (Leonard), 36, 169, 191.
Spangenberg, Rev. A. G., 79, 86, 88, 110, 111, 113, 117.
Spangenberg, *Leben v. Zinzendorf,* 89, 131.
Speiker, Peter, 374, 476.
Sproegel, John Henry, 215, 419.
Sproegel, Widow, 215.
Staehler, John Mich., 479, 480.
Staels, Casper, 25.
Stapleton, *Henckel Memorial,* 215.

Stapleton, *Memorials of Huguenots,* 289, 290.
Stauffer, Christian, 60.
Stedman, Capt. John, 258, 263.
Steinmann, Georg, 293.
Steinmetz, Daniel, 233.
Stephen, Peter, 210, 220.
Stephen, Ulrich, 60, 169, 257, 260, 266, 283, 288, 316, 335, 338.
Stieffel, John G. (Separatist), 87, 92, 117.
Stiettelfreindt, Frantz, 233.
Stoever, Rev. J. C., 106.
Straightforward Account, 107.
Straub, John Wm., 54, 60, 88, 273, 277, 288, 324, 334, 411.
Strecker, Elias, 234.
Streeter, John Philip, 334.
Strohauer, Hans Georg, 234.
Strubel, Frederick, 276.
Stumpf, Adam, 386.
Swatara, 69, 121, 124, 128, 130, 290, 294, 295, 298.
Synod of Berne, 96, 98, 101, 102, 369.
Synod of Dort, 35, 102, 136, 178, 238, 404, 452.
Synod of Phila. (Presb.), 52.

Tempelman, Rev. Conrad, 47, 62-65, 69, 88, 418.
Ten Heuven, Evert, 23, 25, 284, 476.
Ten Heuven, Gerhart, 23, 32, 209, 284.
Ten Heuven, Herman, 23.
Tennent, Rev. Gilbert, 46, 54, 101, 156, 325, 419.
Thomas, George, 332.
Thonis, Gosen, 257.
Tobias, *History,* 81.
Tohickon, 138.
Traxel, Peter, 77.
Treber, Nicolaus, 291.
Trexler, *Skizzen,* 81.
Tricktenhengst, John, 283, 287, 294, 316 (see also Drinktenhengst).

Tulpehocken, 47, 48, 53, 63, 66-70, 106, 121, 123, 124, 130, 133, 205, 250, 251, 252, 274, 275, 276, 277, 278, 281, 294, 295, 296, 298, 316, 326, 342, 379, 380, 385, 398, 409, 412, 413, 416, 449, 450, 466.
Tulpehocken Confusion, 102.

Ulrich, John Caspar, 234, 249, 261, 263, 268, 283, 330, 344, 374, 386, 427.
Unruh, George, 327, 364, 374, 386.
Unruh, Valentine, 68.
Unpartisan Witness, 107.
Uttre, Jacob, 233, 249, 334.

Van Basten, Herman, 54, 260, 342.
Van Bebber, Henry, 109.
Van Horne, *History,* 81, 331.
Van Ostade, Rev. Jacob, 230, 231.
Vende, Frederick, 381, 382.
Vetter, Reichert, 233, 234.
Von Thieren, Rev. B., 66.

Wager, Peter, 332.
Wagner, Abraham, 112.
Walter, Jacob, 234, 261, 269, 283, 317, 334, 363, 395, 396, 397, 404, 407.
Warwick, 121, 124, 127, 128.
Watteville, Bishop, 130.
Weber, Christian, 112.
Webster, *History,* 156.
Weekly Mercury, 20, 215, 246, 329.
Weidler, Michael, 64, 291.
Weis, Andrew, 283.
Weis, Jacob, 290.
Weiss, Rev. Geo. Michael, 26, 29, 31, 32, 33, 37-42, 45, 47, 50, 59, 60, 65, 70, 71, 72, 73, 88, 134, 135, 140, 181, 182, 193, 195, 196, 199, 203, 205-212, 214, 216, 219, 221-227, 229, 230, 231, 232, 236, 240, 243, 254, 259, 273, 274, 277, 281, 300, 304, 315, 316, 327, 328, 336, 344, 392, 410, 411, 430, 432, 439, 444, 447.
Weiss, Rev. George (Schwenk-

INDEX 501

felder), 85.
Weiser, Conrad, 48, 66, 82, 92, 126, 353, 354.
Weiser, C. Z., *Life of C. Weiser,*
Weiser, C. Z., *Monograph,* 33. 354.
Wenrich, Francis, 68.
Weller, Hendrick, 31, 43, 71, 209, 233.
Wentz, Jacob, 112.
Wentz, Peter, 26.
Wentz's Church, 26, 61.
Werner, Henry, 283, 289, 364.
Werns, Conrad, 64.
Wetzel, Jacob, 293.
Western Salisbury, 253.
Whitefield, Rev. George, 89, 112, 113.
Whitemarsh, 21, 23, 24, 25, 28, 29, 58, 59, 155, 160, 190, 215, 238, 250, 257, 261, 264, 273, 281, 292, 293, 294, 295, 297, 298, 340, 398, 399, 408, 409, 413, 414, 423, 430.
Whitney, *Mich. Hillegas,* 216.
White Oaks, 65, 294.
Whitpain, 75-77, 135, 138, 145, 431, 435, 456, 457.
Wilhelm, Jacob, 284, 289, 342.
Wilhelmius, Rev. John, 37, 39, 40, 42, 49, 53, 54, 240, 243, 259, 261, 301, 302, 303, 311, 320, 324, 387, 419.
Wiegner, Christopher, 86, 91, 92, 93, 110, 111, 112, 113.
Willauer, Christian, 293.
Wirtz, (Wuertz), Rev. John C., 78, 89, 445f, 447.
Wiellecken, Rudolf, 233, 234, 316, 341, 363, 395.
Wister, Casper, 68.
Wohlfahrt, Michael, 201.
Wolffmiller, Hans, 36, 191.
Wotring, Abraham, 78.
Wuehrmann, Henry, 316, 340, 363, 395.
Wuehrmann, John, 283, 288.

Yoder, Johannes, 25, 202, 218.
York, 121, 123, 124, 127.
Yost, Anna Maria, 150.

Zeller, Henrich, 342, 364.
Zenger, Peter, 218.
Zetel, Jacob, 234.
Ziegel Church; see Macungy.
Zimmermann, Hans, 121.
Zinzendorf, Count, 70, 79, 82, 87, 89-108, 113, 118, 119, 121, 127, 130, 147, 253, 329, 350, 351-356, 359, 364, 366, 367, 369, 371, 372, 376, 378, 379, 380, 381, 417, 420, 421.
Zinzendorf, *Nachrichten,* 131.
Zinzendorf, *Hirten Lieder,* 131.
Zinzendorf, *Reflexionen,* 114, 131.

Religion in America
Series II

An Arno Press Collection

Adler, Felix. **Creed and Deed:** A Series of Discourses. New York, 1877.

Alexander, Archibald. **Evidences of the Authenticity, Inspiration, and Canonical Authority of the Holy Scriptures.** Philadelphia, 1836.

Allen, Joseph Henry. **Our Liberal Movement in Theology:** Chiefly as Shown in Recollections of the History of Unitarianism in New England. 3rd edition. Boston, 1892.

American Temperance Society. **Permanent Temperance Documents of the American Temperance Society.** Boston, 1835.

American Tract Society. **The American Tract Society Documents,** 1824-1925. New York, 1972.

Bacon, Leonard. **The Genesis of the New England Churches.** New York, 1874.

Bartlett, S[amuel] C. **Historical Sketches of the Missions of the American Board.** New York, 1972.

Beecher, Lyman. **Lyman Beecher and the Reform of Society:** Four Sermons, 1804-1828. New York, 1972.

[Bishop, Isabella Lucy Bird.] **The Aspects of Religion in the United States of America.** London, 1859.

Bowden, James. **The History of the Society of Friends in America.** London, 1850, 1854. Two volumes in one.

Briggs, Charles Augustus. **Inaugural Address and Defense,** 1891-1893. New York, 1972.

Colwell, Stephen. **The Position of Christianity in the United States,** in Its Relations with Our Political Institutions, and Specially with Reference to Religious Instruction in the Public Schools. Philadelphia, 1854.

Dalcho, Frederick. **An Historical Account of the Protestant Episcopal Church, in South-Carolina,** from the First Settlement of the Province, to the War of the Revolution. Charleston, 1820.

Elliott, Walter. **The Life of Father Hecker.** New York, 1891.

Gibbons, James Cardinal. **A Retrospect of Fifty Years.** Baltimore, 1916. Two volumes in one.

Hammond, L[ily] H[ardy]. **Race and the South**: Two Studies, 1914-1922. New York, 1972.

Hayden, A[mos] S. **Early History of the Disciples in the Western Reserve, Ohio;** With Biographical Sketches of the Principal Agents in their Religious Movement. Cincinnati, 1875.

Hinke, William J., editor. **Life and Letters of the Rev. John Philip Boehm:** Founder of the Reformed Church in Pennsylvania, 1683-1749. Philadelphia, 1916.

Hopkins, Samuel. **A Treatise on the Millennium.** Boston, 1793.

Kallen, Horace M. **Judaism at Bay:** Essays Toward the Adjustment of Judaism to Modernity. New York, 1932.

Kreider, Harry Julius. **Lutheranism in Colonial New York.** New York, 1942.

Loughborough, J. N. **The Great Second Advent Movement:** Its Rise and Progress. Washington, 1905.

M'Clure, David and Elijah Parish. **Memoirs of the Rev. Eleazar Wheelock, D.D.** Newburyport, 1811.

McKinney, Richard I. **Religion in Higher Education Among Negroes.** New Haven, 1945.

Mayhew, Jonathan. **Observations on the Charter and Conduct of the Society for the Propagation of the Gospel in Foreign Parts;** Designed to Shew Their Non-conformity to Each Other. Boston, 1763.

Mott, John R. **The Evangelization of the World in this Generation.** New York, 1900.

Payne, Bishop Daniel A. **Sermons and Addresses,** 1853-1891. New York, 1972.

Phillips, C[harles] H. **The History of the Colored Methodist Episcopal Church in America:** Comprising Its Organization, Subsequent Development, and Present Status. Jackson, Tenn., 1898.

Reverend Elhanan Winchester: Biography and Letters. New York, 1972.

Riggs, Stephen R. **Tah-Koo Wah-Kan; Or, the Gospel Among the Dakotas.** Boston, 1869.

Rogers, Elder John. **The Biography of Eld. Barton Warren Stone, Written by Himself:** With Additions and Reflections. Cincinnati, 1847.

Booth-Tucker, Frederick. **The Salvation Army in America:** Selected Reports, 1899-1903. New York, 1972.

Satolli, Francis Archbishop. **Loyalty to Church and State.** Baltimore, 1895.

Schaff, Philip. **Church and State in the United States** or the American Idea of Religious Liberty and its Practical Effects with Official Documents. New York and London, 1888. (Reprinted from *Papers of the American Historical Association,* Vol. II, No. 4.)

Smith, Horace Wemyss. **Life and Correspondence of the Rev. William Smith, D.D.** Philadelphia, 1879, 1880. Two volumes in one.

Spalding, M[artin] J. **Sketches of the Early Catholic Missions of Kentucky;** From Their Commencement in 1787 to the Jubilee of 1826-7. Louisville, 1844.

Steiner, Bernard C., editor. **Rev. Thomas Bray:** His Life and Selected Works Relating to Maryland. Baltimore, 1901. (Reprinted from *Maryland Historical Society Fund Publication,* No. 37.)

To Win the West: Missionary Viewpoints, 1814-1815. New York, 1972.

Wayland, Francis and H. L. Wayland. **A Memoir of the Life and Labors of Francis Wayland, D.D., LL.D.** New York, 1867. Two volumes in one.

Willard, Frances E. **Woman and Temperance:** Or, the Work and Workers of the Woman's Christian Temperance Union. Hartford, 1883.

DATE DUE	
FEB 2 5 1997	
APR 1 4 1997	
GAYLORD	PRINTED IN U.S.A.

GTU Library
2400 Ridge Road
Berkeley, CA 94709
For renewals call (510) 649-2500
All items are subject to recall.